International Migration Outlook
2022

OECD

BETTER POLICIES FOR BETTER LIVES

This work is published under the responsibility of the Secretary-General of the OECD. The opinions expressed and arguments employed herein do not necessarily reflect the official views of the Member countries of the OECD.

This document, as well as any data and map included herein, are without prejudice to the status of or sovereignty over any territory, to the delimitation of international frontiers and boundaries and to the name of any territory, city or area.

The statistical data for Israel are supplied by and under the responsibility of the relevant Israeli authorities. The use of such data by the OECD is without prejudice to the status of the Golan Heights, East Jerusalem and Israeli settlements in the West Bank under the terms of international law.

Note by the Republic of Türkiye
The information in this document with reference to "Cyprus" relates to the southern part of the Island. There is no single authority representing both Turkish and Greek Cypriot people on the Island. Türkiye recognises the Turkish Republic of Northern Cyprus (TRNC). Until a lasting and equitable solution is found within the context of the United Nations, Türkiye shall preserve its position concerning the "Cyprus issue".

Note by all the European Union Member States of the OECD and the European Union
The Republic of Cyprus is recognised by all members of the United Nations with the exception of Türkiye. The information in this document relates to the area under the effective control of the Government of the Republic of Cyprus.

Please cite this publication as:
OECD (2022), *International Migration Outlook 2022*, OECD Publishing, Paris, https://doi.org/10.1787/30fe16d2-en.

ISBN 978-92-64-68412-6 (print)
ISBN 978-92-64-86767-3 (pdf)
ISBN 978-92-64-51165-1 (HTML)
ISBN 978-92-64-87219-6 (epub)

International Migration Outlook
ISSN 1995-3968 (print)
ISSN 1999-124X (online)

Foreword

This publication constitutes the 46th report of the OECD's Continuous Reporting System on Migration. The report is divided into eight chapters plus a statistical annex. Chapter 1 provides a broad overview of recent trends in international migration flows and policies up to 2021 on international movements. It also analyses recent changes on the labour market inclusion of immigrants in OECD countries. Chapter 2 monitors recent changes in migration policies, while Chapter 3 looks at the recent changes in policies that support the integration of immigrants and their children.

Chapter 4 presents a broad overview of the refugee crisis triggered by the unprovoked war of aggression of Russia against Ukraine and of the policy responses in OECD countries. The chapter examines both initial and medium-to-longer term reception support that is available to Ukrainian refugees, focusing specifically on housing, access to immediate assistance and public services, education, and employment.

Chapters 5 to 7 focus on international students. The chapters in turn analyse recent trends, attraction and retention policies, and the economic impact of international students. Chapter 5 provides an overview of international students in OECD countries, their origin and destination countries as well as drivers of their mobility. It discusses how international students differ from domestic students in the OECD and provides the latest enrolment and permit statistics, noting the impact of the COVID-19 pandemic. Chapter 6 reviews OECD countries' policies to attract, admit and retain international students. It provides examples of communication and outreach strategies to international students as well as parameters for their admission. Finally, it discusses policies to monitor the compliance of international students with the regulations set out on their study permit and ensure that institutions and students do not misuse this channel. Chapter 7 provides estimates for the five- and ten-year stay rates of international students, and discusses their importance as a feeder for labour migration during and after study, as well as their economic impact.

Chapter 8 presents succinct country-specific notes and statistics on developments in international migration movements and policies in OECD and selected non-OECD countries in recent years. Lastly, the statistical annex includes a broad selection of recent and historical statistics on immigrant flows, asylum requests, foreign and foreign-born populations, and naturalisations.

This year's edition of the OECD International Migration Outlook is the collective work of the staff of the International Migration Division in the Directorate for Employment, Labour and Social Affairs. Chapter 5 was drafted by Elisabeth Kamm (OECD). Chapter 6 was prepared by Elisabeth Kamm and Jonathan Chaloff (OECD). Chapter 7 was prepared by Elisabeth Kamm and Thomas Liebig (OECD). Jean-Christophe Dumont edited the report. Statistical work was carried out by Philippe Hervé and Nicolas Ortega. Editorial assistance was provided by Dominika Andrzejczak and Charlotte Baer as well as Natalie Corry and Lucy Hulett.

Editorial

We must continue to co-ordinate our responses to the ongoing Ukrainian refugee crisis, as well as plan for their longer-term displacement

The slowdown of international migration witnessed during the COVID-19 pandemic was reversed in 2021, due to a strong bounceback in economic activity and the re-opening of borders, increasing labour needs, and a resumption of visa processing. Yet 2022 has been marked by even greater flows, resulting from Russia's unprovoked war of aggression against Ukraine. Beyond the human tragedy, the war has triggered a refugee and humanitarian crisis at a scale unforeseen in Europe since the Second World War. Close to 5 million Ukrainians have fled to the EU and other OECD countries, while many more have become displaced inside Ukraine.

OECD countries reacted to the Ukrainian refugee crisis decisively and quickly, meeting the sudden and unexpected massive inflows of people seeking protection with unprecedented support. The policy responses by OECD countries built on lessons from previous experiences with large-scale refugee inflows and were adapted to this new situation. Countries co-ordinated their responses, establishing different channels of consultation and collaboration to manage information flows between stakeholders within countries – between ministries, municipalities, and non-governmental organisations – and across borders, allowing for continuous adaptation as the crisis developed. Meanwhile, governments implemented effective and proactive communication strategies to inform both the refugees themselves and the public at large about their actions.

The European Union, by invoking the Temporary Protection Directive for the first time in its history, was able to swiftly mobilise resources to manage the influx in the EU and to ensure the immediate protection and rights of those eligible. Upon registration, beneficiaries of temporary protection immediately received a residence permit, as well as access to employment, accommodation, health, and education for persons under 18 years, alongside many other rights. Outside the EU, other OECD countries also took impressive actions to provide immediate support to Ukrainian refugees. Several countries, including Canada, the United States and the United Kingdom, launched new migration schemes and policies to welcome Ukrainians fleeing the war. Many other exceptional measures have also been taken, as outlined in Chapter 4 of this Outlook.

Alongside governments, citizens and NGOs have stepped forward in many OECD countries to provide support to Ukrainian refugees. The positive impulse for solidarity and the groundswell of civil society action has been broadly acknowledged and often supported by public initiatives. This has allowed countries to do much more with the resources available. The impact has been most visible in relation to providing shelter for new arrivals. Many countries, including Poland, have relied extensively on a system of volunteers to meet the demand for housing.

Overall, OECD countries have managed the early phase of the crisis well, drawing extensively from previous experiences. However, we are entering the next phase of the Ukrainian refugee crisis triggered by Russia's ongoing large-scale aggression against Ukraine. We all hope that those who have fled Ukraine will have the chance to return home shortly and safely. However, considering both the destruction of the country and the traumatic experiences of refugees, we must also think about individuals who are unable to return to their homes, or who wish to remain in the host countries where they have started to rebuild their life. We need to be prepared for the possibility that many refugees will remain in OECD countries for the near future. Considering this, countries need to explore "dual intent" solutions that give refugees quick access to full-scale integration support without hampering a possible return to Ukraine once the situation allows.

Evidence is clear that investing in refugees' language skills is key to facilitating the insertion of Ukrainian children into national school systems as well as ensuring their parents' smooth entry into labour markets. It is also an investment to foster longer-term relationships between Ukraine and its population with the rest of the EU and the OECD.

Education will also play a key role. Access to public education for minor children has been available in all OECD countries from the start of the refugee crisis, but the start of the 2022-23 school year has seen many more Ukrainian children entering national education systems. Host countries made major efforts to scale up their classroom and teaching capacities in time, for instance by recruiting Ukrainian teachers. In parallel, many new initiatives are also being introduced by educational institutions and other stakeholders to facilitate learning opportunities and skills development for adults. Education and training at any age is an important vehicle for integration, with obvious positive spillover effects once these new skills are taken back to Ukraine to rebuild the country.

Ukrainians' existing skills should be fully recognised as well and a quick entry into the labour market promoted. Most of the displaced adults from Ukraine have post-secondary education, so they are well placed to find work, especially at a time when labour and skills shortages are looming in so many sectors (*OECD Employment Outlook 2022*). One crucial area that host countries need to address in relation to this is access to childcare, which is particularly critical considering that most working-age adults from Ukraine are women with children. Capitalising on the skills of Ukrainian refugees will boost not only the economies of host countries but will also help the refugees to be self-reliant. That the skills of Ukrainians are not left idle during their forced displacement is also imperative for the reconstruction of Ukraine.

Different obstacles to integration, however, remain. Access to affordable and durable housing is one of them. Housing is a precondition for refugees to restore some stability in their lives but is of limited availability in many receiving countries, especially in Europe. The rapid influx of Ukrainian refugees happened in the context of significant pre-existing housing challenges, such as insufficient housing supply and rising costs. Solutions to this need to be found soon, as strains on the existing housing stock show no sign of lessening.

It is important to recognise that further migration flows, from Ukraine or other parts of the world, may be triggered by Russia's on-going war against Ukraine. Early lessons from the current crisis can help us prepare. Unified and well-coordinated policy responses across countries allowed us to respond and to adapt quickly to the first refugee wave. The current experience has also stressed the importance of public opinion and support during migration crises. This poses the question of how best to harness and maintain this level of solidarity in the long-term, especially as the indirect economic consequences of the Russian war of aggression against Ukraine are increasingly felt by host countries. The capacity to maintain public support will, at least in part, depend on speedy and successful inclusion of Ukrainian refugees already in host countries.

The Ukrainian refugee crisis will shape international migration for years to come. Undoubtedly, the road ahead will not be easy, but OECD countries are putting past lessons into practice and working together to address the situation. It is important though to continue to take bold actions based on good practice to confront the challenges during the next phase of this humanitarian crisis. This is crucial to provide the necessary support to Ukrainian refugees and pave a way for rebuilding Ukraine.

Stefano Scarpetta,

Director for Employment, Labour and Social Affairs,

OECD

Table of contents

FIGURES

TABLES

Follow OECD Publications on:

https://twitter.com/OECD

https://www.facebook.com/theOECD

https://www.linkedin.com/company/organisation-eco-cooperation-development-organisation-cooperation-developpement-eco/

https://www.youtube.com/user/OECDiLibrary

https://www.oecd.org/newsletters/

This book has...

StatLinks

A service that delivers Excel® files from the printed page!

Look for the *StatLink* at the bottom of the tables or graphs in this book. To download the matching Excel® spreadsheet, just type the link into your Internet browser or click on the link from the digital version.

Executive summary

Migration flows bounced back in 2021

After a record decrease in 2020 due to the COVID-19 crisis, permanent-type migration to OECD countries bounced back by 22% in 2021. First data suggest that the increase in permanent migration flows continued in 2022.

Family migration increased by 40% in 2021 and remained the largest category of inflows, accounting for more than four in ten new permanent immigrants to the OECD. Migration in free mobility areas was less affected by the pandemic, but still fell by 17% in 2020. This trend persisted in 2021, with an estimated decrease of 2%, largely due to Brexit. Free mobility in EU27 countries slightly bounced back with an estimated increase of 4%. Labour migration to OECD countries recovered strongly, by 45%, in 2021 (18% of total permanent-type inflows). Permanent humanitarian migration rose slightly by 4% in 2021, after four consecutive years of decline.

The number of new asylum applications to OECD countries rose by 28% in 2021, to above 1 million. The main origin countries were Nicaragua, Afghanistan and Syria.

Labour market outcomes of immigrants were more resilient than expected

While labour market outcomes for immigrants declined more strongly than those of the native-born in 2020, they also disproportionately improved in 2021. In 2021, around 70% of immigrants were employed, and 9% unemployed, OECD-wide. In almost half of OECD countries, immigrants returned to or exceeded their pre-crisis level of employment in 2021. In particular, the labour market performance of recently arrived immigrants improved more in 2021 compared to their longer-settled counterparts.

The global competition for talent is back on the policy agenda

The global competition for talents continues and new pathways to attract highly educated migrants, remote workers and potential investors have emerged. At the same time, labour shortages, including in low- and middle-skilled occupations, have led several countries to expand temporary labour mobility schemes and bilateral agreements to recruit foreign workers. More generally, COVID-related travel restrictions were gradually lifted in most OECD countries.

Reforms of integration programmes mostly focused on increasing individualisation, improving mentorship, language training, and helping migrants gain rapid and stable access to the labour market. Several countries, notably Germany and the United States, enhanced measures to facilitate or promote naturalisation. A few countries have also put forth National Action Plans to combat discrimination and racism.

Regularisation occurred in 2021/22 in Chile and Italy, and one was announced in Ireland. Colombia launched a far-reaching regularisation for Venezuelans.

Responding to the refugee crisis from Ukraine

Russia's unprovoked war of aggression against Ukraine, which started on 24 February 2022, generated a historic mass flight. OECD countries responded swiftly, granting immigration concessions to Ukrainian nationals, such as visa exemptions, extended stays or prioritisation of immigration applications. The Council of the European Union enacted, for the first time, the Temporary Protection Directive, which provides a set of harmonised rights for the beneficiaries in all EU Member States. Non-EU OECD countries also took, to varying degrees, measures to facilitate the entry and stay of Ukrainian people fleeing the war.

The transition to medium- and longer-term solutions has exposed emerging challenges, including moving away from temporary and other similar subsidiary statuses towards more lasting solutions, mainstreaming support measures, preventing secondary flows and preparing for changes in public mood and support.

International students make a large economic contribution in most OECD countries

In 2020, there were 4.4 million international students enrolled in the OECD, accounting for 10% of all tertiary students. The most important receiving countries are the United States (22% of all international students), the United Kingdom (13%) and Australia (10%). While the destinations of international students have diversified over the past decade, the main origin countries remain China and India (22% and 10% of all international students, respectively).

Over the past decade, almost all OECD countries implemented wide-ranging policies to retain international students after completion of their degree, but the retention of international students varies greatly. Five years after initial admission, more than 60% of international students who obtained a permit for study reasons in 2015 were still present in Canada and Germany, around half in Australia, Estonia and New Zealand, and around two in five in France and Japan. The share of students remaining was below 15% in Denmark, Slovenia, Italy and Norway.

Former international students are an important feeder for labour migration in many countries. Transition from study permits accounted for a large share of total admissions for work in 2019, especially in France (52%), Italy (46%) and Japan (37%). In the United States, former study (F-1) permit holders accounted for 57% of temporary high-skilled (H-1B) permit recipients.

During their studies, between one in three and one in four international students work in the EU, the United Kingdom and the United States, about one in two in Australia and nine in ten in Japan. International students who remain in the host country post-study have long-term employment rates that are on par with those of labour migrants and well above those of migrants overall. Their overqualification rates are half of those of labour migrants or other migrant groups.

While student migration can be of great benefit, the delegation of a gatekeeping role to higher education institutions, and the growing share of economic migration comprised by former students, still carry a number of risks, including distorting migration regulation and undermining labour market regulations.

Key findings

- OECD countries received 4.8 million new permanent-type immigrants in 2021, a 22% increase relative to 2020, but still more than half a million fewer than in 2019.
- The United States remained the largest recipient of permanent immigrants in 2021 (834 000), 43% more than in 2020, and 19% less than in 2019. In the EU, the upturn in permanent-type migration (+15%) was less pronounced.

- By mid-September 2022, close to 5 million individual refugees from Ukraine had been recorded across the EU and other OECD countries, out of whom about 4 million had registered for temporary protection or similar national protection schemes in Europe.

- Across OECD countries, international students made up 7% of students enrolled at bachelor's, 17% at master's, and 26% at the doctoral level in the academic year 2020.

- International students tend to study in their region of origin. In 2020, 29% of international students in OECD countries remained in the same broader geographical region.

- In the OECD as a whole, direct export revenues from international students increased in nominal terms from over EUR 50 billion in 2010 to over EUR 110 billion in 2019.

Key facts and figures

Russia's invasion of Ukraine has led to a historic outflow of refugees

Number of refugees from Ukraine in OECD countries Mid-September 2022

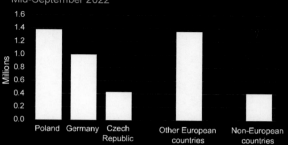

By mid-September 2022, almost 5 million refugees from Ukraine had been recorded in the OECD and the EU.

Many countries responded rapidly to the arrival of Ukrainian refugees

Many OECD countries responded swiftly to the refugee crisis, granting immigration concessions to Ukrainian nationals, such as visa exemptions, extended stays, and temporary protection or private sponsorship programmes.

Temporary protection   Visa exemptions   Extended stays

Migration flows across OECD countries have partially bounced back

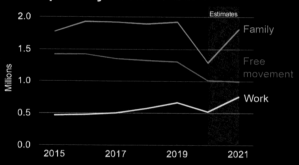

Permanent migration to OECD countries increased in 2021 relative to 2020 by approximately 22%, with family migrants representing 38% of the total.

Employment rates of migrants are almost back to pre-COVID levels

On average in 2021, about 70% of immigrants were employed (only 0.6 percentage points below the pre-Covid-19 level).

70%

The employment rate of immigrants was, on average, 1 percentage point lower than that of the native born.

The number of international students has been rising over the long term

International students as a share of all tertiary students, %

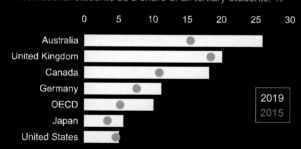

On average across OECD countries, international students make up over 10% of all tertiary educated students.

Revenue from international students continues to increase

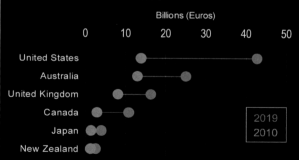

In the OECD as a whole, education-related services from international students, such as tuition & accommodation, increased from €50 billion in 2010 to over €115 billion in 2019.

1 Recent developments in international migration movements and labour market inclusion of immigrants

This chapter provides an overview of recent developments in international migration movements and labour market inclusion of immigrants in OECD countries. The first section analyses the evolution of international migration flows over the last decade, up to 2021. Both permanent and temporary migration flows by category of migration are covered. The chapter then examines recent trends in asylum requests in OECD countries. It then looks at the composition of migration flows and the foreign-born population, as well as trends in acquisition of nationality. The second section of the chapter examines trends in the labour market outcomes of immigrants over the past two decades, with particular attention to the economic crisis provoked by the pandemic. Detailed analysis by sociodemographic characteristics and region of origin is provided.

In Brief

Key findings

Migration trends

- Permanent migration to OECD countries partially bounced back in 2021 after a record decrease in 2020 due to the COVID-19 crisis. OECD countries counted 4.8 million new permanent immigrants in 2021, a 22% increase relative to 2020 but still over half a million short of the 2019 level.

- The increase in permanent migration flows is expected to continue in 2022 as OECD countries lift immigration and travel restrictions.

- The United States remains the OECD country receiving the largest inflows of permanent immigrants in 2021 (834 000, 43% more than in 2020, but still 19% less than in 2019). Canada received a record inflow of over 400 000 new permanent migrants, more than double the inflow in 2020.

- In the EU27, the upturn in permanent-type migration (+15%) was less pronounced. Free mobility was less affected by the pandemic but still fell by 17% in 2020. The estimated rebound in 2021 was modest (+4%).

- The measures against COVID-19 have still severely affected migration flows to Australia, Japan, Korea and New Zealand in 2021.

- Family migration increased by 39% in 2021 in the OECD and remained the largest category of inflows, accounting for more than a third of total permanent-type migration to the OECD. At 1.5 million new family migrants, this is however below the pre-COVID-19 level.

- At nearly 600 000, family migration increased by 30% in the EU, returning to its 2017-19 average level.

- Labour migration to OECD countries rebounded by 45% in 2021 and exceeded 750 000 workers, the highest level in a decade (19% of total permanent-type inflows). This was partly driven by the large increase in the United States, Canada, the United Kingdom and Italy (due to a regularisation programme in this latter country).

- In the EU, permanent labour migration rose in line with family migration (+29% compared to 2020), to reach more than 300 000 new workers.

- Permanent humanitarian migration to OECD countries rose slightly by 3% in 2021, after four consecutive years of decline. The main destination countries for humanitarian migrants were Germany followed closely by Canada (which registered a +136% increase). Significant declines were observed in a few countries such as Australia and New Zealand, the United Kingdom, the United States, and Spain.

- The recruitment of seasonal workers from abroad remained stable at around 460 000 in 2020 and increased by 18% in 2021, mostly driven by the United States, the United Kingdom and France.

- Other types of temporary labour migration were more than halved in 2020 and decreased again in 2021.

- The inflow of working holiday makers to the top 10 OECD receiving countries decreased by 59% in 2020 and then again by 47% in 2021.

- Flows of international trainees decreased by 56% in 2020 in the top 4 OECD receiving countries and again by 69% in 2021. Japan remained the main receiving country despite low inflows (24 000 in 2021 compared with 202 000 in 2019).

- Mobility within multinationals was sharply reduced as a result of the pandemic: intra-company transfers fell by 52% in 2020 and by 24% in 2021.

- In 2020, almost 3.8 million postings were registered in the EU/EFTA, 19% less than the previous year. In Belgium, Germany, Luxembourg and Sweden, more than a quarter of posted workers were providing services in the construction sector. In Slovenia, posted workers sent abroad account for 30% of the construction sector workforce.

- The number of new asylum seekers in OECD countries rebounded by 28% in 2021, to above 1 million. The main origin countries were Nicaragua, Afghanistan and Syria. In the EU, partial figures for 2022 show a further 21% increase compared to 2021.

- Resettlement programmes were able to resume but only 57 000 people in need of international protection were transferred to an OECD country in 2021, around half the pre-COVID-19 average.

- In 2020, two-thirds of OECD countries received more migrant men than women. The share of men among new migrants in OECD countries was 55.5%.

- Despite the pandemic, the foreign-born population living in OECD countries continued to rise in 2021 and reached 138 million, 10.6% of the total population of OECD countries.

- Countries where the share of the foreign-born population has increased the most since 2015 are Iceland (+8 percentage points), Luxembourg (+5 percentage points), Chile (+5 percentage points) and Sweden (+4 percentage points).

- The COVID-19 pandemic and the resulting border closures led to a decrease in inflows from all top 20 countries of origin. China and India, the two top countries of origin in 2019, experienced the sharpest decrease in outflows to OECD countries.

- According to preliminary and partial data, the number of acquisitions of citizenship in OECD countries in 2021 could be the highest ever recorded, at 2.3 million. This represents a 20% increase, partly due to a reduction in the backlogs of applications during the COVID-19 pandemic. Very strong increases have been registered in the United States (+30%), the United Kingdom (+46%), Canada (+22%), Norway (+109%) and Austria (+80%).

Labour market integration

- Overall, labour market outcomes for immigrants worsened more compared to native-born in 2020 but bounced back more strongly in 2021 with the economic recovery.

- Between 2020 and 2021, the employment rate of immigrants improved in over seven out of ten OECD countries. On average in 2021, almost 70% of immigrants were employed, and 9% were unemployed. In almost half of OECD countries, immigrants have returned to or exceeded their pre-crisis level of employment.

- The health crisis caused, for the first time in a decade, an increase in the risk of long-term unemployment in some OECD countries, particularly among immigrants, who have a less developed professional network, poorer language skills, and a higher likelihood of being discriminated against.

- The average number of hours worked by foreign-born persons in employment remains lower than the pre-crisis level.

- The employment of young migrants increased in 2021 but remains on average below pre-crisis levels. The share of young migrants not in education, employment or training has decreased since 2020. Measures put in place by countries to support the labour market integration of young people have helped to mitigate the effects of the crisis.
- The labour market performance of recently arrived immigrants improved more in 2021 compared to their longer-settled counterparts. Among other things, this may be the result of a decrease in the share of inflows of migrants with a weak labour market connection as well as an increase in outflows of recently arrived migrants who have lost their jobs.
- Despite a significant improvement in the employment situation of immigrants from Africa and the Middle East since 2019, they remain the most disadvantaged group in most OECD countries.

Recent trends in international migration

Permanent-type migration to OECD countries partially bounced back in 2021

Permanent migration to OECD countries increased in 2021 relative to 2020 by approximately 22% and stood at 4.8 million (Figure 1.1). Despite this large increase, the inflow is lower than pre-COVID-19 pandemic permanent flows, which averaged 5.3 million between 2017 and 2019.

Permanent-type migration data presented in this section should be interpreted with caution. First, they should not be interpreted as new arrivals as they include not only new entries but also in-country changes of status from a temporary to a permanent status. The terms "permanent-type migration", "permanent inflows/immigration", and "admissions" refer to the same data and are used interchangeably. Border reopenings and the easing of travel restrictions tend to affect in-country transitions less, so these numbers are more stable. Therefore, the observed total increase in permanent flows reflects a larger increase in permanent immigration from abroad. Second, several OECD countries report their migration statistics using fiscal years which do not correspond with calendar years. This is the case for Australia, Ireland and the United States. As a result, the increase in migration flows in calendar year 2021 is only partially reflected in the 2021 national migration statistics for these countries. In this section, however, US data have been adjusted to refer to calendar year from 2019 on.

Third, OECD permanent-type migration includes estimates of migration within free-circulation areas and therefore are not comparable to the total number of new issuances of residence permits.

Figure 1.1. Permanent-type migration to the OECD, 2012-2021

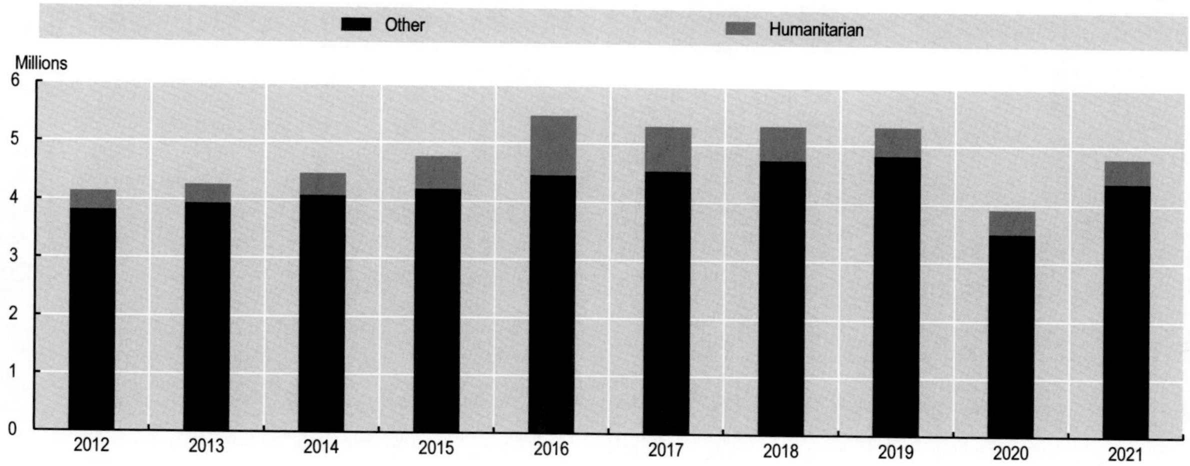

Note: Sum of standardised and unstandardised figures (refer to Table 1.1, not including Colombia, Costa Rica and Türkiye), including status changes and migration within free-circulation areas. 2021 data are partly estimated based on growth rates published in official national statistics.
Source: OECD International Migration Database (available upon request).

StatLink 🔗 https://stat.link/8ibo5c

The 2021 rebound was largely driven by permanent-type migration to major receiving countries such as the United States (+43%), Canada (+117%), Spain (+13%), the United Kingdom (+51%), France (+16%), Italy (+82%) as well as Poland (+37%). The United States remains the OECD country receiving the largest inflows of permanent immigrants in 2021 although inflows were 19% below their pre-pandemic level (Table 1.1).

Canada received a record inflow of over 400 000 new permanent migrants, more than double the inflow in 2020. This makes Canada the third largest receiving country after the United States and Germany. In this latter country, permanent flows remained relatively stable. The unprecedented increased admissions in Canada aim at offsetting the shortfall of 150 000 new permanent residents in 2020 due to the COVID-19 pandemic and at filling critical labour market gaps. The 2022-24 Immigration Levels Plan aims to continue welcoming immigrants at a rate of about 1% of Canada's population, including 431 645 permanent residents in 2022, 447 055 in 2023, and 451 000 in 2024.

Permanent flows rebounded in 2021 in all other OECD countries, with some notable exceptions. The measures against COVID-19 have still severely affected migration flows to Australia, Japan, Korea and New Zealand. Permanent inflows to Australia remained at a similar level in 2021 as in 2020 (fiscal years). In Japan, after continuous growth through 2013-19, the inflow of permanent migrants decreased again in 2021, to 53 400, approximately 40% of the 2019 level. Permanent migration flows to Chile and Colombia continued to decrease. In contrast, permanent migration to Mexico increased again in 2021 (+25% year on year) to a new record level, following a sharp rise in humanitarian admissions.

Table 1.1. Permanent-type migration to selected OECD countries, 2012-21

	2012	2013	2014	2015	2016	2017	2018	2019	2020	2021 (estimates)	2021/20 change
Standardised statistics					Thousands						%
United States	1 031.6	990.6	1 017.2	1 051.0	1 183.5	1 127.2	1 096.6	1 031.0	581.6	833.9	+ 43.4
Germany	425.0	486.2	602.1	708.1	1 077.9	883.1	656.5	643.3	532.1	536.2	+ 0.8
Canada	258.3	262.8	261.5	275.9	296.7	286.5	321.0	341.2	184.6	401.1	+ 117.3
Spain	324.5	275.0	266.0	267.6	290.0	316.8	333.3	388.9	344.7	390.3	+ 13.2
United Kingdom	236.4	283.4	343.9	369.6	354.7	345.4	346.5	346.4	223.4	338.3	+ 51.4
France	246.6	257.3	256.8	261.1	258.7	259.7	281.3	290.9	238.2	276.6	+ 16.1
Italy	308.1	278.7	241.8	221.6	211.0	216.0	223.8	190.6	132.2	241.1	+ 82.3
Australia	249.9	256.9	234.7	227.9	229.4	220.5	195.2	195.7	165.5	169.4	+ 2.4
Netherlands	88.5	92.8	104.0	111.3	125.1	128.2	136.2	153.2	121.1	146.0	+ 20.6
Switzerland	125.6	135.6	134.6	131.2	125.0	118.4	122.1	122.5	118.1	121.2	+ 2.6
Belgium	102.0	104.4	100.5	103.8	106.2	107.7	109.1	113.2	91.6	109.9	+ 19.9
Sweden	96.4	107.0	116.7	120.5	153.2	131.4	121.8	97.8	79.4	83.6	+ 5.3
Portugal	27.9	26.4	30.5	31.2	32.8	39.6	64.0	98.3	80.0	79.8	− 0.3
Austria	70.8	70.8	80.9	103.0	105.7	98.6	87.1	81.9	62.7	73.4	+ 17.1
Mexico	21.0	55.0	43.5	34.4	35.9	32.6	38.7	38.7	54.2	67.7	+ 24.9
Japan	66.5	57.5	65.4	82.0	95.4	100.7	116.5	137.9	85.2	53.4	− 37.3
Denmark	36.0	43.8	50.7	62.3	56.1	52.1	51.1	48.5	41.2	53.0	+ 28.6
Korea	43.9	53.3	61.6	64.5	71.6	70.8	76.1	74.6	53.6	50.6	− 5.5
Norway	57.5	56.6	68.1	61.5	65.1	55.3	46.3	46.6	33.2	38.6	+ 16.2
Ireland	22.4	26.0	27.6	36.6	42.4	40.4	45.5	51.4	42.5	38.1	− 10.4
New Zealand	42.7	45.1	49.9	54.5	55.7	47.2	45.1	38.3	35.7	35.4	− 0.9
Finland	19.7	20.6	19.8	21.6	27.2	24.3	23.7	25.7	24.0	27.5	+ 14.8
Israel	16.6	16.9	24.1	27.9	26.0	26.4	28.1	33.2	19.7	25.0	+ 26.9
Luxembourg	17.2	17.9	18.9	19.4	19.5	21.5	21.6	22.9	19.2	20.6	+ 7.2
All countries	**3 935.1**	**4 020.6**	**4 220.6**	**4 448.5**	**5 044.9**	**4 750.3**	**4 587.5**	**4 612.5**	**3 363.9**	**4 210.7**	**+ 25.2**
EU27 countries included above	1 785.2	1 806.8	1 916.2	2 068.1	2 505.9	2 319.4	2 155.2	2 206.5	1 809.0	2 076.1	+ 14.8
Of which: free movements	899.1	925.4	1 021.1	1 026.8	1 058.6	1 034.2	1 028.5	1 026.8	849.4	884.4	+ 4.1
National statistics (unstandardised)											
Türkiye	..	..	..	..	273.9	364.6	466.9	578.5	470.0	..	..
Poland	47.1	46.6	32.0	86.1	107.0	128.0	137.6	163.5	163.5	224.2	+ 37.1
Chile	65.2	84.4	83.5	101.9	135.5	207.2	339.4	254.1	154.6	96.7	− 37.4
Czech Republic	28.6	27.8	38.5	31.6	34.8	43.5	55.9	63.3	53.8	69.2	+ 28.6
Hungary	20.3	21.3	26.0	25.8	23.8	36.5	49.3	55.3	43.8	49.1	+ 12.1
Colombia	..	..	..	..	..	104.5	217.9	225.8	74.8	40.7	− 45.6
Lithuania	2.5	3.0	4.8	3.7	6.0	10.2	12.3	19.7	22.3	21.1	− 5.1
Slovenia	12.3	11.6	11.3	12.7	13.8	15.5	24.1	27.6	24.8	19.7	− 20.6
Costa Rica	..	..	..	15.7	6.6	8.6	9.2	7.8	..	..	..
Estonia	1.1	1.6	1.3	7.4	7.7	9.1	9.7	11.0	10.3	12.5	+ 20.9
Iceland	2.8	3.9	4.3	5.0	7.9	11.8	11.5	9.5	7.6	8.5	+ 13.0
Latvia	3.7	3.5	4.5	4.5	3.4	5.1	6.5	6.6	4.6	6.5	+ 41.2
Greece	17.7	31.3	29.5	34.0	86.1	80.5	87.3	95.4	63.4	73.6	+ 16.1
Slovak Republic	2.9	2.5	2.4	3.8	3.6	2.9	2.9	2.5	2.8	4.4	+ 56.6
Total (except Colombia, Costa Rica and Türkiye)	**204.4**	**237.6**	**238.2**	**316.4**	**429.6**	**550.3**	**736.5**	**708.4**	**551.3**	**585.5**	**+ 6.2**

Note: Includes only foreign nationals. Data refer to the fiscal year ending in the year of reference for Australia (Jul-Jun) and Ireland (Apr-Mar). For the United States, data refer to fiscal years (Oct-Sep) until 2018 and calendar years from 2019 on. The inflows include status changes, namely persons in the country on a temporary status who obtained the right to stay on a longer-term basis, and migration within free-circulation areas. Series for some countries have been significantly revised. EU averages cover countries stated in the table, excluding the United Kingdom.
Source: OECD International Migration Database (data available upon request).

StatLink ᴍꜱ🔲 https://stat.link/jgivk6

Permanent flows to the European Union countries increased by 15% in 2021 to 2.1 million. All EU countries experienced an increase in permanent inflows with the exception of Portugal and Ireland. In Italy and Poland, 2021 permanent migration flows were higher than in 2019, largely due to new admissions of immigrant workers – in the case of Italy through a regularisation programme (see comments below and in the country note). Several other Eastern European countries experienced large increases in permanent flows. This is the case of the Slovak (+57%) and the Czech (+29%) Republics, and the Baltic States with the exception of Lithuania, and Hungary (+12%).

In the United Kingdom, new permanent-type migration increased by half to 338 000. New programmes for highly skilled migrants (notably health and care workers) as well as flows from the EU and from Hong Kong (China), largely contributed to boost permanent-type migration back to its pre-COVID19 level.

In 2021, OECD countries received on average four new migrants per thousand inhabitants (Figure 1.2). In nearly six in ten OECD countries, the 2021 ratio is higher than the one for the 2012-20 period. The difference is particularly sharp in several Eastern European and Baltic countries, and in Canada. In Norway and Sweden, Australia and New Zealand, as well as Chile and Colombia, this ratio has declined between 2012-20 and 2021.

Figure 1.2. Permanent-type migration to OECD countries as a percentage of the total population, 2021 compared with the 2012-20 average

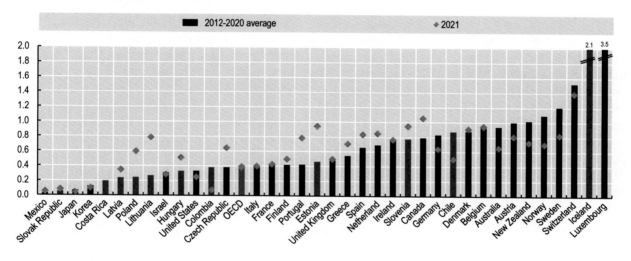

Note: Light blue columns are unstandardised data. OECD weighted average.
Source: OECD International Migration Database (data available upon request).

StatLink ⁛ᵐˢᴸ https://stat.link/3vwn6r

OECD countries received around 1.8 million family migrants in 2021, 40% more than in 2020, but slightly less than pre-COVID-19 (Figure 1.3). Family migration is still the largest category of inflows to OECD countries and accounts for a higher share of the total (43%) compared to 2020 (38%). With more than 610 000 admissions, family migration increased by 30% in the EU, returning to its 2017-19 average level.

Figure 1.3. Permanent-type migration to the OECD area, by category of entry, 2012-21

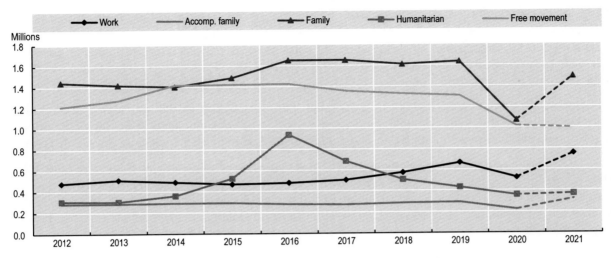

Note: 2021 data are estimates on the basis of preliminary data covering two-thirds of OECD countries.
Source: OECD International Migration Database (data available upon request).

StatLink 🖽📊 https://stat.link/vmjcq0

The United States is the main OECD destination country for family migrants, with an inflow of 532 000 in 2021 (+50%). However, the share of the United States in overall family migration to the OECD went down from 43% in 2019 to 38% in 2021, since family migration increased in a number of other important destination countries. In Italy, family migration nearly doubled in 2021, to 120 000 new migrants, above the 2019 level. The United Kingdom also contributed to the rebound with 105 000 family migrants in 2021, including 59 000 permits delivered under the EU Settlement family Scheme. This is the highest level ever registered, and a 62% increase compared with 2020. Canada saw a similar increase of family migration flows (+64% to 80 000) and recovered pre-COVID-19 levels. The other major increase concerned Australia, which delivered 81% more family visas in 2021 than in 2020. Japan and Korea, in the context of strict travel limitations, together with Portugal and Denmark, are among the few OECD countries where family migration decreased in 2021.

Labour migration to OECD countries rebounded by 45% in 2021 and exceeded 750 000 workers, the highest level in a decade. This was largely driven by Canada where permanent labour migration flows tripled in 2021 to 170 000 and Italy where the increase in labour migration was due to the inclusion of regularised migrants. Several other countries received historically high numbers of permanent migrant workers, in particular the United States (103 000, +60%) and the United Kingdom (82 000, +103%). Overall, permanent labour migration in the EU kept pace with family migration, with more than 300 000 new workers (+29% compared to 2020).

Labour migration to Japan was continuously rising until 2019, but fell by 40% in 2021. Australia, New Zealand, Spain and Sweden also showed declines in labour migration.

Figure 1.4. Composition of permanent-type migration to OECD countries by category of entry, 2020 and 2021

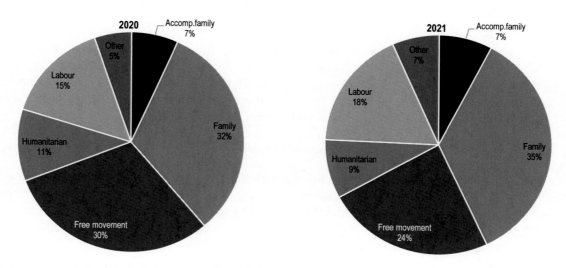

Note: Includes only countries for which data on standardised permanent-type migration are available (refer to Table 1.1).
Source: OECD International Migration Database (data available upon request).

StatLink ᵍ https://stat.link/eqfhvo

Despite being relatively less affected by the COVID-19 pandemic, migration within free-circulation areas nevertheless decreased by 22% in 2020 and by an additional 2% in 2021. The 2021 trend is mainly driven by the end of free circulation between the EU and the United Kingdom due to Brexit, and by the sharp decrease registered over the 2021 fiscal year in Australia. In the EU27, the estimated rebound in 2021 was modest (+4%) and this migration category represented 24% of all permanent flows in 2021 (Figure 1.4). In Germany and in Switzerland, these migration movements declined slightly (by 1% and 3%, respectively), but selected destination countries, such as Spain, Denmark, Sweden and Finland, registered double-digit increases.

Permanent humanitarian migration to OECD countries rose by 3% in 2021, after four consecutive years of decline. The main destination countries for humanitarian migrants were Germany followed very closely by Canada, which registered a +136% increase. Many other major destination countries received more humanitarian migrants in 2021 than in 2020, and the increase was higher than 70% in Italy, Austria, Belgium, Denmark and the Netherlands. The latter was among the few countries where refugee inflows did not drop in 2020. Declines were observed in 2021 in Australia and New Zealand, the United Kingdom, the United States and Spain.

Temporary worker migration has not returned to its pre-COVID-19 level

Inflow of international seasonal workers remained stable during the pandemic

International seasonal workers meet temporary labour needs, especially in agriculture and tourism, but also in construction, care and the agri-food industry, depending on the national programmes in place. Within the EU/EFTA, labour needs are largely met through free movement, but, in the past few years, EU countries have also signed bilateral agreements on seasonal worker recruitment, for example between Germany and Georgia in 2020. Following Brexit, the United Kingdom suffered a shortage of seasonal agriculture and horticulture workers and launched a new Seasonal Workers Pilot in 2019.

The COVID-19 pandemic and the ensuing partial closure of national borders and various lockdown measures barely stopped the recruitment of seasonal workers from abroad, primarily for harvesting activities in OECD countries. In 2020, inflows remained stable at around 460 000. Other types of temporary labour migration more than halved (Annex Table 1.A.2).

In 2021, seasonal worker flows increased by 18%, mostly driven by the United States (+38%), Canada (+10%), the United Kingdom (+11%), New Zealand (+27%) and France (+160%). Poland ranked second as a country of destination for seasonal migrants in 2021, despite a 17% decrease in seasonal flows. This drop is due to a change in the legislation: foreign workers granted access to the Polish labour market after 13 March 2020 no longer need a seasonal work permit to work in seasonal jobs.

Other types of temporary labour migration were significantly impacted by the pandemic

Working holidaymaker programmes help meet low-skilled labour needs mainly in tourism and agriculture. During the COVID-19 pandemic, many receiving countries suspended or reduced these mostly bilateral schemes. The inflow of working holiday makers to the top 10 OECD receiving countries decreased by 59% in 2020 and then again by 47% in 2021. Through these programmes, a total of 106 000 young workers arrived in OECD countries in 2021, four times fewer than in 2019.

In 2021, the decrease in the number of working holiday makers was due to a sharp drop in top receiving countries such as Australia (-73%) and New Zealand (-94%). In most other countries, flows rebounded without however reaching their pre-COVID-19 level (Annex Table 1.A.2). The United States became the most popular destination country for working holidaymakers in 2021, when around 40 000 youth participated in the Summer Work Travel Program. This is less than half of the participants in 2019 (108 000).

Flows of international trainees also continued to decrease sharply in 2021. This trend is driven by the decrease in migration to Japan, the main country of destination for trainees in OECD countries. The inflow of trainees to Japan decreased from 200 000 in 2019 to 86 000 in 2020 and 24 000 in 2021 (Annex Table 1.A.2).

There has also been a marked reduction in mobility within multinationals as a result of the pandemic: intra-company transfers fell by 52% in 2020 and by 24% in 2021. The sole exceptions are Poland, which received 11 to 13 000 ICTs each year since 2019, and Canada, where inflows of ICTs bounced back to their pre-COVID-19 level.

Figure 1.5. Inflows of temporary labour migrants (excluding posted workers), Top OECD receiving countries over the period 2019-21

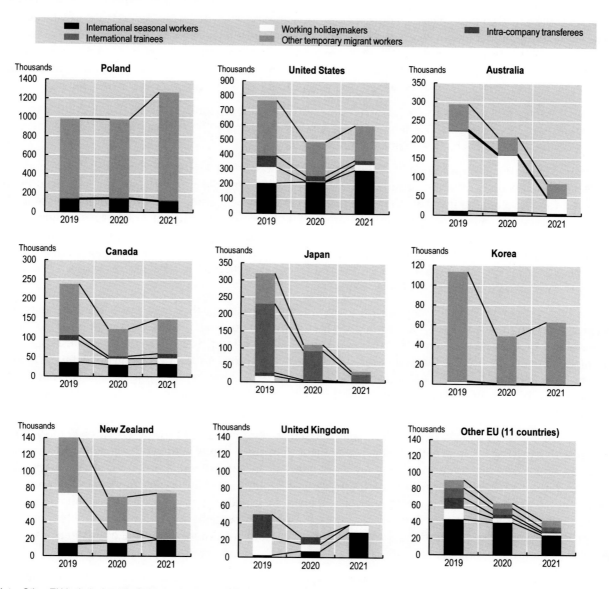

Note: Other EU include Austria, Belgium, Germany, Denmark, Spain, Finland, France, Ireland, Italy, Luxembourg and Sweden.
Source: OECD International Migration Database, https://doi.org/10.1787/data-00342-en.

StatLink https://stat.link/b7ydj2

Other national programmes exist for recruiting foreign workers (Figure 1.5). Poland, for example, has signed bilateral simplified recruitment programmes with Armenia, Belarus, Georgia, Moldova and Ukraine. The great majority of workers employed in Poland under the simplified procedure, in particular in manufacturing, construction and agriculture, as well as administrative services, come from Ukraine. For three years running, Polish employers recruited at least 1 million workers per year other than seasonal or ICTs (refer to Annex Table 1.A.3 for details on categories included), and these flows were not greatly affected by the pandemic. Conversely, all other OECD countries registered a sharp reduction in their temporary labour migration. New recruitments continued falling sharply in Australia and Japan in 2021 due to continuing border restrictions (Figure 1.5).

Contrasting trends in the number of worker postings within the OECD-Europe area in 2020

Inside the European OECD countries, posted workers are defined as salaried or self-employed workers who generally carry out their activity in another member country while staying affiliated to the social security system in their home country. When workers are posted in one single country, the posting cannot exceed 24 months (EC No 987/2009 Article 12), whereas there is no time limit for workers posted in two or more countries (EC No 987/2009 Article 13). Stricter enforcement as well as a better understanding of the rules by the employers contributed to a growing trend in reported worker postings over the past years.

COVID-19 temporarily reversed 15 years of continuous growth in postings, although the 2020 level was still higher than the number of postings any year prior to 2018. In 2020, almost 3.8 million postings were registered in OECD-Europe, 19% less than the previous year.

The bulk of postings (2.4 million out of 3.8 million in 2020) fall under Article 12 of the Regulation and take place in a single other member country. They may not exceed 24 months, and, on average, lasted 100 days (shorter than the average of 115 days in 2019). They concerned around 1.4 million workers who were sent abroad 1.7 times per year on average. In 2020, the total number of Article 12 postings issued by EU/EFTA fell sharply by 23%. The main receiving country remained Germany despite a 19% decrease. The Netherlands jumped as the second receiving country with a 78% increase in postings (mainly due to German workers). France, Austria and Switzerland follow, despite a 28 to 32% loss in Article 12 postings compared with the 2019 numbers (Table 1.2).

For all other postings, only the country of origin is known, as they either take place within at least two destination countries (Article 13), as is the case for 1.2 million postings (-8.8% compared to 2019), or are governed by multilateral agreements (Article 16), for 18 400 postings in 2020. Despite an overall decrease in Article 13 postings in 2020, the main origin countries issued more Article 13 posting notifications in 2020 than in 2019 (Poland: 400 000, +3%; Germany: 115 000, +28%), mainly due to the demand in road freight transport which accounts for nearly one in two postings. This type of posting is not limited in time but, on average, lasts 300 days.

In 2020, two-thirds of Article 12 (single country) postings were issued to provide services in the industry and one-third in services (half in the financial and insurance sectors, half in the education, health and social sectors). Agriculture accounted for less than 1% of total Article 12 postings. A quarter of Article 12 postings were in the construction sector. The sectoral distribution varies widely across destination countries: in Germany, nearly half of posted workers were employed in services, and construction accounted only for 7% of total notifications issued. Conversely, more than half of postings were granted to the construction sector in Romania, Slovenia and the Slovak Republic. Interestingly, more than 20% of postings issued by Belgium, Luxembourg and the Netherlands were granted to temporary employment agencies.

Looking at the sectoral distribution from the perspective of receiving countries, it is noteworthy that in Belgium, Germany, Luxembourg and Sweden, more than a quarter of posted workers were providing services in the construction sector. In Belgium, France and the Netherlands, a relatively high share were employed by a temporary employment agency.

Although the share of postings in total employment is modest (1% or 0.4% in full-time equivalent), the impact on the labour market can be significant in some countries and sectors. For instance, in Slovenia, posted workers sent abroad account for 30% of the workforce in the construction sector. In Croatia, Luxembourg, and the Slovak Republic, the corresponding share is as high as 11 to 13%.

Table 1.2. Postings of workers active under Article 12 in selected European OECD countries, by destination country, 2012-20

Thousands

Destination	2012	2013	2014	2015	2016	2017	2018	2019	2020	2020/2019 change (%)	Average duration 2020 (in days)
Total	**1173.4**	**1275.6**	**1365.9**	**1425.2**	**1539.1**	**1639.1**	**1718.2**	**3076.3**	**2354.2**	**-23**	**101**
Germany	335.9	373.7	414.2	418.9	440.1	427.2	428.9	505.7	410.9	-19	..
Netherlands	99.4	100.4	87.8	89.4	90.9	111.5	126.3	219.3	390.0	+78	..
France	156.5	182.2	190.8	184.7	203.0	241.4	262.1	450.2	307.7	-32	44
Austria	76.4	88.6	101.0	108.6	120.2	141.0	119.9	320.5	232.0	-28	..
Switzerland	64.9	78.1	87.5	97.7	104.3	105.7	113.8	247.0	177.1	-28	..
Belgium	125.3	134.3	159.7	156.6	178.3	167.3	156.7	218.2	168.9	-23	42
Italy	48.7	47.4	52.5	59.1	61.3	64.7	73.9	173.7	90.9	-48	47
Spain	46.1	46.5	44.8	47.4	52.4	60.5	63.9	177.1	82.3	-54	..
United Kingdom	40.4	43.5	50.9	54.3	57.2	59.6	60.8	132.5	62.4	-53	188
Sweden	26.1	29.4	33.0	37.4	39.1	44.0	53.8	85.5	61.5	-28	132
Czech Republic	17.8	18.6	17.2	19.1	22.7	24.2	30.6	101.5	60.5	-40	153
Poland	16.0	14.4	14.5	17.9	17.8	20.6	26.7	93.6	59.0	-37	147
Luxembourg	19.7	20.5	21.8	21.7	26.6	32.7	36.5	52.9	47.5	-10	12
Denmark	11.0	10.8	10.9	13.4	15.7	15.6	20.3	46.3	35.2	-24	..
Hungary	9.9	8.9	9.0	9.7	11.3	12.8	17.1	20.8	29.5	+42	104
Portugal	11.4	10.7	12.8	15.4	18.1	22.6	29.0	50.5	29.2	-42	91
Norway	16.2	18.8	21.3	25.0	23.8	22.9	26.6	38.2	25.0	-34	276
Finland	22.5	19.9	6.6	18.6	21.0	22.3	19.6	35.5	24.9	-30	190
Slovak Republic	6.6	7.0	7.6	8.1	9.7	13.6	14.0	33.2	18.1	-45	116
Greece	6.8	4.8	4.7	5.7	6.4	8.1	11.2	17.4	11.4	-35	..
Slovenia	3.3	4.5	6.6	5.7	5.1	6.2	9.2	17.2	11.3	-34	60
Ireland	4.7	5.6	4.0	4.0	5.8	6.2	7.8	17.2	8.2	-52	256
Lithuania	3.5	2.3	1.9	2.4	2.0	2.3	3.0	10.1	4.7	-54	..
Estonia	2.3	3.0	3.0	2.3	3.7	3.0	3.2	5.0	2.7	-46	256
Latvia	1.5	1.2	1.5	1.4	1.1	1.4	2.2	5.2	2.6	-49	265
Iceland	0.4	0.4	0.3	0.6	1.4	1.7	1.0	2.1	0.9	-59	..

Note: Total weighted average duration per PD A1 issued.

Source: European Commission, Directorate-General for Employment, Social Affairs and Inclusion, De Wispelaere, F., Pacolet, J., De Smedt, L. (2022[1]), *Posting of workers: Report on A1 portable documents issued in 2020*, https://data.europa.eu/doi/10.2767/048597.

StatLink https://stat.link/keomc5

Shifts in origin and destination of asylum seekers

A strong rebound in asylum seeking, but not up to pre-COVID-19 levels

The number of new asylum seekers to OECD countries rebounded by 28% in 2021, to above 1 million (Figure 1.6). Although this is still below the pre-COVID-19 levels, it still exceeds any figure prior to 2015. In the EU, the rise was even sharper (31% to almost 600 000), and partial figures for 2022 show a further 21% increase compared to 2021.

Figure 1.6. New asylum applications since 1980 in the OECD and the European Union

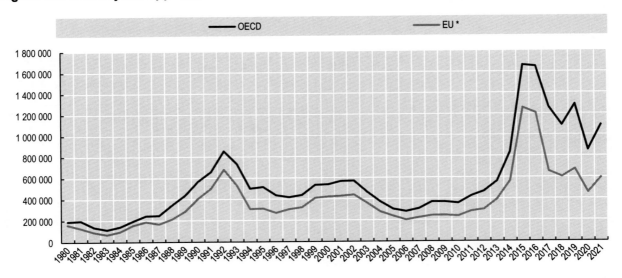

* Includes the United Kingdom.
Source: OECD Secretariat calculations based on data from UNHCR and Eurostat.

StatLink ᵐᵃˢᴸ https://stat.link/ymlb1e

Five OECD countries registered more than 100 000 new asylum applications in 2021. This happened only once before, in 2015. The United States received about 190 000 new asylum applications in 2021, 26% less than in 2020, and 37% less than in 2019. Nevertheless, it remained the main OECD destination country of asylum seekers for the fifth consecutive year (Table 1.3). Citizens from Venezuela accounted for more than 14% of the total and 15% more (27 000) applied for asylum in the United States in 2021 than in 2020. Guatemala, Honduras and El Salvador follow with respectively 23 000, 20 000 and 15 000 new asylum requests. However, these three countries saw a sharp fall, more than third, in comparison to 2020. 13 000 Cuban nationals applied for asylum in 2021, up 35% from 9 500 in 2020. Colombia (11 200) and Haiti (10 000) are the other main origin countries which saw increases. Overall, more than 70% of all asylum seekers in the United States are from Latin America and Caribbean countries.

Germany, second to the United States since 2017, received almost 150 000 new asylum applications in 2021. This represents a surge of about 45% led by asylum requests of citizens of Syria (55 000, +50%), Afghanistan (23 000, +135%) and Iraq (16 000, +58%). Mexico, which prior to 2016 did not appear among the top half of OECD countries in terms of new asylum requests, was third in 2021. Mexico received more than 130 000 applications in 2021, three times more than in 2020. 52 000 of these, or 40%, were Haitian nationals, and 36 000 came from Honduras. Costa Rica follows, confirming the upsurge of the demand for international protection across Central and South America. More than 100 000 of the asylum seekers received by Costa Rica in 2021 came from neighbouring Nicaragua. The number of new asylum applications filed in France reached 104 000 in 2021 (+27%). Countries of origin of asylum seekers in France are relatively diversified as, in addition to the 16 000 requests coming from Afghans, France received more than 3 000 asylum seekers from ten different countries. 62 000 new asylum requests were submitted in Spain (-28%), 56 000 in the United Kingdom (+57%), 44 000 in Italy (+106%) and 37 000 in Austria (+174%).

Table 1.3. New asylum applications by country where application is filed, 2015-21

	2015-18 annual average	2019	2020	2021	Absolute change 2020-21	% change 2020-21	Asylum seekers per million population (2021)	Top three origins of the asylum seekers (2021)
Australia	26 270	27 410	19 220	14 150	- 5 070	-26	549	Malaysia, China, Afghanistan
Austria	39 913	11 010	13 420	36 750	23 330	174	4 064	Syria, Afghanistan, Morocco
Belgium	21 398	23 140	12 930	19 610	6 680	52	1 686	Afghanistan, Syria, Eritrea
Canada	36 180	58 340	19 050	23 370	4 320	23	614	Mexico, India, Colombia
Chile	3 593	770	1 680	2 500	820	49	130	Venezuela, Cuba, Colombia
Colombia	1 670	10 620	11 920	15 940	4 020	34	311	Venezuela, Cuba, Ecuador
Costa Rica	10 243	59 180	21 130	108 430	87 300	413	21 099	Nicaragua, Venezuela, Haiti
Czech Republic	1 240	1 580	800	1 060	260	33	99	Ukraine, Georgia, Afghanistan
Denmark	8 528	2 650	1 440	2020	580	40	347	Afghanistan, Eritrea, Syria
Estonia	143	100	50	80	30	60	60	Afghanistan, Russia, Belarus
Finland	11 225	2 460	1 460	1 370	- 90	-6	247	Afghanistan, Iraq, Somalia
France	87 110	138 290	81 740	103 810	22 070	27	1 587	Afghanistan, Côte d'Ivoire, Bangladesh
Germany	381 125	142 510	102 580	148 240	45 660	45	1 767	Syria, Afghanistan, Iraq
Greece	45 790	74 920	37 860	22 660	- 15 200	-40	2 185	Pakistan, Afghanistan, Syria
Hungary	51 565	470	90	40	- 50	-56	4	Iran, Afghanistan, Ethiopia
Iceland	823	810	630	870	240	38	2 534	Venezuela, Palestinian, Afghanistan
Ireland	3 023	4 740	1 540	2 620	1 080	70	526	Nigeria, Georgia, Somalia
Israel	11 198	9 450	1 890	1930	40	2	220	China, India, Rep. of Moldova
Italy	96 340	35 010	21 340	43 910	22 570	106	727	Pakistan, Bangladesh, Tunisia
Japan	12 055	10 380	3 940	2 410	- 1 530	-39	19	..
Korea	9 835	15 430	6 670	2 330	- 4 340	-65	45	China, Bangladesh, Nigeria
Latvia	303	180	150	580	430	287	311	Iraq, Afghanistan, Belarus
Lithuania	380	630	260	3 910	3 650	1404	1 454	Russia, Belarus, Tajikistan
Luxembourg	2 200	2 200	1 300	1 360	60	5	2 142	Syria, Eritrea, Afghanistan
Mexico	14 105	70 360	41 200	131 420	90 220	219	1 009	Haiti, Honduras, Cuba
Netherlands	24 518	22 540	13 720	24 760	11 040	80	1 442	Syria, Afghanistan, Yemen
New Zealand	440	540	440	420	- 20	-5	86	India, China, Sri Lanka
Norway	9 915	2 210	1 340	1 620	280	21	296	Syria, Afghanistan, Eritrea
Poland	6 378	2 770	1 510	6 240	4 730	313	165	Belarus, Afghanistan, Iraq
Portugal	1 155	1 740	900	1 350	450	50	133	Afghanistan, Morocco, India
Slovak Republic	173	220	270	330	60	22	60	Morocco, Afghanistan, Algeria
Slovenia	1 440	3 620	3 470	5 220	1 750	50	2 511	Afghanistan, Pakistan, Iran
Spain	28 210	115 190	86 390	62 070	- 24 320	-28	1 328	Venezuela, Colombia, Morocco
Sweden	54 803	23 150	13 630	10 180	- 3 450	-25	1 002	Syria, Afghanistan, Ukraine
Switzerland	23 550	12 600	9 770	13 300	3 530	36	1 526	Afghanistan, Eritrea, Algeria
Türkiye	104 715	56 420	31 330	29 260	- 2070	-7	344	Afghanistan, Iraq, Iran
United Kingdom	37 275	44 470	36 030	56 470	20 440	57	828	Iran, Iraq, Eritrea
United States	255 178	301 070	250 940	188 860	- 62 080	-25	567	Venezuela, Guatemala, Honduras
OECD total	**1 423 998**	**1 289 180**	**854 030**	**1 091 360**	**237 330**	**28**	**792**	**Nicaragua, Afghanistan, Syria**
Selected non-OECD countries								
Bulgaria	11 253	2080	3460	10890	7 430	215	1 579	Afghanistan, Syria, Iraq
Romania	2 278	2460	6030	9070	3 040	50	474	Afghanistan, Syria, Bangladesh

Note: Figures for the United States until 2020 refer to "affirmative" claims submitted to the Department of Homeland Security (number of cases, multiplied by 1.5 to reflect the estimated number of persons) and "defensive" claims submitted to the Executive Office for Immigration Review (number of persons). ".." means that figures are not available.
Source: UNHCR; Eurostat; OECD International Migration Database.

StatLink https://stat.link/0p9a6w

For the OECD as a whole, the ratio of new asylum seekers to the total population stood at 792 per million in 2021. Costa Rica remains by far the OECD country with the highest ratio (21 000 per million). According to the UNHCR, in March 2022, Nicaraguan refugees and asylum seekers represented 3% of Costa Rica's population. Austria follows with 4 000, and Greece, Iceland, Luxembourg and Slovenia all received more than 2 000 asylum seekers per million inhabitants. Sweden, which was in the top three until 2019, ranked 16th in 2021 with a ratio of 1 000. Fifteen of the top 20 countries of origin of asylum seekers in 2021 were already in this list in 2019, before the COVID-19 pandemic spread across the world. Countries from Latin America and the Caribbean are found at both extreme of the scale in terms of evolution between 2020 and 2021 (Figure 1.7).

On the one hand, Colombia, Guatemala, El Salvador and Mexico are the only origin countries which saw fewer of their citizens seeking asylum in OECD countries in 2021 than in 2020. On the other hand, the largest increases in new applications are observed for nationals of Nicaragua and Haiti. More than 110 000 Nicaraguans applied for asylum in OECD countries in 2021, six times more than in 2020, and 66 000 Haitians, a fourfold increase. The number of asylum seekers from Afghanistan rose by 55% and exceeded 100 000 for the first time since 2017. 95 000 Syrians submitted an asylum application in an OECD country (+53%), still far from the 2015 and 2016 levels but representing 0.6% of the Syrian population. The number of requests from citizens of Iraq also increased by more than 50% to 39 000. With only 10 000 applications from its citizens, China ranked only 24th in 2021.

Figure 1.7. Top 20 origin countries of asylum applicants in OECD countries, 2020-21

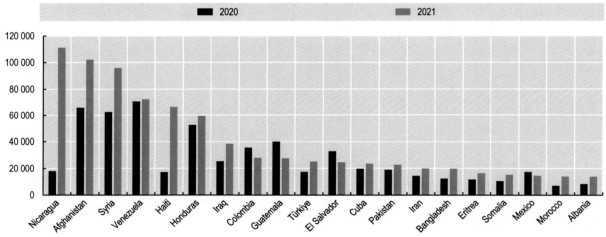

Source: UNHCR, Eurostat.

StatLink ⬛⬛⬛ https://stat.link/cwszq4

After the very sharp drop in 2020, grants of international protection increased by 3% overall in 2021 (Table 1.4), with large variations across destination countries. Indeed, while the number of new refugees more than doubled in Canada to over 60 000, and rebounded by 40% or more in France (+65% to 51 000), Italy (+45% to 31 000), Austria (+45% to 18 800), the Netherlands (+44% to 14 600), Belgium (+74% to 10 700), it fell by 50% or more in Australia, Greece and Spain. Germany remained the main country of new grants for international protection in 2021 with almost 100 000 positive decisions (4%).

Among other countries with over 10 000 new permanent humanitarian migrants, numbers went up in Mexico (+13%) and in Sweden (+4%) and decreased in the United States (-12%), the United Kingdom (-20%) and Switzerland (-7%). In Poland, the number of positive decisions almost reached 3 000, eight times more than in 2020, and the most since data was collection began.

Table 1.4. Positive decisions on applications for international protection and resettlements, 2011-21

	2011	2012	2013	2014	2015	2016	2017	2018	2019	2020	2021	2021/2020 change (%)
Australia	13 976	13 759	20 019	13 768	13 756	17 555	21 968	16 250	18 762	13 171	5 947	-55
Austria	5 870	6 000	6 345	10 425	18 510	31 950	29 510	20 700	13 730	12 985	18 780	+45
Belgium	5 575	5 880	6 810	8 560	11 175	15 850	14 205	11 130	7 180	6 205	10 770	+74
Canada	27 880	23 098	24 139	24 068	32 111	58 914	41 477	45 493	48 533	25 485	60 155	+136
Czech Republic	705	225	365	410	480	445	145	165	155	115	320	+178
Denmark	2 210	2 590	3 935	6 140	10 730	7 715	2 755	1 650	1 785	600	895	+49
Estonia	10	10	10	20	80	140	115	50	50	30	55	+83
Finland	1925	2 600	2 550	2 585	2 815	8 320	5 475	4 565	3 770	2 705	2 980	+10
France	10 870	14 425	16 245	21 090	26 635	35 770	43 190	47 005	47 720	30 725	50 800	+65
Germany	13 190	22 470	26 360	47 835	148 730	446 455	328 400	142 760	121 120	99 720	95 765	-4
Greece	590	625	1 410	3 850	5 875	8 545	12 015	15 805	18 595	35 775	18 420	-49
Hungary	205	460	420	560	470	435	1 290	365	60	130	40	-69
Iceland	10	20	15	45	100	170	220	245	455	580	345	-41
Ireland	195	195	290	590	730	1 145	1 115	1 615	2 335	1 725	2 390	+39
Italy	7 480	22 820	14 465	20 625	29 730	41 220	36 645	49 065	32 365	21 625	31 325	+45
Japan	287	130	175	144	125	143	94	104	101	91		
Korea	38	60	36	633	241	289	442	622	259	204	114	-44
Latvia	30	30	35	25	30	155	310	30	55	25	105	+320
Lithuania	25	60	60	75	90	220	350	160	90	85	450	+429
Luxembourg	85	45	140	160	255	820	1 310	1 015	705	765	860	+12
Mexico	262	389	198	348	615	1 760	3 335	5 756	7 903	18 122	20 403	+13
Netherlands	8 925	6 820	7 355	14 040	17 495	22 520	11 355	6 020	7 720	10 125	14 555	+44
New Zealand	2 741	3 032	3 385	3 551	3 784	4 021	4 149	4 191	3 615	2 289	1 572	-31
Norway	5 995	7 355	7 730	7 155	9 525	16 485	8 085	4 220	4 800	2 840	4 940	+74
Poland	575	590	735	740	695	380	560	435	275	365	2 930	+703
Portugal	95	115	135	125	235	330	670	660	545	95	305	+221
Slovak Republic	120	200	75	175	80	215	60	50	40	45	60	+33
Slovenia	20	35	35	45	50	175	150	135	100	90	20	-78
Spain	1 010	645	555	1 725	1 030	7 250	5 610	3 795	38 525	51 190	20 510	-60
Sweden	12 250	16 975	28 220	35 080	36 470	71 940	34 770	24 635	16 840	10 815	11 330	+5
Switzerland	6 800	4 580	6 605	15 575	14 745	13 955	15 455	16 630	12 055	11 120	10 310	-7
United Kingdom	13 003	11 434	21 274	17 944	20 089	18 854	24 101	30 882	22 700	31 975	25 578	-20
United States	168 460	150 614	119 630	134 242	151 995	157 425	146 003	185 909	107 057	63 888	56 389	-12
All countries	**311 125**	**318 156**	**319 581**	**392 209**	**559 351**	**991 423**	**795 240**	**642 008**	**539 899**	**455 614**	**469 418**	**+3**
All European countries	**97 481**	**127 074**	**151 999**	**215 455**	**356 724**	**751 316**	**577 772**	**383 683**	**353 669**	**332 364**	**324 838**	**-2**

Source: Eurostat, OECD International Migration Database.

StatLink ⧉ https://stat.link/gx4zku

At the regional level, European OECD countries altogether delivered 325 000 positive decisions of international protection in 2021. This is 2% less than in 2020, but only 8% below the 2019 level. Non-European OECD countries, despite a +17% increase to 145 000 grants, are still 22% under the 2019 figure.

Resettlement programmes are designed to transfer the most vulnerable refugees from a country of first asylum to another one which grants them protection. On average, since 1981, 106 000 refugees per year have benefited from resettlement to OECD countries. During the worst of the pandemic, transfers could not take place, so these programmes came to a halt. They were able to resume in 2021 but despite a 67%

jump, only 57 000 people in need of international protection were transferred to an OECD country, around half the pre-COVID-19 average.

Figure 1.8. Refugees admitted under resettlement programmes, 1981-2021

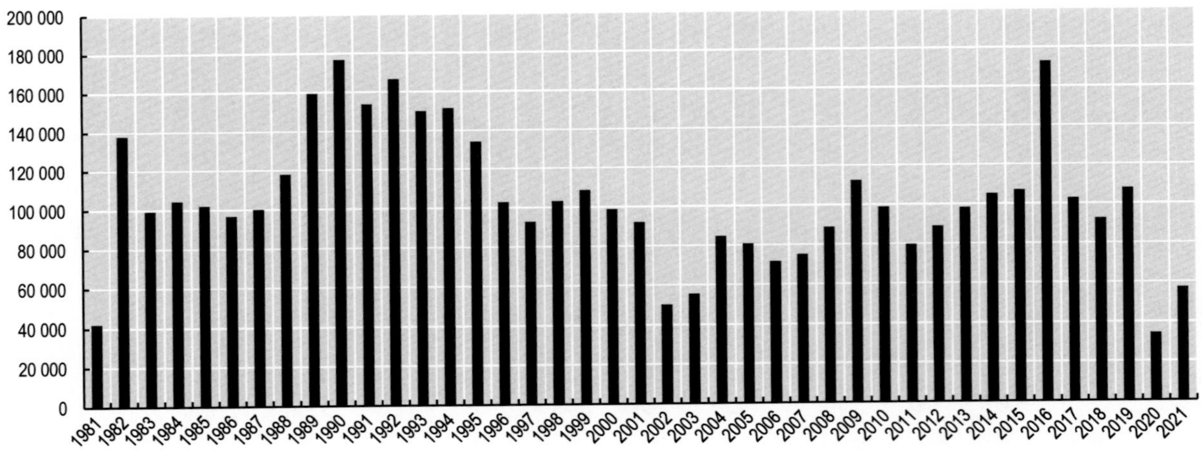

Note: Some data presented may differ from statistics published previously due to retroactive changes or the inclusion of previously unavailable data. More information about UNHCR's resettlement programme can be found at http://www.unhcr.org/resettlement.html.
Source: UNHCR.

StatLink https://stat.link/3tve8m

In 2021, Canada was back on top of the main resettlement countries, with more than 20 000 refugees received through this channel, more than a third of the total. This is also more than double the 2020 figure for Canada. The United States followed with 13 700 resettlement arrivals (+43%). Sweden registered 6 700 resettlements in 2021, twice as many as in the previous year and more than in any year before, and became the third resettlement country. Following the same pattern, Norway received a very high number of resettled refugees in 2021 (3 600, +138%). Australia, where travel restrictions were particularly severe and lasted all of 2021, is the only large destination country which saw a drop in 2021 (-9% to 3 300 resettlements) and was only the fifth main destination country, while it was regularly third in previous years.

China and India start to lose their lead as main origin countries

The COVID-19 pandemic and the resulting border closures led to a decrease in inflows from all top 20 countries of origin (Figure 1.9). This was due to lockdowns in the countries of origin as well as travel restrictions in both countries of origin and countries of destination. China and India, the two top countries of origin in 2019, experienced the sharpest decrease in outflows to OECD countries. In 2020, China and India each represented 5% of all migration flows to OECD countries, compared with 7% and 6% in 2019.

China lost the lead as largest sending country to the OECD to India. The inflow of immigrants from China dropped by more than 50% relative to 2019 to just over 230 000. This represents the lowest inflow of Chinese immigrants to OECD countries since 2000. The inflow of Chinese immigrants decreased by three-quarters to New Zealand and by two-thirds to Japan.

Migrant inflows from India decreased by 41% year on year, to approximately 230 000. The number of Indians received by the main destination countries, Canada and the United Kingdom, halved in 2020, and decreased sharply also in Germany (-44%).

Figure 1.9. Top 20 nationalities of origin of new immigrants to the OECD, 2019-20

Thousands

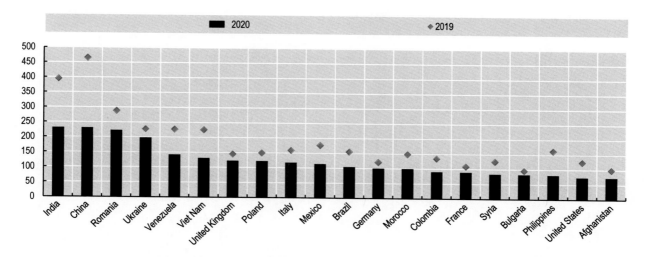

Note: Migration flows to Colombia, Greece and Ireland are not included. Migration flow series to Germany and Korea are adjusted to exclude short-term immigrants. 2020 migration flow data to Türkiye and the United Kingdom are estimated.
Source: OECD International Migration Database, https://doi.org/10.1787/data-00342-en.

StatLink ᠁᠌ https://stat.link/sf05j3

Romania is a close third in the top countries of origin with 223 000 new entries to OECD countries. The decrease in inflows for Romania was small relative to the decrease from China or India (-23%). In particular, the flow of Romanians to Germany, their main country of destination, remained close to 100 000, having decreased only by 11% from 2019 to 2020.

Ukraine displayed a small decline in outflows in 2020 (-12%) and consolidated its position as the fourth country of origin. From 2017 to 2019, inflows to OECD countries from Ukraine increased by more than 40%. Almost 200 000 Ukrainians immigrated to OECD countries in 2020, 55% of them to Poland. Migration flows from Ukraine to Poland remained at a similar level in 2020 relative to 2019 (+2.4%).

Emigration from Venezuela to OECD countries dropped by 37% in 2020 but remained higher than in any year prior to 2019. Other significant drops in flows in 2020 include the sharp decrease of migration from the Philippines, mainly to Canada, and from Cuba, mainly to the United States. Among the top 50 countries of origin, only the Slovak Republic showed an increase in 2020 (+13%), led by a surge in outflows to Hungary (6 000).

Size and composition of foreign-born populations in OECD countries

Foreign-born population continued to rise during the pandemic

Despite the pandemic, the foreign-born population living in OECD countries continued to rise in 2021. The foreign-born population reached 138 million, which represents 10.6% of the total population of OECD countries.

The United States is the main country of residence of immigrants in OECD countries, hosting almost a third of the immigrant population. While the foreign-born population in the United States had plateaued since 2018, it increased from 2020 to 2021, reaching almost 45 million by January 2021. Germany ranks second, hosting almost 14 million immigrants, and the United Kingdom ranks third, with over 9 million foreign-born residents.

Almost half of the foreign-born population in the OECD lives in Europe. EU OECD countries host 37% of the total foreign-born population, and other European OECD countries account for another 10%. A fifth of the foreign-born population lives in a country outside the United States and Europe, mainly in Canada (6%), Australia (5%), Türkiye (2%) and Japan (2%).

Figure 1.10. Distribution of the foreign-born population in OECD countries, 2021

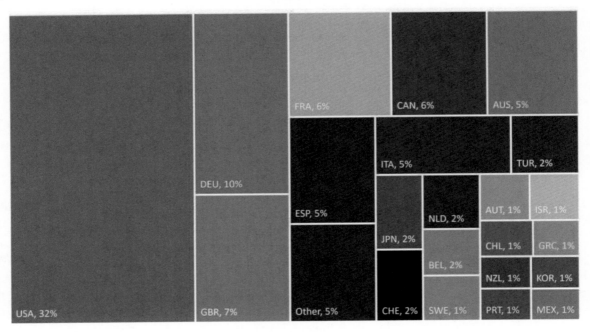

Note: Japanese and Korean data refer to the foreign population.
Source: OECD International Migration Database, https://doi.org/10.1787/data-00342-en.

StatLink 🔗 https://stat.link/1lvthx

Between 2015 and 2021, the share of immigrants in the population increased in almost all OECD countries. The average share was 14.3% in 2021, up from 12.6% in 2015.

In 2021, the foreign-born population represented 20% or more of the total population in nine OECD countries. These are Luxembourg (48%), Switzerland (30%), the settlement countries – Australia (29%), New Zealand (27%) and Canada (21%) – as well as Israel, Austria and Sweden (20%).

The countries with the largest increases since 2015 in the share of the population that is foreign-born are Iceland (+8 percentage points), Luxembourg (+5 percentage points) and Chile (+5 percentage points). The increase in the share of the foreign-born population in Luxembourg follows a longer-term trend. The share of immigrants in the population in Chile tripled in this period, driven partly by the recent arrival of Venezuelans, who now account for a third of the foreign-born population.

The immigrant population increased also significantly in Sweden (+3.7 percentage points) and Germany (+2.9 percentage points), partly due to humanitarian inflows in the mid-2010s. Other countries with a significant increase in the share of immigrants in this period are Austria, New Zealand, Portugal and Spain, with increases close to 3 percentage points.

Figure 1.11. The foreign-born as a percentage of the total population in OECD countries, 2015 and 2021

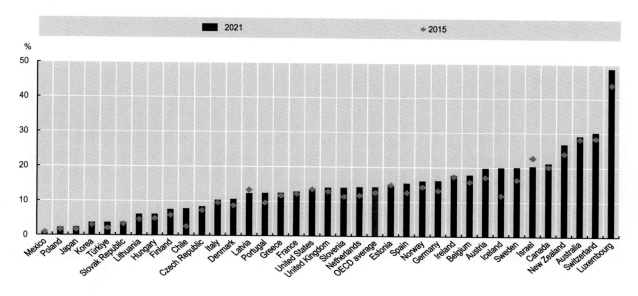

Note: Data refer to 2015, or closest available year, and to 2021, or most recent available year. The OECD average is a simple average of the rates presented in this figure. For Japan and Korea, the data refer to the foreign population rather than the foreign-born population.
Source: OECD International Migration Database, Eurostat, UNDESA.

StatLink 〰️🔢 https://stat.link/o72j9k

Men still account for more than half of migration flows but their share decreased in 2020

In 2020, two-thirds of OECD countries received more migrant men than women. However, the average share of men among new migrants to OECD countries declined and stood at 55.5%, compared with 56.2% over the preceding five-year period.

The gender composition of migrants differs across countries and is partly driven by the composition of migration inflows. Countries with a large share of men among new immigrants are typically countries with relatively large labour migration inflows, such as countries in Central and Eastern Europe and Korea. The United States remained the country with the lowest share of men in its migrant inflows in 2020 (46.2%).

Several countries saw significant declines in the share of men in migration flows. In Slovenia, men represented 64.1% of migration flows in 2020, 3.3 percentage points below the 2015-20 average. In the Slovak Republic, Poland and Iceland the drop stood between 2 and 4 points, and reached 5 points in Greece, which registered the sharpest decline. Among countries with relatively low percentages of men among new immigrants, the largest decline was seen in Korea with 5 points compared to 2015-20, with women now a majority of Korea's inflows (50.9%). Flows to the United Kingdom also comprised fewer men than women in 2020 (48.3% of men, − 2.7 points). In Latvia, on the other hand, the already high proportion of men increased in 2020 to almost 75%.

Figure 1.12. Share of men in overall migration flows to OECD countries, 2015-20

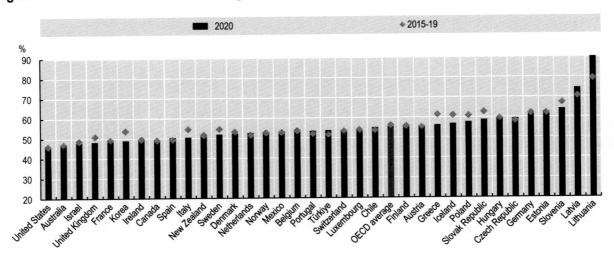

Note: The OECD average is the average of the countries featured in the figure above. For Chile, data refer to 2016 instead of 2020, for Canada, Mexico, Türkiye and the United Kingdom, data refer to 2019 instead of 2020.
Source: OECD International Migration Database, https://doi.org/10.1787/data-00342-en.

StatLink ᐊᗕᔆᒧ https://stat.link/14dowh

Record acquisitions of citizenship in OECD countries in 2021

According to preliminary and partial data, the number of acquisitions of citizenship in OECD countries in 2021 could be the highest ever recorded, at 2.3 million (Figure 1.13). This represents a 20% increase, partly due to a processing of backlogged applications during the COVID-19 pandemic.

Figure 1.13. Acquisitions of citizenships in OECD countries, 2000-21

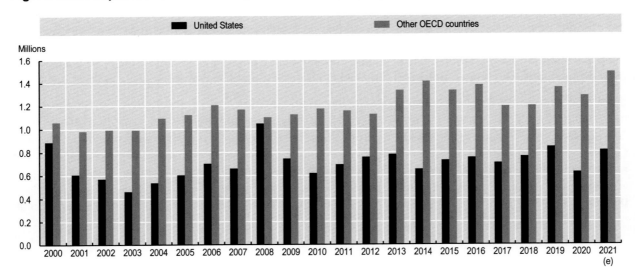

Note: The estimation for 2021 is based on preliminary data for 17 OECD countries accounting for 87% of the 2020 total.
Source: OECD International Migration database, https://doi.org/10.1787/data-00342-en.

StatLink ᐊᗕᔆᒧ https://stat.link/rg4ukb

Among countries for which 2021 data are available, strong increases have been registered in the United States (+186 000, +30%), the United Kingdom (+60 000, +46%), Canada (+24 000, +22%), in Norway – where citizenship acquisitions more than doubled (+21 000, +109%) – and in Austria (+7 000, +80%). Surprisingly, some countries saw declines in naturalisation numbers in 2021. This is the case of Luxembourg (-26%) and Finland (-15%), both countries where naturalisations have been declining for several years, and of Denmark (-8%), which had seen a high level in 2019.

Figure 1.14. Acquisitions of citizenship as a percentage of foreign population, 2019-20

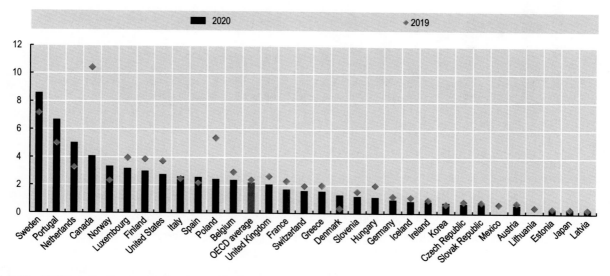

Note: The OECD average is the average of the countries featured in the figure above.
Source: OECD International Migration Database, https://doi.org/10.1787/data-00342-en.

StatLink 🔗 https://stat.link/u9qpnk

Among OECD countries, on average, 2.2% of the foreign population acquired host-country citizenship in 2020 (Figure 1.14). This is a similar share as in 2019.

In 2020, Sweden again became the OECD country in which the largest share of foreigners acquired host country nationality. Almost 9% of its foreign residents became Swedish citizens, substantially more than in 2019. Portugal and the Netherlands followed with respectively 6.7% and 5%, each representing a 1.7 percentage point increase. Canada ranked first in 2019, but the share of foreign residents who became Canadian citizens was only 4% in 2020, down from more than 10% in 2019.

Figure 1.15. Acquisitions of nationality in OECD countries: Top 20 countries of former nationality, 2010 and 2020

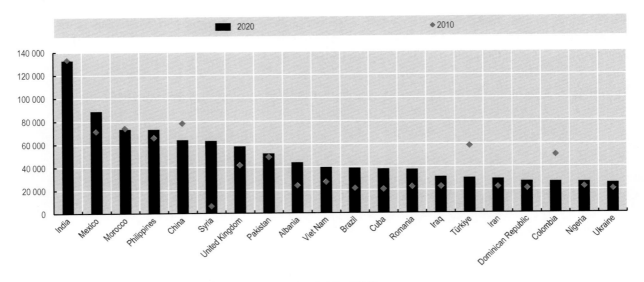

Source: OECD International Migration Database, https://doi.org/10.1787/data-00342-en.

StatLink https://stat.link/xft54k

India has long been the top origin nationality of new citizens of OECD countries and remained in first position in 2020 with over 130 000 grants of citizenship (Figure 1.15). More than half of these grants took place in only three countries: the United States (47 000), Canada (15 000) and the United Kingdom (11 000).

Mexicans remain the second top nationality despite the severe drop of naturalisations in the United States, their main country of destination. Morocco, the Philippines and China follow as the other main nationalities of origin.

The number of Syrians acquiring an OECD citizenship has increased every year between 2014 and 2021 following the large humanitarian inflows around 2015. Over this 8-year period, 100 000 Syrians became citizens in Sweden alone.

Recent trends in labour market outcomes for immigrants in the OECD area

In 2021, the labour market situation of immigrants improved in most OECD countries

Although the COVID-19 pandemic put an end to ten years of continuous improvement in the labour market situation of immigrants in OECD countries, in 2021 the latter had almost fully returned to their pre-crisis employment levels. Overall, the labour market situation of immigrants deteriorated more sharply in 2020 than that of their native-born counterparts, but improved more as the economy recovered in 2021. The employment rate of immigrants in OECD countries increased from 67.9% in 2020 to 69.4% in 2021, 0.5 percentage point lower than before the health crisis. Their unemployment rate fell from 10.3% to 9.1%, but is still 0.7 percentage points higher than before the pandemic (Table 1.5).

In 2021, the employment rate of immigrants in OECD countries was on average 1 percentage point lower than that of the native-born, and the unemployment rate was 3 percentage points higher. However, in more than half of countries, this gap had narrowed significantly in 2021. Indeed, the more prominent increase in the labour market outcomes of immigrants in 2021 – observed in at least two-thirds of OECD countries –

led to a narrowing of the gap with the native-born. One reason for this is the cyclical nature of the jobs held by immigrants (OECD, 2019[2]). Because the labour market outcomes of immigrants are more sensitive to cyclical variations, a period of economic expansion or recovery, such as in 2021, leads to a decrease in the employment and unemployment gaps between immigrants and the native-born.

This trend towards an improvement in the employment situation of immigrants in 2021 varied across host countries, depending in particular on the extent to which each country maintained employment safeguards and health restrictions in 2021. Despite an overall reduction, a gap in the employment rate between immigrants and the native-born still persists, particularly in Western Europe, in contrast to other OECD countries such as the United States and Latin American countries where migrants have higher employment rates than the native-born. In the EU27, the employment rate of the native-born remains 4.5 percentage points higher than that of immigrants. In most OECD countries, immigrants are also more likely to be unemployed than the native-born, again with the exception of the United States where the labour market is particularly flexible, and immigrants are more mobile than their native-born counterparts.

The employment rate of immigrants increased in more than seven out of ten OECD countries between 2020 and 2021, and almost half of OECD countries recorded an increase in the foreign-born employment rate compared to the pre-crisis situation. The increase in the employment rate of the migrant population since 2019 is particularly significant in Poland (+6 percentage points), Denmark (+4 percentage points) and New Zealand (+3 percentage points). In Poland, this dramatic increase can be explained in part by the substantial decrease in the number of immigrants, due to both a reduction in temporary immigration and an increase in out-migration. On the other hand, only eight OECD countries experienced an increase in the employment rate and a concomitant decrease in the unemployment rate (Australia, France, Poland, Portugal, Greece, Luxembourg, New Zealand and Denmark).

In several countries, the improvement in the employment rate of immigrants in 2021 was not enough to offset the negative impact of the 2020 crisis. This is particularly the case in the United States, where employment support mechanisms were limited (OECD, 2022[3]), and immigrants are largely concentrated in sectors and regions with high unemployment. Indeed, despite a substantial increase in the labour market outcomes of immigrants between 2020 and 2021, their employment rate remains significantly lower than in 2019 and their unemployment rate higher (Table 1.5). Nevertheless, in 2021, the number of immigrants fell sharply in areas of high unemployment while it rose in areas of lower unemployment, suggesting greater mobility of migrants to areas with greater employment opportunities (Capps, 2021[4]).

While the situation for the native-born has returned to or exceeded the pre-crisis level, a decline in the employment rate of immigrants compared to 2019 can also be observed in the three Baltic States, Iceland, Switzerland, the Slovak Republic, Italy, Spain, and to a lesser extent Germany (Table 1.5). In most of these countries, this has been accompanied by a worsening of their unemployment rate, as well as a decline in their participation rate. The deterioration of this situation reflects the persistence of the factors that led to the downturn in economic activity during the health crisis, with a greater impact on migrants. In Spain, Italy and Germany, the number of migrants employed in the hospitality sector decreased during the crisis, and the increase in migrant employment in other sectors did not offset this loss. In the Baltic States, the decline in the employment rate of the immigrant population may also be the result of a cohort effect – many 55-64 year-old migrants have left the labour market – and the worsening situation for younger people who have become inactive.

Finally, the employment rate of immigrants residing in Latin American countries, where job retention schemes were limited, remains significantly lower than in 2019. However, the impact of the crisis on the native-born in these countries has been even more acute.

Table 1.5. Labour market situation of immigrants in OECD countries in 2021

| | 2021 | | Change 2021-20 | | Change 2021-19 | | Gap with the native-born in 2021 | |
| | Percentages | | Percentage points | | Percentage points | | Percentage points | |
	Unemployment rate	Employment rate	Unemployment rate	Employment rate	Unemployment rate	Employment rate	Unemployment rate	Employment rate
Australia	5.3	74.2	-1.8	+3.2	-0.2	+1.9	+0.1	-1.5
Austria	11.3	67.6	-0.4	+1.6	+2.5	-1.3	+6.6	-6.3
Belgium	11.0	59.4	+0.4	+1.9	+0.5	+0.7	+5.9	-7.4
Canada	8.5	72.9	-2.4	+4.4	+2.2	-0.3	+1.5	-0.5
Chile*	10.2	69.8	-	-	-	-	-2.8	+16.2
Colombia	6.0	65.5	-11.4	+4.1	-8.8	-2.3	-0.2	+5.1
Costa Rica	18.0	62.1	-2.5	+1.9	+5.6	-5.2	+1.5	+5.5
Czech Rep.	3.3	79.8	+0.3	+0.5	+0.5	+0.6	+0.5	+5.7
Denmark	7.3	70.0	-1.3	+3.3	-1.1	+4.3	+2.6	-6.3
Estonia	9.7	71.2	+1.4	-4.2	+3.5	-4.1	+3.6	-3.2
Finland	13.7	66.2	+0.1	+0.9	+1.6	+2.8	+6.6	-7.2
France	12.3	61.1	-0.3	+1.3	-0.8	+1.5	+5.1	-7.1
Germany**	6.5	68.3	-0.6	+1.4	+0.7	-1.6	+3.5	-9.4
Greece	23.0	54.9	-6.9	+4.2	-6.6	+2.0	+8.8	-2.5
Hungary	3.4	80.3	-1.9	+3.6	+0.8	+0.6	-0.7	+7.4
Iceland	10.8	77.0	-0.9	+1.7	+6.1	-5.4	+5.6	-3.5
Ireland	7.5	71.8	+0.0	+4.4	+1.6	+0.4	+1.6	+2.6
Israel	4.6	77.9	+0.3	-0.4	+1.2	-1.2	-0.0	+13.8
Italy	13.1	59.3	+0.4	+1.5	+0.1	-2.1	+4.0	+1.2
Korea	5.9	67.6	-1.5	+1.3	+0.7	-0.5	+2.2	+0.3
Latvia	8.0	67.1	-1.8	-3.7	+1.0	-3.3	+0.1	-3.1
Lithuania	10.0	68.2	+1.1	-2.4	+4.3	-3.7	+2.7	-4.4
Luxembourg	5.9	72.8	-2.3	+1.8	-0.8	+0.8	+1.8	+8.0
Mexico	5.4	51.7	-1.1	+4.3	+0.1	-1.5	+1.1	-9.4
Netherlands	7.9	66.8	-0.8	-0.5	+0.1	-0.9	+4.3	-15.9
New Zealand	3.2	80.8	-1.2	+2.7	-0.4	+3.0	-1.1	+3.6
Norway	8.9	70.2	+0.1	+2.2	+1.5	+0.4	+5.6	-7.8
Poland	5.1	80.4	+0.3	+4.0	-0.6	+6.2	+1.7	+10.2
Portugal	7.0	76.9	-2.0	+3.2	-1.7	+1.3	+0.4	+7.4
Slovak Republic	8.1	73.7	+1.9	+0.4	-	-7.3	+1.2	+4.3
Slovenia	6.7	67.6	-0.3	-1.0	+0.9	+0.1	+2.1	-4.3
Spain	21.6	60.4	-1.8	+3.0	+2.7	-2.3	+8.3	-2.9
Sweden	19.4	64.9	-0.1	+1.9	+3.4	-0.5	+13.8	-14.1
Switzerland	8.1	75.2	+0.6	-1.8	+0.8	-1.9	+4.3	-6.3
Türkiye***	15.8	40.1	+1.2	-4.1	+1.2	-4.1	+2.5	-7.6
United Kingdom	4.4	75.5	-0.0	-0.2	+1.0	+0.4	+1.2	+0.1
United States	5.6	70.0	-3.4	+3.0	+2.5	-2.2	+0.1	+2.3
OECD average	**9.1**	**69.4**	**+0.7**	**+1.5**	**+0.7**	**-0.6**	**+3.0**	**-1.1**
OECD total	**8.5**	**68.8**	**-1.8**	**+2.3**	**+1.7**	**-1.1**	**+2.6**	**+1.7**
EU27	**11.9**	**64.5**	**-0.7**	**+1.9**	**+0.6**	**-0.3**	**+5.5**	**-4.5**

Note: Gap with the native-born refers to the difference between the corresponding rates of foreign-born and native-born. OECD total is a weighted average and OECD average a simple average. The employment and unemployment rates of the native and foreign-born populations in the European Union countries in 2019 and 2020 have been adjusted for the break in series caused by the change in methodology of the European Union Labour Force Survey (EU-LFS) in 2021. The calculations were made by the OECD Secretariat using the adjusted series for the whole population provided by Eurostat. (*) Data for Chile refers to 2020. (**) Changes in the survey methodology for Germany, as well as technical problems related to the COVID-19 pandemic, led to a break in series in 2020. Accordingly, the German data for 2020 and 2021 are preliminary and may be revised going forward. The unemployment rate in Germany for 2020 is estimated for the population aged 15-74. (***) Data for Türkiye refer to 2020 instead of 2021 and the change refers to 2019 compared to 2020. Rates for Korea are estimated for the population aged 15-59 and refer to foreigners and immigrants who have been naturalised in the past 5 years, versus nationals. The OECD average excludes Chile and Türkiye for which 2021 data are not available, and Germany, for which 2020 data are not available.

Source: European countries and Türkiye: Labour Force Surveys (Eurostat); Australia, Canada, Israel; New Zealand, United Kingdom: Labour Force Surveys; Chile: *Encuesta de Caracterización Socioeconómica Nacional* (CASEN); Colombia: *Gran Encuesta Integrada de Hogares* (GEIH); Mexico: *Encuesta Nacional de Ocupación y Empleo* (ENOE); United States: Current Population Surveys.

StatLink https://stat.link/e2d9vy

While the labour force participation rate of immigrants had declined in 2020, mainly as a result of the many lockdowns that limited their availability and prevented effective job searches, an increase was recorded in 2021 in the majority of OECD countries, except for the Baltic States, Colombia, Slovenia and Switzerland. On average, 75.9% of immigrants were active in the labour market in 2021 compared to 74.6% in 2020. Moreover, the gap with the native-born narrowed slightly in 2021: the labour force participation of migrants is on average 0.6 percentage points higher than that of the native-born and almost half of OECD countries have a higher participation rate among migrants than among the native-born. This gap is particularly high in Poland (12 percentage points), Portugal (8 points), Luxembourg, Hungary and the Czech Republic.

The risk of long-term unemployment for migrants increased as a result of the crisis

Despite this improvement, the COVID-19 pandemic has led to an increase in the risk of long-term unemployment for migrants as well as for the native-born. After a steady decline, the long-term unemployment rate of active immigrants has increased for the first time in a decade in Canada, the United States and Europe. In times of crisis, immigrants face greater difficulties finding a job and are therefore more vulnerable to long-term unemployment because of their less developed networks, their poorer language skills, their concentration in the most exposed sectors, and the hiring discrimination they may face, which increases in times of crisis (OECD, 2009[5]). This last factor also plays a role in the higher probability of migrants being laid off during the pandemic. Auer (2022[6]) highlights the evidence of discrimination in firms in Germany during the first wave of COVID-19: after controlling for sectoral effects, migrants have a higher probability of being fired while people born in Germany are more likely to be included in short-time working schemes. While demand for labour is decreasing, many individuals are discouraged in their job search. These factors favour an increase in long-term unemployment, which can have major repercussions on future labour market outcomes (OECD, 2021[7]).

In the United States, 1.3% of foreign-born were unemployed for more than 12 months in 2021, almost 1 percentage point more than in 2019. More striking is the reversal of the trend: while this proportion was slightly higher among native-born before the crisis, migrants are now more likely to be in long-term unemployment. In the EU27 countries, the incidence of long-term unemployment for immigrants rose from 1.8% in 2020 to 2.3% in 2021, a higher share than that of the native-born population, with immigrant women being even more likely to be in long-term unemployment. In Canada, the long-term unemployment rate has also worsened more significantly for immigrants than for their native-born counterparts.

Box 1.1. Changes in the number of hours worked by migrants since the beginning of the health crisis

A closer look at the changes in the average number of hours worked by migrants since the beginning of the pandemic helps round out the analysis in this chapter. The outbreak of the COVID-19 pandemic led to a substantial decrease in the number of hours worked for the population as a whole, but much more markedly for migrants, who were over-represented in the sectors most affected by the crisis. On average in the EU27 countries, migrants saw the number of hours they worked fall by 17% between the second quarter of 2019 and the second quarter of 2020, compared with 12% for the native-born. In the second quarter of 2020, 20% of employed migrants reported not working (an 8 percentage points increase compared to the first quarter), while this was the case for 16% of the employed native-born population. The number of hours increased in the third quarter of 2020, as the first wave of the pandemic subsided.

By the fourth quarter of 2021, migrants had on average almost regained the number of hours worked pre-crisis: in the EU27 countries, the average number of hours worked by migrants fell by 4% in the fourth quarter of 2019, while it shrank by 3% among the native-born population as a whole. However,

---

44 |

this average hides significant disparities between EU countries. In Belgium, Estonia, Lithuania, Portugal and the Slovak Republic, the average number of hours worked by employed migrants remains 10% to 18% lower than before the crisis (Figure 1.16). In contrast, the native-born in these countries are working almost as much as before the crisis, except in Belgium and Portugal. However, in some countries where migrants have returned to relatively similar working hours as prior to the pandemic (Hungary, Iceland, Luxembourg, Norway and Spain), there has been a reduction in the number of hours worked by the native-born. In addition, the number of hours worked by migrants has increased in Denmark, Poland, Slovenia and Sweden.

In the second quarter of 2020, the number of hours worked by migrant women fell immediately, more significantly than for their male counterparts and for native-born women. Indeed, school closures created an even greater domestic and family workload for women. On the other hand, women, especially migrant women, were over-represented in "front line" jobs, and their working hours increased steeply from the third quarter of 2020 onwards. Nevertheless, in Figure 1.16 the analysis reveals both a continuation of the effects of the crisis on the situation of women in the fourth quarter of 2021 in some European countries (Hungary, Estonia, Portugal, Belgium, Austria) and a substantial increase in the average number of hours worked compared to pre-crisis levels in Nordic countries such as Denmark (+3%), Finland (+17%) or Sweden (+7%) and in Eastern European countries such as Slovenia (+25%) and Poland (+9%). These countries also recorded the highest increases in the participation rate of migrant women, some of whom had to make up for the potential loss of spousal income due to the crisis. These trends could suggest better future labour market integration prospects for migrant women.

Finally, data on changes to the number of hours worked by migrants also indicate a sharper decline in the working hours of young people, individuals with a low level of educational attainment, and those on temporary contracts.

Figure 1.16. Change in the average number of hours worked in OECD European countries, by place of birth and gender, Q4 2019-Q4 2021

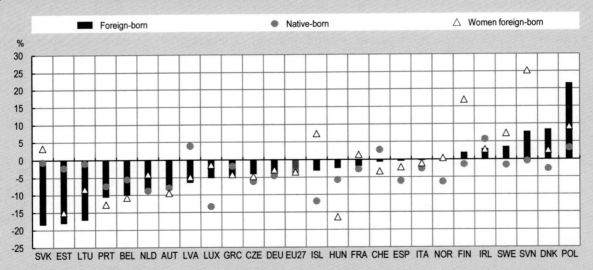

Note: The data correspond to the weekly number of hours actually worked. A change in the methodology of the Labour Force Survey caused a break in series in 2021. The data on the number of hours worked are not adjusted.
Source: Labour Force Surveys (Eurostat).

StatLink https://stat.link/9jw563

Post COVID-19 changes in the labour market outcomes of migrants differ according to certain socio-demographic characteristics

Improved labour market integration of women compared to 2019

Studies have shown that the pandemic has had a greater impact on the employment outcomes of migrant women, mainly due to their over-representation in the sectors most affected by the crisis, but also as a result of the increased domestic workload, school closures and the greater difficulty they have in teleworking (Fasani and Mazza, 2020[8]). That said, an examination of changes in the labour market outcomes of the migrant population by gender between 2019 and 2021 does not reveal any particularly striking differences between women and men, with the exception of the United Kingdom where the employment rate of migrant women is well above its pre-crisis level while that of their male counterparts remains significantly lower (Figure 1.17). In Australia and Canada, the labour market situation of migrant women has also improved more than that of migrant men and native-born women. Conversely, in the EU27 countries, the employment rate of migrant men improved more than for their female counterparts in 2021 (Annex Figure 1.A.3).

The increase in the employment rate of migrant women was particularly significant in the Nordic countries and some Eastern European countries, such as Poland (+13 percentage points) and Slovenia (+6 percentage points), while the employment rate of migrant men increased more strongly in Austria, Greece and the three Baltic States. Likewise, an increase of more than 5 percentage points in the labour market participation rate of migrant women has been observed in several Nordic and Eastern European countries. This could reflect an increase in the number of previously inactive women joining the labour market to make up for the potential loss of spousal income, as is the case in the Nordic countries. (Sánchez Gassen, 2021[9]). Only Colombia, Estonia, Italy and the Slovak Republic recorded a decline in the labour force participation of migrant women of more than 1 percentage point.

Furthermore, foreign-born women residing in Australia and the United Kingdom, have now reached their highest employment rate of the last 20 years. Although the employment rate of migrant men remains substantially higher than that of women, the gap narrowed in 2021 in Australia, Canada and the United Kingdom. This is not the case in the United States, where the gap – of 22 percentage points in 2021 – has always been particularly high (see Annex Figure 1.A.2).

Figure 1.17. Changes in the employment rate by demographic group and country of birth in selected OECD countries, between 2019 and 2021

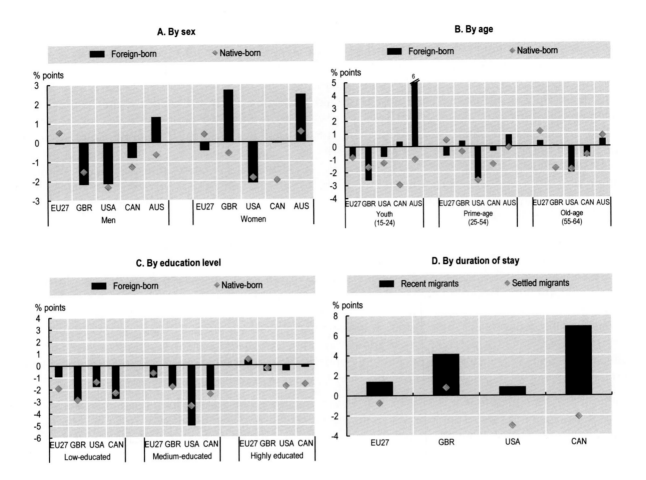

Note: The reference population is the working age population (aged 15-64). "Low-educated" refers to less than upper secondary education, "Medium" to upper secondary and post-secondary non-tertiary education, and "Highly" to tertiary education. The employment rates of the native-born and foreign-born populations in the EU27 countries in 2019 and 2020 have been adjusted for the break in series caused by the change in methodology of the European Union Labour Force Survey (EU-LFS) in 2021. Calculations have been made by the Secretariat using the adjusted series for the whole population provided by Eurostat. EU27 does not include the United Kingdom.

Source: European countries: Labour Force Surveys (Eurostat); Australia, Canada, United Kingdom: Labour Force Surveys; United States: Current Population Surveys.

StatLink 🔗 https://stat.link/0kjv4y

Employment of young migrants has increased compared to 2020 but remains below the pre-crisis level

People aged 15-24, whether native-born or foreign-born, are more vulnerable in the labour market than the general population as a result of the COVID-19 pandemic, mainly because they are over-represented in the sectors most affected by the crisis, are more likely to work on fixed-term contracts, and have less work experience, which puts them at a higher risk of losing their job (OECD, 2021[10]). Disruption to training programmes and apprenticeships is another factor affecting the transition from education to the labour market. In addition to these difficulties, which are common to all young people, young migrants face specific structural barriers. In 2019 and still in 2021, they are for example more likely than their native-born counterparts to work part-time or in temporary jobs.

Generally speaking, despite all these factors, the negative impact of the crisis on the employment rate of young immigrants has not been more marked than for the rest of the immigrant population and their native-born counterparts – except in Australia and Canada (Figure 1.17). Indeed, in Europe, the United Kingdom and to a lesser extent the United States, the employment rate of young people (aged 15-24) has declined to a similar extent to that of non-migrants. In Canada and Australia, the employment rate of migrant youth has even improved and the gap with native-born youth has been narrowing since 2019 (Figure 1.17). Australia put in place a number of measures to support young people during and after the COVID-19 pandemic, including an incentive scheme to hire young people between October 2020 and October 2021 (the JobMaking Hiring Credit), measures to promote the recruitment of apprentices, and the expansion and strengthening of programmes to support the transition to employment (OECD, 2021[10]). Similar measures were put in place in the majority of OECD countries, which has helped to mitigate the lasting effects of the crisis on young people. However, the significant improvement in their labour market situation between 2020 and 2021 (see Annex Figure 1.A.3), has not been enough to offset the negative effects of the crisis, and the employment rate of young immigrants remains, on the whole, below the pre-crisis level.

In the EU27 countries, the share of young people not in education, employment or training (NEET rate) decreased in 2021 among the migrant population while it slightly increased among the native-born population (Figure 1.18). However, the NEET rate for migrants has increased in the Czech Republic, Luxembourg and Norway. In the United States and Canada, the NEET rate for young migrants had increased significantly by 2020 and for the first time in 10 years. In 2021, this rate decreased from 18% to 15% in the United States, a rate still 2 percentage points higher than in 2019. Since the beginning of the crisis, most OECD countries have introduced measures to encourage the hiring of apprentices and vocational training. Some countries, notably France, Sweden, Poland, Austria, Chile and New Zealand, have implemented specific measures targeting vulnerable young people or those from disadvantaged backgrounds – including migrants (OECD, 2021[10]).

Finally, highly educated migrants across OECD countries have almost regained their pre-crisis employment rate, while the situation for low and medium-educated migrants remains significantly worse than in 2019 (Figure 1.17).

Figure 1.18. Share of young people not in education, employment or training ("NEET"), by place of birth, in selected OECD countries, 2019-21

Population aged 15-24

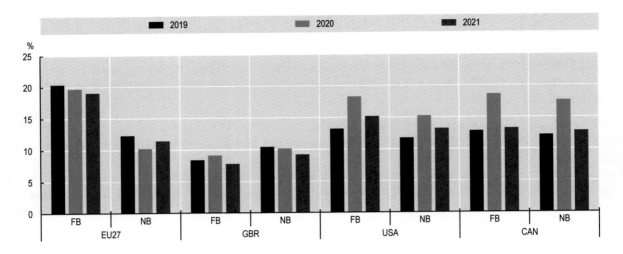

Note: The NEET rates of the native and foreign-born populations in the 27EU countries in 2019 and 2020 have been adjusted for the break in series caused by the change in methodology of the European Union Labour Force Survey (EU-LFS) in 2021. Calculations have been made by the OECD Secretariat taking into account the adjusted series for the whole population provided by Eurostat.
Source: European countries: Labour Force Surveys (Eurostat); Canada: Labour Force Surveys; United States: Current Population Surveys; United Kingdom: National Labour Force Survey.

StatLink ＝￭￭ＳＰ https://stat.link/y1fvrl

The labour market situation of recently arrived migrants significantly improved in 2021

The negative impact of the health crisis on migrant employment in 2020 was, paradoxically, less pronounced for recent immigrants (who arrived in the country less than five years ago) than for settled migrants. Overall, the improvement in the employment situation for recently arrived immigrants in the host country was also much more significant in 2021 (Figure 1.17). In the EU27 countries, the employment rate of recent immigrants increased by 2.3 percentage points between 2020 and 2021, a 1.4 percentage point increase compared to 2019. In contrast, the less marked improvement in the employment situation of immigrants who have been in the country for more than five years in 2021 has not made up for the deleterious effect of COVID-19 in 2020. Similarly, Canada and the United States recorded a dramatic increase of 8 and 6 percentage points respectively in the employment rate of recently arrived immigrants in 2021, exceeding the pre-pandemic level, while the employment rate of longer-settled immigrants declined compared to 2019 (Figure 1.17). In Canada, the number of recently arrived immigrants in employment increased by 71% between 2020 and 2021, while the number of settled migrants in employment increased by only 5%. In the United States, these increases were 35% and 2% respectively.

However, recent immigrants are less likely to remain in employment than their counterparts who have been in the country for more than five years. In European countries, 66% of settled immigrants are in employment compared to 55% of recent immigrants. The unemployment rate of recent immigrants is also higher, with the exception of the United States where it is similar (6%).

There are several factors behind these results. First, the health crisis in 2020 led to a significant decrease in migration flows and in particular in the number of arrivals of migrants with a weak connection to the labour market, such as asylum seekers, refugees and, in several countries, family migrants. In addition, exemptions to the entry restrictions imposed by OECD countries in 2020 and 2021 were granted primarily for work-related reasons, notably in the health, agriculture and transport sectors. In response to labour shortages, some OECD countries have also allowed expansion of work rights for asylum seekers already in the country, particularly in the agricultural sector. This is the case in Spain, where they can be employed six months after submitting an application for international protection. Since December 2020, the United States has also allowed temporary migrants in the agricultural sector to extend their visas and to start working before their new visas are officially approved (EMN/OECD, 2021[11]).

At the same time, the COVID-19 pandemic led to increased outflows of recently arrived immigrants in some OECD countries. Some studies suggest that the immigrants most likely to return to their country of origin are recent immigrants with weaker labour market ties or who lost their jobs during the pandemic. In Norway, the reduction in the number of posted workers during the pandemic mitigated the impact on employment of resident immigrants and native-born (Bratsberg and Raaum, forthcoming[12]).

Disparities in terms of labour market integration based on origins persist in 2021

The labour market situation of foreign-born varies significantly depending on their place of origin. Several factors can explain these variations. The characteristics of the migrant population, such as the share of women, young people, low or highly educated individuals, differ depending on the region of origin. In addition, the degree of language proficiency of migrants and the recognition of foreign diplomas by the host country are other decisive factors for their labour market integration and vary significantly from one region to another. Finally, these disparities also result from the types of migration waves, which influence migrants' status and duration of stay, as for example in the case of humanitarian migration waves. In addition, some studies have revealed a more significant negative effect of the health crisis on ethnic minorities (Fasani and Mazza, 2020[8]; OECD, 2022[13]), which may indicate a higher vulnerability due to labour market discrimination, but also structural effects due to their over-representation in sectors exposed to the crisis. So the effects of the pandemic may not just vary between migrants and native-born, but also between different migrant groups.

The analysis of the changes in employment, unemployment and participation rates by region of origin in 2021 has shown that the employment situation of migrants in 2021 improved in most OECD countries. However, the extent to which this improvement has enabled migrants to regain a similar or better employment situation than before the COVID-19 pandemic varies significantly depending on the region of origin (Table 1.6).

Compared to the pre-crisis level, the employment rate of immigrants from Sub-Saharan Africa, North Africa and the Middle East has increased more than that of other migrant groups in most OECD countries, with the exception of the United States where it has gone down (Table 1.6). Within the EU27, this group has been showing an improvement since 2019. In Europe and Australia, the increase has been accompanied by a decline in their unemployment rate, which has fallen below 10% in Australia for the first time in ten years. Despite this progress, this group remains the most disadvantaged: in 2021, their employment rate was the lowest and their unemployment rate the highest in most OECD countries. In Europe, for example, the gap with immigrants from EU27 countries is substantial: in 2021, 72% of EU27 immigrants were in employment compared to 51.5% of immigrants from North Africa and 56% of those from the Middle East.

Moreover, there has been a significant increase in the employment rate of immigrants from Asia in the United Kingdom and Australia between 2019 and 2021. This can be explained by an increase in departures and a corresponding decrease in entries of international students from Asia due to the pandemic, thus mechanically decreasing their employment rate in these major destination countries for international students.

In the United States, although the employment rate of migrants increased between 2020 and 2021, regardless of their region of birth, no group has managed to regain its pre-crisis level. In particular, despite a significant increase in their employment rate and a significant decrease in their unemployment rate in 2021, the situation of immigrants from Mexico, other Central and South American countries, and the Caribbean has deteriorated significantly compared to 2019. In contrast, the employment rate of immigrants from Asia, Canada and Europe is almost similar (within 0.6 percentage point) to the level observed before the pandemic.

Table 1.6. Employment, unemployment and participation rates by region of origin in selected OECD countries in 2019 and 2021, percentages

	Region of birth	Employment rate		Unemployment rate		Participation rate	
		2019	2021	2019	2021	2019	2021
Australia	Other Oceania	76.9	77.3	5.9	4.8	81.7	81.2
	Europe	78.0	78.3	4.0	3.6	81.2	81.2
	North Africa and the Middle East	52.6	56.7	10.9	9.8	59.0	62.9
	Sub-Saharan Africa	76.2	79.2	6.1	5.2	81.1	83.6
	Asia	69.8	72.8	5.7	5.8	74.0	77.4
	Americas	80.0	80.1	4.5	4.9	83.8	84.2
	Foreign-born (total)	**72.3**	**81.4**	**5.5**	**4.5**	**76.5**	**85.2**
	Native-born	**75.7**	**75.7**	**5.2**	**5.2**	**79.9**	**79.8**
Canada	Sub-Saharan Africa	72.2	73.1	8.7	9.7	79.1	81.0
	North Africa	70.1	70.1	9.6	10.5	77.6	78.4
	Middle East	63.4	64.7	9.0	11.9	69.6	73.4
	Asia	73.3	72.5	5.9	8.4	77.9	79.2
	Europe	77.8	77.4	4.5	6.4	81.5	82.7
	Oceania	82.3	80.5	3.2	4.4	85.0	84.2
	Other North America	69.9	69.5	6.7	7.6	74.9	75.2
	Central and South America and Caribbean	74.7	75.3	6.6	8.5	80.0	82.3
	Foreign-born (total)	**73.2**	**72.9**	**6.3**	**8.5**	**78.1**	**79.6**
	Native-born	**74.9**	**73.4**	**5.5**	**7.0**	**79.3**	**78.9**
EU27 countries	EU27 + EFTA	72.4	72.1	7.5	8.1	78.2	78.4
	Other European countries	66.0	64.5	9.2	9.4	72.7	71.2
	North Africa	50.5	51.5	19.6	19.0	62.8	63.6
	Sub-Saharan Africa	61.3	61.8	16.7	16.2	73.6	73.7
	Middle East	57.3	56.2	14.4	15.2	66.9	66.2
	North America	69.2	66.5	6.8	9.1	74.2	73.2
	Central and South America and Caribbean	65.9	64.1	15.1	17.8	77.6	78.0
	Asia	64.1	63.5	8.6	10.2	70.2	70.7
	Other regions	69.3	68.4	8.2	9.4	75.5	75.5
	Foreign-born (total)	**65.2**	**64.5**	**11.1**	**11.9**	**73.3**	**73.2**
	Native-born	**68.8**	**69.0**	**6.2**	**6.4**	**73.4**	**73.7**
United Kingdom	EU (excluding United Kingdom)	83.0	82.4	2.7	3.0	85.7	85.4
	Other European countries	73.7	73.6	3.4	4.0	77.2	77.6
	North Africa	62.9	63.6	5.0	10.5	67.9	74.2
	Sub-Saharan Africa	75.0	75.0	4.9	5.9	79.9	81.0
	Middle East and Central Asia	51.7	55.1	6.7	10.6	58.4	65.7
	North America	77.0	77.0	2.6	3.8	79.6	80.8
	Central and South America and Caribbean	76.6	75.9	4.8	5.3	81.4	81.3
	Asia	64.7	67.3	3.6	5.3	68.4	72.7
	Other regions	86.2	86.7	1.5	2.5	87.7	89.2
	Foreign-born (total)	**75.7**	**75.5**	**3.5**	**4.4**	**77.9**	**79.9**
	Native-born	**75.6**	**75.4**	**3.0**	**3.3**	**78.1**	**78.7**

	Region of birth	Employment rate		Unemployment rate		Participation rate	
		2019	2021	2019	2021	2019	2021
United States	Mexico	71.0	68.3	3.5	5.3	73.6	72.1
	Other Central American countries	74.0	71.1	3.3	5.9	76.5	75.5
	South America and Caribbean	74.8	70.3	3.5	6.7	77.5	75.4
	Canada	76.2	75.6	2.2	3.4	78.0	78.3
	Europe	74.2	73.6	2.8	4.9	76.3	77.4
	Africa	72.9	69.8	3.7	7.1	75.7	75.2
	Asia and the Middle East	70.6	70.0	2.6	5.1	72.5	73.7
	Other regions	67.5	65.7	2.7	6.0	69.4	69.9
	Foreign-born (total)	**72.2**	**70.0**	**3.1**	**5.6**	**74.6**	**74.2**
	Native-born	**69.8**	**67.8**	**3.9**	**5.5**	**72.7**	**71.7**

Note: The population refers to the working-age population (15-64) for the employment and participation rates and to the active population aged 15-64 for the unemployment rate. The employment, unemployment and participation rates of the native-born and foreign-born populations in the EU27 countries in 2019 and 2020 have been adjusted for the break in series caused by the change in methodology of the European Union Labour Force Survey (EU-LFS) in 2021. Calculations have been made by the OECD Secretariat on the basis of adjusted series for the whole population provided by Eurostat. EU27 does not include the United Kingdom. Regions of birth could not be made fully comparable between countries of residence due to the way the aggregate data provided to the OECD Secretariat is coded. For the United Kingdom, the "Middle East and Central Asia" region only includes the Middle East for 2020 and 2019.
Source: EU27: Labour Force Surveys (Eurostat); Australia, Canada: Labour Force Surveys; the United States: Current Population Surveys.

StatLink ᐧᐧᐧᐧᐧ https://stat.link/xtnlhr

References

Baert, S. (ed.) (2022), "Firing discrimination: Selective labor market responses of firms during the COVID-19 economic crisis", *PLOS ONE*, Vol. 17/1, p. e0262337, https://doi.org/10.1371/journal.pone.0262337. [6]

Bratsberg, B. and O. Raaum (forthcoming), *Bruken av utenlandsk arbeidskraft gjennom COVID-19 pandemien.* [12]

Capps, R. (2021), *Immigrants' U.S. Labor Market Disadvantage in the COVID-19 Economy: The Role of Geography and Industries of Employment*, Washington, DC: Migration Policy Institute. [4]

De Wispelaere, F., L. De Smedt and J. Pacolet (2022), *Posting of workers: Report on A1 portable documents issued in 2019*, Publications Office of the European Union, Luxembourg, https://doi.org/10.2767/487681. [1]

EMN/OECD (2021), *The impact of Covid-19 in the migration area in EU and OECD countries*, European Migrant Network/OECD, https://www.oecd.org/migration/mig/00-eu-emn-covid19-umbrella-inform-en.pdf. [11]

Fasani, F. and J. Mazza (2020), "Being on the Frontline? Immigrant Workers in Europe and the COVID-19 Pandemic", *Institute of Labor Economics (IZA)* IZA Discussion Papers No. 13963. [8]

OECD (2022), "Riding the waves: Adjusting job retention schemes through the COVID-19 crisis", *OECD Policy Responses to Coronavirus (COVID-19)*, OECD Publishing, Paris, https://doi.org/10.1787/ae8f892f-en. [3]

OECD (2022), "The unequal impact of COVID-19: A spotlight on frontline workers, migrants and racial/ethnic minorities", *OECD Policy Responses to Coronavirus (COVID-19)*, OECD Publishing, Paris, https://doi.org/10.1787/f36e931e-en. [13]

OECD (2021), *OECD Employment Outlook 2021: Navigating the COVID-19 Crisis and Recovery*, OECD Publishing, Paris, https://doi.org/10.1787/5a700c4b-en. [7]

OECD (2021), "What have countries done to support young people in the COVID-19 crisis?", *OECD Policy Responses to Coronavirus (COVID-19)*, OECD Publishing, Paris, https://doi.org/10.1787/ac9f056c-en. [10]

OECD (2019), *International Migration Outlook 2019*, OECD Publishing, Paris, https://doi.org/10.1787/c3e35eec-en. [2]

OECD (2009), *International Migration Outlook 2009*, OECD Publishing, Paris, https://doi.org/10.1787/migr_outlook-2009-en. [5]

Sánchez Gassen, N. (2021), *Integrating Immigrants into the Nordic Labour Markets: The impact of the COVID-19 pandemic*, Nordic Council of Ministers. [9]

Annex 1.A. Supplementary tables and figures

Annex Table 1.A.1. Permanent-type flows to OECD countries by category, 2020

Thousands and percentage change compared to 2019

	Work		Accompanying family of workers		Family		Humanitarian		Other		Free movements	
	2020	%	2020	%	2020	%	2020	%	2020	%	2020	%
Australia	43.9	-13	51.9	-12	44.4	-12	13.2	-30	0.1	-30	11.9	-28
Austria	4.6	-24	1.3	-35	5.8	-32	6.8	-8	0.2	-46	43.9	-24
Belgium	3.4	-33	..	..	25.7	-20	5.8	-13	0.1	-23	56.6	-18
Canada	60.0	-42	46.4	-50	49.3	-46	25.5	-47	3.4	-27	..	..
Denmark	7.6	-15	3.3	-32	4.0	24	0.6	-66	0.5	28	25.1	-14
Finland	5.6	-5	..	..	8.6	-16	2.9	-1	..	..	6.8	3
France	43.9	-14	..	..	83.5	-18	27.6	-17	18.9	-27	64.3	-18
Germany	53.7	-32	..	..	72.8	-28	63.6	-14	4.3	-40	337.8	-12
Ireland	13.0	-11	..	-99	1.8	-50	1.6	-9	..	..	26.1	-16
Israel	..	..	..	..	6.3	-2	..	..	13.4	-50	..	..
Italy	8.5	23	..	..	62.3	-38	11.6	-37	2.3	-55	47.6	-20
Japan	56.9	-31	..	..	21.4	-41	0.1	-10	6.9	-64	..	..
Korea	1.4	129	4.3	-21	16.4	6	0.2	-21	31.2	-41	..	..
Luxembourg	1.7	-26	..	..	1.6	-29	0.8	0	0.2	-61	15.0	-13
Mexico	7.3	21	..	..	20.5	21	18.1	129	8.3	6	..	..
Netherlands	14.8	-37	..	..	26.0	-24	5.4	11	..	..	75.0	-17
New Zealand	8.0	-9	10.9	-5	12.2	17	1.6	-57	..	..	2.4	-40
Norway	3.0	-32	..	..	9.0	-24	3.7	-28	..	..	17.6	-30
Portugal	32.6	-6	..	..	28.1	-6	0.1	-49	3.4	-46	15.9	-42
Spain	33.0	-4	..	..	113.1	-16	52.7	32	32.8	18	113.1	-25
Sweden	12.5	-17	12.5	-17	21.7	-6	10.5	-40	..	..	22.3	-18
Switzerland	1.8	-23	..	..	17.2	-12	6.6	2	3.5	-5	89.1	-2
United Kingdom	40.2	-19	27.2	-6	64.9	-17	32.0	41	13.5	-40	45.6	-68
United States	64.4	-7	64.4	-7	354.0	-50	63.5	-41	35.2	-53	..	..
OECD	**521.6**	**-22**	**222.3**	**-23**	**1 070.6**	**-34**	**354.4**	**-18**	**178.2**	**-38**	**1 016.1**	**-22**
EU	**234.8**	**-18**	**17.2**	**-23**	**455.0**	**-22**	**190.0**	**-10**	**62.7**	**-15**	**849.4**	**-17**

Note: EU totals do not include the United Kingdom.
Source: OECD International migration database.

StatLink ᴹˢᴸ https://stat.link/ry8hmi

Annex Table 1.A.2. Inflows of temporary labour migrants (selected categories) 2012-21

Destination	2012	2013	2014	2015	2016	2017	2018	2019	2020	2021	2020/19 change (%)	2021/2020 change (%)
					Thousands							
International seasonal workers												
Total OECD	..	..	..	..	..	..	..	458.3	459.9	543.4	+ 0	+ 18
United States	65.3	74.2	89.3	108.1	134.4	161.6	196.4	204.8	213.4	294.7	+ 4	+ 38
Poland	..	..	..	..	..	..	..	131.4	137.4	113.4	+ 5	- 17
Canada	25.7	27.6	29.8	30.8	34.2	35.2	35.8	36.9	31.2	34.3	- 15	+ 10
United Kingdom	..	..	..	..	..	..	..	2.5	7.2	29.6	+ 189	+ 311
New Zealand	8.0	8.6	8.9	9.6	10.5	11.3	12.2	13.9	15.3	19.4	+ 10	+ 27
Spain	3.8	3.1	3.1	2.9	2.8	5.7	13.8	11.6	18.1	16.0	+ 56	- 12
France	6.4	6.1	6.6	6.7	6.8	7.2	8.1	10.3	5.8	14.9	- 44	+ 160
Australia	1.1	1.5	2.0	3.2	4.5	6.2	8.5	12.2	9.8	6.3	- 19	- 36
Sweden	..	..	..	..	..	..	4.9	6.2	3.5	5.5	- 43	+ 59
Mexico	21.7	15.2	14.7	15.9	14.9	12.4	10.7	10.0	3.7	3.7	- 63	+ 2
Finland	..	..	..	..	..	..	0.9	1.6	1.7	2.0	+ 7	+ 20
Italy	9.7	7.6	4.8	3.6	3.5	3.6	5.6	4.2	1.8	2.0	- 57	+ 9
Norway	2.3	2.5	2.5	2.3	2.4	2.6	2.9	3.4	2.4	1.4	- 31	- 41
Austria	13.2	15.1	7.2	6.9	6.7	6.9	7.6	9.4	8.7	..	..	..
Working holidaymakers												
Total OECD	426.4	475.7	467.6	465.8	470.9	484.0	483.3	482.2	200.0	105.5	- 59	- 47
United States	79.8	86.4	90.3	95.0	101.1	104.9	104.5	108.8	5.0	39.6	- 95	+ 701
Australia	223.0	258.2	239.6	226.8	214.6	211.0	210.5	209.0	149.2	39.6	- 29	- 73
Canada	45.8	44.9	43.2	39.6	44.7	55.8	56.6	55.5	15.8	14.3	- 71	- 10
United Kingdom	19.6	20.9	23.5	25.3	22.3	21.6	20.8	20.1	8.0	8.4	- 60	+ 5
France	2.4	2.7	2.9	3.0	3.8	4.3	5.0	5.2	2.0	2.4	- 61	+ 17
New Zealand	45.2	51.9	58.1	63.5	69.8	69.2	65.9	59.2	14.8	0.9	- 75	- 94
Korea	1.0	1.2	1.3	1.4	1.6	1.9	2.4	2.7	0.9	0.3	- 67	- 64
Denmark	0.4	0.4	0.6	0.8	1.2	1.5	1.8	3.7	1.0	0.0	- 74	- 98
Japan	9.3	9.1	8.1	10.4	11.9	13.8	15.9	18.0	3.3	..	- 82	..
International trainees												
Total OECD	92.6	91.3	106.2	120.5	125.8	148.5	173.5	213.6	93.5	28.7	- 56	- 69
Japan	85.9	83.9	98.7	112.7	121.9	144.1	163.6	201.9	86.2	23.6	- 57	- 73
Germany	4.1	3.9	3.8	4.3	..	..	4.6	5.1	3.1	..	- 39	..
France	1.2	2.0	2.2	2.5	2.6	2.5	3.1	4.2	2.5	3.0	- 41	+ 21
Denmark	1.4	1.4	1.5	1.1	1.3	1.9	2.3	2.4	1.6	2.0	- 30	+ 25
Intra-company transferees												
Total OECD	127.6	134.4	136.1	149.7	141.7	138.9	141.7	150.5	72.1	54.8	- 52	- 24
United States	62.4	66.7	71.5	78.5	79.3	78.2	74.4	77.0	35.9	27.4	- 53	- 24
United Kingdom	29.3	33.2	36.6	36.4	36.0	32.8	31.7	27.1	8.6	0.3	- 68	- 97
Canada	12.4	11.5	11.4	9.8	9.8	11.0	12.7	14.3	5.9	11.3	- 59	+ 91
Poland	..	..	..	..	..	..	..	11.3	12.9	11.9	+ 14	- 7
Japan	6.1	6.2	7.2	7.2	7.7	8.7	9.5	10.0	3.2	0.5	- 68	- 84
Germany	7.2	7.8	9.4	9.1	..	..	8.0	6.7	2.9	1.9	- 56	- 37
Australia	10.1	8.9	..	7.8	8.1	7.6	4.7	2.8	1.8	1.5	- 35	- 17
Ireland	..	..	..	0.9	0.8	0.7	0.8	1.2	0.7	..	- 42	..

Note: For each type of permit, the table presents only the countries for which inflows exceed one thousand in 2021. The number of seasonal workers refers to the number of permits granted, or work authorisations granted in France.
The series on seasonal workers exclude Germany, as no recent data is available.
Source: OECD International Migration Database (data available upon request).

StatLink https://stat.link/78km5h

| 55

Annex Table 1.A.3. Permits considered in the statistics on temporary migration of workers and their characteristics

Country	Name of the programme	Duration of stay / renewability of the contract	Existence of a quota
Australia (Temporary visas granted, fiscal years; excludes New Zealand citizens)	Seasonal workers: Seasonal Worker Programme (within subclass 416 replaced by subclass 403 from Nov 2016)	From 4 to 7 months	Uncapped
	Working holidaymakers: subclasses 417 and 462	Up to 1 year	Subclass 417: uncapped
			Subclass 462: capped except for the United States
	Trainees: The Training visa (subclass 407) introduced in 2016. Former Temporary Work (Training and Research) visa (subclass 402) streams – "Occupational trainee" and "Professional development", closed to new applications from 2016; and the following visas closed to new applications from 24 November 2012: Visiting Academic visa (subclass 419), Occupational Trainee visa (subclass 442), Professional Development visa (subclass 470); and the Trade Training Skills visa (subclass 471) which was repealed in September 2007.	Up to 2 years	
	Intra-company transferees: subclass 457 visas granted (primary applicants)	Up to 4 years	
	Other workers: other temporary work (Short Stay Specialist); International relations (excl. seasonal workers); Temporary Activity; Temporary work (Skilled) (excl. ICTs)		
Austria	Seasonal workers: Winter and Summer tourism; Agriculture; Core seasonal workers; Harvest helpers (number of persons estimated based on the number of permits delivered).	Up to 12 months	
	Intra-company transferees		Uncapped
	Other workers: Researchers, Artists (with document or self-employed), Self-employed workers; Au pair; Other specific paid jobs.		Uncapped
Belgium	Working holidaymakers: top 10 countries of origin (estimation)		
	Trainees (estimation)		
	Other workers: Au Pair; Artists; Sports(wo)men; Invited Professors or trainers; Other temporary workers (estimation)		
Canada (TFWP and IMP programmes – initial permits)	Seasonal workers: Seasonal Agricultural Workers Programme (TFWP): effective entries	Not renewable	
	Working holidaymakers: International Experience Canada Working Holiday and International Youth Program (IMP)	Not renewable	Uncapped
	Intra-company transferees: International Mobility Program (IMP) Work Permit Holders by year in which Initial Permit became effective (Trade – ICT; NAFTA – ICT; GATS professionals; significant benefits ICT)	Varies	
	Other workers: International Mobility Program (IMP): Agreements (excl. ICT); Canadian Interests (excl. working holidaymakers, spouses and ICT); Self-support; Permanent residence applicants in Canada; Humanitarian reason; Temporary Foreign Worker Program: Live-in caregivers; agricultural workers (non seasonal); other TFWP	IMP: varies	Uncapped
		Live-in caregivers: unlimited	
		other TFWP: not renewable	
Colombia	Working holidaymakers		
	Intra-company transferees		
	Other workers		
Denmark	Working holidaymakers		
	Trainees		
	Other workers: De facto status; Au Pair; Volunteers.		

Country	Name of the programme	Duration of stay / renewability of the contract	Existence of a quota
Finland	Seasonal workers: Seasonal work visas	Up to 9 months	
	Trainees		
	Other workers	Up to 12 months	
France (first permits issued)	Seasonal workers: work authorisations issued for each seasonal work contract, including renewals – OFII statistics	Up to 9 months per year (3-year authorisation)	
	Working holidaymakers: *Programme vacances Travail*	Up to 12 months	
	Trainees: *Stagiaires*	Up to 1 year initially (extension up to 3 years in total)	
	Intra-company transferees: *Salarié en mission / Salarié détaché ICT*	Up to 3 years	
	Other workers: Temporary economic migration (visa *"salarié"* < 12 months)	Up to 12 months (renewable)	
Germany (grants of work permits)	Seasonal workers		
	Trainees		
	Intra-company transferees: § 8 BeschV (Praktische Tätigkeiten als Voraussetzung für die Anerkennung ausländischer Berufsqualifikationen), § 10 BeschV (Internationaler Personalaustausch, Auslandsprojekte), § 10a BeschV (ICT-Karte / Mobiler-ICT-Karte)		
	Other workers: § 8 Abs. 2 BeschV (Anerkennung ausländischer Berufsqualifikationen – § 17a AufenthG bis zu 18 Monate), § 8 Abs. 3 BeschV (Anerkennung ausländischer Berufsqualifikationen – sonstige), § 11 Abs. 1 BeschV (Sprachlehrerinnen und Sprachlehrer), § 11 Abs. 2 BeschV (Spezialitätenköchinnen und Spezialitätenköche), § 12 BeschV (Au-Pair-Beschäftigungen), § 13 BeschV (Hausangestellte von Entsandten), § 19 Abs. 2 BeschV (Werklieferverträge), § 25 BeschV (Kultur und Unterhaltung), § 27 BeschV (Grenzgängerbeschäftigung), § 29 Abs. 1 BeschV (Internationale Abkommen – Niederlassungspersonal), § 29 Abs. 2 BeschV (Internationale Abkommen – Gastarbeitnehmer), § 29 Abs. 3 – 4 BeschV (Internationale Abkommen), § 29 Abs. 5 BeschV (Internationale Abkommen – WHO/Europaabkommen)		
Ireland	Working holidaymakers: Working holidaymaker visas		
	Trainees: Internship employment permit		
	Intra-company transferees		
	Other workers: Contract for Services; Exchange Agreement; Sport and Cultural Employment Permits		
Israel (entries excl. Palestinian workers, and stock of Jordanian daily workers working in uncapped sectors)	Working holidaymakers		
	Other workers:		
	Construction: Jordanian workers (daily workers in capped sectors); Tel Aviv city rail project; Sea ports projects; Jordan Valley irrigation project; Foreign Construction Workers (bilateral agreements with Bulgaria, China, Moldova, Romania, Türkiye, Ukraine)	Daily workers: unlimited; other workers: renewable up to 63 months	Capped
	Tourism: Jordanian daily workers in hotel industry and construction in Eilat	Unlimited	Capped
	Agriculture	Not renewable	Capped
	Home care	Renewable up to 63 months (or up to 7 years if no employer change between 5 and 7 years of stay)	Uncapped
	Specialists and skilled (experts working visa)	Unlimited	Uncapped

Country	Name of the programme	Duration of stay / renewability of the contract	Existence of a quota
Italy	Seasonal workers		
	Working holidaymakers		
	Other workers	Up to 12 months	
Japan (New visas, excl. re-entry)	Working holidaymakers: Working holidaymaker visas		
	Trainees: Trainees and Technical intern training		
	Intra company transferees		
	Other workers: Professor; Artist; Religious Activities; Journalist; Researcher; Instructor; Entertainer; Cultural Activities; Designated activities (including some permanent workers and their spouses, such as highly skilled professionals)	1 to 5 years, renewable	Uncapped
Korea (Visas issued)	Industrial trainees: D-3		
	Working holidaymakers: H-1		
	Intra-company transferees: D-7		
	Other workers: visas D-6; D-9; E-1 to E-9; H2		
Luxembourg	Trainees		
	Intra-company transferees		
	Other workers	Up to 12 months	
Mexico	Seasonal workers: Cards of visiting border-worker (*Tarjetas de Visitante Trabajador Fronterizo*)	Up to 5 years	
	Other workers: Temporary residence permit (*Tarjetas de Residente Temporal*) for work		
New Zealand (excludes Australian citizens)	Seasonal workers: Recognised Seasonal Employer Limited Visa; Supplementary Seasonal Employment (extensions)	Up to 7 months (or 9 months for citizen-residents of Tuvalu and Kiribati); extensions possible up to 6 months.	Capped
	Working holidaymakers: Working Holiday Scheme	Up to 12 months (or 23 months for citizens of the United Kingdom or Canada)	Capped for some countries
	Trainees: Work experience for student; Medical & dental trainee; NZ racing conference apprentice; Religious Trainees	Practical training for students not enrolled in New Zealand (or enrolled for 3 months maximum): up to 6 months; Religious trainees: up to 3 years; Apprentice jockeys: up to 4 years	Uncapped
	Other workers:		
	Essential skills	Up to 5 years	Uncapped
	Entertainers and Associated Workers	Contract duration	Uncapped
	Talent (Accredited Employer)	Up to 30 months	Uncapped
	Exchange Work	Up to 12 months	Capped
	Long Term Skill Shortage List Occupation	Up to 30 months	Uncapped
	China Special Work	Up to 3 years	Capped
	Skilled Migrant and Specialist skills	No limit	Uncapped
	Talent – Arts, Culture and Sports	No limit	Uncapped
Norway (non EU/EFTA nationals)	Seasonal workers	Not renewable	
	Working holidaymakers		
	Trainees		
	Intra-company transferees		
	Other workers: Unskilled non seasonal temporary workers		

Country	Name of the programme	Duration of stay / renewability of the contract	Existence of a quota
Poland	Seasonal workers: seasonal work permits (including non-agricultural activities)		Uncapped
	Intra-company transferees	Renewable	
	Other workers:		
	Estimates based on administrative forms from employers for recruiting workers from six countries of origin (Armenia, Belarus, Georgia, Moldova, Russia and Ukraine) under simplified procedures.	Up to 9 months	
	New residence permits (A permits) granted on the ground of work.	6 to 11 months	Uncapped
Portugal	Other workers	Up to 12 months	
Slovenia	Seasonal workers		
	Other workers	Up to 12 months	
Spain	Seasonal workers: Authorisations for temporary employment		
	Intra-company transferees		
	Other workers: Permits for employees with contracts of limited duration; Permits for international service providers; Temporary residence permits for specific professions not requiring a work authorisation; Researchers; Trainees and workers in Research and development		
Sweden	Seasonal workers: Berry pickers		
	Working holidaymakers: Working holiday visas		
	Trainees		
	Other workers: Athletes and coaches; Au Pair; Intra-company transferees; Performers; Visiting researchers.		
Switzerland	Trainees	Up to 18 months	Capped
	Other workers (excluding detached workers):		
	Employed with work permits	Up to 12 months	Capped (contracts of 4 to 12 months duration) or uncapped (permits<4 months)
	Musicians and artists	Up to 8 months	Uncapped
United Kingdom (Entry clearance visas granted)	Seasonal workers in horticulture (from 2019 on)	Up to 6 months	
	Working holidaymakers: Tier 5 – pre–PBS Youth Mobility	Up to 24 months (multi-entry visa)	
	Intra-company transferees:		
	Tier 2 – Intra Company Transfers Short Term (closed on 6 April 2017)		
	Tier 2 – Intra Company Transfers Long Term	Maximum 5 years (9 years if salary > GBP 120 000 per year)	
United States (non-immigrant visa statistics)	Seasonal workers: H-2A – Temporary worker performing agricultural services	Up to 3 years	Uncapped
	Working holidaymakers: J-1 – Exchange visitor, Summer Work Travel Programme	Up to 4 months	Capped
	Trainees: H3	Up to 2 years	
	Intra-company transferees: L-1 – Intracompany transferee (executive, managerial, and specialised personnel continuing employment with international firm or corporation)	Maximum initial stay of one year (3 years for L-1A employees). Extended until reaching the maximum limit of seven years (5 years for L-1B)	
	Other workers:		
	H-2B – Temporary worker performing other services	Up to 3 years	Capped

Country	Name of the programme	Duration of stay / renewability of the contract	Existence of a quota
	H-1B – Temporary worker of distinguished merit and ability performing services other than as a registered nurse	Up to 3 years initially. Maximum limit of six years in total (with some exceptions)	
	H-1B1 – Free Trade Agreement worker (Chile/Singapore)		
	H-1C – Nurse in health professional shortage area (expired in 2009)	Up to 3 years	
	O-1 – Person with extraordinary ability in the sciences, arts, education, business, or athletics	Up to 3 years (extension up to 1 year)	
	O-2 – Person accompanying and assisting in the artistic or athletic performance by O-1	Up to 3 years (extension up to 1 year)	
	P-1 – Internationally recognised athlete or member of an internationally recognised entertainment group	Up to 5 years (1 year for athletic group). Maximum limit of 10 years (5 years for athletic group)	
	P-2 – Artist or entertainer in a reciprocal exchange programme	Up to 1 year initially (extension up to 1 year)	
	P-3 – Artist or entertainer in a culturally unique programme	Up to 1 year initially (extension up to 1 year)	
	R-1 – Person in a religious occupation	Up to 30 months initially	
	TN – NAFTA professional	Up to 3 years	

Annex Table 1.A.4. Top 50 countries of origin of new immigrants to the OECD, 2019-20

	Thousands		Share among total (%)	2020/19 absolute change	2020/19 change (%)	Difference with 2019 rank	Expatriation rate (per '000 population)
	2019	2020	2020				2020
India	395	231	5.0	-164	-41	1	0.2
China	465	231	5.0	-235	-50	-1	0.2
Romania	288	223	4.8	-65	-23	0	11.5
Ukraine	227	199	4.3	-28	-13	0	4.5
Venezuela	227	142	3.1	-85	-37	0	5.0
Viet Nam	226	131	2.8	-94	-42	0	1.4
United Kingdom	145	123	2.6	-22	-15	6	1.8
Poland	150	122	2.6	-28	-19	3	3.2
Italy	159	118	2.5	-41	-26	0	1.9
Mexico	176	113	2.4	-63	-36	-3	0.9
Brazil	155	105	2.3	-51	-33	-1	0.5
Germany	121	101	2.2	-21	-17	5	1.2
Morocco	148	100	2.1	-49	-33	-1	2.7
Colombia	135	90	1.9	-45	-33	0	1.8
France	109	89	1.9	-20	-18	4	1.4
Syria	126	84	1.8	-42	-33	-1	4.9
Bulgaria	96	83	1.8	-13	-14	5	11.8
Philippines	162	82	1.8	-80	-50	-10	0.8
United States	124	74	1.6	-50	-40	-3	0.2
Afghanistan	99	73	1.6	-26	-26	0	1.9
Iraq	119	72	1.5	-47	-40	-3	1.8
Russia	98	66	1.4	-32	-32	-1	0.5
Spain	82	63	1.4	-18	-22	2	1.4
Pakistan	92	63	1.4	-29	-31	-1	0.3
Iran	86	58	1.2	-28	-33	-1	0.7
Türkiye	77	55	1.2	-22	-29	2	0.7
Turkmenistan	81	48	1.0	-32	-40	-1	8.2
Portugal	64	46	1.0	-18	-29	5	4.5
Nigeria	66	43	0.9	-23	-34	0	0.2
Hungary	56	42	0.9	-14	-25	4	4.3
Korea	78	41	0.9	-37	-47	-4	0.8
Peru	65	41	0.9	-24	-37	-1	1.3
Dominican Republic	65	39	0.8	-26	-40	-3	3.7
Albania	52	38	0.8	-14	-27	2	13.2
Croatia	46	37	0.8	-9	-19	7	9.0
Honduras	49	36	0.8	-14	-28	2	3.7
Algeria	46	34	0.7	-12	-26	3	0.8
Haiti	54	33	0.7	-21	-39	-3	2.9
Bangladesh	50	33	0.7	-17	-34	-2	0.2
Greece	46	33	0.7	-13	-29	1	3.1
Canada	44	32	0.7	-12	-27	2	0.9
Cuba	64	31	0.7	-32	-51	-10	2.8
Egypt	49	31	0.7	-18	-37	-4	0.3
Netherlands	41	31	0.7	-10	-24	1	1.8
Serbia	40	30	0.6	-10	-25	3	3.4
Slovak Republic	26	29	0.6	3	13	21	5.3
Bosnia and Herzegovina	40	28	0.6	-12	-31	0	8.4
Argentina	40	26	0.6	-15	-37	-2	0.6
El Salvador	40	24	0.5	-15	-39	1	3.8
Nepal	40	24	0.5	-16	-39	-1	0.8

Source: OECD International Migration Database, https://doi.org/10.1787/data-00342-en.

StatLink ᐃᔑᓚ https://stat.link/sevrpx

Annex Figure 1.A.1. Employment rates by place of birth, 2002-21

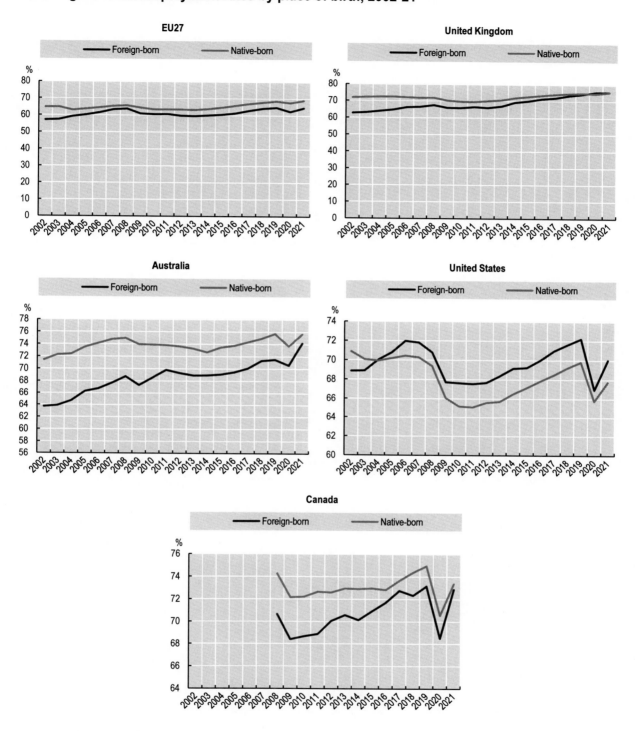

Note: The reference population is the working-age population (15-64). In the EU27, years between 2010- 2020 have been subject to adjustments for the break in series caused by the change in the methodology of the European Labour Force Survey in 2021. Calculations were made by the Secretariat taking into account the adjusted series for the whole population provided by Eurostat. EU27 does not include the United Kingdom.
Source: European Countries: Labour Force Surveys (Eurostat); Australia, Canada and the United Kingdom: Labour Force Surveys; United States: Current Population Surveys.

StatLink ᴍꜱᴸ https://stat.link/n68m5s

Annex Figure 1.A.2. Change in the gap between male and female employment rates, by place of birth, 2002-21

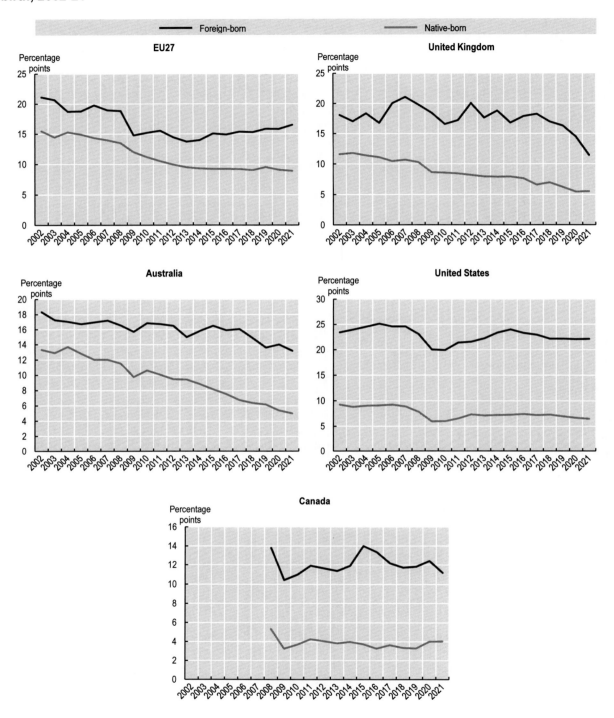

Note: The reference population is the working-age population (15-64). In the EU27, years between 2010- 2020 have been subject to adjustments for the break in series caused by the change in the methodology of the European Labour Force Survey in 2021. Calculations were made by the Secretariat taking into account the adjusted series for the whole population provided by Eurostat. EU27 does not include the United Kingdom.
Source: European Countries: Labour Force Surveys (Eurostat); Australia, Canada and the United Kingdom: Labour Force Surveys; United States: Current Population Surveys.

StatLink ⬛ https://stat.link/ap45ki

Annex Figure 1.A.3. Changes in employment rates by demographic group and country of birth, in selected OECD countries, 2021 compared to 2020

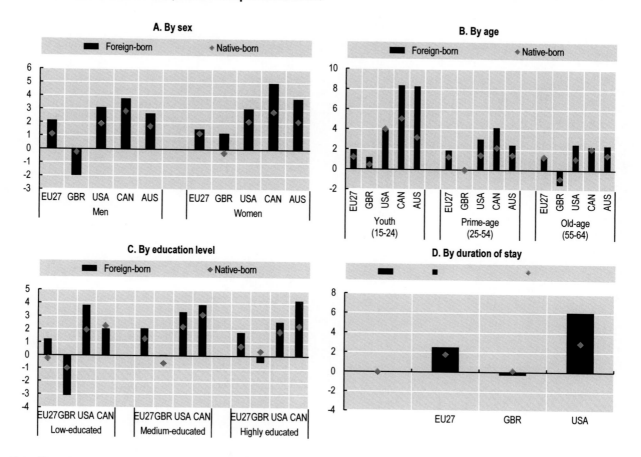

Note: The reference population is the working-age population (15-64). "Low-educated" here refers to less than upper secondary attainment, "Medium-educated" to upper secondary and post-secondary non-tertiary, "Highly educated" to tertiary. The employment rates of native-born and foreign-born populations in the EU27 countries in 2019 and 2020 have been subject to adjustments for the break in series caused by the change in the methodology of the European Labour Force Survey in 2021. Calculations were made by the OECD Secretariat taking into account the adjusted series for the whole population provided by Eurostat. EU27 does not include the United Kingdom.
Source: EU27: Labour Force Surveys (Eurostat); Australia, Canada and the United Kingdom: Labour Force Surveys; United States: Current Population Surveys.

StatLink ⬛⬛ https://stat.link/zq7y8b

Annex Table 1.A.5. Employment rates of persons aged 25-64 by place of birth and education level, OECD countries, 2021

	Foreign-born			Native-born		
	Low	Medium	High	Low	Medium	High
Austria	51.4	70.4	77.8	45.5	74.6	86.9
Belgium	37.4	60.9	77.3	32.7	65.1	85.5
Canada	44.2	64.7	79.7	45.4	70.7	82.4
Chile	73.7	81.7	85.1	61.2	74.1	82.2
Czech Republic	61.3	82.8	82.2	23.9	79.6	85.0
Denmark	57.5	79.7	89.3	53.9	80.1	88.4
Estonia	50.6	70.0	75.1	39.5	76.7	89.1
Finland	46.5	69.4	81.4	39.9	74.4	87.8
France	48.4	60.5	74.6	35.2	68.7	85.6
Germany	54.7	75.5	78.0	47.8	80.7	90.2
Greece	50.6	54.9	61.6	37.7	55.0	75.8
Hungary	67.6	78.5	87.0	38.6	77.0	90.1
Iceland	73.0	76.1	80.7	64.3	81.5	90.6
Ireland	33.6	70.9	85.2	36.2	68.6	86.3
Israel	65.8	76.7	85.0	41.9	69.2	87.4
Italy	54.9	62.5	66.5	40.2	63.9	80.5
Latvia	39.5	62.9	77.7	31.4	70.7	86.5
Lithuania	34.8	62.5	80.5	24.9	69.6	89.7
Luxembourg	56.7	63.5	84.1	33.4	68.7	84.7
Mexico	70.1	64.1	71.2	65.6	71.6	79.7
Netherlands	53.5	69.3	78.2	68.9	83.2	90.2
New Zealand	66.4	79.5	86.3	71.9	83.0	89.3
Norway	51.5	72.5	81.9	54.9	79.7	90.0
Poland	-	76.0	88.6	24.7	70.7	89.9
Portugal	71.4	77.3	91.0	59.5	68.6	85.9
Slovak Republic	-	75.6	84.7	13.7	74.9	85.5
Slovenia	41.3	72.9	81.7	29.3	69.7	88.9
Spain	52.4	62.0	70.2	48.1	58.2	81.2
Sweden	41.8	72.5	80.7	40.7	81.8	90.9
Switzerland	63.6	74.7	83.3	54.8	80.7	91.4
Türkiye	-	-	-	-	-	-
United Kingdom	67.3	77.6	85.0	55.4	77.6	87.0
United States	58.9	67.4	77.9	29.0	65.4	81.6
EU27	52.1	67.8	76.3	41.9	71.4	86.2
OECD average	54.7	70.5	79.9	45.1	72.9	86.4

Note: For Mexico, data refer to 2019. For New Zealand, data refer to 2020. For Chile data refer to 2017. For Israel, data refer to 2020. The OECD average does not include Poland, Türkiye and the Slovak Republic as data are not available for all levels of education in these countries.
Source: European countries: Labour Force Surveys (Eurostat); Canada, Israel; New Zealand: Labour Force Surveys; Mexico: Encuesta Nacional de Ocupación y Empleo (ENOE); the United States: Current Population Surveys.

StatLink ᴍᴸ https://stat.link/g4en7v

Annex Table 1.A.6. Employment of foreign-born persons by industry, 2021

	Agriculture and fishing (%)	Mining, manufacturing and energy (%)	Construction (%)	Wholesale and retail trade (%)	Hotels and restaurants (%)	Education (%)	Health (%)	Activities of households as employers (%)	Admin. and ETO (%)	Other services (%)	Total (%)	Total foreign-born employed (thousands)	Foreign-born in total employment (%)
Australia	1.3	11.0	7.4	11.8	9.0	6.7	14.8	-	9.0	29.1	100	-	30.3
Austria	1.5	19.0	9.4	15.4	10.4	5.4	10.5	-	9.4	18.9	100	914	22.3
Belgium	-	12.1	8.2	11.7	5.3	6.6	14.5	-	20.7	20.9	100	820	17.9
Czech Republic	2.3	34.6	11.2	12.1	4.7	4.5	6.6	0.5	6.0	17.6	100	229	4.7
Denmark	-	13.8	5.0	14.4	8.4	9.8	19.6	-	11.6	17.3	100	259	9.9
Estonia	-	30.4	10.4	12.6	-	11.0	-	-	-	35.5	100	49	8.5
Finland	1.8	13.4	9.2	10.6	8.6	8.5	15.7	0.0	11.6	20.8	100	221	9.5
France	1.0	10.5	11.1	12.1	6.7	6.3	13.7	2.3	13.7	22.5	100	3 017	11.8
Germany	0.6	24.3	7.3	13.6	6.7	4.8	12.7	0.8	10.6	18.6	100	7 172	18.6
Greece	9.0	15.0	11.6	15.4	18.3	2.2	4.4	4.2	7.3	12.5	100	263	7.1
Hungary	3.7	20.9	10.0	16.0	7.2	10.7	6.8	0.0	7.9	16.9	100	142	3.2
Iceland	3.5	15.1	8.9	10.3	13.7	10.4	11.9	-	8.6	17.7	100	29	16.2
Ireland	-	16.8	5.0	14.7	9.9	6.8	16.7	0.0	8.2	21.9	100	501	24.1
Israel	0.5	15.5	3.7	10.6	3.2	8.5	16.1	5.3	10.6	26.0	100	801	27.8
Italy	6.5	20.3	9.7	10.4	7.9	2.4	6.0	15.0	7.1	14.8	100	3 024	14.3
Latvia	-	19.4	12.2	18.4	-	8.5	7.5	-	8.1	25.9	100	59	7.6
Lithuania	-	33.7	-	19.4	-	14.8	-	-	-	32.0	100	33	2.7
Luxembourg	-	3.9	7.9	10.7	4.8	4.6	9.0	2.3	20.4	36.3	100	152	58.2
Netherlands	1.7	12.4	4.0	14.9	6.9	6.5	14.5	0.3	14.5	24.2	100	1 093	13.0
Norway	1.3	11.4	9.4	12.1	7.5	7.3	21.8	0.0	12.7	16.6	100	500	19.8
Portugal	-	17.3	4.9	14.9	5.1	11.2	12.7	2.6	12.3	19.1	100	387	8.8
Slovak Republic	1.0	21.4	8.0	19.5	6.1	4.0	7.7	-	9.3	22.9	100	23	1.0
Slovenia	-	26.9	15.7	11.3	5.1	5.7	7.6	-	9.9	17.9	100	87	9.5
Spain	6.5	10.3	9.5	14.3	15.2	3.2	6.6	9.7	8.8	15.9	100	3 411	18.1
Sweden	-	11.2	5.0	10.2	5.5	13.9	20.1	0.0	13.1	21.0	100	956	21.3
Switzerland	0.6	15.3	7.9	12.3	6.2	6.5	14.6	2.1	8.7	25.8	100	1 231	32.1
United Kingdom	0.4	10.5	5.4	11.9	8.5	9.7	16.1	0.3	10.8	26.2	100	5 052	17.0
United States	1.8	12.1	11.7	12.5	8.2	6.2	12.7	1.2	9.2	24.6	100	23 494	18.6
EU27	2.6	17.4	8.4	13.0	8.3	5.2	11.2	4.2	10.7	19.0	100	23 399	12.7

Note: A dash indicates that the estimate is not reliable enough for publication. ETO stands for extra-territorial organisations. The population refer to the employed population aged 15 to 64. Data for Australia refer to 2017. Data for the United Kingdom refer to the first three-quarters of 2020. Data for Israel and the Slovak Republic refer to 2020.
Source: Australia, Israel, United Kingdom: Labour Force Surveys; European countries: Labour Force Surveys (Eurostat); United States: Current Population Surveys.

StatLink 🔗 https://stat.link/ismtq0

2 Recent developments in migration policy

This chapter provides an overview of the changes in the immigration policies in OECD countries during the period 2021-22 with a particular focus on post COVID-19 innovative schemes and solutions as well as humanitarian admission programmes in response to conflicts and geo-political instability.

In Brief

Key findings

- The increasing vaccination rates resulted in fewer travel restrictions throughout 2021.
- COVID-related travel restrictions were gradually lifted, with, until then, exceptional measures and derogations maintained for some categories (students, seasonal workers, remote workers, health care professionals, etc.). Essential and frontline workers continued to receive increased attention during the COVID-19 recovery period.
- The global competition for talents continued despite the impact of the pandemic. New pathways to attract highly educated migrants, remote workers and potential investors have become more widespread among OECD countries.
- At the same time, acute labour shortages, including in low- and middle-skilled occupations, have led many governments to expand their temporary labour mobility schemes and bilateral agreements to help alleviate hiring challenges and offer better working conditions to precarious foreign workers.
- In many OECD countries, national retention strategies regarding temporary workers include streamlined (renewal or change of status) processes and new permanent residency schemes.
- By comparison, few changes were made to family migration policy. Recent legal amendments either tighten the requirements on sponsors or simplify the family reunification procedure for beneficiaries of international protection.
- Besides the resumption of asylum-related processes and resettlement activities across OECD countries, major policy and legal changes were introduced in 2021-22 in the field of international protection and humanitarian admission, inter alia in response to large-scale emergency situations and political crises.
- Similarly, exceptional circumstances have prompted several countries to strengthen their borders and concentrate their efforts on fighting irregular migration, on a temporary basis or in a more lasting manner.

Introduction

The COVID-19 pandemic had far-reaching effects on migration and border management throughout 2020-21. One year later, the widespread use of exemptions, extensions, ad hoc concessions and facilitations to mitigate the impact of the pandemic are slowly coming to an end. Immigration policy changes are now returning to focus on structural reforms, whether large or small scale. In 2021-22, attracting skilled and highly skilled professionals remained a political priority for a large number of OECD countries, leading to specific policy initiatives (digital nomad visas, modernised migration management tools, extended job-search permits, etc.) meant to last beyond the recovery period. Tapping temporary foreign workers to ease persisting labour shortage is another long-term challenge for countries heavily dependent on tourism, agriculture and other critical sectors. Other recent developments related to international protection and humanitarian admission, shifting in some cases from previous approaches, are part of broader policy responses to crises and geopolitical considerations.

Changes to COVID-19 mitigation measures

Border requirements and travel restrictions

Restrictive immigration policies continued to apply across OECD countries in 2021-22, although governments gradually relaxed restrictions for cross-border and domestic travel and progressively stepped away from "Zero-COVID" approaches.

On 1 July 2021, the European Union's Digital COVID-19 Certificate (EUDCC) went into effect and was nationally implemented in 27 EU Member States and all four non-EU Schengen Area countries. The Council of the European Union adapted several times its epidemiologically safe third countries list throughout the year. In accordance with subsequent recommendations, the EU/EEA Member States significantly eased restrictions on entry and quarantine rules for certain categories of travellers and visa holders, especially those fully vaccinated. In Europe and beyond, concessions were granted between neighbouring countries, with relaxed rules for cross-border and essential workers.

In many OECD countries, exceptional measures introduced to ensure continued legality of stay for migrants affected by restrictions on travel and immigration services have been repeatedly extended. In Norway, mitigation measures for seasonal workers unable to return to their home countries were prolonged through the end of 2021. Extension of residence permits and expiring visas was also granted to residing migrants in Portugal, until June 2022, and in Costa Rica, until September 2022. Flexible work arrangements (e.g. simplifying remote working activities of foreigners) were maintained in Poland and in Italy (even beyond the end of the State of Emergency announced by the Italian Government in March 2022) and bilateral tax agreements concluded by Luxembourg with Germany, Belgium and France for the telework of cross-border workers were automatically extended until 30 June 2022.

While some countries progressively reopened their borders to foreign nationals in the course of 2021, others maintained COVID-related travel restrictions for a few months longer before announcing their lifting from early 2022. Australia announced full reopening of borders in February 2022, as did Iceland and Switzerland (except for third-country nationals coming from high-risk countries). Conditions and rules for entry were updated by the Czech Ministry of Health on 18 March 2022. Entry restrictions for all travellers were lifted in Israel on 21 May 2022. Despite a gradual reopening of its borders (notably with Venezuela) from June 2021, the Health Emergency State in Colombia has been extended until the end of June 2022. Chile presented its "Protected Borders Plan" (with updates on entry requirements for foreign travellers) in April 2022 and New Zealand announced in August 2021 a national plan "Reconnecting New-Zealanders to the world" to safely and progressively reopen its borders, with a phased approach towards a full reopening expected in July 2022. While no general entry bans applied in Mexico and Korea, the latter applied until June 2022 a special entry procedure and tight border screenings with a quarantine requirement for unvaccinated travellers.

Despite the overall ease (or end) of travel bans and restrictions in OECD countries, vigilance remains while transitioning out of the acute COVID-19 phase. In April 2022, the European Parliament (LIBE Committee) supported a proposal of the EU Commission to extend the EU Digital COVID-19 Certificate framework for another year until June 2023 and pursue a co-ordinated approach by then to ensure free and safe travel of foreigners, within the EU and across its borders.

Recovery strategies

National border closures and travel restrictions enacted to limit the spread of the COVID-19 pandemic deeply impacted many countries' economies and led to significant delays and disruptions. Some backlogs, e.g. in processing applications, persisted despite the progressive resumption of consular activities and reopening of immigration services in the course of 2021. The United States Citizenship and Immigration Services (USCIS), for instance, is striving to reduce processing delays caused by the pandemic while improving services, e.g. by reusing previously submitted biometrics, waiving in-person visa interview requirements when possible, or extending deadlines for applicants and employers to respond to various agency actions. In Israel, an automatic extension of six months is granted by the Population and Immigration Authority (PIBA) to certain categories of visa holders and residents due to the growing demand for appointments. In the Netherlands, a dedicated Asylum Task Force was set up by the Ministry of Immigration to support the work of the Immigration and Naturalisation service (IND) and eliminate the backlog of more than 15 000 asylum applications that had accrued up to April 2020. New working methods and practical arrangements were needed to clear this initial backlog as well as applications lodged after that date, leading to an extended deployment of the Task Force until the end of 2021. Significant delays in processing visa and permits applications were also reported in Portugal.

National responses to, and recovery from, COVID-19 include concrete measures and actions towards foreign workers and/or vulnerable categories of migrants. Australia, for instance, established a Global Business and Talent Attraction task force to support the post-COVID-19 recovery and better attract talented workers and innovative companies to the domestic labour market. As an additional measure to support the COVID-19 recovery plan and help fill shortages (especially in agricultural sectors) the government also committed to bringing an additional 12 500 Pacific workers to Australia under the Seasonal Worker Programme (SWP) and the Pacific Labour Scheme (PLS) by March 2022. Colombia specifically addressed migration and integration issues in its 2022 six-point response plan to prevent risks of abuses and exploitation of vulnerable and strongly affected population (including migrants and IDPs).

In the EU, most governments adopted national recovery and resilience plans (NRRP), setting out their reform and investment agendas until 2026, in accordance with the Regulation establishing the Recovery and Resilience Facility (RRF), adopted on 11 February 2021.

While many of these national plans do not explicitly refer to migration management as a key response to the post-COVID-19 recovery, a few NRRPs contain measures to support inter alia social and economic cohesion or digital transformation, likely to directly or indirectly impact immigration policies. The NRRP in Greece will include investments for the digitalisation of the migration and asylum system. Several NRRPs, especially from countries heavily reliant on tourism (e.g. Spain), plan to diversify and massively invest in digitalisation of public administration, including with regard to border control and migration management. Increased focus on health care systems, access, and security, in the formulated long-term strategies, is also likely to impact and reshape existing immigration policies. As part of its national recovery plan, approved by the European Commission on 1 June 2021, Poland intends to introduce measures to facilitate the hiring of migrant workers for longer periods of time to tackle unemployment and improve the situation of the Polish labour market post-crisis. Similarly, the NRRP of the Slovak Republic, approved in June 2021, proposes reforming existing policies and legislation on migration and integration in the Slovak Republic, and working to attract a qualified labour force from abroad as a response to increasing shortages in the country's own qualified labour force.

As part of the government's efforts to recover from the COVID-19 crisis, Ireland has now extended its five-year multiple entry short-stay visas to all visa-required third-country nationals (an option previously available only to Chinese nationals).

Managing labour migration

Throughout 2021-22, the global competition for talents continued despite the impact of the pandemic. Immigration pathways for skilled professionals have been developed in many countries with a view to facilitate international recruitment, better attract, and retain foreign talents with sought-after skills. In fact the so-called "Great Resignation", an economic trend illustrated by a record number of people quitting their jobs after the COVID-19 pandemic, obliged decision-makers to rethink their immigration policies and a vast majority of companies to adapt their employee retention strategies in an innovative way.

Many OECD countries continue to see an important role for foreign workers, especially in shortage occupations. Alongside the German Skilled Immigration Act, which entered into force in March 2020, the Coalition Agreement presented by the government in Germany in December 2021 called for further immigration routes and streamlined procedures for skilled workers, in particular in shortage occupations. Similarly, the New Migration Policy for 2021-25 adopted by the Slovak Republic on 8 September 2021 emphasises the need for well-managed labour migration in order to prevent social, economic and environmental tensions. In the United States, the Executive Order presented by the Biden Administration in February 2021[1] unveiled several policy changes aimed at easing the recruitment of foreign workers and better retaining talents and highly educated professionals (e.g., in STEM occupations). Similarly, in Bulgaria, both the Migration Strategy (2021-25) and the Employment Strategy (2021-30) set up labour migration as a political priority, especially highly skilled workers.

But highly skilled professionals are not the only ones that OECD countries seek to attract. Efforts to facilitate the entry, hiring and the working conditions of temporary workers, in "essential" or critical occupations, such as the agricultural or health sector, have been pursued in 2021-22. A number of OECD countries introduced new admission schemes, flexibilities, and even, in some cases, dedicated pathways for permanent residency to help retain this valuable workforce and reduce the risk of abuses and exploitations.

Attracting talent

While many countries were already engaged in the global competition for talent before the crisis started, the impact of the COVID-19 on the existing talent shortage has been considerable. Due to the strict travel and mobility restrictions, working conditions have shifted from an office-centric culture to more flexible and hybrid options. This new trend, combined with more systemic demographic and socio-economic challenges, spurred many countries to further enhance their attractiveness strategies for foreign talents (e.g. highly educated foreign national, entrepreneurs and international students) and adopt new measures to address skills needs in the long term. Since 2020-21, digital nomads and foreign remote workers have received increased attention, with emerging schemes and programmes dedicated to this growing category of remote workers, employed or self-employed in companies abroad (Box 2.1).

Box 2.1. "Digital nomads" and cross-border remote workers

COVID-19, combined with the digital transformation across all business areas, fundamentally changed working conditions. Office closures and travel restrictions led to a massive global expansion of teleworking to which many countries and employers have had to adapt. While 2020 marked the emergence of new "digital nomad visa schemes" within OECD countries, initiated by Estonia in August, remote workers policies continued to spread throughout 2021 and their number is rising.

To date, 6 OECD countries and at least 22 non-OECD countries offer specific visas for digital nomads (DNVs) which allow foreign workers to stay in the country and work remotely for a company abroad. Costa Rica and Greece introduced remote worker visa schemes at the end of 2021. Hungary launched, in February 2022, the "White Card", a one-year permit for digital nomads to reside in Hungary while working for a foreign employer or foreign clients. On 29 June 2022, Latvia introduced a digital nomad visa that allows foreign nationals (self-)employed in an OECD country to work remotely from Latvia for up to one year, renewable for another year, without local sponsorship. Proposals are working their way through the legislative process in Italy, Spain and Colombia; in Italy, Parliament passed it in March 2022.

Justifications put forward by countries to develop dedicated pathways for digital nomads and international remote workers vary. Tourism-dependent economies, severely harmed by the pandemic, launched DNV programmes as part of their recovery strategies to replenish their lost revenue and attract potential consumers/taxpayers. Others see a benefit in issuing DNVs to combat misuse of pre-existing migration schemes (e.g. tourist visas, non-active statuses or freelance permits) and clarify the legal status of foreigners who only have income from abroad, mostly from employed or self-employed activities.

As most DNV schemes were adopted in the midst – or after the peak- of COVID-19, the clear benefits (relative to the efforts required to manage them) as well as the risk associated (e.g. compliance and possible misuses) of these schemes remain uncertain. However, there is considerable interest in monitoring how newly implemented DNVs develop over time.

Source: OECD (2022[1]), "Should OECD countries develop new Digital Nomad Visas?", https://www.oecd.org/migration/mig/MPD-27-Should-OECD-countries-develop-new-Digital-Nomad-Visas-July2022.pdf.

To better attract and retain skilled migrants from across the world, several OECD countries are planning to adopt points-based immigration systems (PBS), a model already used in Australia, Canada, Japan and New Zealand, where foreigners have to score above a certain threshold of "points" in order to obtain a residence or work permit. In the United Kingdom, a so-called "Points-Based Immigration System" introduced in early 2021 became the main immigration route for foreign skilled workers, although it is rather a checklist of mandatory criteria. Germany and the Czech Republic are both exploring the possibility to develop PBS criteria in the near future. In Germany, while the exact criteria haven't been defined yet, a PBS is meant to run parallel to existing channels and include a "points-based opportunity card" for job-hunting workers from third countries.

At the EU level, attracting skills and talents from abroad also became a political priority to improve overall migration management in a sustainable and ambitious manner. The revised "EU Blue Card" Directive (2021/1883) introduced new rules for the entry and residence of highly skilled workers, including more flexible admission conditions, enhanced rights and the possibility to move and work more easily between EU Member States. In addition, the European Commission announced on 27 April 2022 a set of policy actions and legal proposals aimed at better attracting talents to the EU while addressing serious labour markets shortages, including an EU Talent Pool initiative aimed at matching EU employers with the talent they need.

Job-search permits and smooth recruitment processes of graduates and young professionals

Since April 2022, researchers and graduates who completed their projects or studies can apply in Finland for a new two-year residency permit to seek work or start a business (in 2018, the extension was allowed for up to one year). The new permit can also be requested within five years of graduation or the completion of research. Pending new legislation, the Spanish Government also announced in June 2022 its intention to grant residence permits to foreign students for the duration of their studies and to extend work rights for one to two years after graduation.

Additional facilitations for international students and researchers were also introduced in Lithuania in March 2021, with relaxed requirements for work-related residence permits and the possibility for young graduates to start to work immediately while waiting for a decision on their application. In March 2022, the Israeli Hi-Tech Work visa regulation was revised to allow high tech domestic companies to more easily recruit international students and young graduates. According to the revision, these companies can now request work visas for university students or recent graduates for certain high-tech professions within three years of their graduation.

Recent policy shifts on (highly-)skilled workers

In Australia, policy priority focuses on the Employer Sponsored and Skilled Independent programme. As a result, while the planning level of the 2022-23 Migration programme remains at 160 000 places, 109 900 are allocated to skilled workers compared to 79 600 in the previous year. In order to address the shortfall of immigration in 2020, Immigration, Refugees and Citizenship Canada (IRCC) increased the targets for permanent admission to Canada to 401 000 in 2021 (the prior plan foresaw 351 000), to 411 000 in 2022, and to 421 000 in 2023.

New Zealand is also rebalancing its immigration system to make it easier to attract and hire high-skilled migrants, while supporting some sectors to transition to more productive and resilient ways of operating, instead of relying on lower-skilled migrant workers. A new Accredited Employer Work Visa (AEWV) was introduced 4 July 2022, enabling accredited employers to easily hire skilled migrant workers where genuine skills or labour shortage exist. This streamlined single visa process is meant to replace six work visas previously in place. Although border restrictions remained in place in New Zealand until August 2022, a number of exceptions were announced in December 2021. Among them, a border class exception has been put in place for the technology sector, enabling 600 specialist tech workers and their family members to come to New Zealand.

As part of a broader legal reform, Sweden introduced in June 2022 a new residence permit for highly qualified jobseekers and start-up founders, allowing eligible foreign nationals to stay in the country for up to nine months to seek employment or start a business in Sweden. In Lithuania, highly qualified workers are entitled since March 2021 to start to work pending the examination of their application for a residence permit. In the United Kingdom, from 2022, a single sponsored Global Business Mobility route opened for workers based outside the United Kingdom who are undertaking a temporary work assignment in the United Kingdom as a Senior or Specialist Worker, Graduate Trainee, UK Expansion Worker, Service Supplier or Secondment Worker. A new unsponsored route for the "High Potential Individual" has also been announced by the United Kingdom in May 2022, allowing graduates from top-ranked universities abroad to apply for an unsponsored two- to three-year work visa, bring their family members with them and switch to longer-term employment visas if the conditions are met.

In Spain, the forthcoming "Start-ups Law", aimed at attracting international talents and remote workers, is presented as a major milestone of the government's Recovery, Transformation and Resilience Plan. In June 2022, Finland launched a new fast-track service for specialists, start-up entrepreneurs, EU Blue Card applicants, and their family members (with a maximum processing period of two weeks). In addition, an expanded long-term visa (D) for specialists and high-growth start-up entrepreneurs has been announced for April 2023, as part of the government's commitment to increase education-based and work-based immigration to the country. In its roadmap released in September 2021, the Finnish Government plans to double the current volume of work-based immigration by 2030 to attain the overall increase of at least 50 000 work-based immigrants. The number of new foreign degree students is expected to triple to 15 000 by 2030, with the aim that 75% of them find employment in Finland.

In the United States, the latest USCIS H-1B processing data show increasing admission rates for new employment petitions, extensions, amendments and change of employers. The premium processing programme that guarantees expedited visa processing for certain employer-based visa petitions is also about to be expanded to several additional immigration benefit case-types.

Talent retention strategies

Effective July 2022, Australia will grant additional concessions to employers wishing to retain (highly-) skilled foreign workers holding a Temporary Skills Shortage (TSS) visa. For these categories, the "onshore renewal restriction" is removed, allowing applications lodged from within Australia for the short-term stream to continuously reside and work in the country. Starting between June and August of 2022, individuals in

Canada who completed a Canadian post-secondary degree and hold a post-graduate work permit expiring in 2022 will be eligible for a work permit extension of up to 18 months. In Sweden, foreign workers can now renew their temporary work permits even after a cumulative permit duration of four years; they were previously required to apply for permanent residence and, if not eligible, to leave the country.

Retaining foreign doctors and health care professionals represented a major challenge for countries facing serious workforce shortages in these critical occupations. In Ireland and in Poland, relaxed rules have been recently introduced not only to ease their recruitment (e.g. work permit exemptions for doctors, nurses, dentists or midwives amid the COVID-19 crisis and further administrative simplifications since November 2021 in Poland) but also to facilitate their settlement in the host country through reduced burdens and additional pathways to residency. In Ireland, a temporary scheme (active from March to April 2022) allowed non-EU medical doctors who had been working for more than two years in Ireland (under a General Employment permit) to apply for a "Stamp 4" residence permit, offering them (and their partners) the right to work without preconditions for a specified period, which counts as residence for subsequent citizenship application requirements.

Supporting business and investors

From 2021 onwards, several OECD countries revised their regulatory frameworks to adjust conditions for foreign investors and business owners/travellers. To support Australia's post-COVID-19 economic recovery, the Business Innovation and Investment Program (BIIP) and the Complying Investment Framework (CIF) have been updated and streamlined. Key changes, entered into force on 1 July 2021, include the reduction from nine to four visa streams and newly open pathways to permanent residency for these categories. At the same time, some eligibility requirements have been tightened and the investment amount threshold for the investor streams increased significantly. Similarly, the threshold amounts for obtaining a "golden visa" in Portugal increased from January 2022 (e.g. from EUR 350 000 to EUR 500 000 for the investment fund option and from EUR 1million to EUR 1.5 million for capital transfers), except for real estate investments, yet subject to geographical restrictions.

By comparison, a new law approved in June 2021 in Costa Rica reduced the minimum investment required for foreign investors, streamlined processes and provided tax benefits to holders of Temporary resident visas, including retirees. In the course of 2021, several developments took place in Lithuania aimed at improving the investment environment in Lithuania and helping foreign investors (and their family members) to relocate in the country and enter the labour market. Amendments to the Investment Law, which took effect in June 2021, include the issuance of temporary residence permits (for up to three years) to foreign employees, shareholders or chief executives of an eligible investor, arriving in Lithuania under an investment agreement. From May 2022, foreign nationals hired by "growth companies" in Estonia are no longer subject to the annual immigration quota. Travellers seeking to conduct short-term business activities in Chile can now apply for a Consular short-term authorisation, granted for up to ten years, for single or multiple entries.

Addressing pressing labour shortage in the agriculture sector...

The agriculture sector is heavily dependent on foreign workforce in many countries. With the COVID-19, mobility restrictions, border closures and suspension of immigration services led to a disruption of traditional labour supplies, affecting more particularly countries characterised by periods of peak seasonal labour demand or labour-intensive production. In a bid to address significant labour shortages due to the drop in migrant arrivals, most of these countries adopted complementary solutions and dedicated policy measures.

Korea mobilised inactive population groups as additional sources of labour in agriculture. Between 2 March 2021 and 31 March 2022, the country extended its Temporary Seasonal Worker Program allowing all foreign residents with non-employment status to legally engage in seasonal work. Previously opened to

E-9 foreign workers with expiring work permits, this temporary scheme was later expanded to other categories of visa holders (e.g. family visitors, work and visit status holders) with the aim to enrol in the programme up to 79 000 eligible foreign residents. A new regulation entered into force in Austria on 1 January 2022 allowing those who registered with the Public Employment Service (AMS) to be issued a seasonal employment permit for an initial period of six months, outside of the quota and without a labour market test.

Other countries implemented measures or agreements to facilitate or maintain the admission of temporary foreign workers filling in specific labour shortages. On 23 August 2021, Australia introduced a new sponsored visa stream (the Australian Agriculture Visa, AAV) open to workers from countries with bilateral agreements. On 28 March, an agreement with Viet Nam was reached. The AAV was meant to be temporary supplementing the existing Pacific Australia Labour Mobility (PALM) which remains the primary scheme for meeting agricultural workforce shortages in Australia. In 2021, the United Kingdom extended its Seasonal Workers Pilot Scheme (launched in 2019) for horticulture, allowing up to 30 000 foreigners per year to come and work in this field for up to six months. Costa Rica extended its bilateral agreement with Nicaragua on the temporary hiring of Nicaraguan agricultural workers in Costa Rica for an additional seven months to cover the 2021-22 harvesting season. In July 2021, Germany concluded new bilateral labour agreements with the Republic of Moldova on employment of seasonal workers in agriculture for 2022.

In 2021-22, Austria, Italy and Israel increased their annual quotas of seasonal workers, notably in the agricultural sector. In Israel, an additional 2 500 work permits will be issued in 2022 to temporary migrant workers for the agricultural sector, compared to the previous year. In Italy, an additional quota of 14 000 is reserved for non-EU workers in the farming sector for 2022. This amount is likely to increase with a revision of the annual "Flow Decree", announced in June 2022 by the Italian Government, that will raise the number of admissions for contract, seasonal and self-employment to 75 000 for 2021-22 (from 69 700 previously). While continuously increasing since 2016, the seasonal workers quota in Austria was raised by 636 places in 2022. Access to residency and employment of "regular" seasonal workers, notably in agriculture/forestry, is also facilitated. Seasonal workers recruited in Estonia are exempt from the annual immigration quota and the labour market test requirements. By contrast, Korea reduced quotas for nonprofessional workers under the E-9 visa from 56 000 in 2020 to 52 000 for 2021. Since March 2021, the Flemish Region (Belgium) reduced the minimum salary threshold requirement for seasonal workers.

... While further protecting seasonal workers from exploitation

Due to the temporary nature of their activity, seasonal workers may be particularly vulnerable to precarious working conditions and exploitation. As of 17 June 2021, it became easier for foreign seasonal workers in Finland to change employers. The amendment to the Seasonal Workers Act tightened, at the same time, sanctions for non-compliant employers. Greater protection is also ensured, since June 2021, for foreign berry pickers with an Act on the legal status of foreigners picking natural products. The new law lays down the rights of pickers of natural products, clarifies their status and specifies the obligations of operators and the legally-binding sanctions/penalties in case of non-compliance. In Sweden, employment contracts must now be attached to the application for a work permit in order for the Swedish Migration Agency to control the working conditions of the position offered. The Agency may also oblige the employer to report any (less favourable) change in the terms of the employment contract – subject to a fine in case of non-compliance. In July 2021, a new temporary visa (Migrant Exploitation protection work visa) became available for workers who have a report of exploitation assessed by Employment New Zealand and have been given a Report of Exploitation Assessment letter. The visa is valid for six months and allows the holder to leave their current job during the investigation and change employer easily.

Streamlined entry and recruitment of temporary workers

Entry facilitations for temporary workers are not limited to (non-)seasonal workers working in the field of agriculture. Starting in 2022, Germany concluded several bilateral labour agreements e.g. for the placement of nurses with Indonesia and India or the placement of electricians and gardeners with Colombia. In Israel, the bilateral agreements signed by the government with third countries over the past few years (e.g. with China, Moldova, Ukraine (construction) or the Philippines (caregiving sector), are expected to become the only way of recruiting temporary migrant workers subject to annual quotas. In December 2021, an additional 20 000 H-2B visas for temporary non-agricultural employment were authorised by the United States' relevant departments for the first half of 2022.

Further flexibilities to ease the recruitment of temporary workers were introduced in Italy (with the so-called "Sostegni Ter" Decree) and in Australia (with the consolidation of the two existing PALM – Pacific Australia Labour Mobility – schemes into one single scheme on 4 April 2022). The Knesset (Israeli Parliament) voted in January 2022 the abolishment of the 15-20% wage levy paid by all employers of foreign workers in construction – the last sector to be subject to this levy. This change was made to reduce construction and infrastructure project costs. The Act on Foreigners of Poland was amended in January 2022 to simplify and facilitate the recruitment of foreign workers. Changes include a reduced number of supporting documents, the possibility to change employers and/or easily review the terms and conditions of employment, such as the length of employment, based on the sole declaration of the employer for workers from six countries. To enhance companies' competitiveness, Estonia plans to ease restrictions on third-country workers from 2023 by extending the length of work permits from one year to three years.

In the Czech Republic, demand exceeds processing capacity at many foreign consulates; a quota system is used together with criteria for priority processing. The quotas for Employee Cards were raised in 2021 (i.e. up to 3 600 highly qualified and 50 000 qualified foreign employees). Romania also saw sharp demand for foreign workers; the initial quota for 2021, 25 000 workers, was supplemented in August 2021 with another 25 000. The quota announced for 2022 is 100 000. Actual inflows are below this number due to processing capacity.

COVID-19 travel restrictions also greatly impacted youth mobility schemes and working holiday programmes (WHP) in many countries. As infection rates overall declined, several OECD countries concluded bilateral agreements to attract (young) travellers and/or temporary visitors likely to help fill shortages.

As of 1 January 2022, a new bilateral youth mobility scheme between the United Kingdom and Iceland became applicable. This scheme provides opportunities for young citizens of the two countries to experience culture and general way of life in each other's countries. Iceland had already reached a similar agreement with Japan. Applicants are granted a one-year residence permit (not renewable) and an unlimited work permit. In February 2021, France opened its working holiday programme to the Republic of Peru (with a quota of 300 beneficiaries per year). The Netherlands extended its Working Holiday Programme to Japan (becoming the 9th participating country) and Swiss young citizens were given access to the WHP in Australia in 2022.

As of September 2021, Canada further eased the eligibility requirements for vaccinated *International Experience Canada* (IEC) candidates who weren't required to submit a proof of a valid job offer to receive an invitation to apply for the Working Holiday Pool. Foreign youth whose applications were approved in 2020 but were unable to come to Canada due to border control measures benefitted from an additional 12 months to activate their work permit. Similarly, the Working Holiday Schemes reopened in New Zealand in March 2022 as part of the government's plan to "reconnect" the country to the rest of the world.

Besides working holidaymakers, international students and graduates also benefit in some countries from temporary mobility programmes. The "Young generation as change agents" programme (YGCA), a European-funded project in Spain, which ended in June 2021, allowed 98 Moroccan graduates to complete a master's degree in Spain in one of the strategic sectors pre-identified by the Moroccan authorities. France implemented a Partnership Agreement on Migration and Mobility with India in October 2021 to facilitate inter alia temporary circular migration and mobility of Indian students and researchers. But these projects require beneficiaries and participants to return to their country after the completion of their studies with dedicated assistance for their integration in the local labour market.

Pathways to permanent residency for temporary residents

As part of their efforts to retain and further integrate temporary workers, several OECD countries announced newly created or extended pathways to permanent residency for certain visa or permits holders, with a focus on occupations deemed essential or critical during the COVID-19 crisis. Some of these pathways are employer-driven, introduced on a temporary or a long-term basis.

From July 2022, a new permanent residency pathway will become available in Australia for certain short-term visa holders under the existing Employer Nomination scheme visa programme. For two years, employers will benefit from facilitations to retain foreign employees. Following the Federal election in May 2022, these policy measures are set to continue, with expected changes regarding streamlined access to permanent residency for visa holders working under successful arrangements and those that have priority skills that are in shortage in Australia.

On 1 January 2022, the Atlantic Immigration Pilot Program in Canada became the permanent Atlantic Immigration Program (AIP). This pathway enables skilled workers and international graduates who want to live and work in one of the four Canadian Atlantic Provinces to obtain permanent residence. This change is meant to help employers hire and retain qualified candidates while filling local and community needs. In addition, Canada launched, between May and November 2021, a "Temporary Resident to Permanent Resident Pathway" for temporary essential workers (e.g. health care) and young graduates already present in Canada, with a cap set at 90 000 applications. Further flexibilities include the possibility for applicants to leave Canada from June 2022 while waiting for a decision and the extended validity of the Bridging Open Work Permit (BOWP) until 2024, allowing applicants to keep working while waiting for the results of their permanent residence application. In September 2021, New Zealand announced its new Resident Visa, a one-off, simplified pathway to residency for around 165 000 work-related visa holders (including essential skills, post-study work visas and their immediate family members). For these eligible applicants, a Permanent Resident Visa is usually the next step after being granted a Resident Visa.

As part of the intraregional agreement between the member countries of the Andean Community, Colombia offers, since January 2022, a new nationality-based visa (the Andean Migrant visa) to eligible nationals of Bolivia, Ecuador and Peru and their families, valid for two years. Under this scheme, visa holders benefit from a streamlined access to permanent residency after this two-year period, without the need for employer sponsorship.

In some other countries, acquiring permanent residency is subject to stricter requirements. In Sweden, an amendment made in July 2021 to the Aliens Act subject the permanent residency status to a "maintenance requirement", i.e. proof of a sufficiently high and stable income deriving either from permanent employment in Sweden, or from a fixed-term employment lasting at least 18 months from the date on which the application is examined. These changes entered into force without transitional rules, applying also to post-graduates and researchers. In Canada, the minimum amount of funds required to apply for permanent residence through the Express Entry (Federal Skilled Worker Program) increased from 9 June 2022. In Chile, holders of temporary residence permits who wish to stay in Chile permanently must have resided in the country for at least 24 months and not having left the country for more than 60 days (against 180 previously) during the previous year of residence. However, after becoming permanent residents, foreigners benefit from relaxed rules allowing them to leave Chile for up to two years (instead of one) without losing their immigration status.

As part of a package of measures proposed as a follow-up to the New Pact on Migration and Asylum, the European Commission presented on 27 April 2022 a recast of Directive 2003/109/EC on long term-residents. This proposal aims to create a more effective, coherent and fair system to acquire EU long-term resident status, e.g. by strengthening the rights of long-term residents and their family members including those who have cumulated residence in different Member States. The proposal additionally puts in place a mechanism to ensure a level playing field between the EU long-term residence permit and national permanent residence permits in terms of procedures, equal treatment rights, and access to information. While negotiations are ongoing, the recast is expected to improve EU's overall attractiveness to foreign talent and enhance the integration of third-country nationals who settled legally and on a long-term basis in the EU.

Family migration

While recent changes regarding the admission of family migrants are mainly procedural, either to relax or tighten eligibility requirements, some of these may have major implications for the main applicants and their family members. With regard to family reunification, targeted legal changes in Australia, Norway, Slovenia or Luxembourg were meant to tighten the eligibility requirements for sponsors (requiring for instance greater proof of self-sufficiency or higher salary thresholds). Luxembourg and Germany, on the contrary, overall relaxed the rules and conditions for beneficiaries of international/subsidiary protection while applying for family reunification. In November 2021, the USCIS issued policy guidance to address automatic extension of employment authorisation for certain H-4, E (treaty traders) and L (ICTs), non-immigrant dependent spouses.

More substantially, the Canadian Minister of Immigration, Refugees and Citizenship announced improvements to Canada's super visa programme, which allows parents and grandparents to visit their Canadian or permanent resident children or grandchildren in Canada for an extended period of time. Starting 4 July 2022, the allowable length of stay for Super visa holders will increase to five years per entry, up from the current allowable stay of two years per entry. Visa holders will also have the option to extend their stay by up to two years at a time while in Canada.

International protection and geopolitical considerations

Recent changes in asylum-related policies

The extraordinary and emergency measures adopted by most OECD countries to contain the spread of the COVID-19 virus deeply impacted asylum seekers whose access to protection was, in some cases, highly restricted. In Greece, the Emergency Legislative Decree adopted on 2 March 2020 temporarily suspended the asylum process for one month. On 21 November 2021, after more than one year of border restrictions, Canada removed the temporary measure restricting asylum claims from foreign nationals seeking entry from the United States between designated land ports of entry.

More fundamentally, the successive crises that have hit many parts of the world over recent years (e.g. economic, migration and, more recently sanitary) led a large number of countries to reform their asylum policy frameworks. Key changes in 2021 include legislative amendments intended to accelerate and streamline asylum procedures (in Luxembourg and Slovenia) and targeted revisions of national lists of safe countries of origin. While the French Council of State withdrew, on 2 July 2021, several countries from the French list of safe countries of origin (Benin, Senegal and Ghana), the Greek Government announced on 7 June 2021 its decision to list the Republic of Türkiye as a safe third origin country for asylum seekers from Syria, Afghanistan, Pakistan, Bangladesh and Somalia. Following the transposition of the Recast Asylum Procedure Directive into its national legislation, in May 2021, Sweden adopted its own list of safe countries of origin, resulting in an accelerated procedure on the assumption that persecution is unlikely to occur in these designated countries. In Austria and Luxembourg, independent bodies have been appointed to closely monitor the rights and well-being of children in immigration and asylum cases.

Policy shifts occurred in Denmark and the United Kingdom with regard to asylum claims processing and international protection. On 3 June 2021, Denmark passed a legislative amendment allowing for the transfer of asylum seekers to a third country, framed by a prior bilateral agreement, for the purposes of both asylum processing and protection of refugees outside Europe. Announced in March 2021, the asylum system reform in the United Kingdom, embodied by the Nationality and Borders Act, became an Act of Parliament on 28 April 2022. Beside the proposals for differential treatment of refugees through "a two tier-system", depending on their mode of arrival, the new Bill puts into statute provisions allowing to remove asylum seekers whose claims are inadmissible to a "safe third country" with which an agreement has been concluded. To date, only one agreement of this nature has been signed, with Rwanda.[2] In Sweden, changes made to the Aliens Act in July 2021, maintaining several restrictions introduced by the previous law, include a shift to temporary residence permits for beneficiaries of international protection, permanent residence being only granted to resettled refugees.

Humanitarian admission

Most resettlement and humanitarian admission activities, paused or suspended during the COVID-19 pandemic, resumed in 2021, albeit often only slowly. While implementing these programmes, many countries had to adopt new working methods, e.g. to select refugees or assess individual cases, in order to comply with COVID-19 health measures. Furthermore, the challenges raised by the long-running conflicts, emerging unrests and political crises in various parts of the world, have led more and more OECD countries to (re)open humanitarian pathways either through resettlement schemes or (temporary) admission programmes.

The outflow of Venezuelan refugees, the second-largest external displacement crisis in the world, remains a serious matter of concern, in particular for neighbouring countries. From 8 October 2021, Venezuelans are granted a ten-year Temporary Protection Permit in Colombia. This unprecedented programme, complementary to international protection, applies to those currently living in the country and those entering via official checkpoints over the next two years. Over 2.1 million Venezuelans are expected to benefit from this programme over the next decade.

In response to the internal repression in Belarus, Poland launched in 2020 the initiative "Solidarity with Belarus", a 5-point aid plan including commitments to provide support and simplification of entry procedures for people who needs to arrive to Poland, by means of an exceptional national humanitarian visa procedure. Lithuania adopted a similar approach, introducing several changes to facilitate the entry of Belarussian nationals (who could obtain multiple-entry visas under facilitated conditions and cross the border on humanitarian grounds). What is more, in the second half of 2021 the EU took a number of specific measures to counter the instrumentalisation of migration by Belarus at its external borders (Box 2.2).

Box 2.2. EU policy response to the border and humanitarian crisis triggered by Belarus

Starting in the summer of 2021, an instrumentalisation of migrants sponsored by Belarus at the EU external borders particularly affected Lithuania, Poland and Latvia. In response to the emergency situation that resulted from the unprecedented increase in border crossings from Belarus, the European Commission offered both immediate material and political support that led to several measures including a decision on emergency aid of EUR 36.7 million from the Asylum, Migration and Integration Fund (AMIF) to enhance the implementation of asylum procedures and the reception conditions in these countries, including for vulnerable persons.

In December 2021, upon request from the European Council, the Commission put forward a set of temporary asylum and return measures of an extraordinary and exceptional nature to assist Latvia, Lithuania and Poland in managing migration flows. The measures, which remained in force for a period of six months, included extended registration deadlines for asylum applications, swift border procedures and practical support from EU agencies.

Following the Taliban offensive in August 2021, rescue operations and evacuations of Afghan citizens were carried out by OECD and non-OECD countries. Many EU/EEA countries granted humanitarian admissions to evacuees from Afghanistan during the second half of 2021. Some of them included these evacuations in their resettlement quotas (Norway) while others launched dedicated resettlement pathways for Afghan nationals in need of protection. The Irish "Afghan Admission Programme" allows Afghans already residing in Ireland to nominate four family members to join them, even if they are currently in the neighbouring countries of Iran, Pakistan, Turkmenistan, Uzbekistan and Tajikistan. Invited by the European Commission to make pledges for the next ad hoc resettlement Programme in 2022, 15 EU Member States agreed to help almost 40 000 Afghans through resettlement and humanitarian admission.

In the United Kingdom, where a Minister for Afghan Resettlement was specifically appointed to oversee the "Operation Warm Welcome", a dedicated resettlement pathway for Afghan citizens (ACRS) opened in January 2022. The scheme, which differs from the Afghan Relocation and Assistance Policy (ARAP) scheme, provides a safe and legal way for some of the most vulnerable and at-risk people from Afghanistan to come to the United Kingdom and benefit from indefinite leave to remain (ILR) in the country.

Canada committed to welcome at least 40 000 refugees through a special humanitarian programme to resettle vulnerable Afghan nationals outside of Afghanistan. Beginning in July 2021, the United States evacuated and offered humanitarian parole to nearly 80 000 Afghans through Operation Allies Welcome, granting them the right to live and work in the country, but no pathway to lawful permanent residence status. In March 2022, Afghanistan was designated for Temporary Protected Status (TPS). Under TPS, eligible foreign nationals can apply for employment authorisation and are permitted to remain in the United States as long as they benefit from the policy. In April and May 2022, the United States added Cameroon, South Sudan, Sudan, and Ukraine to the list of countries from which individuals are eligible for TPS protection.

For clarification purposes, New Zealand renamed in November 2021 its humanitarian border exception category, established in March 2020 to facilitate entry of people who have a compelling humanitarian reason to enter New Zealand, as the "compassionate entry border exception category".

In addition, several legislative amendments were introduced with regard to the reception of resettled refugees. In Slovenia, where a pre-departure orientation programme replaced, in November 2021, the three-month introductory activities post-arrival, or in Ireland, where the Department of Children, Equality, Disability, Integration and Youth is now responsible for refugee resettlement. On 24 February 2021, guidelines for the reception policy for resettled refugees were issued by the French Government, enhancing the decentralisation of the system and the key role played by the regional prefectures in this process.

More generally, the United States Government announced the resettlement of 20 000 refugees from the Americas during fiscal years 2023 and 2024, a three-fold increase over projected arrivals in FY2022. Within this context, more referrals of displaced Haitians will be received into the US Refugee Admissions Program (USRAP). In March 2021, the Department of State and Homeland Security announced the reopening of the Central American Minors (CAM) Programme, which from 2014-18 allowed certain parents with pre-defined categories of lawful presence in the United States to petition on behalf of their children for access to USRAP processing for potential refugee resettlement in the United States while still in their home country (El Salvador, Guatemala, or Honduras). In Germany, the "New Start in a Team" (NesT) programme, a community-based sponsorship of refugees pilot project launched in 2019, will become an integral part of the German resettlement programme as of 1 January 2023. Within this context, 200 additional resettlement places for particularly vulnerable refugees will be available.

The Canadian Minister of Immigration announced in 2021 a dedicated resettlement stream for Human rights defenders with an annual quota of 250 spaces. In Australia, the latest public consultations on the Humanitarian Programme, which offers resettlement for refugees and people overseas who are in humanitarian need (e.g. Myanmar citizens), highlighted a certain number of key issues, regarding notably the size and objectives of the programme, the cohorts of prioritisation and the impact of COVID-19 and border restrictions on resettlement activities.

Making use of innovative digital tools

Digitalisation in migration management processes is an increasing trend. During the pandemic, innovative tools and solutions had to be developed to support third-country nationals' admission and/or further integration. While most in-person services were halted due to national lockdowns and social distancing measures, policy makers across OECD countries established new – or further modernised – digital tools for identification, information or processing purposes. Canada, for instance, enhanced its IRCC digital service to receive electronic permit applications and provided dedicated training to staff supporting applicants remotely.

In Chile, an implemented Act adopted in February 2022 led to the centralisation of immigration case adjudication in the National Immigration Service (NIS). Within this context, access to the NIS online portal has been extended to all foreign nationals, including in-country applicants, with the immediate issuance of a receipt allowing eligible applicants to reside (and, in some case, work) while their application is being processed. In an effort to simplify and modernise its legislation (unchanged since 1975), Chile also restructured its visa categories, issuing Temporary resident visas to foreign workers who previously had to apply for distinct residence and work permits. In Belgium, the online platform "Working in Belgium", a one-stop-shop based on inter-regional agreement and co-ordinating relevant information for single permit applicants and holders, became effective on 31 March 2021. The online application service residence permits for foreigners in France (ANEF), initially opened for international students, was progressively rolled out across other work and residence authorisations categories throughout 2021. Greece also pursued the digital transformation of its migration and asylum processes with the issuance, from March 2021, of an online tax identification number for beneficiaries of international protection and the launch, on 15 April 2021, of a new online platform for the submission of certain residence permit applications. Other functional and technological improvements have been reported in Latvia, Poland, New Zealand and Türkiye (e-appointment system for beneficiaries of temporary protection). Revoking a previous decision, the Swedish Migration Agency allows employers and foreigners to submit employment contracts and assignment letters with digital signatures in support of work permit applications.

From September 2021, visa-free foreign visitors (from 102 countries) need to obtain an electronic travel authorisation (K-ETA), subject to a full online process, before entering Korea.

Digital transformation is also at the core of European migration and asylum policies with various objectives set by the European Commission, such as the full digitalisation of the visa procedure by 2025 or the interoperability of EU information systems in the field of police and judicial co-operation, asylum and migration to be achieved by the end of 2023.

Return and readmission policies

Ongoing negotiations on the New Pact on Migration and Asylum may lead to some new EU regulations in the future. The "screening" regulation would put in place pre-entry screening applicable to all non-EU country nationals who are present at the external border without fulfilling the entry conditions while a revised Eurodac regulation would modernise the database of asylum seekers and irregular migrants. Meanwhile several EU/EEA Member States adopted concrete measures in 2021 to accelerate the removal processes or to better define conditions for voluntary return (Denmark, Germany, Greece) of irregular migrants.

While these targeted revisions were already planned in policy frameworks or part of comprehensive legislative reforms, other changes, of an exceptional nature, resulted in OECD countries from emergency situations and acute political crises. The Greek authorities announced in March 2020 a tougher approach towards migrants and asylum seekers attempting to cross land and sea borders irregularly from Türkiye, deploying a joint military and police operation at its eastern land border in the Evros region. In July 2021, in response to the sudden influx of migrants from Belarus, an "Extreme Situation" was declared in Lithuania, resulting in a Resolution on "Countering Hybrid Aggression" adopted by the parliament on 13 July and inviting the government to take all measures to contain and prevent the threat, e.g. by deploying the Lithuanian Armed Forces to protect the Lithuanian-Belarus borders. Latvia declared a State of Emergency over the migrant influx at the Belarus border on 10 August, authorising border guards, armed forces and police to protect its borders and prevent irregular entry. Poland also deployed border guard officers and soldiers from the Polish army at its borders. Walls and fences were erected in these countries as well as in other parts of the world, e.g. Türkiye's border wall with Iran extended in September 2021 by Türkiye to block new arrivals of Afghans. Terminated in 2021, the US Government programme "Migrant Protection Protocols" (MPP) with Mexico, was reinstated by court order in 2022, with new guidelines.

References

OECD (2022), "Should OECD countries develop new Digital Nomad Visas?", *Migration Policy Debates*, No. 27, OECD, Paris, https://www.oecd.org/migration/mig/MPD-27-Should-OECD-countries-develop-new-Digital-Nomad-Visas-July2022.pdf. [1]

Notes

[1] Executive Order on Restoring Faith in Our Legal Immigration Systems and Strengthening Integration and Inclusion Efforts for New Americans, 14012.

[2] UK-Rwanda Migration and Economic Development Partnership, MoU signed on 14 April 2022.

3 Recent developments in migrant integration policy

This chapter provides an overview of the changes in the integration policies in OECD countries during the period 2021-22. Notably, global instability and the accompanying large-scale movements have renewed attention to policies of regularisation and naturalisation. The chapter addresses this attention as well as policy changes designed to improve labour-market integration and to meet the needs of specific migrant groups. It further examines the system reorganisations that have been pursued to improve service delivery.

In Brief

Key findings

- While most countries have relaxed COVID-19 related restrictions on gatherings, several have taken measures to integrate flexible learning arrangements from the period, especially for language, over the long term, as they have been well received by migrants participating in integration measures.

- Large numbers of migrants, particularly those fleeing instability in their home country, were regularised in 2021 and 2022. Regularisation programmes in Chile and Italy were well underway, and a new regularisation was announced in Ireland. Colombia has launched a particularly far-reaching regularisation to meet large inflows from Venezuela.

- OECD countries generally encourage naturalisation as an important lever of integration and have introduced measures to increase flexibility. Germany announced an intention to make broad changes to naturalisation laws, including facilitating dual citizenship, and the United States implemented several measures as part of an interagency strategy to promote naturalisation.

- Large-scale reforms of integration programmes, for example in Belgium, were focused on increasing individualisation, improving mentorship, and helping migrants gain rapid, but stable, access to the labour market.

- Countries have sought to improve access to education for both youth and adult migrants. The European Union Action Plan on Integration and Inclusion (2021-27) will also specifically promote measures for inclusive education and training.

- While few OECD countries have launched comprehensive programmes targeting women and young migrants, an increasing number of countries have recognised the disproportionate impact of COVID-19 on these groups, particularly in terms of labour-market insertion. Germany has launched several programmes aimed to integrate migrant parents of young children.

- Recognition of skills remains high on the integration policy agenda. Germany introduced an accelerated administrative procedure for recognition procedures in professions governed by federal law or by equivalent state regulations. Israel and Luxembourg have also introduced measures to recognise the skills of specific migrant groups.

- While few countries have made significant changes to language training schemes for adult migrants, those who have done so have increased target language levels in recognition of the fact that migrants need greater proficiency than they have previously achieved to maximise their potential.

- Reorganisation and clearer delineation of functions related to integration has been pursued, but countries have taken a wide variety of approaches, from the creation of co-ordination bodies and one-stop-shops to further delegation to municipal governments.

- Several countries, notably Ireland, the Netherlands, Finland and Sweden, have put forth National Action Plans to combat discrimination and racism, with a particular focus on better integrating immigrants into working life and increasing public participation.

Introduction

As the need to focus on pandemic-related supports has receded, OECD countries have been examining the essential question that motivates integration measures for new arrivals and for those who have been present over the longer term: what action can the government take to increase cohesion and improve equality of opportunity for migrants? COVID-19 remained relevant throughout much of 2021, but countries have gradually adjusted to a "new normal". In some cases, this has meant carrying out structural reforms with a focus on increased flexibility, individualisation, and participation. Countries have also continued the work of reducing discrimination and dismantling barriers for women and other vulnerable migrants. Aside from the rapid policy actions and upscaling that have been necessary – particularly in Europe – to respond to the integration needs of a large influx of migrants from Ukraine (addressed in detail in the special chapter), a substantial area of focus has been on integrating migrants more effectively and, in many cases, on encouraging their eventual naturalisation.

Flexibility introduced in response to COVID-19 may remain as the pandemic ebbs

Many of the restrictions put in place in response to the COVID-19 pandemic were gradually relaxed throughout 2021, but countries were still faced with the need to mitigate the barriers to migrant integration and reduce the potential for delays that were caused by the pandemic. Reduced availability of public transport, over exposure to COVID-19 and restricted access disincentivised migrant participation in integration courses. Transportation subsidies were introduced, for example in Germany, where migrants who attended in-person classes were eligible for reimbursement of travel expenses. Countries also improved the flexibility of their migration courses to create favourable conditions for migrants to continue participation in programmes. For example, the Netherlands granted an extension to all migrants required to attend integration programmes. In January 2021, an additional four-month extension was made available to migrants who were participating voluntarily in the programme as well, but limited to participants who had fewer than six months remaining to complete the course. In Germany, deadlines were extended by six months for those who first enrolled in courses between March 2018 and June 2021. In addition to relaxing time constraints, governments also introduced flexibility in the modalities of teaching. Given the limited availability of in-person teaching, most OECD countries accelerated the digital transformation of their integration courses. In Germany, during periods of high infection rates, numerous vocational language courses were held fully or partially in virtual classrooms. Throughout 2021, nearly 70% of new vocational language courses were delivered through mixed modality. The Immigrant Council of Ireland moved its social integration activities online to guarantee continuity. Throughout 2021, the "Migrant Leadership Academy" programme that aims at bringing together socially engaged migrants was delivered remotely.

As restrictions have relaxed, countries continue to consider whether some of the policies introduced during the pandemic should be made permanent. In Austria, for example, migrants can still subscribe to online and mixed format language classes on the national integration portal. Increased availability of online classes and greater flexibility have proven popular with migrants, particularly those who work or have young children. Instituting such changes on a more permanent basis can also improve the resilience of course provision in the event of future unexpected challenges. The pandemic also accentuated certain weaknesses in integration programmes for which governments may compensate going forward. Sweden, for example, doubled its budgetary allocation for 2022-24 to improve Swedish language learning for employees in elderly care and related fields. It also reinforced subsidised employment and will continue to introduce entry jobs so that jobseekers can demonstrate their skills to an employer more easily.

Regularisation has seen a new impetus in several countries

Regularisation is frequently carried out in countries facing acute migration pressures. Greece, Italy, Spain, and the United States are among those countries with a history of enacting periodic regularisations, but regularisation initiatives are not at all rare, having been carried out in the majority of OECD and EU countries. Regularisation reduces migrants' vulnerability in a number of domains and provides them access to mainstream services. In 2021 and early 2022, regularisation policies – whether temporary or longer term – have been implemented across a large number of OECD countries. In this period, most governments introduced regularisation initiatives, either to respond to humanitarian needs or to improve the integration of existing populations of migrants.

For certain countries, specifically those that have not traditionally been countries of immigration but have large populations of unregulated or transitory migrants, regularisation has been a key component of their fledgling integration policies. This approach reduces strain on asylum systems and acknowledges the challenges inherent in conducting large-scale removals. In April 2021, Chile has implemented a new immigration law that encompasses a regularisation mechanism targeted at irregular stayers arrived before March 2020. Those who arrived through irregular pathways can leave the country without being penalised and apply abroad for a temporary visa allowing them to work in Chile. The law also aims at reducing irregularity by issuing receipts of in-process residence and visa application, which grant staying and working in the country immediately after submitting the application.

In February 2021, Colombia announced a ten-year Temporary Protection Status to the 1.8 million Venezuelans present on its territory or those entering via official checkpoints over the following two years. Beneficiaries can access a broad range of Colombian social services – education, health care, as well as recognition of professional titles, permission to work and other financial services. The Colombian efforts with Venezuelan refugees signal a focus on the longer-term integration of immigrants, particularly in meeting needs that arise given the long-term stay. Indeed, one early initiative, a measure enacted in 2019, concerns the grant of Colombian citizenship to Venezuelan children born in the country on or after 18 August 2015. The framework is intended to avoid child statelessness that results from the difficulty of acquiring Venezuelan citizenship once abroad.

Additional OECD countries have pursued regularisation, albeit on a smaller scale. In April 2021, Korea introduced a regularisation programme targeted at minors. Unregistered children of irregular foreign residents who are born in Korea and lived in the country for 15 years or more can stay in the country until completing their upper secondary education with a D-4 visa, accompanied by their parents. The programme runs until February 2025. Ireland announced a new regularisation scheme in July 2021 that is expected to affect up to 17 000 undocumented immigrants. The scheme will accept applications from 31 January 2022 until 31 July 2022. The programme is specifically meant to reduce delays for individuals who have been in an immigration process for at least two years and covers undocumented migrants who have lived in the country for four years without permission (three years in the case of those with children). Beneficiaries have access to the labour market and can start the naturalisation procedure. Italy has continued the implementation of an employment-specific regularisation scheme announced in early 2020 for migrant workers in the fishery, agri-food, care and domestic sectors. The purpose of the measure was to reduce tax evasion and migrant worker exploitation by enabling undocumented workers who were previously employed to receive a residence permit and by encouraging the regularisation of existing labour contracts.

With every regularisation scheme, the government must consider what mechanisms are necessary for smooth implementation. Italy has experienced delays, with only 26% of applicants receiving regular status two years after the start of the programme. It thus announced in March 2021 a decision to hire temporary workers and labour inspectors to accelerate the evaluation of submitted applications and address staffing issues. Chile took the approach of completely digitalising its application procedures to ease processing.

Countries continue to take disparate approaches toward naturalisation

Naturalisation can have important implications for immigrants' social integration and labour market outcomes (OECD/European Union, forthcoming[1]), and the overall trend amongst OECD countries has been to take steps to encourage more migrants to pursue citizenship. While few OECD countries have made broad changes to their naturalisation requirements in 2021 and 2022, many countries have actively considered the question of how best to transition migrants to citizens.

Some countries have acted to encourage increased naturalisation…

Germany announced the intention to enact significant reforms to nationality law in its new coalition agreement. Changes would focus on simplification of requirements, for example lowering the number of years of residency to five years (or three in the case of special integration achievements) and lowering the required level of German-language proficiency. Notably, changes would include the recognition of dual citizenship in addition to granting children birthright citizenship if their parents resided in Germany for at least five years prior to their birth. Additionally, on 20 August 2021, an amendment to the Nationality Act entered into force that provides those who lost or were unable to acquire German citizenship due to Nazi persecution a recourse to naturalisation, both for themselves and for their descendants. The Act also excludes from naturalisation anyone convicted of anti-Semitic, racist, xenophobic, or other misanthropic acts.

The United States has taken several actions to build on the February 2021 Executive Order: "Restoring Faith in Our Legal Immigration System and Strengthening Integration and Inclusion Efforts for New Americans". On 2 July 2021, the Interagency Naturalization Working Group (NWG) published the Interagency Strategy for Promoting Naturalization. The strategy has three focus areas: 1) immigrant, community, and education outreach initiatives; 2) capacity building and partnerships; and 3) citizenship education materials and inclusion language. Since publishing the strategy, the United States has instituted several projects to reach groups such as current and former military members and their families, geographically isolated groups, and the elderly. US Citizenship and Immigration Services has developed a digital naturalisation eligibility tool and has co-operated with the Social Security Administration to improve the process of issuance of social security numbers.

Estonia has also taken measures to encourage naturalisation. The Integration Foundation invites people with undetermined citizenship to take part in a series of events in Tallinn and Ida-Viru County. At the meetings, they introduce the possibilities of acquiring citizenship, discuss obstacles and advantages, share detailed information on how to apply for citizenship, and give advice on how to prepare for exams.

…others have introduced flexibility…

Some OECD countries have sought to increase flexibility for migrants seeking to acquire citizenship. Latvia took steps to digitalise the application process and to create tools for potential applicants to test their knowledge in advance of the interview. In September 2021, Australia introduced flexibility regarding the residence requirement for Global Talent Visa holders, significantly reducing the number of days that they must be physically present in Australia to seek Australian citizenship. The government also updated citizenship application fees for the first time since 2016, increasing the fee from AUD 285 to AUD 490 to reflect the cost of processing applications. Luxembourg recently extended the deadline to apply for recovery of Luxembourgish nationality and introduced an amendment allowing migrants to change their name upon naturalisation.

Colombia, Lithuania, and Sweden considered issues specific to migrant children. Lithuania amended its Law of Citizenship to establish that a child of a stateless person lawfully residing in Lithuania would have "birthright" Lithuanian citizenship, regardless of the actual place of birth. One proposal presented in

Sweden in July 2021 would concern protection of children in the cases of renunciation of citizenship and further measures to limit the occurrence of statelessness.

… while still others have considered restrictions or additional requirements

While countries have generally sought to offer greater flexibility or to clarify rights of naturalisation, there have been outliers. Denmark moved to tighten access to naturalisation, including by adding questions to the citizenship test and an additional waiting period of two years after obtaining permanent residence (one year for refugees and stateless persons). Additionally, applicants must now demonstrate they have had a full-time job or been self-employed for 3.5 of the previous 4 years. The Danish Parliament reintroduced the constitutional ceremony that was paused due to COVID-19 and is considering retroactive revocation of nationality in the case of action that is prejudicial to the vital interests of Denmark.

Greece established strict economic criteria for naturalisation in 2021, requiring that foreign nationals who wish to acquire Greek citizenship prove an adequate standard of living equal to at least the national minimum wage for all years of prior legal residence upon which the application for naturalisation is based. This change follows amendments to the Greek Citizenship Code passed in 2019 and 2020 that required applicants to demonstrate knowledge of Greek language and political life in addition to being integrated into Greek economic life. The Swedish Government has proposed introduction of tests of the Swedish language and knowledge of Swedish society as a condition for the acquisition of Swedish citizenship, though this has not yet entered into effect. In 2022, Israel renewed the Law of Citizenship and its restriction on citizenship based on marriage between Israelis and residents of the Palestinian territory following the law's failure to pass in 2021.

While a requirement to demonstrate oral Norwegian skills at a Level B1 (up from the previous level A2) under the Common European Framework of Reference for Languages (CEFR) has not yet been implemented, Norway did introduce additional requirements. Amendments to the Nationality Act increase the residence requirements for naturalisation from seven to eight years after permanent residence (with the exception of refugees) and introduces the requirement that individuals with a specified minimum income level must have resided in Norway six out of the previous ten years.

Reforms to the composition of and eligibility for integration measures

OECD countries have dedicated increased attention to creating integration measures that meet the needs of migrants and encourage their participation. In some cases, this has taken the form of obligatory measures. Belgium (Flanders) has made significant changes to its integration policy, to take effect in September 2022. Under the new programme, each migrant who participates will develop an individualised pathway, benefit from intervention by the Flemish employment and vocational training services, and be matched to a "Flemish buddy" for 40 hours of mentoring. This individual will act as a sponsor who can provide new arrivals with a network, ideally increasing their chances of finding a job or lodging. The programme will also be fee based. Most migrants will be expected to pay EUR 360 for introduction measures (EUR 90 for language and civics courses and EUR 90 per examination). The Flemish Government continues to offset the full cost of integration, valued at EUR 4 500 per individual. Few categories of migrants – eligible but not obliged to take up the programme – will be exempted from fees. In Brussels, where migrants may choose between French and Dutch programmes, Flemish integration programmes remain available free of charge (the latter being under the responsibility of Flanders).

The Netherlands also instituted changes to its integration measures in 2022. The new civic integration programme introduces individually tailored integration measures through a Civic Integration and Participation Plan. Work placements and volunteer work play a major role in the new system, which includes a Labour Market and Participation module. Additionally, three new learning pathways for the Dutch language have been developed. A Knowledge of Dutch Society module is standardised across all pathways. The government bears the cost of civic integration for humanitarian migrants. Family and other migrants are eligible to participate in the various modules, but they must arrange and finance their learning independently.

Sweden introduced the Intensive Introduction Year programme for certain participants in the Introduction Programme, which began on 15 April 2021. The Intensive Introduction Year Initiative enables participants to take part in a combination of measures, based on the individual's needs as well as those of potential employers, to include language training and work practice, but also matching activities and skills validation. The aim of this full-time programme is that migrants will enter employment within one year. Participants are encouraged to take part in activities in their spare time such as additional language training and mentorship programmes. A gender equality perspective must be included in all aspects of the intensive year, with the intention of enabling both women and men to enter the workforce to an equal extent.

In 2021, Estonia reorganised its work and entrepreneur module, creating in its stead two separate modules based on the migrant's interest either to start employment or to set up a business. The work module provides information about looking for a job, writing a resume, and about the services provided by the Estonian Unemployment Insurance Fund. The entrepreneurship module focuses on the nuances of founding a company but also answers questions about laws and taxes. Japan has also introduced a training course, as part of its Comprehensive Measures, to promote stable employment for migrants, focused on necessary training and reemployment, where relevant.

Denmark, Poland, the Slovak Republic, and Slovenia made certain relatively discrete changes to their integration measures. Denmark introduced an exemption from payment requirements for vocational education for unaccompanied minors and migrants with temporary stay permits. Poland announced for the first time that foreigners married to Polish citizens have the right to participate in individual integration programmes. On 12 January 2022, the Slovak Government amended its Act on Asylum to allow for earlier access to integration support, particularly for asylum seekers. The waiting period for access to the labour market was shortened from nine to six months, and asylum seekers will now have access to social and psychological counselling and integration courses. Integration allowances were also increased for holders of international protection. Slovenia modified its integration programme beginning in June 2022 by allowing asylum seekers increased access to integration allowances, sociocultural programmes, and counselling. Additionally, New Zealand announced the extension of eligibility for resettlement support from 12 months to 24 and announced the inclusion of support for family sponsors under the Refugee Quota programme.

Access to education and skills recognition remains high on the integration policy agenda

Nearly all countries enable access to mainstream early schooling for young children, and recent national actions serve to cement that policy preference. In 2021, Norway shifted the lower boundary age of its integration programme from 16 to 18 years of age to make clear that all migrant youth should achieve an education. The Costa Rican Ministry of Public Education and the General Directorate recently enacted a co-ordination protocol to regularise migrant children in the public education system, aiming to decrease dropout rates of migrant minors by providing better access to scholarships and degrees. Poland's West Pomerania region ran a programme designed to facilitate integration of children aged 5 to 18 into the school system, including by building the intercultural competencies of teachers. The Netherlands has also reconfigured its integration programme with the intention of facilitating education for young people, offering this group a specific integration pathway designed to prepare them for further education at secondary vocational, professional, or academic level. In New Zealand, children of eligible work visa holders will benefit from domestic tertiary student status prior to their application for residency.

For adult migrants, there is recognition that more needs to be done to facilitate access to education where necessary. Across the OECD, 37% of the foreign-born are highly educated, a larger share than among the native-born (32%). With the exception of Iceland and the Latin American OECD countries, the share of highly educated individuals among immigrants has increased by 7 percentage points over the past decade. However, a significant number of the foreign-born are poorly educated (27%). The share of the immigrant population that is poorly educated is higher in Europe, surpassing 35% in Belgium, Italy, France, Greece, Malta, and Spain. In the Republic of Türkiye, the share is over 50% (OECD/European Union, 2018[2]). In OECD countries with large numbers of high-skilled jobs, a lack of education can present a significant integration barrier. The year 2021 marked the initial implementation of the European Union Action Plan on Integration and Inclusion (2021-27), which proposes targeted integration support that takes into account specific challenges for people with a migrant background. Main actions supported by the EU under the plan include promoting inclusive education and training, bridging programmes, faster recognition of qualifications, and improved skills recognition. Specific emphasis is placed on improving digital solutions under the Digital Education action plan. The Commission will work with social and economic partners, as well as employers, to support entrepreneurship and make it easier to recognise and assess skills. Additionally, countries such as Norway have sought to make it easier for adult migrants to use their integration benefit to access formal education. Norway also removed a requirement that a migrant already have basic skills to participate in its integration programme. To help skilled workers and specialists bridge the integration gap, the Finnish long-term action plan contemplates offering education programmes through higher education institutions and mentorship support.

Member countries also enacted specific changes to their policies of skills recognition. In keeping with provisions of the Skilled Workers Immigration Act adopted in 2020, Germany furthered its work on shortening deadlines for recognition procedures in a number of professions. The newly introduced, accelerated administrative procedure covers professions governed by federal law or equivalent regulations under state law. Israel introduced a policy allowing doctors working in hospitals under the supervision of an experienced mentor to receive a license without examination. In Luxembourg, a new law on recognition of diplomas issued in the United Kingdom entered into force on 1 January 2021. In March 2022, New Zealand launched the Former Refugees, Recent Migrants, and Ethnic Communities Employment Action Plan, which is focused on skills recognition and matching. Among its objectives is the intention to collaborate more effectively with the private sector.

Language for adult migrants is an increasingly universal pillar of integration measures

Language remains one of the key pillars of integration, and several countries have recognised the need to place increased focus on host-country language proficiency. Estonia has identified language teaching and learning as a key pillar for integration. As part of its Language Strategy for 2021-35, Estonia has announced the goal that every Estonian resident be proficient in the Estonian language and that more opportunities and better tools be developed to pursue this goal. In Japan, the Ministry of Education, Culture, Sports, Science and Technology (MEXT) has been promoting the establishment of a comprehensive system through which local governments can improve offerings of the Japanese language. Additionally, MEXT has developed language-learning materials using digital solutions for foreign nationals living in locations where it is difficult to set up in-person classes. To improve the quality of education, MEXT has published a report on a new framework based on the CEFR and is considering a qualification system for Japanese language teachers. In Australia, several states made additions or improvements to their English as an Additional Language programmes. South Australia notably introduced a 6-module online course to support language teachers. Sweden announced an intention to increase the possibility for migrants to combine language and vocational training.

Only a small number of OECD countries made changes to the target level for host-country language proficiency in 2021. In Flanders (Belgium), migrants in the mandatory integration programme who are not in work or study two years after receiving their integration certificate will be obligated to reach CEFR level B1 in spoken Dutch. In the Netherlands, the New Civic Integration Act 2021, with its separate integration tracks, will require most migrants to speak and write Dutch at level B1 (in both the B1 pathway and the educational pathway). Migrants in the empowerment pathway are expected to learn Dutch at CEFR A1 to prepare for a basic level of participation in the Netherlands. Prior to this change, the target level for all migrants was CEFR A2. These increases are in keeping with a recent trend in the OECD, suggesting that host countries have recognised not only the need to look at a migrant's specific circumstances, but also that their target language levels have been insufficient to integrate certain migrants. Slovenia introduced for the first time a requirement that migrants reach CEFR level A2 as a condition for seeking permanent residence. The change will be applied on 27 April 2023 after a two-year transition period. Legislative changes to the Aliens Act also included a move from the provision of free civics and language courses to a co-financing model, whereby, after the two-year transition period, migrants will cover 50% of the cost for language courses out-of-pocket.

Related to the issue of language, some countries have taken steps to increase and improve access to interpretation and translation services. Norway, for instance, clarified the obligation for public bodies to use qualified interpreters to provide services within its 1 January 2022 Interpretation Act.

Countries have continued their attention to anti-discrimination policies, including in the context of broader anti-racism strategies

With the support of the European Union and its Action Plan on Integration and Inclusion, several EU countries have launched follow-up national plans on diversity and anti-racism. In June 2021, Belgium (Flanders) announced the need for a new organisation designed to encourage and participate in integration. The goal of this participatory organisation is to defend the rights of minorities and strive for inclusiveness and participation. The organisation's main areas of work are housing, labour, education, policy participation, and social cohesion. In April 2022, the new organisation, called LEVL, announced that it was operational.

Ireland, the Netherlands, and Sweden made progress in developing their national action plans. Ireland published an interim report of the Anti-Racism Committee and commenced work on a Traveller and Roma inclusion strategy in 2021. The Committee targeted May 2022 for submission of the National Action Plan against Racism to the Minister for Children, Equality, Disability, Integration and Youth. Sweden launched a nationwide index on the socio-economic status of residential areas as part of its long-term strategy. On 15 October 2021, the Netherlands appointed a National Co-ordinator against Discrimination and Racism, tasked with drawing up a multi-year national programme with clear targets. Additionally, the Netherlands announced the formation of a four-year State Commission to evaluate and propose solutions to reduce discrimination in government. Germany also appointed its first-ever federal anti-racism Commissioner in February 2022. The Commissioner's office is charged with developing a diversity strategy for the federal administration and with co-ordinating the government's measures to combat racism.

Promotion of diversity in working life has become a particular priority. In Finland, a programme to ensure that companies and organisations benefit from diversity was launched in 2021. The programme is linked to the objective of raising the employment rate and promoting employment and advancement of immigrants, and it includes initiatives to match immigrants to their skills. Finland adopted the recommendations published in its Action Programme against Racism in September 2021 and has also undertaken a campaign to amplify refugee voices.

Beyond the European Union, other OECD countries have taken similar actions to combat discrimination against individuals with a migrant background. Canada has issued a call to action on diversifying the public service. Additionally, in 2022, Immigration, Refugees and Citizenship Canada announced that anti-racism representatives would be placed in every sector of its department, in part to ensure that anti-discrimination principles are well respected when it comes to processing immigrant applications. Japan formulated "Comprehensive Measures" for fiscal year 2021 in recognition of the need to enhance acceptance of foreign nationals, a challenge that was laid bare as it responded to the spread of COVID-19. Switzerland has also sought to support and reinforce anti-discrimination and diversity institutions. In 2022, a particular focus has been on preventing discrimination in the labour market. In Australia, the state of Victoria launched an Anti-Racism Taskforce in June 2021 to develop and implement its first state-wide Anti-Racism Strategy. New Zealand established a new Ministry for Ethnic Communities in July 2021 to ensure equitable provision of government services and the promotion of inclusion of ethnic communities.

Specific needs of women and young migrants

Countries seek to reduce gender barriers to increase equality of outcomes

The disproportionate impact of the COVID-19 pandemic on outcomes for migrant women drew increased attention to the need for gender mainstreaming in project design in addition to certain targeted measures. OECD countries have taken particular efforts to strengthen opportunities for foreign-born women to enter the domestic labour market. For example, Sweden's Public Employment Service will put forward a plan to improve outcomes for women for 2022-25, co-ordinated with the national Gender Equality Agency. The Agency is principally focused on those women who are far from the labour market and do not participate in integration measures. Canada extended the Racialised Newcomer Women Pilot that was first launched in December 2018 with a CAN 31.9 million commitment to projects on employment and career advancement of women. The government had observed that the unemployment rate of visible minority or non-white newcomer women (9.7%) was higher than that of racialised (8.5%) and non-racialised (6.4%) newcomer men (Immigration, Refugees and Citizenship Canada, 2021[3]). In 2021, Canada announced an additional CAN 15 million to support the labour market integration of this group, with projects continuing to receive funds until 31 March 2022. The projects are located throughout the Canadian territory and focus on diverse issues, such as building confidence, networking, enhancing computer skills, and entrepreneurship.

As part of the Women's Safety Package, the Australian Government will provide AUD 29.3 million over 3 years beginning in July 2021 to support safety, social and economic inclusion of migrant women. The additional funding will support women through the Settlement Engagement and Transition programme. Innovative projects to address identified employment needs will also be supported. Sweden announced an additional SEK 4 million in funding for its Gender Equality Agency in 2022, partially in response to inflows of women and children from Ukraine. The funding is intended to strengthen work against exploitation and trafficking.

Germany has specifically identified the needs of migrants with childcare obligations, many of whom are women. Germany's Federal Ministry of Labour and Social Affairs is developing programmes to allow women to participate more frequently in qualification and training measures. In January 2022, the Federal Ministry for Family Affairs, Senior Citizens, Women and Youth launched the federal programme, "Integration Course with Child: Building Blocks for the Future". In addition to offering childcare programmes concurrently with integration courses, the German Government notes the importance of providing support both during and after participation in integration measures.

Recognition of issues specific to migrant youth has increased

Recognising the challenges and sacrifices of young people during the COVID-19 pandemic, the EU declared 2022 to be the Year of Youth. The flagship initiative is the ALMA (Aim, Learn, Master, Achieve) programme, which supports youth from disadvantaged backgrounds seeking work experience in member states other than their own home country. Sweden extended the mandate of its Delegation for the Employment of Young People and Newly Arrived Migrants through February 2023. The aim of the delegation is to improve co-ordination between municipalities and the central government on measures against youth unemployment. More generally, there has been a continued shift in integration programmes toward acknowledging the importance of education for young people. One of the tracks available under the reformed integration programme in the Netherlands (discussed above) is specifically designed for young people who are in the Netherlands attending tertiary education or who wish to receive their school diploma. New Zealand announced the creation of a pilot for former refugee youth, intended to support young refugees in accessing higher education and/or occupational skills training, such as apprenticeships. Refugee youth will work with Immigration New Zealand and other relevant agencies in the co-design phase.

Countries reorganise and delineate responsibilities to improve co-ordination

Several OECD countries reorganised their provision of integration services in 2021 and 2022, with some making large-scale changes. Such reforms reflect increasing awareness of the need to involve all of the actors engaged in integration of migrants to develop a cohesive and well-co-ordinated plan. In the Netherlands, Slovenia, and several Nordic countries, reorganisation took the form of clearer designation of responsibility, either on the national or municipal level. In Norway, responsibility for integration was transferred to the Ministry of Labour, while in Sweden, a new Ministry for Migration and Integration was established, with authority over integration, anti-segregation, and reception of asylum seekers. The Minister for Employment and Gender Equality continues to be responsible for labour market integration of newly arrived immigrants. At the same time, Norway has sought to increase the role of civil society for 2021-24, primarily by providing grant support to organisations. The Finnish Government announced the transfer of responsibility for integration to municipalities as part of its Act on the Promotion of Immigrant Integration. Additionally, Romania published a new methodology based on its Integration Act that stresses the interconnected responsibilities of its ministries on housing, education, and employment. In contrast, demonstrating slight shift toward a more localised approach, in December 2021, Australia announced an AUD 37.3 million investment in a community support programme for humanitarian migrants, under which community-based sponsorship of refugees would be piloted. A significant portion of the funds was designated to social enterprise grants for refugee employment.

As part of the changes introduced under the 2021 Civic Integration Act, the Netherlands sought to delineate municipal responsibility for the supervision of new arrivals more clearly. Under the new Act, while the Ministry of Social Affairs and Employment leads the governance of integration, and civic integration exams are co-ordinated by the Ministry of Education and the Institute for the Implementation of Education, municipalities have taken on an even greater number of tasks, with the goal of providing a more individualised offering. Municipalities have responsibility for housing, asylum shelters, social assistance, employment services and education in addition to implementation of three civic integration paths. The municipality now also covers the cost of integration courses for humanitarian migrants. This represents a significant divergence from the largely market-driven private sector integration offerings that have been previously available.

Estonia and Belgium took action to improve co-ordination mechanisms. Estonia launched the plan "Cohesive Estonia 2021-30," a joint venture between the Ministry of Culture, Ministry of Interior, and the Foreign Ministry. Belgium's Council of Ministers approved the establishment of the Inter-Ministerial Conference on Migration and Integration in February 2021, with the aim to contribute to consultation and coherent policy making across the federal and regional governments.

The one-stop-shop model has gained popularity as a way to co-ordinate referring migrants to appropriate services. To assist migrants with integration issues, Lithuania established the International House Vilnius in September 2021. This centralised location provides integration services, advice, and referrals in English and Russian to highly qualified migrants and their family members. Prior to the invasion of Ukraine by Russia, Poland had announced a project under the Asylum, Migration and Integration Fund (AMIF) to open pilot Integration Centres for Foreigners in two voivodeships, Wielkopolska and Opolska. The first centre was opened in Kalisz on 8 March 2022. These centres were designed to offer advice regarding the labour market, Polish language learning, cultural assistance, and psychological and legal help. The project was co-ordinated with the National Network for the Integration of Foreigners, which is designed to bring together a variety of institutions and offices concerned with issues facing migrants.

Other countries have continued to refine national action plans and improve co-ordination. Ireland extended its migrant integration strategy to the end of 2021. As part of this strategy, several government departments were restructured, and responsibility for migrant integration and refugee resettlement was transferred to the Department of Children, Equality, Disability, Integration and Youth. Policies implemented as part of this restructuring include establishment of a new international protection support service to be phased in from 2021-24. Latvia's Cabinet of Ministers approved a Ministry of Culture policy-planning document that created guidelines for building a cohesive society. These "Guidelines for the Development of a Cohesive and Active Civil Society 2021-27" emphasise integration of migrants through the learning of Latvian language and history.

References

Immigration, Refugees and Citizenship Canada (2021), *Government announces new initiatives to help racialized newcomer women succeed in Canada*, https://www.canada.ca/en/immigration-refugees-citizenship/news/2021/08/government-announces-new-initiatives-to-help-racialized-newcomer-women-succeed-in-canada.html (accessed on 8 June 2022). [3]

OECD/European Union (2018), *Settling In 2018: Indicators of Immigrant Integration*, OECD Publishing, Paris/European Union, Brussels, https://doi.org/10.1787/9789264307216-en. [2]

OECD/European Union (forthcoming), *Settling In 2023: Indicators of Immigrant Integration*, OECD Publishing, Paris/European Union, Brussels. [1]

4 Responding to the Ukrainian refugee crisis

This chapter provides an overview of the Ukrainian refugee crisis and the policy responses in OECD countries. Discussing the scale and nature of migration flows triggered by the unprovoked war of aggression of Russia against Ukraine, it covers information on migration permits and rights granted to Ukrainians. The chapter then examines both initial and medium-to-longer term reception support that is available to Ukrainian refugees, focusing specifically on housing, access to immediate assistance and public services, education, and employment. As countries are beginning to transition towards integration efforts, new challenges are emerging. These are explored in the last section of the chapter.

In Brief

Key findings

- Russia's unjustifiable, unprovoked, and illegal war of aggression against Ukraine has generated a historic mass outflow of people fleeing the war. By mid-September 2022, close to 5 million individual refugees from Ukraine had been recorded across the EU and other OECD countries, out of whom about 4 million had registered for temporary protection or similar national protection schemes in Europe.

- OECD countries in Europe and beyond responded swiftly to the refugee crisis, granting immigration concessions to Ukrainian nationals, such as visa exemptions, extended stays or prioritisation of immigration applications.

- The Council of the European Union enacted, for the first time, the Temporary Protection Directive 2001/55/EC (TPD), which provides a set of harmonised rights for the beneficiaries in all EU Member States.

- Non-EU OECD countries also responded swiftly to the Ukraine crisis and took, to varying degrees, measures to facilitate the entry and stay of Ukrainian people fleeing the war. In some cases, non-EU countries use existing pathways to admit Ukrainians. Other countries, however, have established new Ukraine-specific schemes and policies, including Canada, the United States and the United Kingdom. The scope of these policies is often limited to Ukrainian citizens and their immediate family members with preference given to people with existing connections to the host country.

- OECD countries extended different types of support and assistance to new arrivals to mitigate the risk of social and economic exclusion of refugees and to assist them in meeting basic needs. These measures generally include providing emergency shelter, financial subsidies and cash benefits, as well as ensuring access to education and health services. The extent of different formal reception measures in countries often depends on the type of permit granted.

- Although there is a widespread expectation that Ukrainians fleeing the war will return after its end, countries are increasingly extending access to different integration measures.

- Ensuring access to housing has been a major challenge in many receiving countries. The rapid influx of Ukrainian refugees to Europe happened in the context of significant pre-existing housing challenges, such as insufficient housing supply and rising costs. This is limiting available options for housing refugees both in the short and medium-to-long term in many host countries, including Poland.

- Access to public education for minor children is available in all OECD and EU countries, yet in the first months of the crisis, many students continued to follow a Ukrainian curriculum online. Most countries are now looking to integrate students fully into national systems and have made efforts to scale up their classroom and teaching capacities to facilitate this, including by hiring Ukrainian teachers.

- Outside compulsory education, providing VET to Ukrainian refugees is often seen as a particularly promising pathway with high expected returns, which is why many countries have taken special measures to facilitate access to both upper secondary and adult vocational training.

- While immediate access to higher education is not common, most countries have introduced some support measures to help Ukrainian refugees with this. These include host language training, academic guidance, financial assistance and grants, and reserved study places. Moreover, many higher education institutions in OECD countries have implemented their own exceptional measures to support Ukrainian students and scholars.

- Some of the characteristics of Ukrainian refugees, especially their educational profile, are likely to improve their labour market integration prospects and employability compared to other refugees, while others, namely that most arrivals are women with children, may hinder them.

- Ukrainian refugees have been granted the right to work in most host countries. Despite this, they have been relatively slow to enter the labour force, though the number of people wanting to do so is expected to rise.

- Many OECD countries offer help with finding a job, although the degree and nature of the support provided varies significantly. Focus has been on facilitating successful matching: many online portals have been launched or are in development with varying degrees of in-built matching systems to connect Ukrainian refugees to companies and suitable jobs.

- The transition to medium- and longer-term solutions has exposed emerging challenges, including moving away from temporary and other similar subsidiary statuses towards permanent statuses, mainstreaming support measures, addressing secondary flows and preparing for changes in public opinion and support.

Introduction

The large-scale unprovoked aggression of Russia against Ukraine that started on 24 February 2022 has created a massive refugee[1] crisis unseen in Europe since World War II. While it took two years to reach 3 million Syrian refugees, this number was hit in less than three weeks in the case of Russia's war of aggression against Ukraine. By mid-September 2022, close to 5 million individual refugees from Ukraine had been recorded across the EU and other OECD countries, out of whom about 4 million had registered for temporary protection or similar national protection schemes in Europe. OECD countries in Europe and beyond responded swiftly to the new situation, opening their doors and extending support to new arrivals. The duration of inflows, however, remains unknown and countries are only beginning to grasp and address longer-term challenges related to this massive influx.

Many OECD countries have faced displacement crises over the last decade, notably in 2014-17 in Europe and in the context of the Venezuelan migration and refugee crisis in South America. The Ukrainian refugee crisis, however, has many unique characteristics. First, pre-existing visa facilitations for Ukrainian nationals in Europe greatly promoted orderly cross-border movements. Second, compared to other refugee flows, the profile of arrivals is atypical: it is highly skewed, as mostly women with children are leaving the country, and a higher share of arrivals are tertiary educated. Third, there is a widespread expectation that Ukrainians fleeing the war will return after its end. And finally, in many respects, the response in receiving countries has also been unique. The crisis has attracted unprecedented political and public support from host populations, and there has been an exceptional mobilisation of institutions and host communities.

The policy responses built on lessons from previous experiences with large-scale refugee inflows. In addition to ensuring the immediate needs of new arrivals are met (e.g. temporary shelter and subsistence), most governments have introduced further measures. Such measures include financial subsidies (e.g. cash benefits), free services (e.g. transport), and facilitating access to education, health services and employment. The extent of such measures, however, has varied between countries and depended on the type of permit granted. As the war drags on and the task of rebuilding Ukraine is still ahead, countries are recognising that a quick return of displaced persons is unlikely and are transitioning from providing short-term immediate support to medium- and long-term responses. Such transitions towards more durable solutions have been particularly pressing in the case of housing, where reception capacities in many countries and regions are severely challenged. Yet the need to adapt and revise approaches goes beyond that. As people stay for longer, the availability of meaningful learning and career opportunities becomes critical, as does general integration support.

In the context of this transition, a number of new challenges are also emerging. The majority of Ukrainian refugees in OECD countries have temporary and subsidiary statuses, which may raise issues in the event of protracted war and displacement. As many exceptional measures introduced in the outbreak of the refugee crisis have sunset clauses, countries need to devise ways for providing sufficient support to Ukrainian refugees through mainstream measures without overburdening general social security systems. At the same time, the questions about possible implications of secondary movements to other countries and changes in public opinion and support are also becoming key policy considerations.

This chapter gives an overview of the nature and scope of the refugee crisis and the policy responses in OECD countries. It covers information on associated migration flows, permits and rights granted to Ukrainians as well as immediate and medium-to-longer term support available to the new arrivals, including measures related to housing, education, and employment. Finally, the main challenges ahead are discussed.

Migration flows triggered by the Russian large-scale invasion of Ukraine

Russia's unprovoked war of aggression against Ukraine generated a historic mass flight. Daily outflows from Ukraine increased rapidly during the first days of the war, peaking at over 200 000 border crossings on 6 March 2022. The numbers have, however, declined progressively since then and net migration from Ukraine is currently zero or even slightly negative as the number of returns to Ukraine increased. By mid-September 2022, close to 5 million individual refugees from Ukraine had been recorded across the EU and other OECD countries, out of whom about 4 million had registered for temporary protection or similar national protection schemes in Europe.

The majority of people fleeing Ukraine went to Poland, which has recorded more than 6 million border crossings from the country since February. During this period, 1.3 million people also entered Hungary, 1.2 million Romania, followed by the Slovak Republic (780 000) and Moldova (600 000). Many Ukrainian refugees continued to travel towards other destination countries and cross-border travel remains substantial in both directions. Consequently, despite the large number of border crossings, there are only about 29 000 refugees in Hungary and 86 000 in Romania.

As of mid-September 2022, Poland is the main receiving country in absolute numbers with 1.38 million refugees from Ukraine recorded for temporary protection in the country (Figure 4.1). Poland is followed by Germany with about 1 million and the Czech Republic with more than 400 000 refugees.

Outside the EU, more than 550 000 Ukrainian nationals and family members have applied through the Canada-Ukraine authorisation for emergency travel (CUAET) for a temporary resident visa to travel to and stay in Canada. Almost 240 000 have been approved and more than 82 000 people have arrived in the country. In the United States, since 25 April, 124 000 people have applied to financially sponsor Ukrainian refugees through a private sponsorship programme (United for Ukraine) and almost 51 000 Ukrainians have arrived through this initiative. Tens of thousands of additional Ukrainians obtained a non-immigrant or an immigrant visa or were admitted along the Mexico US border. In the United Kingdom, total arrivals of Ukrainians through the Ukraine sponsorship scheme or the Ukraine family scheme has now reached 126 000.

Figure 4.1. Number of refugees from Ukraine recorded in OECD countries, absolute numbers and per thousand of total population, mid-September 2022

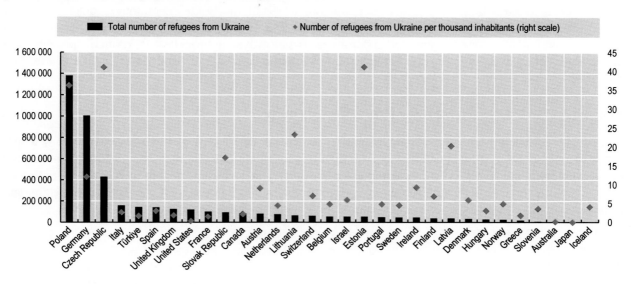

Source: OECD Secretariat calculations.

StatLink 📊 https://stat.link/1e98r7

As a percentage of total population, across OECD countries, the main receiving countries are Estonia and the Czech Republic with more than 40 refugees per thousand inhabitants. They are followed by Poland (36 ‰), Lithuania (23 ‰) and Latvia (20 ‰) (Figure 4.1).

The general mobilisation in Ukraine prevents most men aged 18 to 60 from leaving the country. As a result, mostly women with children, some elderly people but very few working age men have left the country so far. As a result, in virtually all host countries, at least 70% of the adults are women and over a third of all refugees are children. Shares of both groups are larger in countries geographically closer to Ukraine. In Poland, for instance, children account for over 40% of refugees and about 87% of all adults are female. Similarly, in Lithuania, about 36% of all Ukrainian refugees are minor children and 83% of the adults are women. In Spain, 33% of the arrivals have been minors and 70% women, while in Italy the figures are respectively 30% and 75%.

The limited information currently available on the level of education of Ukrainian refugees suggests not only that a higher share of them are tertiary educated than among other refugee groups, but that they are also more highly educated than the general Ukrainian active population (among which 34% were tertiary educated in 2019). The exact figures, however, vary across countries. According to administrative data from Spain, 62% of Ukrainian adults have a tertiary degree, 28% upper secondary or a professional qualification, 9% a secondary degree, while around 1% have no more than primary education. Two non-representative studies from Germany found even higher educational levels among the refugee population in the country: less than 2% of the respondents were low-educated, while the share of tertiary-educated exceeded 73% (INFO GmbH, 2022[1]; Panchenko, 2022[2]).

In the same vein, data collected by the European Union Agency for Asylum (EUAA) and the OECD across several EU countries found that 71% of respondents overall had a completed tertiary degree with 41% holding a master's degree or higher. A further 11% have completed professional (vocational) education. There are, however, some differences in qualification levels of respondents by their region of origin, with Ukrainians fleeing from Kyiv City having a higher education level than other groups.

Immigration permits and rights granted to Ukrainians

When Russia began its war of aggression against Ukraine, many OECD countries quickly granted immigration concessions to Ukrainian nationals, such as visa exemptions, extended stays or prioritisation of immigration applications. Significant differences in pathways, approaches to granting permits and associated rights, however, prevail between the European Union (EU) and non-EU OECD member countries.

The EU activated the Temporary Protection Directive

Since 2017, Ukrainian citizens holding biometric passports can travel to the Schengen Zone, which includes Iceland, Switzerland and Norway, without a visa for a period of 90 days, which allowed the majority of Ukrainians to enter the EU through regular pathways. The visa requirement for Ukrainian nationals travelling to Ireland was also lifted as an emergency measure on 25 February 2022. While some Ukrainian refugees continue onwards to non-EU countries, most have stayed in Europe.

On 4 March 2022, the Council of the European Union enacted by means of the Implementing Decision (EU) 2022/382, for the first time ever, the Temporary Protection Directive 2001/55/EC (TPD). The EU Member States (MSs) are bound to grant TPD status to both Ukrainian nationals who resided in Ukraine before or on 24 February 2022, as well as stateless people and foreign citizens who benefited from international (or equivalent national) protection in Ukraine before that date. Although some national variations may apply (e.g. scope extended to other categories, varying registration processes, longer permit validity, wider rights and benefits), MSs are bound by this legal framework and cannot offer a lower set of rights than those foreseen by the Directive to the beneficiaries of temporary protection (BTPs).

Denmark, while not bound by the TPD, mirrored the directive in its Special Act except for a few differences: stateless persons from Ukraine are not included, and a permit will be given for two years at first, with the possibility of extension for a further year. Switzerland, Norway and Iceland also offer similar protection schemes to Ukrainians through, respectively, the special "S permit" visa programme, the temporary collective protection scheme and a residence permit on humanitarian grounds.

Poland and Hungary distinguished from the beginning beneficiaries of protection arriving from Ukraine according to their nationality under national law. In both countries, the national temporary protection regime (provided in Poland by the Special Law adopted on 7 March 2022 and by the Gov. Decree 86/2022 in Hungary) only applies to Ukrainian nationals and their family members, while third-country nationals or permanent residents in Ukraine are subject to a distinct protection scheme, with different status or registration process. In July 2022, the Netherlands stopped granting temporary protection to third-country nationals with a temporary Ukrainian residence permit.

Moreover, people fleeing Ukraine have been able to apply for international protection. The availability of alternative protection routes is particularly important for those Ukrainian nationals who may not be eligible for temporary protection but are still in need of protection. This includes, for instance, Ukrainian nationals who were already present on the territory of a current host country prior to 24 February 2022 and thus are outside the scope of temporary protection in several EU MSs.

Approaches in other OECD countries

Other OECD countries outside the EU/EFTA responded to the Ukraine crisis and took, to varying degrees, measures to facilitate the entry and stay of people fleeing the war. The scope of these policies is often limited to Ukrainian citizens and their immediate family members with preference given to people with existing connections to the host country.

In some cases, non-EU/EFTA countries have established new Ukraine-specific schemes and policies. The primary pathway for Ukrainians into the United States is through the Uniting for Ukraine (U4U) programme. While not a visa programme, this humanitarian parole option, launched on 25 April 2022, allows Ukrainian citizens and their immediate family members, who have a US sponsor, to travel to the United States and stay there for up to two years. During their stay, they are permitted to apply for work authorisation, and benefits including food stamps, Supplemental Security Income and Medicaid. The Canada-Ukraine Authorization for Emergency Travel (CUAET) offers Ukrainians and their family members free, extended temporary status for up to 3 years, allowing them to stay, work and study in Canada. Unlike applications for resettlement as a refugee and streams for permanent residence, there is no cap on the number of applications accepted under the CUAET. The 2022 Special Ukraine Visa scheme in New Zealand allows New Zealanders of Ukrainian origin to apply to bring family members still in Ukraine to the country. The United Kingdom meanwhile administers multiple parallel Ukraine-specific schemes based on the applicants' existing links to the country (the Ukraine Family Scheme, the Ukraine Extension Scheme, and the Homes for Ukraine Sponsorship Scheme).

Other non-EU/EFTA OECD countries use existing pathways to admit Ukrainians. Japan is granting the new arrivals 90-day visas and the opportunity to switch to Designated Activities Visa for a year. Israel admits as immigrants Ukrainians approved to enter under the Law of Return. Those who are eligible but have not been approved may enter provisionally and complete their immigration process after arrival. In Australia, the Temporary Humanitarian Concern (THC) visa was made available for all Ukrainian nationals between February and the end of July. After this pathway expired, Ukrainian nationals who have entered Australia on a temporary visa and are unable to access normal visa pathways or return to Ukraine, may seek asylum by applying for a Protection Visa.

While the provisions of the TPD allowed the EU Member States to speed up administrative processes significantly, most non-EU countries did not introduce major changes to their processing procedures. The growth in applications has led to processing delays in some countries, including Australia, Canada, and the United States. In some instances, these delays were not caused just by the Ukrainian refugee crisis but also by an increase in applications after the resumption of visa processing following COVID-19 lockdowns. In the United Kingdom, for instance, the number of visa applications for the year ending in March 2022 had been almost two and half times higher (+145%) than during the year before (Home Office, 2022[3]). The increase in applications from Ukrainians looking to enter and stay in the United Kingdom via one of the three new Ukraine-specific schemes put further strain on the system, resulting in significant visa delays.

Initial support measures in OECD countries

OECD countries have also extended different types of support and assistance to new arrivals. The extent of formal reception measures in countries often depends on the type of permit granted. In the European Union, the EU TPD provides a set of harmonised rights for the beneficiaries, including rights to work (although restrictions may apply), accommodation, health care, and education for children under 18. As many arrivals are minors, the accompanying EU Commission (2022[4]) guidelines call for special attention to be paid to the child's best interest and well-being during the initial response and later. In non-EU OECD countries, in most cases, sponsored arrivals are not eligible for the same levels of reception support as those seeking asylum or protection. The treatment of Ukrainians already present in a country's territory prior to 24 February 2022 also varies widely across OECD countries. In most cases, these individuals are eligible for full reception support only if they seek asylum.

The unprecedented scale of the crisis prompted the European countries to co-operate closely to manage the response to the Ukrainian refugee crisis. In March, the European Commission (EC) set up a "Solidarity Platform" to co-ordinate the operational response among the EU Member States. It is used to collect information about the needs in host countries and to co-ordinate the operational follow-up. The European Commission also supports non-EU neighbouring countries like the Republic of Moldova in strengthening their response by providing emergency support at border crossing points and transit points, funding to cover basic living conditions in accommodation centres and multipurpose cash assistance for vulnerable displaced people to cover their basic needs in Moldova. Moreover, 18 EU Member States and Norway have offered in-kind assistance to Moldova through the EU Civil Protection Mechanism (UCPM).

Emergency shelter

Ensuring access to housing has been one of the main challenges in most receiving countries. The rapid influx of Ukrainian refugees soon exhausted existing reception facilities, especially as the numbers of other asylum arrivals did not decrease during the first half of 2022. Most host countries in Europe had to adapt and scale up their reception capacity. To house the large number of individuals fleeing Ukraine as quickly as possible, countries have relied on a mix of accommodation options, supplementing existing or newly-created reception centres or other emergency solutions with programmes supporting reception by private households (OECD, 2022[5]).

Many Ukrainian refugees found shelter in private accommodation. From the outset, private hosts and households in Europe opened their homes to displaced persons, in an unprecedented show of solidarity. Poland has relied extensively on a system of volunteers to meet housing needs. During first months of the refugee crisis, around half of those who arrived in Norway found shelter in private homes. Finland and Latvia estimated that the share of displaced persons in temporary private accommodation was around two-thirds, while in Belgium and Italy it reached at times 85-90%. Acknowledging the financial burden of hosting arrangements, some governments provide financial support to private hosts, including France, Poland, the Czech Republic, the Slovak Republic, Slovenia and the United Kingdom. Ukrainians entering the non-EU OECD countries using sponsorship-based models (e.g. the United Kingdom and the United States) are also typically housed in private homes with the costs for this housing covered by the sponsor. Canada also foresees sponsors being responsible for housing, but some arrivals may be housed for two weeks in emergency accommodation.

Alongside private hosts and households, countries, including Germany, Greece, Ireland, and Sweden, have also relied on existing centres for asylum seekers. Many other countries, including Belgium, Croatia, Finland, Poland and Spain, have had to open new reception centres to cope with the demand. In Norway, more than 85 temporary emergency centres were opened across the country to house 20 000 refugees, with plans to dismantle them as demand dissipates (UDI, 2022[6]). An additional source of accommodation has been found in hotels, hostels, and schools. Some countries have even turned to emergency solutions, such as cruise ships, containers, tents, or mobile sheds.

Unlike previous large refugee flows, most people fleeing Ukraine are women and children. This composition raises specific challenges to the provision of adequate accommodation and countries are looking to mitigate different risks that these groups might face in relation to housing, including the risk of exploitation and gender-based violence. In Luxembourg, for instance, the Red Cross and Caritas organise house visits because of an identified risk of labour and sexual exploitation.

Developing housing solutions for children arriving from Ukraine unaccompanied or separated (accompanied by adults other than their parents) is an area of particular focus, especially in the EU (OECD, 2022[5]). Taking into account the best interest of the child, accommodation options are considered in close consultation with the competent child protection departments and other relevant social services. In the case of unaccompanied minors, these include foster placements, safe houses and specialised centres for minors or private accommodations (of family friends or acquaintances). In Poland and Germany, co-ordination units have been set up to arrange accommodation of larger groups of unaccompanied minors and orphans, mainly in facilities of youth welfare services, youth hostels or recreation centres.

Access to assistance and public services

Measures have been taken across OECD countries to mitigate the risk of social and economic exclusion of refugees from Ukraine and to assist them in meeting their basic needs. Most host countries provide financial assistance, but levels and mechanisms vary widely across countries. The EU Member States, Norway, Switzerland and the United Kingdom, for instance, provide a financial subsidy enabling Ukrainian refugees to cover daily basic living expenses and to access decent accommodation. In Italy, BTPs may receive EUR 300 per person per month (EUR 150 per child) for a period of three months; in the Netherlands, the financial allowance is EUR 260 per person per month. Spain has a two-phase system. During the first phase, BTPs receive maintenance aid (EUR 170/month for an individual) and pocket money, separately from a rental allowance. The second phase covers an allowance for basic needs. The total cost of providing assistance to Ukrainian refugees for the European OECD countries is estimated to be EUR 26.6 billion in 2022 (Box 4.1).

Outside the EU, financial support and subsidies may be available to Ukrainians only under certain conditions. In Canada, some provinces provide income support. In Korea, arrivals designated as refugees have access to financial support. In New Zealand, sponsoring family must commit to covering expenses for arriving Ukrainians.

All OECD countries offer access to health care, but similarly to financial assistance, the levels vary. Some countries offer access only to urgent primary health care while others have opened their social security systems more broadly to Ukrainians. The Slovak Republic provides access to emergency and necessary care. In Sweden, children have full access to health care, but adults may access only emergency health and dental care. In Australia, recipients of temporary humanitarian visa have access to Medicare. In Canada, Ukrainian arrivals are generally eligible only for urgent primary health care through the Interim Federal Health Program, but some provinces have extended access to include also other health care services (e.g. Quebec, British Columbia and Alberta). Most OECD countries have also recognised the need to provide access to mental health care. Often this is provided via hotlines, for instance in Belgium, Portugal and Poland. The Czech Republic also offers first psychological aid in reception centres.

As many arrivals are minors, access to public education for children has been a priority and it is available in all the EU and other OECD countries. Some countries also reported offering enrolment opportunities to pre-schoolers, including Finland, France, Hungary and Latvia. The magnitude of inflows during the first months of the crisis, however, was significantly larger than anything some education systems had previously experienced, causing severe strains on classroom capacities, notably in Poland. In turn, several countries have sought to hire Ukrainian teachers to facilitate the teaching of large numbers of Ukrainian children, including Germany, Spain and the Czech Republic. For adults, immediate access to training and education is less common and regular entry requirements of educational institutions apply.

Box 4.1. Preliminary estimates of the financial impact of the Ukrainian refugee crisis in Europe triggered by Russia's large-scale war of aggression against Ukraine

While it remains difficult to assess the overall economic consequences of this unprecedented crisis, it is possible to estimate the costs associated with welcoming and supporting Ukrainian refugees in the European OECD countries. The estimates below cover a 10-month period in 2022 and include direct financial support and housing, as well as education and health care costs. The methodology used follows that adopted in the OECD Brief on "The potential contribution of Ukrainian refugees to the labour force in European host countries" (OECD, 2022[7]). The distribution and demographic composition of the Ukrainian refugee population across these countries is assumed to remain fixed at the level observed in each country at the end of April 2022. However, it appears that the numbers of refugees from Ukraine in Hungary, the Slovak Republic and Romania used for this estimation are an overestimation for these countries as many people have either moved on or returned to Ukraine.

Living costs

The biggest share of all costs in Europe are related to the provision of accommodation and financial subsidies to Ukrainian refugees. Based on the refugee population estimates and the information collected on the financial support that people living in reception centres and private accommodation receive, as well as considering the financial transfers provided to hosting families, we can estimate that the total cost of providing housing and direct financial assistance in Europe is EUR 17.2 billion. The variation between countries, however, is significant. As expected, total costs are expected to be the highest for Poland at EUR 6.2 billion. In Germany, public expenditure on living costs is EUR 4.4 billion, while in Spain it is expected to reach almost a billion – EUR 981 million.

Education costs

To estimate the total cost of education, we assume that the average cost of education per grade equals the marginal cost. This is clearly an overestimation, but at the same time, including Ukrainian children in national school systems will require language training and other additional support for which costs are difficult to estimate at this stage.

The cost of ensuring educational access to Ukrainian refugees is estimated at about EUR 5.1 billion. Countries bordering Ukraine and those with the largest Ukrainian diaspora (i.e. Czech Republic, Italy, Germany and Spain) are expected to have the highest costs. In the Czech Republic, different education costs are estimated at EUR 352 million. In Poland, total educational expenditure is expected to reach EUR 1.5 billion.

Health care costs

On average, Ukrainian refugees are younger than both the general population in Ukraine and in the host countries. The calculations take this into account in relation to health costs. Overall, the health care costs are estimated to be about EUR 4.4 billion. Germany ranks first at EUR 1.4 billion, followed by Poland – which has lower per capita health care costs – at EUR 664 million. The Czech Republic ranks third at EUR 341 million.

Total costs

In total, the mass inflow of refugees from Ukraine is estimated to cost the European OECD countries about EUR 26.6 billion in 2022 (Table 4.1). The related costs are expected to be over EUR 1 billion in five countries – Germany, Poland, the Czech Republic, Spain and Romania. Germany and Poland are estimated to bear more than 50% of all costs. The highest expenditure per refugee, however, is expected in Switzerland, Belgium and Luxembourg, while the lowest cost per capita are in Hungary, Greece and Romania.

Table 4.1. Component costs (living, education, health) and total costs per country

Country	Living costs, million EUR	Primary education costs, million EUR	Secondary education costs, million EUR	Health costs, million EUR	Total cost, million EUR	Per capita cost, EUR
Austria	263	78	88	163	592	7 360
Belgium	400	51	47	91	589	12 626
Croatia	49	7	11	17	84	4 210
Czech Republic	1 265	144	208	341	1 957	5 028
Denmark	86	66	23	82	257	8 288
Estonia	90	31	16	30	166	3 898
Finland	74	20	27	45	166	6 379
France	391	56	73	186	706	8 031
Germany	4 428	553	466	1 361	6 808	11 347
Greece	45	11	8	15	78	2 707
Ireland	176	29	23	69	297	10 064
Italy	418	98	80	141	737	5 710
Latvia	70	15	8	14	107	3 339
Lithuania	153	14	24	32	223	3 581
Luxembourg	24	13	10	16	63	12 487
Netherlands	241	62	53	132	488	8 549
Norway	106	43	13	73	236	12 491
Portugal	95	24	17	31	168	4 028
Slovenia	41	4	3	5	53	8 978
Spain	981	115	81	181	1 359	8 009
Sweden	75	114	21	115	325	7 525
Switzerland	394	71	73	177	714	13 452
United Kingdom	96	16	31	63	207	6 073
Poland	6 207	1 133	356	664	8 360	5 225
Hungary	104	84	96	87	372	1 730
Slovak Republic	411	68	68	94	642	4 217
Romania	499	149	148	207	1 002	3 012
Total	**17 182**	**3 069**	**2 072**	**4 432**	**26 756**	
Average						**6 173**

Source: OECD Secretariat calculations.

StatLink 🔗 https://stat.link/v86bsk

Transitioning towards medium and long-term responses

With no clear end to the refugee crisis in sight, most host countries have started adjusting policies and activities to better address medium to long-term needs of their new Ukrainian communities. Early integration of refugees has many known benefits, particularly for helping newcomers become self-supporting, yet in the context of this refugee crisis, countries are balancing this consideration with their understanding that many Ukrainians intend to go home and will remain in the host country only temporarily. Moreover, the return and reintegration of Ukrainian nationals is seen as vital for rebuilding Ukraine when the time comes. Consequently, the long-term integration of newcomers has not been a priority in most countries.

As a speedy return to Ukraine is becoming less likely, a growing number of OECD countries have expanded Ukrainians' access to integration measures. Language courses for Ukrainian refugees are now available in most host countries, and several countries, including Australia, Germany, and Canada, offer Ukrainian arrivals similar access to all integration measures – including civics education – as other refugee groups. In July, Estonia made attendance in the Settle in Estonia adaptation programme compulsory for Ukrainian BTPs. Other countries are offering programmes adapted to the circumstances of Ukrainian refugees. Norway, for instance, offers the Norwegian Introduction Programme (NIP) and language training for Ukrainians in English. The English language classes are supposed to prepare Ukrainian refugees for further studies in Norway, as many higher educational programmes require a certain level of English but not necessarily Norwegian.

Securing durable housing

Access to safe, secure and affordable housing is a precondition for refugees to restore stability in their lives, seek new opportunities and to connect with their new host community. Private citizens have stepped forward in many OECD countries, alongside NGOs, the private sector and government services to provide housing for Ukrainian refugees. Most of these solutions, however, are short-term. The transition to more durable accommodation is a looming challenge (OECD, 2022[5]).

Capacity constraints and dispersal

The rapid influx of Ukrainian refugees and the associated demand for housing is occurring in the context of significant pre-existing capacity constraints and affordability challenges. Housing costs have been increasing in many OECD countries for the last decade with even further increases expected given inflationary pressures (OECD, 2022[8]; OECD, 2021[9]). This has not only limited available short-term housing options but will also have medium-to-long term implications.

The housing capacities are particularly strained in OECD countries bordering Ukraine, but also in countries further afield. The Netherlands, for instance, is one of the countries that identified housing shortages as a main challenge for hosting BTPs. Capacity constraints are particularly severe in metropolitan areas, where migrants generally tend to concentrate. In Poland, this led to a rapid growth of urban populations between February and April: the population of Warsaw grew by 15%, Kraków by 23%, Gdańsk by 34% and Rzeszów – closest to the Ukrainian border – increased by 53% (Wojdat and Cywiński, 2022[10]).

These severe housing pressures require countries to think about how best to distribute BTPs throughout their territory to alleviate regional pressures. Latvia announced that the number of refugees accommodated in each municipality will be in proportion to the municipality's declared population and when a municipality reaches its capacity, the state will be entitled to transfer BTPs to other municipalities. Germany is using its existing dispersal system and plans to condition access to social assistance on the BTPs' presence in their designated location. In Switzerland, the reliance on private hosts for housing in the early stages of reception circumvented the traditional cantonal dispersal system, but cantons are increasingly seeking to reclaim responsibility for dispersal to limit unequal pressures on specific municipalities. Some countries (e.g. France) have reported that dwellings in rural areas are unattractive to Ukrainians and remain vacant. Norway compensates municipalities for costs incurred in cases when the designated refugee never arrives.

Assistance with finding and securing accommodation

Alongside capacity constraints, Ukrainian refugees also suffer from an information gap, lack of proper documentation and sufficient income, and in some cases, negative prejudice against foreigners by landlords (OECD, 2022[5]). In this context, assistance with finding and securing accommodation is essential and many countries have implemented support measures. In many cases, financial assistance is provided to support with initial costs of arranging independent housing. Spain has provided funding to BTPs who wish to hire a real estate agent to help with the housing search. In Belgium, the Public Centres for Social Welfare provide an installation allowance that can be used to purchase furniture, among other things. Many countries, including Austria, Luxembourg, the Netherlands, Slovenia and Switzerland, provide rent support if Ukrainian refugees do not have their own means of support.

Countries have also sought to address the information gap among arrivals, given their lack of familiarity with the local housing market. Some, for example France and Iceland, have made housing information available at reception centres or on their dedicated online information portals. Most OECD and EU countries have also created online platforms on which Ukrainians can access information about their housing options and their rights. *Portugal for Ukraine*, for instance, serves as a centralised forum for BTPs to receive information on how to access housing and other support in Portugal.

Ensuring educational continuity

The start of the 2022-23 school year has seen many more refugee children entering national education systems in host countries, prompting countries to make significant efforts to scale up their classroom and teaching capacities. The implementation of multi-phased and long-term plans to integrate Ukrainian refugees into regular education systems is now a priority in most OECD and EU countries.

During the first months of the refugee crisis, many refugee students continued to follow a Ukrainian curriculum remotely (see Box 4.2). In Latvia, nearly half of all school-aged children continued distance learning until the end of the 2021-22 school year. This meant that alongside facilitating integration into national systems for some, education ministries in many receiving countries also had to find ways in which to support Ukrainian school leavers, who wished to complete their studies with the Ukrainian high school exam.

Most host countries, however, are now looking to integrate Ukrainian students fully into national systems and classrooms, at least for compulsory education. Education systems are essential vehicles for integration as they provide opportunities for social interactions with locals, help to learn and practice local language and to understand the cultures of the host country. Integrated education systems also help the native population with being open to diversity and change.

Despite this, prior research suggests that the specific needs of refugee students are not always met by education systems in receiving countries, especially as refugees may also suffer from post-traumatic stress due to displacement, family bereavement and separation, and daily material stress (Spaas et al., 2022[11]). There are, however, ways to promote better outcomes, which include applying a holistic model responding to refugees' learning, social and emotional needs, teaching them the host country's language while also developing their mother tongue, providing flexible learning options and pathways, and creating opportunities for social interactions between refugee and other students (Cerna, 2019[12]).

It is also important to support learning outside classrooms, especially for children. Some OECD countries, including Austria, Canada, Estonia, Lithuania, Italy, and the United Kingdom, offered summer camps and schools for Ukrainian refugees to support language learning, build social networks and facilitate integration more broadly. Targeted measures to expand early childhood education and care (ECEC) to Ukrainian refugees, including offering financial assistance as most ECEC services still require at least a partial fee payment from parents, are also being considered.

Primary and secondary education

The pressures on education systems have been particularly severe in Europe, where the majority of Ukrainian refugees are located. In June 2022, the European Commission published a Staff Working Document, developed in consultation with the United Nations High Commissioner for Refugees (UNHCR) and the United Nations Children's Fund (UNICEF), as well as other stakeholders, outlining good practices and practical insights to support the EU Member States in the inclusion of displaced children from Ukraine in education during the 2022-23 school year (European Commission, 2022[13]). The European Union law requires that migrant students enrol in the host country schools within three months of moving to the country and the EU Member States are encouraged to actively prepare displaced children to enter non-segregated mainstream education as soon as possible, as opposed to segregated or special schools.

This has not prevented schools from providing additional support to students when deemed necessary, whether by implementing individualised pathways or offering temporary reception classes, especially for pupils in higher grades. Many countries, including Belgium, Denmark, France, the Slovak Republic and Spain, offer some form of reception classes, which involve providing additional language training, psychological support, competency and knowledge assessments or some other assistance that should ease students' transition into regular classes. In Portugal, a televised distance learning programme has been developed with 14 classes, each co-led by a Ukrainian teacher and a Portuguese teacher, and Ukrainian textbooks are made available to refugee students to provide continuity of learning (OECD, 2022[14]).

Despite the decision to prioritise integration into national education systems, host countries are still faced with a challenge of developing compatible systems and flexible pathways in education that would allow for a possible return to Ukraine in the future. An important element in this needs to be the maintenance of pupils' mother tongue. In some countries, the teaching of origin-country language is embedded in formal education, for instance, in Sweden, where pupils who do not speak Swedish as their first language have the right to receive tuition in their mother tongue. Other countries, including Estonia, Latvia and Romania, have special Ukrainian schools, where students follow a national curriculum, but study some subjects in Ukrainian. In some Canadian provinces (e.g. Alberta and Manitoba), Ukrainian refugee students have been able to enrol in pre-existing Ukrainian-English bilingual study programmes.

Box 4.2. Remote learning offered educational continuity for Ukrainian students

Refugees often face interruptions in schooling due to displacement, yet many Ukrainians enrolled in education were able to resume their studies remotely. Similarly to other countries, Ukraine had scaled up its digital learning modalities in response to COVID-19 pandemic and was able to shift to remote teaching already in March 2022.

Ukraine's main platform for distance learning is the All-Ukrainian Online School (grades 5-11), offering lessons in 18 core subjects and methodological support for teachers, but many other resources are also available for all educational levels, including early childhood education. For example, the NUMO online kindergarten, developed in collaboration between UNICEF and the Ministry of Education and Science of Ukraine, offers video classes for children aged 3 to 6. Online learning is also possible at Ukrainian universities.

Many host countries supported the dissemination of digital tools and resources through their platforms, including the School Education Gateway and the New Ukrainian School Hub. Sometimes these sources became part of educational integration. In Germany, some federal states such as Berlin and Saxony offer the possibility to follow online courses of the Ukrainian Ministry of Education for the duration of reception classes, while receiving German language and in-person teaching support.

These existing digital resources are also used to support maintaining a link with Ukraine to support possible return to the country. Ukrainian policy makers view the refugee situation as temporary and the Ukrainian Ministry of Education and Science stresses the need for students to continue their studies in Ukrainian language, culture and history instead of, or at least in addition to, attending schools in host countries (OECD, 2022[15]).

Vocational education and training (VET)

Governments and other interested parties are also laying foundations for more lasting measures that go beyond compulsory education. Providing VET in host countries can be a particularly promising pathway, as occupations typically entered through VET are in high demand. These occupations can grant high expected returns to Ukrainian refugees, host country labour markets, and for the rebuilding of Ukraine (OECD, 2022[16]). The European Commission (2022[17]), in its guidance published on 14 June 2022, invited the EU MSs to ensure swift access to initial VET, including apprenticeships, and to provide, as quickly as possible, targeted upskilling and reskilling opportunities, including VET and/or practical workplace experience.

Refugees, however, often face barriers to entering VET and tend to be less successful in completing their studies than their native peers (Jeon, 2019[18]). Specific challenges include relatively weak language skills, lack of relevant social networks and knowledge about labour market functioning, as well as possible discrimination in the apprenticeship market, which need to be addressed to make VET systems work for all Ukrainian refugees.

Several countries have taken specific measures to facilitate and ease access to both upper secondary and adult vocational training for Ukrainian refugees, including waiving some entry requirements (OECD, 2022[19]). Latvia, for instance, exempts Ukrainian minors from the mandatory state examination for admission in a VET programme. The majority of European OECD countries, as well as Australia and the United States, offer Ukrainians access to adult vocational training as part of job training through public employment services or adult education courses. Countries are also adopting policies to make the hiring of Ukrainian VET teachers easier, for instance Germany and the Netherlands.

Tertiary education

Most host countries have sought to facilitate access to higher education institutions for Ukrainian refugees, yet there is a significant variety in policy responses. In many cases, Ukrainian students have been able to benefit from pre-existing policies and measures in place for refugee students. In Portugal, for instance, Ukrainian students were able to benefit from the existing framework for the admission of students in humanitarian emergency to Higher Education Institutions with full access to social grants, including scholarships, and equality to national students' status for the purpose of tuition fees. Most EU countries use and develop measures and instruments already in place, which generally include host language training or support, psychological counselling, academic guidance, introductory courses, scholarships, and reserved study places (European Commission/EACEA/Eurydice, 2022[20]). Some countries have also introduced exceptional policies such as full tuition fee exemption for Ukrainian refugees, including Austria, Ireland, Poland, Romania, Slovenia and Sweden.

Higher education institutions (HEIs), however, have a substantial degree of autonomy in most countries and have implemented their own exceptional measures to support Ukrainian students and scholars. These have included opening up of university and research positions, scholarships, and different types of assistance for Ukrainian citizens as well as pledges to enrol students and reducing and in some cases waiving tuition fees. For instance, more than 50 universities and research institutions in France offer Ukrainian refugees different types of assistance, including financial, to resume their studies. Such HEI-led initiatives aimed at Ukrainian tertiary students are to varying degrees in place in most OECD countries.

Measures have also been put in place to support Ukrainian international students, who were already studying in host countries prior to February. The United States announced changes in work rights for Ukrainian students (e.g. suspending certain employment authorisation rules for Ukrainian students who are experiencing severe economic hardship as a direct result of the war). The Canadian Government launched a fund to support research trainees from Ukraine currently in Canada or who wish to come to

Canada to study or do their research. The Norwegian Government has also established a grant scheme for Ukrainian students in Norway who are struggling financially due to the war.

Some financial support provided to university students is conditional on return to Ukraine and contributing to reconstruction, most notably that provided by the Ukrainian Global University (UGU). The Ukrainian Global University is a vast network of educational institutions, who, in partnership with the Office of the President of Ukraine, support Ukrainian high school and university students, scholars, tutors to take up studies in host countries by providing them with scholarships and fellowships. The initiative requires all students to return to Ukraine after finishing their studies to help rebuild the country post-war.

Promoting employment and employability

Since the start of this refugee crisis, only a relatively small number of those of working age fleeing Ukraine have entered the labour market in the EU and other OECD countries, though the number of people wanting to do so is expected to rise. This will impact both employment levels and expand labour force in host countries in the coming years. By the end of 2022, between 850 000 and 1.1 million working-age people are expected to enter the labour market in Europe, with the estimated impact on labour force being about 0.5%, about twice as large as that of the 2014-17 inflows (OECD, 2022[7]). Considering the strong geographical concentration of Ukrainian refugees, most of the impact on labour force will be observed in a few countries, reaching the highest levels in the Czech Republic (2.2%), Poland (2.1%), and Estonia (1.9%). Ensuring a swift and effective labour market integration is essential for allowing refugees to rebuild their lives and achieving stable livelihoods, yet refugees often struggle with finding employment or remain underemployed. Some of the characteristics of Ukrainian refugees are likely to improve their integration prospects and employability, including their educational profile, existing social networks, and immediate labour market access in many host countries, while others on the contrary may hinder them, namely that most arrivals are women with children and other dependents.

Job search and matching

Over the last decade, the global community has been taking steps to improve refugees' labour market outcomes (OECD/UNHCR, 2018[21]). It remains a priority also during this crisis and Ukrainian refugees have been granted the right to work almost immediately in most host countries – even if this right remains subject to applicable professional rules and national labour-market policies (OECD, 2022[19]). In the EU Member States, the right to work is covered by the Temporary Protection Directive, with the European Commission (2022[17]) encouraging MSs to provide the broadest possible access to the labour market. Other European countries not bound by the directive and non-EU countries, including Canada, Denmark, Japan, Norway and Switzerland, have introduced their own national regulations to ensure immediate labour market access for Ukrainian refugees.

Access to the labour market, however, is not sufficient to guarantee employment and countries choose to offer further support to Ukrainians for finding a job, although the degree and nature of support provided varies significantly. In many countries, including most EU countries, Australia, New Zealand, Switzerland and the United Kingdom, public employment services play a key role when it comes to providing information on jobs, offering necessary training and acting as matchmakers between refugees and employers. In some countries, specific units have been created for this. For instance, Portugal's Institute of Employment and Vocational Training has mobilised a task force to co-ordinate skills matching between Ukrainian arrivals and Portuguese businesses.

Different matching tools are also available to ease the process. Several countries have created online portals with varying degrees of in-built matching systems to connect BTPs to companies and suitable jobs, including Estonia, France, Poland and Portugal. At the EU level, the European Commission is currently developing a web-based EU Talent Pool for displaced people from Ukraine to post profiles, following a scenario developed by the OECD (2022[22]). Employers will be able to consult an overview of the registered profiles via appointed national contact points to learn if the skills they are looking for are represented in the Ukrainian community in their area.

As with housing provision, many ad hoc matching pages sprung up on social media with private citizens and business owners offering job opportunities to Ukrainian refugees. Despite the general goodwill associated with these initiatives, there are also clear risks. Considering their vulnerabilities, including psychological trauma, lack of financial resources, inability to speak the local language and limited awareness of their rights, Ukrainian refugees are at high risk of exploitation, prompting both labour inspectorates and law enforcement agencies to enforce preventive and corrective interventions. The Ombudsman's Office in the Czech Republic has warned that Ukrainian refugees should trust only official information and avoid labour brokers.

Entrepreneurship is another pathway for self-reliance among Ukrainian refugees and some host communities and countries provide entrepreneurship training courses for new arrivals (e.g. Ireland). This has also been supported at times by the Ukrainian Government. For instance, the Ministry of Digital Transformation of Ukraine, the Ministry of Economic Development and Technology of Poland and the Polish Investment and Trade Agency with the support of Mastercard have opened a support centre (Diia.Business) in Warsaw, where Ukrainian refugees can learn how to start a business in Poland.

Skills assessment and recognition

The information currently available on the educational levels of Ukrainian refugees suggests a higher share of them are tertiary educated compared to most other refugee groups. Recognising their qualifications and educational credentials thus plays a particularly important role in ensuring their successful integration in the labour market. Many Ukrainians arrive with all or partial educational documents, aiding the recognition processes immensely. Ukraine has also been at the forefront in digitalising student data and host countries have been able to call on Ukrainian authorities to verify national educational documents. Despite this, a destruction of infrastructure has increased response times and receiving countries have also used alternate measures to speed up skills assessment and recognition processes.

Numerous tools are available to facilitate skills assessment and recognition in these instances, most of which have been developed in the context of prior refugee crises. The European Qualifications Passport for Refugees (EQPR), developed by the Council of Europe, is a standardised document that explains the qualifications a refugee is likely to have based on the available evidence. While not a formal recognition act, it summarises and presents available information on the applicant's educational level, work experience and language proficiency. Drawing on similar methodology, the UNESCO Qualifications Passport (UQP) is also available for non-European countries. Different means are also available at national levels. For instance, MYSKILLS test in Germany, available for 30 professions in six languages, allows job seekers to identify and demonstrate their professional skills without corresponding documentation. The European Commission is also working with the European Training Foundation (ETF), Ukrainian authorities and the EU MSs to compare the Ukrainian national qualification framework and the European Qualifications Framework (EQF), to make Ukrainian qualifications more easily understandable across borders for employers, education and training providers alike.

Another form of support available is the removal of qualification requirements or the expedition of skills evaluations and credential recognition. In the case of the Ukrainian refugee crisis, this has been used mainly in relation to teaching and health care professions, where regular recognition procedures can be very lengthy. Poland has shortened the timeline for recognition of medical qualifications for this group, and Spain is undertaking fast-track assessment of medical degrees and other qualifications. Lithuania exempts BTPs from language requirements for employment (including teaching) for a period of two years. Sweden has not introduced a special programme for Ukrainian refugees, but BTPs are able to take advantage of the existing fast-track for teachers, pre-school teachers and medical professionals.

Addressing gender-specific needs

Despite the often-immediate access, Ukrainian refugees have been relatively slow to enter the labour force in host countries. In Austria, as of June 2022, only about 10% of all eligible working age BTPs had signed up with the Austrian Public Employment Service. There are several possible reasons behind this, including the uncertainty about the length of stay, but the gender profile of arrivals may also play a role. Immigrant women in general are more prone than native-born women to be in long-term unemployment, in involuntary inactivity and at risk of over-qualification, yet the risk is even higher for refugee women (Liebig and Tronstad, 2018[23]). Moreover, refugee women can be particularly vulnerable to labour market exploitation and gender-based violence. Authorities uncovered evidence of human trafficking already in the early weeks of the Ukrainian refugee crisis (Hoff and de Volder, 2022[24]). These and other gender-based risks and challenges need to be addressed to facilitate meaningful access to employment for Ukrainian refugees.

A major barrier to labour market entry is access to affordable dependent care, especially as the majority of arrivals are women with children or other dependents. Some host countries have sought to address this. In France, for instance, children up to the age of three have access to public day-care, free of charge until the end of 2022. Poland has opened hundreds of new childcare centres. Yet many countries were facing severe shortages of care places and staff even prior to the new influx, so ensuring longer-term access to affordable care services remains a challenge.

In addition, targeted counselling and job training can help women participate in host countries' labour market. Access to job training, work placements and professional networks is particularly important to ensure their labour market integration at appropriate skill levels. Immigration Refugees and Citizenship Canada, for instance, sponsors Her Mentors project (Women's Economic Council) that connects migrant women (including Ukrainians arriving under the CUAET) to mentors, also offering skills training to advance employment or self-employment opportunities and supporting women in joining professional associations.

Emerging challenges

Phasing out temporary protection in the EU and beyond

Considering the scale of flows, rapid activation of the Temporary Protection Directive helped avoid overwhelming national asylum systems, better manage unprecedented levels of arrivals and ensure the immediate protection and rights of those eligible in the EU. Yet as its name indicates, this is by design a temporary solution and intended to last initially for a year. After that, it may be extended for further periods (from six months to a two-year maximum). A further extension for up to a third year is also possible, but on a qualified majority vote on a proposal from the European Commission. Once the temporary protection regime ends, the regular rules and regulations on protection and on foreigners again apply. Considering the total numbers of BTPs to date, transitioning from temporary protection to other legal bases for stay will be a major administrative undertaking in many countries, requiring them to start preparing for this transition as soon as possible.

Temporary and subsidiary statuses also come with several embedded challenges that countries need to take into account as the refugee crisis continues. They make sense for short-lived crises, but are less appropriate in the event of long-term displacement as temporary protection generally grants fewer rights than conventional refugee status. Displaced persons may find themselves living with precarious situations with limited integration prospects (OECD, 2016[25]). Moreover, temporary protection is based on an expectation of eventual return. It can be, however, nearly impossible to predict return flows. Returns can vary significantly between groups. In the context of large-scale displacement experienced in Europe due to armed conflicts during the Yugoslav Wars from 1991 to 2001, which led to the adoption of the TPD in 2001, the majority of Bosnian refugees did not go home after active warfare ended in Bosnia, while in contrast, most Kosovar refugees returned to Kosovo *en masse* (Koser and Black, 1999[26]; OECD, 2016[25]). The return decisions within Ukrainian refugee groups will most likely vary significantly as well, depending on a range of factors, including the region of origin, cultural background, economic and family circumstances. While many will return, there is a need to ensure that alternative pathways for settlement are available for those who cannot return or who decide against returning to Ukraine when temporary protection regime ends.

Some EU countries, most notably Poland, are already taking first steps towards phasing out temporary protection. Legal amendments have been introduced stipulating that Ukrainians who left their homeland because of Russian aggression can apply directly for a three-year temporary residence permit. The application may be submitted no earlier than 9 months from the date of entry and no later than 18 months from 24 February 2022. This is in place to ensure continuity regardless of whether temporary protection is extended or not. This pathway, however, is not available to those Ukrainians who already have another legal basis for staying in Poland independently from temporary protection, including recipients of international protection.

Challenges with transitioning away from temporary solutions may also arise elsewhere. Initial steps to phase out such systems have already been taken also outside the European Union. In particular, Australia has closed its Temporary Humanitarian Stay pathway, guiding Ukrainian nationals who have arrived on a temporary visa and are unable to return to Ukraine to apply for asylum. However, with some temporary schemes it is unclear if and how Ukrainians could transition to other statuses if these programmes were to end before return to Ukraine is possible. In the United States, Ukrainians arriving through the Uniting for Ukraine (U4U) parole programme are not provided with an immigration status and in most cases are not eligible for immigration status or lawful permanent residence after their parole ends. In Norway, contrary to other humanitarian permits, temporary collective protection granted to Ukrainians does not count towards a permanent residence and there is no clear pathway to long-term residence.

Transitioning from exceptional measures to mainstream solutions

Most host countries have introduced temporary exceptional measures to support the reception of new arrivals. In some cases, such measures have been directed at refugees themselves, for instance, as one-time or temporary cash assistance or as free services. Many European countries, for instance, have made provisions for temporary free travel for Ukrainian displaced persons, including Austria, Belgium, France, Germany Lithuania, Italy, Poland and Sweden. In other cases, host communities have been the recipients, e.g. financial support provided for hosting private households. In many cases, such exceptional measures have been essential for managing the influx. Poland and the Slovak Republic, for instance, report that the provision of financial compensation for hosting has been an increasingly important consideration for private hosts over time and has helped to ensure the availability of temporary housing options in otherwise over-strained market conditions (OECD, 2022[5]).

These temporary measures, however, are not expected to last forever. Many of them have already expired or are expected to end later in 2022. As the refugee crisis continues, countries either need to extend these measures or provide support through mainstream measures and social security systems. Some EU countries have tried to mainstream general support measures from the start. In the Czech Republic, Estonia, Latvia, Lithuania and Luxembourg, for instance, BTPs access social services on the same basis as other residents. Since 1 June, Ukrainian BTPs also have access to the general social security system in Germany.

While mainstreaming should be a longer-term goal in most contexts, supplementary exceptional measures may still be needed medium-term to prevent general social security systems from becoming overwhelmed. This is particularly important in the context of housing. In July, several Latvian cities, including Riga, stopped accepting Ukrainian refugees, as the previous state allocation for the accommodation of the refugees was substantially reduced (to EUR 3.5 per day) and municipalities deemed this to be insufficient to secure private housing in local market conditions. There are also limited alternatives available in such cases. Access to social housing is generally not an option as available stocks are limited and under great pressure. Social housing stock ranges from over 20% of the housing stock in the Netherlands, Denmark and Austria, to less than 2% in Latvia, the Slovak Republic, Spain, Estonia, Lithuania and the Czech Republic (OECD, n.d.[27]). Stock is particularly sparse in the main countries of first reception for Ukrainians, and allocation is already managed by waitlists in many countries. In this situation, giving priority placement to Ukrainian refugees in social housing ahead of other eligible groups is unlikely to be an option.

Addressing secondary movements

Mobility inside and outside the EU of Ukrainians has remained at a high level ever since 24 February. Right from the start, cross-border movements went in both directions, as people fleeing the country crossed those from the diaspora returning to fight. Meanwhile visa-free travel in the EU allowed refugees to move between the EU Member States before registering for temporary protection or seeking protection outside Europe. Many Ukrainians are also beginning to return to Ukraine – whether temporarily or permanently – and in July 2022, about the same number of Ukrainian citizens were crossing the border in both directions for the first time since early February.

While expected, these movements can become a source of concern for many host countries, especially in Europe and the Schengen Area. In recent years, the EU Member States have seen an increase in secondary movements by beneficiaries of international protection and limiting secondary movements of asylum seekers has been a policy priority since the 2015-16 crisis (EASO, 2021[28]). In the context of temporary protection and the current crisis, concerns may arise that some individuals could abuse the system by registering for protection and collecting social assistance in one or more EU Member States, while residing elsewhere, including Ukraine.

The European Commission has developed an EU platform for the exchange of information on BTPs, allowing the EU MSs to exchange information on registered persons in real time, including addressing instances of double or multiple registrations and limiting possible misuse of the system. Some countries are also taking steps to manage secondary movements of Ukrainian arrivals. In Switzerland for example, protection status S may be revoked in case of prolonged travel home or abroad. Following consultation with the cantonal and city authorities, the State Secretariat for Migration (SEM) decided that it may revoke the protection status of persons if they return to their home country for more than 15 days in a quarterly period. This also applies if a Ukrainian refugee spends more than two months in a third country. While there are no plans to revoke residence permits granted on the grounds of protection under the TPD, Sweden and some other EU Member States have stated that BTPs may lose the right to aid (including housing and financial support) if they leave the country for extended periods.

Preparing for changes in public opinion and support

Across host countries, Ukrainian refugees have been welcomed with unprecedented and overwhelming support. During the first months of the refugee crisis, many host governments were able to rely heavily on civil society and private citizens, who volunteered their time and resources to help Ukrainian refugees, ensuring that reception systems did not collapse under the influx of new arrivals. Public opinion and support for displaced populations, however, tends to wane over time, making it unlikely that host governments can rely on this high level of public support in the long term. Incoming evidence is already suggesting that compassion fatigue is beginning to set in as donations and volunteering efforts are declining, and public anxieties are on the rise in response to record inflation in Europe and beyond.

Changes in public mood and support are not necessarily a sign for governments to change their policies towards Ukrainian refugees, but, instead, an indicator that more attention needs to be paid to addressing public anxieties and restoring confidence in migration and integration systems. Public narratives around migration tend to be depicted as swaying from one extreme to another: from full solidarity to anti-immigrant hostility. In reality, public opinions are less binary and people hold multiple, competing beliefs and opinions at the same time, creating opportunities to prepare for changes by promoting solidarity and defusing tensions (Banulescu-Bogdan, 2022[29]).

Perceptions of unfairness in particular can undermine solidarity and harm public support for refugees. Resentment is easily triggered in response to perceived privileged treatment of newcomers compared to other groups. For instance, some political parties in Ireland have already voiced their opposition to housing Ukrainian refugees ahead of existing long-term housing applicants. To minimise possible backlash, some countries (e.g. Belgium) are deliberately avoiding introducing Ukraine-specific social programmes and measures where possible to minimise the appearance of special treatment.

Countries are also taking steps to demonstrate that the concerns of local citizens are treated seriously and that there are long-term plans in place to manage these pressures on host societies. Several countries, such as Australia, Denmark, Ireland and Italy, already follow a co-ordinated approach to communicating their crisis response to the public as well as presenting a coherent long-term strategy for Ukrainians' integration (OECD, 2022[30]). In other countries, regular exchanges and close communication with local communities to identify turning points in public opinion are a core part of their longer-term response plans to the refugee crisis. Estonia, for instance, is planning to start organising regular community-based roundtables to hear and respond to the concerns people may have in relation to the Ukrainian refugee crisis. While it is impossible to entirely allay the fears of the public, addressing these anxieties head on can prevent them from growing into existential threats fuelling anti-immigrant sentiment.

References

Banulescu-Bogdan, N. (2022), *From Fear to Solidarity: The Difficulty in Shifting Public Narratives about Refugees.*, Migration Policy Institute, Washington, DC, https://www.migrationpolicy.org/sites/default/files/publications/refugee-narratives-report-2022_final.pdf. [29]

Cerna, L. (2019), "Refugee education: Integration models and practices in OECD countries", *OECD Education Working Papers*, No. 203, OECD Publishing, Paris, https://doi.org/10.1787/a3251a00-en. [12]

EASO (2021), *EASO Asylum Report 2021*, European Asylum Support Office, Valletta, https://euaa.europa.eu/sites/default/files/EASO-Asylum-Report-2021.pdf. [28]

European Commission (2022), *Communication from the Commission on Guidance for access to the labour market, vocational education and training and adult learning of people fleeing Russia's war of aggression against Ukraine*, European Commission, Brussels, https://ec.europa.eu/commission/presscorner/detail/en/IP_22_3620. [17]

European Commission (2022), *Communication from the Commission on Operational guidelines for the implementation of Council implementing Decision 2022/382*, European Commission, https://eur-lex.europa.eu/legal-content/EN/TXT/PDF/?uri=CELEX:52022XC0321(03)&from=EN. [4]

European Commission (2022), *Supporting the inclusion of displaced children from Ukraine in education : considerations, key principles and practices for the school year 2022-2023*, Publications Office of the European Union, https://doi.org/10.2766/310985. [13]

European Commission/EACEA/Eurydice (2022), *Supporting refugee learners from Ukraine in higher education in Europe*, Eurydice report. Luxembourg: Publications Office of the European Union. [20]

Hoff, S. and E. de Volder (2022), *Preventing human trafficking of refugees from Ukraine: A rapid assessment of risks and gaps in the anti-trafficking response*, La Strada International and The Freedom Fund, https://freedomfund.org/wp-content/uploads/UkraineAntiTraffickingReport_2022_05_10.pdf. [24]

Home Office (2022), *Immigration statistics, year ending March 2022*, https://www.gov.uk/government/statistics/immigration-statistics-year-ending-march-2022 (accessed on 24 August 2022). [3]

INFO GmbH (2022), *Geflüchtete aus der Ukraine*. [1]

Jeon, S. (2019), *Unlocking the Potential of Migrants: Cross-country Analysis*, OECD Reviews of Vocational Education and Training, OECD Publishing, Paris, https://doi.org/10.1787/045be9b0-en. [18]

Koser, K. and R. Black (1999), ""Limits to Harmonization: The 'Temporary Protection' of Refugees in the European Union"", *International Migration*, Vol. 37/3, http://onlinelibrary.wiley.com/doi/10.1111/1468- 2435.00082/abstract. [26]

Liebig, T. and K. Tronstad (2018), "Triple Disadvantage?: A first overview of the integration of refugee women", *OECD Social, Employment and Migration Working Papers*, No. 216, OECD Publishing, Paris, https://doi.org/10.1787/3f3a9612-en. [23]

OECD (2022), *Feasibility Study on the Development of an EU Talent Pool: Final Report*, OECD, Paris, https://www.oecd.org/migration/mig/Report-Feasibility-Study-on-the-Development-of-an-EU-Talent-Pool-2022.pdf. [22]

OECD (2022), "Housing support for Ukrainian refugees in receiving countries", *OECD Policy Responses on the Impacts of the War in Ukraine*, OECD Publishing, Paris, https://doi.org/10.1787/9c2b4404-en. [5]

OECD (2022), "How to communicate on the Ukrainian refugee crisis and build on the support of host communities?", *OECD Policy Responses on the Impacts of the War in Ukraine*, OECD Publishing, Paris, https://doi.org/10.1787/db78fd32-en. [30]

OECD (2022), "How vocational education and training (VET) systems can support Ukraine: Lessons from past crises", *OECD Policy Responses on the Impacts of the War in Ukraine*, OECD Publishing, Paris, https://doi.org/10.1787/e8e86ce2-en. [16]

OECD (2022), *OECD Economic Outlook, Volume 2022 Issue 1*, OECD Publishing, Paris, https://doi.org/10.1787/62d0ca31-en. [8]

OECD (2022), *Rights and Support for Ukrainian Refugees in Receiving Countries*, OECD Publishing, Paris, https://doi.org/10.1787/09beb886-en. [19]

OECD (2022), "Supporting refugee students from Ukraine in host countries", *OECD Policy Responses on the Impacts of the War in Ukraine*, OECD Publishing, Paris, https://doi.org/10.1787/b02bcaa7-en. [14]

OECD (2022), "The potential contribution of Ukrainian refugees to the labour force in European host countries", *OECD Policy Responses on the Impacts of the War in Ukraine*, OECD Publishing, Paris, https://doi.org/10.1787/e88a6a55-en. [7]

OECD (2022), "The Ukrainian Refugee Crisis: Support for teachers in host countries", *OECD Policy Responses on the Impacts of the War in Ukraine*, OECD Publishing, Paris, https://doi.org/10.1787/546ed0a7-en. [15]

OECD (2021), *Building for a better tomorrow: Policies to make housing more affordable*, Employment, Labour and Social Affairs Policy Briefs, OECD Publishing, Paris, http://oe.cd/affordable-housing-2021. [9]

OECD (2016), "International migration following environmental and geopolitical shocks: How can OECD countries respond?", in *International Migration Outlook 2016*, OECD Publishing, Paris, https://doi.org/10.1787/migr_outlook-2016-7-en. [25]

OECD (n.d.), *OECD Affordable Housing Database*, OECD, Paris, http://www.oecd.org/social/affordable-housing-database.htm (accessed on 10 July 2022). [27]

OECD/UNHCR (2018), *Engaging with employers in the hiring of refugees: A 10-point multi-stakeholder action plan for employers*, UNHCR Publishing, Geneva, https://www.unhcr.org/5adde9904. [21]

Panchenko, T. (2022), *Prospects for Integration of Ukrainian Refugees into the German Labor Market: Results of the ifo Online Survey*, https://www.cesifo.org/en/publikationen/2022/article-journal/prospects-integration-ukrainian-refugees-german-labor-market (accessed on 2 August 2022). [2]

Spaas, S. et al. (2022), "Mental Health of Refugee and Non-refugee Migrant Young People in European Secondary Education: The Role of Family Separation, Daily Material Stress and Perceived Discrimination in Resettlement", *J Youth Adolescence*, Vol. 51, pp. 848–870, https://doi.org/10.1007/s10964-021-01515-y. [11]

UDI (2022), *Avtaler om akuttinnkvartering*, https://www.udi.no/aktuelt/nye-avtaler-om-akuttinnkvartering/ (accessed on 7 June 2022). [6]

Wojdat, M. and P. Cywiński (2022), *"Urban hospitality: Unprecedented growth, challenges and opportunities"*, Union of Polish Metropolises, Warsaw, https://metropolie.pl/fileadmin/user_upload/UMP_raport_Ukraina_ANG_20220429_final.pdf. [10]

Notes

[1] The term "refugee" is used in this chapter to refer to persons who are fleeing from Russia's war against Ukraine and have obtained some sort of international protection, including not only formal refugee status (as per the Geneva Convention) but also subsidiary and temporary protection (as in the case of most arrivals from Ukraine).

5 International students: A growing group of migrants in the OECD

Elisabeth Kamm

This chapter provides an overview of international students in OECD countries, their origin and destination countries as well as drivers of their mobility. It discusses how international students differ from domestic students in the OECD and provides the latest enrolment and permit statistics, in part impacted by the COVID-19 pandemic.

In Brief

- In 2020, there were 4.4 million international students enrolled in the OECD, accounting for 10% of all tertiary students. The most important receiving countries are the United States (22% of all international students), the United Kingdom (13%) and Australia (10%).

- The share of international students is higher at higher levels of education. Across OECD countries, international students make up 7% of students enrolled at bachelor's, 17% at master's, and 26% at the doctoral level in the academic year 2020.

- Since 2010, there has been a strong increase in international students in the OECD virtually everywhere. The absolute increase was largest in the United States, Canada and Australia, followed by Germany and the Republic of Türkiye, while the relative growth was largest in smaller destinations such as the Baltic countries and Slovenia.

- While the destinations of international students have diversified over the past decade, the main origin countries have largely remained stable, with China and India accounting for 22% and 10% of all international students, respectively. One in twelve international students in the OECD is a Chinese student in the United States.

- International students tend to study in their region of origin. In 2020, 29% of international students in OECD countries originated from the same broader geographical region. This was notably the case for three-quarters of international or foreign students in Austria, the Czech Republic, Denmark, Slovenia and the Slovak Republic (Europe); Chile, Colombia and Costa Rica (Latin America) and Japan and Korea (Asia).

- In most OECD countries, international students are more likely to study STEM subjects than domestic students, especially natural sciences, mathematics and statistics, and ICT subjects. In turn, international students are less likely to study subjects in the fields of education, health, and welfare. National data indicate a preference for studies in the field of engineering among Indian students.

- Despite the strong increase in recent years, international students enrolled account for only about 3% of all foreign-born people in an OECD country. In some destinations, however, this share is twice as high, as is the case in Japan, Poland and Türkiye, at around 7%.

Introduction

In the academic year 2020, 4.4 million international students[1] were studying in an OECD country, 70% more than a decade ago. International students are thus a rapidly expanding group of foreign-born.

For the individuals concerned, studying abroad is often an opportunity to access higher quality education and acquire new skills. International study experience is also a way to improve employability, not only in the origin and host countries, but also in alternative destinations. It also helps international students to expand their knowledge of other societies and to improve their language skills, especially English.

From a migration policy perspective, international students are a unique group of migrants, as they are often seen as pre-integrated migrants who have domestic credentials that are easily recognisable by employers and who have at least some experience and knowledge with respect to the host country, including the language.

Against this backdrop, this chapter provides an overview of the state of international student migration to OECD countries.[2] It begins with a comprehensive overview of international student populations in OECD countries, their fields of study, destinations, and origin countries, and how these evolved over time. It provides the latest data, including enrolment and permit data, and discusses impacts of the COVID-19 pandemic. Chapter 6 of this publication looks into specific policies to attract and retain international students, and Chapter 7 investigates the retention of international students and their economic impact.

Overview of international students in OECD countries

What is an international student?

For the purposes of this chapter, international students are individuals who left their country of origin to move to another country for study. This chapter therefore takes a broad definition of international students that goes beyond the one used in international education statistics (see Box 5.1). Indeed, from a migration management perspective, any type of study abroad that may affect the migration pathway is of interest, as long as the entry category is associated with educational purposes.

That notwithstanding, the focus of this chapter is on students enrolled in an educational course classified as ISCED5 and higher. This includes everyone enrolled in tertiary education, regardless of age, notably also in short-cycle tertiary education which is often more practically based, occupationally-specific or prepares for a degree programme. However, in some cases, other types of students from abroad may also be included, if they are covered by the same permit regime. The term international students may thus encompass students in non-university education such as VET and individuals attending specific language courses.

Specific language institutes and schools that offer intensive language training exist across the OECD. In many countries, it is enough to obtain a regular tourist visa to attend a language course, which is often only for a few months. In other countries, language programmes serve as a preparatory course to enrol in a full-degree programme and persons enrolled in such courses are considered international students. This is common in Specialised Training Colleges, post-secondary courses of Japan and in some Eastern European countries, where such preparatory courses allow international students to be able to study in the national languages of the host country. For example, the share of international students that are in Japanese language schools was 16% in 2011 and went up to 30% in 2018, although it declined slightly since (27% in 2019, 22% in 2020). In most countries, however, these groups of international students are rather small. In Germany for example, language courses and visa for non-tertiary education account for about 8% of the total international student visas. In practice, who is considered an "international student" depends on the data source used. In particular, education statistics build on enrolment data and may not well capture the underlying migration category (see Box 5.1).

A key distinction with respect to international students is between credit and degree mobility. Credit mobility refers to a situation where international students study abroad for a short period not leading to a specific degree. They then obtain educational credits from the host institution and thereafter return to their sending institution to complete their degree. In contrast, the term degree mobility refers to individuals who move to a country to obtain a full degree (such as a master's degree) at the destination. The lines between the two are increasingly blurring, however, due to dual degree programmes, which give a degree in both host and sending countries.

Box 5.1. Data and statistics on international students

Enrolment versus permit data

The most important data source on international students is the OECD-UNESCO database, which is based on enrolment statistics in education institutions and mainly focuses on tertiary degrees. Countries are requested to determine as country of origin of students the country in which they obtained the upper secondary qualification that provides access to tertiary education. When countries do not have access to this information, alternative measures may be used. These include, in order of preference, the country of permanent or usual residence, or citizenship. The term foreign student is used for students who do not have the citizenship of the country in which they study and is only used as an approximation in some countries when data on the other mentioned grounds is not available. This is notably the case in Colombia, Costa Rica, the Czech Republic, Hungary, Israel, Italy, Korea, the Slovak Republic and Türkiye (see Annex Table 5.A.1).

OECD countries also record residence permits issued for study or educational purposes. This permit data works to capture international students who do not benefit from free mobility zones (such as within the EU) as well as their families. Permits are issued for both credit and degree mobility, as well as sometimes for language courses, and can include students attending other educational programmes such as au pairs.

The COVID-19 pandemic and its impact on 2020 international students data

The COVID-19 pandemic had a major impact on international student migration, as is evidenced in the permit data presented below. However, it had only a minor impact on most enrolment statistics reported in this chapter. This is because reported enrolment data for 2020 generally refers to the academic year 2019/20, which in most OECD countries started in the fall of 2019. However, in a few OECD countries, the academic year 2020 started in February to April 2020, i.e. the early phase of the pandemic. This is the case in Japan, Australia and New Zealand. Especially the two latter countries registered a large decline in student enrolment in 2020.

A profile of international students

Few origin countries dominate an increasingly diverse set of destinations

In 2010, less than one in four international students was enrolled in an OECD country outside of the United States, the United Kingdom, Australia, Germany, France, Canada and Japan. However, the share of international students enrolled in an OECD country outside these top-7 destinations has grown constantly, having increased to almost 30% by 2020 (Figure 5.1).

In 2020, 4.4 million international students were enrolled in the OECD area, more than a third of these (1.4 million) in a European OECD country. In the same year, more than one in five (22%) international students in the OECD studied in the United States, followed by more than one in ten in the United Kingdom and Australia. Despite a slight decline in the dominance of these destinations, in 2020 almost half of all international students (45%) in the OECD were still studying in these top-3 English-speaking countries. Germany and France are the major recipient countries in Europe, hosting about 14% of international students to the OECD as a whole, and 45% of those studying in a European OECD country. Among the top-7 destinations, Canada has seen the sharpest increase in its popularity among international students; 7% of all international students in the OECD studied in Canada in 2020, up from just 3% in 2010.

Figure 5.1. Main OECD destinations remain but others are increasing their market share

International students enrolled in OECD countries by destination, 2010 and 2020

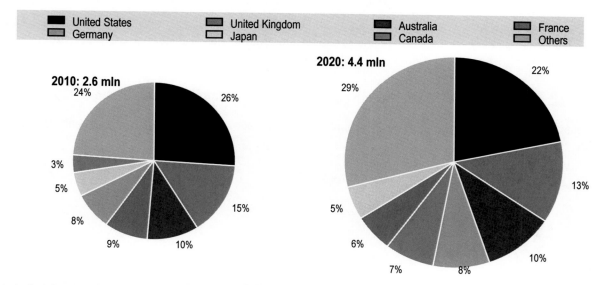

Note: In the left chart, data for France and Japan refer to data from 2013.
Source: OECD Education at a Glance Database, 2022.

StatLink ᵃˢ᷅ https://stat.link/csu9eg

Most international students in OECD countries come from Asia. In 2020, about three in five international students in the OECD came from the continent, with half of the Asian students originating from two main origin countries: China (overall 22%) and India (overall 10%). Compared to 2013, the earliest year for which origin country data is available, the share of students from Asia has increased, while the share of Europeans remained stable (Figure 5.2).

Figure 5.2. International students in the OECD mainly come from Asia and Europe

Share of international students enrolled in an OECD country by continent of origin, 2013 and 2020

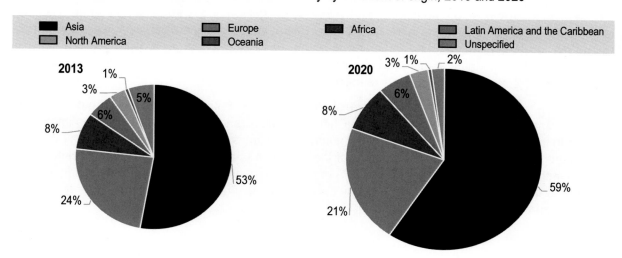

Note: For comparability reasons, data in 2013 include data from all OECD member countries as of 2022, to the extent available.
Source: OECD Education at a Glance Database, 2022.

StatLink ᵃˢ᷅ https://stat.link/z3apdv

In 2020, 86% of international students in Australia originated from Asia, their share tops 76% in the United States, and 59%, in the United Kingdom. Taken together, these top-3 receiving countries alone host 57% of all international students from Asia.

A cross-tabulation by destination and origin shows China as the key origin and the United States as the key destination country. About 1 in 12 international students in the OECD is a Chinese student in the United States. This share has remained constant over the past decade.

Figure 5.3. China and India are key origin countries of international students in the OECD

Students enrolled in OECD countries by origin country and percentage relative to in-country enrolment, 2013 and 2020

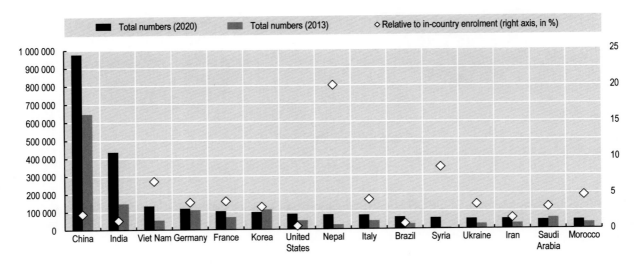

Note: Relative to in-country enrolments refer to data from 2019 for Viet Nam, 2016 for Syria and 2014 for the United States.
Source: OECD Secretariat calculations based on OECD Education at a Glance Database, 2022 and UNESCO tertiary enrolment data.

StatLink 🔗 https://stat.link/4liya3

In spite of their large absolute numbers, relative to their overall in-country enrolment in tertiary education, numbers of international students in the OECD from China and India are not particularly high (Figure 5.3). Among the top-15 origin countries, Nepal, on the other hand, stands out as a country with a significant proportion of international students. The number of Nepalese students enrolled in the OECD in 2020 is equivalent to 20% of all tertiary students enrolled domestically in Nepal.

An estimation based on the global youth population aged 20-29 confirms this picture. About a third of the world's population in this age group lives in China and India, and thus their presence as international students in the OECD relative to their national youth population is not high. In contrast, among the top-15 origin countries, Syria has the highest share of the country's total youth cohort residing as international students in the OECD (2%). Among these, 62% of Syrian students in the OECD were studying in Türkiye and a further 26% in Germany. Indeed, in some cases taking up studies can be a complementary pathway for humanitarian migration (Box 5.2).

Box 5.2. Study as a complementary pathway for humanitarian migration

Complementary pathways for humanitarian migration, while no substitute for asylum, are an additional way for individuals in need of international protection to be admitted. Such regulated pathways include family reunification, work, and study permits. Particularly during periods of large-scale influx of (highly-educated) refugees (e.g. the current crisis in Ukraine), granting visas for educational purposes to humanitarian migrants provides host countries with an additional avenue of admission. Across OECD countries, study permits and visas for academic scholarships are primarily issued for tertiary programmes, although secondary programmes and apprenticeships are also not uncommon.

Since 2017, the OECD and the UNHCR provide a joint monitoring of such pathways. The latest edition shows that, in 2019, study permits made up 15% of the permits granted for non-humanitarian reasons to the seven populations in the study (Afghanistan, Eritrea, Iran, Iraq, Somalia, Syria, Venezuela), less than for work (17%) and family reasons (67%). In 2019, the 24 000 new study permits delivered to the seven populations considered amounted to 2% of the total number of study permits delivered by OECD countries.

Complementary pathways are generally associated with legal and administrative hurdles for refugees. Study permits, with eligibility (often) tied to educational attainment, are particularly difficult to access for humanitarian migrants. As such, while the number of visas granted for educational purposes was very low among the (low-educated and younger) refugee populations from Somalia, Eritrea and Afghanistan, it was comparatively higher among (better-educated) humanitarian migrants from Iran and Venezuela.

Overall, data from 2010 to 2019 show however that the number of study permits granted was stable over the decade (between 20 000 to 30 000) apart from a peak in 2014 and even declined in 2019. This is in contrast to the steady increase of work permits over the same period and a strong increase until 2017 among family permits. This suggests that study as a complementary pathway for migrants from these countries was not used to the same extent as other pathways.

Source: OECD-UNHCR (2021[1]), *Safe Pathways for Refugees II – OECD-UNHCR Study on Third-country Solutions for Refugees: Admissions for family reunification, education, and employment purposes between 2010 and 2019*, https://www.oecd.org/els/mig/Safe-Pathways-for-Refugees_2021.pdf.

Countries in Central Asia (Turkmenistan, Uzbekistan, Afghanistan), the Near East (Azerbaijan, Syria), as well as Sub-Saharan Africa (Somalia and Guinea-Bissau) are the origin countries with at least 1 000 international students in the OECD in 2020 which have seen the strongest increase compared to 2013. Among the top-15 in 2020, as shown in Figure 5.3, the increase was strongest in Syria (a 12-fold increase), followed by Nepal and India, where numbers tripled. By contrast, the numbers of international students from Saudi Arabia slightly declined.

International students are of varying, yet overall increasing, importance in the OECD

In almost all OECD countries, the share of international students in tertiary education has increased over the last decade (Figure 5.4). Italy, Belgium, France and New Zealand stand out as the only OECD countries with a slight drop in the share of international students over this period, and only in Italy and Greece was the absolute number of enrolled international students in 2020 lower than in 2010.[3] In most countries, one observes a parallel increase in absolute numbers of international students and their share of the student population. While the absolute increase since 2010 was largest in the United States, Canada and Australia, followed by Germany and Türkiye, the relative increase was largest in the Baltic countries and Slovenia.

Figure 5.4. International student mobility has been expanding virtually everywhere

International students as a share of all tertiary students (in percentages), 2010, 2015, and 2020

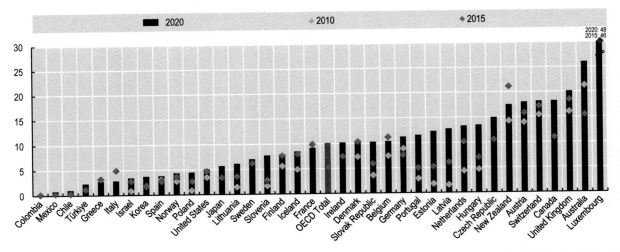

Note: Divergence in data sources and definitions can lead to shares different from those reported by national sources. 2020 data typically refer to the academic year 2019/20 and thus the impact of COVID-19 is most visible in countries where the data refer to 2020, notably Australia and New Zealand.
Source: OECD Education at a Glance Database, 2022.

StatLink 🔗 https://stat.link/5s839r

The share of international students is higher at upper levels of education, but this pattern varies across countries. On average across OECD countries, international students make up 7% of students enrolled at the bachelor's level, 17% at the master's level, and 26% at the doctoral level for academic year 2020 (Table 5.1).

In most countries, an increase in international students at the master and doctoral levels drives the overall growth observed over the last years. Relative to 2015, the increase among those enrolled in a PhD programme was largest in Hungary, Estonia and Germany. The increase among master's students was largest in Latvia, Estonia and Ireland. There is virtually no decline in shares of international students by education level observed between 2015 and 2020 with the exception of the United States, the only OECD country to experience a strong decline in the share of international students in PhD programmes. In 2020, 26% of PhD students in the United States were international students, down from 38% in 2015. Data suggest, however, that the drop actually occurred as early as in the academic year 2017.

Despite the increase in recent years, stocks of international students only account for a small share of the overall foreign-born population in OECD countries, on average 3% in 2019.[4] In some destinations, however, this share is twice as high, reaching approximately 7% in Poland, Japan and Türkiye. Moreover, in countries that have a comparatively small foreign-born population, international students make up a larger share of the foreign-born. In contrast, in countries that have a large foreign-born population such as Luxembourg and Israel, or which have received large numbers of humanitarian migrants in recent years, the share of international students relative to the overall foreign-born population is small, below 2%.

Table 5.1. The share of international students is higher at higher levels of tertiary education

International students enrolled in OECD countries, 2020

	International tertiary students		International students as a share of all (%)			Top three countries of origin in 2020
	Total (thousands)	2020/19 change (%)	Total tertiary education	Master's or equivalent level	Doctoral or equivalent level	
Australia	458	-11	26	50	33	China, India, Nepal
Austria	76	2	18	23	37	Germany, Italy, Bosnia and Herzegovina
Belgium	53	2	10	20	33	France, Netherlands, Cameroon
Canada	323	14	18	20	36	India, China, France
Chile	13	20	1	4	19	Peru, Colombia, Venezuela
Colombia	5	-5	0	1	2	Venezuela, Ecuador, Mexico
Costa Rica	3	48				
Czech Republic	48	4	15	18	22	Slovak Republic, Russia, Ukraine
Denmark	31	-4	10	20	36	Germany, Norway, Romania
Estonia	6	16	12	18	26	Finland, Russia, Nigeria
Finland	24	1	8	10	25	Viet Nam, Russia, China
France	252	2	9	13	38	Morocco, China, Algeria
Germany	369	10	11	17	23	China, India, Syria
Greece	22	-26	3	1	2	Cyprus, Albania, Germany
Hungary	38	7	13	21	25	Germany, China, Romania
Iceland	2	23	9	11	42	United States, Philippines, Germany
Ireland	24	-4	10	23	36	India, China, United States
Israel	13	14	3	5	9	United States, Russia, France
Italy	59	7	3	4	16	China, India, Iran
Japan	223	10	6	10	21	China, Viet Nam, Nepal
Korea	112	13	4	11	17	China, Viet Nam, Uzbekistan
Latvia	10	16	13	27	12	India, Uzbekistan, Germany
Lithuania	7	4	6	12	7	Belarus, India, Ukraine
Luxembourg	4	14	48	75	89	France, Germany, Belgium
Mexico	43	23	1	2	8	
Netherlands	125	13	13	19	48	Germany, Italy, China
New Zealand	44	-20	17	34	49	China, India, Australia
Norway	13	5	4	7	23	China, Sweden, Germany
Poland	62	11	4	5	8	Ukraine, Belarus, India
Portugal	44	19	12	14	33	Brazil, Cabo Verde, Guinea-Bissau
Slovak Republic	14	9	10	12	12	Ukraine, Czech Republic, Serbia
Slovenia	6	15	8	9	20	
Spain	82	6	4	11	19	France, Colombia, Ecuador
Sweden	32	3	7	12	36	China, India, Finland
Switzerland	58	4	18	29	57	France, Germany, Italy
Türkiye	185	16	2	8	7	Syria, Azerbaijan, Turkmenistan
United Kingdom	551	11	20	40	41	China, India, United States
United States	957	-2	5	12	26	China, India, Korea
OECD Total	**4390**	**17**	**10**	**17**	**26**	**China, India, Viet Nam**
OECD – Europe	1388	8	11	18	27	China, Germany, India

Note: Stocks of international students: Data for Colombia, Costa Rica, the Czech Republic, Hungary, Israel, Italy, Korea, the Slovak Republic and Türkiye refer to foreign students instead of international students; exclude Erasmus students in European countries.
Source: OECD Education at a Glance Database, 2022.

StatLink https://stat.link/twzh78

In 2020, the number of enrolled students OECD-wide roughly corresponded to about 14% of the foreign-born youth cohort aged 15 to 34. Thus, about one in seven young immigrants in the OECD is an international student. In Eastern European countries with small migrant populations, such as Poland, and in countries where the foreign-born population is rather old, as in Latvia and Lithuania, international students account for more than half of all young foreign-born. In Estonia, they account for over a third and more than one in five young foreign-born in Canada, Australia, Finland, the Netherlands and Portugal is an international student.

In terms of socio-demographics, international students are more likely to be male and slightly older than the national student population. In 2019, 52% of international students in the OECD were men, which contrasts with the prevalence of women in OECD tertiary education systems. Male students account for over 55% of international students in some countries, including the Baltic countries, Finland, Japan and Türkiye. In contrast, in Belgium, Iceland, Israel, Korea, the Slovak Republic and Slovenia, at least 55% of international students are women. Research has also shown that female students are over-represented in the European ERASMUS+ credit mobility programme (Böttcher et al., 2016[2]). There is no standardised age data available on international students in the OECD, but data from the EUROSTUDENT VII survey show that, on average, international students in Europe are somewhat older than the overall student population in their host country, a fact related to their likelihood to enrol in more advanced degree programmes. These survey data do not, however, include PhD students. In France, where the overall student population is the youngest in Europe at a median age of just 21, international students have a median age of 24 years. In the Nordic countries, by contrast, the median age of students is the highest, reaching 25 years and even higher. International students in these countries have a median age between 25 and 32.

International students make distinct academic choices

Figure 5.5. Field-of-study-choices within countries are often similar

Dissimilarity index between international and domestic students, by broad field of study, percentages, 2020

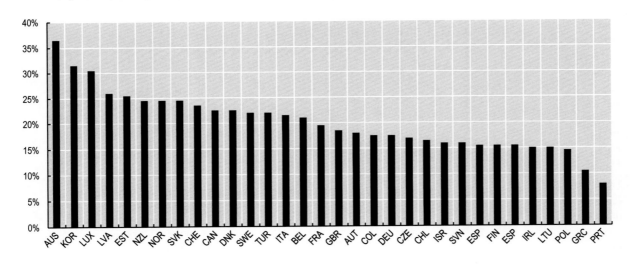

Note: The dissimilarity index measures the percentage of international students that would need to change their study field to mirror the study choice distribution of domestic students in the host country. A 100% score would reflect complete mismatch between the study choices of international students and domestic students, a 0% would reflect full overlap. The percentage score is calculated by summing the absolute percentage differences for each study field between international students and domestic students, divided by two.
Source: OECD Secretariat calculations.

StatLink https://stat.link/aeus1p

International students enrol in different study subjects from domestic students. A dissimilarity analysis shows that, overall, the differences are not very large. In most countries, around 20% of international students would need to change their study field to mirror the study choice distribution of domestic students in the host country (Figure 5.5). The countries that stand out for the most unequal study choices between international and domestic students are Australia, Korea and Luxembourg, where more than 30% of international students would have to change fields of study to match the distribution of domestic students across fields. However, the dissimilarity index does not provide a complete picture of subject-specific differences, given the fact that different fields of study are more popular overall in certain countries.

In most OECD countries, international students are somewhat more likely (29% vs. 24%) to study science, technology, engineering, mathematics (the so-called STEM subjects) and Information and Communication Technologies (ICT) (Figure 5.6). However, this is not the case in Colombia, Italy, Korea, Lithuania, Portugal, the Slovak Republic and Spain. In Australia, the difference in those enrolled in the field of ICT is particularly large: while 14% of international students are enrolled in ICT subjects, this share is only 4% among domestic students. Across OECD countries, international students are less likely to study subjects in the fields of education, health, and welfare. Large differences exist in several countries (see Annex Table 5.A.2 for an overview). For example, in Austria and Korea, international students are more than twice as likely as domestic students to study a subject in the field of social sciences, journalism, and information. This is also true, though less pronounced, in Lithuania and Slovenia. In Iceland, Norway, Sweden and Switzerland, international students are about three times more likely to study natural sciences, mathematics, and statistics than domestic students (in Chile, Israel, France and Türkiye, they are about twice as likely to do so). Finally, international students are about twice as likely as domestic students to study a subject in art and humanities in Belgium, Colombia, Israel, Italy and Norway.

Figure 5.6. International students are overrepresented in natural sciences and ICT

Share of international students and domestic students, by field of study, OECD total, 2020

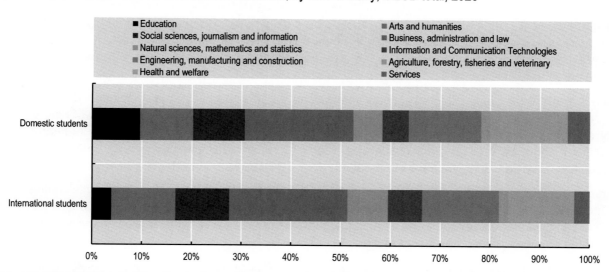

Note: International students include nationals who pursued upper-secondary studies abroad and returned to their home country.
Source: OECD Education at a Glance Database, 2022.

StatLink 🔗 https://stat.link/1kljar

National data[5] on field or subject choice by origin country reveal large differences, with few patterns by origin or destination. They suggest, however, that Indian students are strongly overrepresented in STEM subjects, particularly in engineering. In the United States, in the 2017/18 school year, almost half of international students were studying STEM subjects. This share was around 45% for Chinese students and 79% for Indian students (Congressional Research Service, 2019[3]). In the Netherlands in 2016/17, over half of Indian students were enrolled in engineering degree programmes, a strong overrepresentation compared to other origin countries (Nuffic, 2017[4]). The three largest groups of international students in Germany predominantly study subjects in the field of engineering, with about 66% of Indian, 61% of Syrian, and 50% of Chinese students enrolled in 2021. Overall, about 40% of international students studied engineering in Germany, while the share was only 24% among domestic students (Destatis, 2022[5]). In France, in 2018/19, almost two in three (63%) Indian students were enrolled in a science course. This concentration is higher than that of any other top-20 origin country in France. Moroccan and Algerian students also often chose a subject in the field of sciences, each at 44%, and only a few (5-6%) were studying law and political sciences. Chinese students in France are more equally distributed across study fields, including economics, social, and natural sciences but seldom study law or political science (2%) or health and medicine (1%). Students from Sub-Saharan Africa, by contrast, are most likely to study political sciences and law (15-20%) than students from other top-20 origin countries (Campus France, 2020[6]). In Luxembourg, non-EU students enrolled in masters' programmes account for half of all enrolled students in disciplines related to science, technology, and medicine, while they comprise only 17% of the overall enrolled student population.

In Germany, international students[6] appear less likely than the overall student population to change their study subject. An analysis based on the course of study statistics shows that, of all the students who began their first year at German universities in the 2018/19 semester, while 14% of all bachelor's level students changed their study subject by their third semester, only 9% of international bachelor's students had done so. The change rate for those starting a bachelor's degree was highest for those studying mathematics and natural sciences, for all students (19%) as well as international students (14%). Overall, the change rate at the master's level was much lower, at 4% for all and 3% for international students (Destatis, 2022[7]).

The COVID-19 pandemic profoundly impacted on international student migration

In 2020, there was a strong decline in permits issued to international students across almost all OECD countries (Table 5.2). However, in those countries where 2021 data are already available, these numbers are back to pre-pandemic levels in about half of the countries. The full picture of the impact of COVID-19 on international students has not yet emerged, as the pandemic is not reflected in most of the 2020 enrolment data (Box 5.1).

The COVID-19 pandemic affected not only international student numbers but also influenced the decision-making processes of receiving institutions and countries. This includes the development of new policies for attraction, study, and retention, but also a shift in the general focus on the salience of international study for countries of origin and destination. Many of these consequences are still unfolding, as the temporary provisions in place have often ended.

Across the OECD, specific measures were put in place to ensure that international students could still be eligible for student visas as well as to prevent visas and permits from being withdrawn. To limit delays in the application procedure for international student visas, many OECD countries allowed online application for visas or submission of application documents.

From an attraction perspective, the COVID-19 pandemic challenged in-person outreach efforts. In some cases, for example in Japan, the work of national agencies and universities to attract students shifted to virtual formats including virtual student fairs. Reports from higher education institutions suggest that, while there is a desire to develop a hybrid approach, virtual outreach is likely to shape recruitment in the future, given that it allows institutions to reach additional audiences at lower costs.

Table 5.2. Inflows of international tertiary-level students in OECD countries, 2016-21

Number of residence permits issued for study purposes

	Number of residence permits issued					
	2016	2017	2018	2019	2020	2021
	Thousands					
Australia	136.8	156.6	162.9	173.4	122.6	65.6
Austria	4.5	4.1	3.8	3.6	2.2	4.0
Belgium	6.3	6.9	6.9	8.7	5.7	9.2
Canada	105.9	134.7	151.9	171.4	50.8	216.7
Chile	1.5	1.5	..	..	..	..
Czech Republic	5.7	2.9	3.5	6.1	..	..
Denmark	9.2	8.9	8.9	8.5	5.0	5.3
Estonia	0.9	1.1	1.2	1.3	..	..
Finland	6.3	5.2	5.2	5.2	3.2	5.8
France	71.2	78.1	80.9	86.5	70.2	82.0
Germany	37.3	39.5	48.0	49.2	12.4	..
Greece	0.3	0.3	0.3	0.3	..	..
Hungary	7.8	10.8	10.8	..	..	..
Iceland	0.4	0.5	0.5	0.4	..	..
Ireland	21.4	27.6	30.2	34.7	14.7	..
Italy	8.5	2.9	3.2	2.9	0.7	..
Japan	108.1	123.2	124.3	121.6	49.7	11.7
Korea	65.1	72.7	82.7	86.6	52.4	65.9
Latvia	1.3	1.6	2.3	2.4	..	..
Lithuania	0.9	0.9	1.1	1.2	..	..
Luxembourg	0.2	0.4	0.3	0.4	0.2	..
Mexico	4.3	3.7	6.1	5.7	2.8	4.6
Netherlands	15.8	17.0	18.3	20.2	11.8	20.4
New Zealand	39.5	39.1	37.5	38.6	8.8	1.1
Norway	3.2	3.8	3.6	3.8	2.0	3.4
Poland	21.3	21.6	26.0	6.1	..	..
Portugal	3.5	4.9	8.4	13.4	12.3	10.9
Slovak Republic	1.5	1.7	2.0	2.6	..	..
Slovenia	1.3	1.3	1.5	1.8	..	..
Spain	35.6	39.7	42.0	45.0	28.1	..
Sweden	9.0	10.4	10.2	10.8	6.6	8.5
Switzerland	11.3	11.2	11.2	11.4	11.4	..
United Kingdom	270.7	305.8	330.6	376.1	221.9	368.6
United States	471.7	393.6	362.9	364.2	111.4	366.3
Total	**1 488.5**	**1 534.0**	**1 589.1**	**1 663.9**	..	..
Total EU/EFTA	**285.0**	**303.1**	**330.2**	**326.4**	..	..

Note: Data refer to international tertiary-level students, including students enrolled in language courses (excluding free mobility students). The data do not include professional training courses.
Source: OECD International Migration Database, 2022.

StatLink 🔗 https://stat.link/1co0l3

In many countries, it was – and remains – impossible to obtain a residence permit for purely online studies. However, given the pandemic, Israel admitted international students for 2020/21 whether or not classes were online. In Australia, the shift to remote studies did not have an impact on compliance with visa conditions, and in the United States, international students enrolled for the fall semester 2020 were allowed to remain in the country even though studies were remote. Periods of online study have also been counted for access to post-graduation permits in some countries. This was possible in Australia, Austria, Canada, Denmark, Greece, Hungary, Japan, Korea, Lithuania and Poland. In Switzerland, online study from abroad was excluded from this calculation, but online study from within the country was allowed to access post-graduation permits.

In most OECD countries, provisions for labour market access during study differed by type of study (in-person or virtual). It was only in the Netherlands, Poland, the Slovak Republic and Switzerland that periods of online studies were treated the same way as in-person for the purpose of work, provided the student was physically present in the national territory.

Many countries also lifted restrictions on maximum allowable work hours during the study period and opened up international students' access to national funds and other financial support mechanisms. Australia, Ireland, New Zealand, and the United Kingdom were four countries that lifted working hour limits, with certain exceptions. In the United Kingdom, the lifting of restrictions only applied to certain jobs in the health sectors for example. Norway and Poland introduced specific scholarships for students in financial hardship.

Given the all-online study environment, the pandemic also raised questions about the connection between student fees and international students' ability to benefit from services. Notably, only a few countries adapted their student fees during the COVID-19 pandemic, among them Hungary, Italy, Korea, the Netherlands, Poland, and the United States, though to varying degrees (OECD, 2020[8]). Survey evidence suggests that a large majority of prospective international students (80%) feels that fees should be discounted if students are unable to study in person (Quacquarelli Symonds, 2021[9]). It is not yet clear if this has led to an actual shift in international students' destination choices.

From a retention perspective, a decline in incoming international students implies a decreased potential talent pool in the years to come. In reaction, some countries where international students are a core feeder to high-skilled migration schemes provided specific temporary provisions. From May to November 2021, Canada temporarily granted 40 000 international graduates already in Canada eligibility to apply for permanent residency.

The special case of intra-European study exchange and Erasmus+

Erasmus+ is the EU's programme to support, among other objectives, international student migration. By the end of 2020, Erasmus+ and its predecessor programmes[7] have reached close to 12 million overall participants (European Commission, 2021[10]).

The higher education programme allows students to spend 2-12 months, typically one or two academic semesters abroad, generally without obtaining a degree in the higher educational institution abroad. Hence, international students in the programme are credit seeking, in contrast to degree seeking students, which are the focus of the remainder of this chapter.

A relatively easy access through an established institutional framework of co-operation between universities via an inter-institutional agreement characterise the higher education programme. A student can benefit from Erasmus+ mobility for up to 12 months at each level of studies (bachelor, master, PhD) and receives a scholarship for covering additional costs connected to living abroad. The amount depends on the country and contributes to covering costs of living abroad and related travel.

The higher education programme has grown enormously over the past decades, in part due to new countries accessing the programme and an inclusion of new forms of mobility such as traineeship in its framework. Created in the academic year 1987/88 and supporting around 3 200 students across the initial 11 participant countries back then, annual participation in tertiary student mobility was 350 000 participants in 2018/19. This figure includes both students enrolled for one or two semester in higher education (about 2/3 of the total) as well as more practical learning experiences such as traineeships (European Commission, 2020[11]).

Five large European OECD countries accounted for the bulk of the higher education programme in recent years: Spain, Germany, France, the United Kingdom and Italy (Figure 5.7). In 2018/19, half of all incoming students stayed in one of these five countries, and 58% of those outgoing came from one of these countries.

Figure 5.7. Most countries welcome more students than they send abroad with Erasmus+

Inbound and outbound Erasmus+ students in higher education, call 2018/19

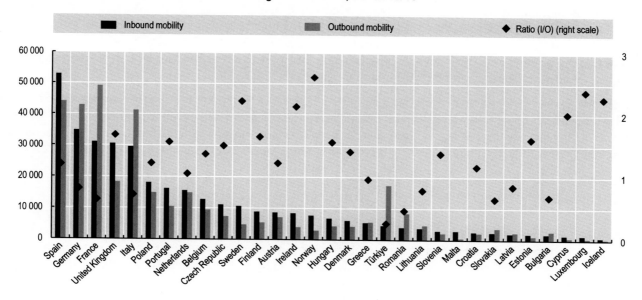

Note: The data includes student mobility for studies and traineeships. Partner countries are not included in the graph. 96% of outbound and 99% of inbound mobility in 2018 was realised between the programme countries included in the figure.
Source: Data adjusted from ANNEX 15 – KA103/KA107 – Higher Education student mobility under Call 2018 – Mobility periods summary per country, European Commission (2020[12]), "Erasmus+ annual report 2019: statistical annex", https://data.europa.eu/doi/10.2766/431386.

StatLink 🔗 https://stat.link/185jno

Some countries show a strong imbalance in regards to numbers going abroad (outbound mobility) and numbers arriving (inbound mobility). Türkiye and Romania, for example, send much more students abroad then they receive under Erasmus+, while the opposite is the case for Norway, Ireland and Sweden.

In 2019/20, Germany, France and Italy were net sending countries, while Spain and the United Kingdom were net receiving countries. Since the start of the new Erasmus+ programme cycle in 2021-27, the United Kingdom is no longer participating in the programme.

Among the 2 million student mobilities realised in higher education over the latest Erasmus+ programme cycle (2014-20), 64% were bachelor and 31% at master level. Only 3% were from the short study cycle (ISCED 5) and 1.4% from doctoral level (European Commission, 2021[10]).

Eurostudent[8] data shows that overall credit-mobility for tertiary study in Europe is more common during the master than bachelor cycle. About 8% of respondents have realised at least a temporary enrolment abroad; 14% of respondents in master degrees and 7% of respondents in bachelor degrees. Among all students in Europe covered by the survey that went to another country for study, two-thirds (64%) took part in Erasmus+. In total, 19% of the surveyed students have realised study-related stays abroad during tertiary education below PhD level, when other forms of mobility such as internships or work placements are included (Hauschildt et al., 2021[13]).

Some other characteristics of Erasmus+ participants are noteworthy. Participants are more likely to study humanities and arts, social sciences, business and law, as well as engineering, manufacturing and construction. In addition, women are more likely to participate in Erasmus+ than men, 58% over the period 2014-20, and this figures has remained relatively stable over time (European Commission, 2021[10]). The gender gap is observed across countries and subjects (Böttcher et al., 2016[2]; Benedictis and Leoni, 2020[14]). What is more, students with low socio-economic background are less likely to participate (European Commission, 2019[15]; Netz and Grüttner, 2020[16]). In particular, students with high-educated parents more often indicate intending or preparing a temporary study abroad, and financial support by parents is mentioned as a contributing factor (Hauschildt et al., 2021[13]; Meng, Wessling and Mühleck, 2020[17]). The latest impact study identified the Erasmus+ scholarship as particularly important for students from Eastern Europe. One in three participating students from Eastern European Programme countries reported the grant to be a main driver for participation, compared with one in four for participating students from a disadvantaged background[9] (European Commission, 2019[15]).

For the current programme cycle 2021-27, the Erasmus+ programme budget almost doubled to EUR 26.2 billion, compared with EUR 14.7 billion for 2014-20. The aim is to triple the number of beneficiaries, reach out to students from all social backgrounds, build stronger relations with the rest of the world, focus on promoting forward-looking study fields, and promote a European identity (European Commission, 2021[18]).

Who studies where? Drivers of international student migration

Many factors drive an individual's decision to study abroad and to select a specific destination. This section discusses macro factors beyond the control of policy makers as well as selected determinants of individuals' destination choice that can be directly influenced by national policy. Hence, the focus is on key "pull" factors in the host countries, rather than on economic and social forces within the home country, which "push" students abroad. Various other factors, including personal liberty and safety, lifestyle and climate preferences, family and network ties, as well as the perceived educational quality, drive destination choices but are not covered here. The attractiveness of certain OECD countries to particular students is a result of the interplay of various driving factors, as well as policies in place (Box 5.3).

Box 5.3. The attractiveness of OECD countries to university students

In 2019, the OECD assessed for the first time how OECD countries fare in attracting talented migrants. Three different profiles of talent were considered: workers with graduate (master's or doctorate) degrees, entrepreneurs, and university students. The top-5 most attractive countries to university students in this exercise were Switzerland, Norway, Germany, Finland, and the United States. The analysis highlighted how international university students are attracted to a different set of countries than workers or entrepreneurs and examined the key role of policies.

In the assessment, most English-speaking countries (United States, Canada, Australia, the United Kingdom and New Zealand) score high due to language environment in addition to their tertiary education spending. By contrast, Norway, Germany and Switzerland rank high as they allow international students broad access to work during studies, as well as applying the same or no (Norway) tuition fees to domestic and foreign students. Future prospects are also considered, favouring countries like France and Italy, which allow easy transition to work permits after graduation.

Note: An update of the OECD Indicators of Talent Attractiveness is forthcoming.

Macro factors shape international students' destination choices

Several macro factors beyond the control of policy makers shape international students' destination choice. Key among them are geographical proximity, shared official languages, and the presence of a diaspora community.

Geographical distance from the country of origin has been found to have a significant negative effect on international student flows in several cross-national studies (Abbott and Silles, 2015[19]; Beine, Noël and Ragot, 2014[20]; Didisse, Nguyen-Huu and Tran, 2018[21]; Kaushal and Lanati, 2019[22]). Many students remain in their region of origin even when seeking an international experience (Figure 5.8). Overall, in 2020, 29% of international students in OECD countries originated from the same geographical region as their country of study. This share is particularly high in some countries. In Korea and Japan, over 90% of international or foreign students originated from Asia. Similarly, 95% of international students studying in Mexico are from the American continent. Fellow Europeans dominate the share of international students throughout European OECD countries. They account for at least three in four international students in Austria, the Czech Republic, Denmark, the Slovak Republic and Slovenia. New Zealand is the only OECD country with a sizeable share of international students from Oceania (7%), mostly from Australia. In about two-thirds of OECD countries, at least half of the international student population originates from only one world region. However, the international student population is somewhat more diverse in Finland, France, Germany, Ireland, Israel, Portugal and Türkiye, where at least 10% originate from three different continents.

Figure 5.8. Most international students stay in their region of origin

Percentage of international students in OECD countries by broad region of origin, 2020

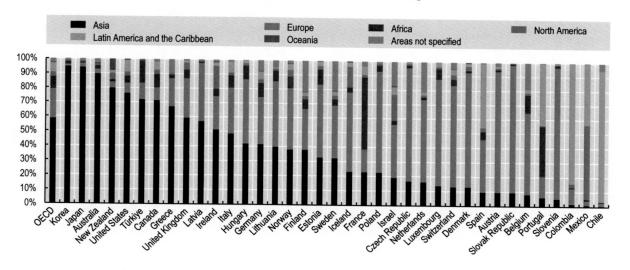

Note: The OECD average is based on the weighted average of countries included in the graph.
Source: OECD Education at a Glance Database, 2022.

StatLink ⌁⌁⌁ https://stat.link/7z3pmo

In addition to geographic distance, shared first language is a key factor in international tertiary educational mobility. In 2020, half of the international students in France came from the African continent, with French-speaking Morocco (13%) and Algeria (9%) accounting for by far the largest shares. Overall, one in three students from an African country studying in an OECD country was studying in France. The same pattern is evident for Brazilian (41%) and Portuguese-speaking African international students (22%) enrolled in

Portugal and for Latin American students in Spain (46%). However, this might reflect a broader set of factors beyond language, including economic ties and existing networks. Indeed, previous studies have shown a positive network effect – an increasing share of international students studying in a country with a diaspora of the same origin country (Perkins and Neumayer, 2014[23]). The literature has described the presence of country nationals at the destination as a "magnet for international students", the effect of which increases with the level of education of the network at the destination (Beine, Noël and Ragot, 2014[20]). National evidence, for example from the United States, shows that skilled work visa issuances to a country are positively and significantly related to the number of international students from that country (Shih, 2016[24]).

Figure 5.9. Shares of Chinese- and Indian-born students correlate with their migrant population

The share of Chinese- and Indian-born students relative to their share of the foreign-born population, 2019

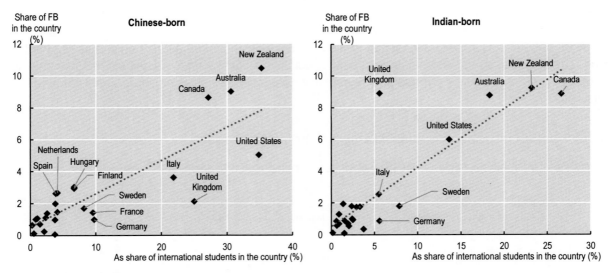

Note: All data refer to the year 2019. Indian-born students in Latvia were excluded from the graph.
Source: OECD Secretariat based on Education and Migration Databases, 2022.

StatLink https://stat.link/n4ucya

For the two main countries of origin, a strong correlation between the share of foreign-born population and the share of international students is only visible for English-speaking countries (Figure 5.9). The United Kingdom provides an interesting case of contrasts. The share of international students from China is high (25%), while the share of Chinese-born among the overall foreign-born population is low (2%). Available evidence for the United Kingdom suggests that many Chinese do not stay in the United Kingdom following their studies (UK Department for Education, 2022[25]). For Indian-born, this picture is reversed. The United Kingdom has a rather low number of Indian international students relative to the United Kingdom's large Indian-born population. Key factors, in addition to language and historic ties, seem to be study fees and options to stay in the country after studies. Data from Australia, for instance, suggest that Indian students enrol at universities that charge lower course fees relative to the top universities for the same courses but provide the same access to a post-study work visa and potential to obtain a permanent visa (Birrell, 2019[26]). Generally, it may be that Indian students tend to choose countries with good stay prospects after graduation but comparatively lower study fees.

Tuition fees and admission

The role tuition fees play in attracting international students is not clear-cut. Student fees can act as a signal of the quality of education, in particular in those countries with a positive reputation. In such cases, higher fees tend to attract international students. A reverse causality effect also exists, whereby those countries and universities that already attract high numbers of international students, predominantly English-speaking OECD countries, can afford to charge high fees based on their popularity (Beine, Noël and Ragot, 2014[20]). Charging tuition fees allows universities to maintain a constant funding stream, which, in turn, allows them to improve their educational rankings, increase in prestige and research output, and subsidise the cost of enrolling additional domestic students (Chen, 2021[27]).

Changes in study fees for international students have led to a variety of outcomes. For instance, the introduction of tuition fees in Sweden for students of countries outside the EU and EEA in 2011 led to a sharp decrease of new enrolments from this group the first year, down by 80%. The sharp decrease in new students consisted for the most part of fewer students from Bangladesh, Ethiopia, Türkiye and Ukraine. A similar reform in Denmark in 2006 introduced tuition fees for foreign students and led to a reduction by 20% in the first year (Sanchez-Serra and Marconi, 2018[28]). After the first year, the number of new international enrolments started to increase in both Denmark and Sweden and have since then returned to about the same levels as before the respective reforms. One important reason for this is the expansion and introduction of new scholarships. An evaluation of the Swedish reform has shown that the long-term impact of the reform has been on the composition of incoming student groups, with fewer students from poorer or/and less democratic countries seeking entry. Without scholarships, it is estimated that only a fraction of students would likely originate from these countries (Bryntesson and Börjesson, 2019[29]). A recent evaluation of a similar reform in Finland in 2017 showed that while the number of international students in Finland initially declined as well, the number now exceeds the level preceding the introduction of fees. Here the reform coincided with an increase in the provision of foreign-language degrees as well as enhanced efforts to attract and support international students, likely explaining the different outcome (Ministry of Education and Culture, 2022[30]).

In Germany, throughout the years 2006-14, 7 out of the 16 federal states introduced a fee only to repeal it soon thereafter. Analysis of these reforms shows that only one state (Lower Saxony) significantly reduced its international student intake upon introducing fees, while the remaining fee-reintroducing states did not lose international students (Zullo and Churkina, 2021[31]). Recent evidence from Italian universities shows a robust and negative effect of fees on international student intake (Beine, Delogu and Ragot, 2020[32]). Offering foreign students the same subsidies to tuition fees as domestic students (and also granting them and their partners some rights to work) more than doubled the number of new entrants to doctoral programmes in New Zealand in 2006, the year the changes took effect, compared to a slight decline in other tertiary programmes (OECD, 2017[33]).

The existence of affordable tuition options is usually listed in international student surveys as a key decision factor when choosing a course (Quacquarelli Symonds, 2021[9]). However, the definition of "affordable" is origin country-specific. For example, survey data from the Czech Republic suggest that the main reason North Americans choose to study in the Czech Republic is the comparatively low tuition fee (57%), while for the Slovaks, who face similar if not cheaper costs in their home country, this is among the least important reasons (13%) (Michaela Kudrnáčová et al., 2020[34]). Tuition fees can also be an obstacle to attracting students from lower socio-economic backgrounds. Previous work has shown that students from wealthier socio-economic groups are more likely to go abroad for their tertiary education (Waters and Brooks, 2010[35]; Hauschildt et al., 2015[36]). In the latest EUROSTUDENT survey wave, 60% of respondents identified financial burden as the main obstacle to (temporary) enrolment abroad. Likewise, 37% of respondents to a special Eurobarometer in 2018 identified lack of financial means as a key reason not to study abroad, though this ranked as a third concern, behind the lack of an opportunity and family, personal, and work reasons.

An additional admission factor that appears relevant, though understudied in the academic literature, is how quickly international students receive a response after submitting their application. Survey data show that international students have high expectations, and among over 100 000 respondents, 71% claim that it is extremely or very important that they hear back quickly from a university after making an enquiry. Indeed, 31% of prospective international students expect their application to be processed within three days (Quacquarelli Symonds, 2021[9]).

The role of language of instruction

Language affects tertiary education mobility decisions in multiple ways. First, a common official language has been shown to be a key explanatory variable for bilateral student mobility (Abbott and Silles, 2015[19]), a connection also evident in OECD stock data, as discussed above. Second, the goal of improvement of host-country language skills is a key factor for student mobility, in particular for those choosing English-speaking destinations. English language improvement has been shown to be among the top-3 influential factors for picking the United States as the destination (Nicholls, 2018[37]), and improving foreign language skills has been found to be one important reason for Chinese students to study abroad, especially in the United Kingdom (Counsell, 2011[38]).

On the other hand, research on the role of language learning in students' motivation to study in non-English-speaking destinations is limited. A study of ERASMUS (internal European) mobility found that language improvement was ranked only sixth on a 14-item scale, and so can be considered as relatively unimportant (Lesjak et al., 2015[39]). A survey examining students' decision to enrol in international exchange programmes in Spain or Germany specifically, however, found that language improvement and practice ranked third and second on a list of 26 key motivations (Castillo Arredondo et al., 2017[40]).

A perceived lack of foreign language skills has been shown as an obstacle to the individual decision to study abroad (see (Netz, 2015[41]) for examples of European countries). In a 2018 Eurobarometer survey, one-third of young European respondents, across all education levels, declared themselves unable to study in more than one language. Nevertheless, 77% of young Europeans say they would like to learn a new language, while 84% would like to improve the knowledge of a foreign language they had previously acquired.

The language of instruction – and in particular, English as the medium of instruction (EMI) – in higher education has become a dominant theme of discussion, both in academic literature and the political sphere (for an overview see (Unangst, Altbach and de Wit, 2022[42]). Debates include discussion of perceived advantages, such as attracting more international students and opportunities for national students through improved English knowledge, as well as concerns about language quality and the risk of exclusion of certain groups (Macaro et al., 2017[43]). For example, recent survey data from the Czech Republic suggest that almost a quarter of international students (23%) are dissatisfied with the quality of teaching, mainly due to a low standard of English spoken by teachers, whereas among those studying in Czech, only 7% are dissatisfied with their course (Michaela Kudrnáčová et al., 2020[34]).

International students are strongly overrepresented in English-course programmes. In Denmark for example, in 2020, international students made up 40% of those studying in English-language programmes compared to just 2% in programmes taught in Danish. In Poland, in the academic year 2020/21, foreign students made up 4% of the programmes thought in Polish, but 65% of those taught in English. Overall, however, about 61% of foreign students studied in Polish, a high share. Hungary is an interesting case, as it offers higher education programmes in English, French, Hungarian and German. Data on enrolment rates by the language of education in Hungarian higher education from the 2021/22 winter semester show that only 4% of students studying in Hungarian are international students. By contrast, 95% of those studying in German are international students, whereas just 5% are Hungarian. Among those enrolled in English and French programmes, about four in five are international students.

Labour market access during and after studies

The possibility to work while pursuing studies can be a driver for international students to select a country. According to a 2018 survey by the Canadian Bureau for International Education, 62% of international post-secondary students stated that they chose Canada because of the possibility to work during their studies (CBIE, 2018[44]). A 2017 survey on 2 000 current and former international students in the United States found that 46% of the respondents considered the ability to work while studying important in selecting an institution (World Education Service, 2017[45]).

International students also consider their staying prospects when deciding where to study. A 2019 survey of international graduates in Australia showed that as many as 76% considered access to post-study work rights an important factor in their decision to choose Australia as their study destination (Nghia, 2019[46]). Likewise, research from Canada shows that three in four international students consider the opportunity to work in Canada following their studies as an important factor in destination choice (CBIE, 2018[44]). In addition, international survey data suggest that about half of prospective international students want to remain in the country of their studies at least temporarily after they graduate (Quacquarelli Symonds, 2021[9]).

Overall, many factors influence international students' destination choices. Notably some of them including geographical proximity and the presence of a diaspora are outside of the immediate control of policy. Others, including tuition fees and the language of instruction are concrete policy choices, though not necessarily of migration policy makers. Then again, other policy in particular granting labour market access during and after study, admitting family members and efforts to retain international graduates for work in the country allow countries to stir international student migration – though to varying degrees. This chapter provided an overview of the state of international student migration to the OECD. It serves as the background for the two following chapters; one on attraction, admission and retention policies, another on stay rates and the economic impact of international students.

References

Abbott, A. and M. Silles (2015), "Determinants of International Student Migration", *The World Economy*, Vol. 39/5, pp. 621-635, https://doi.org/10.1111/twec.12319. [19]

Beine, M., M. Delogu and L. Ragot (2020), "The role of fees in foreign education: evidence from Italy", *Journal of Economic Geography*, Vol. 20/2, pp. 571-600, https://doi.org/10.1093/JEG/LBY044. [32]

Beine, M., R. Noël and L. Ragot (2014), "Determinants of the international mobility of students", *Economics of Education Review*, Vol. 41, pp. 40-54, https://doi.org/10.1016/J.ECONEDUREV.2014.03.003. [20]

Benedictis, L. and S. Leoni (2020), "Gender bias in the Erasmus network of universities", *Applied Network Science*, Vol. 5/1, https://doi.org/10.1007/s41109-020-00297-9. [14]

Birrell, B. (2019), "Overseas students are driving Australia's Net Overseas Migration tide", https://tapri.org.au/wp-content/uploads/2019/04/Overseas-students-are-driving-NOM-final-18-April-2019.pdf (accessed on 11 April 2022). [26]

Bryntesson, A. and M. Börjesson (2019), "Internationella studenter i Sverige Avgiftsreformens påverkan på inflödet av studenter", http://www.delmi.se (accessed on 4 May 2022). [29]

Campus France (2020), *Key figures 2020*, http://www.campusfrance.org/en/resource/key-figures-2020 (accessed on 11 May 2022). [6]

Castillo Arredondo, M. et al. (2017), "Motivations of educational tourists in non-English-speaking countries: the role of languages", *Journal of Travel & Tourism Marketing*, Vol. 35/4, pp. 437-448, https://doi.org/10.1080/10548408.2017.1358238. [40]

CBIE (2018), *The Student's Voice: National Results of the 2018 CBIE International Student Survey*, Canadian Bureau for International Education, https://cbie.ca/wp-content/uploads/2018/08/Student_Voice_Report-ENG.pdf. [44]

Chen, M. (2021), "The Impact of International Students on US Colleges: Higher Education as a Service Export", *SSRN Electronic Journal*, https://doi.org/10.2139/ssrn.3859798. [27]

Congressional Research Service (2019), *Foreign STEM Students in the United States*, https://crsreports.congress.gov/product/pdf/IF/IF11347 (accessed on 10 May 2022). [3]

Counsell, D. (2011), "Chinese students abroad: Why they choose the UK and how they see their future", *China: An international journal*, Vol. 9/1, pp. 48-71, https://muse.jhu.edu/article/423826. [38]

Destatis (2022), *Sonderauswertung. Studienverlaufsstatistik.* [7]

Destatis (2022), "Studierende an Hochschulen - Fachserie 11 Reihe 4.1 - Sommersemester 2021", https://www.destatis.de/DE/Themen/Gesellschaft-Umwelt/Bildung-Forschung-Kultur/Hochschulen/Publikationen/_publikationen-innen-hochschulen-studierende-endg.html (accessed on 9 May 2022). [5]

Didisse, J., T. Nguyen-Huu and T. Tran (2018), "The Long Walk to Knowledge: On the Determinants of Higher Education Mobility to Europe", *The Journal of Development Studies*, Vol. 55/6, pp. 1099-1120, https://doi.org/10.1080/00220388.2018.1475647. [21]

European Commission (2021), *Erasmus+ annual report 2020*, Publications Office of the European Union, https://data.europa.eu/doi/10.2766/36418. [10]

European Commission (2021), *The new Erasmus+ programme for 2021-2027 has launched!*, https://www.eacea.ec.europa.eu/news-events/news/new-erasmus-programme-2021-2027-has-launched-2021-03-25_en (accessed on 2 August 2022). [18]

European Commission (2020), *Erasmus+ annual report 2019*, Publications Office of the EU, https://data.europa.eu/doi/10.2766/651849. [11]

European Commission (2020), *Erasmus+ annual report 2019: statistical annex*, Publications Office, https://data.europa.eu/doi/10.2766/431386. [12]

European Commission (2019), *Erasmus+ higher education impact study*, Publications Office of the EU, https://data.europa.eu/doi/10.2766/162060. [15]

Hauschildt, K. et al. (2015), "Social and economic conditions of student life in Europe : synopsis of indicators : EUROSTUDENT V 2012-2015". [36]

Hauschildt, K. et al. (2021), *Social and Economic Conditions of Student Life in Europe. Eurostudent VII 2018-2021 | Synopsis of Indicators*, https://doi.org/10.3278/6001920dw. [13]

Kaushal, N. and M. Lanati (2019), "International student mobility: Growth and dispersion", *NBER working paper series*, http://www.nber.org/papers/w25921.   [22]

Lesjak, M. et al. (2015), "Erasmus student motivation: Why and where to go?", *Higher Education*, Vol. 70/5, pp. 845-865, https://doi.org/10.1007/s10734-015-9871-0.   [39]

Macaro, E. et al. (2017), "A systematic review of English medium instruction in higher education", *Language Teaching*, Vol. 51/1, pp. 36-76, https://doi.org/10.1017/s0261444817000350.   [43]

Meng, C., K. Wessling and K. Mühleck (2020), *Eurograduate pilot study: key findings*, European Commission, Directorate-General for Education, Youth, Sport and Culture, https://www.eurograduate.eu/results (accessed on 12 April 2022).   [17]

Michaela Kudrnáčová et al. (2020), *Studying and living in the Czech Republic from the perspective of foreign students: Report on Research at Czech Universities*, Czech National Agency for International Education (DZS), https://www.dzs.cz/sites/default/files/2020-09/DZS_zprava_o_zahranicnich_studentech_BOOK_EN_nahled3%20%281%29.pdf.   [34]

Ministry of Education and Culture (2022), *Introduction of tuition fees did not halt the internationalisation process of higher education institutions – room for growth in tuition fee revenue - OKM - Ministry of Education and Culture, Finland*, https://okm.fi/en/-/introduction-of-tuition-fees-did-not-halt-the-internationalisation-process-of-higher-education-institutions-room-for-growth-in-tuition-fee-revenue (accessed on 27 April 2022).   [30]

Netz, N. (2015), "What deters students from studying abroad? Evidence from four european countries and its implications for higher education policy", *Higher Education Policy*, Vol. 28/2, pp. 151-174, https://doi.org/10.1057/HEP.2013.37.   [41]

Netz, N. and M. Grüttner (2020), "Does the effect of studying abroad on labour income vary by graduates' social origin? Evidence from Germany", *Higher Education*, Vol. 82/6, pp. 1195-1217, https://doi.org/10.1007/s10734-020-00579-2.   [16]

Nghia, T. (2019), "Motivations for Studying Abroad and Immigration Intentions", *Journal of International Students*, Vol. 9/3, https://doi.org/10.32674/jis.v0i0.731.   [46]

Nicholls, S. (2018), "Influences on international student choice of study destination: Evidence from the United States", *Journal of International Students*, Vol. 8, pp. 597-622, https://doi.org/10.5281/zenodo.1249043.   [37]

Nuffic (2017), *International degree students in the Netherlands: a regional analysis*, http://www.nuffic.nl/en/publications/international-degree-students-in-the-netherlands-a-regional-analysis (accessed on 10 May 2022).   [4]

OECD (2020), *Education at a Glance 2020: OECD Indicators*, OECD Publishing, Paris, https://doi.org/10.1787/69096873-en.   [8]

OECD (2017), "Tuition fee reforms and international mobility", *Education Indicators in Focus*, No. 51, OECD Publishing, Paris, https://doi.org/10.1787/2dbe470a-en.   [33]

OECD-UNHCR (2021), *Safe Pathways for Refugees II - OECD-UNHCR Study on Third-country Solutions for Refugees: Admissions for family reunification, education, and employment purposes between 2010 and 2019*, https://www.oecd.org/els/mig/Safe-Pathways-for-Refugees_2021.pdf.   [1]

Perc, M. (ed.) (2016), "Gender Gap in the ERASMUS Mobility Program", *PLOS ONE*, Vol. 11/2, p. e0149514, https://doi.org/10.1371/journal.pone.0149514. [2]

Perkins, R. and E. Neumayer (2014), "Geographies of educational mobilities: exploring the uneven flows of international students", *The Geographical Journal*, Vol. 180/3, pp. 246-259, https://doi.org/10.1111/GEOJ.12045. [23]

Quacquarelli Symonds (2021), "EU International Student Survey 2021", in *Supporting recovery and driving growth in global higher education*, Quacquarelli Symonds, London. [9]

Sanchez-Serra, D. and G. Marconi (2018), "View of Increasing International Students' Tuition Fees: The Two Sides of the Coin", *International Higher Education*, https://ejournals.bc.edu/index.php/ihe/article/view/10278/8953 (accessed on 19 April 2022). [28]

Shih, K. (2016), "Labor market openness, H-1B visa policy, and the scale of international student enrollment in the United States", *Economic Inquiry*, Vol. 54/1, pp. 121-138, https://doi.org/10.1111/ecin.12250. [24]

UK Department for Education (2022), *Graduate outcomes (LEO), Tax Year 2018-19*, https://explore-education-statistics.service.gov.uk/find-statistics/graduate-outcomes-leo/2018-19#dataBlock-cb5bd289-e28a-4996-93f3-d2c70e9fc52b-tables (accessed on 11 April 2022). [25]

Unangst, L., P. Altbach and H. de Wit (2022), "English as medium of instruction in non-Anglophone countries : A global comparative analysis of policies, practices, and implications", in *International Student Recruitment and Mobility in Non-Anglophone Countries*, Routledge, https://doi.org/10.4324/9781003217923-3. [42]

Waters, J. and R. Brooks (2010), "Accidental achievers? International higher education, class reproduction and privilege in the experiences of UK students overseas", *British Journal of Sociology of Education*, Vol. 31/2, pp. 217-228, https://doi.org/10.1080/01425690903539164. [35]

World Education Service (2017), "Career Prospects and Outcomes of U.S.-Educated International Students: Improving Services, Bolstering Success", https://knowledge.wes.org/wes-research-report-career-outcomes. [45]

Zullo, M. and O. Churkina (2021), "A quasi-experiment in international student mobility: Germany's fee re-introductions", *https://doi.org/10.1080/21568235.2021.1983451*, https://doi.org/10.1080/21568235.2021.1983451. [31]

Annex 5.A. Supplementary tables

Annex Table 5.A.1. Criteria used for defining international students (or foreign students)

	Criterion	Date of data collection	Additional Notes
AUS	Residence	5 August 2020	
AUT	Upper secondary diploma	1 October 2019	In case country of upper secondary diploma is not available, occurrence in the statistical database on enrolments in former years is used instead
BEL	Upper secondary diploma	1 February 2020	Data on international tertiary students do not include students of social promotion education in the French Community, and students of the Open University, the Institute for Tropical Diseases and the Evangelic Theological Faculty in the Flemish Community. Therefore, the coverage of international and foreign students is different and the data cannot be compared. Data for ISCED 5 – associate degree – higher vocational adult education – only includes data from the Flemish Community and use information on citizenship rather than on the country of upper secondary completion
CAN	Residence	21 April 2021	Non-Canadian citizens excluding landed immigrants (permanent residents)
CHE	Prior education	15 November 2019	
CHL	Residence	30 June 2020	Tertiary Education Institutions report if students are non-foreign, foreign residents or foreign non-residents. As of 2018, it is considered that mobile students are those who obtained an upper secondary education diploma in a country different from Chile. For cases when the country of upper secondary diploma is not available, it is considered that mobile students are those who are classified as non-residents
COL	Citizenship	31 December 2020	
CRI	Citizenship		
CZE	Citizenship	30 September 2019	
DEU	Prior education	1 September 2019	The number of mobile students in professional programmes in ISCED 554 and 655 is negligible and reported with the value zero
DNK	Upper secondary diploma	1 October 2019	International students are defined as students who have obtained their upper secondary education abroad. If the country of origin is unknown, citizenship is used as a proxy for the country of prior education
ESP	Residence	31 October 2019	The country of upper secondary diploma is used as a criterion at ISCED Level 5.
EST	Residence	10 November 2019	Country of origin
FIN	Upper secondary diploma	20 September 2019	A mobile/international student is a student who has taken upper secondary diploma abroad (outside Finland). If the data on the specific country of origin is not available based on upper secondary diploma it is defined based on the citizenship of the student
FRA	Upper secondary diploma		A "mobile student" is the one who obtained her/his upper secondary diploma abroad. As her/his country (of origin) is unknown, her/his citizenship is used as a proxy for the country
GBR	Residence	16 January 2020	
GRC		20 May 2020	
HUN	Citizenship	1 October 2019	Citizenship is used to determine the country of origin
IRL	Residence	30 September 2019	
ISL	Prior education	15 October 2019	Citizenship, for a minority of cases where country of prior education is missing
ISR	Citizenship	30 June 2020	
ITA	Citizenship	1 March 2020	
JPN	Student Visa	1 May 2019	
KOR	Citizenship	1 April 2020	
LTU	Upper secondary diploma	1 September 2019	
LUX	Upper secondary diploma	30 October 2020	Country of upper secondary diploma is used for mobile students in ISCED 5 to 8

	Criterion	Date of data collection	Additional Notes
LVA	Prior Education	10 October 2019	
MEX	Place of birth	30 September 2019	
NLD	Upper secondary diploma	31 December 2019	Country of upper secondary diploma only distinguishes between The Netherlands and "abroad". Among that second category, citizenship is used to determine the country of origin. Data on international and foreign students do not include those enrolled at the Open University
NOR	Upper secondary diploma	1 October 2019	
NZL	Residence	1 July 2020	A student is considered mobile if he, or she, is a non-resident. For mobile students, citizenship is used to determine the country of origin
POL	Upper secondary diploma	30 September 2019	Country of upper secondary diploma for ISCED 7 and ISCED 6, not postgraduate. Lack of data on country of upper secondary diploma on some programmes at ISCED 6 and 8 level. As a best national estimate Poland used data on: ISCED 6 (postgraduate studies) and ISCED 8 level – country of prior education (country of master's diploma); ISCED 6 – postgraduate studies – country of prior education
PRT	Upper secondary diploma	31 December 2019	Definition of the international student is "Country of upper secondary diploma" from 2013/14. Until 2013/14, it was defined on the basis of their country of prior education (meaning "previous education": in case of a student at ISCED 7 level, the country of origin is the country where the ISCED 6 degree has been awarded)
SVK	Citizenship	15 September 2019	Citizenship is used to determine the country of origin
SVN	Residence	15 September 2019	
SWE	Residence	15 October 2019	International students are defined as students who have a student residence permit or are either non-residents or have moved to Sweden not more than six months before starting their studies. For students at ISCED 8 the time limit is 24 months. Students with student residence permit are reported by country of citizenship while other students are reported by country of birth. Exchange students (credit mobile students) are not included in the definition above
TUR	Citizenship	1 December 2019	Turkish citizens who live abroad and study in high school there and then study in Türkiye can also apply for foreign student admission quota
USA	Residence	1 September 2019	Students who are not citizens of the United States and who are in the country on a temporary basis and do not have the right to remain indefinitely

Source: Adjusted from Education at a Glance, Metadata, 2022.

Annex Table 5.A.2. International and domestic students by subject

Share of international students and domestic students enrolled by field of study, 2020 (%)

		Education	Arts and humanities	Social sciences, journalism and information	Business, administration and law	Natural sciences, mathematics and statistics	Information and Communication Technologies (ICTs)	Engineering, manufacturing and construction	Agriculture, forestry, fisheries and veterinary	Health and welfare	Services
AUS	International	4	6	3	46	4	14	12	1	11	1
	Domestic	11	12	9	23	7	4	8	1	24	2
AUT	International	5	14	16	20	11	5	16	2	9	1
	Domestic	14	9	7	25	8	5	17	1	9	4
BEL	International	3	14	13	12	6	2	12	5	32	2
	Domestic	10	8	10	24	4	4	11	2	26	2
CAN	International	1	7	9	28	13	10	18	1	5	5
	Domestic	5	10	12	20	11	5	10	1	17	5
CHE	International	5	13	12	19	17	5	18	0	9	3
	Domestic	11	8	8	26	7	4	14	1	18	3
CHL	International	5	4	5	34	5	6	18	2	17	4
	Domestic	11	4	5	22	2	4	21	3	22	5
COL	International	6	9	15	28	2	3	17	2	16	2
	Domestic	8	4	12	36	2	5	21	3	7	3
CZE	International	2	10	10	21	8	11	13	3	18	4
	Domestic	14	9	9	19	6	5	14	4	13	7
DEU	International	2	14	8	18	11	10	29	2	7	1
	Domestic	9	12	8	24	9	7	19	1	9	3
DNK	International	2	10	9	28	7	8	21	2	9	4
	Domestic	8	10	9	23	5	5	11	1	25	2
ESP	International	4	9	12	26	5	3	12	2	22	5
	Domestic	12	11	10	20	6	6	13	1	16	6
EST	International	3	14	10	36	7	12	11	4	4	0
	Domestic	8	13	6	20	6	10	15	2	14	6
FIN	International	3	10	4	23	6	19	19	2	11	4
	Domestic	6	11	7	18	5	9	19	2	19	4
FRA	International	1	16	10	29	13	6	16	0	7	2
	Domestic	3	13	7	25	7	3	16	2	15	10
GBR	International	2	13	14	34	9	6	13	1	7	0
	Domestic	6	14	16	21	10	5	8	1	17	0
GRC	International	5	16	13	16	12	4	15	3	12	3
	Domestic	4	13	13	20	10	4	21	4	8	3
IRL	International	1	11	7	20	10	11	12	1	24	2
	Domestic	8	15	6	22	10	6	11	2	17	4
ISL	International	8	41	10	8	15	2	8	2	4	1
	Domestic	15	8	17	19	4	6	9	1	17	4
ISR	International	13	13	16	14	14	6	12	1	11	0
	Domestic	20	8	18	14	6	8	17	0	9	0
ITA	International	1	31	12	15	6	2	21	2	9	1
	Domestic	8	16	14	18	8	2	15	3	14	3

		Education	Arts and humanities	Social sciences, journalism and information	Business, administration and law	Natural sciences, mathematics and statistics	Information and Communication Technologies (ICTs)	Engineering, manufacturing and construction	Agriculture, forestry, fisheries and veterinary	Health and welfare	Services
KOR	International	3	22	13	31	2	4	11	1	4	11
	Domestic	6	16	6	13	5	6	23	1	14	9
LTU	International	1	10	16	23	2	4	15	2	26	1
	Domestic	4	9	9	27	4	6	17	3	19	2
LUX	International	5	7	13	37	11	11	9	6	2	0
	Domestic	19	13	10	24	6	7	9	0	12	0
LVA	International	1	3	4	38	1	10	11	1	25	7
	Domestic	8	8	8	25	3	7	16	2	15	9
NOR	International	4	20	11	15	15	6	12	1	11	4
	Domestic	17	10	11	19	4	5	10	1	18	5
NZL	International	5	8	7	33	9	11	13	2	8	4
	Domestic	8	13	13	19	10	5	10	2	18	3
POL	International	2	12	16	27	4	6	9	2	17	7
	Domestic	9	10	11	23	4	5	15	2	14	8
PRT	International	4	12	13	25	5	2	20	2	12	5
	Domestic	3	10	11	22	6	3	21	2	16	6
SVK	International	9	8	6	11	3	4	11	2	42	3
	Domestic	13	8	10	19	5	5	13	2	18	7
SVN	International	4	10	15	18	8	9	20	1	7	9
	Domestic	10	9	8	19	6	5	19	3	14	8
SWE	International	3	14	13	11	14	7	25	1	11	1
	Domestic	14	14	11	14	5	4	17	1	18	2
TUR	International	5	12	13	20	5	2	24	2	14	3
	Domestic	4	13	10	39	2	2	10	2	13	5
OECD	**International**	**4**	**12**	**10**	**23**	**8**	**7**	**15**	**2**	**13**	**3**
	Domestic	**9**	**10**	**10**	**21**	**6**	**5**	**14**	**2**	**15**	**4**

Source: Adjusted from Education at a Glance Database, 2022.

StatLink ⬛⬛⬛ https://stat.link/23xlhm

Notes

[1] The term *international student* in the following refers to individuals coming from abroad for studying a full-time degree at a tertiary learning institution.

[2] This work was produced with the financial support of the German Federal Ministry of Education and Research. It includes a contribution by Ewa Krzaklewska (Jagiellonian University of Krakow).

[3] In part, these changes are due to changing methodology of the definition of international student. For a detailed overview, see *Education at a Glance*, yearly details of Annex 3.

[4] This share is calculated based on national definitions of international students (i.e. foreign students) in each country. For the stock of foreign-born, the data refers to foreigners in Japan and Korea.

[5] Unless mentioned otherwise, data and policy evidence were collected via a questionnaire on international student attraction, admission and retention policies, from January 2022 as well as from the national reports of the OECD Expert Group on Migration.

[6] Nationally defined as foreign students who have acquired their university entrance qualification abroad or at a preparatory college.

[7] Since 2014, the programme incorporates previously separate programmes key among them the higher education programme, previously known and sometimes still referred to as "Erasmus". The higher education programme has been introduced under changing frameworks (Socrates I (1994-99), Socrates II (2000-2006), Lifelong Learning 2007-2013, Erasmus+ 2014-00 and Erasmus+ 2021-27). Before 2014, student mobility was under the Lifelong Learning Programme. Herein, the name Erasmus referred to the higher education exchange. Other programmes covered other target groups, such as the Leonardo da Vinci programme for vocational education, the Comenius for pupils and the Grundtvig programme for adult education. Since 2014, the Erasmus+ programme brings together programmes that previously operated separately; the Lifelong Learning Programme, the Youth in Action programme, Erasmus Mundus, and adds the area of sports activities. Erasmus+ allows students to go abroad not only in the EU but also beyond, as mobility may take place between 33 programme countries, or programme and worldwide partner countries. Programme countries include all EU member states: Belgium, Bulgaria, the Czech Republic, Denmark, Estonia, Ireland, Greece, Spain, France, Croatia, Italy, Cyprus, Latvia, Lithuania, Luxembourg, Hungary, Malta, the Netherlands, Austria, Poland, Portugal, Romania, Slovenia, the Slovak Republic, Finland, Sweden and the United Kingdom until 2020. It further includes third countries associated to the programme, namely: Iceland, Liechtenstein, North Macedonia, Norway, Serbia and Türkiye.

[8] The EUROSTUDENT project collects and analyses comparable data on the social dimension of European higher education. It is a European-wide survey on the social and economic conditions of student life in Europe. The seventh round of the EUROSTUDENT project took place from June 2018 to August 2021. In total, 26 countries of the European Higher Education Area participated and about 270 000 students were surveyed.

[9] The Erasmus+ Programme Guide defines participants with disadvantaged backgrounds and fewer opportunities based on the following criteria: disability, educational difficulties, economic obstacles, cultural differences, health problems, social obstacles and geographical obstacles.

6 Attraction, admission and retention policies for international students

Elisabeth Kamm and Jonathan Chaloff

This chapter reviews OECD countries' policies to attract, admit and retain international students. It provides examples of communication and outreach strategies to international students as well as parameters for their admission. It outlines policies in place that support international students during their stay, such as through labour market access and the admission of family members. It looks at international students' stay prospects to search for a job upon graduation. It finally discusses policies to monitor the compliance of international students with the regulations set out on their study permit and ensure that institutions and students do not misuse this channel.

In Brief

- In all OECD countries, a study permit requires proof of acceptance by a university, proof of financial means to support living expenses, and health insurance. Despite similar core requirements, rejection rates for study visas vary greatly, ranging from 2% to 40% in OECD countries with available data.

- Estonia, Lithuania, Poland, Slovenia and Sweden are the only OECD countries where international students enjoy full access to the labour market during their study programme with no restrictions. In all other countries, labour market access is restricted in some way, most commonly via an hourly limit of work permitted during classes. Only in Colombia are all international students prohibited from working.

- Over the last decade, OECD countries have implemented wide-ranging policies to retain international students after completion of their degree. In particular, international students can remain in the country upon graduation to look for a job in almost all OECD countries. Most of these postgraduate extension schemes have a duration between 12 and 24 months, though they extend to three years or more in Australia, Canada, New Zealand, and the United Kingdom.

- To monitor that international students comply with the provisions set out in their study permit, some countries require the Higher Education Institutions to report on their students' progress or lack thereof, while in other OECD countries this obligation rests with the student themselves in order to prolong their permit. Other integrity concerns include misuse of the visa to overstay, to engage in unauthorised employment, and to conduct technological or military espionage.

- While student migration can be of great benefit to the student, the host institution and the host country, the delegation of a gatekeeping role to higher education institutions, and the growing share of economic migration comprised by former students, still carry a risk of distorting migration regulation, ensuring respect of labour market regulations, and in extreme cases, of malicious misuse.

Introduction

Over the last decade, OECD countries have taken active measures to attract, support and retain international students. The attraction and admission of international students involves many actors, including universities and agencies specialising in higher education marketing. Higher Education Institutions (HEI) carry most of the costs of informing and pre-screening prospective students. In this respect, the role of national authorities in the attraction and admission process is more limited than for other migrant groups.

While international students have to meet certain self-sufficiency and insurance criteria, once accepted, they often do not undergo the same skills assessment as labour migrants. This is despite the fact that in most OECD countries international students can work (part-time) during studies and stay in the country upon graduation to look for a job. In many countries, they also face facilitations to enter the labour market and stay in the mid to long term.

Against this backdrop, this chapter provides an overview of the policies in place in OECD countries along five key areas: i) outreach and communication to international students; ii) parameters for admission; iii) support during studies; iv) retention after graduation; and v) monitoring of compliance.[1, 2]

Outreach policy and communication strategies

A first step for attracting international students is to inform relevant target audiences about the unique advantages of study, research, and live in their respective countries and institutions. International student outreach across the OECD is characterised by a diversity of communication initiatives on an institutional, national, and regional level, as well as by a diversity of actors involved, including ministries and higher education agencies, universities, and private agencies specialising in higher education marketing.

Communication channels

All OECD countries have official national websites to inform international students about the higher education programmes offered and to provide relevant information regarding the migration process. In some countries, such as in Sweden, the website content on fees, residence permits, and scholarships changes depending on the target audience. It utilises the IP address of the connection and allows potential applicants to choose the information relevant to their nationality.

These websites and related outreach efforts are either managed by a designated ministry, such as the Ministry of Education in Denmark and Italy, or by specialised independent agencies and organisations in charge of promoting the country as a destination of international study, such as DAAD in Germany and Campus France in France (Table 6.1).

Table 6.1. Outreach platforms and communication channels

Country	Online							Offline	
	National website	Operated by	Social Media					Study fairs in the last 3 years	Promotion offices abroad
			Facebook	Twitter	YouTube	LinkedIn	Instagram		
AUS	www.studyaustralia.gov.au	Australian Government	X	X	X	X	X	Yes	Yes
AUT	www.studyinaustria.at/en/	Austrian Agency for Education and Internationalisation	X	X	X			Yes	Yes
BEL	www.studyinbelgium.be/ www.studyinflanders.be/ www.ahs-ostbelgien.be/	The three communities have separate agencies in charge of promoting international study	X	X			X	Yes	n/a
CAN	www.educanada.ca/study-plan-etudes/before-avant/guide.aspx?lang=eng	EduCanada, a collaboration between the provinces and territories through the Council of Ministers of Education (CMEC) and Global Affairs Canada	X	X		X		Yes	Yes
CZE	www.studyin.cz/ www.dzs.cz	Czech National Agency for International Education and Research (DZS)	X	X	X	X	X	Yes	n/a
DEU	www.study-in-germany.de/en/ https://www.daad.de/en/	German Academic Exchange Service (DAAD)	X	X	X	X	X	Yes	Yes
DNK	www.studyindenmark.dk	Danish Ministry of Education and Science	X					Yes	n/a

Country	Online							Offline	
	National website	Operated by	Social Media					Study fairs in the last 3 years	Promotion offices abroad
			Facebook	Twitter	YouTube	LinkedIn	Instagram		
EST	www.studyinestonia.ee/ www.educationestonia.org/	Education and Youth Board of Estonia	X	X		X	X	Yes	n/a
FRA	www.campusfrance.org/fr	Campus France	X	X	X	X	X	Yes	Yes
GBR	www.study-uk.britishcouncil.org/	British Council	X	X	X	X	X	Yes	Yes
GRC	www.studyingreece.edu.gr/el/archiki/	Ministry of Education and Religious Affairs, Ministry of Foreign Affairs, Ministry of Tourism and Ministry of Culture and Sports	X	X		X		Yes	n/a
HUN	http://studyinhungary.hu/	The non-profit organisation Tempus Public Foundation (TPF)	X		X			Yes	n/a
ISR	https://studyisrael.org.il/	The Council for Higher Education (CHE)	X	X	X	X	X	Yes	n/a
ITA	www.studiare-in-italia.it/studentistranieri https://www.universitaly.it www.studyinitaly.esteri.it	Italian Ministry of Education, University and Research (MIUR)	X		X	X		n/a	n/a
JPN	www.studyinjapan.go.jp/ja/	Japan Student Services Organization (JASSO)	X		X		X	Yes	Yes
KOR	www.studyinkorea.go.kr	National Institute for International Education (NIIED)	X				X	Yes	Yes
LTU	https://studyin.lt/	Education Exchange Support Foundation (SMPF)	X		X	X	X	Yes	n/a
LVA	www.studyinlatvia.lv/	The State Education Development Agency in partnership with the Ministry of Education and Science	X	X	X		X	Yes	n/a
MEX	https://upn.mx/index.php/comunidad-upn/intercambio-academico	Department of Academic Exchange and International Relations	X				X	n/a	n/a
NLD	www.studyinholland.nl/	Nuffic, a state-funded non-profit organisation for internationalisation of education						n/a	n/a
NOR	www.studyinnorway.no/	The Norwegian Directorate for Higher Education and Skills (HKDir)	X		X	X	X	Yes	n/a
NZL	www.studywithnewzealand.govt.nz/en	Government of New Zealand	X	X	X	X	X	Yes	Yes

Country	Online								Offline	
	National website	Operated by	Social Media						Study fairs in the last 3 years	Promotion offices abroad
			Facebook	Twitter	YouTube	LinkedIn	Instagram			
POL	https://study.gov.pl/	Polish National Agency for Academic Exchange (NAWA)	X	X	X	X	X		Yes	n/a
PRT	https://www.study-research.pt/	Portuguese Directorate General for Higher Education and Fundação para a Ciência e Tecnologia (Portuguese Public Agency for Science, Technology and Innovation support)	X	X		X	X		Yes	No
SVK	www.studyinslovakia.saia.sk	Slovak Academic Information Agency (SAIA)	X	X	X	X	X		Yes	n/a
SWE	www.studyinsweden.se/	The Swedish Institute, a public agency tasked with promoting Sweden abroad	X		X		X		n/a	Yes
TUR	www.studyinturkey.gov.tr	Turkish Council of Higher Education (YOK)	X	X	X				Yes	n/a
USA	www.studyinthestates.dhs.gov	US Department of Homeland Security	X	X	X	X	X		n/a	n/a

Note: Study fairs include those done virtually. Responses that were left blank are marked with n/a.
Source: OECD Policy questionnaire, 2022.

One important channel to promote international study are student fairs and the presence of overseas offices. Over the last three years, about two-thirds of OECD countries have arranged or participated in (virtual) student fairs in origin countries (Annex Table 6.A.1). The main OECD destination countries (Australia, Canada, United Kingdom, New Zealand, Germany, France and Japan) have agency offices in origin countries, but so do Austria, Korea and Sweden. Campus France has, for example, more than 250 offices and branches located in over 120 countries.

Social media have become an increasingly important communicational tool for student attraction. Given that international students constitute a particularly diverse audience in terms of nationality, degree level, study interest, culture, language, and income, with different media usage habits and access to technology, OECD countries use a diverse mix of communication channels and platforms. Most OECD countries have social media presence on Facebook, Twitter, Instagram, YouTube and LinkedIn. In some cases, the governments use more nationally specific social media platforms. Australia and Korea are, for example, using the social platform Sina Weibo to target Chinese students.

Reports from communication officers on higher education[3] highlight that using social media to engage discussions and dialogue, rather than just "broadcast" information, is especially important to build trust and to respond to information needs.

Another channel to reach potential students are student and alumni networks. They provide the opportunity to reach possible international students through intermediaries who can share their personal experience and answer questions in the languages of the specific target audiences. In an effort to build a stronger community of international students, the Czech National Agency for International Education and Research (DZS) invited student ambassadors and alumni to use their social media channels. During the COVID-19 pandemic, the United Kingdom launched student-led communication campaigns to reassure and support prospective EU and international students to continue with their plans to study in the United Kingdom. The campaign produced more than 100 student testimony videos where students gave their view on their experience of studying at a British university during the pandemic. Of more than 2 000 prospective international students surveyed, 67% said that the campaign had made them feel more confident to continue their plans to study in the United Kingdom. In France, the communication campaign *Bienvenue en France*, launched, in 2020 uses actual students not only for testimonies on their website, but also as ambassadors at student fairs.

Overall, OECD countries and their national student agencies use a multi-channel approach, reaching out to audiences in different places at different times, online and offline, allowing for feedback from audiences as well as the inclusion of alumni networks and ambassadors.

Effective messaging

To attract international students, countries also adjust their messaging to the identified reasons and preferences of the international students to choose their country. While some countries highlight the international reputation and quality of education, others highlight additional and increasingly valued elements such as the diversity of students in the study location, their culture, quality of life, or general safety. For example, Sweden developed a new communication and brand strategy after surveying 7 000 international students in Sweden and discovering that two main factors determining the choice of Sweden were the Swedish lifestyle and its education system.

Estonia's main message revolves around the strong recruitment and employability perspectives granted by Estonian diplomas. Canada highlights the prospects for international students to eventually become residents. In contrast, the outreach of Hungary and the United States makes no mention of retention.

Targeting specific students

Some countries target international students from certain countries and backgrounds. The British Council has, for example, run specific campaigns targeting China, particularly promoting the United Kingdom as a destination to learn English to prepare for an international job market. Among other groups, Latvia and the Slovak Republic also target their own nationals living abroad. Most countries target multiple countries. For example, New Zealand has a list with currently 13 countries on which the marketing activity is focused. In Israel, a similar list exists but is limited to four countries: Canada, China, India, and the United States. Spain targets students from countries of Latin America, the Mediterranean basin and North Africa.

Targeting international students based on characteristics other than their country of origin is less common. Attracting individuals with particular language skills, if considered at all, is mostly done in the context of particular scholarship programmes for studying in the national language, for example in the Slovak Republic. Canada also expanded a specific programme (Student Direct Stream), which provides faster processing for applicants resident in certain countries, to include prospective students from Morocco and Senegal and to encourage more young French speakers to choose to study in Canada.

Only a handful of OECD countries target international students based on their intended field of study or broader labour market needs as in the case of Australia. Among those who do, sectors include information technology and communication (ICT) in Estonia and STEM subjects in the United States. In Lithuania and the Slovak Republic, targeting the field of studies appears only in the context of government scholarships. Policies to attract international students despite or particularly because of socio-economic factors are limited. The most common tools to do so are grants and scholarships, discussed below.

Parameters for admission

Admission process

In all OECD countries, a study permit requires proof of acceptance by a university, proof of financial means to support living expenses, and health insurance. Beyond these minimum requirements, the admission process differs between countries, and often also from one higher education institution to the next.

In the majority of OECD countries, university sponsorship is restricted to accredited institutions. In Australia, for example, applicants can only enrol in a full-time course registered on the Commonwealth Register of Institutions and Courses for Overseas Students. In Denmark, applicants are restricted to publicly accredited educational institutions or specific state-approved programmes.

In most cases, verification of prior education is conducted by individual academic institutions as a condition for admission, rather than by migration authorities as a condition for issuance of the visa for studies. Several OECD countries, however, request verification of previous educational outcomes before issuance of residence permits. How this is done varies. For example, in Germany, public authorities require prior education to be provided by a state-recognised body of the home country. In France, credentials are inspected and authenticated by a national academic information centre.

Other policy changes simplify the admission procedure. In Spain, for example, since 2018, international students can fill out immigration forms from abroad and from within Spain, and task a representative to deliver their application, eliminating the obligation to go themselves to the consulate. In addition, authorisations to stay for studies in higher education institutions can be submitted by the institution itself. In this way, universities participate in the admission process of international students.

Duration of study permit

In about half of OECD countries, the study permit is issued for the full duration of studies (Table 6.2). In several of these countries, the permit is valid for a few months longer such as in Canada (+90 days), Latvia (+4 months), the Netherlands (+3 months), and the United Kingdom (+4 months, if the study course is longer than 12 months). In Japan, the period is designated individually by the Ministry of Justice and can be up to 4 years and 3 months. In Estonia, it can be between 12 months up to the entire duration of the study. In Lithuania, the permit is for the duration of studies but not longer than two years. In Poland, the first permit is valid for 15 months, but for three years upon renewal. In the rest of the OECD, the permit or visa is usually valid for about one year. In the Czech Republic, Luxembourg and Slovenia, the permit is valid for a maximum of one year or the duration of the study course, whichever is shorter.

Table 6.2. Permit characteristics

| | Duration of permit | | Labour market access | | |
	Maximum duration of single issuance/ renewals	Maximum duration (including renewals)	Automatic	Following request	No
AUS	60 months	5 years (for one permit)	X		
AUT	12 months	No limit		X	
BEL	12 months, renewable for duration of studies	No limit	X		
CAN	Duration of studies + 90 days	n/a	X		
CHE	12 months, renewable for duration of studies	8 years		X	
CHL	12 months	n/a		X	
COL	36 months	n/a			X
CZE	12 months or duration of studies, whichever is shorter	No limit		X	
DEU	24 months	10 years	X		

	Duration of permit		Labour market access		
	Maximum duration of single issuance/ renewals	Maximum duration (including renewals)	Automatic	Following request	No
DNK	Duration of studies + 12 months	No limit	X		
ESP	12 months		X		
EST	12 months up to entire period of the study	No limit	X		
FIN	Duration of studies		X		
FRA	Duration of studies, 3 years for bachelor's, 2 years for master's, and 4 years for PhD	No limit	X		
GBR	Duration of studies and degree + 4 months (if studies are longer than 12 months)	3 years or 5 years depending on degree	X		
GRC	12 months, renewable for duration of studies	Duration of studies + extra year for Greek language	X		
HUN	Duration of studies	Duration of studies	X		
IRL	Duration of studies	7 years	X (full-time students of at least 1 year)		
ISR	12 months	Duration of studies		X	
ITA	Up to 12 moths, renewable for duration of studies. Not more than 3 years beyond legal length of degree	Duration of studies + 3 years beyond legal length of degree	X (with limitations)		
JPN	Period designated individually by the Minister of Justice, but single issuance is maximum 51 months	No limit		X	
KOR	24 months	Depending on degree		X	
LTU	Duration of studies but no longer than 24 months	No limit	X		
LUX	12 months or duration of studies, whichever is shorter	No limit	X		
LVA	12 months, renewable for duration of studies + 4 months	Duration of studies + 4 months	X		
MEX	12 months	Duration of studies		X	
NLD	Duration of studies + 3 months	5 years		X	
NOR	Duration of studies	Duration of studies	X.		
NZL	Duration of studies	4 years	X.		
POL	15 months for first issuance, 3 years for renewal	n/a	X		
PRT	12 months. Annually renewable until conclusion of studies	Not relevant as long all legal requirements are fulfilled, since after concluding the current degree, the applicant can enroll in a next level higher education degree.		X (upon written notification)	
SVK	Duration of studies	6 years	X		
SVN	12 months or duration of studies, whichever is shorter	Duration of studies		X	
SWE	First permit 13 months than 12 months for renewals	No limit	X (after 30 ECTS)		
TUR	12 months, renewable for duration of studies	n/a		X	
USA	Duration of studies	7 years	X		

Note: Table does not include CRI and ISL.
Source: OECD Policy questionnaire, 2022.

Against this backdrop, international students in some countries have to renew their permit annually, while in others, the maximum duration for a single issuance of a permit is for many years (as for PhD studies in France, 60 months in Australia, 51 months in Japan). This does not mean that students once admitted do not need to provide proof of their study progress, but rather that they do not have to resubmit paperwork and pay fees for renewal or extension.

In about two-thirds of OECD countries, there is a limit on how long someone can hold a student permit (including renewals). This ranges from 3-5 years in the United Kingdom (degree vs below degree level) and 5 years in Australia to 10 years in Germany. Other countries fall in between, such as 6 years in the Slovak Republic, 7 years in the United States, and 8 years in Switzerland, where exceptions are possible. By contrast, in about a quarter of OECD countries, no such restrictions are in place, and a student visa can be prolonged as long as its conditions are met.

Tuition fees

In most OECD countries with available data, international students at public institutions pay different fees than national students enrolled in the same programme. Differences are most pronounced in France and the English-speaking OECD countries. In the latter, also nationals pay comparatively high amounts, but foreign students pay on average about twice or more the tuition fees charged to national students (Figure 6.1). By contrast, fees are identical for both foreign and national students in Chile, Italy, Japan and Spain. There are no tuition fees for any students at public universities in Norway.

Several European countries apply lower or no fees for EEA students but apply increased fees for those from outside the EEA. In Denmark, Finland and Sweden, higher education is tuition-free for nationals and EEA citizens, but international students from outside EEA countries are charged. While this policy has been in place for over a decade in Denmark (2006/07) and Sweden (2011), it was introduced only in 2017 in Finland. Similarly, France introduced a fee regime at public universities, which, as of 2019, applies different tuition fees to European and non-European students. From the start of the 2019/20 academic year, annual fees for a bachelor's and master's degrees increased more than 15-fold to EUR 2 770 for bachelor's and EUR 3 770 for master's annually for international students. In international comparison as shown above, they are nevertheless low and universities can waive part or all of the higher study fees for specific groups and may do so for a maximum of 10% of the total number of students (including national and European ones). Most French institutions grant exemption to international students coming from less developed as well as French-speaking countries (Campus France, 2019[1]). Other European countries that distinguish between EEA and non-EEA students include Austria, Estonia, Hungary, Ireland, the Netherlands, and the Flemish Community in Belgium.

Figure 6.1. Annual tuition fees are twice as high in key destination countries

Annual average (or most common) tuition fees in equivalent USD converted using PPPs, for full-time students, charged by public tertiary institutions to national and foreign students (ISCED 7), 2019/20

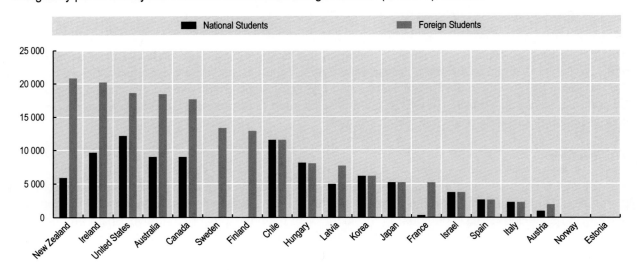

Note: See Annex 3 of Education at a Glance 2021 for notes.
Source: Adjusted from OECD Education at a Glance (2021).

StatLink 🔗 https://stat.link/bfcr8x

Australia, Canada, and Israel apply differentiated fees for national and foreign students. In Israel, the average tuition fees charged by public institutions for international bachelor's students are more than three times the fees charged for national students.

In some countries, the tuition fees vary depending on the language of instruction, with higher tuition fees for programmes in non-national languages. For example, in the Czech Republic, Estonia, Greece and the Slovak Republic, international students studying in the national language pay the same fees as nationals. The concept of different study fees by the language of instruction is also applied in Hungary, Israel, Italy, Latvia, and Poland, though to varying degrees (Table 6.3).

Language requirements

International students in OECD countries typically need to demonstrate study language knowledge before enrolment (Table 6.3). In most countries, requirements and levels are set by the HEI or the academic programme via the enrolment procedure and not by immigration policy. In some countries such as Estonia and Hungary, however, proof of sufficient knowledge of the language of the study programme is required in the framework of the immigration procedure.

Only in a few countries are international students required to learn or attend classes in an official national language during their studies. These requirements are usually tied to scholarships. In Hungary, for instance, *Stipendium Hungaricum* beneficiaries have scholarships covering their tuition fees for studying in Hungary including for all English-taught programmes. However, scholarship holders need to study Hungarian language and culture as a subject in their first year. In Latvia, international students who have the Latvian State Scholarship are required to understand some degree of the Latvian language.

In almost all OECD countries that provided information on the subject, at least some full-degree programmes at public universities are offered in English. In most cases, English is the only non-national language that is available as the language of instruction in addition to the national languages. However, in some Eastern European countries, other offers exist. These include programmes in German and French in Hungary, in Russian in Lithuania, and in German, French, Russian and Hungarian in the Slovak Republic. Mexico is an exception in the OECD, as no full degree programmes at public universities are available in English. Notably, the English-speaking countries, here Australia, Canada, Ireland, New Zealand, the United Kingdom, and the United States do not offer full programmes in another language than their national language(s).

Table 6.3. Language requirements and policies for international students in OECD countries

	Do students need to demonstrate language skills before enrolment? If yes, at what level?	Full degree programmes at public universities offered in non-national language(s)	Do study fees differ by language of instruction?
AUS	Yes, depending on institution	No	n/a
AUT	Yes, no level specified	Yes	No
BEL	Yes, English, French and Dutch at CEFR B2 level for programmes taught in the respective languages, exceptions apply	Yes, English	No
CAN	Yes, depending on institution	No	n/a
CHE	Yes, depending on institution	English	No
CHL	n/a	English	No
CZE	Yes, but no specific level of language knowledge is set	Yes	No
DEU	Yes, certificate of German language proficiency or proof of intend to attend a language course in Germany, or English language skills for a degree programme taught in English	English	No
DNK	n/a	English	N
EST	Yes, applicants need to present a certificate of English skills. Usually, the required minimum test result is 6 in IELTS and 72 in TOEFL (IBT). Depending on the institution and programme, there might be additional entrance tests such as an interview, written essay, portfolio etc.	English	Yes
FIN	Yes, no level specified	n/a	
FRA	Yes, mandatory for undergraduates in public universities; may vary in other HEI and levels	Yes	No
GBR	n/a	No	n/a
GRC	Yes, depending on institution	English	Yes
HUN	Yes, CEFR B2 minimum	English, French and German	Yes
ISR	Yes, high English level (knowing Hebrew or Arabic helps)	English	Yes
ITA	Yes, CEFR B2 minimum	Mostly English	Yes
JPN	Yes, Post-secondary course of specialised training college: N1 or N2 (The Japanese-Language Proficiency Test (JLPT)) University, graduate school and junior college: Not known	Post-secondary course of specialised training college: No. University, graduate school and junior college: Not known	Post-secondary course of specialised training college: No. University, graduate school and junior college: Not known
KOR	Yes, depending on institution	Yes	No
LTU	Yes, depending on institution	English and Russian	No
LUX	Yes	English (in addition to French and German)	No
LVA	Yes, the level of knowledge must be equal or higher than standard B2	English	Yes

	Do students need to demonstrate language skills before enrolment? If yes, at what level?	Full degree programmes at public universities offered in non-national language(s)	Do study fees differ by language of instruction?
MEX	Yes, no level specified	No	No
NLD	Yes, CEFR B1 minimum	English	No
NOR	Yes, no level specified	English	No
NZL	Yes, no language requirement to obtain a student visa. Level required depends on institution. For some courses there is a requirement to an English course, in those cases schools often offer these classes	No	No
POL	Yes, no level specified	Yes	Yes
PRT	Yes, depending on institution	English, French	No, but may depend on the student being covered by the international student status
SVK	Yes, depending on institution	English, Hungarian, German, French and Russian	Yes
SWE	Yes, the general English requirement for English language studies in higher education in Sweden is the equivalence of the Swedish upper secondary school course English 6	English	No
TUR	Yes	English, German, French, Arabic	No
USA	Yes, depending on institution	No	No

Note: Table does not include COL, CRI, ESP, FIN, IRL, ISL, SVN, and TUR.
Source: OECD Policy questionnaire, 2022.

Many OECD countries have increased their offers of English language programmes over the last years. In Norway, for example, in 2020, 90% of undergraduate offers but only 44% at a higher degree are registered to be taught in Norwegian. In addition, while in 2011 just 11% of courses were registered with English as the language of instruction, this share had increased to 19% in 2020 (Diku, 2022[2]). In Sweden, 64% of all programmes at master's level are taught in English. This is an increase of 26 percentage points from 2007 (Malmström and Pecorari, 2022[3]). In Italy, the number of programmes in English increased from 143 to 245 between 2013/14 and 2015/16 (Rugge, 2018[4]). In Israel, English-taught programmes offered have doubled for bachelor's degrees, 25 instead of 13 in 2016, and increased by 25% for master's programmes, 85 instead of 63 in 2016. The number of English-language degree programmes at German higher education institutions has increased more than six-fold from 258 (2008) to 1 550 (2020). The proportion of all degree programmes they account for also rose considerably during this period, from 2% to 8%, and the vast majority of these programmes (86%) were offered at the master's degree level. In 2020, English-taught programmes accounted for 2% of bachelor's degree programmes, but 14% of master's degree programmes. In the Netherlands in 2018/19, about 28% of bachelor's programmes at research universities were exclusively offered in English, and another 15% were offered in multiple languages. For master's programmes, there were 76% offered in English only, and another 10% offered in multiple languages, typically Dutch and English. Engineering, liberal arts, and sciences master's courses were only offered in English (Nuffic, 2019[5]). Also in cross-national surveys, and aside from the national language(s), English is the most frequent language of study, mentioned by four in ten respondents (38%) in a recent Eurobarometer on the topic. Analysing data from 19 European countries, Sandström and Neghina (2017[6]) report a 50-fold increase in the number of English-taught bachelor's programmes in Europe.

Support policies during studies

Employability and labour market access during studies

In most OECD countries, the student permit automatically grants access to the labour market (Table 6.2). International students in Australia, Belgium, Canada, Germany, Denmark, Estonia, Finland, France, Greece, Hungary, Latvia, Lithuania, Luxembourg, Norway, Poland, the Slovak Republic, Sweden, and the United Kingdom do not require a separate permit for employment. In most other OECD countries, including Austria, the Czech Republic, Israel, Italy, Japan, Korea, Mexico, the Netherlands, Slovenia, Switzerland, Türkiye, and the United States, international students need to obtain an authorisation, typically a work permit, before the start of their employment. In New Zealand, only some programmes qualify for part-time work rights. Likewise, in Israel, employment is only possible for a small group of international students, those enrolled in a high-tech related field of study. Colombia is an exception in the OECD, as the employment of international students is generally not possible.

Estonia, Lithuania, Poland, Slovenia, and Sweden are the only OECD countries where international students can work full-time during their study programme with no hourly restrictions, provided that this does not interfere with their study progress. In all other countries, labour market access is restricted in some way, most commonly via an hourly limit of work permitted during classes.

In about two-thirds of OECD countries, international students can only work part-time, when university courses are in session (Figure 6.2).[4] In some countries, this limit is slightly more flexible such as 40 hours per fortnight in Australia, 60% of the statutory maximum for full-time employment in France, and 120 full days or 240 half days in Germany. In Austria, Denmark, Korea, Latvia, Lithuania, Luxembourg, and the United Kingdom, the maximum work hours depend on the study level, with stricter limits in place for lower levels of study. About half of the countries that apply an hourly limit to employment during academic terms lift this during academic breaks. This is the case in Australia, Belgium, Canada, Denmark, Italy, Korea, Luxembourg, New Zealand, Norway, the United Kingdom, and the United States. In the Netherlands, international students can either work 16 hours per week during academic terms or full-time during the summer break from June to August.

Beyond an hourly limit, the second most common restriction is the sector of employment. For example, in Korea, international students who have obtained a part-time work permit must not work in a non-skilled sector, but are allowed to work in a skilled sector if the sector is related to their field of study, or translation. In Luxembourg and Mexico, the job must be related to the international student's field of study. In the latter, work is only possible to carry out postgraduate and research studies. In France, the job must be related to the course of study if the work hours exceed the 60% limit.

Finally, specific requirements and restrictions are in place in some countries. For example, in Austria, employment permits for more than 20 hours per week require a labour market test. In the United States, off-campus employment is possible only after one year of studies through Curricular Practical Training (CPT) and only by sponsoring employers through co-operative agreements with the school; more than 12 months of full-time work under CPT precludes later use of post-graduate Optional Practical Training (OPT). In Switzerland, non-EU students are allowed to start working alongside studies only after 6 months of staying in the country.

Figure 6.2. In most countries international students can work part-time during academic session

Maximum working hours per week allowed in selected OECD countries (during the semester), 2022

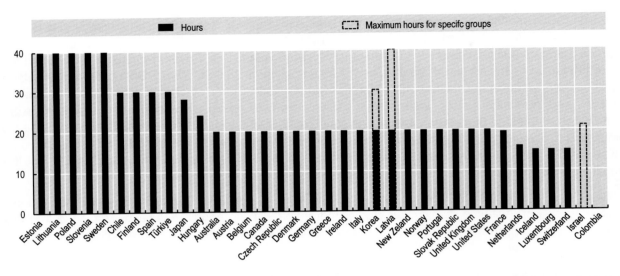

Note: The figure includes OECD countries for which data are available. In Australia, international students can work 40 hours per fortnight. In Denmark, the limit is 20h/week for BA/MA students and full time for PhD students. In Israel, only international students in High-Tech related fields of study can request part-time employment in relevant companies during their studies. In the United States, employment is only allowed on-campus or in an off-campus worksite affiliated with the institution. In Latvia, the limit is 20h/week for BA students and 40h/week for master's/PhD students. In Luxembourg, the limit is 10h/week for BA students and 15h/week for master's/PhD students. In Korea, the limit is 20h/week for bachelor's students and 30h/week for master's/PhD students. The data for Denmark, Portugal, and Spain refer to non-EU students, whereas there is no limit on the maximum number of working hours alongside studies for EU and domestic students. Estonia, Lithuania, Poland, Slovenia and Sweden set no limits on the maximum hours of working alongside studies.
Source: OECD policy questionnaire and desk research on official websites, 2022.

StatLink ⫘ https://stat.link/bh35pu

Housing support and access to student loans and scholarships

In addition to labour market access, OECD countries can support international students also indirectly, via publicly subsidised student housing and access to public loans.

Access to publicly subsidised student housing is a common support measure in this context, at least in European OECD countries, as well as Japan and Korea. However, some specifications apply, often at the individual programme level. Regarding national policies, for example in Greece, undergraduate third-country national students have access to student dormitories in the same way as national students, but housing allowance is provided only to Greek and EU nationals. By contrast, access to subsidised housing is not available in English-speaking OECD countries, including Australia, Canada, New Zealand, the United Kingdom, and the United States.

National students' loans are only available to international students in the same way as to nationals in a few OECD countries. Partly this is because such a support system does not exist in all countries. Among the countries that do offer access to national students' loans are Chile, Hungary, Italy, Mexico, and Switzerland. In Lithuania, Luxembourg, and Sweden, access to national student loans is only possible for EU/EEA nationals and only under certain conditions. In Estonia, an application to study loans is possible only for those with a long-term residence permit or permanent right of residence.

In about half of OECD countries, international students have access to public scholarships in the same way as national students do. This is the case in Austria, Chile, the Czech Republic, Estonia, Germany,

Greece, Hungary, Italy, Japan, Korea, Latvia, Lithuania, Luxembourg, Mexico, the Netherlands, Poland, Switzerland, and the United Kingdom. Many countries offer public scholarships under a specific framework. An example is the Latvian State Scholarship, to which prospective students of over 40 eligible countries can apply based on bilateral agreements.

Family admission and their labour market access

Family reunification is an important factor to attract migrants and foster their integration into the host society. International students are no exception. In all but four OECD countries, partners of international students can join international students (Table 6.4). Only in Ireland, Lithuania, Luxembourg, and Türkiye are international students not allowed to have spouses join them abroad as they move. Lithuania is the most open among these four, where partners can join international students after two years of residence, while PhD students can immediately reunite. In Luxembourg instead, only PhD students are allowed to reunite with their spouses/partners, and only if their contract is longer than one year. In Ireland and Türkiye, international students are not allowed to have their spouses join them at all. The terms and conditions of admission or reunification of partners of international students vary. For example, in the Czech Republic, Portugal, the Slovak Republic, and Slovenia, applications can be filed only after arrival. The specific type of visa (visitor, family reunification, or residence) and its duration differ as well.

In most OECD countries, partners of international students can work. In Austria, Denmark, Estonia, Germany, Italy, Lithuania, New Zealand, Norway, Portugal, the Slovak Republic (after one year of residence), Sweden, Switzerland, and the United Kingdom, they automatically have access to the labour market. By contrast, in Australia, Belgium, Canada, the Czech Republic, Hungary, Japan, Korea, Latvia, Mexico, Slovenia, and the United States, they must apply for a work permit, whose requirements differ by country. For example, in Australia, partners of international students need to pass a labour market test and Austria limits the number of hours spouses/partners are allowed to work. In other countries, income parameters apply, such as personal income thresholds in Finland and the Netherlands, while in the United States, the income earned by the spouse/partner must not be required for the financial support of the student visa beneficiary. Only in eight countries where partners can join international students, they are generally not allowed to work. This is the case in Chile, Colombia, France, Greece, the Netherlands, Poland and Spain.

Table 6.4. Family admission and their labour market access

Country	Partners can join international students	Partners labour market access			Comments
		Automatically	Upon request	No	
AUS	Yes	X			Work up to 40 hours per fortnight; spouse/partner of master's and PhD can work unlimited hours. All only once the primary student visa holder has commenced their course.
AUT	Yes		X		
BEL	Yes		X		
CAN	Yes		X		
CHE	Yes	X			
CHL	Yes			X	Immediate family members can get a temporary visa for the duration of the studies as dependents.
COL	Yes			X	
CRI	Yes				n/a
CZE	Yes		X		
DEU	Yes	X			
DNK	Yes	X			
ESP	Yes			X	

Country	Partners can join international students	Partners labour market access			Comments
		Automatically	Upon request	No	
EST	Yes	X			Student family members can apply for a residence permit for the same period as student.
FIN	Yes				n/a
FRA	Yes			X	
GBR	Yes	X			Only Tier 4 students studying a post-graduate course 12 months or + at a university, or a Government sponsored student on a course of longer than 6 months can bring their partners and/or dependents.
GRC	Yes			X	
HUN	Yes	X			
IRL	No				n/a
ISR	Yes			X	
ITA	Yes	X			General conditions for family reunification apply, subject to minimum income and housing criteria. Family permit holders can work (no limitations). Duration is linked to the holder of the study permit.
JPN	Yes	X			
KOR	Yes	X			
LTU	No/Yes	X			General conditions for family reunification apply to bachelor students (2 years of res.). Family permit holders can work. Students who come for master degree studies can immediately bring their family.
LUX	No				Only PhD students with work contracts longer than one year.
LVA	Yes	X			
MEX	Yes	X			
NLD	Yes			X	Yes, subject to regular income criteria (i.e. principal must earn EUR 867.68 per month).
NOR	Yes	X			The person with whom the family member is applying for family immigration must be a student at a higher level. This means a master's or PhD programme at a university college or a university.
NZL	Yes	X			Open work visa if the partner student is studying at master's level or above. For bachelor's and post-grad students the course must be a skilled shortage course in order for the partner to gain a work visa.
POL	Yes			X	They may only enter if they have own purpose of stay / residence title.
PRT	Yes	X			If the spouse has obtained a residence permit, he/she can automatically enter the labour market.
SVK	Yes	X	X		Automatic only after 12 months of stay with a temporary residence for the purpose of family reunification. Before 12 months, an authorisation is required.
SVN	Yes	X			
SWE	Yes	X			If the residence permit is valid for more than 6 months.
TUR	No				n/a
USA	Yes		X		Dependent spouse and unmarried children under the age of 21 under F2, M2, and J2 visa classifications. Work authorisation is subject to approval: the income earned by the spouse must not be required for the support of the F1/J1/M1 visa beneficiary.

Source: OECD policy questionnaire, 2022.

Stay prospects after graduation

Over the last decade, OECD countries have implemented wide-ranging policies to retain international students. These include options to change residence permits before graduation, (automatic) study permit extensions or specific post-graduation permits to search for, and start, a job. Other facilitating measures include facilitating employment by, for example, removing the labour market test. Some policies also foster long-term stay, for example when countries count (part of) the duration of study in the application process for permanent residence and naturalisation. In the context of the COVID-19 pandemic, some countries extended these policies to international students enrolled in full-time online courses.

In almost all OECD countries, international students can change their study permit to another residence permit already prior to graduation, provided they meet its requirements. In some countries, this is restricted to certain categories, such as only to family permits as in Luxembourg. Sweden requires international students to demonstrate proof of study activity and to have completed at least half a year of coursework (30 ECTS) prior to changing status to a permit for employment. In some countries, it may be difficult for students who have not graduated to qualify for any of the work permits available if they all require higher education qualifications.

Most OECD countries have policies to enable international students to stay on and look for a job upon graduation. However, access to and duration of these postgraduate extensions vary (Table 6.5). In Denmark, Estonia, Greece and Luxembourg, the extension of a study permit is automatic, without request. In some countries, international graduates can stay for a limited period, such as 60 days in the United States, three months in Poland, four months in Latvia (based on their study permit), but have to apply for an extension if they want to stay longer.

Table 6.5. Post-graduation policies

| | Is there a post-graduate extension for seeking employment/self-employment? | | | | Is employment under a post-graduate job-search permit restricted? | Status change prior to graduation? | Favourable conditions for change of status to employment post-graduation? | Does study time count towards permanent residence / naturalisation? |
	Automatically	Upon request	No	Max. length (months)				
AUS		X		48	No	Yes	Yes	Yes
AUT		X		24	Yes	Yes	Yes	Yes
BEL		X		12	No	Yes	Yes	Yes
CAN		X		36	No	Yes	Yes	Yes
CHE		X		6	No	Yes	Yes	Yes
CHL		X		24	n/a	Yes		Yes
COL			X			Yes	No	Yes
CZE		X		9	No	Yes		Yes
DEU		X		18	No	Yes	Yes	Yes
DNK	X			6	Yes, working hours cap (except in June, July and August)	Yes	Yes	Yes
ESP		X		12			Yes	Yes
EST	X			9	No		No	Yes
FIN		X		24	No	Yes	Yes	Only exceptions
FRA		X		12	Yes, working hours cap	Yes	Yes	No
GBR							Yes	No
GRC	X			12	No	No	Yes	No
HUN		X		9	Yes, only job search	Yes	No	Yes
IRL		X		24	No	Yes	Yes	
ISR		X				Yes	Yes	No

	Is there a post-graduate extension for seeking employment/self-employment?				Is employment under a post-graduate job-search permit restricted?	Status change prior to graduation?	Favourable conditions for change of status to employment post-graduation?	Does study time count towards permanent residence / naturalisation?
	Automatically	Upon request	No	Max. length (months)				
ITA		X		12	No		Yes	Yes
JPN		X		12	Yes	Yes	Yes	Yes
KOR		X		24	Yes	No	Yes	Yes
LTU		X		12	No	Yes	Yes	Yes
LUX	X			9	Yes, employment must be related to field of study		Yes	Yes
LVA	X	X		4 – thereafter upon request	Yes, only job search		No	Yes
MEX			X			Yes	Yes	No
NLD		X		12	No	Yes	Yes	Yes
NOR		X		12	No	Yes	Yes	No for a permanent residence permit Yes for Norwegian citizenship if study period was one year or longer
NZL		X		36	Yes, self-employment not allowed	Yes	Yes	No
POL	X	X		3 – thereafter upon request		Yes	Yes	Yes
PRT		X		12	No. Upon notification, the applicant can work.	No	No.	Yes
SVK		X		9	Yes, working hours cap	Yes	Yes	Yes
SVN		X					Yes	Yes
SWE		X		12	No	Yes	Yes	No
TUR		X		12	No	Yes	No	Yes
USA	X	X				Yes	Yes	No

Note: Table does not include CRI and ISL.
Source: OECD policy questionnaire, 2022.

The post-graduate extension is typically between one and two years of duration (Figure 6.3). In some countries, the extension is tied to the duration of prior studies, such as in Canada, or to the level of the newly obtained qualification, as in Australia, New Zealand, and the United Kingdom. Notably, in all European OECD countries that transposed the EU Directive (2016/801), third-country nationals are allowed to stay for at least nine months upon graduation. In Finland, graduates can apply for the permit for job search within five years of the expiration of their residence permit for studies. Hence, international students can leave the country and still have favourable conditions to return to Finland for several years. A similar provision is in place in France, for up to four years after graduation. Mexico and Colombia are exceptions in the OECD, as they do not offer post-graduation extensions to international students.

Figure 6.3. Most postgraduate extension schemes are between 12 and 24 months

Minimum and maximum duration of stay, typically to search for a job following graduation, in months, 2022

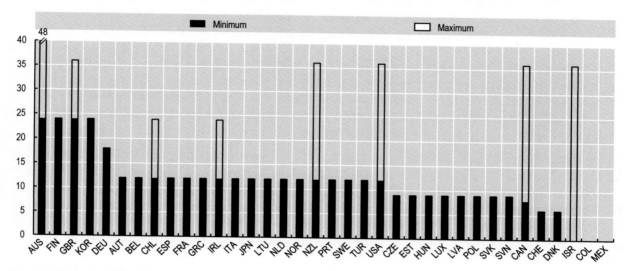

Note: AUS: Graduate Work stream, usually up to 18 months (increased to 24 months as a COVID-19 concession); Post-Study Work stream, two years for bachelor's and up to four years for PhD graduates. GBR: two years for bachelor's and master's, three years for PhD. NZL: one to three years depending on level and duration of prior programme. CAN: equal to the prior duration of studies. USA: refers to post-completion Optional Practical Training (OPT), can be extended by additional 24 months for graduates in STEM subjects. IRL: Graduates with an award at Level 8 or above can apply for 12 months, those with Level 9 or above can renew for additional 12 months. EST: 270 days. ISR: only for graduates in High Tech related fields of study. Spain is planning to increase the postgraduate extension to two years.
Source: OECD Secretariat questionnaire, 2022.

StatLink https://stat.link/842exm

International graduates can usually work to finance their living expenses during their period of job search. In some countries including Belgium, Canada, the Czech Republic, Estonia, Germany, Greece, Lithuania, the Netherlands and Sweden, international graduates have full labour market access during this period. In Japan, international graduates need to apply for a permit to engage in activities other than those allowed under the status of residence previously granted. In Denmark and the Slovak Republic, the employment is restricted to 20h/week, similarly to during studies, and likewise in France, it is restricted to 60% of normal working hours. New Zealand prohibits self-employment and employment in commercial sexual services. In Luxembourg, the job must be in graduates' prior field of study. By contrast, in Austria, Estonia, Hungary, Latvia, and Poland, work is not allowed while on a job search permit.

Countries also offer other forms of facilitation to employment for international graduates. For example, in Germany, after the job-seeking period, graduates are exempt from the labour market test, provided that their sector and qualification level of employment corresponds to their field and degree of study. In Italy, international graduates from an Italian educational institution are exempt from the annual quotas set on issuance of a residence permit for work purposes. In Austria, graduates who have at least completed a bachelor's programme are exempt from passing the points system and can apply directly for the Red-White-Red Card to settle temporarily in Austria and to work for a specified employer. In the Slovak Republic, employers can employ international graduates without the need to apply for a work permit or a labour market test. Also in Finland, no labour market test is needed. In Lithuania, international graduates applying for a residence permit for work are exempted from the 1-year work experience requirement and the labour market test if they are applying within 2 years after completing their studies. In Belgium, international graduates can apply for a single permit from within the territory.

The time international students spend studying in the host country often counts fully or partially towards permanent residence or naturalisation. In Colombia, Denmark, Japan, Korea and Türkiye, study time counts entirely as residence for such purposes. In Switzerland, stays for study purposes are counted when, at the end of their studies, the foreigner has been in possession of a permanent residence permit for two years without interruption. For long-term residence under the EU Directive 2003/109/EC, at least half of the periods of residence for study purposes may be taken into account in the calculation of the five-year legal continuous residence requirement.[5] This is reflected in the national legislation in countries that are covered by the Directive, for example, Austria, Belgium, the Czech Republic, Germany, Hungary, Latvia, Lithuania and Slovenia. The same conditions apply in these countries to the national permanent residence scheme. In Chile, international graduates can apply for permanent residency after only one additional year of stay in the country, so in total at after at least two years of stay in Chile.

By contrast, in several key destination countries, including France, Israel, Italy and Mexico, study years do not count towards permanent residence applications. This is also true in Sweden, except for doctoral students who can count the period with a temporary residence permit towards obtaining a permanent one. In Australia, Canada, New Zealand, and the United States, permanent residency is issued separately from residence requirements on a temporary status, so the question of counting years as a student is less relevant. However, in some countries, a period of international study or a national degree allow for favourable access for long-term stay (Box 6.1).

Box 6.1. Retaining international students through access to options for long-term stay

In **Australia**, international students who completed at least two academic years can earn 5 points (10 if in rural Australia) of the currently required 60 points pass mark to express their interest in migrating permanently. Engineering, accounting, and computer science graduates can complete a one-year Professional Year Program upon graduation, which earns them an extra five points in the skilled migrant visa points test.

In **Canada**, applicants to the high-skilled permanent migration programme earn additional points for their post-secondary Canadian education. What is more, the Canadian Experience Class is an immigration stream that allows those with just one year of Canadian skilled work experience to make an expression of interest, a pathway open to all those who have worked in the country on a post-graduation permit.

In **Chile**, international graduates can apply for permanent residency after only one additional year of stay in the country, so in total at after at least two years of stay in Chile.

In **France**, while all international students are allowed to stay in France for 12 months after the completion of their post-graduation or higher degrees from a French institute to look for employment, bilateral agreements with Benin, Burkina Faso, India, and some other countries extend this privilege to two years. Students who have left France may apply for this permit as well, within a maximum of four years from obtaining their diploma in France.

Ensuring system integrity and preventing abuse

Alongside the arguments for expanding the number of international students and supporting their bridge to residence following study, there are also concerns about programme integrity and oversight of international student programmes. International student programmes can be misused by students, intermediaries and institutions in bad faith, for purposes other than those for which they were designed and for illicit gain. Even when institutions are in good faith, they can be defrauded or exploited by bad-faith students; even when students are in good faith, they can be duped into paying for programmes which are not legitimate (e.g. not accredited) or even fictitious (Figure 6.4).

Figure 6.4. Examples of compliance concerns in international study programmes

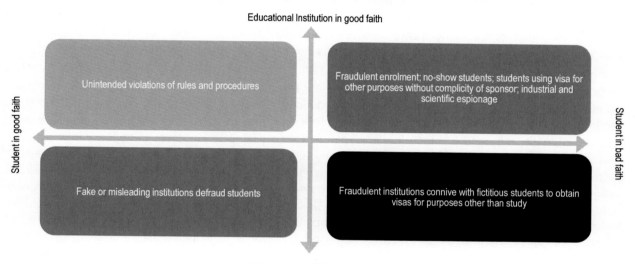

Concerns in regulation centre on separate areas. These include misuse of the student visa, primarily to circumvent restrictions on labour migration, but also related forms of fraud. In addition, there is growing discussion of the risk to protection of intellectual property and strategic knowledge represented by international students conducting espionage. This section addresses the following compliance areas:

- The risk of applicants for student visas use the visa to enter the territory and overstay after expiration, with no intention of ever studying;
- The related issue of fraudulent or bogus schools, set up to defraud international students or to knowingly serve only as vehicles for visa issuance, conniving with students to sponsor a visa in exchange for payment;
- The risk that applicants use the student visa to come to work, and remain in student status indefinitely while employed but not graduating;
- The risk that legitimate students violate restrictions on employment by working excess hours or in jobs or locations not allowed under their status;
- The risk that international students conduct technological or industrial espionage on behalf of their origin country or other malicious actors.

There are other concerns that countries may have about misuse of student visas, such as the potential for criminal or terrorist activity, but these are not specific to international student visas and apply to all admissions.

Each concern has its own set of policy responses.

Issuing student visas only to bona fide students

Combating entry with no intention to take up studies – and the related risk of overstay – generally concentrates on pre-admission screening.

Even before a student applied for a visa, they must be enrolled in an institution. These sponsor institutions are expected, in return for "gatekeeping" privileges, to conduct reasonable verification of the good intentions of students. Indeed, the fact that it is often schools which verify the authenticity of documents attesting prior education means that risk management is partially delegated to them.

Many countries use not only accreditation but a separate system of recognised or ranked institutions granted rights to enrol international students. Usually these systems take into account the capacity of the school to support and report on students, as well as the observed behaviour of their students. A recognition or ranked sponsor system provides an incentive for schools to carefully review applicants to identify risk factors, rather than blindly enrol all applicants; if they can lose the privilege of sponsoring international students, they must exercise more care. In countries where international students are a significant source of income for higher education institutions there may be additional compliance mechanisms.

In the United States, HEIs must be approved by USCIS for attendance by F-1 foreign students. Only schools certified by the Student and Exchange Visitor Program (SEVP) can enrol F or M non-immigrant students. Schools must meet recordkeeping, retention, reporting and other requirements to remain certified, as well as renew certification every two years. In Australia, HEIs must be in the Commonwealth Register of Institutions and Courses for Overseas Students (CRICOS) in order to sponsor students; the Department of Education oversees this Register, although review and monitoring is conducted by state-level bodies. Registration is valid for up to seven years and can be renewed. The United Kingdom requires Student Sponsor Licences of education providers (previously Tier 4 Sponsors). Student Sponsor Licences are valid for four years and renewable. HEIs with the required rating in the pre-existing statutory education inspections generally qualify. Initially, applicants are probationary until they pass a first Basic Compliance Assessment. Since 2011, Korea has used a ranking system called the International Education Quality Assurance System (IQEAS) to ease document requirements for foreign students enrolling in these institutions. IQEAS is based on the share of overstaying and non-compliant students, as well as a subjective evaluation of the capacity of the institution to support international students (OECD, 2019[7]).

Fraudulent and bogus institutions are also a concern. It may not be sufficient to require accreditation if educational institutions can easily obtain accreditation. The approved sponsor requirements – which may involve an often expensive review process and ongoing auditing – is one means to filter out fraudulent institutions. Violations, as well as a record of poor compliance, lead to withdrawal of the right to sponsor students.

The proliferation of intermediary recruiting agents in certain origin countries, who draw a commission from the institution, means that there is a layer of agents with an incentive to place students with sponsor institutions in the destination country. Fraudulent institutions may take advantage of this ready supply of agents to enrol international students, and agents may seek institutions willing to sponsor bogus students. One notable operation to identify and combat this phenomenon was in the United States, where authorities created a fictitious university in 2013 – complete with accreditation – and waited for agents in origin countries to propose students. The operation concluded in 2016 with charges against these agents, who were aware that the institution was bogus but still enrolled more than 1 000 students. Some of these students may have believed they were attending a real institution, while others may have sought a visa allowing admission and access to employment.

Institutions may also be legitimate but exist primarily to place students into employment rather than to provide education. This has been a concern in a number of countries primarily with language schools, leading some (e.g. the United Kingdom, Ireland) to restrict labour market access to students enrolled in higher education institutions.

Once a potential student has enrolled, they still must apply for and receive a student visa. Proof of sufficient resources and insurance are generally required, subject to consular review. Document verification and in-person interview are the principal means used in European countries (European Migration Network, 2022[8]), although some may also contact HEIs to confirm enrolment and payment of fees. Language ability certificates may be checked, and some authorities even test language skills. The consulate may also require authentication of prior education documents. Rejection rates for visas show how consular review can lead to refusal of some applicants. The rejection rate varies widely among the countries that provided or publish official data. For instance, the rejection rate of study visas was 2% for Greece, for the period 2019-21, 7% in 2021 for Denmark, and 4% in 2021 in the Netherlands. In other OECD countries, rates are higher, with about 21% of student visas being refused in 2021 in Belgium, 40% in Canada, and around 40-50% in Sweden. Rejection rates may reflect many factors, including the accessibility and the complexity of the procedure, risk assessment approaches, and the types of programmes to which potential students apply. Therefore, they are not comparable across countries as an indicator of the level of scrutiny or the legitimacy of applicants, or even the ease of admission of international students.

Monitoring of compliance with educational progress

A key question for managing the migration of international students is monitoring that students comply with the conditions specified in their permit; the main concern is that the primary purpose of stay is to pursue education. To deal with the risk of use of the student visa for employment, without graduating, authorities require academic progress (Table 6.6) and impose a maximum stay (Table 6.2). These requirements are meant to ensure that students take their education commitments seriously.

Who is responsible for reporting and providing evidence of study progress varies between OECD countries. Only Sweden has no reporting requirements in place for institutions or students.

The HEI is responsible for reporting and providing proof of study progress in Australia, Denmark, Italy, Latvia, Lithuania, Luxembourg, the Netherlands, the Slovak Republic, Slovenia, the United Kingdom and the United States. In the United Kingdom, for example, a licensed sponsor must inform the Border Agency if a student does not arrive for their course, is absent or leaves the course earlier than expected. In the Slovak Republic, universities are obliged to inform the authorities in case a student has prematurely cancelled their study or has been repelled from the study.

By contrast, in Austria, France, Germany, Greece, Hungary, Israel, Japan and Switzerland, the students themselves have to provide proof of their study progress. In Austria, this is due when students apply for an extension of the residence permit, when they must provide evidence of sufficient academic success (at least 16 ECTS per academic year). Similarly, in Israel, students must provide yearly written proof from the recognised educational institution of continued registration in order to renew their visa.

In Belgium, Canada, Colombia, the Czech Republic, Estonia, Korea, Mexico, New Zealand, Norway, Poland, Portugal and Türkiye the monitoring obligation is shared. Thus, both the host institutions and the international students themselves have to report on study progress or if the conditions under which they received their permit have changed. For example, in Canada international students may be requested to complement the HEI report by providing evidence that they are enrolled in a designated learning institution and are actively pursuing their studies. In Belgium, the Immigration Office can send a demand for proof of continued progress to both the applicant or the HEI and they have 15 days to send in the required documents.

In almost all OECD countries, the student permit can be revoked during its duration for school-related reasons. The most common reason is the absence and discontinuation of studies. Some countries, such as Belgium, Latvia, Lithuania, and the United States, specify that a lack of progress may also be a reason for revoking the permit. The EU Students and Researchers Directive provides for the possibility to withdraw an authorisation if there is evidence that the third-country national is residing for another purpose than study. Also in Türkiye the permit can be revoked if there is evidence that the permit has been used for a purpose other than that for which it was granted. In Mexico and New Zealand a study permit cannot be revoked, although other administrative measures or sanctions may be in place.

Table 6.6. Monitoring of compliance of students after admission

	Who is responsible for reporting?			For permit renewal/extension, which of the following evidence, if any, is required:			Can the permit be revoked during its duration for school related reasons?	
	Host-institutions	International students	Both	Proof of continued study / progress	Proof of attendance	Other	Yes/No	Comments
AUS	X			X			Yes	
AUT		X		X			Yes	Discontinuation of studies
BEL			X	X			Yes	Lack of academic progress
CAN			X	X			Yes	
CHE		X		X	X		Yes	Initial conditions are no longer fulfilled
COL			X	X			Yes	Absence
CZE			X	X		Accommodation, financial means and medical insurance	Yes	Discontinuation of studies
DEU		X		X			Yes	Lack of academic progress
DNK	X			X	X		Yes	Lack of academic progress and high absence
EST			X	X		Same as first issuance	Yes	Lack of academic progress
FRA		X		X		Financial means and insurance	Yes	
GRB	X			X	X	Financial means	Yes	Lack of academic progress and absence
GRC		X		X	X		Yes	Lack of academic progress or initial conditions are no longer fulfilled
HUN		X		X	X		Yes	
ISR		X		X			Yes	Lack of academic progress
ITA			X	X	X		Yes	Lack of academic progress
JPN		X		X	X		Yes	Absence
KOR			X	X	X	In some cases financial means	Yes	Absence
LTU	X			X	X		Yes	
LUX	X			X	X		n/a	
LVA	X			X			Yes	Lack of academic progress and absence
MEX			X	X			No	
NLD	X			X	X		Yes	
NOR			X	X	X	Financial means	n/a	
NZL			X	X	X			The permit cannot be revoked, but the holder can be served a deportation liability notice for breaching conditions such as absence, lack of academic progress or working unlawfully
POL			X	X	X		Yes	The permit has been used for other than studying

	Who is responsible for reporting?			For permit renewal/extension, which of the following evidence, if any, is required:			Can the permit be revoked during its duration for school related reasons?	
	Host-institutions	International students	Both	Proof of continued study / progress	Proof of attendance	Other	Yes/No	Comments
PRT		X		X		Proof of paid enrollment and tuition fees	Yes	In cases where the applicant dropped out, didn't attend classes or had no viable justification for not concluding successfully its curricular plan.
SVK	X			X			Yes	Discontinuation of studies
SVN	X			X			n/a	
SWE	No reporting required						Yes	Discontinuation of studies
TUR			X	X			Yes	Lack of academic progress or the permit has been used for other purposes than studying
USA	X			Renewal or extension is not necessary as permit is valid for study duration			Yes	Lack of academic progress and absence

Source: OECD Policy questionnaire, 2022.

Monitoring compliance with employment restrictions

In addition to checking academic progress, most countries also impose restrictions on employment to ensure that students focus on their education (Figure 6.2). The risk of working more hours than allowed, or in jobs not permitted by the work authorisation, may be difficult to address since it requires either reporting or data monitoring. In a number of countries, employers must report hiring, so it is possible for authorities to manually or automatically check if contract conditions comply with the restrictions of the student status. In the case of multiple employers of a single student, each contract may fall within maximum hours, but to check whether hours cumulatively exceed the limit, compliance checks must also sum hours worked in all job sites. If employers declare the employment relationship and pay social contributions, it may also be possible to use social security contribution information to assess whether hours are exceeded, although employment contribution data does not always contain hours worked. Illegal employment – undeclared by the employer, with or without the awareness of the student – is harder to detect.

The more complex the restrictions, such as in field of study or type of occupation, the more challenging the compliance effort. In the United States, for example, post-graduate Optional Practical Training must be in the major area of study; the institution is responsible for approving placements in employment and the extension of student status is contingent on this approval. It is only with inspections by field agents that US Immigration and Customs Enforcement identified cases where approval was given to placement in jobs outside the student's area of study.

Preventing use of student visas to conduct espionage

Industrial and technological espionage using international students and researchers recruited by the origin country have become of increasing concern in some major OECD destination countries. Concern has focused primarily on students from China – in particular, from military-linked universities and from government-funded programmes for researchers sent abroad (CSET, 2021[9]; NIDS, 2020[10]). Transfer of technology – patents and intellectual property – is the main concern, both in military and civilian industries.

However, misuse of student visas by others – such as Russians – performing military espionage and intelligence gathering has also been identified.

While much of the compliance check occurs in the visa issuance process, there are also measures taken by universities and research institutions to examine the source of funding for applicants and to report to the government on research activities in fields considered of strategic importance. Not all countries have specific reporting procedures. In the United States, students are required to disclose ties to military and government as part of their visa applications. The White House Office of Science and Technology Policy (OSTP) published guidelines in 2021 for institutions to examine sources of funding for foreign researchers (National Science and Technology Council, 2021[11]). In the United Kingdom, the Academic Technology Approval Scheme (ATAS) requires students and researchers in certain fields and from certain countries to obtain an ATAS certificate in order to study or do research in the United Kingdom. In 2022, the national intelligence agency reported that 50 Chinese students left due to ATAS (MI5, 2022[12]).

Conclusion

There is a clear policy trend across OECD countries to attract and retain international students, and many countries have increased facilitations for international students by providing longer residence permits, broader employment opportunities, and easier transition to employment after graduation. International students who graduate are explicitly seen as a desirable component of labour migration inflows. The effect of these policies is to give greater gatekeeping power to higher education institutions, since their enrolment choices affect the downstream composition of migrants – potentially even crowding out other labour migrants when admission is subject to caps and ceilings. This gatekeeping responsibility has also meant greater compliance obligations to combat the misuse of student routes to circumvent migration regulations. It also means greater supervision of education institutions to ensure that none exploit this gatekeeping role. Further, the broader employment rights granted to students are often subject to complex restrictions, which can be difficult to enforce. While student migration is clearly of great benefit to the student, the host institution and the host country, this chapter has also noted some of the risks to the migration framework, with respect of labour market regulations, and even national security. These risks must be taken into account as countries compete to have the most attractive policies for international students.

References

Campus France (2019), *Introduction of differentiated enrolment fees for non-EU students. Comprehensive overview of the measure*, https://www.campusfrance.org/en/droits-inscription-2019-2020-etudiants-internationaux (accessed on 19 April 2022). [1]

CSET (2021), "Assessing the Scope of U.S. Visa Restrictions on Chinese Students", Center for Security and Emerging Technology (CSET) Issue Brief, Washington, DC., https://cset.georgetown.edu/wp-content/uploads/CSET-Assessing-the-Scope-of-U.S.-Visa-Restrictions-on-Chinese-Students.pdf. [9]

Diku (2022), *Dikus rapportserie 07/2021 Tilstandsrapport for høyere utdanning 2021*, https://diku.no/rapporter/dikus-rapportserie-07-2021-tilstandsrapport-for-hoeyere-utdanning-2021 (accessed on 6 May 2022). [2]

European Migration Network (2022), *EMN inform: Preventing, detecting, and tackling situations where authorisations to reside in the EU for the purpose of study are misused*, European Migration Network, Brussels, https://eur-lex.europa.eu/ (accessed on 13 July 2022). [8]

Malmström, H. and D. Pecorari (2022), *Språkval och internationalisering Svenskans och engelskans roll inom forskning och högre utbildning*, Rapporter från Språkrådet, https://www.isof.se/sprakrapport19 (accessed on 4 May 2022). [3]

MI5 (2022), *Joint address by MI5 and FBI Heads*, MI5, London. [12]

National Science and Technology Council (2021), *Recommended Practices for Strengthening the Security and Integrity of America's S&T Research Enterprise*, U.S. Government, Washington, D.C., http://www.whitehouse.gov/ostp. (accessed on 15 July 2022). [11]

NIDS (2020), "NIDS China Security Report 2021: China's Military Strategy in the New Era", *National Institute for Defense Studies (NIDS)*, http://www.nids.mod.go.jp/publication/chinareport/pdf/china_report_EN_web_2021_A01.pdf. [10]

Nuffic (2019), *Incoming degree student mobility in Dutch higher education 2018-2019*, http://www.nuffic.nl/en/publications/incoming-degree-student-mobility-in-dutch-higher-education-2018-2019 (accessed on 10 May 2022). [5]

OECD (2019), *Recruiting Immigrant Workers: Korea 2019*, Recruiting Immigrant Workers, OECD Publishing, Paris, https://doi.org/10.1787/9789264307872-en. [7]

Rugge, F. (2018), *L'internazionalizzazione della formazione superiore in Italia.*, Fondazione CRUI, https://www2.crui.it/crui/crui-rapporto-inter-digitale.pdf (accessed on 6 May 2022). [4]

Sandström, A. and C. Neghina (2017), "English-taught bachelor's programmes Internationalising European higher education", http://www.eaie.org (accessed on 6 May 2022). [6]

Annex 6.A. Supplementary tables

Annex Table 6.A.1. Outreach and communication efforts

	Participation in study fairs in origin countries/regions in the last 3 years	Agency offices in origin countries/regions
AUS	Yes – Chinese Taipei, India, Japan, Mongolia, Korea, Hong Kong (China)	Argentina, Bangladesh, Brazil, Chile, China, Colombia, Fiji, Ghana, Hong Kong (China), India, Indonesia, Japan, Kenya, Korea, Malaysia, Mexico, Mongolia, Pakistan, Papua New Guinea, Peru, Philippines, Singapore, Sri Lanka, Chinese Taipei, Thailand and Viet Nam
AUT	Yes	Yes
BEL	Yes – Participation in various study fairs organised by for example Study in Europe, embassies or other entities. Due to COVID-19, many of these fairs have taken place virtually in the past years	n/a
CAN	Yes	IRCC offices may conduct outreach to students and are located in: Australia, Austria, Brazil, China, Colombia, Egypt, France, Ghana, Haiti, Hong Kong (China), Indonesia, Israel, Italy, Jamaica, Jordan, Kenya, Lebanon, Mexico, Peru, Poland, Romania, Russia, Saudi Arabia, Senegal, Singapore, South Africa, Sri Lanka, Tanzania, Thailand, Trinidad and Tobago, Tunisia, Türkiye, Ukraine, Viet Nam, the Philippines, the UAE, the United Kingdom, the United States.
CZE	Yes – Latin America (Colombia, Ecuador, Chile), Ukraine, Kazakhstan, China and Albania	n/a
DEU	Yes.	DAAD regional offices in 19 countries
DNK	Yes – The agency participates in EAIE and NASFA fairs together with relevant HEIs, however, the purpose of the participation is not to attract international students but to connect the Danish HEI's with their international partners	n/a
EST	Yes – Russia, Ukraine, India, Finland, Türkiye, Georgia, Japan and some regions worldwide- Central Asia, Latin America	n/a
FRA	Yes – In 2021, the student fairs organised were concentrated around Asia and Latin America.	The 259 Campus France offices are part of the French diplomatic network and are present in 127 countries.
GBR	Yes – in China, India, Indonesia, Malaysia, Pakistan, Nigeria, Türkiye, Thailand, and the EU (region-wide).	China, India, Indonesia, Malaysia, Pakistan, Nigeria, Türkiye, Thailand, France, Germany.
GRC	Yes – United States, China, Canada, France, Japan, Georgia.	n/a
HUN	Yes – South-East Asia, Latin-America, Singapore, Japan, India, South-Korea, Canada.	n/a
ISR	Yes – Through NAFSA, EAIE, IGSF and Virtual study fairs (targeting United States, Argentina, Russia, India, United Kingdom, Germany, Canada)	n/a
ITA	n/a	n/a
JPN	Yes	In Indonesia, Thailand, Viet Nam, Korea, Malaysia, Peru, Brazil, Russia, Türkiye, Egypt, Kenya, Zambia, Uzbekistan, Kazakhstan, India, Sri Lanka, Myanmar and Thailand.
KOR	Yes – both online and offline study fairs: Chinese Taipei, Kazakhstan, Canada, Malaysia, Uzbekistan, Viet Nam, Mexico, Colombia, Indonesia, France, Mongolia, the Netherlands, Japan, Chile, Peru, Colombia and Indonesia	In the United States, China, Japan, Russia, Paraguay, United Kingdom., France, Germany, Canada, Argentina, Brazil, Australia, Kazakhstan, Uzbekistan, Kyrgyzstan, New Zealand, Thailand, Viet Nam, Ukraine and Malaysia
LTU	Yes – online events, but also participated in study fairs in Sakartvelo, Ukraine, United Kingdom, Germany, Latvia, Poland and the Netherlands	n/a
LVA	Yes – on-site fair in Ukraine and online fairs in Latin/South America, Japan	n/a
MEX	n/a	n/a
NLD	n/a	n/a

	Participation in study fairs in origin countries/regions in the last 3 years	Agency offices in origin countries/regions
NOR	Yes – in the United States, Canada and Singapore	n/a
NZL	Yes – Pre-Covid-19, NZL hosted (and with third parties) fairs in locations such as India, Thailand, Viet Nam, Japan, Korea, China, Brazil, Colombia and across Europe	Brazil, Chile, China, Germany, India, Indonesia, Japan, Republic of Korea, Singapore, Thailand, the United States of America and Viet Nam. NZL has staff in offices in some countries cover bordering markets (e.g. Staff member in Berlin covers France, Italy and the United Kingdom)
POL	Yes	n/a
SVK	Yes – Physical Fairs: Ukraine; Ethiopia; Malaysia; Finland (EAIE) and virtual Fairs: Africa; Asia; Eurasia; Europe; Indian Subcontinent; Latin America; Morocco & Tunisia, Philippines; Singapore; South America; Sub-Saharan Africa; Türkiye, Russia and Central Asia; Study in Europe Webinar Series Africa; ASEAN (Association of Southeast Asian Nations); EAIE	
SWE	n/a	France
TUR	Yes – online fairs for all over the world	n/a
USA	n/a	n/a

Note: Table only includes countries that provided at least partial answers; n/a means that the country left this answer blank.
Source: OECD Policy questionnaire, 2022.

Notes

[1] This work was produced with the financial support of the German Federal Ministry of Education and Research. It includes a contribution by Hedvig Heijne (Consultant to the OECD).

[2] Unless cited otherwise, data and policy evidence were collected via a questionnaire on international student attraction, admission and retention policies, from January 2022 as well as from the national reports of the OECD Expert Group on Migration.

[3] Many examples in this section are based on a meeting of communications experts in June 2021, as part of the OECD Network of Communication Officers on Migration (NETCOM). Additional good practise examples can be found on the network's website: https://www.oecd.org/migration/netcom/.

[4] This is notably the case in all EU countries that transposed the EU Students and Researchers Directive, which specifies that students shall be able to work at least 15 hours a week.

[5] In April 2022, the European Commission presented a proposal for a Recast Long-Term Residents Directive (COM(2022) 650 final). The proposal would fully count any period of residence spent as holder of a long-stay visa or residence permit for acquiring the EU long-term resident status. This will cover cases where a third-country national who previously resided in a capacity or under a status excluded from the scope of the Directive (e.g. as a student), subsequently resides in a capacity or under a status falling within the scope (e.g. as a worker). In those cases, it will be possible to fully count the periods of residence as a student, towards the completion of the five years period.

7 Retention and economic impact of international students in the OECD

Elisabeth Kamm and Thomas Liebig

This chapter discusses the retention of international students, their importance as a feeder for labour migration, and their economic impact. It starts by providing estimates for their stay rates, five and ten years after admission. It follows with a discussion of the magnitude of international students as a source to labour migration. The chapter ends with a discussion of the economic impact of international students in the host country.

In Brief

- The retention of international students varies greatly across OECD countries. Five years after initial admission to the country, more than 60% of international students who obtained a permit for study reasons in 2015 were still present in Canada and Germany, around half in Australia, Estonia and New Zealand, and around two in five in France and Japan. This is the case for one in six in the United Kingdom, and less than one in seven in Denmark, Italy, Norway and Slovenia.

- Retention rates of international students tend to be higher for more recent cohorts of international students, coinciding with greater efforts to enable them to stay on and change status after study.

- Students from China and India, the two largest groups of international students in the OECD, show remarkably different retention behaviours. Indian students tend to have a higher stay rate than the overall international student population. The retention behaviour of Chinese students is more diverse, with overall larger shares leaving after their education.

- Former international students are an important feeder for labour migration in many countries. The share of educational permits changed to a work permit accounted for a large share of total admissions for work in 2019, especially in France (52%), Italy (46%) and Japan (37%). In the United States, former study (F1) permit holders accounted for 57% of temporary high-skilled (H1B) permit recipients.

- In the OECD as a whole, direct export revenues in nominal terms from international students increased from over EUR 50 billion in 2010 to over EUR 115 billion in 2019. These education-related services exports include the direct contribution of international students to the host country's economy during studies for tuition, food, accommodation, local transport, and other services.

- In English-speaking OECD countries, education-related services are important export items. In Australia and New Zealand, exports of education-related services accounted for 8% and 5% of total exports, respectively, in 2019. Canada, the United Kingdom, and the United States follow at around 2% of total exports.

- During their studies, between one in three and one in four international students work in the EU, the United Kingdom and the United States, about one in two in Australia and nine in ten in Japan. International students can thus be an important contributor to local labour markets, especially in large cities and in the hospitality and education sectors in where they are overrepresented compared with domestic students. For example, data from the European Labour Force suggest that a quarter of working non-EU students were employed in the hospitality sector in 2020, compared with one in ten among native-born students.

- Scholarships and in-country costs for international students often account for a large share of Official Development Assistance (ODA). In 2020, this item accounted for 24% of the total ODA in Austria, 45% in Hungary, and over half of all ODA in Poland and Slovenia. While Germany was the country with the highest amount of ODA allocated to in-country international students, with USD 1.8 billion, this accounted for only 7% of the country's total ODA.

- International students who remain in the host country post-study have long-term employment rates that are on par with those of labour migrants and well above those of migrants overall. Their overqualification rates are half of those of labour migrants or other migrant groups.

Introduction

International students are a unique group of migrants. Given their domestic study experience, international students are often considered a pre-integrated source of future labour supply. It is thus no surprise that most OECD countries have created specific or facilitated pathways for international students to remain in the country after study to take up employment. Indeed, despite their initial admission for temporary stay, many remain in their country of study supported by policies to retain them for work. Yet, little is known with respect to how many actually stay on across OECD countries, and with respect to the importance of this channel for labour migration overall.

Already during study, many international students work or otherwise contribute to the economy. In countries with high tuition fees, international students are an important factor for financing the higher education system, as student fees are often higher for international students than for domestic students. In contrast, in countries where tertiary education is tuition free, imputed student costs for international students from developing countries can be an important factor of official development assistance.

Against this backdrop, this chapter provides a comparative assessment of the stay rates of international students across OECD countries using national permit data. It first reviews the available evidence and then presents novel data with respect to both retention and the contribution of international students as a feeder to overall labour migration. This is followed by a brief look at the economic impact of international students. The chapter concludes with a discussion of the role of international study for migration policy.[1]

Staying on: Retention of international students

Retention as a policy focus

How to retain international students after graduation is a key question in many OECD countries. Nearly half the countries covered in a study by the European Migration Network consider attracting and retaining international students a policy priority (European Migration Network, 2018[1]). For example, the Government of Latvia has set a goal of increasing the share of international students staying in the country after graduation to 10% by 2030 (OECD, 2017[2]). The Estonian strategy for the international promotion of Estonian higher education includes an indicator on employment in Estonia after graduation. The objective is that 30% of international students at master or doctoral level remain to work in Estonia. Australia, Canada, New Zealand, and the United Kingdom highlight in their international education strategies the role of international graduates to fill vacancies (Australian Department of Education, Skills and Employment, 2021[3]; Government of New Zealand, 2018[4]).

Available evidence

Available evidence on the retention of international students is mostly country-specific. In recent years, about a third of OECD countries have looked into this issue. The most common approach in these studies has been to calculate the share of individuals remaining in the country a specified number of years after the initial study permit or, alternatively, after their graduation. These estimations use different methodological approaches, reference periods, and data sources. Results are thus not comparable across countries. Table 7.1 provides an overview.

Table 7.1. Available evidence of student stay rates in OECD countries

Country	Approach and data	Results	Source
Australia	Follow-up of student/temporary or permanent permit holders, pooled from 2000/01 and 2013/14 (1.6 million individuals).	16% of all international students eventually transitioned to permanent residence.	(The Treasury and the Department of Home Affairs, 2018[5])
Austria	Pooling graduation cohorts from 2008/09 to 2018/19. Based on residence status at graduation, 1, 2, 3 years later. Report lists numbers by nationality and separated by type of study and years since graduation.	Master's graduates 2016/17 who had left the country ("Wegzugsquoten"): Austrian nationals: 5%; German nationals: 64%; other EU: 53%; other non-EU (includes UK): 43%.	(Statistics Austria, 2021[6])
Belgium	Belgian National Register, individuals residing for study reasons in 2010. Socio-economic position in 2014 (4 years later).	43% had an active labour market status in Belgium (working or job seeking) in 2014.	(Federale Overheidsdienst, 2017[7])
Canada	Share of international students obtaining a post-graduation work permit after their study permit expired. 2008-17 cohorts.	43% of international students whose study permit had expired in 2017 obtained a post-graduation work permit within one year. This share was 48% for the 2012 cohort five years after their first study permit had expired.	(Crossman, Lu and Hou, 2022[8])
Czech Republic	Survey of graduates who studied in the Czech Republic between 2012 and 2021. 3 136 responses.	45% of the graduates of full-degree programmes have been staying in the Czech Republic for work purposes.	(DZS, 2022[9])
Denmark	–	42% of graduates from English-language programmes at Master level left Denmark within 2 years of completing their studies. Only about a third remain in the Danish workforce after 2 years.	(Danish Ministry of Higher Education and Science, 2018[10])
Estonia	Immediate transition to work after graduation.	Graduates with master or doctoral degree who worked immediately after graduation; 56% in 2016/17; 58% in 2017/18.	(Statistics Estonia, 2019[11])
Finland	Tracking 13 (years) graduating cohorts across national data registries. Stay rates 3 years after graduation international students graduating in Finland between 1999 and 2011.	67% of bachelor's, 64% of master's graduates were residing in Finland three years after graduation. Sample excludes those who lived in Finland before enrolment.	(Mathies and Karhunen, 2020[12])
France	Metropolitan France, nationals of third countries having obtained a first student permit in 2015, follow-up in subsequent years until 2020.	One year after first permit, 37% had left France (or became nationals); 5 years after first permit, 57% had left (or became nationals).	(Ministère de l'Intérieur, 2021[13])
Germany	Pooling third-country nationals who had studied in Germany in the period January 2005 – October 2013, follow-up in October 2014.	In October 2014, 54% of the former students were still living in Germany.	(Hanganu, 2015[14])
Korea	Immediate transition to work after graduation.	12% of master's and PhD graduates worked immediately after graduation in 2021.	(Ministry of Education Korea, 2021[15])
Luxembourg	Place of first registered employment.	46% of international master and PhD graduates of 2014-19 had a first registered employment in Luxembourg.	Data provided by the University of Luxembourg, 2022
Netherlands	Stay rates of international graduates cohorts of 2006/07 and 2012/13 based on linked data by Statistics Netherlands.	Almost 25% of the international students who studied in the Netherlands still live there 5 years after graduating.	(NUFFIC, 2022[16])
Norway	Immigrants who graduated with a bachelor or master degree in Norway in 2007 and 2012, and their labour market status five years later.	78% of international graduates of 2007 were still living in Norway five years after graduation – 88% among these were in employment. 76% of international graduates of 2012 were still living in Norway in 2017, 85% of these were employed.	(Statistics Norway, 2020[17])
New Zealand	Follow-up five years after initial permits.	Two-thirds (66%) of all first student permit (FSV) holders in 2009 are overseas five years after they obtain their FSV.	(New Zealand Ministry of Education, 2017[18])
Switzerland	Place of residence of graduates of Swiss universities one year after the year of graduation.	36% of international students (bachelor graduates of a university of applied sciences, graduates of a pedagogical university as well as master and PhD graduates) were residing abroad in 2015.	(Bundesamt für Statistik, 2017[19])
United Kingdom	Longitudinal Educational Outcomes dataset to link higher education and tax data, and to chart the transition of graduates from higher education into the workplace.	Five years after graduation of the graduation cohort of 2013-14, about 39% of EU and 15% of non-EU graduates were recorded in "sustained employment", further studies, or both.	(UK Department for Education, 2022[20])

Note: National research presented in this table uses differing methodologies, years and target groups. Shares are thus not comparable between countries and do not necessarily refer to international students with a permit based on education, as used in the OECD estimations below.

Research has also looked at the share of residents who initially arrived for the purpose of education. Data from Canada show that in 2021, more than a third (39%) of new permanent immigrants admitted in that year held a Canadian study permit at some point in the past. This share has substantially increased in the past years, up from just 16% in 2017. Data from Australia show that about 21% of the over 160 000 permanent residence permits issued in 2017/18 were obtained by applicants who held, or previously had held, an Australian student permit (Birrell, 2019[21]).

In contrast to the growing amount of country-specific evidence on retention rates, internationally comparable evidence is scarce. In virtually all OECD countries, international students[2] who do not benefit from free mobility receive a study permit to take up their studies, but student permit statistics do not incorporate information on whether or not a student has graduated. Therefore, while a proxy for entries (issued permits) exists, the calculation for staying on is less straightforward. Previous estimations, including by the OECD and the European Commission, do not allow for tracing international students over time, but rather provide a snapshot of staying behaviour one year after enrolment in studies (see Box 7.1).

Box 7.1. Previous international evidence

An approach previously taken by the OECD (2011[22]), was to calculate the share of student permit holders changing to a status other than "education", relative to the number of international students not renewing their student permit in the same year, which includes both people changing status or leaving the host country. The number of students not renewing their permit was proxied by subtracting the difference in observed stocks of international students between year *t* and year *t-1* from the number of inflows (measured in permits). The number of status changes relative to this overall number gave an indication of the overall share of students staying on in the country. In 2008/09, this share was between 17-33% for the countries covered. However, it is important to acknowledge the potential drawbacks of this approach in a context of changing intakes of students, different study durations and lags involved in their potential permit changes.

There have also been estimates for the EU as a whole, based on data from Eurostat on permits. Focusing on non-EU origin countries, for the EU as a whole, aggregate stay rates of previously studying non-EU citizens were estimated to be between 16% and 29%, depending on the assumptions taken regarding study duration and other parameters not observed in the data. A report by the European Commission (2018), using the European Union Labour Force Survey (EU-LFS) and focussing on staying behaviour of intra-European students, calculated the shares of respondents who were EU citizens with a different citizenship than their country of residence, had lived in the host country for more than a year, and were a student in that country the year before the reference year. Estimates were only obtained for the United Kingdom, the Netherlands and Sweden. In each of these countries, stay rates were estimated of 40% or higher for those who finished their studies.

Source: OECD (2011[22]), *International Migration Outlook 2011*, https://doi.org/10.1787/migr_outlook-2011-en; Weisser (2016[23]), "Internationally mobile students and their post-graduation migratory behaviour: An analysis of determinants of student mobility and retention rates in the EU", https://doi.org/10.1787/5jlwxbvmb5zt-en; European Commission (2018[24]), *Study on the movement of skilled labour: Final report*, https://doi.org/10.2767/378144.

The OECD and Eurostat collect data on the type of permits given to previous study permit holders by year (EUROSTAT, 2021[25]). These numbers also show that the channel through which retention occurs differs widely. In Belgium, Lithuania, Poland and Slovenia, more than 40% of international study permit holders who change status change to a family permit. In contrast, in Denmark, France, Germany, Italy, the Netherlands, and the Slovak Republic, more than three in four status changes are towards work-related permits.

Relating these numbers to the annual education permits issued in previous years provides a first indication of retention. The data show that about one in three student permit holders change their initial education permit to a different type of permit in subsequent years. As visible in Figure 7.1, these data are sensitive to changes in student numbers over time.

Figure 7.1. About one in three study permit holders extend their stay

Estimated share of education permits changed to a different permit (or accessing post-study work) in 2019, relative to average annual education permits issued from 2016 to 2018

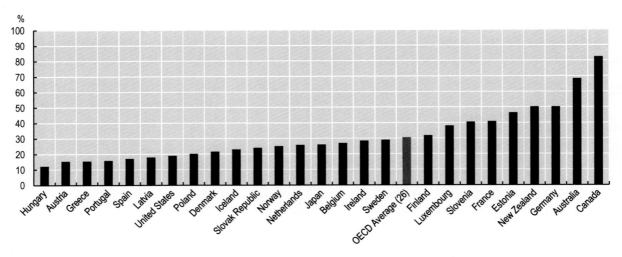

Note: Shares are calculated as the number of educational permit holders who changed their permit in 2019 to any other permit, relative to the average annual number of new permits issued to international students from 2016 to 2018. The OECD average is the simple average of countries included in the graph. Australia and Canada: transition to post-graduation permits for job search as well as direct transitions to permanent residence. United States: Students with an F1 visa who transitioned into H1B in the United States. Japan: transition from education/study to work.
Source: OECD Secretariat based on International Migration Database and Eurostat data, 2022.

StatLink https://stat.link/x0bdnc

Methodological considerations and limitations

A retention rate analysis typically starts with a cohort admitted or graduated and considers their retention in the country at different time intervals. The graduation year or time since first permit are both possible reference points. A disadvantage of the latter is that duration of study varies, making it difficult to have a clear cut-off year for post-study retention. While the graduation year provides a clear cut-off date, this information is generally not available in permit data. What is more, not all international students graduate. The following analysis takes the issuance of the first study permit as the starting point for analysis. Many, though not all, OECD countries record permit data and mark these permits with a unique person-specific identifier. Based on this unique identifier, it is possible to connect a permit recipient who initially arrived for educational purposes with all his/her subsequent permits. In some countries, it is not possible to make this link, and thus estimations here cannot follow individual permit receivers but only look at transitions to other categories in a given year and relate them to other variables of interest, such as prior admissions for education or current admission for work.

Permit statistics have some methodological shortcomings. First, they only give an indication of a person's presence in a country in a given year and serve as an approximation of actual staying behaviour. Many countries do not distinguish between degree students and exchange or language students, so initial permits include many students who stay only a few months or one academic year. What is more, in some countries, the study permit is simply prolonged for those who want to search for a job. Hence, individuals might appear in the statistics as if they are still studying, while they are in fact already looking for a job. Moreover, international students who transition to permanent residence or become naturalised in some countries drop out of permit statistics and cannot be distinguished from those who leave the country. In other countries, these individuals can be identified and separately tabled. These limitations can lead to bias, as one of the main assumptions of the permit identifier approach is that individuals for whom no data is recorded have left the country.

Calculation of retention requires a decision as to who is to be included in the "retained" group. Retention rates can focus solely on former international students currently in the country as labour migrants or can also include former international students who have transitioned to other categories, such as family permits. The following analysis examines all subsequent permits, including labour, family, and humanitarian permits.

Estimations based on permit data do not allow for any information on individuals who benefit from free mobility rights. Therefore, the calculations below exclude student movements in free mobility zones such as the EU/EEA and the New Zealand-Australian Trans-Tasman Agreement.

Results

Stay rates over time

Overall, five years after receiving their first education permit in 2015, around 30% of international students still hold a valid permit in their host country, though there are strong differences across OECD countries (Figure 7.2). Ten years after first admission, this share drops strongly in most countries, but remains at almost 50% in Canada and Germany and around 30% in Australia and New Zealand.

Figure 7.2. Five-year retention rates are often higher for the cohort of 2015 than the cohort of 2010

Share of first study permit receivers in 2010 and 2015, recorded with valid permit in 2020

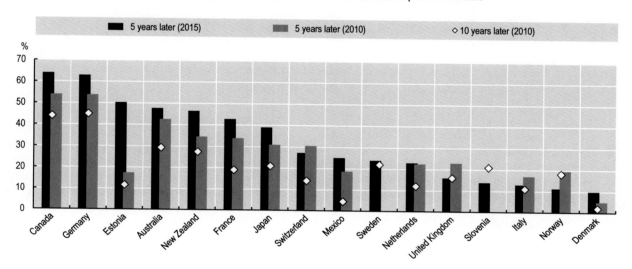

Note: Data include individuals on a valid permit, including those with an education permit. Data from Denmark, Sweden and Switzerland include returning individuals. Data for Germany includes persons already resident who obtained a first time education permit. Data from Italy and Mexico refer to the 2011 cohort instead of 2010, and thus to 4 years after admission in the year 2015 and 9 years later in 2020. Data do not include individuals who have become citizens in France, New Zealand and the Netherlands. Data from the United Kingdom refer to out-of-country visa grants with no valid leave in the prior 12 months, are based on nationality and include a small number of minors arriving for secondary education. This graph refers to permit statistics and does not include individuals benefiting from free mobility.
Source: OECD Secretariat calculations, 2022.

StatLink ᵃˢᵖ https://stat.link/g2574d

The available data suggest that retention has tended to increase for more recent cohorts. With the exception of Switzerland, the United Kingdom, Norway and Italy, the cohort of 2015 is more likely to remain in the country five years later than the 2010 cohort. The most striking difference is visible in Estonia, where retention rates increased from less than one in five to about one in two. The small numbers for the Nordic countries need to be interpreted in the context of large shares of students admitted for education purposes coming from other high income OECD countries.

It should be noted that the figures shown above include individuals who are still, or again, on a study permit. In some countries, this group is considerable. For example, in Canada and Germany, about a quarter of initial permit receivers in 2015 were still recorded to have a study permit in 2020. A similar figure has been observed in Australia (20%). In contrast, in the United Kingdom and New Zealand, this was only the case for 10% and 6%, respectively, of the 2015 cohort. Excluding current study permit holders from the baseline leads to a reduction in retention rates. Not surprisingly, the decline is largest in Australia (14 percentage points), Canada (by 12 percentage points) and Germany (by 11 percentage points). It is also large in France (10 percentage points) and the United Kingdom (9 percentage points). However, the overall ranking of countries in terms of retention remains largely the same (Figure 7.3).

Figure 7.3. Excluding individuals with education permit decreases retention rates

Share of first study permit receivers in 2015, recorded with valid permit in 2020, including and excluding education permits

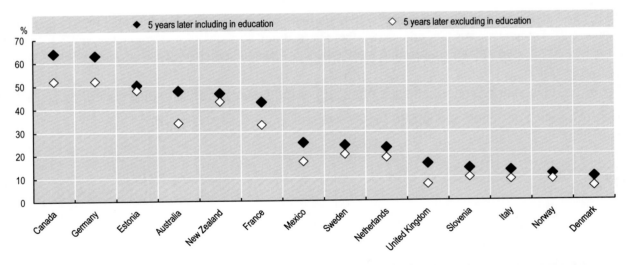

Note: Data include individuals on a valid permit. Data from Denmark and Sweden include returning individuals. Data for Germany includes persons already resident who obtained a first time education permit. Data do not include citizens in France, New Zealand and the Netherlands. Data from the United Kingdom refer to out-of-country visa grants with no valid leave in the prior 12 months, are based on nationality and include a small number of minors arriving for secondary education. This graph refers to permit statistics and does not include individuals benefiting from free mobility.
Source: OECD Secretariat calculations, 2022.

StatLink ᴍᴷ https://stat.link/z43hbm

Detailed data on the annual trajectory of permit holders are available only from a few OECD countries (Figure 7.4). These data show that individuals in Australia, France and Germany remain on a student permit for a relatively long time. By contrast, in New Zealand, Italy and Norway, students transition much faster to other permit categories. In New Zealand, two years after admission, 16% hold a job-search permit, which accounts for about a third of all those who remained after study. In other countries where this data is available, shares are below 5% in all years. Italy does not have a job-search permit.

Figure 7.4. The retention of international students over a decade

Permit recorded for individuals who received their first educational permit in 2010, from 2010 to 2020

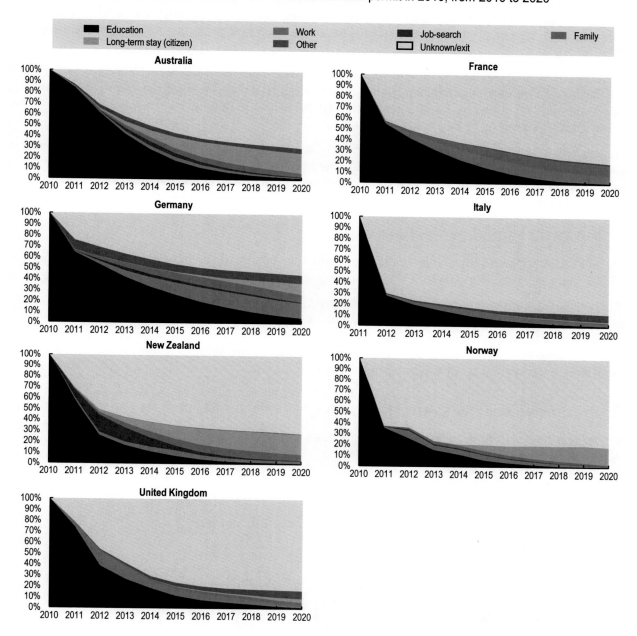

Note: Data only include individuals who received a permit, thus excluding individuals benefiting from free mobility schemes. Long-term stay category includes long-term / permanent work classes in New Zealand and Australia. Data from New Zealand and France do not include individuals who transitioned to citizenship. These are included in the unknown/exit category. Data from the United Kingdom refer to out-of-country visa grants with no valid leave in the prior 12 months. They are based on nationality and include a small number of child students arriving for secondary education.
Source: OECD Secretariat calculations, 2022.

StatLink 🏝️ https://stat.link/y2hn8w

Data from Australia suggest that international students complete their studies faster than nationals, and are also more likely to successfully graduate.[3] Data from Canada point in a similar direction. Almost two-thirds (65%) of international master's degree students who started their programme in 2013 had graduated within two years, compared with 58% of Canadian students. Most international (87%) and Canadian (83%) master's students had graduated within four years of starting the programme (Statistics Canada, 2020[26]).

Ten years after the first education permit, former international students in Australia, Canada, New Zealand, Norway, and Sweden are predominantly on a long-term permit if they are still in the country.[4] In Germany, this is the case for only about one-quarter of those still in the country, and most who still reside in the country have a permit for work.

Transition to a family permit is overall less common. Less than one in ten initial student permit receivers in 2010 hold a family permit ten years later, with shares reaching 10% in France, 7% in Germany, 6% in New Zealand, 2% in Sweden and in the Netherlands, and only 1% in Canada, Italy, Norway, Denmark and the United Kingdom.

Stay rates of Chinese and Indian students

As seen in Chapter 5, China and India are key origin countries for international students in most OECD countries, accounting for 22% and 10%, respectively, of the total in the academic year 2020.

International students from India have a higher stay rate than international students overall. For Chinese students, the pattern is more diverse. In most countries, they have a lower stay rate than the overall student population, with the exceptions of Canada, Japan, the Netherlands and New Zealand (Figure 7.5). Likewise, data from the United States show that Indians are more likely to remain in the country for an initial work experience than Chinese students (Box 7.2).

Figure 7.5. Indian students have higher stay rates than other permit holders

Stay rates in 2020 of Chinese, Indian, and all permit holders with first education permit in 2015

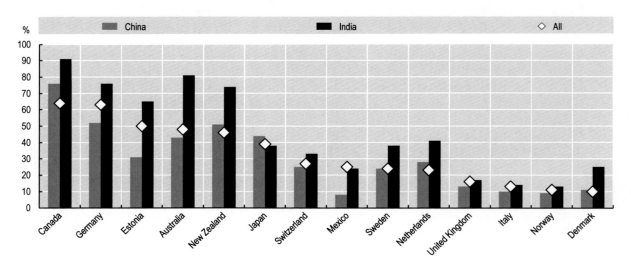

Note: Stay rate includes individuals still enrolled as students. Data with less than 40 nationals in the base year are excluded. Data from Denmark and Sweden include returning individuals. Data from New Zealand do not include individuals who transitioned to citizenship. Data from the United Kingdom refer to out-of-country visa grants with no valid leave in the prior 12 months and include a small number of child students arriving for secondary education.
Source: OECD Secretariat calculations, 2022.

StatLink 🖼️ https://stat.link/eczur3

Data on the retention behaviour of Chinese and Indian students also show differences in speed of transition to other categories, especially work permits. In Germany, where international students remain on a study permit for a relatively long time, the share of Chinese among the 2015 cohort still on an education permit in 2020 was slightly higher than the overall share, 27% compared with 23% overall. In contrast, only 10% of Indians admitted in 2015 for study were still on a student permit in 2020. A similar picture regarding differences between the two groups emerges in New Zealand, where just 6% of all first-time admissions in 2015 were still on a study permit in 2020. Seventeen percent of Chinese students admitted in 2015 were still on an education permit five years later, whereas this was only the case for 2% of Indian students. Instead, 45% of Indians were on a short- or long-term (including permanent) work permits. The share of Chinese students with a work permit was just 14%. In the United Kingdom, while overall about 4% of 2015 admissions held a work permit in 2020, this was the case for only 2% of Chinese, but 9% of Indian students. In Canada, 54% of Chinese but only 9% of Indian students were still on a study permit in 2020, 5 years after admission, compared with 29% among all study permit receivers. In the same year, 71% of the Indians admitted in 2015 held a work permit, compared with 18% of Chinese, and 26% of all 2015 admissions. Numbers from Estonia are too small for publication, but indicate a similar difference between the two groups. However, this pattern does not hold everywhere. In Australia, 5 years after admission in 2015, 24% of Chinese and 27% Indians were still recorded with an educational permit.

In Sweden, only 5% of all students remained on a study permit five years after first admission. For both China (9%) and India (7%), the shares are slightly higher. However, in 2020, a comparatively large share of former Indian students in Sweden held a work permit (23%) against much lower shares among Chinese (6%) and among all students (7%) admitted five years earlier. In the Netherlands, five years after admission in 2015, only 4% of all permit recipients were still recorded on a study permit. In contrast, 14% held a work permit. This share was slightly higher among Chinese (16%) and significantly higher among Indian nationals (36%). In Denmark, just 4% of all admitted in 2015 held a work permit in 2020. This share was 5% among Chinese nationals and 14% among Indians.

In sum, available country-specific evidence by nationality suggests that Indian students are more likely than the overall international student population to stay following their initial permit in the host country. They are also more likely in most countries to hold a work permit five years after first admission than Chinese and other peers.

In this context, it is key to note that international students from India are more likely enrolled at the master or PhD (ISCED 7 or 8) level than Chinese students, which might explain their quicker transition to the labour market and shorter period on an education permit. Overall, 58% of Indian students study at a master or PhD level in OECD countries, compared to just 45% of Chinese international students in 2020.

Box 7.2. Indian students account for the bulk of post-study work authorisations in the United States

International students who pursue a tertiary degree in the United States are generally not allowed to work off-campus during the first academic year but may take up on-campus employment. After the first academic year, students may engage in off-campus employment via Optional Practical Training (OPT). An OPT authorisation allows temporary employment that is directly related to a student's major area of study for up to 12 months total employment. This can be used pre- or post-completion of studies. Since 2008, students with STEM degrees may apply for an additional 24-month of post-graduate OPT. Data on OPT authorisations show that virtually all OPTs are obtained for post-graduate work. Indian students are overrepresented among students who receive both a general OPT and a STEM extension.

Indian nationals also have long accounted for the bulk of direct transitions from a study permit (F1) to a temporary high-skilled permit (H1B). In 2019, they accounted for 60% of such transitions, up from around 40% in 2010. By contrast, at their peak over the past decade in 2015, Chinese nationals made up 31% of direct transitions, while in 2019 their share reached only 23%. This is true despite the fact that there have been approximately two to three times as many Chinese students in the United States as Indians over this decade. These data thus indicate that, as in other countries, Indian students are more likely to remain in the United States, at least compared to Chinese students.

Source: United States Immigration and Customs Enforcement (2022[27]), *Homeland Security Investigations: Student and Exchange Visitor Program*, data shared with the OECD June 2022.

International students as future labour migrants

It is not possible to quantify the importance of international students as a feeder to labour migration through stay rates alone, due to variations in overall numbers and composition of the international student cohort in different OECD countries, as well as the scale of overall labour migration and national populations.

To assess the impact of international students as a feeder to labour migration, one needs to relate the transition from an educational to a work permit to the overall numbers admitted for work. Doing so shows considerable differences across countries (Figure 7.6). In France, Italy and Japan, the share of educational permits changed to a work permit account for 30% or more of the total admissions for work in 2019, while this figures is below 10% in countries like Austria, Norway, Portugal and Spain.

In the settlement countries, international students can transition directly to permanent residence, but most of those who remain stay initially on temporary permits. In 2019, 14% of permits for work in New Zealand were obtained by individuals initially admitted for study. This share was 9% in Canada. The large majority of these temporary work permits to international students were for post-graduation work (81% in New Zealand and 73% in Canada). In Australia, 17% of permanent residency visas were granted to former international students in Australia in 2019-20. In the United States, former study (F1) permit holders accounted for 57% of high-skilled temporary (H1B) permit recipients in 2019.

Figure 7.6. International students are a feeder to labour migration, to varying degrees

Education permits changed to a work permit in 2019, relative to admission for work 2019 (left); Permits issued relative to specified migration class, 2019 (right), in %

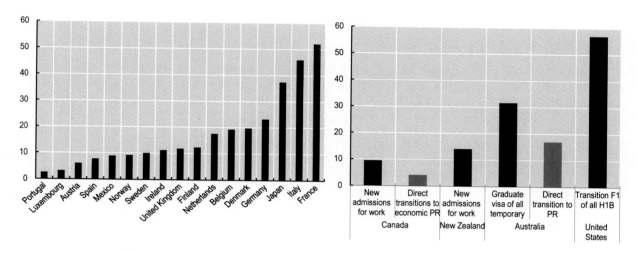

Note: Data for European OECD countries and Japan (left graph) refer to education permits changed to permits for work. Australia (light blue): permanent residency (PR) visas granted to former international students in Australia relative to all permanent residency visas granted for work in 2019-20. Australia (dark blue): Temporary Graduate visas (subclass 485) granted relative to all temporary permits. New Zealand (dark blue): New admissions for work of persons who were first admitted on a study/education permit, relative to all new admissions for work. Canada (dark blue): Initial work permit holders who were first admitted as study permit holders, relative to all Initial work permit holders with permit that became effective in 2019. Canada (light blue): direct transitions of former students to economic category of permanent residency (PR). United States: Former F1-study permit holders relative to share of H1B recipients, 2019.

Source: European OECD countries: OECD Migration database and Eurostat, permit statistics national data for Japan. New Zealand: Ministry of Business, Innovation & Employment, 2022. Canada: IRCC, CDO, 2022 Data. Australia: Australian Government Migration Statistics, 2022.

StatLink ᵐˢ𐊏 https://stat.link/rq73fk

Economic impact

The presence of international students affects host countries' economies in a variety of ways. This section assesses three different dimensions of the economic impact, that is, the macroeconomic impact as measured in the national accounts, the impact on Official Development Assistance (ODA) and on the labour market. The section ends with a short discussion on the long-term outcomes of previous international students in the host-country labour market, based on novel data for the OECD EU countries.

Previous evidence on the economic impact of international students comes primarily from country-specific studies. Given the growing importance of international study, in-depth research is surprisingly scarce and often dated (see the overview in Annex Table 7.A.1). For example, evidence from France and Germany, the two main destination countries for international students in continental Europe, is limited to only one dated study per country (Campus France, 2014[28]; Prognos, 2013[29]).

The OECD countries with the most frequent assessment of the economic impact of international students are the English-speaking OECD countries: Australia, Canada, New Zealand, the United Kingdom, and the United States. Several studies have also been carried out for Belgium (particularly for the Flanders region), Estonia, Ireland, the Netherlands, Spain and Sweden. Half of the OECD countries have no available studies on the economic impact of international students.

Estimates of the macroeconomic impact

The estimate of the macroeconomic impact is based on an export data analysis, which has two advantages. First, despite not being able to quantify the indirect and induced economic contributions, it provides an accurate measure of the direct economic contribution (tuition fee + non-tuition fee spending) during studies. Second, it allows to have comparable statistics for most OECD countries over the last decade, while most of the previous evidence is country-and-year specific and hardly comparable.

An internationally comparable estimate of the macroeconomic impact of international students is available from the national accounts. The data on the exports of education-related services cover expenditure by international students on tuition fees, food, accommodation, local transport, and health services. These data are collected by the OECD as part of the national accounts statistics on international trade.

Figure 7.7 shows general growth of exports of education-related services across most OECD countries, with total revenues in the OECD area increasing from EUR 50 billion in 2010 to over EUR 115 billion in 2019.

Figure 7.7. From 2010 on to 2019, revenues from international students increased almost everywhere

Education-related services exports (gross) in millions of EUR, 2010 and 2019, current values

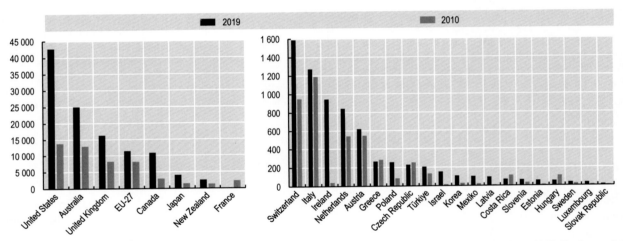

Note: For Austria, data for 2010 refer to 2012. For France, data for 2010 refer to 2011. For Ireland, data for 2010 refer to 2012. For Japan, data for 2010 refer to 2014. For the Netherlands, data for 2010 refer to 2014. For the Slovak Republic, data for 2010 refer to 2013. For Türkiye, data for 2019 refer to 2018.
Source: Data from OECD EBOPS 2010 – Trade in Services by Partner Economy database. Data for Switzerland are from the Swiss National Statistical Office (BFS). Data for the United Kingdom are from The Pink Book time series by the Office of National Statistics.

StatLink https://stat.link/cyfqib

English-speaking OECD countries, including the United States, Australia, the United Kingdom, Canada and New Zealand, rank as the top five countries by gross revenues, accounting for more than 80% of the total revenues from the exports of education-related services in the OECD area in 2019. The figures for the United States and Canada have more than tripled over the past decade, while Australia, New Zealand, and the United Kingdom saw a twofold increase. The growth in exports of education-related services has been particularly strong in Japan, whose revenues from international students almost tripled from 2014 to 2019, as well as in Ireland (20-fold increase), Israel and Latvia (both tenfold). Virtually all Central and Eastern European OECD countries experienced significant increases in their education-related services exports, often doubling or tripling over the past decade. The EU-27 average growth rate has been significantly lower (+42%), as large recipient countries such as Austria and Italy experienced more modest growth rates.

The gross values of exports of education-related services can be compared with total exports (Figure 7.8). Again, the English-speaking OECD countries show the highest shares, and all recorded increases over the past decade. In Australia, the share increased from 6% to 8.5%, and, in New Zealand, from 4% to 5%. Canada, the United Kingdom and the United States have seen their shares of education-related services increase to 2% of their total exports. In the remainder of OECD countries, exports of education-related services remain well below 1% of total exports. Among these, Estonia, Ireland, Israel, Japan and Latvia have seen strong increases. In contrast, Costa Rica, the Czech Republic, Greece, Hungary and Italy have seen sizeable decreases as a share of total exports from 2010 to 2019.

Figure 7.8. English-speaking countries have the highest exports of education-related services

Education-related services exports (gross) as percentage of total exports, 2010 and 2019

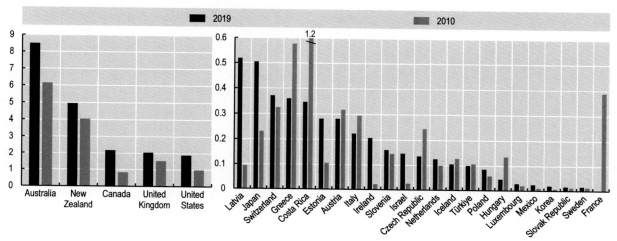

Note: For Austria, data for 2010 refer to 2012. For France, data for 2010 refer to 2011. For Iceland, data for 2010 refer to 2013 and data for 2019 refer to 2018. For Ireland, data for 2010 refer to 2012. For Japan, data for 2010 refer to 2014. For the Netherlands, data for 2010 refer to 2014. For the Slovak Republic, data for 2010 refer to 2013. For Türkiye, data for 2019 refer to 2018. Calculations based on current prices and current exchange rates.
Source: Data from OECD EBOPS 2010 – Trade in Services by Partner Economy database. Data for Switzerland are from the Swiss National Statistical Office (BFS). Data for the United Kingdom are from The Pink Book time series by the Office of National Statistics.

StatLink 📊 https://stat.link/z2k0r1

Official Development Assistance

The implicit counterpart to revenue from high tuition fees are scholarships and subsidised study for international students. For students from developing countries, the two items are considered Official Development Assistance (ODA). The rationale behind counting these towards a country's ODA has been that international students will return home with additional human capital, which contributes to development. This accounting has been questioned in recent years, given the enhanced efforts of most OECD countries to retain international graduates in the host country.

Figure 7.9. ODA to international students is highest in countries with low or no study fees

ODA to scholarships and student costs in donor countries, USD millions in constant prices (left) 2010, and 2020 and relative to total ODA in 2020 (right)

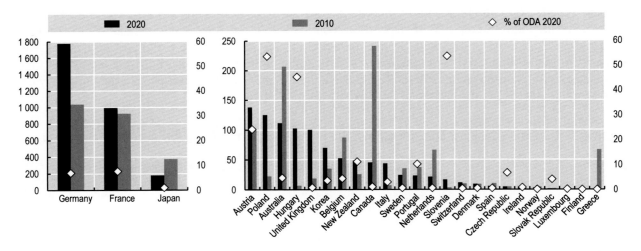

Note: Data include both scholarships and in-country student costs. For Austria, data for 2010 refer to 2014. For Canada, data for 2020 refer to 2019. For Norway and the United Kingdom, data for 2010 refer to 2013. For Switzerland, data for 2010 refer to 2011.
Source: OECD ODA Database, 2022.

StatLink https://stat.link/w4crmt

Not surprisingly, this part of ODA is highest in countries with many international students and low tuition fees (Figure 7.9). As a result, in 2020 as in 2010, Germany was the country with the highest amount of ODA allocated to in-country international students, with almost USD 1.8 billion in 2020. France reported the second highest figure, with USD 1 billion. However, the growth over the past decade was much less marked in that country, as education fees for international students experienced a substantial increase in 2019. All other countries have values below USD 400 million in both years.

ODA to international students is also a substantial share of total ODA in some countries. In 2020, scholarships and student costs accounted for 24% of total ODA in Austria, 45% in Hungary, and over half of all ODA in Poland and Slovenia. By contrast, the share of ODA provided via scholarships and student costs in the donor country was rather low in Germany (7%), France (8%) and Japan (1%), despite the overall large amounts. Most of the English-speaking OECD countries that ranked in the top for revenues from international students (see above) did not provide a substantial share of their total ODA to international students. Only New Zealand devolved slightly more than 11% of its total ODA to international students. Most other countries also provided only small shares of their total ODA to in-country international students.

As mentioned, ODA to international students consists of two components: scholarships and student costs in donor countries. In countries with high tuition fees, scholarships account for the bulk of ODA to international students. This is the case for most OECD countries. Only in a few countries do the estimated student costs account for the bulk of ODA to international students. This is notably the case in Germany (95%), Austria (95%), Belgium (93%), Poland (93%) and Slovenia (96%). In France, about 18% of the ODA to international students goes to scholarships and about 82% to student costs. Considering only scholarships, France donated the largest total amount to international students in 2020 (USD 186 million), followed by Japan (USD 178 million) and Australia (USD 111 million).

Labour market impact at national and local level

In most OECD countries, upon their arrival, international students have the right to work alongside their studies, at least part-time. The contribution of students to the host country's employed population is bound by the country-specific rules on student work, but also depends on students' decision to take up employment.

In the 2019 International Migration Outlook, the OECD estimated for the first time the potential contribution of international students to the labour market (OECD, 2019[30]). This methodology has also been used for this section. The contribution is estimated in full-year and full-time equivalent (FY/FTE) terms. An upper-bound estimate is that all international students work the maximal hours allowed by the rules of their permit. In full-year full-time equivalent terms, in the academic year 2020, international students added up to 1.2% to the working age population in Australia and 0.5% in Austria. In other countries, their maximal potential contribution is below 0.5%. This estimation represents the upper bound of the contribution of international students to the employed population.

Relative to the employed youth, this number is significantly higher in all countries and reaches a full 5% in Australia (Figure 7.10).

Figure 7.10. International students add up to 1% and more to the employed youth population in many countries

Estimation of the contribution of international students to employed population and employed youth, 2020

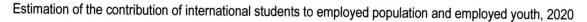

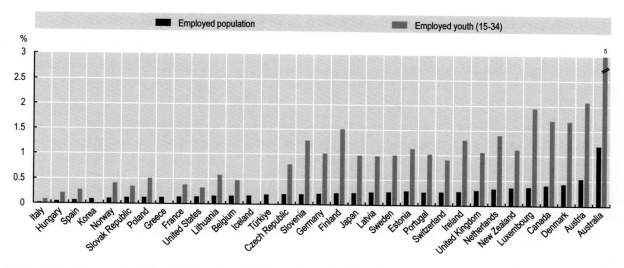

Notes: The estimated contribution of international students to the employed population assumes that the average international student works 34% of the maximal hours of work allowed per year by the permit rules. Available shares of international students working are used for Australia, Austria, Belgium, Denmark, France, Germany, Hungary, Ireland, Italy, Japan, Luxembourg, the Netherlands, Portugal, Spain, Sweden, United Kingdom and Unites States.
Source: OECD Migration Database.

StatLink https://stat.link/1lk7i2

Within this bound, the actual choice of international students to take up employment alongside their studies varies across countries. A proxy for European OECD countries can be obtained from labour force data on the employment of foreign-born students in tertiary education who arrived less than five years ago. These data show that about a third of all students in the EU are employed, with similar levels among foreign-born (34%) and native-born (35%), but higher shares among EU-born (42%) than non-EU-born (31%). Using the same approximation, about a third of international students in the United States are working (35%). In France and the United Kingdom, about one in four work. In Australia, according to the 2016 Census, about half of international students were in employment, mostly working part-time. The highest shares are observed in Switzerland and Denmark, where around 60% of international students are in employment, as well as in Japan, where this figure reaches 90%.

The labour market impact is not equally distributed across the country. It is strongly concentrated locally in the municipalities with tertiary education institutions, and within these, in the proximity of the areas where international students reside. Data from the 2019 European Labour Force Survey show that foreign-born students aged 15-34 in tertiary education who arrived less than five years ago are strongly overrepresented in urban areas. Eighty percent live in cities, compared with 53% of their native-born peers. Likewise, labour force data from the United States from 2019 show that among foreign-born students aged 15-34 in tertiary education who arrived less than five years ago, 53% lived in a principal city against 32% of their native-born peers.

International students are also concentrated in certain sectors, especially hospitality as this is a sector where labour needs are often outside of the regular university schedule and where entry barriers are low. According to the European labour force survey in 2019, a quarter of working non-EU students was employed in the accommodation and food service sector, compared with one in five EU-born students and one in ten native-born students. While native-born students are thus twice as likely to work in this sector than the overall population (10% vs 5%), non-EU-born international students are five times as likely (25% versus 5%). Compared to the overall population, international students are also strongly over-represented in the education sector, at 16% versus 11% for native-born students and 8% for the total population.

Long-term outcomes of international students who remain in the host country

Some tentative evidence on the long-term outcomes of international students is available from the 2021 European Labour Force Survey, which includes information on the (self-declared) reason for migration of immigrants for most major international student destinations in Europe. This information is synthesised in (Table 7.2).

In most countries for which data are available, five years after arrival, immigrants who arrived for education reasons (i.e. predominantly international students) have higher employment rates than the overall foreign- and native-born populations, but slightly below those who arrived as labour migrants. Overall in European OECD countries for which these data are available, three out of four of those who arrived for education purposes are in employment.

These data also show that international students, when in employment, tend to be able to put their formal qualifications in good use. The incidence of overqualification, which is the share of tertiary-educated who are working in jobs requiring only lower levels of education, is much lower for this group than for labour migrants or for migrants overall, in all countries with available data. Indeed, overall their overqualification rates are roughly the same as for their native-born peers and half of those of labour migrants or other migrant groups.

Likewise, a recent report by Statistics Canada has shown that shortly after admission as permanent labour migrants, those with previous Canadian study earned considerably more than those who did not study in Canada (Crossman, Lu and Hou, 2022[8]). This advantage was entirely due to their better language skills and higher likelihood to have worked in Canada. When compared only with immigrants who had similar language knowledge and Canadian work experience, those with Canadian study initally earned less, mostly because of their higher tendency to pursue further schooling in the early years after immigration. The benefit of Canadian study grew over time and around 10 years after immigration, permanent labour migrants with at least one year of Canadian study had significantly higher earnings than their peers with foreign degrees, even after controlling for other factors.

Table 7.2. Outcomes of previous international students who remain in the host country compared with other migrant groups

Selected European OECD countries, 2021

	Arrived for education	Arrived for work	All Foreign-born	Native-born
	Employment rate			
All (EU in OECD)	74.9%	75.6%	65.7%	68.3%
Germany	77.5%	81.1%	70.9%	77.8%
France	75.4%	73.4%	62.5%	67.2%
Italy	68.2%	74.9%	61.0%	58.1%
Spain	67.5%	72.1%	61.8%	63.1%
Sweden	72.4%	84.1%	66.1%	77.9%
	Overqualification rate			
All (EU in OECD)	19.3%	37.5%	33.1%	20.8%
Germany	15.1%	30.8%	30.5%	17.7%
France	18.6%	26.0%	28.1%	19.6%
Italy	23.1%	65.9%	49.3%	18.5%
Spain	32.0%	56.4%	51.9%	34.7%

Note: Employment rate for the foreign-born refers to individuals with at least 5 years of residence in the country. Overqualification is defined as persons in employment working in a job at ISCO Level 4-9 who have completed a tertiary degree (ISCED 5-8) and are not in education.
Source: OECD Secretariat calculations on the basis of data from the European Labour Force Survey (EU-LFS).

In Europe, the long-term impact of participation in the Erasmus programme (see Chapter 5) on later employment outcomes has also been relatively well studied. A recent overview of the literature found that participants tended to enjoy higher wages, were more likely to hold a managerial position, and undergo an international career (Crăciun, Orosz and Proteasa, 2020[31]). Likewise, for international students from Spain, participation in the Erasmus programme was found to have a positive effect on the probability of becoming an entrepreneur (Conti, Heckman and Pinto, 2016[32]).

Conclusion

International students are an increasingly important part of international migration flows. In the decade preceding the COVID-19 pandemic, the intake of international students rose significantly in most countries. International students have emerged as a key feeder for labour migration, with large and growing shares staying on for employment in their host countries after graduation.

Compared with other migrant groups, international students have a number of advantages in accessing to labour migration channels in host countries. They are "pre-integrated" in the host-country society and have often tied contacts with host-country labour markets due to part-time employment or internships. In addition, they have domestic credentials that are familiar to employers, facilitating labour market entry. Concerns about "Brain Drain", whether or not justified, are also less pressing than for other groups of educated workers recruited from less developed countries, as international students have acquired at least part of their human capital in host countries.

The above analysis has also provided a number of insights into the importance of specific policy levers. For example, countries approach tuition fees for international students in various ways. In countries with high fees, international student expenditure often accounts for a large share of services exports and for financing the tertiary education system. Countries with minimal or no fees, while not benefitting from the presence of international students in terms of the public purse, are able to declare the associated costs as official development assistance. The rationale behind counting costs for hosting international students towards ODA has been that international students will return home with their newly formed human capital, which is means of development assistance. The increasing numbers of students remaining, and the efforts of countries to retain international graduates, might however come into conflict with this objective.

Overall, there seem to be clear benefits associated with international student migration, notably in terms of labour market integration. At the same time, their rising importance as a feeder for labour migration, both in absolute terms and relative to other channels, also raises questions whether international students are meeting the exact skills needs for which labour migration pathways are designed. While labour migration through this channel is greatly facilitated, actual work skills have not been "tested" in any meaningful way. International student migration is also not a solution to the shortages in mid- and lower-skilled segments of the labour markets that many OECD countries are facing. Likewise, the high concentration of international students in capital cities in many countries suggests that international student migration could often exacerbate regional disparities.

A balance should be maintained in the migration system to avoid that countries become overly dependent on this particular channel, and are aware of its specificities. That notwithstanding, attracting international students has broad economic payoff, including through better post-study outcomes of international students compared with other migrant groups. The available evidence shows that countries are becoming better at retaining students who have studied in their countries.

References

Australian Department of Education, Skills and Employment (2021), *Australian Strategy for International Education 2021-2030 - Department of Education, Skills and Employment, Australian Government*, https://www.dese.gov.au/australian-strategy-international-education-2021-2030/resources/australian-strategy-international-education-2021-2030 (accessed on 20 May 2022). [3]

Birrell, B. (2019), "Overseas students are driving Australia's Net Overseas Migration tide", https://tapri.org.au/wp-content/uploads/2019/04/Overseas-students-are-driving-NOM-final-18-April-2019.pdf (accessed on 11 April 2022). [21]

Bundesamt für Statistik (2017), *Hochschulabsolventinnen und -absolventen mit Migrationshintergrund - Arbeitsmarktintegration und Abwanderung in 2015*, http://www.bfs.admin.ch/bfs/de/home/statistiken/kataloge-datenbanken/publikationen.assetdetail.4104529.html (accessed on 10 May 2022). [19]

Campus France (2014), *Beyond Influence: the Economic Impact of International Students in France*, http://www.campusfrance.org (accessed on 19 May 2022). [28]

Centraal Plaanbureau (2019), *De economische effecten van internationalisering in het hoger onderwijs en mbo*, https://www.cpb.nl/de-economische-effecten-van-internationalisering-het-hoger-onderwijs-en-mbo-0 (accessed on 19 May 2022). [42]

Choi, Y., E. Crossman and F. Hou (2021), "International students as a source of labour supply: Transition to permanent residency", https://doi.org/10.25318/36280001202100600002-eng. [46]

Conti, G., J. Heckman and R. Pinto (2016), "The Effects of Two Influential Early Childhood Interventions on Health and Healthy Behaviour", *The Economic Journal*, Vol. 126/598, https://doi.org/10.1111/ecoj.12420. [32]

Crăciun, D., K. Orosz and V. Proteasa (2020), "Does Erasmus Mobility Increase Employability? Using Register Data to Investigate the Labour Market Outcomes of University Graduates", in *European Higher Education Area: Challenges for a New Decade*, Springer International Publishing, Cham, https://doi.org/10.1007/978-3-030-56316-5_8.   [31]

Crossman, E., Y. Lu and F. Hou (2022), *International students as a source of labour supply: Engagement in the labour market after graduation*, Statistics Canada, https://doi.org/10.25318/36280001202101200002-eng.   [8]

Danish Ministry of Higher Education and Science (2018), *More international graduates must stay and work in Denmark*, http://ufm.dk/en/newsroom/press-releases/2018/more-international-graduates-must-stay-and-work-in-denmark (accessed on 8 April 2022).   [10]

De Witte, K. and M. Soncin (2021), "Do international classes pay off? A cost-benefit analysis of the internationalisation of higher education in Flanders", *Higher Education*, Vol. 82/3, pp. 459-476, https://doi.org/10.1007/s10734-021-00737-0.   [34]

Deloitte Access Economics (2015), *The value of international education to Australia*, http://www.internationaleducation.gov.au. (accessed on 19 May 2022).   [33]

Domnïca Certus (2016), *Number of foreign students in Latvia has trebled in 3 years :: The Baltic Course | Baltic States news & analytics*, International Internet Magazine, http://www.baltic-course.com/eng/education/?doc=121527 (accessed on 19 May 2022).   [41]

DZS, C. (2022), *Survey among international alumni of Czech universities*, http://www.dzs.cz/sites/default/files/2022-06/Survey%20among%20international%20alumni%20of%20Czech%20universities_2022_0.pdf (accessed on 5 August 2022).   [9]

European Commission (2018), *Study on the movement of skilled labour: Final report*, European Commission, Brussels, https://doi.org/10.2767/378144 (accessed on 15 April 2022).   [24]

European Migration Network (2018), *Attracting and retaining international students in the EU*, http://ec.europa.eu/home-affairs/system/files/2019-09/00_eu_international_students_2018_synthesis_report.pdf (accessed on 18 May 2022).   [1]

EUROSTAT (2021), *Residence permits (migr_res)*, https://ec.europa.eu/eurostat/cache/metadata/en/migr_res_esms.htm (accessed on 11 April 2022).   [25]

Federale Overheidsdienst (2017), "Socio-economische monitoring 2017", https://werk.belgie.be/nl/publicaties/socio-economische-monitoring-2017-arbeidsmarkt-en-origine.   [7]

Global Affairs Canada (2020), *Economic impact of international education in Canada 2017-2018*, Canmac Economics Limited, https://www.international.gc.ca/education/report-rapport/impact-2018/index.aspx?lang=eng (accessed on 19 May 2022).   [35]

Government of New Zealand (2018), *International Education Strategy 2018 – 2030 » He Rautaki MĀtauranga A Ao*, http://www.enz.govt.nz/assets/Uploads/International-Education-Strategy-2018-2030.pdf (accessed on 23 May 2022).   [4]

Grasset and Menéndez (2020), "The Economic Impact of International Students in Spain", http://agrilife.org/cromptonrpts/files/2011/06/3_4_7.pdf (accessed on 19 May 2022).   [36]

Hanganu, E. (2015), "Bleibequoten von internationalen Studierenden im Zielstaaten-Vergleich", http://www.bamf.de/SharedDocs/Anlagen/DE/Forschung/Forschungsberichte/Kurzberichte/artikel-auswertung-zu-absolventenstudiefb23.pdf?__blob=publicationFile&v=12 (accessed on 10 August 2022). [14]

Indecon International Economic Consultants (2019), *Indecon Independent Assessment of the Economic and Social Impact of Irish Universities*, http://www.indecon.ie (accessed on 19 May 2022). [40]

London Economics (2021), *The costs and benefits of international higher education students to the UK economy*, https://londoneconomics.co.uk/blog/publication/the-costs-and-benefits-of-international-higher-education-students-to-the-uk-economy-september-2021/ (accessed on 19 May 2022). [38]

Market Economics Limited (2018), *Economic Valuation of International Education in NZ 2018*, m.e consulting. [43]

Mathies, C. and H. Karhunen (2020), "Do they stay or go? Analysis of international students in Finland", *Globalisation, Societies and Education*, Vol. 19/3, pp. 298-310, https://doi.org/10.1080/14767724.2020.1816926. [12]

Ministère de l'Intérieur (2021), *Les chiffres clés de l'immigration 2020*, https://www.immigration.interieur.gouv.fr/Info-ressources/Actualites/Focus/Nouveaute-les-chiffres-cles-de-l-immigration-2020-en-28-fiches (accessed on 7 April 2022). [13]

Ministry of Education Korea (2021), *Education Statistics Analysis 2021 - Higher Education Statistics. Table | 표 Ⅰ-2-35 | 연도별 성별 국내 비학위과정 외국인 연수생수(2004~2021)*, https://moe.go.kr/boardCnts/viewRenew.do?boardID=351&boardSeq=90276&lev=0&searchType=null&statusYN=W&page=1&s=moe&m=0310&opType=N (accessed on 17 June 2022). [15]

Nafsa (2021), *New NAFSA Data Show Largest Ever Drop in International Student Economic Contributions to the U.S.*, https://www.nafsa.org/about/about-nafsa/new-nafsa-data-show-largest-ever-drop-international-student-economic (accessed on 19 May 2022). [45]

New Zealand Ministry of Education (2017), *Moving places. Destinations and earnings of international graduates*, Ministry of Education, http://www.educationcounts.govt.nz/__data/assets/pdf_file/0004/179959/Moving-Places-Destinations-and-earnings-of-international-graduates.pdf (accessed on 7 March 2022). [18]

NUFFIC, T. (2022), *Stayrates of international graduates*, https://www.nuffic.nl/en/subjects/facts-and-figures/stayrates-of-international-graduates (accessed on 7 April 2022). [16]

OECD (2019), *International Migration Outlook 2019*, OECD Publishing, Paris, https://doi.org/10.1787/c3e35eec-en. [30]

OECD (2017), *OECD Economic Surveys: Latvia 2017*, OECD Publishing, Paris, https://doi.org/10.1787/eco_surveys-lva-2017-en. [2]

OECD (2011), *International Migration Outlook 2011*, OECD Publishing, Paris, https://doi.org/10.1787/migr_outlook-2011-en. [22]

Oxford Economics (2020), *Multiplying Economic Value: The Impact of Swedish Universities*, Oxford Economics, London, https://suhf.se/app/uploads/2020/10/Multiplying-Economic-Value-The-Impact-of-Swedish-Universities-Oxford-Economics-2020.pdf. [44]

Prognos (2013), *The Financial Impact of Cross-border Student Mobility on the Economy of the Host Country*, https://siesca.uned.ac.cr/images/publicaciones/Financial_impact_of_cross-border_student.pdf. [29]

Statistics Austria (2021), *Wegzüge und Berufseinstieg von Universitätsabsolventinnen und -absolventen 2021*, Statistics Austria. [6]

Statistics Canada (2020), "Student pathways through postsecondary education", https://www150.statcan.gc.ca/n1/en/daily-quotidien/200917/dq200917b-eng.pdf?st=tuKON83D (accessed on 9 May 2022). [26]

Statistics Estonia (2022), *International students and graduates continue to contribute more in taxes to the Estonian economy*, https://www.stat.ee/en/uudised/valisuliopilaste-ja-vilistlaste-maksupanus-eesti-majandusse-suurenes-taas. [37]

Statistics Estonia (2019), *Välisüliõpilase majanduslik mõju. Eesti tööturul osalemine 2019*, Statistics Estonia, http://www.stat.ee/sites/default/files/2021-01/v%C3%A4lis%C3%BCli%C3%B5pilaste%20majanduslik%20m%C3%B5ju_bl3mm.pdf (accessed on 8 April 2022). [11]

Statistics Norway (2020), *Hvordan går det med innvandrere som fullfører en bachelor- eller mastergrad i Norge?*, http://www.ssb.no/utdanning/artikler-og-publikasjoner/hvordan-gar-det-med-innvandrere-som-fullforer-en-bachelor-eller-mastergrad-i-norge (accessed on 25 March 2022). [17]

Tempus Public Foundation (2020), *Measuring the economic impacts of inbound higher education mobility*, https://tka.hu/publication/14367/measuring-the-economic-impacts-of-inbound-higher-education-mobility (accessed on 19 May 2022). [39]

The Treasury and the Department of Home Affairs (2018), *Shaping a Nation*, http://research.treasury.gov.au/external-paper/shaping-a-nation (accessed on 16 June 2022). [5]

UK Department for Education (2022), *Graduate outcomes (LEO), Tax Year 2018-19*, https://explore-education-statistics.service.gov.uk/find-statistics/graduate-outcomes-leo/2018-19#dataBlock-cb5bd289-e28a-4996-93f3-d2c70e9fc52b-tables (accessed on 11 April 2022). [20]

United States Immigration and Customs Enforcement (2022), *Homeland Security Investigations. Student and Exchange Visitor Program. Data shared with the OECD June 2022.* [27]

Weisser, R. (2016), "Internationally mobile students and their post-graduation migratory behaviour: An analysis of determinants of student mobility and retention rates in the EU", *OECD Social, Employment and Migration Working Papers*, No. 186, OECD Publishing, Paris, https://doi.org/10.1787/5jlwxbvmb5zt-en. [23]

Annex 7.A. Supplementary table

Annex Table 7.A.1. Recent studies on the economic impact of international students in OECD countries

	Approach and data	Estimated economic impact	Years analysed	Author
AUS	To model the economic contribution from student expenditure on fees and living expenses, different lines of revenues were considered.	International education was estimated to contribute AUD 17.1 billion to Australia's GDP in 2014/15. The export revenues were estimated to support over 130 700 Full Time Equivalent (FTE) employees in 2014/15,, accounting for 1.3% of Australia's total employment.	2014/15	(Deloitte Access Economics, 2015[33])
AUT	Based on an analysis of the literature, an input-output model was developed to quantify the economic contribution of international students.	The value added calculated for international students amounted to around EUR 8 000 per head. Every 10 international students, 15 jobs were estimated to be added to the economy (8 800 in aggregate). The aggregate value added contributed by each graduate amounted to around EUR 74 000.	2011	(Prognos, 2013[29])
BEL (Flanders)	The methodology used a cost-benefit analysis, by which the direct and indirect benefits and costs of international students are calculated. The long-term impact of international students is examined by estimating the stay rate after graduation and the subsequent contribution to the national economy. Data on students from the Flemish Ministry of Education and stay rates data are from the Flemish Government Social Security Data.	Regarding direct contribution: the private social contribution made by students (e.g. due to student jobs) is close to EUR 48 million, tuition fee income is close to EUR 57 million, while the non-tuition fee income from spending amounts to nearly EUR 630 million. Furthermore, long-term benefits outweigh the costs, with a long-term net benefit estimated between EUR 4.2 and 5.6 billion.	2015/16	(De Witte and Soncin, 2021[34])
CAN	An input-output model was built upon extensive secondary research involving reviewing literature, collecting existing statistical data and information, as well as consultations with representatives from the provincial and territorial education sectors, and representatives from organisations promoting and researching trends in international education in Canada and/or its provinces.	In 2018, the combined direct and indirect GDP contribution of all student expenditures amounted to CAD 19.7 billion, considering not only the sectors directly impacted by international student spending, but also the many other industries in the supply chain of those directly impacted. In terms of employment, 218 577 jobs were associated with international students.	2020	(Global Affairs Canada, 2020[35])

	Approach and data	Estimated economic impact	Years analysed	Author
CHE	Based on an analysis of the literature and a survey, an input-output model was developed to quantify the economic contribution of international students.	The gross value added per student amounted to EUR 17 500. For every 10 international students, 18 jobs are estimated to be added to the economy (4 100 in aggregate). The aggregate gross value-added effect per head was estimated around EUR 24 400.	2011	(Prognos, 2013[29])
DEU	Based on an analysis of the literature and national data, an input-output model was developed to quantify the economic contribution of international students.	International students generated EUR 400 million in tax revenues and created 22 000 jobs. Public expenditure is estimated to amortise if 30% of international graduates stay and work in Germany for at least five years.	2011	(Prognos, 2013[29])
DNK	A cost-benefit analysis was carried out by the Danish Ministry of Education from national registry data. The average net contribution per international student are calculated on the basis of students from the period 2004-15 with a focus on the year groups that started in the period 2004-07. This follows the behaviour of the international students for up to 11 years after the start of their studies.	Approximately one in four international students in the business academy and professional bachelor programs, respectively, was estimated to make a positive net contribution to public finances. In the master's programs, a little more than one in three was estimated to make a positive net contribution. Overall,, including also those who left Denmark immediately after graduating, each student contributed on average between DKK 2000-7 500 per year from the start of studies.	2004 to 2016	(Danish Ministry of Higher Education and Science, 2018[10])
ESP	The estimation technique was based on an input-output model. Data are from various public and private educational institutions in Spain.	International students made an overall economic contribution to the Spanish economy amounting to EUR 3.7 billion (with a multiplier effect of 2.27).	2018/19	(Grasset and Menéndez, 2020[35])
EST	Calculations were made from population census data collected by Statistics Estonia.	International students paid EUR 3.6 million in income tax and EUR 7.8 million in social contributions. The total tax receipts from international students who graduated in academic year 2019/20 and continued working in Estonia was estimated EUR 4.5 million.	2019/20	(Statistics Estonia, 2022[37])
FRA	Exports approach built on survey data. 4 200 questionnaires were answered by a representative sample of the international students who had studied in France for at least 3 months in the previous 3 years, or who had started their study programs more than 3 months before the survey.	International students contributed EUR 4 billion to the French economy and 11 000 jobs to the tourism industry.	2013	(Campus France, 2014[28])
GBR	The approach adopted was an input-output model. The analysis focused on the aggregate economic benefits and costs to the UK economy associated with the 272 920 international students commencing their studies in 2018/19, taking account of the impact associated with these students over the entire duration of their study in the United Kingdom (adjusted for completion rates).	The 2018/19 cohort of international students delivered a net economic benefit of GBP 25.9 billion to the United Kingdom. This is a 19% increase in real terms from the net benefit found for the 2015/16 cohort of international students reported in previous studies.	2018/19	(London Economics, 2021[38])

	Approach and data	Estimated economic impact	Years analysed	Author
HUN	Mixed methodology, using expert interviews and focus group studies as well as a survey and administrative data.	Overall, the direct economic contribution by the students and their guests was around HUF 181 billion (about EUR 543 million) through fees, living expenses, and tourism. Through their spending, students have an average employment effect of 8.37 workers added per 100 students. Considering the indirect effects and the intersectoral relations, the employment effect is close to 20 000 added jobs. Besides, students' spending also generated public revenues of around HUF 11 billion (EUR 33 million).	2019/20	(Tempus Public Foundation, 2020[39])
IRL	Contribution of tuition fees to the economy was estimated with export data from the Irish University Authority, while non-tuition fee expenses come from the Higher Education Authority's student survey.	Net contribution of international students from tuition fees was around EUR 216 million. The estimated total non-tuition expenditure by international students was of EUR 119.5 million. The total annual export income generated for the Irish economy by international students was around EUR 336 million.	2017/18	(Indecon International Economic Consultants, 2019[40])
LVA	The approach used was an input-output model built on a survey of students in Latvia in the 2015/16 academic year. For the analysis of the indirect effects, OECD multipliers have been used.	International students directly contributed around EUR 73 million to the Latvian economy. The indirect contribution was estimated around EUR 75 million. The total impact of international students on the Latvian economy was estimated to be around EUR 148 million (0.61% of GDP). Also, they contributed about EUR 20 million a year to the Latvian budget in taxes and created about 1 474 jobs (2.7 for every 10 students).	2015/16	(Domnica Certus, 2016[41])
NLD	Microdata from the Dutch Central Bureau of Statistics were used to calculate the chances of staying and subsequent labour market outcomes. For the calculation of costs and benefits, a distinction was made according to type of education and origin (EEA or non-EEA).	The balance of income and costs during and after the study is positive for both EEA and non-EEA students, but the positive balance is much larger for students from non-EEA countries. The labour market participation rate of foreign vocational school and university graduates who continue to live in the Netherlands after studies is lower than the labour participation rate of Dutch-born graduates.	2006 to 2017	(Centraal Plaanbureau, 2019[42])
NZL	The economic contribution associated with international students' spending was estimated using a multi-regional input-output model. The assessment was delivered using a staged approach with a survey to collect information.	International education was estimated to deliver an economic contribution of NZD 5.1 billion to the New Zealand economy (4.8 on-shore and 0.3 off-shore) and supported an estimated 47 490 jobs. Visiting guests added a further NZD 460 million to the economy.	2017	(Market Economics Limited, 2018[43])

	Approach and data	Estimated economic impact	Years analysed	Author
POL	Based on an analysis of the literature, an input-output model was developed to quantify the economic contribution of international students.	The gross value added per student amounted to EUR 3 900. Every 10 international students add 23 jobs to the economy (5 700 in aggregate). The aggregate gross value-added effect per head was EUR 22 100. The long-term tax revenues from indirect taxes on consumer goods and services as well as direct taxes on the earnings arising from job creation were around EUR 1 200.	2011	(Prognos, 2013[29])
SWE	For the calculations, an input-output model built on Swedish Higher Education Authority's data was employed.	International students' expenditure amounted to an estimated SEK 2.4 billion in the year under study, supporting around 2 900 jobs. The economic activity and employment sustained by international students' subsistence spending generated SEK 660 million in tax revenues for the Swedish national and municipal government.	2017/18	(Oxford Economics, 2020[44])
USA	The approach adopted was exports-based. Tuition and living expense data come from the U.S. Department of Education's National Center of Educational Statistics Integrated Postsecondary Education Data System (IPEDS). Datasets used to calculate the number of jobs created or supported came from the U.S. Department of Commerce, specifically International Trade Administration and Bureau of Economic Analysis.	International students contributed USD 28.4 billion to the economy and supported 306 308 jobs. For every three international students, one US job is created and supported by spending occurring in the higher education, accommodation, dining, retail, and transportation sectors.	2020/21	(Nafsa, 2021[45])

Notes

[1] This work was produced with the financial support of the German Federal Ministry of Education and Research. It includes a contribution by Giacomo Boffi (Consultant to the OECD).

[2] For the calculation of retention data, international students are defined as foreign individuals who obtained a permit for study purposes. The use of permit statistics generally does not allow to include data on individuals benefiting from free mobility schemes, such as intra-European mobility.

[3] Data from the Australian Government Department of Education, Skills and Employment show that international students in Australia are more likely to graduate than domestic students, and to have shorter durations of study. Overall, 70% of international students at bachelor level who started in 2016 had graduated four years later. This compares to just 43% of domestic students. Nine years after starting their bachelor's degree studies in 2011, 73% of domestic students had graduated, compared with 80% for international students.

[4] These findings for Canada are in line with earlier results that show that about three in ten international students who arrived in Canada between 2005 and 2009 became permanent residents within ten years of arrival (Choi, Crossman and Hou, 2021[46]).

8 Country notes: Recent changes in migration movements and policies

Australia

Foreign-born population – 2021	29.2% of the population	Main countries of birth:
Size: 7.5 million, 51% of women	Evolution since 2011: +25%	United Kingdom (16%), China (9%), India (9%)

In 2020, Australia received 165 000 new immigrants on a long-term or permanent basis (including changes of status), -15.4% compared to 2019. This figure comprises 7.2% immigrants benefitting from free mobility, 26.6% labour migrants, 58.2% family members (including accompanying family) and 8% humanitarian migrants. Around 123 000 permits were issued to tertiary-level international students and 207 000 to temporary and seasonal labour migrants.

India, China and the United Kingdom were the top three nationalities of newcomers in 2020. Among the top 15 countries of origin, Nepal registered the strongest increase (800) and New Zealand the largest decrease (-9 400) in flows to Australia compared to the previous year.

In 2021, the number of first asylum applicants decreased by -26%, to reach around 14 100. The majority of applicants came from Malaysia (2 100), China (2000) and Afghanistan (1 100). The largest increase since 2020 concerned nationals of Afghanistan (800) and the largest decrease nationals of Malaysia (-1 900). Of the 22 000 decisions taken in 2021, 10% were positive.

For 2021-22, the Migration Program planning level was maintained at 160 000 places. The number will remain the same for 2022-23, but the allocation will shift to favour the Skilled category (109 900 compared to 79 600 for 2021-22) to ease critical workforce shortages and support the economic recovery from COVID-19. To support social cohesion outcomes and family reunification, from 2022-23 the Partner visa category will move to a demand driven model and, consequently, will no longer be subject to a ceiling.

On 23 May 2022, the Hon. Anthony Albanese MP was sworn in as the 31st Prime Minister of Australia. The Australian Government is giving active consideration to the size and composition of the Permanent Migration Program for 2022-23 and beyond.

Australia's international border measures were progressively introduced from February 2020 and were a key tool in keeping COVID-19 at manageable levels. Australia's international border remained largely closed until 1 November 2021 when it began a staged reopening to fully vaccinated Australian citizens and permanent residents. On 15 December 2021, certain fully vaccinated visa holders no longer needed to apply for a travel exemption to enter Australia. On 21 February 2022, Australia implemented the third major step in reopening to all remaining fully vaccinated visa holders, predominantly tourists. The final stage of reopening occurred on 6 July 2022 when the remaining border restrictions for entering Australia ceased.

Visa extensions (through 31 December 2022) were made available for Prospective Marriage visa holders who were unable to travel to Australia due to travel restrictions.

To support international students impacted by COVID-19, the relaxation of the working hours requirement was extended. Temporary Graduate Visa holders were eligible for visa extensions or a second visa if they lost time in Australia. The stay period for Masters by Coursework applicants was increased from two to three years. Graduate Work Stream applicants no longer need to nominate an occupation from the skilled occupation list.

Two new visa streams for eligible Hong Kong and British National (Overseas) passport holders opened on 5 March 2022, providing more pathways to permanent residence in Australia.

Effective from 1 July 2022, certain Temporary Work and Temporary Skill Shortage visa holders currently working in Australia are able to apply for permanent residency under the Employer Nomination Scheme.

In line with its commitment under the Global Compact on Refugees to expand access to third-country solutions, Australia is a core member of the Global Task Force on Refugee Labour Mobility and is committed to working with the international community to foster global dialogue on labour complementary pathways for refugees and displaced people.

In 2021, the government, working in collaboration with Talent Beyond Boundaries, commenced the Skilled Refugee Labour Agreement pilot programme aimed at providing skilled refugees with a pathway to live and work in Australia.

The 2021-22 Humanitarian Program was set at 13 750 places maintaining Australia's long-term commitment to resettlement while also taking account of the challenges associated with COVID-19.

For further information: https://immi.homeaffairs.gov.au/

Key figures on immigration and emigration – Australia

Long-term immigration flows
2020 (Source: OECD)

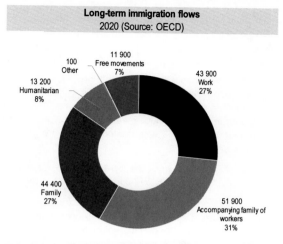

Temporary migration
(Sources: OECD, UNHCR)

Temporary labour migration

	2020	2020/19
Working holidaymakers	149 250	- 29%
Seasonal workers	9 820	- 19%
Intra-company transfers	1 840	- 35%
Other temporary workers	43 400	- 35%

Education

	2020	2020/19
International students	122 600	- 29%
Trainees	2 960	- 9%

Humanitarian

	2021	2021/20
Asylum seekers	14 150	- 26%

Inflows of top 10 nationalities
(national definition)

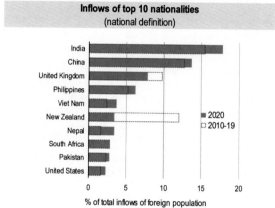

% of total inflows of foreign population

Emigration of Australians to OECD countries
(national definition)

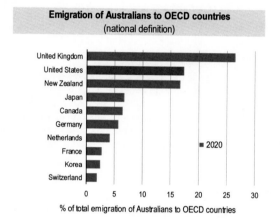

% of total emigration of Australians to OECD countries

Components of population growth

	2021 Per 1 000 inhabitants	2021/20 difference
Total	5.0	+0.6
Natural increase	5.4	+0.3
Net migration plus statistical adjustments	-0.4	+0.3

Annual remittances

	Million current USD	Annual change %	Share in GDP %
Inflows (2021)	922	-47.4	+0.1
Outflows (2021)	3 804	-12.7	+0.2

Labour market outcomes
2021

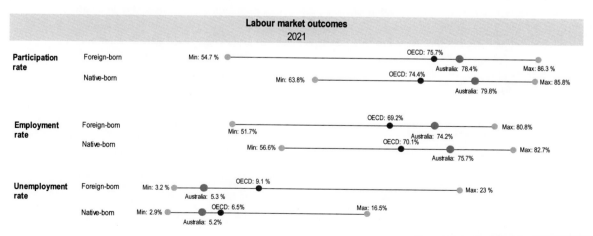

Austria

Foreign-born population – 2021	19.9% of the population	Main countries of birth:
Size: 1.8 million, 51% of women	Evolution since 2011: +39%	Germany (14%), Bosnia and Herzegovina (10%), Türkiye (9%)

In 2020, Austria received 63 000 new immigrants on a long-term or permanent basis (including changes of status and free mobility), -23.5% compared to 2019. This figure comprises 70% immigrants benefitting from free mobility, 7.4% labour migrants, 11.4% family members (including accompanying family) and 10.9% humanitarian migrants. Around 2 200 permits were issued to tertiary-level international students and 9 300 to temporary and seasonal labour migrants (excluding intra-EU migration). In addition, 232 000 intra-EU postings were recorded in 2020, a decrease of -28% compared to 2019. These posted workers are generally on short-term contracts.

Germany, Romania and Hungary were the top three nationalities of newcomers in 2020. Among the top 15 countries of origin, Syria registered the strongest increase (2 100) and Romania the largest decrease (-2 800) in flows to Austria compared to the previous year.

In 2021, the number of first asylum applicants increased by 200%, to reach around 37 000. The majority of applicants came from Syria (16 000), Afghanistan (7 800) and Morocco (1 800). The largest increase since 2020 concerned nationals of Syria (10 600) and the largest decrease nationals of Russia (-20). Of the 19 000 decisions taken in 2021, 65% were positive.

In January 2022, the revised shortage list for red-white-red (R-W-R) cards came into force, extending the federal list by 21 occupations. With the exception of Vienna, individual provinces added other occupations to their shortage lists in recognition of local conditions.

A reform package of the R-W-R-Card, the system in place for the recruitment of (highly) skilled third-country citizens, is planned for summer 2022. The aim is to accelerate the one-stop-shop (while procedures still remain with the residence authorities and Public Employment Service) and establish a digital platform via the existing Austrian Business Agency (ABA-Unit "Work in Austria") to provide co-ordinated information and support services to potential employers as well as job seekers. A monitoring system will control the duration and efficiency of search processes using digital procedures, thereby reducing bureaucracy and speeding-up matching. Some aspects of the reform package were in place by the end of 2021, with the expectation of being in full operation by mid-2022.

The existing Austrian Business Agency has been linked to EURES and can thus access job offers anywhere in the European Economic Area and Switzerland. This will be an important facilitator for job-matching of migrant workers and especially of Ukrainians in their current situation as displaced persons.

In December 2021, an amendment to the Foreign Worker Act was accepted by parliament, facilitating access to annual employment permits for third-country "permanent" seasonal workers who work regularly (three years within the last five years: 2017-21) in tourism or agriculture/forestry. Until end of 2022, "permanent" seasonal workers may register for their special status with the Public Employment Service. These registered seasonal workers may access seasonal work for a maximum of 9 months without labour market testing. They are not included in the seasonal worker quota. Within the reform package of the R-W-R-Card of summer 2022, it is planned that this group of workers may even apply for a special Red-White-Red Card under facilitated conditions if a few additional requirements have been fulfilled.

In March 2022, implementing an EU Council decision, the Austrian Government introduced regulation to issue, upon application, special residence permits to displaced persons from Ukraine receiving relevant temporary protection in Austria. Since then Austrian employers may be issued work permits for holders of such a residence permit without labour market test/quota.

For further information: www.migration.gv.at | www.bmeia.gv.at | www.bmi.gv.at | www.sozialministerium.at

Key figures on immigration and emigration – Austria

Long-term immigration flows
2020 (Source: OECD)

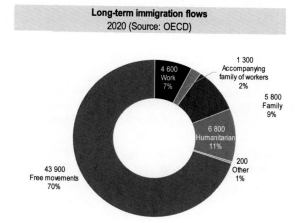

- 4 600 Work 7%
- 1 300 Accompanying family of workers 2%
- 5 800 Family 9%
- 6 800 Humanitarian 11%
- 200 Other 1%
- 43 900 Free movements 70%

Temporary migration
(Sources: OECD, Eurostat)

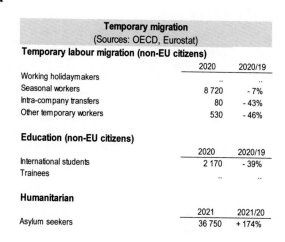

Temporary labour migration (non-EU citizens)

	2020	2020/19
Working holidaymakers	..	
Seasonal workers	8 720	- 7%
Intra-company transfers	80	- 43%
Other temporary workers	530	- 46%

Education (non-EU citizens)

	2020	2020/19
International students	2 170	- 39%
Trainees	..	..

Humanitarian

	2021	2021/20
Asylum seekers	36 750	+ 174%

Inflows of top 10 nationalities
(national definition)

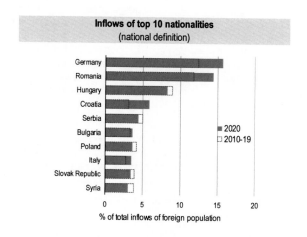

Germany, Romania, Hungary, Croatia, Serbia, Bulgaria, Poland, Italy, Slovak Republic, Syria

■ 2020
□ 2010-19

% of total inflows of foreign population

Emigration of Austrians to OECD countries
(national definition)

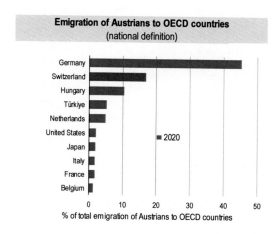

Germany, Switzerland, Hungary, Türkiye, Netherlands, United States, Japan, Italy, France, Belgium

■ 2020

% of total emigration of Austrians to OECD countries

Components of population growth

	2021 Per 1 000 inhabitants	2021/20 difference
Total	5.2	+1.7
Natural increase	-0.7	+0.2
Net migration plus statistical adjustments	5.8	+1.4

Annual remittances

	Million current USD	Annual change %	Share in GDP %
Inflows (2021)	3 167	+7.3	+0.7
Outflows (2021)	7 016	+13.1	+1.5

Labour market outcomes
2021

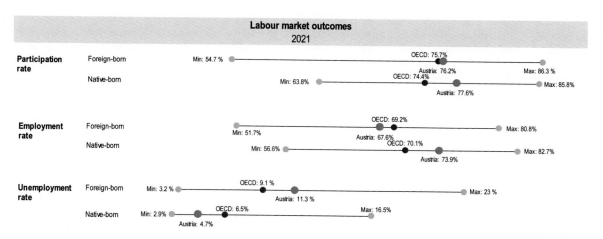

Participation rate
- Foreign-born: Min: 54.7 %, OECD: 75.7%, Austria: 76.2%, Max: 86.3 %
- Native-born: Min: 63.8%, OECD: 74.4%, Austria: 77.6%, Max: 85.8%

Employment rate
- Foreign-born: Min: 51.7%, OECD: 69.2%, Austria: 67.6%, Max: 80.8%
- Native-born: Min: 56.6%, OECD: 70.1%, Austria: 73.9%, Max: 82.7%

Unemployment rate
- Foreign-born: Min: 3.2 %, OECD: 9.1 %, Austria: 11.3 %, Max: 23 %
- Native-born: Min: 2.9%, OECD: 6.5%, Austria: 4.7%, Max: 16.5%

StatLink ⁜ℐ⌁ https://stat.link/45v7p6

Belgium

Foreign-born population – 2021	17.9% of the population	Main countries of birth:
Size: 2.1 million, 51% of women	Evolution since 2011: +28%	Germany (14%), Bosnia and Herzegovina (10%), Türkiye (9%)

In 2020, Belgium received 92 000 new immigrants on a long-term or permanent basis (including changes of status and free mobility), -19% compared to 2019. This figure comprises 61.8% immigrants benefitting from free mobility, 3.7% labour migrants, 28.1% family members (including accompanying family) and 6.4% humanitarian migrants. Around 5 700 permits were issued to tertiary-level international students. In addition, 169 000 intra-EU postings were recorded in 2020, a decrease of -23% compared to 2019. These posted workers are generally on short-term contracts.

Romania, France and the Netherlands were the top three nationalities of newcomers in 2020. Among the top 15 countries of origin, Romania registered the largest decrease (-3 000) in flows to Belgium compared to the previous year.

In 2021, the number of first asylum applicants increased by 51.6%, to reach around 20 000. The majority of applicants came from Afghanistan (5 200), Syria (1 800) and Eritrea (1 500). The largest increase since 2020 concerned nationals of Afghanistan (2 800) and the largest decrease nationals of Brazil (-400). Of the 21 000 decisions taken in 2021, 44% were positive.

The Belgian Government plans to adopt a new Migration Code in order to ensure greater clarity of the Belgian Aliens Act, to safeguard legal certainty and to avoid inconsistencies. Furthermore, extra funding was granted to the State Secretary to recruit staff for the Asylum and Migration Services and to deal with the shortage of reception places. This shortage, due to numerous reasons (backlog in processing applications for international protection, influx after the Taliban takeover in Afghanistan, floods in Wallonia damaging reception places, etc.), hindered people to apply for international protection, thus unable to receive the rights pertaining to this (so called "bed, bath, bread"). An Inter-Ministerial Conference on Migration and Integration was set up to establish greater coherence across policy levels. A website providing a one-stop shop platform to launch an application for a single permit as well as a website providing information on migration and asylum have been established. Last but not least, COVID-19 travel restrictions in Belgium were gradually relaxed throughout the year.

On 11 July 2021, the Belgian Aliens Act was amended. The new provisions amended chapter II of the Alien Act on International Students in order to implement the Directive EC/2016/801 into Belgian law. The main change is the introduction of a "Search Year" residence card allowing third-country nationals who have completed their higher education studies in Belgium to stay for an additional year to seek employment or start a business.

On 16 December 2021, Belgium fully implemented the EU Directive to grant intra-corporate transferees (ICT) permits. A partial implementation of the Directive in October 2020 had allowed applications to be submitted.

Following the Taliban takeover in Afghanistan, the Belgian Government decided in August 2021 to suspend any forced or voluntary return of irregular migrants to the country until the situation improves. The Commissioner General for Refugees and Stateless Persons (CGRS) announced a temporary suspension of decisions, initially until the end of September, then renewed several times, until it was lifted in March 2022.

On 23 May 2021, 475 undocumented migrants, mostly from South Asia and North Africa, went on a hunger strike to obtain legal residency in Belgium. The Secretary of State appointed a Special Envoy to act as conciliatory figure between the government and the hunger strikers. On 22 July, the strike ended after authorities signalled their willingness to renegotiate individual situations. In June 2022, the 422 applications for regularisation (for 516 individuals) were examined; 55 applications (for 90 individuals) received a positive result.

In July 2021, the Flemish Government approved a decree to implement a new civic integration programme. The programme includes four main steps: learning Dutch, becoming economically independent, learning Flemish culture, and taking part in a 40-hour tandem-team programme with a Flemish citizen, followed by a final integration exam. Participation in the programme is upon payment of a fee. The legislation came into force in March 2022.

For further information: www.dofi.ibz.be | www.emploi.belgique.be | www.myria.be | www.statbel.fgov.be

Key figures on immigration and emigration – Belgium

Long-term immigration flows
2020 (Source: OECD)

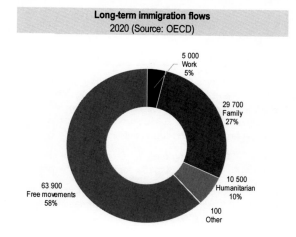

- 5 000 Work 5%
- 29 700 Family 27%
- 10 500 Humanitarian 10%
- 100 Other
- 63 900 Free movements 58%

Temporary migration
(Source: Eurostat)

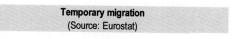

Temporary migration (non-EU citizens)

	2020	2020/19
Employment reasons	650	- 54%
Family reasons	7 190	- 24%
Education reasons	1 200	+ 10%
Other reason	4 720	- 15%

Humanitarian

	2021	2021/20
Asylum seekers	19 610	+ 52%

Inflows of top 10 nationalities
(national definition)

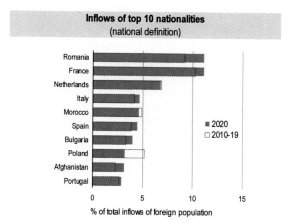

Romania, France, Netherlands, Italy, Morocco, Spain, Bulgaria, Poland, Afghanistan, Portugal

■ 2020
□ 2010-19

% of total inflows of foreign population

Emigration of Belgians to OECD countries
(national definition)

France, Netherlands, Spain, Germany, Switzerland, Luxembourg, United States, Italy, Canada, Austria

■ 2020

% of total emigration of Belgians to OECD countries

Components of population growth

	2021 Per 1 000 inhabitants	2021/20 difference
Total	6.6	+3.8
Natural increase	0.5	+1.6
Net migration plus statistical adjustments	6.1	+2.2

Annual remittances

	Million current USD	Annual change %	Share in GDP %
Inflows (2021)	15 883	+29.3	+2.6
Outflows (2021)	7 794	+25.2	+1.3

Labour market outcomes
2021

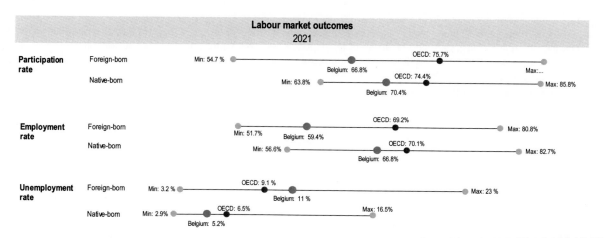

Participation rate	Foreign-born	Min: 54.7 %	OECD: 75.7% — Belgium: 66.8% — Max:...
	Native-born	Min: 63.8%	OECD: 74.4% — Belgium: 70.4% — Max: 85.8%
Employment rate	Foreign-born	Min: 51.7%	OECD: 69.2% — Belgium: 59.4% — Max: 80.8%
	Native-born	Min: 56.6%	OECD: 70.1% — Belgium: 66.8% — Max: 82.7%
Unemployment rate	Foreign-born	Min: 3.2 %	OECD: 9.1 % — Belgium: 11 % — Max: 23 %
	Native-born	Min: 2.9 %	OECD: 6.5% — Belgium: 5.2% — Max: 16.5%

StatLink 🔗 https://stat.link/5d6jqk

Bulgaria

Foreign-born population – 2021	3% of the population	Main countries of birth:
Size: 0.2 million, 50% of women	Evolution since 2011: +160%	Russia (17%), Türkiye (9%), Germany (8%)

In 2020, 5 000 new immigrants obtained a residence permit for longer than 12 months in Bulgaria (excluding EU citizens), -25.1% compared to 2019. This figure comprises 15.2% labour migrants, 20.8% family members (including accompanying family), 8.6% who came for education reasons and 55.4% other migrants. Around 600 short-term permits were issued to international students and 1 500 to temporary and seasonal labour migrants (excluding intra-EU migration). In addition, 6 015 intra-EU postings were recorded in 2020, a decrease of 57% compared to 2019. These posted workers are generally on short-term contracts.

Türkiye, Russia and Ukraine were the top three nationalities of newcomers in 2020. Among the top 15 countries of origin, Ukraine registered the strongest increase (400) and Türkiye the largest decrease (-1 100) in flows to Bulgaria compared to the previous year.

In 2021, the number of first asylum applicants increased by 200%, to reach around 11 000. The majority of applicants came from Afghanistan (5 000), Syria (3 700) and Iraq (500). The largest increase since 2020 concerned nationals of Afghanistan (4 300) and the largest decrease nationals of Lebanon (-10). Of the 3 270 decisions taken in 2021, 62% were positive.

The period 2020-21 was one of political uncertainty, with four different parliaments and four different governments which precluded substantial long-term migration policy changes. Some changes to the Foreigners Act concerning migration were introduced during this period, most designed to improve and simplify the procedures relating to labour market access for seasonal and highly skilled foreign labour. Other changes addressed criticism by the European Commission (EC) for noncompliance with EU requirements.

The possibilities for company representation offices to obtain long-term residence permits were tightened in response to fraudulent activity. Changes to the legislation stipulate that no more than three representatives per foreign company may obtain a long-term residence permit. The permits may be granted only after assessment of submitted documents regarding the economic activity and tax compliance of the foreign company for a period of two years, as well as assessment of documents concerning its planned activities. A new "start-up visa" for entrepreneurs was introduced in 2021 after discussions for more than a year. It allows foreigners to obtain a Bulgarian long-term visa and residence permit on the grounds of participation in high-tech and/or innovative projects.

Several changes aimed at reducing the administrative burden of accessing the labour market by seasonal and highly qualified foreign workers. When changing an employer, seasonal workers can receive a new residence permit that remains valid until the expiration date of the initial permit.

Other amendments to the Act put more preconditions on family reunion reasons for granting residence permits for the partners of refugees. The legislation now states that permits for long-term residence can be granted to family members of individuals granted asylum, temporary protection or humanitarian status only when the documents certifying family ties are recognised under Bulgarian legislation. Unaccompanied foreign children and foreigners under 18 years old who entered Bulgaria with a guardian but who were abandoned may now receive a permit to stay until the age of 18.

Changes coming into force in February 2021 harmonised Bulgarian legislation with EU Directives on a single application procedure and intra-company transfers. Foreign students from third countries who reside and study in another EU member state were given the right to enter Bulgaria and continue their education in Bulgaria. This change is designed to facilitate students' mobility and have a positive impact on the Bulgarian education system. Foreign students who complete their education in Bulgaria will no longer need to return to their home countries in order to apply for a residence permit. This change should facilitate the integration of highly skilled third-country citizens who graduated in Bulgaria.

In 2021, a new Employment Strategy (2021-30) was adopted by the Council of Ministers. It includes labour migration in which policy will focus mainly on ensuring a balanced reception of third-country nationals in Bulgaria, including facilitating access for qualified third-country nationals and the promotion of bilateral intergovernmental agreements.

For further information: www.aref.government.bg | www.nsi.bg | www.mvr.bg

Key figures on immigration and emigration – Bulgaria

Grants of long-term residence permits
2020 (Source: Eurostat)

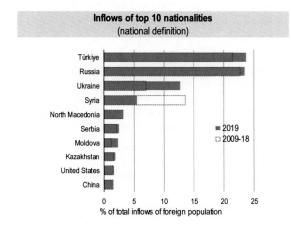

- 500 Studies 9%
- 900 Work 15%
- 1 200 Family 21%
- 3 300 Other 55%

Temporary migration
(Source: Eurostat)

Temporary migration (non-EU citizens)

	2020	2020/19
Employment reasons	1 480	+ 8%
Family reasons	1 660	- 29%
Education reasons	640	- 27%
Other reason	510	- 45%

Humanitarian

	2021	2021/20
Asylum seekers	10 890	+ 215%

Inflows of top 10 nationalities
(national definition)

Türkiye
Russia
Ukraine
Syria
North Macedonia
Serbia
Moldova
Kazakhstan
United States
China

■ 2019
□ 2009-18

0 5 10 15 20 25
% of total inflows of foreign population

Emigration of Bulgarians to OECD countries
(national definition)

Germany
Netherlands
Austria
Belgium
Spain
Türkiye
Switzerland
United Kingdom
Italy
France

■ 2020

0 10 20 30 40 50 60
% of total emigration of Bulgarians to OECD countries

Components of population growth

	2021 Per 1 000 inhabitants	2021/20 difference
Total	-11.3	-6.3
Natural increase	-13.1	-3.6
Net migration plus statistical adjustments	1.8	-2.6

Annual remittances

	Million current USD	Annual change %	Share in GDP %
Inflows (2021)	786	-43.0	+1.0
Outflows (2021)	157	-16.9	+0.2

Labour market outcomes
2021

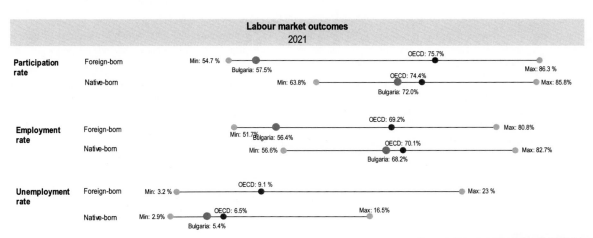

Participation rate	Foreign-born	Min: 54.7 % · Bulgaria: 57.5% · OECD: 75.7% · Max: 86.3 %
	Native-born	Min: 63.8% · OECD: 74.4% · Bulgaria: 72.0% · Max: 85.8%
Employment rate	Foreign-born	Min: 51.7% · Bulgaria: 56.4% · OECD: 69.2% · Max: 80.8%
	Native-born	Min: 56.6% · OECD: 70.1% · Bulgaria: 68.2% · Max: 82.7%
Unemployment rate	Foreign-born	Min: 3.2 % · OECD: 9.1 % · Max: 23 %
	Native-born	Min: 2.9% · OECD: 6.5% · Bulgaria: 5.4% · Max: 16.5%

StatLink 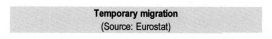 https://stat.link/xaousj

Canada

Foreign-born population – 2018	21.3% of the population	Main countries of birth:
Size: 7.9 million, 52% of women	Evolution since 2011: +17%	India (8%), China (8%), Philippines (7%)

In 2020, Canada received 185 000 new immigrants on a long-term or permanent basis (including changes of status), -45.9% compared to 2019. This figure comprises 32.5% labour migrants, 51.8% family members (including accompanying family) and 13.8% humanitarian migrants. Around 51 000 permits were issued to tertiary-level international students and 53 000 to temporary and seasonal labour migrants.

India, China and the Philippines were the top three nationalities of newcomers in 2020. Among the top 15 countries of origin, India registered the largest decrease (-42 000) in flows to Canada compared to the previous year.

In 2021, the number of first asylum applicants increased by 23%, to reach around 23 400. The majority of applicants came from Mexico (2 300), India (1 700) and Colombia (1 400). The largest increase since 2020 concerned nationals of Iran (700) and the largest decrease nationals of Nigeria (-300). Of the 48 000 decisions taken in 2021, 54% were positive.

Canada's 2022-24 Immigration Levels Plan aims to continue welcoming increasing amounts of new permanent residents. Planned admissions include 431 645 in 2022, 447 055 in 2023, and 451 000 in 2024. These targets represent a growth rate of about 1% of Canada's population per year.

At the beginning of 2022, Canada established the Atlantic Immigration Program as a permanent programme, replacing the Atlantic Immigration Pilot, initially launched in 2017.

Several changes addressed disruptions caused by COVID-19. In response to border closures the expedited one time TR to PR Pathway, in effect from May to November 2021, enabled more than 90 000 temporary workers and student graduates in Canada to apply for permanent residence with over 45 000 approved to date. To ease family reunification despite the economic difficulties during the pandemic, COVID-19 and employment insurance benefits could be included to meet the income requirements for family class sponsorship for the 2020 tax year. In addition, the overall income requirement for sponsors of parents and grandparents was reduced.

In December 2021, Canada launched the second phase of its Economic Mobility Pathways Pilot, which helps skilled refugees to access Canada's existing economic immigration pathways. The EMPP helps to fill labour shortages in high-demand sectors such as health care, while providing refugees with a durable solution. The EMPP aims to admit 500 skilled refugees and their family members under Phase 2 and to expand even further in the future.

In June 2021, the Citizenship Act was amended to include a reference to Indigenous and Treaty Rights in the Oath of Citizenship to support newcomers' awareness of Indigenous rights and history.

In August 2021, IRCC announced a special resettlement initiative for Afghan nationals to help resettle at least 40 000 Afghan nationals over the next two years. In addition, Canada launched a new resettlement stream for human rights defenders with an annual quota of 250 resettlement spaces for 2021 and 2022.

As of March 2022, the Canada-Ukraine Authorization for Emergency Travel was launched to help Ukrainians and their family members receive extended stay in Canada, as well as work and study options. Additionally, federal settlement services, such as language training and a one-time benefit of USD 3 000 for each adult and USD 1 500 for each child are offered. This is an extraordinary measure aimed at supporting Ukrainians arriving under this special, accelerated temporary residence pathway.

During the pandemic, the majority of settlement services, including language training, were shifted to online delivery. This ensured continued support to newcomers and refugees, while respecting public health guidelines, and included resources to address the increase in gender-based violence during the pandemic. In response to the need for flexibility, the validity period of language assessment results was extended, and remains, from one to two years.

Canada will invest close to CAD 830 million in the next five years to modernise its business practices and implement an enterprise-wide digital migration management platform. This new platform will support greater use of data and digital tools to improve application processing across lines of business and better support applicants.

For further information: www.canada.ca/en/services/immigration-citizenship

Key figures on immigration and emigration – Canada

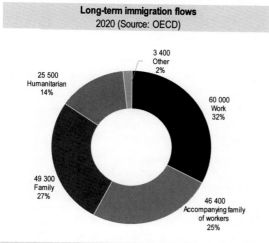

Long-term immigration flows
2020 (Source: OECD)

- 60 000 Work 32%
- 46 400 Accompanying family of workers 25%
- 49 300 Family 27%
- 25 500 Humanitarian 14%
- 3 400 Other 2%

Temporary migration
(Sources: OECD, UNHCR)

Temporary labour migration

	2020	2020/19
Working holidaymakers	15 850	- 71%
Seasonal workers	31 190	- 15%
Intra-company transfers	5 930	- 59%
Other temporary workers	..	..

Education

	2020	2020/19
International students	50 780	- 70%
Trainees	..	..

Humanitarian

	2021	2021/20
Asylum seekers	23 370	+ 23%

Inflows of top 10 nationalities
(national definition)

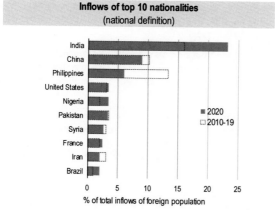

India, China, Philippines, United States, Nigeria, Pakistan, Syria, France, Iran, Brazil

■ 2020
□ 2010-19

% of total inflows of foreign population

Emigration of Canadians to OECD countries
(national definition)

United States, United Kingdom, Korea, Australia, Germany, Mexico, France, Netherlands, Japan, New Zealand

■ 2020

% of total emigration of Canadians to OECD countries

Components of population growth

	2021 Per 1 000 inhabitants	2021/20 difference
Total	12.0	+7.7
Natural increase	1.5	+0.2
Net migration plus statistical adjustments	10.4	+7.6

Annual remittances

	Million current USD	Annual change %	Share in GDP %
Inflows (2021)	807	-38.5	+0.0
Outflows (2021)	7 193	+6.0	+0.4

Labour market outcomes
2021

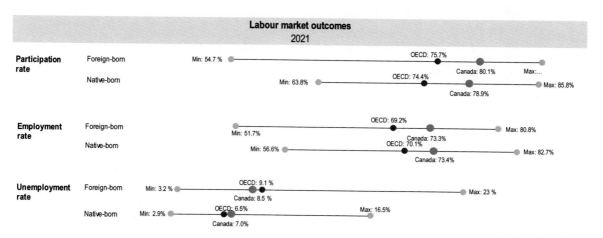

Participation rate

Foreign-born: Min: 54.7 % — OECD: 75.7% — Canada: 80.1% — Max:...
Native-born: Min: 63.8% — OECD: 74.4% — Canada: 78.9% — Max: 85.8%

Employment rate

Foreign-born: Min: 51.7% — OECD: 69.2% — Canada: 73.3% — Max: 80.8%
Native-born: Min: 56.6% — OECD: 70.1% — Canada: 73.4% — Max: 82.7%

Unemployment rate

Foreign-born: Min: 3.2 % — OECD: 9.1 % — Canada: 8.5 % — Max: 23 %
Native-born: Min: 2.9% — OECD: 6.5% — Canada: 7.0% — Max: 16.5%

StatLink ᴍSL https://stat.link/3tmzcy

Chile

Foreign-born population – 2020	7.8% of the population	Main countries of birth:
Size: 1.5 million, 53% of women	Evolution since 2011: +305%	Venezuela (31%), Peru (16%), Haiti (12%)

Venezuela, Haiti and Colombia were the top three nationalities of newcomers in 2020. Among the top 15 countries of origin, Venezuela registered the largest decrease (-67 000) in flows to Chile compared to the previous year.

In 2021, the number of first asylum applicants increased by 49% to reach around 2 500. The majority of applicants came from Venezuela (2 100), Cuba (150) and Colombia (100). The largest increase since 2020 concerned nationals of Venezuela (1 700) and the largest decrease nationals of Colombia (-600). Of the 640 decisions taken in 2021, 2% were positive.

A new immigration law was approved by the Chilean Congress in December 2020 and published in April 2021 in the official gazette. The law establishes a new immigration framework and restructures the existing visas and permits. The National Immigration Services is henceforth responsible for all visa and residence applications, with the exception of tourist visas.

In the first half of 2022, several implementing regulations have been published. One of the key changes is the expansion of the Temporary Residence Visa, phasing out, among others, the Work Contract Visa. The revised Temporary Residence Visa has 16 subcategories: workers performing remunerated activities, foreign nationals seeking job opportunities, seasonal workers, studies, international agreements, humanitarian reasons among others. It has an initial duration of two years and is renewable in two-year increments. Previously, some temporary visas were issued with an initial duration of one year. This was the case of the Mercosur Temporary Residence Visa, which was issued for one year and renewable only once.

For migrant workers employed in Chile, obtaining the new Temporary Residence Visa instead of the Work Contract Visa implies that their visa is no longer tied to the validity of the work contract, which means that they may change employers or companies in Chile without affecting their work-authorised status. Furthermore, dependent family members of temporary residence holders will automatically receive a work authorisation, which was not the case previously.

Foreign nationals seeking to work and reside in Chile need to remain outside the country while completing their work and residence process. It is no longer possible to enter on a tourist visa and apply through an in-country process. Exceptions apply for migrants with family ties to a Chilean citizen or permanent resident. In-country applications can be submitted through the National Immigration Service's online portal. In these cases, immigrants receive a receipt that allows them to reside, and in some cases to work, in Chile immediately.

An extraordinary regularisation process took place in 2021. For 180 days starting 20 April 2021, migrants who entered Chile through authorised crossing points before 18 March 2020 and who did not have a criminal record could apply for regularisation. Migrants who entered Chile illegally had until the end of the regularisation period to depart Chile without facing penalties.

COVID-19 measures delayed immigration processes in 2021. Permanent residence applications had to be submitted online only for all nationalities. The Ministry of Foreign Affairs suspended non-urgent legalisation and authentication services.

The Ministry of Interior has extended the concession allowing Venezuelan nationals with expired passports or identification cards to enter and regularise their status in Chile. The documents must have been issued in or after 2013 and will now be considered valid until 22 April 2023.

For further information: www.extranjeria.gob.cl

Key figures on immigration and emigration – Chile

Long-term and temporary immigration flows
2018 (Source: OECD)

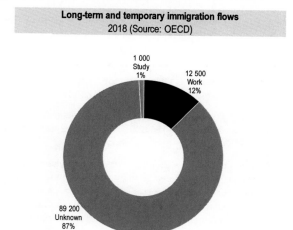

1 000
Study
1%

12 500
Work
12%

89 200
Unknown
87%

Asylum seekers
(Source: UNHCR)

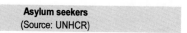

	2021	2021/20
Asylum seekers	2 500	+ 49%

Inflows of top 10 nationalities
(national definition)

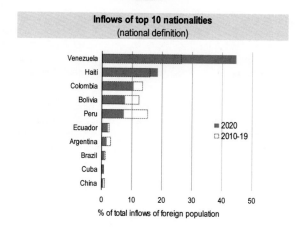

Emigration of Chileans to OECD countries
(national definition)

Components of population growth

	2020 Per 1 000 inhabitants	2020/19 difference
Total	18.0	+0.0
Natural increase	3.6	-1.7
Net migration plus statistical adjustments	14.5	+1.8

Annual remittances

	Million current USD	Annual change %	Share in GDP %
Inflows (2021)	71	+2.2	+0.0
Outflows (2020)	774	+7.1	+0.3

Labour market outcomes
2020 compared to 2021 OECD average

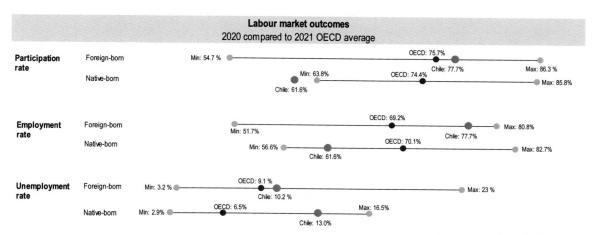

StatLink https://stat.link/dnq34h

China

Foreign-born population – 2021	0.04% of the population	Main countries of birth:
Size: 0.53 million, 45.6% of women		Korea (14%), United States (12%), Viet Nam (12%)

At the end of 2021 there were a total of 531 000 foreign residents in the People's Republic of China. The top three countries of origin for foreign nationals in China were the Republic of Korea (13.6%), the United States (12.5%) and Viet Nam (12.2%).

In 2021, there was a total of 2.2 million entries from foreign nationals. The top five origin countries of foreign nationals were the Philippines (450 000), Viet Nam (379 000), Mongolia (217 000), Russia (166 000), and Korea (134 000). The Chinese National Public Security authorities issued 38 000 visas, 170 000 short-term stay permits, and 508 000 long-term residence permits.

In April 2021, The National Immigration Administration of China (NIA) officially launched the China Immigration Service Hotline and English version website to provide useful information and government services to Chinese citizens and foreign nationals. The hotline, which provides 24-hour service in both Chinese and English, provides a range of services to Chinese and foreign nationals including guidance on current immigration policies and facilitates feedback on services. NIA has also developed an English language website to provide information on China's immigration management system, and deliver a range of online services to foreign nationals and businesses both in and outside of China.

China has expanded the scope of online booking services at the Exit and Entry Administration, including allowing foreign nationals to book appointments and fill in application materials online. There have also been six specific measures for elderly applicants to submit documents required for exit and entry procedures. To facilitate better service for the elderly, the NIA established a fast track "green channel" for document handling, promoted the use of self-service and online "smart services", simplified the photo-collecting process, increased the number of payment options, improved the user experience for online procedures, and established an online platform for express service.

In September 2021, China announced improvements in the management of long-term foreign residents in China by strengthening information sharing between relevant government ministries, optimising administrative processes, and promoting a "single service window" for residence and work permits for skilled migrants. Additionally, foreign nationals in China holding a work-type residence permit are no longer required to change their residence status to undertake professional training and development courses.

For further information: https://en.nia.gov.cn/

Key figures on immigration and emigration – China

Long-term immigration flows
(Source: National Immigration Administration)

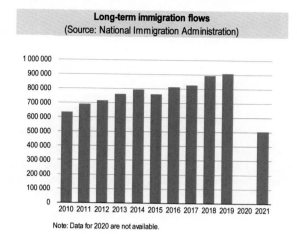

Note: Data for 2020 are not available.

Temporary migration
(Sources: UIS, UNHCR)

Education

	2020	2020/19
International students	225 100	+ 12%

Humanitarian

	2021	2021/20
Asylum seekers	350	- 1%

Inflows of top 10 nationalities
(national definition)

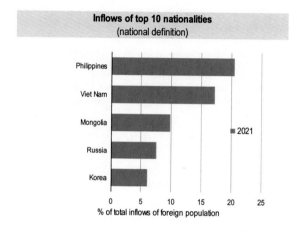

% of total inflows of foreign population

Emigration of Chinese to OECD countries
(national definition)

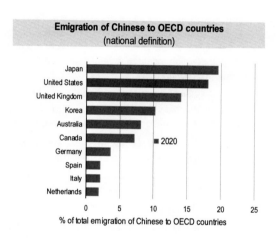

% of total emigration of Chinese to OECD countries

Components of population growth

	2021 Per 1 000 inhabitants	2021/20 difference
Total	0.7	-1.5
Natural increase	..	..
Net migration plus statistical adjustments	..	..

Annual remittances

	Million current USD	Annual change %	Share in GDP %
Inflows (2021)	53 000	-10.9	+0.3
Outflows (2021)	22 903	+25.2	+0.1

StatLink ⬛͢ⅢＳᴸ https://stat.link/i7osm0

Colombia

Foreign-born population – 2020	3.7% of the population	Main countries of birth:
Size: 1.9 million, 49.9% women		Venezuela (93%), United States (1%), Ecuador (1%)

Venezuela, the United States and Ecuador were the top three nationalities of newcomers in 2020. Among the top 15 countries of origin, Venezuela registered the largest decrease (-121 000) in flows to Colombia compared to the previous year.

In 2021, the number of first asylum applicants increased by 34% to reach around 16 000. The majority of applicants came from Venezuela (12 000). The largest increase since 2020 concerned nationals of Venezuela (4 000). Of the 6 950 decisions taken in 2021, 8% were positive.

Since 2015, Colombia has received massive migratory flows, including an estimated 1.7 million Venezuelan migrants as of January 2021. This prompted the Colombian Government to adopt different measures for migrants such as the Temporary Protected Status for Venezuelan Migrants (TPSV) in March 2021.

This far-reaching protection mechanism grants a legal status for migrants to stay in the national territory, and the possibility to apply for a permanent resident visa after ten years.

The regularisation consists of a registry process in the Unified Registry for Venezuelan Migrants (RUMV, for its acronym in Spanish), which consists of an online pre-registry (in which biographical, demographic, facial biometrics, immediate family members and preliminary evidence of permanence in the territory are collected), an online socio-economic characterisation survey, and an on-site biometric registry (which includes facial, fingerprint and signature data, as well as the validation of the information provided by the migrant during pre-registration).

After completing the RUMV, the next step is authorisation and issuance of the Temporary Protection Permit (TPP), which accords the holder a valid identification document granting rights and duties within the Colombian territory, including the possibility to exercise any legal activity or occupation and access to a variety of public and private services.

As of May 2022, 2.3 million Venezuelan migrants filled out the socio-economic survey, there were over 1.2 million granted TPPs and over 1 million permits were delivered to Venezuelans.

The Colombian Government lifted the border restrictions implemented as a response to the COVID-19 crisis with neighbouring countries and has reopened its borders progressively with Peru, Ecuador, Brazil and Panama, which had been closed since March 2020. In June 2021, there has been a gradual reopening of all borders with Venezuela.

In August 2021, the Colombian and Panamanian authorities concluded a binational agreement on border management co-operation. It establishes a daily quota system to control the flow of irregular migrants transiting through the common border of the two countries. The measure seeks to regulate migrant flows, mainly from Cuba, Venezuela, and Haiti on their way to the United States through the Darien Gap. Furthermore, it aims at facilitating the exchange of information on migration flows between the two countries.

Moreover, the Colombian Government enacted the new Integrated Migration Policy (IMP) law in August 2021, which establishes a permanent legal framework on migration policy in Colombia. It aims, inter alia, to promote regular migration, improve the socio-economic integration of migrants and offer a better protection to vulnerable migrant populations and also includes an entire section of Colombians living abroad. In line with the objectives of the IMP, the Colombian Ministry of Foreign Affairs and the Office for the Attention and Socio-economic Integration of the Migrant Population of the Presidency of the Republic adopted a new mechanism to facilitate the recognition of foreign qualifications.

For further information: www.migracioncolombia.gov.co

Key figures on immigration and emigration – Colombia

Long-term immigration flows by category
2019 (Source: OECD)

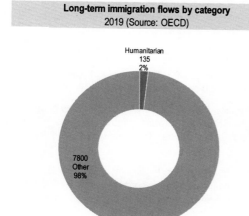

Humanitarian
135
2%

7800
Other
98%

Temporary migration
2019 (Sources: OECD, UNHCR)

Temporary labour migration

	2019	2019/18
Working holidaymakers	230	+ 14%
Seasonal workers	..	..
Intra-company transfers	130	- 4%
Other temporary workers	21 000	- 3%

Education

	2019	2019/18
International students	4 060	- 13%
Trainees	..	..

Humanitarian

	2021	2021/20
Asylum seekers	15 940	+ 34%

Inflows of top 10 nationalities
(national definition)

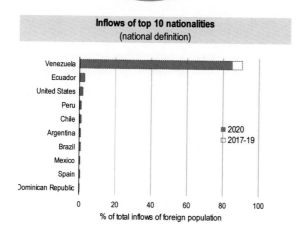

% of total inflows of foreign population

Emigration of Colombians to OECD countries
(national definition)

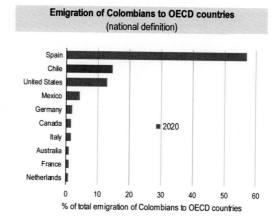

% of total emigration of Colombians to OECD countries

Components of population growth

	2021 Per 1 000 inhabitants	2021/20 difference
Total	13.3	-6.1
Natural increase	4.9	-1.6
Net migration plus statistical adjustments	8.4	-4.5

Annual remittances

	Million current USD	Annual change %	Share in GDP %
Inflows (2021)	8 606	+24.0	+2.7
Outflows (2021)	387	+49.1	+0.1

Labour market outcomes
2021

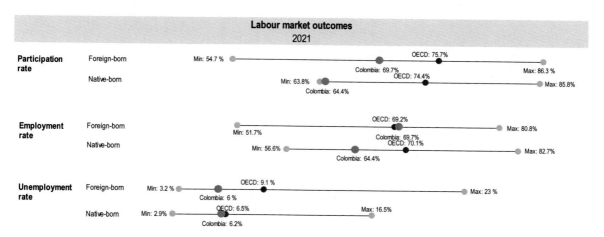

StatLink https://stat.link/frdzgb

Costa Rica

Foreign-born population – 2020	10.2% of the population	Main countries of birth:
Size: 0.5 million, 49% women	+28% since 2010	Nicaragua (67%), Venezuela (5%), Colombia (5%)

In 2021, the number of first asylum applicants increased by 413%, to reach around 108 000. The majority of applicants came from Nicaragua (102 000), Venezuela (3 000), Haiti (900). The largest increase since 2020 concerned nationals of Nicaragua (92 500).

Migration policy in Costa Rica is largely shaped by efforts to regulate immigration from its Central American neighbours and from Venezuela. In 2021, the Costa Rican Government implemented a new protection mechanism for irregular migrants. The measure aims to provide temporary protection to Venezuelan, Nicaraguan or Cuban nationals who entered the country between January 2010 and March 2020 and whose asylum applications have been rejected.

Specific measures are in place for people from neighbouring countries near border areas. In January 2021, the Government of Costa Rica enacted a decree to allow indigenous Nicaraguan and Panamanian nationals living in bordering areas with Costa Rica to work on specific activities. They are authorised by the General Directorate to enter and leave the national territory on a daily basis.

In August 2021, the Costa Rican Government implemented a one-year working visa aimed at foreign nationals working remotely and extendable for an additional year under specific requirements. Under this "digital nomad" scheme, foreign nationals will be able to obtain a one-year remote work permit that is extendable for an additional year if they meet certain salary, health insurance and other requirements. Workers under this scheme are exempt from local income taxes.

In November 2020, the Costa Rican and Nicaraguan Governments signed a binational agreement to regulate the temporary hiring of Nicaraguan workers in Costa Rica for the harvesting season 2020-21. The agreement was implemented to offset labour shortages in the agricultural sector during the pandemic. In 2020-21, around 6 700 seasonal migrant workers benefited from this measure. The bilateral agreement was extended in September 2021 for an additional seven months to cover the 2021-22 harvesting season.

In July 2021, the Costa Rican Government adopted a new law that lowers investment requirements for obtaining temporary residence, encouraging the attraction of investors, pensioners and retirees. Among other measures, the law reduces the minimum investment amount to obtain temporary residence under the investor category from USD 200 000 to USD 150 000.

In the context of COVID-19, Costa Rica decided to prolong all permits that expired after 1 October 2021 until 30 September 2022.

On the integration side, the Ministry of Public Education and the General Directorate enacted a co-ordination protocol in January 2021, to regularise migrant children in the public education system. The protocol aims to decrease the dropout rates of migrant minors by providing better access to scholarships and degrees. Successful applicants will receive a legal status under the category of students.

In February 2021, the Costa Rican Government and UNHCR established a new agreement to provide medical coverage to refugees and asylum seekers in Costa Rica, starting in early 2021. The agreement expanded the previous medical insurance already implemented in 2020.

On 23 May 2022, the Government of the Republic published a decree which provides foreigners a special category for the migratory regularisation in order to work temporarily in the agricultural sector, averaging 18 000 permits annually.

Further information: https://www.migracion.go.cr

Key figures on immigration and emigration – Costa Rica

Emigration of Costa Ricans to OECD countries
(Source OECD, national definition)

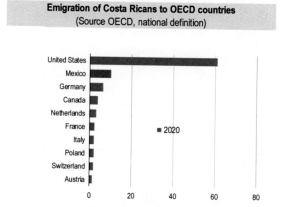

% of total emigration of Costa Ricans to OECD countries

Temporary migration to Costa Rica
(Sources: UIS, UNHCR)

Education

	2020	2020/19
International students	2 668	+ 3%

Humanitarian

	2021	2021/20
Asylum seekers	108 430	+ 413%

Components of population growth

	2021 Per 1 000 inhabitants	2021/20 difference
Total	10.0	-0.4
Natural increase	4.4	-1.9
Net migration plus statistical adjustments	5.6	+1.5

Annual remittances

	Million current USD	Annual change %	Share in GDP %
Inflows (2021)	594	+12.1	+0.9
Outflows (2021)	549	+10.5	+0.9

Labour market outcomes
2021

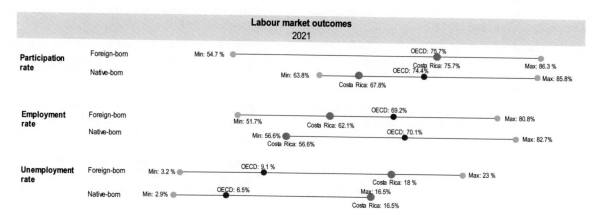

Czech Republic

Foreign population – 2021	5.9% of the population	Main countries of nationality:
Size: 0.6 million, 43% of women	Evolution since 2011: +49%	Ukraine (26%), the Slovak Republic (20%), Viet Nam (10%)

In 2020, 49 000 new immigrants obtained a residence permit for longer than 12 months in the Czech Republic (excluding EU citizens), - 49.4% compared to 2019. This figure comprises 57.1% labour migrants, 24.7% family members (including accompanying family), 11.3% who came for education reasons and 6.9% other migrants. Around 2 100 short-term permits were issued to international students and 1 500 to temporary and seasonal labour migrants (excluding intra-EU migration). In addition, 60 000 intra-EU postings were recorded in 2020, a decrease of -40% compared to 2019. These posted workers are generally on short-term contracts.

Ukraine, the Slovak Republic and Russia were the top three nationalities of newcomers in 2020. Among the top 15 countries of origin, the Slovak Republic registered the strongest increase (1 400) and Ukraine the largest decrease (-1 700) in flows to the Czech Republic compared to the previous year.

In 2021, the number of first asylum applicants increased by 33.3% to reach around 1 100. The majority of applicants came from Ukraine (300), Georgia (200) and Afghanistan (200). The largest increase since 2020 concerned nationals of Afghanistan (170) and the largest decrease nationals of Azerbaijan (-30). Of the 940 decisions taken in 2021, 28% were positive.

In 2021, the Czech Republic was tackling persisting impacts of the COVID-19 pandemic on migration flows. Restrictions on all non-essential travel to the Czech territory that had been introduced in 2020 as a response to the COVID-19 pandemic outbreak and that followed the recommendation of the European Commission remained applicable but they were gradually eased during 2021. The requirement to complete an electronic Public Health Passenger Locator Form when travelling from countries with a medium or high risk of COVID-19 transmission was introduced in February 2021. In August 2021, entry conditions were eased for fully vaccinated third-country nationals. The Czech Republic finally lifted all remaining border epidemiological measures related to COVID-19 in April 2022.

Despite the pandemic, the Czech Republic granted 199 000 short-term visas and 58 500 long-term visas and residence permits to third-country nationals, mainly labour migrants. 14 500 citizens of the EU/EEA Member States and 4 000 of their family members moved to the Czech Republic in 2021.

The salary threshold for admission of labour migrants from third countries increased in 2021. The basic threshold for an Employee Card – a single permit for long-term labour migrants – and the short-term work permit corresponds with the national minimum wage. In January 2022, the national monthly minimum wage was raised from CZK 15 200 to CZK 16 200 (approx. EUR 650). The new minimum wage is around 41.7% of average national wage.

A new amendment to the Act on Residence of Foreign Nationals, approved in August 2021, introduced new requirements concerning identification and health insurance of migrants in the country. Following the EU regulation the security of identity cards was strengthened. Residence permits issued by the Czech Republic to all third-country nationals including family members of EU citizens must now contain biometric data. If already residing in the Czech Republic, migrants are required to exchange their current permit for a biometric permit. According to the new health insurance requirements, all third-country nationals must be insured in the scope of comprehensive health care (from Pojišťovna VZP, a subsidiary of the General Health Insurance Company of the Czech Republic). This requirement does not apply to migrants covered by the Czech public health insurance or insurance paid for on the basis of international agreement.

In April 2022, the Ministry of Labour and Social Affairs in co-operation with Mendel University launched "Smart Migration", a mobile application that provides information to migrants on living in the Czech Republic and navigating government services, including health, education, housing, and migration matters. Users can thereafter generate tasks and the application will remind them what needs to be done. It also provides contacts of relevant authorities and organisations in the Czech Republic and allows migrants to talk directly to personal virtual assistant (Chatbot).

For further information: www.mvcr.cz/mvcren | www.czso.cz | www.mpsv.cz | www.uradprace.cz | www.cizinci.cz

Key figures on immigration and emigration – Czech Republic

Grants of long-term residence permits
2020 (Source: Eurostat)

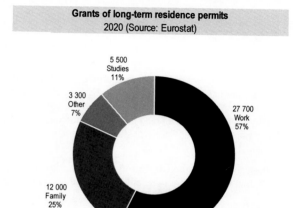

- 5 500 Studies 11%
- 3 300 Other 7%
- 27 700 Work 57%
- 12 000 Family 25%

Temporary migration
(Source: Eurostat)

Temporary migration (non-EU citizens)

	2020	2020/19
Employment reasons	1 490	- 69%
Family reasons	1 400	- 71%
Education reasons	2 060	- 72%
Other reason	800	- 79%

Humanitarian

	2021	2021/20
Asylum seekers	1 060	+ 33%

Inflows of top 10 nationalities
(national definition)

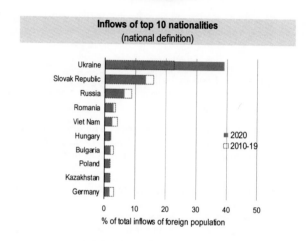

% of total inflows of foreign population

Emigration of Czechs to OECD countries
(national definition)

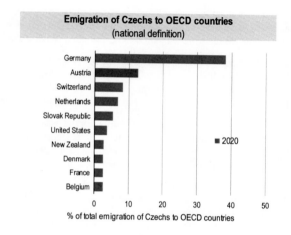

% of total emigration of Czechs to OECD countries

Components of population growth

	2021 Per 1 000 inhabitants	2021/20 difference
Total	2.1	+1.4
Natural increase	-2.7	-0.9
Net migration plus statistical adjustments	4.8	+2.3

Annual remittances

	Million current USD	Annual change %	Share in GDP %
Inflows (2021)	4 387	+13.6	+1.6
Outflows (2021)	4 069	+24.6	+1.4

Labour market outcomes
2021

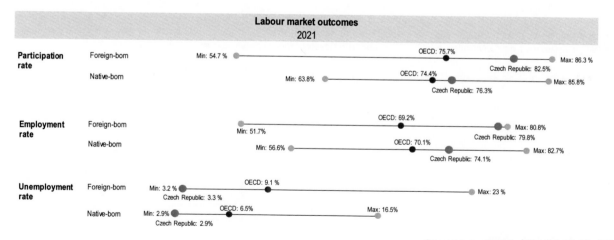

Participation rate	Foreign-born	Min: 54.7% — OECD: 75.7% — Czech Republic: 82.5% — Max: 86.3%
	Native-born	Min: 63.8% — OECD: 74.4% — Czech Republic: 76.3% — Max: 85.8%
Employment rate	Foreign-born	Min: 51.7% — OECD: 69.2% — Czech Republic: 79.8% — Max: 80.8%
	Native-born	Min: 56.6% — OECD: 70.1% — Czech Republic: 74.1% — Max: 82.7%
Unemployment rate	Foreign-born	Min: 3.2% — Czech Republic: 3.3% — OECD: 9.1% — Max: 23%
	Native-born	Min: 2.9% — Czech Republic: 2.9% — OECD: 6.5% — Max: 16.5%

StatLink https://stat.link/igcjmh

Denmark

Foreign-born population – 2021	10.6% of the population	Main countries of birth:
Size: 0.6 million, 50% of women	Evolution since 2011: +44%	Poland (7%), Syria (6%), Türkiye (5%)

In 2020, Denmark received 41 000 new immigrants on a long-term or permanent basis (including changes of status and free mobility), -15% compared to 2019. This figure comprises 61% immigrants benefitting from free mobility, 18.4% labour migrants, 17.9% family members (including accompanying family) and 1.5% humanitarian migrants. Around 5 000 permits were issued to tertiary-level international students and 3 800 to temporary and seasonal labour migrants (excluding intra-EU migration). In addition, 35 000 intra-EU postings were recorded in 2020, a decrease of -24% compared to 2019. These posted workers are generally on short-term contracts.

Romania, Poland and Germany were the top three nationalities of newcomers in 2020. Among the top 15 countries of origin, Sweden registered the strongest increase (100) and India the largest decrease (-800) in flows to Denmark compared to the previous year.

In 2021, the number of first asylum applicants increased by 40%, to reach around 2000. The majority of applicants came from Afghanistan (600), Eritrea (400) and Syria (300). The largest increase since 2020 concerned nationals of Afghanistan (500) and the largest decrease nationals of Morocco (-30). Of the 1 550 decisions taken in 2021, 50% were positive.

The Positive List for Skilled Work is a list of skilled professions experiencing a shortage of qualified professionals that was introduced in 2020. Foreigners who have been offered a job included in this list can apply for a Danish residence permit of up to four years. As of January 2021, a fee was imposed on working holiday visa applications.

While beneficiaries of temporary subsidiary protection status in Denmark were required to wait three years for family reunification, that delay has been administered since October 2021 as a two-year waiting period due to the judgment of 9 July 2021 from the European Court of Human Rights in the case of M.A. v. Denmark. In April 2022, the Danish Government proposed an amendment to the Aliens Act to consolidate that practice (adopted in June 2022, effective 1 July 2022).

On 3 June 2021, the Danish Parliament adopted a law introducing the possibility of transferring asylum seekers for asylum application processing and subsequent protection in third countries. The transfer scheme will only enter into effect when Denmark secures an agreement with a third country. A Danish Return Agency was established in August 2020 and a new Return Act came in to force on 1 June 2021 and regulates the voluntary return procedure.

In April 2021, the Danish Parliament revised the criteria for naturalisation. The agreed criteria applicants must fulfil are in general: 1) speak and write Danish at a satisfying level (Danish 3 or 2 for applicants who have been self-supporting; 2) pass the Danish citizenship test; 3) sign a solemn declaration; 4) reside in Denmark for nine years with a permanent residence permit for at least the last two years, 5) been a full-time employee or self-employed for at least three years and six months within the last four years and at the time of the submission of the bill of notification of naturalisation; 6) participate in a "constitutional ceremony" and exchange a handshake with a representative of the public authorities at the ceremony. Applicants must also be self-supporting (not receiving major social benefits) and cannot be convicted of certain crimes or have received certain sanctions.

In December 2020, the government and social partners agreed to extend the target group of the *Integrationsgrunduddannelse (igu)* programme to refugees and their family for up to ten years after obtaining a residence permit (formerly up to five years). *Igu* is a job and training programme, by which new arrivals are brought into regular employment for a period of two years on special wage-conditions.

Following the national action plan against parallel societies, the Danish Government has received and accepted 17 development plans for housing areas with social and integrational challenges. In June 2021, the government, together with a large majority in the parliament, have agreed on new initiatives ensuring that all social housing neighbourhoods will be *Mixed Residential Areas*. The initiatives includes new rental rules, which will prevent the development of new vulnerable residential areas.

For further information: www.uim.dk | www.newtodenmark.dk | www.integrationsbarometer.dk

Key figures on immigration and emigration – Denmark

Long-term immigration flows
2020 (Source: OECD)

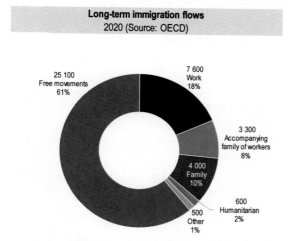

Temporary migration
(Sources: OECD, Eurostat)
Temporary labour migration (non-EU citizens)

	2020	2020/19
Working holidaymakers	1 320	- 64%
Seasonal workers	..	..
Intra-company transfers	..	..
Other temporary workers	830	- 42%

Education (non-EU citizens)

	2020	2020/19
International students	5 000	- 41%
Trainees	1 640	- 30%

Humanitarian

	2021	2021/20
Asylum seekers	2 020	+ 40%

Inflows of top 10 nationalities
(national definition)

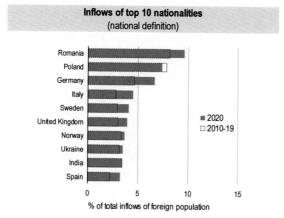

Emigration of Danish citizens to OECD countries
(national definition)

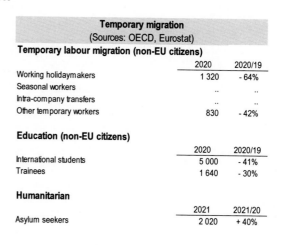

Components of population growth

	2021 Per 1 000 inhabitants	2021/20 difference
Total	5.7	+2.7
Natural increase	1.1	+0.0
Net migration plus statistical adjustments	4.6	+2.7

Annual remittances

	Million current USD	Annual change %	Share in GDP %
Inflows (2021)	1 492	+2.8	+0.4
Outflows (2020)	3 327	+0.4	+0.9

Labour market outcomes
2021

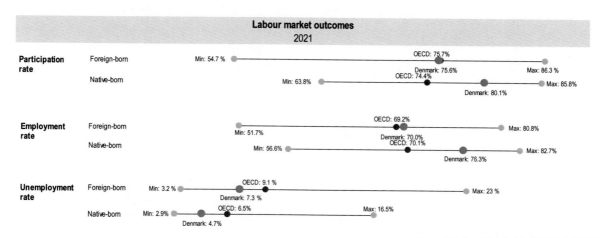

StatLink https://stat.link/6p5yn9

Estonia

Foreign-born population – 2021	15% of the population	Main countries of birth:
Size: 0.2 million, 56% of women	Evolution since 2011: -7%	Russia (57%), Ukraine (13%), Belarus (5%)

In 2020, 4 800 new immigrants obtained a residence permit for longer than 12 months in Estonia (excluding EU citizens), -19.3% compared to 2019. This figure comprises 41.5% labour migrants, 43.5% family members (including accompanying family), 10.2% who came for education reasons and 4.7% other migrants. In addition, 2 700 intra-EU postings were recorded in 2020, a decrease of -46% compared to 2019. These posted workers are generally on short-term contracts.

Ukraine, Russia and Finland were the top three nationalities of newcomers in 2020. Among the top 15 countries of origin, Russia registered the largest decrease (-300) in flows to Estonia compared to the previous year.

In 2021, the number of first asylum applicants increased by 66.7% to reach around 75. The majority of applicants came from Afghanistan (15), Russia (10) and Belarus (5). The largest increase since 2020 concerned nationals of Afghanistan (15). Of the 75 decisions taken in 2021, 67% were positive.

Starting from August 2020, an amendment to the Aliens Act enables applications for the digital nomad visa. Under this scheme, visa holders will be able to work remotely from Estonia for an employer in another country, or as freelancers. Digital nomads can only come to work in Estonia through a mediator who assumes responsibility for their stay. Granting a visa to a digital nomad is subject to the general terms, including having sufficient funds for staying in Estonia. The implementation of the digital nomad visa programme will be phased. In the first stage, foreigners who can prove they are digital nomads will be allowed to apply for the visa.

The preparation of a new national integration plan for 2021-30 is underway, which will formulate the objectives of the integration policy of Estonia and the activities needed to achieve them. The state wishes to recognise the value of everyone in society, support cultural diversity, and promote the Estonian language and culture. The new integration plan will include activities designed for native Estonians as well as the long-term foreign residents of Estonia. More attention will also be paid to new immigrants and refugees, as well as compatriots living outside Estonia.

New regulations aimed at preventing disregard for employment rules in Estonia entered into force in July 2020. Under these amendments, the lawfulness of the employment of a foreigner is the responsibility of the company in Estonia that gains actual benefit from the foreigner's work. The obligation to prove the lawful grounds of employment extends to companies using temporary agency staff. These amendments also ensure that the income tax payable by foreigners working in Estonia is received in Estonia.

The government approved an amendment to the Citizenship Act, which allows the Estonian citizenship to be removed from a person who has committed a crime against the state, such as treason or terrorist offences. This amendment only applies to people having acquired Estonian citizenship through naturalisation.

The government approved a draft act concerning the creation of a national automated biometric identification system (ABIS) database. In the first stage, biometric data collected in offence proceedings will be transferred to ABIS. In the second stage, biometric data from the Identity Documents Database, the Database of Prohibitions on Entry and the Visa Register, will be transferred to ABIS.

As of April 2021, background checks on e-residency applicants were reinforced, in the context of the programme's growth. An e-resident's digital ID may not be issued to a person who is a threat to public order or national security.

For further information: www.politsei.ee | www.stat.ee | www.siseministeerium.ee | www.workinestonia.com | www.tootukassa.ee

Key figures on immigration and emigration – Estonia

Grants of long-term residence permits
2020 (Source: Eurostat)

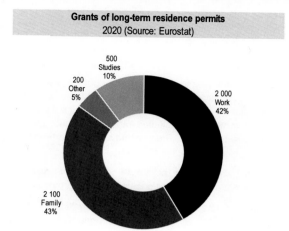

- 500 Studies 10%
- 200 Other 5%
- 2 000 Work 42%
- 2 100 Family 43%

Temporary migration
(Source: Eurostat)

Temporary migration (non-EU citizens)

	2020	2020/19
Employment reasons	50	- 55%
Family reasons	40	- 38%
Education reasons	70	+ 100%
Other reason	60	+ 11%

Humanitarian

	2021	2021/20
Asylum seekers	80	+ 60%

Inflows of top 10 nationalities
(national definition)

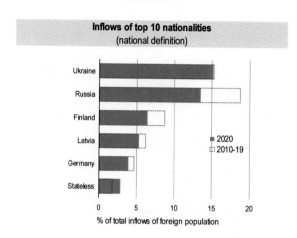

- Ukraine
- Russia
- Finland
- Latvia
- Germany
- Stateless

■ 2020
□ 2010-19

% of total inflows of foreign population

Emigration of Estonians to OECD countries
(national definition)

- Finland
- Germany
- Netherlands
- Australia
- Sweden
- Norway
- United States
- Switzerland
- Denmark
- Austria

■ 2020

% of total emigration of Estonians to OECD countries

Components of population growth

	2021 Per 1 000 inhabitants	2021/20 difference
Total	1.3	+0.5
Natural increase	-4.0	-2.0
Net migration plus statistical adjustments	5.3	+2.5

Annual remittances

	Million current USD	Annual change %	Share in GDP %
Inflows (2021)	580	+4.8	+1.6
Outflows (2021)	258	+26.4	+0.7

Labour market outcomes
2021

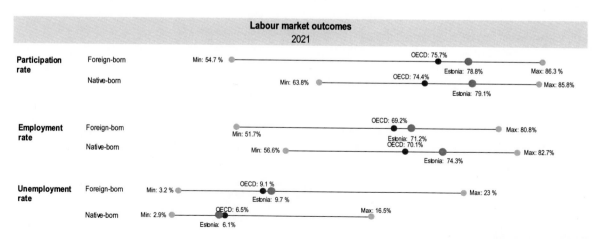

Participation rate

Foreign-born — Min: 54.7% — OECD: 75.7% — Estonia: 78.8% — Max: 86.3%

Native-born — Min: 63.8% — OECD: 74.4% — Max: 85.8% — Estonia: 79.1%

Employment rate

Foreign-born — Min: 51.7% — OECD: 69.2% — Estonia: 71.2% — Max: 80.8%

Native-born — Min: 56.6% — OECD: 70.1% — Max: 82.7% — Estonia: 74.3%

Unemployment rate

Foreign-born — Min: 3.2% — OECD: 9.1% — Estonia: 9.7% — Max: 23%

Native-born — Min: 2.9% — OECD: 6.5% — Max: 16.5% — Estonia: 6.1%

StatLink ⏷ https://stat.link/6l423z

Finland

Foreign-born population – 2021	7.6% of the population	Main countries of birth:
Size: 0.4 million, 48% of women	Evolution since 2011: +70%	Estonia (11%), Sweden (8%), Iraq (5%)

In 2020, Finland received 24 000 new immigrants on a long-term or permanent basis (including changes of status and free mobility), -6.8% compared to 2019. This figure comprises 28% immigrants benefitting from free mobility, 23.6% labour migrants, 35.9% family members (including accompanying family) and 12.2% humanitarian migrants. Around 3 200 permits were issued to tertiary-level international students and 2 900 to temporary and seasonal labour migrants (excluding intra-EU migration). In addition, 25 000 intra-EU postings were recorded in 2020, a decrease of -30% compared to 2019. These posted workers are generally on short-term contracts.

Russia, Estonia and Iraq were the top three nationalities of newcomers in 2020. Among the top 15 countries of origin, Ukraine registered the strongest increase (200) and India the largest decrease (-400) in flows to Finland compared to the previous year.

In 2021, the number of first asylum applicants decreased by -6.2%, to reach around 1 400. The majority of applicants came from Afghanistan (200), Iraq (200) and Somalia (100). The largest increase since 2020 concerned nationals of Georgia (50) and the largest decrease nationals of Iraq (-300). Of the 2 310 decisions taken in 2021, 46% were positive.

In September 2021, Finland introduced for the first time quantitative targets to education and work-based immigration: at least doubling work-based immigration from its current level by 2030; and tripling the number of new foreign students to 15 000 students a year. The aim is that 75% of them stay in Finland for work after graduation.

The introduction of a fast-track plan for specialists, start-up entrepreneurs and their family came into force in June 2022 in the form of a long-term visa (visa D). It is now proposed to extend this plan to researchers, students and their family. Since April 2022, international students have extended work opportunities (from 25 to 30 hours per week) and graduates have new opportunities to stay in Finland to settle and work. The job-search visa for graduates saw its duration extended from one to two years after graduation.

An Act to improve the legal status and earnings of foreigners picking natural products and to ensure equal treatment with other companies providing the same services, entered into force in June 2021. It defines these workers' rights and obligations.

The government submitted a proposal on 21 April 2022 to amend the Act on Foreigners and enable Finland to make use of the support from the European Union Agency for Asylum in the event of a mass influx of migrants. This is the second part of a broader project launched by the Ministry of the Interior. The first part was an amendment to the Reception Act that entered into force on 1 January 2022. The Finnish Immigration Service is now fully responsible for planning and organising reception services in case of a mass influx of migrants. The third part should concern the use of additional personnel in detention units.

A new Act to foster the integration of immigrants has been proposed to Parliament in May 2022 and could possibly enter into force at the end of 2024. Municipalities and other local actors would get more responsibilities to assess service needs related to skills and integration, at an early stage, as well as multilingual orientation to Finnish society, education, guidance and information to promote integration. Integration plans would be shortened and more tailored to individual needs.

Adopted in October 2021, the government Action Plan for Combating Racism will be carried out in different branches of government until 2023. The Action Plan aims to dismantle structural inequalities in society, promote non-discrimination in the Finnish working life, strengthen the authorities' equality competence, raise awareness of racism and its various forms, and develop research and data collection related to racism.

For further information: www.tem.fi/en/labour-migration-and-integration | www.migri.fi | www.stat.fi | www.intermin.fi

Key figures on immigration and emigration – Finland

Long-term immigration flows
2020 (Source: OECD)

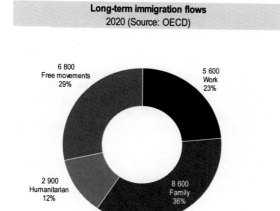

- 6 800 Free movements 29%
- 5 600 Work 23%
- 8 600 Family 36%
- 2 900 Humanitarian 12%

Temporary migration
(Sources: OECD, Eurostat)

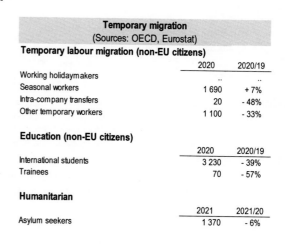

Temporary labour migration (non-EU citizens)

	2020	2020/19
Working holidaymakers	..	..
Seasonal workers	1 690	+ 7%
Intra-company transfers	20	- 48%
Other temporary workers	1 100	- 33%

Education (non-EU citizens)

	2020	2020/19
International students	3 230	- 39%
Trainees	70	- 57%

Humanitarian

	2021	2021/20
Asylum seekers	1 370	- 6%

Inflows of top 10 nationalities
(national definition)

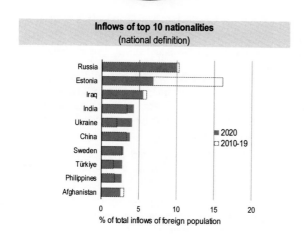

Russia, Estonia, Iraq, India, Ukraine, China, Sweden, Türkiye, Philippines, Afghanistan

■ 2020
□ 2010-19

% of total inflows of foreign population

Emigration of Finnish citizens to OECD countries
(national definition)

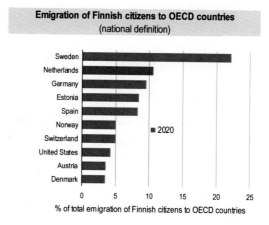

Sweden, Netherlands, Germany, Estonia, Spain, Norway, Switzerland, United States, Austria, Denmark

■ 2020

% of total emigration of Finnish citizens to OECD countries

Components of population growth

	2021 Per 1 000 inhabitants	2021/20 difference
Total	2.6	+1.1
Natural increase	-1.5	+0.1
Net migration plus statistical adjustments	4.1	+0.9

Annual remittances

	Million current USD	Annual change %	Share in GDP %
Inflows (2021)	842	+5.5	+0.3
Outflows (2021)	1 013	+3.7	+0.3

Labour market outcomes
2021

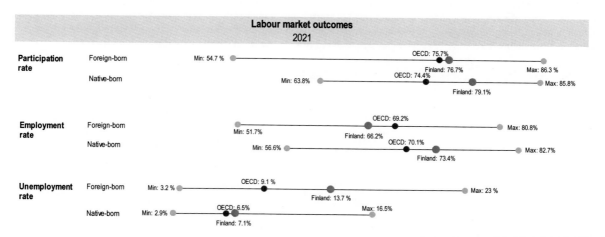

Participation rate
- Foreign-born: Min: 54.7 %, OECD: 75.7%, Finland: 76.7%, Max: 86.3 %
- Native-born: Min: 63.8%, OECD: 74.4%, Finland: 79.1%, Max: 85.8%

Employment rate
- Foreign-born: Min: 51.7%, OECD: 69.2%, Finland: 66.2%, Max: 80.8%
- Native-born: Min: 56.6%, OECD: 70.1%, Finland: 73.4%, Max: 82.7%

Unemployment rate
- Foreign-born: Min: 3.2 %, OECD: 9.1 %, Finland: 13.7 %, Max: 23 %
- Native-born: Min: 2.9%, OECD: 6.5%, Finland: 7.1%, Max: 16.5%

StatLink https://stat.link/vhro47

France

Foreign-born population – 2021	13.3% of the population	Main countries of birth:
Size: 8.6 million, 52% of women	Evolution since 2011: +16%	Algeria (16%), Morocco (12%), Portugal (7%)

In 2020, France received 238 000 new immigrants on a long-term or permanent basis (including changes of status and free mobility), -18.1% compared to 2019. This figure comprises 27% immigrants benefitting from free mobility, 18.4% labour migrants, 35% family members (including accompanying family) and 11.6% humanitarian migrants. Around 70 000 permits were issued to tertiary-level international students and 14 000 to temporary and seasonal labour migrants (excluding intra-EU migration). In addition, 308 000 intra-EU postings were recorded in 2020, a decrease of -32% compared to 2019. These posted workers are generally on short-term contracts.

Algeria, Morocco and Italy were the top three nationalities of newcomers in 2020. Among the top 15 countries of origin, Guinea registered the strongest increase (1 000) and Morocco the largest decrease (-5 100) in flows to France compared to the previous year.

In 2021, the number of first asylum applicants increased by 27%, to reach around 104 000. The majority of applicants came from Afghanistan (16 000), Côte d'Ivoire (6 200) and Bangladesh (6 200). The largest increase since 2020 concerned nationals of Afghanistan (6 000) and the largest decrease nationals of Angola (-900). Of the 137 000 decisions taken in 2021, 25% were positive.

An online residence permit application service was opened for international students in 2020. On 24 March 2021, a new online application platform has been implemented for some other types of residence permits based on digitalised documents. The deployment of this e-service will be gradual and will eventually concern all applications. As of 6 April 2021, work authorisations must also be submitted through a new Online Application Platform. Processing criteria have been adapted, especially lifting the qualification-occupation matching and focusing on the employers' efforts rather than on shortage indicators. The Shortage Occupation List, which was last published in 2008, has been updated in 2021 with some regional specificities. The lists, which exempt an extended number of occupations from the labour market test, are planned to be updated regularly. The Labour Authorities ("DIRECCTE") are no longer involved in application processing and are replaced by interregional platforms.

In 2021, France signed an agreement with Peru on the implementation of a working holiday programme, and a partnership agreement with India to facilitate the mobility of students, academics, researchers, as well as other labour migration and to encourage the mobility of skills and talents.

A national plan for reception of asylum seekers and integration of refugees has been launched for 2021-23. The plan includes concrete actions to better identify vulnerable groups and improve their support. Accordingly, the accommodation capacity has been increased, alongside a better spread across the territory. Following the increase in the numbers of unaccompanied minors in France, a new system registering individual data was also gradually deployed in 2020 in order to better guarantee child protection and avoid transfers between departments. In addition, clearer instructions facilitating the residence permit applications of unaccompanied minors at 18 years old have been provided.

France is continuing to assess measures to strengthen integration of newly arrived third-country nationals and to suggest complementary measures to the Republican Integration Contract, with a growing priority on French language courses. Those complementary schemes focus on the labour market integration of immigrant women, tackling the digital divide, promoting internal mobility of humanitarian migrants from the capital region to other regions and improving their access to mental health support. Projects enabling relationships between newcomers and the host-country society are receiving special attention, in particular those involving young French nationals in the reception and integration of immigrants of the same age and mentorship programmes with volunteers. In addition, training programmes towards reception services and language learning professionals are encouraged. As regards French citizenship applications, the level of French language required was increased in 2020.

For further information: https://www.immigration.interieur.gouv.fr/Immigration | https://accueil-integration-refugies.fr/

Key figures on immigration and emigration – France

Long-term immigration flows
2020 (Source: OECD)

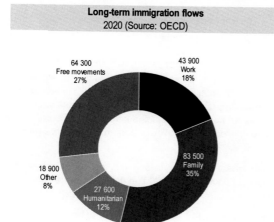

Temporary migration
(Sources: OECD, Eurostat)

Temporary labour migration (non-EU citizens)

	2020	2020/19
Working holidaymakers	2 040	- 61%
Seasonal workers	5 760	- 44%
Intra-company transfers	..	..
Other temporary workers	3 290	- 42%

Education (non-EU citizens)

	2020	2020/19
International students	70 200	- 19%
Trainees	2 500	- 41%

Humanitarian

	2021	2021/20
Asylum seekers	103 810	+ 27%

Inflows of top 10 nationalities
(national definition)

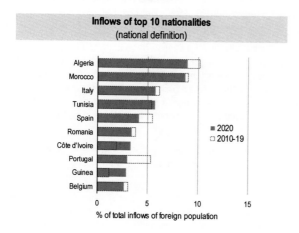

Emigration of French to OECD countries
(national definition)

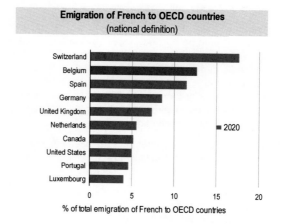

Components of population growth

	2021 Per 1 000 inhabitants	2021/20 difference
Total	2.7	+0.2
Natural increase	1.2	+0.2
Net migration plus statistical adjustments	1.5	+0.0

Annual remittances

	Million current USD	Annual change %	Share in GDP %
Inflows (2021)	26 291	+0.6	+0.9
Outflows (2021)	15 050	+2.9	+0.5

Labour market outcomes
2021

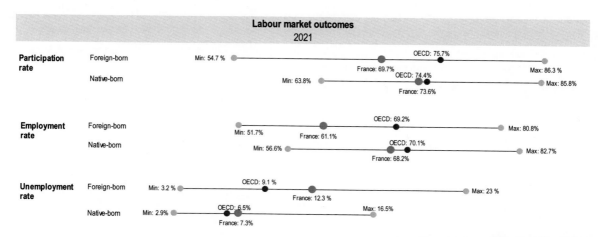

StatLink https://stat.link/cme1ly

Germany

Foreign-born population – 2021	16.2% of the population	Main countries of birth:
Size: 13.6 million, 49% of women	Evolution since 2011: +29%	Poland (11%), Türkiye (9%), Russia (7%)

In 2020, Germany received 532 000 new immigrants on a long-term or permanent basis (including changes of status and free mobility), -17.3% compared to 2019. This figure comprises 63.5% immigrants benefitting from free mobility, 10.1% labour migrants, 13.7% family members (including accompanying family) and 12% humanitarian migrants. Around 12 000 permits were issued to tertiary-level international students and 6 100 to temporary and seasonal labour migrants (excluding intra-EU migration). In addition, 411 000 intra-EU postings were recorded in 2020, a decrease of -19% compared to 2019. These posted workers are generally on short-term contracts.

Romania, Poland and Bulgaria were the top three nationalities of newcomers in 2020. Among the top 15 countries of origin, Afghanistan registered the strongest increase (1 100) and Romania the largest decrease (-46 000) in flows to Germany compared to the previous year.

In 2021, the number of first asylum applicants increased by 44.5% to reach around 148 000. The majority of applicants came from Syria (55 000), Afghanistan (23 000) and Iraq (16 000). The largest increase since 2020 concerned nationals of Syria (18 500) and the largest decrease nationals of Nigeria (-800). Of the 133 000 decisions taken in 2021, 45% were positive.

In November 2021, the German Government adopted its coalition agreement, which codifies the objectives for the upcoming four years. The agreement envisages several measures aimed at facilitating labour migration. These include the introduction of a points-based opportunity card providing entry to job seekers from third countries, an expansion of the EU Blue Card to non-academic professionals and the possibility for holders of a residence permit to stay abroad temporarily. In addition, the Western Balkan regulation, currently limited in time until 2023, will no longer be subject to this limit. According to this regulation, the Federal Employment Agency can allow nationals from the countries of the Western Balkans with a job offer to take up employment in Germany. The coalition agreement also includes the aim to facilitate the participation of international students in higher education as well as vocational education and training.

The coalition agreement further seeks to offer integration courses to new arrivals immediately and to shorten the qualifying period of prior residence for naturalisation and settlement permits to five and three years respectively. In addition, dual citizenship will generally be permitted.

In the area of humanitarian migration, the agreement foresees the removal of employment bans for people already living in Germany and an easier path to family reunification for persons under subsidiary protection. Several measures seek to facilitate residence for persons with a toleration status, i.e. a temporary suspension of deportation. For example, people with this status will be able to obtain residence permits when undergoing vocational training. The government also plans a number of legislative and other measures to facilitate the return of persons who have no right to stay in Germany.

The Skilled Workers Immigration Act, which came into force in March 2020, introduced an accelerated administrative procedure for skilled workers and their family members. This procedure shortens the deadline for recognition procedures for professions under federal law. Throughout 2020 and 2021, the federal states adopted equivalent regulations for professions governed by federal state law. Furthermore, the Skilled Workers Immigration Act enables the Federal Employment Agency to conclude placement agreements with third countries for skilled foreign professionals. Workers recruited via these agreements can initiate the recognition procedure of their qualifications while taking up employment in Germany in parallel. In July 2021, the Federal Employment Agency signed the first agreement for nurses with Indonesia. In December 2021, it concluded further agreements with the Indian state Kerala for nurses, with Mexico for nurses and chefs, with Colombia for electricians and gardeners and in May 2022 with Jordan for nurses.

Other bilateral labour agreements concluded with Georgia in January 2020 and with Moldova in July 2021 allow nationals of these third countries to engage in seasonal agricultural work in Germany.

In February 2022, the German Government appointed its first national anti-racism commissioner. The commissioner plans, inter alia, to establish a consultation centre for victims of racism, draft a national action plan and co-ordinate the actions of the different ministries against racism.

For further information: www.bmas.de | www.bmi.bund.de | www.bamf.de | www.destatis.de

Key figures on immigration and emigration – Germany

Long-term immigration flows
2020 (Source: OECD)

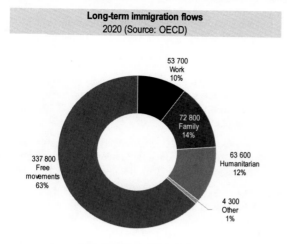

Temporary migration
(Sources: OECD, Eurostat)

Temporary labour migration (non-EU citizens)

	2020	2020/19
Working holidaymakers	..	..
Seasonal workers	..	..
Intra-company transfers	2 940	- 56%
Other temporary workers	..	..

Education (non-EU citizens)

	2020	2020/19
International students	12 360	- 75%
Trainees	3 120	- 39%

Humanitarian

	2021	2021/20
Asylum seekers	148 240	+ 45%

Inflows of top 10 nationalities
(national definition)

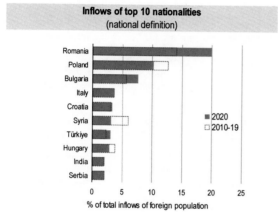

% of total inflows of foreign population

Emigration of Germans to OECD countries
(national definition)

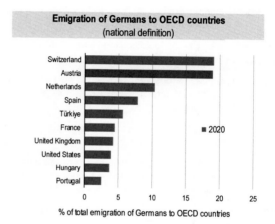

% of total emigration of Germans to OECD countries

Components of population growth

	2021 Per 1 000 inhabitants	2021/20 difference
Total	1.0	+1.1
Natural increase	-2.7	-0.1
Net migration plus statistical adjustments	3.7	+1.3

Annual remittances

	Million current USD	Annual change %	Share in GDP %
Inflows (2021)	20 412	+11.7	+0.5
Outflows (2020)	22 024	-8.0	+0.6

Labour market outcomes
2021

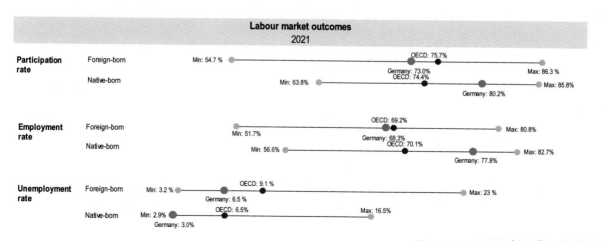

StatLink 🔗 https://stat.link/bhn29y

Greece

Foreign-born population – 2021	13.1% of the population	Main countries of birth:
Size: 1.4 million, 54% of women	Evolution since 2011: +3%	Albania (48%), Georgia (7%), Russia (5%)

In 2020, 20 000 new immigrants obtained a residence permit longer than 12 months in Greece (excluding EU citizens), -53.2% compared to 2019. This figure comprises 8.2% labour migrants, 42% family members (including accompanying family), 3.5% who came for education reasons and 46.3% other migrants. In addition, 11 000 intra-EU postings were recorded in 2020, a decrease of -35% compared to 2019. These posted workers are generally on short-term contracts.

In 2021, the number of first asylum applicants decreased by -40.1% to reach around 23 000. The majority of applicants came from Pakistan (3 400), Afghanistan (3 200) and Syria (2 900). The largest increase since 2020 concerned nationals of Bangladesh (860) and the largest decrease nationals of Afghanistan (-7 900). Of the 37 000 decisions taken in 2021, 44% were positive.

In June 2021, Greece started COVID-19 vaccinations in migrant camps of Lesbos, Samos and Chios islands. On mainland camps, the authorities launched a dedicated vaccination campaign available to all those without social or health security number. To ensure that everyone can access vaccination, Greek authorities issued a temporary social security number (AMKA) to all foreigners and uninsured individuals TCNs. In August 2021, the Ministry of Migration and Asylum activated the online platform for automatic renewal of residence permits until December 2021.

In March 2021, in the context of the digital transformation of the asylum process, the Ministry of Migration and Asylum proceeded to digital issuance of a Tax Identification Number (AFM) to TCNs or stateless persons who are holders of the International Protection Applicant Status.

In September 2021, a one-year renewable visa was created for digital nomads working from Greece, whether self-employed or employed by a foreign company. This visa grants holders immigration status, under income conditions, but does not allow to change status or work in Greece.

As of 1 October 2021, the Ministry of Migration and Asylum took the responsibility for implementing the financial assistance programme for applicants for international protection implemented until then by UNHCR.

In August 2021, the Greek Government introduced a new legislation initiative aiming to accelerate deportations of irregular migrants. The new legislation reduces the period for deportations from 30 days to between a week and 25 days and make it more difficult for migrants to challenge a deportation order by applying a stricter definition to what can be regarded as "humanitarian grounds".

In 2021, new provisions relating to residence permits for investors were put in place, allowing investors to apply for a residence permit without coming to Greece. They still have to come to Greece to submit biometric data within one year from the application date.

In October 2020, the citizenship code was amended (Ministerial Decision Prot. No. 2984/2021) and established for the first time specific and strict economic criteria for applicants for Greek citizenship. The decision clarifies that applicants must prove that their annual income ensures an adequate standard of living without burdening the Greek welfare system.

Further information: www.migration.gov.gr | www.astynomia.gr | www.statistics.gr

Key figures on immigration and emigration – Greece

Grants of long-term residence permits
2020 (Source: Eurostat)

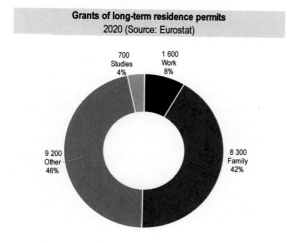

700 Studies 4%
1 600 Work 8%
9 200 Other 46%
8 300 Family 42%

Asylum seekers
(Source: Eurostat)

	2021	2021/20
Asylum seekers	22 660	- 40%

Inflows of top 10 nationalities
(national definition)

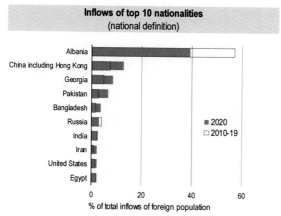

% of total inflows of foreign population

Emigration of Greeks to OECD countries
(national definition)

% of total emigration of Greeks to OECD countries

Components of population growth

	2021 Per 1 000 inhabitants	2021/20 difference
Total	-7.0	-3.3
Natural increase	-5.5	-1.2
Net migration plus statistical adjustments	-1.6	-2.2

Annual remittances

	Million current USD	Annual change %	Share in GDP %
Inflows (2021)	689	+4.7	+0.3
Outflows (2021)	2 938	+7.8	+1.4

Labour market outcomes
2021

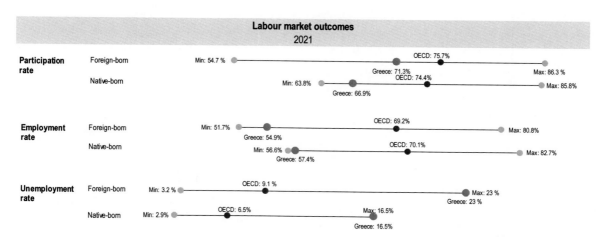

Participation rate	Foreign-born	Min: 54.7 %	OECD: 75.7%	Greece: 71.3%	Max: 86.3 %
	Native-born	Min: 63.8%	OECD: 74.4%	Greece: 66.9%	Max: 85.8%
Employment rate	Foreign-born	Min: 51.7%	OECD: 69.2%	Greece: 54.9%	Max: 80.8%
	Native-born	Min: 56.6%	OECD: 70.1%	Greece: 57.4%	Max: 82.7%
Unemployment rate	Foreign-born	Min: 3.2 %	OECD: 9.1 %	Greece: 23 %	Max: 23 %
	Native-born	Min: 2.9%	OECD: 6.5%	Greece: 16.5%	Max: 16.5%

StatLink https://stat.link/6vmyrf

Hungary

Foreign-born population – 2021	6.2% of the population	Main countries of birth:
Size: 0.6 million, 48% of women	Evolution since 2011: +36%	Romania (35%), Ukraine (12%), Serbia (7%)

In 2020, 44 000 new immigrants obtained a residence permit longer than 12 months in Hungary (excluding EU citizens), -0.3% compared to 2019. This figure comprises 62% labour migrants, 6.1% family members (including accompanying family), 13% who came for education reasons and 18.9% other migrants. Around 3 300 short-term permits were issued to international students and 4 600 to temporary and seasonal labour migrants (excluding intra-EU migration). In addition, 29 000 intra-EU postings were recorded in 2020, an increase of 42% compared to 2019. These posted workers are generally on short-term contracts.

Ukraine, the Slovak Republic and Germany were the top three nationalities of newcomers in 2020. Among the top 15 countries of origin, the Slovak Republic registered the strongest increase (4 500) and Ukraine the largest decrease (-12 000) in flows to Hungary compared to the previous year.

In 2021, the number of first asylum applicants decreased by -55.6% to reach around 40. The majority of applicants came from Iran (10), Afghanistan (5) and Ethiopia (5). The largest increase since 2020 concerned nationals of Iran (5). Of the 60 decisions taken in 2021, 67% were positive.

In 2020 and 2021, no legislative or administrative changes occurred relating to the status, conditions of access to the labour market and entitlement for jobseeker's benefit of foreign workers.

In August 2021, Hungary carried out its own rescue operation from Afghanistan to bring Hungarian, allied and EU citizens, as well as Afghan citizens and their families who have been working with Hungarian troops in recent years, to Hungary. As a result of the operation, a total of 540 people were evacuated, including 57 Afghan families and 180 Afghan children. Evacuated Afghan citizens are offered the opportunity to restart their lives in Hungary. There are no plans to admit additional Afghan nationals.

Third-country nationals legally in Hungary and unable to leave during the COVID-19 pandemic and after the expiry of a visa were granted a temporary residence certificate. This was extended during successive waves of the pandemic until 28 February 2022.

For further information: www.bmbah.hu

Key figures on immigration and emigration – Hungary

Grants of long-term residence permits
2020 (Source: Eurostat)

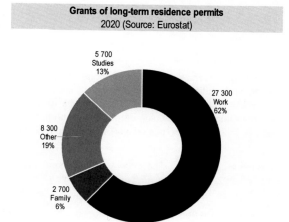

- 5 700 Studies 13%
- 27 300 Work 62%
- 8 300 Other 19%
- 2 700 Family 6%

Temporary migration
(Source: Eurostat)

Temporary migration (non-EU citizens)

	2020	2020/19
Employment reasons	4 560	- 33%
Family reasons	940	..
Education reasons	3 260	- 28%
Other reason	2 070	- 10%

Humanitarian

	2021	2021/20
Asylum seekers	40	- 56%

Inflows of top 10 nationalities
(national definition)

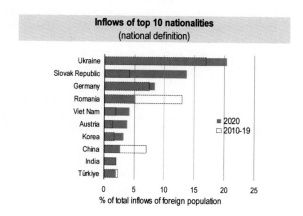

Ukraine, Slovak Republic, Germany, Romania, Viet Nam, Austria, Korea, China, India, Türkiye

■ 2020 ☐ 2010-19

% of total inflows of foreign population

Emigration of Hungarians to OECD countries
(national definition)

Germany, Austria, United Kingdom, Netherlands, Switzerland, Czech Republic, United States, Denmark, Canada, Belgium

■ 2020

% of total emigration of Hungarians to OECD countries

Components of population growth

	2021 Per 1 000 inhabitants	2021/20 difference
Total	-4.3	-0.3
Natural increase	-6.4	-1.5
Net migration plus statistical adjustments	2.1	+1.2

Annual remittances

	Million current USD	Annual change %	Share in GDP %
Inflows (2021)	3 487	-25.0	+1.9
Outflows (2021)	1 623	+19.9	+0.9

Labour market outcomes
2021

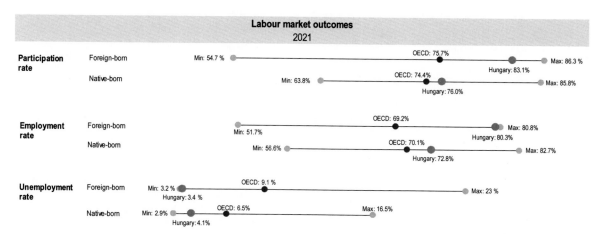

Participation rate
- Foreign-born: Min: 54.7 % — OECD: 75.7% — Hungary: 83.1% — Max: 86.3 %
- Native-born: Min: 63.8 % — OECD: 74.4% — Hungary: 76.0% — Max: 85.8 %

Employment rate
- Foreign-born: Min: 51.7% — OECD: 69.2% — Hungary: 80.3% — Max: 80.8%
- Native-born: Min: 56.6% — OECD: 70.1% — Hungary: 72.8% — Max: 82.7%

Unemployment rate
- Foreign-born: Min: 3.2 % — Hungary: 3.4 % — OECD: 9.1 % — Max: 23 %
- Native-born: Min: 2.9% — Hungary: 4.1% — OECD: 6.5% — Max: 16.5%

StatLink https://stat.link/knqj6m

Ireland

Foreign-born population – 2016	17.3% of the population	Main countries of birth:
Size: 0.8 million, 51% of women	Evolution since 2011: +6%	United Kingdom (34%), Poland (14%), Lithuania (4%)

In 2020, Ireland received 43 000 new immigrants on a long-term or permanent basis (including changes of status and free mobility), -17.2% compared to 2019. This figure comprises 61.3% immigrants benefitting from free mobility, 30.5% labour migrants, 4.3% family members (including accompanying family) and 3.8% humanitarian migrants. Around 15 000 permits were issued to tertiary-level international students and 900 to temporary and seasonal labour migrants (excluding intra-EU migration). In addition, 8 200 intra-EU postings were recorded in 2020, a decrease of -52% compared to 2019. These posted workers are generally on short-term contracts.

In 2021, the number of first asylum applicants increased by 70.4% to reach around 2 600. The majority of applicants came from Nigeria (500), Georgia (300) and Somalia (300). The largest increase since 2020 concerned nationals of Georgia (300) and the largest decrease nationals of Brazil (-30). Of the 1 550 decisions taken in 2021, 94% were positive.

A new centre-right-Green coalition government formed following the general election in February 2020 introduced two main migration policy initiatives. First, a White Paper to End Direct Provision and to Establish a New International Protection Support Service was published in February 2021. The white paper proposed that newly arrived asylum seekers would spend a maximum of four months in state-owned reception and integration centres. In a second phase, accommodation would be offered in own-door self-contained units. Asylum applicants would be allowed access to the labour market after six months and would otherwise be eligible for mainstream social welfare support payments. Reforms are to be achieved by 2024. The main progress up to March 2022 has been the provision of several hundred self-contained apartment units for applicants in the system.

Second, following the commitment in the 2020 programme for government to develop policy for the regularisation of long-term undocumented migrants, a regularisation scheme was announced in July 2021 for those who had been resident and undocumented for four or more years, or three years in the case of those with children in Ireland. The scheme, launched in January 2022, provides for successful applicants to receive an immigration permission, access to the labour market and to be able to begin the naturalisation process.

Eligible applicants include individuals who have been undocumented (i.e. without an immigration permission) for at least four years; individuals who have dependent children living with them will be eligible to apply after three years of being undocumented in the State; international protection applicants who have been in the international protection process for at least two years are also eligible to apply.

For further information: www.inis.gov.ie | www.ria.gov.ie | www.enterprise.gov.ie

Key figures on immigration and emigration – Ireland

Long-term immigration flows
2020 (Source: OECD)

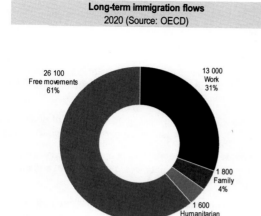

- 26 100 Free movements 61%
- 13 000 Work 31%
- 1 800 Family 4%
- 1 600 Humanitarian 4%

Temporary migration
(Sources: OECD, Eurostat)

Temporary labour migration (non-EU citizens)

	2020	2020/19
Working holidaymakers	..	..
Seasonal workers	..	..
Intra-company transfers	720	- 42%
Other temporary workers	140	- 42%

Education (non-EU citizens)

	2020	2020/19
International students	14 730	- 58%
Trainees	20	- 39%

Humanitarian

	2021	2021/20
Asylum seekers	2 620	+ 70%

Inflows of top 10 nationalities
(national definition)

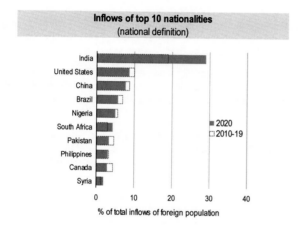

India, United States, China, Brazil, Nigeria, South Africa, Pakistan, Philippines, Canada, Syria

■ 2020
□ 2010-19

% of total inflows of foreign population

Emigration of Irish citizens to OECD countries
(national definition)

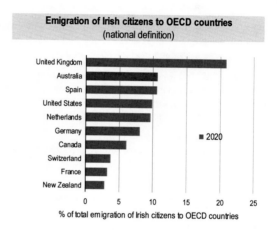

United Kingdom, Australia, Spain, United States, Netherlands, Germany, Canada, Switzerland, France, New Zealand

■ 2020

% of total emigration of Irish citizens to OECD countries

Components of population growth

	2021 Per 1 000 inhabitants	2021/20 difference
Total	10.7	+2.3
Natural increase	5.0	+0.3
Net migration plus statistical adjustments	5.6	+1.9

Annual remittances

	Million current USD	Annual change %	Share in GDP %
Inflows (2021)	180	-69.3	+0.0
Outflows (2020)	..	..	..

Labour market outcomes
2021

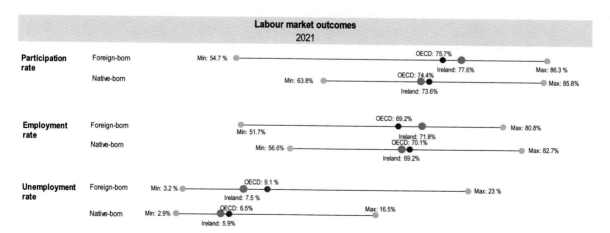

Participation rate
- Foreign-born: Min: 54.7 % — OECD: 75.7% — Ireland: 77.6% — Max: 86.3 %
- Native-born: Min: 63.8% — OECD: 74.4% — Ireland: 73.6% — Max: 85.8%

Employment rate
- Foreign-born: Min: 51.7% — OECD: 69.2% — Ireland: 71.8% — Max: 80.8%
- Native-born: Min: 56.6% — OECD: 70.1% — Ireland: 69.2% — Max: 82.7%

Unemployment rate
- Foreign-born: Min: 3.2 % — OECD: 9.1 % — Ireland: 7.5 % — Max: 23 %
- Native-born: Min: 2.9% — OECD: 6.5% — Ireland: 5.9% — Max: 16.5%

StatLink https://stat.link/5oj90f

Israel

Foreign-born population – 2021	20.4% of the population	Main countries of birth:
Size: 1.8 million, 55% of women	Evolution since 2011: -4%	Former USSR (50%), Morocco (7%), United States (6%)

In 2020, Israel received 20 000 new immigrants on a long-term or permanent basis (including changes of status), -40.8% compared to 2019. This figure comprises 32% family members (including accompanying family). Around 26 000 permits were issued to temporary and seasonal labour migrants.

Russia, Ukraine and France were the top three nationalities of newcomers in 2020. Among the top 15 countries of origin, France registered the strongest increase (200) and Russia the largest decrease (-9 200) in flows to Israel compared to the previous year.

In 2021, the number of first asylum applicants increased by 2.2% to reach around 1900. The majority of applicants came from China (400), India (268) and Republic of Moldova (190). The largest increase since 2020 concerned nationals of China (320) and the largest decrease nationals of Russia (-270). Of the 7 290 decisions taken in 2021, 0% were positive.

Permanent migration to Israel picked up in 2021 after a COVID-related decline. The Ministry of Immigration and Integration reported 29 000 new immigrants under the Law of Return, back to the 2018 level but lower than in 2019. The leading origin countries were Russia, United States, Ukraine, France and Ethiopia.

The formation of a government in mid-2021 led to several policy changes regarding temporary foreign workers. The main changes were increases in the ceilings and the elimination of the employer levy. The ceiling on the number of temporary foreign workers in construction was increased in 2021, to 30 000 non-Israeli workers and 80 000 Palestinian cross-border workers.

In February 2022, the levy – an employment tax imposed on employers of foreign workers was eliminated. The levy applied to all foreigners employed in Israel, except for temporary workers in care and agriculture. The levy was eliminated primarily to respond to requests to reduce employment costs of construction workers but will also affect lower employer costs of temporary workers and asylum seekers in tourism and services, for example.

The number of temporary foreign workers rose to 104 000 at the end of 2021, up from 98 200 a year earlier. The main sectors of employment were care (57 500), agriculture (23 200) and construction (17 000). There were also 19 200 foreigners admitted for temporary work who were no longer compliant with their permit conditions, mostly workers who entered for care work and either overstayed or left their employers.

The temporary foreign work programme operates increasingly through bilateral labour agreements (BLAs). This procedure does not apply to experts and construction workers employed by authorised non-Israeli companies. As of June 2021, some foreign homebased caregivers arrived under BLA's. By the end of 2021, 50% of new homebased caregivers arriving in Israel arrived under BLA's.

As of 31 December 2021, 87 900 Palestinians holding permanent work permits and 12 500 holders of seasonal work permits were employed in Israel, an increase in the total number of active permit holders and of workers over the previous year. The total quotas for these workers were set at 98 250 regular permits and 12 500 seasonal permits. The quota has been largely steady since 2018, although it increased by about 13 000 (to allow additional construction workers) in August 2021.

In December 2021, the government proposed a quota for up to 500 international students to remain up to three years after their studies for employment in the technology sector, on the condition that they earn 150% the average salary after six months employment. This would extend the previous one-year maximum post-study work period, but would apply a salary threshold albeit being lower than the 200% threshold imposed on foreign experts.

For more Information: www.gov.il

Key figures on immigration and emigration – Israel

Long-term immigration flows
2020 (Source: OECD)

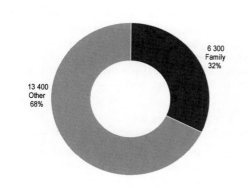

6 300
Family
32%

13 400
Other
68%

Temporary migration
(Sources: OECD, UNHCR)

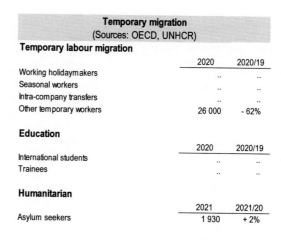

Temporary labour migration

	2020	2020/19
Working holidaymakers	..	..
Seasonal workers	..	..
Intra-company transfers	..	..
Other temporary workers	26 000	- 62%

Education

	2020	2020/19
International students	..	..
Trainees	..	..

Humanitarian

	2021	2021/20
Asylum seekers	1 930	+ 2%

Inflows of top 10 nationalities
(national definition)

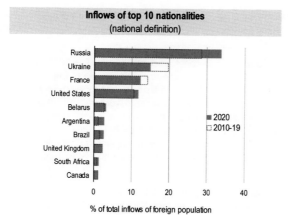

% of total inflows of foreign population

Emigration of Israelis to OECD countries
(national definition)

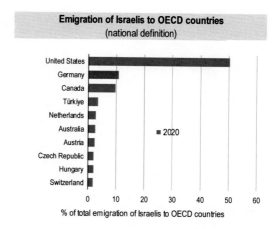

% of total emigration of Israelis to OECD countries

Components of population growth

	2021 Per 1 000 inhabitants	2021/20 difference
Total	17.4	+1.2
Natural increase	14.3	+0.4
Net migration plus statistical adjustments	3.1	+0.8

Annual remittances

	Million current USD	Annual change %	Share in GDP %
Inflows (2021)	6 096	-0.2	+1.3
Outflows (2020)	5 843	-6.4	+1.4

Labour market outcomes
2020 compared to 2021 OECD average

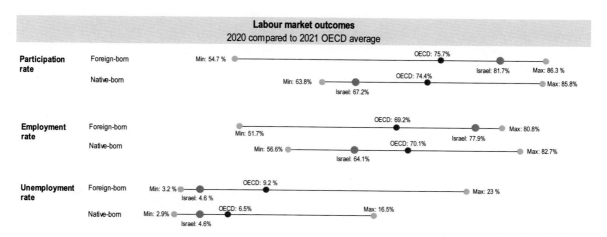

Italy

Foreign-born population – 2021	10.4% of the population	Main countries of birth:
Size: 6.3 million, 54% of women	Evolution since 2011: +9%	Romania (15%), Albania (8%), Former USSR (7%)

In 2020, Italy received 132 000 new immigrants on a long-term or permanent basis (including changes of status and free mobility), - 30.6% compared to 2019. This figure comprises 36% immigrants benefitting from free mobility, 6.4% labour migrants, 47.1% family members (including accompanying family) and 8.8% humanitarian migrants. Around 700 permits were issued to tertiary-level international students and 2 100 to temporary and seasonal labour migrants (excluding intra-EU migration). In addition, 91 000 intra-EU postings were recorded in 2020, a decrease of -48% compared to 2019. These posted workers are generally on short-term contracts.

Romania, Albania and Morocco were the top three nationalities of newcomers in 2020. Among the top 15 countries of origin, Nigeria registered the strongest increase (1 600) and Brazil the largest decrease (-11 000) in flows to Italy compared to the previous year.

In 2021, the number of first asylum applicants increased by 100% to reach around 44 000. The majority of applicants came from Pakistan (6 900), Bangladesh (6 600) and Tunisia (6 400). The largest increase since 2020 concerned nationals of Tunisia (5 400) and the largest decrease nationals of El Salvador (-450). Of the 44 000 decisions taken in 2021, 50% were positive.

Two major developments should be mentioned in 2021. First, the implementation of the regularisation of unregistered migrant workers in Italy prior to 8 March 2020 continued. The process was accelerated by the recruitment of temporary workers to deal with tens of thousands of applications.

The second development was a change in the annual quota decree for seasonal and non-seasonal workers. The 2021 quota decree – passed at the end of 2021 and applicable to entries in 2022 – allowed an increase in the legal admission of foreign workers to 69 700. The ceiling had been set at about 31 000 annually in the previous five years. The quota also assigned the number of seasonal and non-seasonal workers and those admitted in different economic sectors. The number of seasonal workers was set at 42 000, up from 18 000 in previous years. Employers' organisations in the agricultural sector were directly involved in managing the available entry quotas for seasonal workers. The number of workers in transport, construction and tourism/hospitality was set at 20 000, only from countries which have signed or are negotiating migration management co-operation agreements with Italy. Other parts of the quota are set aside for status changes. There is also a possibility the government may update the number of entries for seasonal and non-seasonal workers during the same year through the issue of new decrees.

In January 2022, the Ministry of Labour and Social Policies released a multi-year integrated plan for work, integration and inclusion, following consultations with different actors. The plan, covering 2021-27, follows on the previous 7-year plan. There are seven action areas: supporting co-operation among integration actors; fighting undeclared and exploitative work and promoting dignified work and a culture of legality; inclusion of vulnerable migrants; leveraging the full potential of school-age foreigners and other migrants in accessing the labour market; promoting social and work inclusion of migrant women; social, sport and cultural participation; and promotion of legal migration channels.

Faced with the crisis that followed the invasion of Ukraine by Russia, the Italian Government responded with a decree declaring a state of humanitarian emergency until 31 December 2022 and adopting urgent measures to counter its economic and humanitarian effects. These include increasing the resources available to the fund for national emergencies and expanding the national reception network. In addition, recognition of health professional qualifications for Ukrainian doctors and health workers has been relaxed, allowing them temporarily to practise professionally if residing in Ukraine before 24 February 2022.

For further information: www.interno.gov.it | www.integrazionemigranti.gov.it | www.istat.it

Key figures on immigration and emigration – Italy

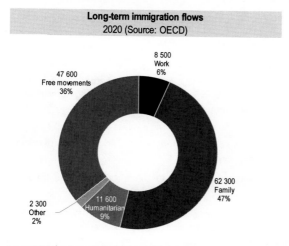

Long-term immigration flows
2020 (Source: OECD)

- 8 500 Work 6%
- 47 600 Free movements 36%
- 62 300 Family 47%
- 11 600 Humanitarian 9%
- 2 300 Other 2%

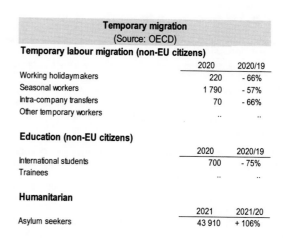

Temporary migration
(Source: OECD)

Temporary labour migration (non-EU citizens)

	2020	2020/19
Working holidaymakers	220	- 66%
Seasonal workers	1 790	- 57%
Intra-company transfers	70	- 66%
Other temporary workers	..	..

Education (non-EU citizens)

	2020	2020/19
International students	700	- 75%
Trainees	..	..

Humanitarian

	2021	2021/20
Asylum seekers	43 910	+ 106%

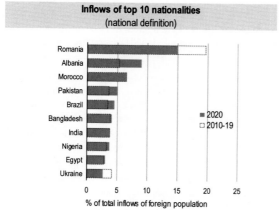

Inflows of top 10 nationalities
(national definition)

Romania, Albania, Morocco, Pakistan, Brazil, Bangladesh, India, Nigeria, Egypt, Ukraine

■ 2020 □ 2010-19

% of total inflows of foreign population

Emigration of Italians to OECD countries
(national definition)

Germany, Spain, Switzerland, France, United Kingdom, Netherlands, Belgium, Portugal, Austria, United States

■ 2020

% of total emigration of Italians to OECD countries

Components of population growth

	2021 Per 1 000 inhabitants	2021/20 difference
Total	-4.3	+2.5
Natural increase	-5.2	+0.4
Net migration plus statistical adjustments	1.0	+2.2

Annual remittances

	Million current USD	Annual change %	Share in GDP %
Inflows (2021)	10 258	-2.0	+0.5
Outflows (2021)	12 195	+19.6	+0.6

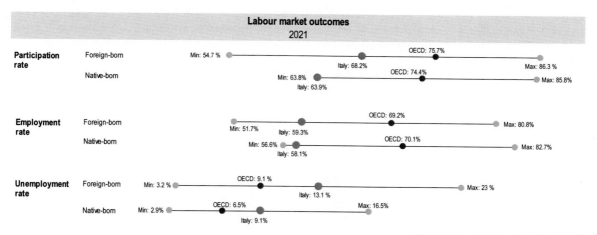

Labour market outcomes
2021

Participation rate
- Foreign-born: Min: 54.7% — Italy: 68.2% — OECD: 75.7% — Max: 86.3%
- Native-born: Min: 63.8% — Italy: 63.9% — OECD: 74.4% — Max: 85.8%

Employment rate
- Foreign-born: Min: 51.7% — Italy: 59.3% — OECD: 69.2% — Max: 80.8%
- Native-born: Min: 56.6% — Italy: 58.1% — OECD: 70.1% — Max: 82.7%

Unemployment rate
- Foreign-born: Min: 3.2% — OECD: 9.1% — Italy: 13.1% — Max: 23%
- Native-born: Min: 2.9% — OECD: 6.5% — Italy: 9.1% — Max: 16.5%

StatLink https://stat.link/7fa4dx

Japan

Foreign population – 2021	2.3% of the population	Main countries of birth:
Size: 2.9 million, 51% of women	Evolution since 2011: +35%	China (26%), Korea (16%), Viet Nam (11%)

In 2020, Japan received 85 000 new immigrants on a long-term or permanent basis (including changes of status), -38.2% compared to 2019. This figure comprises 66.7% labour migrants, 25.1% family members (including accompanying family) and 0.1% humanitarian migrants. Around 50 000 permits were issued to tertiary-level international students and 111 000 to temporary and seasonal labour migrants.

Viet Nam, China and Indonesia were the top three nationalities of newcomers in 2020. Among the top 15 countries of origin, China registered the largest decrease (-86 000) in flows to Japan compared to the previous year.

In 2021, the number of first asylum applicants decreased by -38.7% to reach around 2 400. Of the 14 000 decisions taken in 2021, 5% were positive.

Between 2021 and 2022, a few changes were made to the Specified Skilled Workers (SSW) Program, a status of Residence newly created in 2019, initially allowing foreign workers to work in 14 industry fields. The application procedures for the SSW Program were amended in 2021 to merge three manufacturing fields (Machine parts and tooling; Industrial machinery; and Electric, electronics and information) into a single field. Therefore, the SSW Program is to be re-organised under 12 industry fields.

As of May 2022, Japan has signed Memoranda of Co-operation related to the Status of Residence of SSW with 14 countries: the Philippines, Cambodia, Nepal, Myanmar, Mongolia, Sri Lanka, Indonesia, Viet Nam, Bangladesh, Uzbekistan, Pakistan, Thailand, India, and Malaysia.

The Immigration Services Agency started accepting online applications by foreign residents themselves by identifying the applications through the use of the individual certification function of the Individual Number Card in March 2022. All foreign nationals with an Individual Number Card can now apply for residence procedures online, such as acquisition of status of residence, extension of period of stay, change of status of residence, issuance of certificate of eligibility, issuance of certificate of authorised employment, re-entry permission and permission to engage in an activity other than that permitted under the status of residence previously granted. Only the status of residence "Diplomat" and "Temporary Visitor" are not eligible for online applications.

The Project to Promote Foreign National Entrepreneurial Activities, which started in December 2018, allows foreign entrepreneurs receiving support for entrepreneurial activities from local governments to stay in Japan to prepare for starting a business for a maximum of one year. The government decided to take necessary measures in 2022 to allow foreign nationals who were not able to start a business within the same period of stay (up to one year) to engage in entrepreneurial activities in Japan for additional six months maximum by making use of the Project for Facilitation of Acceptance of Foreign Entrepreneurs in the National Strategic Special Zones.

In December 2021, the Immigration Services Agency announced the current status of the 12 improvement measures shown in the investigation report on the death of the detainee in Nagoya Regional Immigration Bureau. Subsequently, as a part of the improvement measures, "Mission and principles of the Officials at the Immigration Services Agency of Japan" was formulated in order to reform mind and organisation of Immigration Services Agency and recommendations were compiled at the Advisory Committee to strengthen the medical system of detention facilities.

In response to the COVID-19 pandemic, Japan has imposed restrictive border control measures. Since March 2022, some restrictions were lifted, allowing mainly short-term business travellers and new mid to long-term residents, including exchange students, to enter the country. The Immigration Services Agency made an announcement of the termination of the special measures for the visa status of persons who have difficulty in returning home country due to the effects of the spread of COVID-19 in May 2022.

Further information: https://www.mhlw.go.jp/english/ | https://www.isa.go.jp/en/ | https://www.moj.go.jp

Key figures on immigration and emigration – Japan

Long-term immigration flows
2020 (Source: OECD)

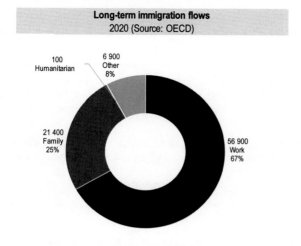

- 6 900 Other 8%
- 100 Humanitarian
- 21 400 Family 25%
- 56 900 Work 67%

Temporary migration
(Sources: OECD, UNHCR)

Temporary labour migration

	2020	2020/19
Working holidaymakers	3 330	- 82%
Seasonal workers	..	..
Intra-company transfers	3 190	- 68%
Other temporary workers	18 380	- 79%

Education

	2020	2020/19
International students	49 750	- 59%
Trainees	86 220	- 57%

Humanitarian

	2021	2021/20
Asylum seekers	2 410	- 39%

Inflows of top 10 nationalities
(national definition)

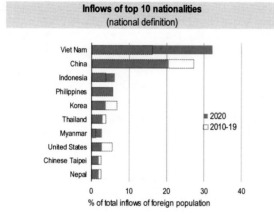

Viet Nam, China, Indonesia, Philippines, Korea, Thailand, Myanmar, United States, Chinese Taipei, Nepal

■ 2020
□ 2010-19

% of total inflows of foreign population

Emigration of Japanese to OECD countries
(national definition)

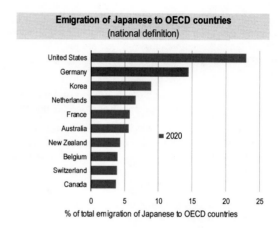

United States, Germany, Korea, Netherlands, France, Australia, New Zealand, Belgium, Switzerland, Canada

■ 2020

% of total emigration of Japanese to OECD countries

Components of population growth

	2021 Per 1 000 inhabitants	2021/20 difference
Total	-5.1	+0.0
Natural increase	-4.8	+0.0
Net migration plus statistical adjustments	-0.3	+0.0

Annual remittances

	Million current USD	Annual change %	Share in GDP %
Inflows (2021)	5 291	+8.8	+0.1
Outflows (2021)	6 133	-25.6	+0.1

Labour market outcomes - Foreign population
2020 compared to 2021 OECD averages

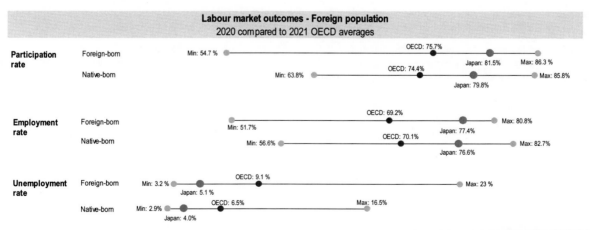

Participation rate
- Foreign-born: Min: 54.7%, OECD: 75.7%, Japan: 81.5%, Max: 86.3%
- Native-born: Min: 63.8%, OECD: 74.4%, Japan: 79.8%, Max: 85.8%

Employment rate
- Foreign-born: Min: 51.7%, OECD: 69.2%, Japan: 77.4%, Max: 80.8%
- Native-born: Min: 56.6%, OECD: 70.1%, Japan: 76.6%, Max: 82.7%

Unemployment rate
- Foreign-born: Min: 3.2%, Japan: 5.1%, OECD: 9.1%, Max: 23%
- Native-born: Min: 2.9%, Japan: 4.0%, OECD: 6.5%, Max: 16.5%

StatLink ᵐˢᴸ https://stat.link/6o1qx8

Korea

Foreign population – 2021	3.7% of the population	Main countries of birth:
Size: 1.9 million, 45% of women	Evolution since 2011: +88%	China (47%), Viet Nam (10%), United States (4%)

In 2020, Korea received 54 000 new immigrants on a long-term or permanent basis (including changes of status), -28.2% compared to 2019. This figure comprises 2.5% labour migrants, 38.9% family members (including accompanying family) and 0.4% humanitarian migrants. Around 28 000 permits were issued to tertiary-level international students and 49 000 to temporary and seasonal labour migrants.

China, Viet Nam and the United States were the top three nationalities of newcomers in 2020. Among the top 15 countries of origin, the United States registered the strongest increase (500) and Thailand the largest decrease (-44 000) in flows to Korea compared to the previous year.

In 2021, the number of first asylum applicants decreased by -65.1% to reach around 2 300. The majority of applicants came from China (300), Bangladesh (230) and Nigeria (160). The largest increase since 2020 concerned nationals of Myanmar (40) and the largest decrease nationals of Russia (-1 000). Of the 11 000 decisions taken in 2021, 1% were positive.

In 2021, reforms in labour migration policy were made to address sectoral labour shortages under the COVID-19 pandemic. In November 2021, limits on daily and weekly entries of Employment Permit System (EPS) workers were lifted and the Korea resumed issuing EPS permits in "high-risk" countries. The restrictions had led annual entries of EPS workers to drop to 6-7 000 in 2020 and 2021, while the total number of E-9 workers fell from 252 100 in May 2020 to 216 600 in May 2021. The number of H-2 workers fell from 160 500 to 122 800 over the same period, although this was largely due to a corresponding increase in permanent residents (F-4 and F-5).

Admission quotas for E-9 workers in 2022 were set at 59 000, primarily for manufacturing (44 500). Foreign workers are subject to ten days of quarantine in government-run facilities upon arrival regardless of vaccination.

The amended Employment of Foreign Workers Act affected the EPS in October 2021. H-2 workers are now allowed to work in the mining sector. For E-9 and H-2 workers granted a four-year and ten-month extension, the minimum period abroad before re-entry was reduced from three to one month, and it now requires four years and ten months employment in the same sector rather than workplace.

The Korean Government introduced a number of visa extensions. Initially these responded to the difficulty of visiting offices in person, or of departing during the pandemic. Later, extensions compensated for fewer entries of foreign workers by extending the stay of those already present. In 2021, extensions were granted for three-month periods. In December 2021, about 40 000 EPS workers with permits expiring before 12 April 2022 were granted a one-year extension. In March 2022, an additional 130 000 workers with permits expiring between 13 April and 31 December 2022 were granted a one-year extension. Those who have already been granted a one-year extension received an additional 50 days.

The Social Integration programme was modified to count COVID-19 vaccination and testing as training hours, as well as online classes under Gyeonggi province's free Korean language training.

Exceptional temporary residence and work permits for foreign residents stranded in Korea due to political unrest in origin countries are available for Burmese, Afghans and Ukrainians from March and August 2021 and February 2022 respectively. Amendments to the Enforcement Decree of the Immigration Control Act in October 2021 allow foreigners with exceptional contributions to the Korean Government (e.g. Afghan Special Contributors) to receive an F-2 residence visa. Also, Korean Ukrainians and families of Ukrainian residents in Korea can apply for a fast-track visa from any Korean Embassy since March 2022.

In April 2021, a regularisation regarding unregistered children of irregular foreign residents was introduced for those born in Korea and who have lived for 15 years or more, running until February 2025. Children can stay in the country with a D-4 visa until completing their upper secondary education, accompanied by their parents.

For further information: www.eps.go.kr | www.immigration.go.kr | www.kostat.go.kr

Key figures on immigration and emigration – Korea

Long-term immigration flows
2020 (Source: OECD)

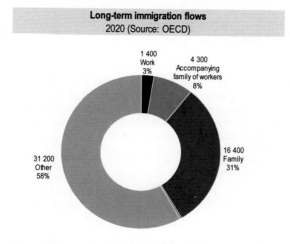

- 1 400 Work 3%
- 4 300 Accompanying family of workers 8%
- 16 400 Family 31%
- 31 200 Other 58%

Temporary migration
(Sources: OECD, UNHCR)

Temporary labour migration

	2020	2020/19
Working holidaymakers	880	- 67%
Seasonal workers	..	..
Intra-company transfers	..	..
Other temporary workers	47 650	- 57%

Education

	2020	2020/19
International students	28 340	- 20%
Trainees	300	- 64%

Humanitarian

	2021	2021/20
Asylum seekers	2 330	- 65%

Inflows of top 10 nationalities
(national definition)

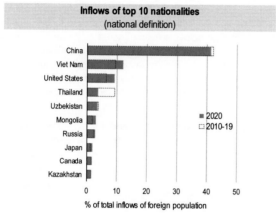

China, Viet Nam, United States, Thailand, Uzbekistan, Mongolia, Russia, Japan, Canada, Kazakhstan

■ 2020 ☐ 2010-19

% of total inflows of foreign population

Emigration of Koreans to OECD countries
(national definition)

United States, Japan, Canada, Australia, Germany, Hungary, New Zealand, Poland, Netherlands, Mexico

■ 2020

% of total emigration of Koreans to OECD countries

Components of population growth

	2021 Per 1 000 inhabitants	2021/20 difference
Total	-1.8	-3.1
Natural increase	-1.1	-0.5
Net migration plus statistical adjustments	-0.7	-2.7

Annual remittances

	Million current USD	Annual change %	Share in GDP %
Inflows (2021)	7 704	+3.8	+0.4
Outflows (2021)	9 758	+0.8	+0.5

Labour market outcomes
2021

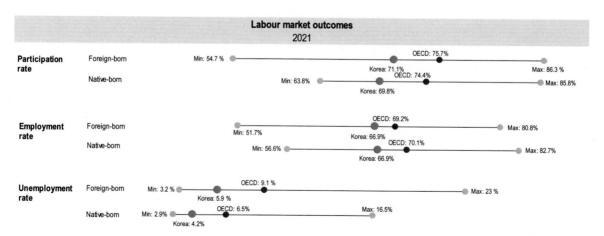

Participation rate
- Foreign-born: Min: 54.7%, OECD: 75.7%, Korea: 71.1%, Max: 86.3%
- Native-born: Min: 63.8%, OECD: 74.4%, Korea: 69.8%, Max: 85.8%

Employment rate
- Foreign-born: Min: 51.7%, OECD: 69.2%, Korea: 66.9%, Max: 80.8%
- Native-born: Min: 56.6%, OECD: 70.1%, Korea: 66.9%, Max: 82.7%

Unemployment rate
- Foreign-born: Min: 3.2%, OECD: 9.1%, Korea: 5.9%, Max: 23%
- Native-born: Min: 2.9%, OECD: 6.5%, Korea: 4.2%, Max: 16.5%

StatLink https://stat.link/h9wbgn

Latvia

Foreign-born population – 2021	12.3% of the population	Main countries of birth:
Size: 0.2 million, 61% of women	Evolution since 2011: -24%	Russia (48%), Belarus (17%), Ukraine (14%)

In 2020, 3 400 new immigrants obtained a residence permit longer than 12 months in Latvia (excluding EU citizens), -53.8% compared to 2019. This figure comprises 51.2% labour migrants, 22.3% family members (including accompanying family), 19.9% who came for education reasons and 6.6% other migrants. Around 500 short-term permits were issued to international students and 800 to temporary and seasonal labour migrants (excluding intra-EU migration). In addition, 2 600 intra-EU postings were recorded in 2020, a decrease of -49% compared to 2019. These posted workers are generally on short-term contracts.

Ukraine, Russia and Uzbekistan were the top three nationalities of newcomers in 2020. Among the top 15 countries of origin, Ukraine registered the largest decrease (-400) in flows to Latvia compared to the previous year.

In 2021, the number of first asylum applicants increased by 300% to reach around 600. The majority of applicants came from Iraq (400), Afghanistan (70) and Belarus (55). The largest increase since 2020 concerned nationals of Iraq (350) and the largest decrease nationals of Syria (-10). Of the 200 decisions taken in 2021, 45% were positive.

In 2020, new procedures were adopted to speed up the registration of an asylum seeker's application and to introduce a uniform system for issuing an identity document, as well as indicating their place of accommodation or stay. Further improvements to the asylum register were made in 2021, including centralised updating of data and extending the amount of data to be included. In June 2021, the parliament adopted amendments to the Asylum Law to facilitate employment and access to health and education services for asylum seekers. Amendments to the Law on the Register of Natural Persons include information on asylum seekers and ensures that included and updated data will be centrally available to all institutions, resulting in faster service of asylum seekers in the institutions. Further amendments of the Immigration Law in September 2021 provide that a third-country national who has submitted an asylum application in Latvia has the right to employment if a decision on the granting of status has not been taken within three months.

In 2020, the mandatory requirement to prove sufficient financial resources was temporarily abolished if the third-country national entered Latvia and applied for a temporary residence permit by 10 June 2020. For persons applying for a first temporary residence permit after 10 June 2020, the requirements for meeting the national salary threshold or sufficient financial resources for third-country nationals are applied in full.

In December 2020, amendments to the Labour Law governing the posting of third-country workers were adopted to ensure more effective protection of the rights of posted employees in accordance with the legal norms of the European Union.

In June 2021, amendments to the Personal Identification Documents Law came into force, which introduced personal electronic ID cards for foreigners, allowing them to access government e-services, use an e-address, verify their identity and sign documents electronically, serving as a gateway to a wide range of public administration services offered by Latvia.

The rules regarding foreign students residing temporarily in Latvia were tightened in September 2021, putting greater focus on higher education institutions to report adverse behaviour or attendance. Further amendments were designed to improve the efficiency and infrastructure of border control.

For further information: www.pmlp.gov.lv | www.csp.gov.lv | www.emn.lv

Key figures on immigration and emigration – Latvia

Grants of long-term residence permits
2020 (Source: Eurostat)

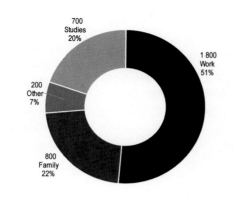

700
Studies
20%

1 800
Work
51%

200
Other
7%

800
Family
22%

Temporary migration
(Source: Eurostat)

Temporary migration (non-EU citizens)

	2020	2020/19
Employment reasons	790	- 23%
Family reasons	630	- 40%
Education reasons	530	+ 53%
Other reason	160	- 43%

Humanitarian

	2021	2021/20
Asylum seekers	580	+ 287%

Inflows of top 10 nationalities
(national definition)

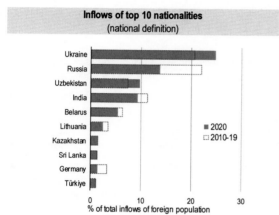

■ 2020
□ 2010-19

% of total inflows of foreign population

Emigration of Latvians to OECD countries
(national definition)

Germany
Netherlands
Norway
Estonia
Sweden
Denmark
Finland
Iceland
Switzerland
Austria

■ 2020

% of total emigration of Latvians to OECD countries

Components of population growth

	2021 Per 1 000 inhabitants	2021/20 difference
Total	-9.3	-1.7
Natural increase	-9.1	-3.2
Net migration plus statistical adjustments	-0.2	+1.5

Annual remittances

	Million current USD	Annual change %	Share in GDP %
Inflows (2021)	1 317	+9.5	+3.4
Outflows (2021)	398	+127.9	+1.0

Labour market outcomes
2021

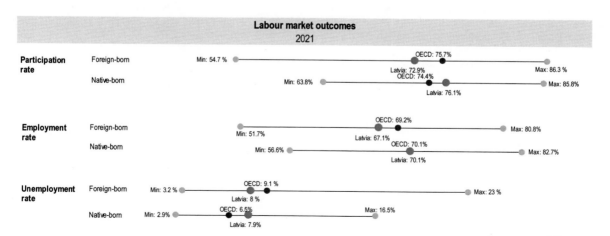

Participation rate	Foreign-born	Min: 54.7 %	OECD: 75.7% Latvia: 72.9%	Max: 86.3 %
	Native-born	Min: 63.8%	OECD: 74.4% Latvia: 76.1%	Max: 85.8%
Employment rate	Foreign-born	Min: 51.7%	OECD: 69.2% Latvia: 67.1%	Max: 80.8%
	Native-born	Min: 56.6%	OECD: 70.1% Latvia: 70.1%	Max: 82.7%
Unemployment rate	Foreign-born	Min: 3.2 %	OECD: 9.1 % Latvia: 8 %	Max: 23 %
	Native-born	Min: 2.9%	OECD: 6.5% Latvia: 7.9%	Max: 16.5%

StatLink 🔗 https://stat.link/q7j2o9

Lithuania

Foreign-born population – 2021	6.1% of the population	Main countries of birth:
Size: 0.2 million, 44% of women	Evolution since 2011: -21%	Russia (29%), Belarus (24%), Ukraine (19%)

In 2020, 22 000 new immigrants obtained a residence permit for longer than 12 months in Lithuania (excluding EU citizens), 5.2% more than in 2019. This figure comprises 87.9% labour migrants, 4.1% family members (including accompanying family), 5.3% who came for education reasons and 2.8% other migrants. Around 200 short-term permits were issued to international students and 200 to temporary and seasonal labour migrants (excluding intra-EU migration). In addition, 4 700 intra-EU postings were recorded in 2020, a decrease of -54% compared to 2019. These posted workers are generally on short-term contracts.

Ukraine, Belarus and Russia were the top three nationalities of newcomers in 2020. Among the top 15 countries of origin, Belarus registered the strongest increase (900) and Russia the largest decrease (-47) in flows to Lithuania compared to the previous year.

In 2021, the number of first asylum applicants increased by 1 400% to reach around 3 900. The majority of applicants came from Iraq (2 400), Belarus (250) and Congo (150). The largest increase since 2020 concerned nationals of Iraq (2 400). Of the 3 280 decisions taken in 2021, 13% were positive.

Migration policy underwent significant changes in 2021 and 2022. Widespread labour shortages meant most social and economic policy measures were directed towards facilitating labour and business migration and attracting investors. They included allowing foreigners to acquire the status of an electronic resident (e-resident), giving them access to Lithuanian administrative, public or commercial services by remote means.

In 2021 a quota was set for foreigners entering Lithuania to work in an occupation included in the List of Shortage Occupations. Once the quota is exhausted, foreigners whose occupation is included in the List are required to obtain a work permit.

In January 2021, and again in June, the Law on Investment was amended to speed up the issuance of residence permits for investors and make it easier to transfer employees into Lithuania.

To facilitate the entry into Lithuania for highly qualified workers, the Law on Legal status of foreigners was amended in March 2021 to foresee the possibility for highly qualified workers to start their employment after they applied for temporary residence permit.

Amendments to the Law on the Legal Status of Foreigners in March 2021 eased requirements and improved conditions for third-country nationals who study or have completed their studies or research in Lithuania. Changes included exemptions from work experience requirements, permission to start working immediately after study and the right to work with the permit issued for the purpose of job searching.

Foreigners whose period of legal stay in Lithuania expired when Lithuania introduced quarantine period in response to the pandemic (from 16 March 2020 to 16 August 2020) and who were unable to leave the country were allowed to stay up to two additional months.

As a result of the political crisis triggered by the presidential elections in Belarus, the Lithuanian Government took steps to facilitate labour immigration for citizens from there, including issuing temporary residence permits and introducing measures to encourage the transfer of Belarus business to Lithuania. The sudden increase in the flow of irregular migrants from Belarus in July 2021 led the Lithuanian Government to declare a state of emergency, strengthen border protection, including the installation of a physical barrier, and initiate a wide range of changes in the Law on the Legal Status of Foreigners.

On 30 June 2022, Seimas adopted amendments to the Law on Legal Status of Foreigners. Amendments foresee simplification of immigration rules for (highly qualified) workers, students, and start-ups from 1 August 2022, and the possibility to apply for temporary residence permit while abroad via intermediaries (external service provider) from 1 January 2023.

For further information: www.migracija.lt | www.stat.gov.lt | https://www.emn.lt/en/

Key figures on immigration and emigration – Lithuania

Grants of long-term residence permits
2020 (Source: Eurostat)

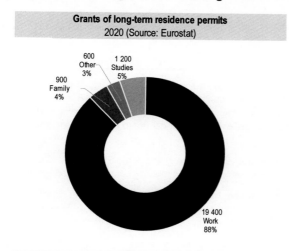

600 Other 3%
1 200 Studies 5%
900 Family 4%
19 400 Work 88%

Temporary migration
(Source: Eurostat)

Temporary migration (non-EU citizens)

	2020	2020/19
Employment reasons	180	+ 16%
Family reasons	80	- 2%
Education reasons	190	- 15%
Other reason	40	+ 67%

Humanitarian

	2021	2021/20
Asylum seekers	3 910	+1 404%

Inflows of top 10 nationalities
(national definition)

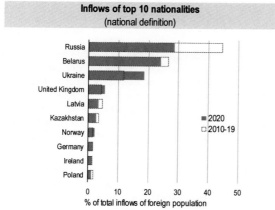

% of total inflows of foreign population

■ 2020
□ 2010-19

Emigration of Lithuanians to OECD countries
(national definition)

Germany
United Kingdom
Norway
Netherlands
Denmark
Sweden
Spain
Iceland
United States
Switzerland

■ 2020

% of total emigration of Lithuanians to OECD countries

Components of population growth

	2021 Per 1 000 inhabitants	2021/20 difference
Total	3.7	+3.1
Natural increase	-8.7	-2.1
Net migration plus statistical adjustments	12.4	+5.2

Annual remittances

	Million current USD	Annual change %	Share in GDP %
Inflows (2021)	778	-4.2	+1.2
Outflows (2021)	403	+10.2	+0.6

Labour market outcomes
2021

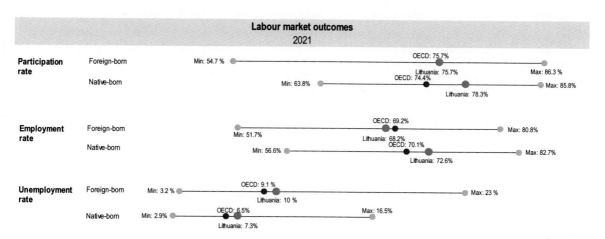

Participation rate	Foreign-born	Min: 54.7 %	OECD: 75.7% Lithuania: 75.7%	Max: 86.3 %
	Native-born	Min: 63.8%	OECD: 74.4% Lithuania: 78.3%	Max: 85.8%
Employment rate	Foreign-born	Min: 51.7%	OECD: 69.2% Lithuania: 68.2%	Max: 80.8%
	Native-born	Min: 56.6%	OECD: 70.1% Lithuania: 72.6%	Max: 82.7%
Unemployment rate	Foreign-born	Min: 3.2 %	OECD: 9.1 % Lithuania: 10 %	Max: 23 %
	Native-born	Min: 2.9%	OECD: 6.5% Lithuania: 7.3%	Max: 16.5%

StatLink https://stat.link/jrakqs

Luxembourg

Foreign-born population – 2021	48.2% of the population	Main countries of birth:
Size: 0.3 million, 49% of women	Evolution since 2011: +47%	Portugal (24%), France (14%), Belgium (7%)

In 2020, Luxembourg received 19 000 new immigrants on a long-term or permanent basis (including changes of status and free mobility), -16.2% compared to 2019. This figure comprises 77.9% immigrants benefitting from free mobility, 8.8% labour migrants, 8.4% family members (including accompanying family) and 4.1% humanitarian migrants. Around 200 permits were issued to tertiary-level international students. In addition, 47 000 intra-EU postings were recorded in 2020, a decrease of -10% compared to 2019. These posted workers are generally on short-term contracts.

France, Portugal and Italy were the top three nationalities of newcomers in 2020. Among the top 15 countries of origin, Syria registered the strongest increase (11) and France the largest decrease (-500) in flows to Luxembourg compared to the previous year.

In 2021, the number of first asylum applicants increased by 5% to reach around 1 400. The majority of applicants came from Syria (400), Eritrea (300) and Afghanistan (100). The largest increase since 2020 concerned nationals of Syria (90) and the largest decrease nationals of Iran (-30). Of the 1 180 decisions taken in 2021, 73% were positive.

In September 2021, the Ministry of Foreign and European Affairs announced the extension of temporary entry restrictions for third-country nationals in the context of COVID-19 until 31 December 2021. The exception for international students and cross-border workers continued to apply. Tax agreements concluded with Belgium, France and Germany for the telework of this latter category were automatically extended.

On 16 June 2021, the Immigration Law was amended to comply with the requirements arising from Regulation (EU) 2019/1157 on strengthening the security of identity cards of EU citizens and residence documents issued to citizens of the EU and their family members exercising their right to free movement. The amendment also introduces administrative simplification measures and procedural safeguards related to international protection (e.g. an extended deadline from three to six months granted to beneficiaries who wish to apply for family reunification, suspensive appeals against Dublin transfer decisions or status withdrawal etc.). Finally, the amendment also stipulates that only Luxembourgish citizens who do not depend financially on the social assistance system are entitled to sponsor the legal entry and residence of third-country nationals. Residence permits granted to victims of human trafficking are renewable every six months until the end of the investigation.

The Interdisciplinary Commission, in charge of evaluating the best interest of the child for unaccompanied minors in return cases, established by Law of 4 December 2019, entered into force on 1 January 2020 and members were appointed in April 2021. This collegial body assesses whether it is in the best interest of unaccompanied minors to remain in Luxembourg until they reach the age of majority.

In 2021, the Ministry of Family Affairs, Integration and the Greater Region (MIFA) launched the "Pact of living together". Since then, 28 municipalities have signed the pilot project with the ministry and the SYVICOL, and commit to focus on communication, the access to information and participation at the local level.

The number of Welcome and Integration Contracts (CAI) designed to foster integration and involvement of foreigners in the social, economic and political life of Luxembourg rose significantly in 2021 and 2022 after a decrease due to the health situation in 2020. The MIFA has organised additional online classes on Luxembourg and virtual orientation events to allow signatories to obtain updated information from public authorities and associations. Efforts are made to raise awareness of the benefits of the CAI programme through communication and dissemination strategies, leaflets distributions and an ambassador network.

Following the publication of a European Union Agency for Fundamental Rights' report, a parliamentary debate on racism and discrimination took place in July 2020. It led especially to a commitment from the Chamber of Deputies to increase the resources of the Center for Equal Treatment (CET) and to a motion inviting the government to "commission a study on the phenomenon of racism in Luxembourg in order to develop a coherent strategy to combat it". Co-ordinated by the MIFA, the study report "Racism and ethno-racial discrimination in Luxembourg" was released in March 2022.

For further information: www.guichet.public.lu | www.ona.gouvernement.lu | www.maee.gouvernement.lu

Key figures on immigration and emigration – Luxembourg

Long-term immigration flows
2020 (Source: OECD)

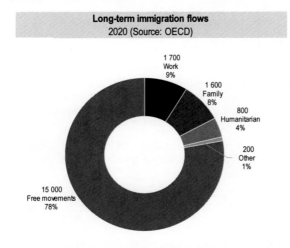

- 1 700 Work 9%
- 1 600 Family 8%
- 800 Humanitarian 4%
- 200 Other 1%
- 15 000 Free movements 78%

Temporary migration
(Sources: OECD, Eurostat)

Temporary labour migration (non-EU citizens)

	2020	2020/19
Working holidaymakers	..	..
Seasonal workers	..	..
Intra-company transfers	10	- 54%
Other temporary workers	..	..

Education (non-EU citizens)

	2020	2020/19
International students	220	- 47%
Trainees	10	- 70%

Humanitarian

	2021	2021/20
Asylum seekers	1 360	+ 5%

Inflows of top 10 nationalities
(national definition)

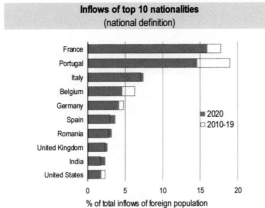

% of total inflows of foreign population

Emigration of Luxembourgers to OECD countries
(national definition)

% of total emigration of Luxembourgers to OECD countries

Components of population growth

	2021 Per 1 000 inhabitants	2021/20 difference
Total	16.7	+3.0
Natural increase	3.4	+0.5
Net migration plus statistical adjustments	13.2	+2.5

Annual remittances

	Million current USD	Annual change %	Share in GDP %
Inflows (2021)	2 273	+10.4	+2.6
Outflows (2021)	15 563	+8.6	+17.9

Labour market outcomes
2021

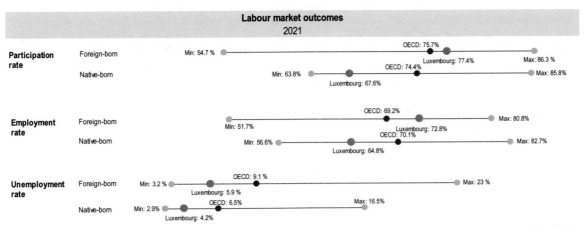

Participation rate
- Foreign-born — Min: 54.7 % — OECD: 75.7% — Luxembourg: 77.4% — Max: 86.3 %
- Native-born — Min: 63.8% — OECD: 74.4% — Luxembourg: 67.6% — Max: 85.8%

Employment rate
- Foreign-born — Min: 51.7% — OECD: 69.2% — Luxembourg: 72.8% — Max: 80.8%
- Native-born — Min: 56.6% — OECD: 70.1% — Luxembourg: 64.8% — Max: 82.7%

Unemployment rate
- Foreign-born — Min: 3.2 % — OECD: 9.1 % — Luxembourg: 5.9 % — Max: 23 %
- Native-born — Min: 2.9% — OECD: 6.5% — Luxembourg: 4.2% — Max: 16.5%

StatLink https://stat.link/werb9a

Mexico

Foreign-born population – 2020	0.9% of the population	Main countries of birth:
Size: 1.2 million, 50% of women	Evolution since 2010: +25%	United States (66%), Guatemala (5%), Venezuela (4%)

In 2020, Mexico received 54 000 new immigrants on a long-term or permanent basis (including changes of status), 40.1% more than in 2019. This figure comprises 0% immigrants benefitting from free mobility, 13.4% labour migrants, 37.8% family members (including accompanying family) and 33.4% humanitarian migrants. Around 2 800 permits were issued to tertiary-level international students and 13 600 to temporary and seasonal labour migrants.

Venezuela, Honduras and the United States were the top three nationalities of newcomers in 2020. Among the top 15 countries of origin, Honduras registered the strongest increase (4 300) and China the largest decrease (-200) in flows to Mexico compared to the previous year.

In 2021, the number of first asylum applicants increased by 220%, to reach around 130 000. The majority of applicants came from Haiti (52 000), Honduras (36 000) and Cuba (8 300). The largest increase since 2020 concerned nationals of Haiti (46 000). Of the 58 000 decisions taken in 2021, 48% were positive.

Mexico's migration policy aims at guaranteeing safe, orderly and regular migration with full respect for the human rights of migrants of people in human mobility. Although Mexico has collaborated with the United States at preventing northward irregular migrants from Guatemala, El Salvador and Honduras from arriving at the US border, Mexico has been defending migrants' rights and taking a humanitarian approach to economic development in order to address the structural causes of migration.

The Migrant Protection Protocols (MPP), was started under the Trump Administration, in early 2019, to have asylum seekers who sought to stay in the United States be sent back to Mexico while they waited for a solution to their cases in US courts. In December 2021, the Mexican Administration accepted a second phase and resumed taking the returned migrants. Faced with such decision, Mexico expressed its interest to obtain more resources for shelters, protection for vulnerable groups, consideration of local conditions of security and, shelter and care capacity of the National Institute of Migration, as well as the application of measures against COVID-19.

During 2021, there were several initiatives with the aim of reducing irregular transit, including a marked increase in the number of detentions. The National Guard, created by a presidential decree, has a clear mandate to collaborate with the National Migration Institute to carry out the migratory control, verification, and review functions in national territory.

In 2021 there was a significant increase in the volume of permanent residents in the country, compared to the volume registered in the previous four years. There was also an exponential increase in children and adolescents in an irregular migratory situation, possibly as a result of the legal reforms on children that were published in November 2020.

Additionally, Mexico and the United States announced in December 2021 *Sembrando Oportunidades*, a scholarship and training programme for young people from Honduras, El Salvador, and Guatemala that allows them to find stable employment in their countries of origin.

In response to the rising number of asylum seekers, in 2021 there was in increase in the budget allocated to the Mexican Commission to Aid Refugees (Comar) mostly coming from aid from the United Nations' High Commissioner for Refugees and donor countries. It has largely been civil society organisations that have assumed the humanitarian tasks of operating shelters along the route, giving medical assistance, helping with legal aid, and many other forms of assistance.

Furthermore, there was progress in the actions promoted for the reintegration of Mexican returnees. In that year the Inter-institutional Strategy for Comprehensive Care for Repatriated and Returning Mexican Families was established, which aims to strengthen the public policy of the Mexican State oriented to the reintegration of repatriated and returning Mexican families.

Finally, in 2021 Mexico chaired the Regional Conference on Migration enhancing dialogue on irregular migration and promoting the International Migration Review Forum sharing good practices on its implementation.

For further information: www.gob.mx | www.inegi.org.mx | www.politicamigratoria.gob.mx

Key figures on immigration and emigration – Mexico

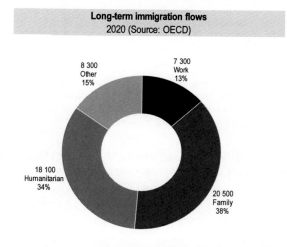

Long-term immigration flows
2020 (Source: OECD)

- 8 300 Other 15%
- 7 300 Work 13%
- 18 100 Humanitarian 34%
- 20 500 Family 38%

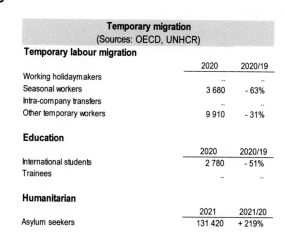

Temporary migration
(Sources: OECD, UNHCR)

Temporary labour migration

	2020	2020/19
Working holidaymakers	..	..
Seasonal workers	3 680	- 63%
Intra-company transfers	..	..
Other temporary workers	9 910	- 31%

Education

	2020	2020/19
International students	2 780	- 51%
Trainees	..	..

Humanitarian

	2021	2021/20
Asylum seekers	131 420	+ 219%

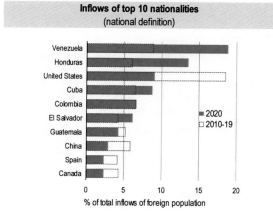

Inflows of top 10 nationalities
(national definition)

Venezuela, Honduras, United States, Cuba, Colombia, El Salvador, Guatemala, China, Spain, Canada

■ 2020
□ 2010-19

% of total inflows of foreign population

Emigration of Mexicans to OECD countries
(national definition)

United States, Spain, Canada, Germany, France, Netherlands, Switzerland, Italy, Japan, Chile

■ 2020

% of total emigration of Mexicans to OECD countries

Components of population growth

	2020 Per 1 000 inhabitants	2020/19 difference
Total	7.2	-1.3
Natural increase	4.3	-6.4
Net migration plus statistical adjustments	2.9	+5.1

Annual remittances

	Million current USD	Annual change %	Share in GDP %
Inflows (2021)	54 130	+25.3	+4.2
Outflows (2020)	899	-8.4	+0.1

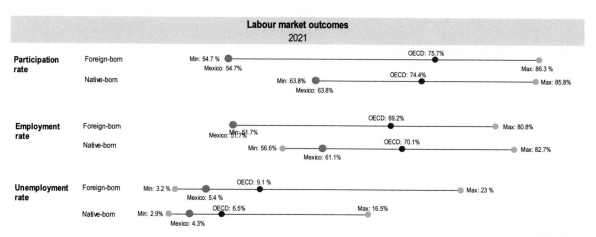

Labour market outcomes
2021

Participation rate
- Foreign-born: Min: 54.7 %, Mexico: 54.7%, OECD: 75.7%, Max: 86.3 %
- Native-born: Min: 63.8%, Mexico: 63.8%, OECD: 74.4%, Max: 85.8%

Employment rate
- Foreign-born: Min: 51.7%, Mexico: 51.7%, OECD: 69.2%, Max: 80.8%
- Native-born: Min: 56.6%, Mexico: 61.1%, OECD: 70.1%, Max: 82.7%

Unemployment rate
- Foreign-born: Min: 3.2 %, Mexico: 5.4 %, OECD: 9.1 %, Max: 23 %
- Native-born: Min: 2.9 %, Mexico: 4.3%, OECD: 6.5%, Max: 16.5%

StatLink 🔗 https://stat.link/ekbd61

Netherlands

Foreign-born population – 2021	14.3% of the population	Main countries of birth:
Size: 2.5 million, 52% of women	Evolution since 2011: +31%	Türkiye (8%), Suriname (7%), Morocco (7%)

In 2020, the Netherlands received 121 000 new immigrants on a long-term or permanent basis (including changes of status and free mobility), -21% compared to 2019. This figure comprises 61.9% immigrants benefitting from free mobility, 12.2% labour migrants, 21.4% family members (including accompanying family) and 4.4% humanitarian migrants. Around 12 000 permits were issued to tertiary-level international students. In addition, 390 000 intra-EU postings were recorded in 2020, an increase of 78% compared to 2019. These posted workers are generally on short-term contracts.

Poland, Romania and Germany were the top three nationalities of newcomers in 2020. Among the top 15 countries of origin, Syria registered a slight increase (+69) and India the largest decrease (-6 400) in flows to the Netherlands compared to the previous year.

In 2021, the number of first asylum applicants increased by 81% reaching around 25 000. The majority of applicants came from Syria (8 400), Afghanistan (3 000) and Türkiye (2 500). The largest increase since 2020 concerned nationals of Syria (4 300) and the largest decrease nationals of Nigeria (-220). Of the 17 000 decisions taken in 2021, 73% were positive.

In July 2021, amendments to the Aliens Employment Act were designed to make Dutch labour market policies more flexible so as to cope better with future uncertainties. One of the measures introduces a work permit for a maximal duration of three years. Other measures included proposals to strengthen the position of the employee (e.g. requirements regarding the monthly payment of salary and payment by giro). The amendments entered into force on 1 January 2022.

In early 2021 a new residence scheme came into force initially in the form of a four-year pilot. It followed the announcement in July 2019 by the Minister for Migration of such a scheme for essential staff of start-ups founded in the Netherlands. The new regulation allows innovative start-ups to hire highly skilled migrants from third countries who are essential to their growth. The start-up staff attracted via this scheme must meet a lowered salary criterion compared to that for highly skilled migrants; in addition, they must be given a small share (minimum of 1%) in the company. A start-up may attract a maximum of five employees via the new scheme.

In response to the COVID-19 crisis, several measures were taken in 2020 in support of knowledge migrants. Employers temporarily unable to meet the income criterion were not fined and there were no implications for the residence permit of the employee. Additionally, self-employed persons, even with a non-permanent right of residence, may make use of the support measures for entrepreneurs, although this is contrary to the conditions attached to their right of residence.

The crisis exacerbated the already unfavourable position of many EU workers in the Netherlands in terms of housing and dependency on their employer. In 2020 and 2021, the government provided a budget of EUR 100 million for the housing of vulnerable groups, including labour migrants. Measures to support international students were also taken. Any delay to their studies due to the COVID-19 pandemic would have no consequences for their residence permit. In addition, specific measures were introduced to allow registration for a study programme with an online language test or to use this test when applying for visa documents.

Under the Withdrawal Agreement, UK nationals and their family members who were legally resident in the Netherlands before 1 January 2021 had until 30 June 2021 (later extended to 1 October 2021) can apply for a residence document. They may be eligible for a temporary residence document (5 years validity) or a permanent residence permit (10 years validity), depending on their period of residence in the Netherlands.

Chinese Taipei, Uruguay and Japan joined the Working Holiday Programme in 2020. Those aged 18 to 30 can reside in the Netherlands temporarily in the context of the cultural exchange programme.

For further information: www.ind.nl/ www.cbs.nl

Key figures on immigration and emigration – Netherlands

Long-term immigration flows
2020 (Source: OECD)

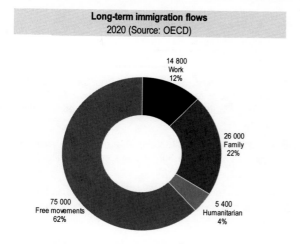

14 800
Work
12%

26 000
Family
22%

5 400
Humanitarian
4%

75 000
Free movements
62%

Temporary migration
(Source: Eurostat)

Temporary migration (non-EU citizens)

	2020	2020/19
Employment reasons	2 570	- 31%
Family reasons	3 330	- 26%
Education reasons	960	- 86%
Other reason	30	- 17%

Humanitarian

	2021	2021/20
Asylum seekers	24 760	+ 80%

Inflows of top 10 nationalities
(national definition)

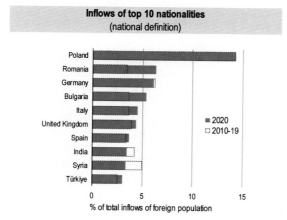

Poland
Romania
Germany
Bulgaria
Italy
United Kingdom
Spain
India
Syria
Türkiye

■ 2020
□ 2010-19

0   5   10   15

% of total inflows of foreign population

Emigration of Dutch to OECD countries
(national definition)

Belgium
Germany
Spain
United Kingdom
France
Switzerland
Portugal
United States
Austria
Sweden

■ 2020

0   5   10   15   20   25

% of total emigration of Dutch to OECD countries

Components of population growth

	2021 Per 1 000 inhabitants	2021/20 difference
Total	6.6	+2.7
Natural increase	0.5	+0.5
Net migration plus statistical adjustments	6.1	+2.2

Annual remittances

	Million current USD	Annual change %	Share in GDP %
Inflows (2021)	2 593	+15.8	+0.3
Outflows (2021)	15 242	+12.4	+1.5

Labour market outcomes
2021

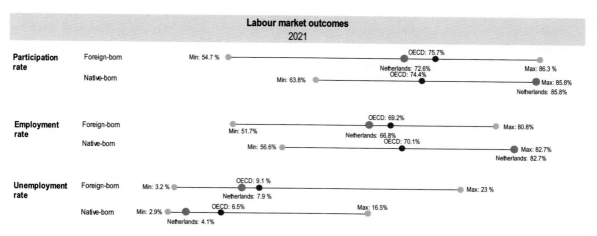

Participation rate

Foreign-born — Min: 54.7 % — OECD: 75.7% — Netherlands: 72.6% — Max: 86.3 %

Native-born — Min: 63.8% — OECD: 74.4% — Max: 85.8% — Netherlands: 85.8%

Employment rate

Foreign-born — Min: 51.7% — OECD: 69.2% — Netherlands: 66.8% — Max: 80.8%

Native-born — Min: 56.6% — OECD: 70.1% — Max: 82.7% — Netherlands: 82.7%

Unemployment rate

Foreign-born — Min: 3.2 % — OECD: 9.1 % — Netherlands: 7.9 % — Max: 23 %

Native-born — Min: 2.9% — OECD: 6.5% — Netherlands: 4.1% — Max: 16.5%

StatLink ⌗Ⅲᴸˢᴸ https://stat.link/e3o87l

New Zealand

Foreign-born population – 2018	27.4% of the population	Main countries of birth:
Size: 1.3 million, 51% of women	Evolution since 2011: +33%	United Kingdom (21%), China (10%), India (9%)

In 2020, New Zealand received 36 000 new immigrants on a long-term or permanent basis (including changes of status), -6.8% compared to 2019. This figure comprises 6.8% immigrants benefitting from free mobility, 22.3% labour migrants, 64.5% family members (including accompanying family) and 6.4% humanitarian migrants. Around 16 000 permits were issued to tertiary-level international students and 70 000 to temporary and seasonal labour migrants.

India, the United Kingdom and South Africa were the top three nationalities of newcomers in 2020. Among the top 15 countries of origin, Vanuatu registered the strongest increase (400) and China the largest decrease (-11 000) in flows to New Zealand compared to the previous year.

In 2021, the number of first asylum applicants decreased by -4.4% to reach around 400. The majority of applicants came from India (100), China (68) and Sri Lanka (29). The largest increase since 2020 concerned nationals of India (100) and the largest decrease nationals of Indonesia (–90). Of the 550 decisions taken in 2021, 29% were positive.

Throughout the COVID-19 pandemic, border restrictions have been a key pillar of New Zealand's COVID-19 response. Border exceptions were therefore implemented to fill critical roles in New Zealand, including health workers, construction and infrastructure workers, and targeted exceptions for specified occupations. Onshore work visa holders were also supported to remain working in New Zealand through a series of targeted visa extensions.

In early 2022, New Zealand announced a plan for a phased reconnection with the world. This included border exceptions for critical workers and family reunification, and staged border reopening for visitors, students, and remaining visa categories. The final stage of the reopening was in July 2022 and included remaining work visas followed by all other visa categories including visitors and students.

To provide greater certainty to onshore temporary workers, New Zealand introduced the 2021 Resident Visa for holders of specified work visas, in September 2021. Criteria included living in New Zealand for three or more years, or earning above the median wage, or working in a role that is considered "scarce" by Immigration New Zealand. Estimated to cover about 165 000 onshore temporary migrants, this residence pathway was also open to Critical Purpose Visa holders who came to NZ for a longer-term role.

In July 2022, the Accredited Employer Work Visa (AEWV) went live with a maximum duration of three years, replacing six types of temporary work visas. There are three steps to hiring a migrant on the AEWV. The employer must be granted accreditation, confirm the position meets salary and job advertising requirements, and the actual visa application. The AEWV generally requires jobs to pay at least the median wage, with some exceptions for recruitment below this threshold. New residence pathways will also become available: A straight to residence pathway will be available for specified occupations from 5 September 2022. Work to residence pathways will be available to migrant workers who have spent two years on an AEWV in specified occupations or in roles paying at least twice the median wage.

In response to developments in Afghanistan in August 2021, over 1 250 Afghan nationals were issued visas, allowing them to resettle in New Zealand. This offer was available to Afghan nationals who assisted the New Zealand Defence Force (NZDF) or other government agencies during New Zealand's deployment to Afghanistan, and their immediate families.

In March 2022, New Zealand and Australia jointly agreed that New Zealand will resettle up to 150 refugees per year for three years who have been subject to Australia's regional processing legislation. The resettlement arrangement will be implemented under New Zealand's existing Refugee Quota Programme and covers both refugees who are in Nauru as well as those who have been taken onshore to Australia.

In response to the war in Ukraine, New Zealand announced the Ukraine Special Visa in March 2022, allowing Ukrainian-born New Zealand citizens and residents to sponsor family members to come to New Zealand. Successful applicants are granted two-year work visas with work rights, and children can attend school.

For further information: www.immigration.govt.nz

Key figures on immigration and emigration – New Zealand

Long-term immigration flows
2020 (Source: OECD)

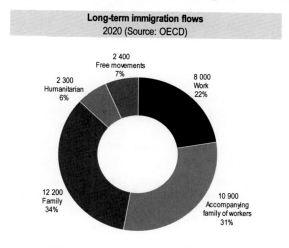

- 8 000 Work 22%
- 10 900 Accompanying family of workers 31%
- 12 200 Family 34%
- 2 300 Humanitarian 6%
- 2 400 Free movements 7%

Temporary migration
(Source: OECD)

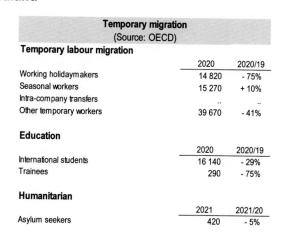

Temporary labour migration

	2020	2020/19
Working holidaymakers	14 820	- 75%
Seasonal workers	15 270	+ 10%
Intra-company transfers	..	..
Other temporary workers	39 670	- 41%

Education

	2020	2020/19
International students	16 140	- 29%
Trainees	290	- 75%

Humanitarian

	2021	2021/20
Asylum seekers	420	- 5%

Inflows of top 10 nationalities
(national definition)

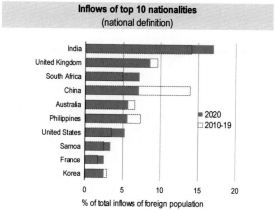

Emigration of New Zealanders to OECD countries
(national definition)

Components of population growth

	2020 Per 1 000 inhabitants	2020/19 difference
Total	19.9	+3.0
Natural increase	4.7	-0.3
Net migration plus statistical adjustments	15.2	+3.4

Annual remittances

	Million current USD	Annual change %	Share in GDP %
Inflows (2021)	148	+0.0	+0.1
Outflows (2021)	872	-0.3	+0.4

Labour market outcomes
2021

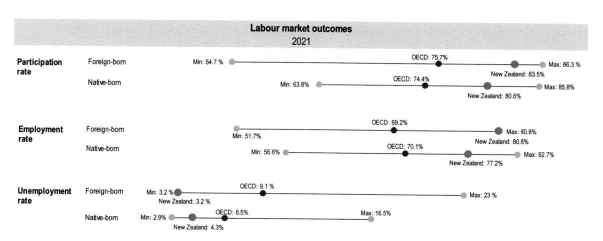

Participation rate	Foreign-born	Min: 54.7 %	OECD: 75.7%	Max: 86.3 % / New Zealand: 83.5%
	Native-born	Min: 63.8%	OECD: 74.4%	Max: 85.8% / New Zealand: 80.6%
Employment rate	Foreign-born	Min: 51.7%	OECD: 69.2%	Max: 80.8% / New Zealand: 80.8%
	Native-born	Min: 56.6%	OECD: 70.1%	Max: 82.7% / New Zealand: 77.2%
Unemployment rate	Foreign-born	Min: 3.2 % / New Zealand: 3.2 %	OECD: 9.1 %	Max: 23 %
	Native-born	Min: 2.9% / New Zealand: 4.3%	OECD: 6.5%	Max: 16.5%

StatLink https://stat.link/plhotk

Norway

Foreign-born population – 2021	16.1% of the population	Main countries of birth:
Size: 0.9 million, 48% of women	Evolution since 2011: +54%	Poland (12%), Sweden (5%), Lithuania (5%)

In 2020, Norway received 33 000 new immigrants on a long-term or permanent basis (including changes of status), -28.7% compared to 2019. This figure comprises 52.9% immigrants benefitting from free mobility, 8.9% labour migrants, 27% family members (including accompanying family) and 11.2% humanitarian migrants. Around 2 000 permits were issued to tertiary-level international students and 4 800 to temporary and seasonal labour migrants.

Poland, Sweden and Lithuania were the top three nationalities of newcomers in 2020. Among the top 15 countries of origin, India registered the largest decrease (-1 300) in flows to Norway compared to the previous year.

In 2021, the number of first asylum applicants increased by 20.5% to reach around 1 600. The majority of applicants came from Syria (600), Afghanistan (300) and Eritrea (200). The largest increase since 2020 concerned nationals of Afghanistan (200) and the largest decrease nationals of Russia (-15). Of the 1 340 decisions taken in 2021, 83% were positive.

Due to the COVID-19 pandemic, Norway reintroduced previously lifted entry restrictions in January 2021 for the first half of 2021. Since then they were gradually removed.

From January 2021 on, British citizens and their family members, who were in Norway before the end of 2020 maintain their rights to reside, work or study in Norway.

Norway's new Integration Act entered into force in January 2021. Among the major changes, the Introduction Programme for refugees and their families became more flexible to last between six months to four years instead of the previous two years. The new provisions ease the completion of upper secondary education during participation, via the inclusion of counties that also received more co-ordination and planning responsibilities.

The new Act replaced the previous requirement of hours of training in the Norwegian language with a requirement to achieve a minimum level between A2 and B2 depending on prior education and skills. Two other policy changes relate to language abilities. Amendments to the Social Services Act in 2021 made completed language training a condition for receiving financial assistance. From January 2022 onwards, public sector institutions must use qualified interpreters when necessary to provide public services.

Due to the COVID-19 pandemic, adaptations to the new Integration Act provided more flexibility for participants and additional funding to increase the use of online Norwegian language training and strengthen the Job Opportunity Program. To enhance the skills and qualifications among all unemployed and the temporarily laid-off, a scheme allowed combining training with unemployment benefits, which was replaced by permanent regulations in October 2021.

Norway introduced several new Action Plans, including for the Freedom from Negative Social Control and Honour Based Violence (2021-24), a new Action Plan against Antisemitism (2021-23), and a revised strategy for combating work-related crime. A new strategy to strengthen the role of civil society in developing and implementing the integration policy (2021-24) includes a commitment to increased economic support to NGOs.

From December 2020, the required period of residence to achieve a permanent residence permit for humanitarian migrants was extended from three to five years. From October 2021, the introduction benefit can no longer count towards the income requirement for family migration. At the same time, students in primary and secondary education can be exempt from the self-sufficiency requirement. From January 2022, Norway raised the general duration required for naturalisation from seven years of residence in the last ten years to eight of the last 11 years. The requirement can be six years for applicants with a high income.

A temporary regularisation scheme from June to December 2021 allowed refused asylum seekers who fulfilled several conditions, including having lived in Norway for at least 16 years by October 2021 and a combined age and time spent in Norway of at least 65 years to regularise.

For further information: www.udi.no | www.imdi.no | www.ssb.no

Key figures on immigration and emigration – Norway

Long-term immigration flows
2020 (Source: OECD)

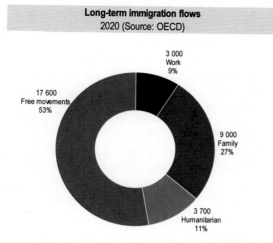

- 3 000 Work 9%
- 17 600 Free movements 53%
- 9 000 Family 27%
- 3 700 Humanitarian 11%

Temporary migration
(Sources: OECD, Eurostat)

Temporary labour migration

	2020	2020/19
Working holidaymakers	170	- 27%
Seasonal workers	2 360	- 31%
Intra-company transfers	860	- 46%
Other temporary workers	1 360	- 44%

Education

	2020	2020/19
International students	2 010	- 48%
Trainees	50	- 78%

Humanitarian

	2021	2021/20
Asylum seekers	1 620	+ 21%

Inflows of top 10 nationalities
(national definition)

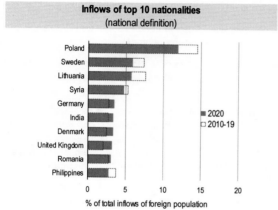

% of total inflows of foreign population

Emigration of Norwegians to OECD countries
(national definition)

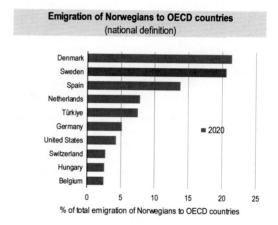

% of total emigration of Norwegians to OECD countries

Components of population growth

	2021 Per 1 000 inhabitants	2021/20 difference
Total	6.3	+1.9
Natural increase	2.6	+0.3
Net migration plus statistical adjustments	3.7	+1.6

Annual remittances

	Million current USD	Annual change %	Share in GDP %
Inflows (2021)	671	+9.0	+0.1
Outflows (2020)	..	..	..

Labour market outcomes
2021

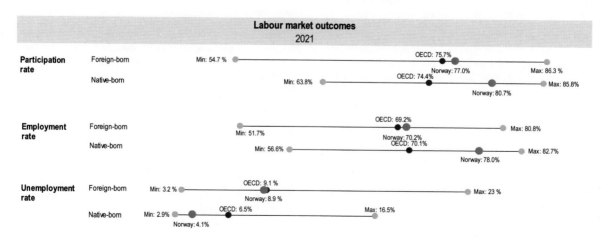

StatLink https://stat.link/q6tvfa

Poland

Foreign-born population – 2020	2.2% of the population	Main countries of birth (2011):
Size: 0.8 million, 59% of women	Evolution since 2011: +26%	Ukraine (27%), Germany (10%), Belarus (10%)

In 2020, 69 000 new immigrants obtained a residence permit longer than 12 months in Poland (excluding EU citizens), -26.1% compared to 2019. This figure comprises 60% labour migrants, 15.2% family members (including accompanying family), 0.1% who came for education reasons and 24.7% other migrants. Around 27 000 short-term permits were issued to international students and 461 000 to temporary and seasonal labour migrants (excluding intra-EU migration). In addition, 59 000 intra-EU postings were recorded in 2020, a decrease of -37% compared to 2019. These posted workers are generally on short-term contracts.

Ukraine, Belarus and India were the top three nationalities of newcomers in 2020. Among the top 15 countries of origin, Ukraine registered the strongest increase (2 600) and Belarus the largest decrease (-1 000) in flows to Poland compared to the previous year.

In 2021, the number of first asylum applicants increased by 310%, to reach around 6 200. The majority of applicants came from Belarus (2 100), Afghanistan (1 600) and Iraq (1 300). The largest increase since 2020 concerned nationals of Belarus (1 700) and the largest decrease nationals of Russia (-150). Of the 3 610 decisions taken in 2021, 60% were positive.

In August 2021, the Department of Migration Analysis and Policy was merged with the Department of International Affairs into a new Department of International Affairs and Migration to improve co-ordination in international, border and migration policy.

Due to the COVID-19 pandemic, the validity of various types of residence permits, Schengen and national visas were automatically extended from March 2020, although this did not entitle to stay or travel to other Schengen countries.

In September 2020, the government launched a new programme and simplified visa procedure, "Poland. Business Harbour", aimed at supporting ICT sector entrepreneurs from Belarus considering relocation to Poland. In July 2021, the programme was expanded to include Armenia, Georgia, Moldova, Russia, and Ukraine.

From December 2020, foreigners in Poland with a humanitarian or "Poland. Business Harbour" visa may be employed without a work permit. Exemption was also granted to medical professionals and private domestic staff of diplomats and consular officers. In November 2021, new rules entered into force which make it easier for doctors who have gained their professional qualifications in non-EU countries to practice in Poland. Foreign doctors can work under the simplified rules for a maximum of five years, under condition they confirm knowledge of the Polish language and have obtained a promise of employment from the future employer.

New rules on posting of workers, in force from September 2020, resulted from the implementation of EU Directive 2018/957/EU provisions into Polish law. The key change was to guarantee posted workers remuneration rights covering all components under labour law, not only a minimum wage.

On 29 January 2022, an amendment to the Act on Foreigners came into force, which aims to simplify and accelerate procedures for the employment of foreigners, prioritising salary level.

In October 2021, in response to the situation on the Polish-Belarusian border, the Foreigners Act and International Protection Act were amended. According to the new provisions, applications for international protection lodged by foreigners apprehended immediately after crossing illegally the external EU border *may* not to be examined unless they arrived directly from a territory, where their life or freedom was threatened and they presented credible reasons for illegal entry. New Article 303b in the Foreigners Act, provides that people illegally crossing the border may be issued an order to leave the territory and will be temporarily banned from entering Poland and the Schengen area. The entry ban included in the order will be issued for a period of six months to three years.

Art. 18c in the Act on Protection of the State Border, introduces a criminal provision with regard to destroying border infrastructure. A person who "takes away, destroys, damages, removes, moves or makes unusable elements of infrastructure, located in the border zone and intended for the protection of the state border, in particular fences, entanglements, barriers or turnpikes" will be subject to a punishment of six months to five years imprisonment. However, in the case of lesser gravity, the offender will be subject to a fine.

For further information: www.emn.gov.pl | www.udsc.gov.pl | www.stat.gov.pl | www.cudzoziemcy.gov.pl | www.fundusze.mswia.gov.pl

Key figures on immigration and emigration – Poland

Grants of long-term residence permits
2020 (Source: Eurostat)

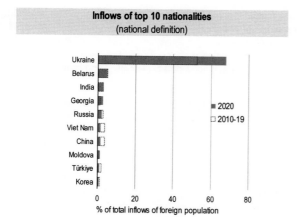

- 50 Studies
- 41 200 Work 60%
- 10 400 Family 15%
- 17 000 Other 25%

Temporary migration
(Source: Eurostat)

Temporary migration (non-EU citizens)

	2020	2020/19
Employment reasons	461 130	- 19%
Family reasons	1 810	- 24%
Education reasons	27 200	+ 45%
Other reason	39 250	- 7%

Humanitarian

	2021	2021/20
Asylum seekers (2018)	6 240	+ 313%

Inflows of top 10 nationalities
(national definition)

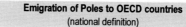

Ukraine, Belarus, India, Georgia, Russia, Viet Nam, China, Moldova, Türkiye, Korea

■ 2020
□ 2010-19

% of total inflows of foreign population

Emigration of Poles to OECD countries
(national definition)

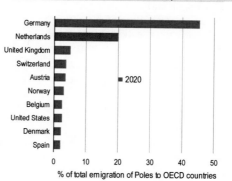

Germany, Netherlands, United Kingdom, Switzerland, Austria, Norway, Belgium, United States, Denmark, Spain

■ 2020

% of total emigration of Poles to OECD countries

Components of population growth

	2021 Per 1 000 inhabitants	2021/20 difference
Total	-4.9	-1.8
Natural increase	-5.0	-1.8
Net migration plus statistical adjustments	0.1	+0.0

Annual remittances

	Million current USD	Annual change %	Share in GDP %
Inflows (2021)	7 131	+5.2	+1.1
Outflows (2021)	9 419	+19.0	+1.4

Labour market outcomes
2021

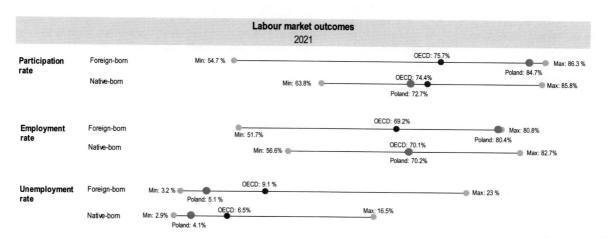

Participation rate
- Foreign-born: Min: 54.7 % — OECD: 75.7% — Poland: 84.7% — Max: 86.3 %
- Native-born: Min: 63.8% — OECD: 74.4% — Poland: 72.7% — Max: 85.8%

Employment rate
- Foreign-born: Min: 51.7% — OECD: 69.2% — Poland: 80.4% — Max: 80.8%
- Native-born: Min: 56.6% — OECD: 70.1% — Poland: 70.2% — Max: 82.7%

Unemployment rate
- Foreign-born: Min: 3.2 % — Poland: 5.1 % — OECD: 9.1 % — Max: 23 %
- Native-born: Min: 2.9% — Poland: 4.1% — OECD: 6.5% — Max: 16.5%

StatLink https://stat.link/d8an6j

Portugal

Foreign population – 2021	6.5% of the population	Main countries of nationality:
Size: 0.7 million, 53% of women	Evolution since 2011: +49%	Brazil (28%), United Kingdom (7%), Cape Verde (6%)

In 2020, Portugal received 80 000 new immigrants on a long-term or permanent basis (including changes of status and free mobility), -18.6% compared to 2019. This figure comprises 19.9% immigrants benefitting from free mobility, 40.7% labour migrants, 35.1% family members (including accompanying family) and 0.1% humanitarian migrants. Around 12 000 permits were issued to tertiary-level international students. In addition, 29 000 intra-EU postings were recorded in 2020, a decrease of -42% compared to 2019. These posted workers are generally on short-term contracts.

Brazil, the United Kingdom and India were the top three nationalities of newcomers in 2020. Among the top 15 countries of origin, the United Kingdom registered the strongest increase (4 800) and Brazil the largest decrease (-6 600) in flows to Portugal compared to the previous year.

In 2021, the number of first asylum applicants increased by 50% to reach around 1 400. The majority of applicants came from Afghanistan (600), Morocco (100) and India (80). The largest increase since 2020 concerned nationals of Afghanistan (600) and the largest decrease nationals of Gambia (-90). Of the 510 decisions taken in 2021, 60% were positive.

In May 2022 Portugal published the final report of the National Implementation Plan of the Global Compact for Migration, a document that takes stock of the progress made since 2020, including some relevant achievements such as the significant growth of the decentralised response network to support migrants, the development of a management system to collect information to better understand the needs and profiles of migrants in order to formulate better intervention responses, and the launching of the Migrant Reception Guide, which is intended to facilitate the work of public and private institutions and civil society and to support migrants wishing to live in Portugal.

Reflecting Portugal's continued commitment to promoting safe, orderly and regular migration and the 23 GCM objectives, a new version of the National Plan is being prepared. The new document will heed the best practices implemented, but also the ongoing challenges. The document will also be informed by the outcome of the civil society consultation process conducted in 2021 by the High Commission of Migration in partnership with the International Organisation for Migration.

The Decree-Law 14/2021 went into force on 1 January 2022, and stricter requirements to obtain a "golden visa" came into effect. Residence permits for investment will no longer be possible based on real estate investment in Lisbon, Porto, Algarve and coastal regions, once properties acquired that are intended for housing, only allow access to this regime if they are located in the Autonomous Regions of the Azores and Madeira or in the territories of interior. There is no change, however, on the threshold amounts for real estate investment that remain at EUR 500 000 or EUR 350 000 if the building is older than 30 years.

Residence applications for investment on other grounds will be subject to higher investment thresholds. The threshold for capital transfers increased from EUR 1 to 1.5 million.

The minimum requirement for transfers for research activities, holdings in investment and/or venture capital funds, and the incorporation of commercial companies increased from EUR 350 000 to 500 000.

Due to the COVID-19 pandemic, many immigrants have not been able to renew their visas or permits. In February 2022, the government prolonged the exceptional measures taken the previous years. All documents and visas related to the stay in national territory that have expired since early March 2020 are deemed valid until 30 June 2022. These documents will continue to be accepted after 30 June 2022, as long as the holder provides proof that he/she has scheduled an appointment to renew the documents. Furthermore, all foreign citizens with cases pending at the Foreigners and Borders Service (SEF), who filed a request by 31 December 2021, are temporarily in a situation of regular stay in the country and have access to health, social support, employment and housing.

For further information: www.acm.gov.pt | www.om.acm.gov.pt | www.sef.pt

Key figures on immigration and emigration – Portugal

Long-term immigration flows
2020 (Source: OECD)

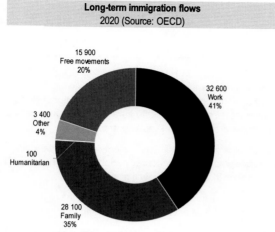

32 600
Work
41%

15 900
Free movements
20%

3 400
Other
4%

100
Humanitarian

28 100
Family
35%

Temporary migration
(Source: Eurostat)

Temporary migration (non-EU citizens)

	2020	2020/19
Employment reasons	70	- 82%
Family reasons	..	..
Education reasons	..	..
Other reason	340	- 53%

Humanitarian

	2021	2021/20
Asylum seekers	1 350	+ 50%

Inflows of top 10 nationalities
(national definition)

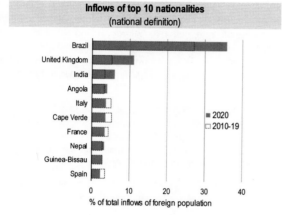

Brazil
United Kingdom
India
Angola
Italy
Cape Verde
France
Nepal
Guinea-Bissau
Spain

■ 2020
□ 2010-19

0   10   20   30   40
% of total inflows of foreign population

Emigration of Portuguese to OECD countries
(national definition)

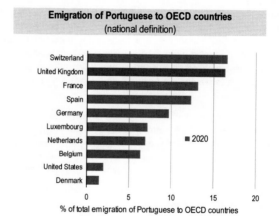

Switzerland
United Kingdom
France
Spain
Germany
Luxembourg
Netherlands
Belgium
United States
Denmark

■ 2020

0   5   10   15   20
% of total emigration of Portuguese to OECD countries

Components of population growth

	2021 Per 1 000 inhabitants	2021/20 difference
Total	5.2	+5.0
Natural increase	-4.4	-0.6
Net migration plus statistical adjustments	9.6	+5.6

Annual remittances

	Million current USD	Annual change %	Share in GDP %
Inflows (2021)	4 760	+10.0	+1.9
Outflows (2020)	240	-7.4	+0.1

Labour market outcomes
2021

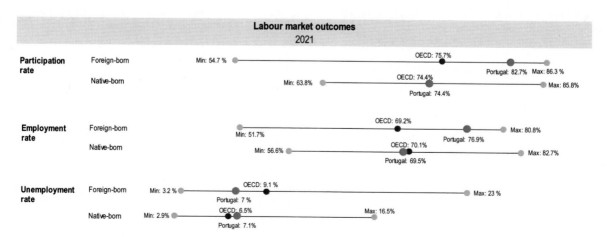

Participation rate

Foreign-born: Min: 54.7 % OECD: 75.7% Portugal: 82.7% Max: 86.3 %
Native-born: Min: 63.8% OECD: 74.4% Portugal: 74.4% Max: 85.8%

Employment rate

Foreign-born: Min: 51.7% OECD: 69.2% Portugal: 76.9% Max: 80.8%
Native-born: Min: 56.6% OECD: 70.1% Portugal: 69.5% Max: 82.7%

Unemployment rate

Foreign-born: Min: 3.2 % OECD: 9.1 % Portugal: 7 % Max: 23 %
Native-born: Min: 2.9% OECD: 6.5% Portugal: 7.1% Max: 16.5%

StatLink ⟐ https://stat.link/ad5fi6

Romania

Foreign-born population – 2021	3.6% of the population	Main countries of birth:
Size: 0.7 million, 46% of women	Evolution since 2011: +309%	Moldova (40%), Italy (11%), Spain (9%)

In 2020, 16 000 new immigrants obtained a residence permit longer than 12 months in Romania (excluding EU citizens), -29.2% compared to 2019. This figure comprises 64.4% labour migrants, 15.3% family members (including accompanying family), 13.8% who came for education reasons and 6.5% other migrants. Around 900 short-term permits were issued to international students and 700 to temporary and seasonal labour migrants (excluding intra-EU migration). In addition, 18 000 intra-EU postings were recorded in 2020, an increase of 12% compared to 2019. These posted workers are generally on short-term contracts.

In 2021, the number of first asylum applicants increased by 50.5% to reach around 9 100. The majority of applicants came from Afghanistan (3 900), Syria (1 200) and Bangladesh (900). The largest increase since 2020 concerned nationals of Afghanistan (1 500) and the largest decrease nationals of Syria (-250). Of the 4 100 decisions taken in 2021, 28% were positive.

The National Strategy on Immigration 2021-24 was published in September 2021. Priority was given to ensuring the legality of foreign residence, combating illegal migration and undeclared work, and ensuring unrestricted access to the asylum procedure.

The Strategy has three general objectives. The first concerns migration for economic reasons. The emphasis is on limiting entries rather than on the integration of those who are already in the country. Specific aims include simplifying the means of access by foreigners for work, posting or investment and combating illegal migration. The second objective deals with international protection. Among specific measures are an asylum applications system in accordance with national, European and international legal standards, better conditions of reception and assistance for asylum seekers, relocation of refugees and asylum seekers and greater co-operation with other European and international bodies concerned with asylum. The third objective concerns procedures for dealing with large-scale migration waves generated by crises, such as those in Syria or Afghanistan, and is focused on avoiding security threats.

Specific Government Orders in 2021: introduced changes to improve the protection of residence permits against counterfeiting, including the use of biometrics; set out annual quotas of work authorisations for foreigners, including a doubling of foreign workers newly admitted to the Romanian labour market; amended conditions for posting of workers to Romania and for Romanians working abroad; transposed EU Directive 2016/801 on conditions of entry and residence of third-country nationals for the purposes of research, studies, training, voluntary service, pupil exchange schemes or educational projects and au pairing.

In November 2020, Romania adopted measures relating to Brexit. UK citizens and their family members who resided in Romania and wished to remain there after 31 December 2020 were required to register with the Romanian immigration authorities for the new residence status before 31 December 2021.

In response to the COVID-19 crisis, immigrants with temporary visas who were unable to return had their visas automatically extended. The validity of all documents which expired during the national emergency/alert state was extended for 90 days following the cessation of restrictions. Asylum applications continued to be lodged and processed as usual.

Emergency Ordinance no. 20/2022, effective from 11 March 2022, outlined measures dealing with the inflows resulting from the war in Ukraine. Ukrainian citizens can work in Romania based on a full-time individual work agreement without a work permit and without observing the nine months in a year limit for an employment agreement, as under the normal rules. In addition, the right of residence for work purposes is extended without the need to obtain a long-stay working visa. Ukrainians may also receive free emergency medical care and qualified first aid treatment through the national health care system and be included in national public health programmes. Individuals hosting foreign citizens or stateless persons coming from the area of the armed conflict in Ukraine may be reimbursed for food expenses on a per diem basis.

For further information: www.alba.insse.ro | www.mai.gov.ro | www.igi.mai.gov.ro

Key figures on immigration and emigration – Romania

Grants of long-term residence permits
2020 (Source: Eurostat)

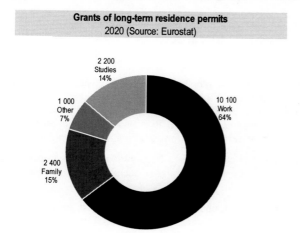

Temporary migration
(Source: Eurostat)

Temporary migration (non-EU citizens)

	2020	2020/19
Employment reasons	730	- 65%
Family reasons	410	- 35%
Education reasons	870	- 52%
Other reason	220	- 55%

Humanitarian

	2021	2021/20
Asylum seekers (2018)	9 065	+ 50%

Inflows of top 10 nationalities
(national definition)

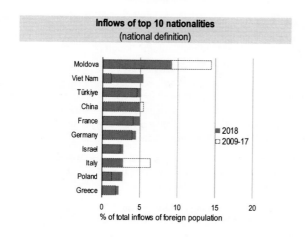

Emigration of Romanians to OECD countries
(national definition)

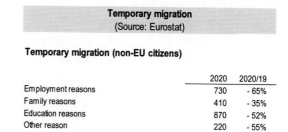

Components of population growth

	2021 Per 1 000 inhabitants	2021/20 difference
Total	-8.6	-2.0
Natural increase	-8.2	-3.0
Net migration plus statistical adjustments	-0.4	+1.0

Annual remittances

	Million current USD	Annual change %	Share in GDP %
Inflows (2021)	9 160	+15.3	+3.2
Outflows (2021)	634	+18.2	+0.2

Labour market outcomes
2021

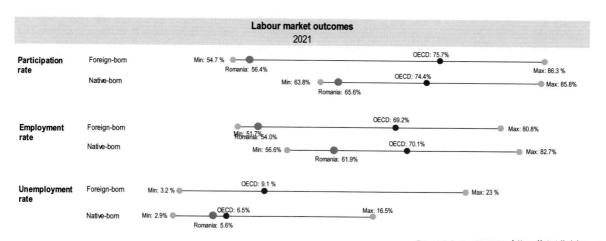

Slovak Republic

Foreign-born population – 2021	3.7% of the population	Main countries of birth:
Size: 0.2 million, 48% of women	Evolution since 2011: +38%	Czech Republic (44%), Hungary (8%), Ukraine (6%)

In 2020, 15 000 new immigrants obtained a residence permit for longer than 12 months in the Slovak Republic (excluding EU citizens), -30.3% compared to 2019. This figure comprises 67.1% labour migrants, 14.4% family members (including accompanying family), 13% who came for education reasons and 5.5% other migrants. Around 300 short-term permits were issued to international students and 1 700 to temporary and seasonal labour migrants (excluding intra-EU migration). In addition, 18 000 intra-EU postings were recorded in 2020, a decrease of -45% compared to 2019. These posted workers are generally on short-term contracts.

The Czech Republic, Hungary and Ukraine were the top three nationalities of newcomers in 2020. Among the top 15 countries of origin, the Czech Republic registered the strongest increase (300) and Romania the largest decrease (-78) in flows to the Slovak Republic compared to the previous year.

In 2021, the number of first asylum applicants increased by 24.5% to reach around 300. The majority of applicants came from Morocco (100), Afghanistan (90) and Algeria (20). The largest increase since 2020 concerned nationals of Morocco (65) and the largest decrease nationals of Syria (-25). Of the 130 decisions taken in 2021, 35% were positive.

In September 2021 a new migration policy for the period until 2025 was adopted, replacing a policy adopted in 2011. The document focuses on economic migration and humanitarian migration. Family reunification and migration of students are not explicitly dealt with. The return of emigrants is among the priorities of the new policy, including continuation of return support programmes; however, recently adopted return schemes for highly qualified experts attracted very few returnees.

As a response to the COVID-19 pandemic, amendments to the Act on the Residence of Aliens extended the validity of temporary residence, permanent residence or tolerated residence until two months after the revocation of the crisis. A third-country national who had legally entered the territory of the Slovak Republic but was not yet granted a residence permit could stay until one month after the revocation of the crisis. A third-country national outside the Slovak Republic could submit an application for the renewal of temporary residence or an application for permanent residence for an indefinite period at the embassy.

In effect from 21 May 2020, an amendment of the Employment Services Act in connection with the Residence of Aliens Act extended the validity of the relevant confirmations of the possibility of filling a vacancy or employment permits for the third-country nationals. It would expire at the time of the declared COVID-19 emergency, within two months of its withdrawal.

Free circulation of workers in border regions has been regulated by various ad hoc acts of the Public Health Agency during the pandemic. In general, the goal was to ease the movements of "pedlars" from neighbouring EU countries (Czech Republic, Austria. Hungary, Poland) by stipulating various exemptions (from quarantine, COVID-19 testing, etc.). The measures were focused on the population living within 30 km from borders, or on persons with an employment contract in one country and residence in another. Many issues remained problematic, notably for the Slovak citizens living in neighbouring areas in Austria and Hungary who experienced difficulties commuting to work or schools during border closures. The problems were particularly intensive in the neighbourhood of the capital Bratislava, close to the Austrian and Hungarian borders.

In order to attract talents and professionals, a governmental decree, with effect from 1 April 2022, facilitates access to the labour market for selected occupations for highly qualified third-country nationals who are graduates of top universities. Visas are issued for the purpose of seeking employment for up to 90 days; or for the purpose of employment for a maximum period of one year.

Another governmental decree, with effect from 1 April 2022, regulates the issuance of visas in occupations with labour force shortage such as bus and heavy truck drivers for third-country nationals from Belarus, Serbia, North Macedonia, Bosnia and Herzegovina, Montenegro, Georgia, Armenia, Moldova and Ukraine, for maximum period of one year.

For further information: www.minv.sk

Key figures on immigration and emigration – Slovak Republic

Grants of long-term residence permits
2020 (Source: Eurostat)

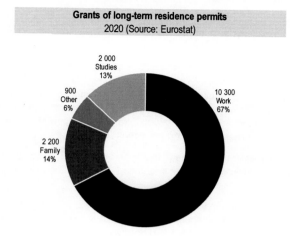

- 2 000 Studies 13%
- 900 Other 6%
- 10 300 Work 67%
- 2 200 Family 14%

Temporary migration
(Source: Eurostat)

Temporary migration (non-EU citizens)

	2020	2020/19
Employment reasons	1 740	- 68%
Family reasons	690	- 2%
Education reasons	330	- 37%
Other reason	90	- 6%

Humanitarian

	2021	2021/20
Asylum seekers (2018)	330	+ 22%

Inflows of top 10 nationalities
(national definition)

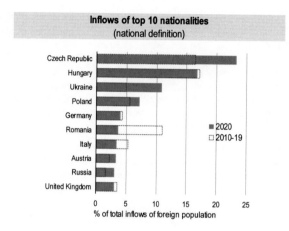

% of total inflows of foreign population

■ 2020
□ 2010-19

Emigration of Slovaks to OECD countries
(national definition)

% of total emigration of Slovaks to OECD countries

■ 2020

Components of population growth

	2021 Per 1 000 inhabitants	2021/20 difference
Total	-4.6	-4.9
Natural increase	-3.1	-2.7
Net migration plus statistical adjustments	-1.5	-2.3

Annual remittances

	Million current USD	Annual change %	Share in GDP %
Inflows (2021)	2 235	-11.8	+1.9
Outflows (2021)	453	+10.4	+0.4

Labour market outcomes
2021

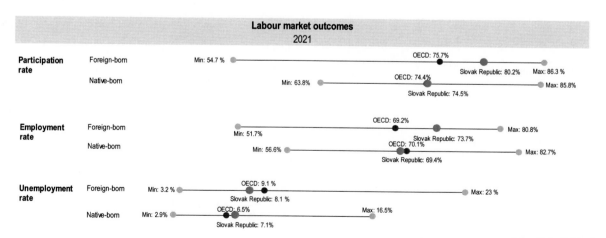

Participation rate

Foreign-born — Min: 54.7 % — OECD: 75.7% — Slovak Republic: 80.2% — Max: 86.3 %

Native-born — Min: 63.8% — OECD: 74.4% — Slovak Republic: 74.5% — Max: 85.8%

Employment rate

Foreign-born — Min: 51.7% — OECD: 69.2% — Slovak Republic: 73.7% — Max: 80.8%

Native-born — Min: 56.6% — OECD: 70.1% — Slovak Republic: 69.4% — Max: 82.7%

Unemployment rate

Foreign-born — Min: 3.2 % — OECD: 9.1 % — Slovak Republic: 8.1 % — Max: 23 %

Native-born — Min: 2.9% — OECD: 6.5% — Slovak Republic: 7.1% — Max: 16.5%

StatLink ᴍˢᴸ https://stat.link/zp2aqn

Slovenia

Foreign-born population – 2021	14.1% of the population	Main countries of birth:
Size: 0.3 million, 41% of women	Evolution since 2011: +28%	Bosnia and Herzegovina (45%), Croatia (15%), Serbia (10%)

In 2020, 12 000 new immigrants obtained a residence permit longer than 12 months in Slovenia (excluding EU citizens), -37.5% compared to 2019. This figure comprises 56.5% labour migrants, 41.8% family members (including accompanying family), 0.5% who came for education reasons and 1.1% other migrants. Around 1 800 short-term permits were issued to international students and 3 000 to temporary and seasonal labour migrants (excluding intra-EU migration). In addition, 11 000 intra-EU postings were recorded in 2020, a decrease of -34% compared to 2019. These posted workers are generally on short-term contracts.

Bosnia and Herzegovina, Serbia and Croatia were the top three nationalities of newcomers in 2020. Among the top 15 countries of origin, Italy registered the strongest increase (500) and Bosnia and Herzegovina the largest decrease (-4 100) in flows to Slovenia compared to the previous year.

In 2021, the number of first asylum applicants increased by 50.6% to reach around 5 200. The majority of applicants came from Afghanistan (2 600), Pakistan (500) and Iran (300). The largest increase since 2020 concerned nationals of Afghanistan (1 900) and the largest decrease nationals of Morocco (-1 100). Of the 180 decisions taken in 2021, 9% were positive.

An amendment to the Foreigners Act, which took effect in May 2021, tightened the conditions for all types of residence permits in Slovenia. The government will no longer consider reimbursements for work-related expenses as well as a number of other social benefits when assessing whether applicants possess sufficient means of substance. The amendment further envisages a Slovenian language requirement at A1 level under the Common European Framework of Reference for Languages (CEFR) for the extension of a temporary residence permit for family reunification and at A2 level for permanent residence permits after a two-year transitional period. In addition, public language and integration courses will only be offered to certain categories of migrants and participants will have to bear half of the costs. Another major change allows applicants, on certain conditions, to collect their first residence permit in Slovenia instead of at a consular post abroad. Furthermore, the mandate for all integration measures for third-country nationals (TCNs) was transferred from the Ministry of the Interior to the Office for Support and Integration of Migrants.

The amendment transposed the Students and Researchers Directive 2016/801/EU by introducing new types of residence permits for, inter alia, trainees and volunteers as well as a mobility scheme for researchers and students with residence permits from other EU member states. In addition, scholarships are included in the assessment of sufficient means of substance required for a study permit.

In November 2021, an amendment to the International Protection Act aimed at better enforcing international protection procedures became applicable. It introduced the possibility to appeal against resolutions to the Supreme Court and imposed requirements on legal counsellors to disclose information about the identity of asylum seekers. To incentivise a better integration of refugees, the amendment conditions certain rights on integration achievements. In addition, it shortened the period during which refugees are entitled to integration assistance from three to two years. Finally, the amendment extended the accommodation possibilities for unaccompanied minors.

As of 2021, an amendment to the Labour Market Regulation Act requires that unemployed TCNs who have not received any formal education in the country pass an A1 level Slovenian language exam within one year of registration in the unemployment register. Due to COVID-19 related difficulties in the implementation of the exam, the Ministry of Labour, Family and Social Affairs granted a six-month extension of the deadline to people unable to take the exam before December 2021.

To contain the spread of COVID-19 infections, Slovenia implemented a number of entry and quarantine requirements for nationals and foreigners. As of February 2022, these conditions no longer apply when entering the country.

For further information: www.stat.si | www.gov.si/podrocja/drzava-in-druzba | www.infotujci.si

Key figures on immigration and emigration – Slovenia

Grants of long-term residence permits
2020 (Source: Eurostat)

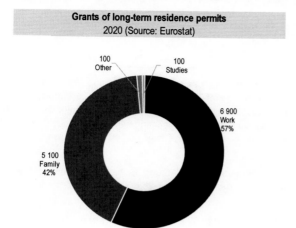

- 100 Other
- 100 Studies
- 6 900 Work 57%
- 5 100 Family 42%

Temporary migration
(Source: Eurostat)

Temporary migration (non-EU citizens)

	2020	2020/19
Employment reasons	3 020	- 59%
Family reasons	1 990	- 5%
Education reasons	1 770	- 28%
Other reason	10	+ 0%

Humanitarian

	2021	2021/20
Asylum seekers (2018)	5 220	+ 50%

Inflows of top 10 nationalities
(national definition)

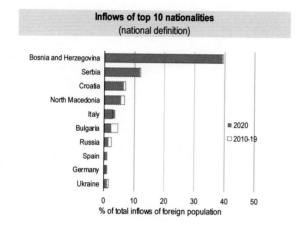

% of total inflows of foreign population

- ■ 2020
- □ 2010-19

Emigration of Slovenes to OECD countries
(national definition)

Austria, Germany, Switzerland, Netherlands, Italy, Belgium, United States, Australia, Japan, Hungary

- ■ 2020

% of total emigration of Slovenes to OECD countries

Components of population growth

	2021 Per 1 000 inhabitants	2021/20 difference
Total	-0.9	-7.1
Natural increase	-2.0	+0.5
Net migration plus statistical adjustments	1.2	-7.5

Annual remittances

	Million current USD	Annual change %	Share in GDP %
Inflows (2021)	736	+8.9	+1.2
Outflows (2021)	317	+13.0	+0.5

Labour market outcomes
2021

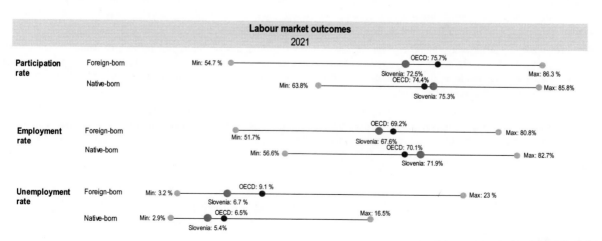

Participation rate	Foreign-born	Min: 54.7 % — OECD: 75.7% — Slovenia: 72.5% — Max: 86.3 %
	Native-born	Min: 63.8% — OECD: 74.4% — Slovenia: 75.3% — Max: 85.8%
Employment rate	Foreign-born	Min: 51.7% — OECD: 69.2% — Slovenia: 67.6% — Max: 80.8%
	Native-born	Min: 56.6% — OECD: 70.1% — Slovenia: 71.9% — Max: 82.7%
Unemployment rate	Foreign-born	Min: 3.2 % — OECD: 9.1 % — Slovenia: 6.7 % — Max: 23 %
	Native-born	Min: 2.9% — OECD: 6.5% — Slovenia: 5.4% — Max: 16.5%

StatLink https://stat.link/24nsgu

Spain

Foreign-born population – 2021	15.4% of the population	Main countries of birth:
Size: 7.2 million, 52% of women	Evolution since 2011: +15%	Morocco (11%), Romania (8%), Colombia (8%)

In 2020, Spain received 345 000 new immigrants on a long-term or permanent basis (including changes of status and free mobility), -11.4% compared to 2019. This figure comprises 32.8% immigrants benefitting from free mobility, 9.6% labour migrants, 32.8% family members (including accompanying family) and 15.3% humanitarian migrants. Around 28 000 permits were issued to tertiary-level international students and 19 000 to temporary and seasonal labour migrants (excluding intra-EU migration). In addition, 82 000 intra-EU postings were recorded in 2020, a decrease of -54% compared to 2019. These posted workers are generally on short-term contracts.

Colombia, Morocco and Venezuela were the top three nationalities of newcomers in 2020. Among the top 15 countries of origin, the United Kingdom registered the strongest increase (200) and Venezuela the largest decrease (-28 000) in flows to Spain compared to the previous year.

In 2021, the number of first asylum applicants decreased by -28.2%, to reach around 62 000. The majority of applicants came from Venezuela (16 000), Colombia (11 000) and Morocco (6 400). The largest increase since 2020 concerned nationals of Morocco (5 500) and the largest decrease nationals of Colombia (-16 100). Of the 71 000 decisions taken in 2021, 29% were positive.

In October 2021, the Spanish Government enacted Decree 903/2021 on the rights and freedoms of foreigners in Spain. It provides protection and regular status to former unaccompanied migrant minors upon reaching legal age. The new regulation amends the previous decree 557/2011 which left many young migrants without legal documentation and at risk of social exclusion after turning 18. The decree extends the initial residence permit from one to two years, and extends the validity of renewals, and guarantees access to work for minors who are of working age when they reach the age of majority, thus favouring their integration into Spanish society.

On 2 November 2021, the Spanish Government approved a new procedure for the entry and stay of third-country nationals working in the audiovisual sector with the aim of creating an agile, flexible and simple system that facilitates the recruitment professionals in the sector. This new procedure is part of the "Spain Audiovisual Hub of Europe" Plan approved by the Government on 23 March 2021, which aims to improve Spain's attractiveness as a European platform for business, work and investment in the audiovisual sector.

In December 2021, the Spanish Government approved the National Refugee Resettlement Programme for 2022. The programme aims to relocate and integrate 1 200 refugees in Spain, mainly from Syria, Afghanistan, Iran and Iraq. In collaboration with UNHCR, regional governments promote the reception of refugee families and their accompaniment during 2022.

In March 2022, the decree 220/2022 on the international protection reception system was passed by the Spanish Government. The aim was to complement the Asylum Law provisions with regard to reception conditions of asylum seekers and beneficiaries of international protection. In accordance with Directive 2013/33/EU, the new system aims to increase its efficiency in both quantitative and qualitative terms. Likewise, it includes a new funding model for collaborating entities, thereby increasing the stability, predictability and effective evaluation of the system.

In March 2022, Spain launched *Wafira*, a skills-mobility partnership with Morocco that will turn 250 circular migrant women into financially independent rural actors. It is funded by the European Union through the Migration Partnership Facility Mechanism and promotes the training of women in the agricultural sector in Spain. The programme provides further support to them in their own business initiatives in Morocco by providing financial and technical assistance.

The Spanish authorities have expanded circular migration policies to fulfil labour shortages in the agricultural sector during the harvesting season in Andalucía, southern Spain. In October 2021, the Spanish authorities launched a circular migration programme with the Ecuadorian and Honduran authorities allowing approximately 250 Ecuadorian and Honduran agricultural labourers to work in Spain between December and June 2022.

On 17 May 2022, the land border between Morocco and Spain was officially reopened after its closure in March 2020 due to the COVID-19 health crisis. The reopening takes place progressively, allowing EU and Schengen area residents as well as cross-border workers to enter Spain in a first phase and gradually allowing other groups of individuals in subsequent stages.

For further information: www.extranjeros.inclusion.gob.es | www.mites.gob.es | www.ine.es

Key figures on immigration and emigration – Spain

Long-term immigration flows
2020 (Source: OECD)

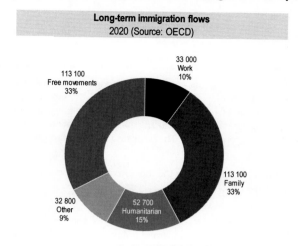

33 000 Work 10%

113 100 Free movements 33%

113 100 Family 33%

52 700 Humanitarian 15%

32 800 Other 9%

Temporary migration
(Sources: OECD, Eurostat)
Temporary labour migration (non-EU citizens)

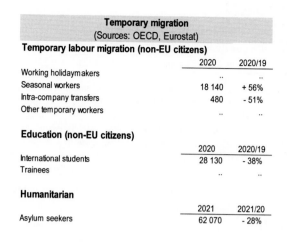

	2020	2020/19
Working holidaymakers	..	..
Seasonal workers	18 140	+ 56%
Intra-company transfers	480	- 51%
Other temporary workers	..	..

Education (non-EU citizens)

	2020	2020/19
International students	28 130	- 38%
Trainees	..	..

Humanitarian

	2021	2021/20
Asylum seekers	62 070	- 28%

Inflows of top 10 nationalities
(national definition)

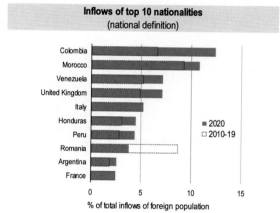

- Colombia
- Morocco
- Venezuela
- United Kingdom
- Italy
- Honduras
- Peru
- Romania
- Argentina
- France

■ 2020
□ 2010-19

% of total inflows of foreign population

Emigration of Spanish to OECD countries
(national definition)

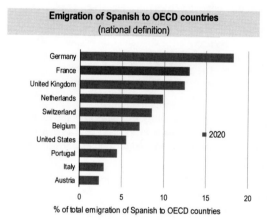

- Germany
- France
- United Kingdom
- Netherlands
- Switzerland
- Belgium
- United States
- Portugal
- Italy
- Austria

■ 2020

% of total emigration of Spanish to OECD countries

Components of population growth

	2021 Per 1 000 inhabitants	2021/20 difference
Total	0.7	-0.7
Natural increase	-2.4	+0.8
Net migration plus statistical adjustments	3.1	-1.5

Annual remittances

	Million current USD	Annual change %	Share in GDP %
Inflows (2021)	9 000	+5.8	+0.6
Outflows (2020)	349	-23.9	+0.0

Labour market outcomes
2021

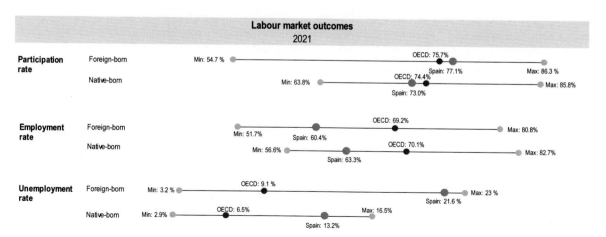

Participation rate

Foreign-born — Min: 54.7 % — OECD: 75.7% — Spain: 77.1% — Max: 86.3 %

Native-born — Min: 63.8% — OECD: 74.4% — Spain: 73.0% — Max: 85.8%

Employment rate

Foreign-born — Min: 51.7% — Spain: 60.4% — OECD: 69.2% — Max: 80.8%

Native-born — Min: 56.6% — Spain: 63.3% — OECD: 70.1% — Max: 82.7%

Unemployment rate

Foreign-born — Min: 3.2 % — OECD: 9.1 % — Spain: 21.6 % — Max: 23 %

Native-born — Min: 2.9% — OECD: 6.5% — Spain: 13.2% — Max: 16.5%

StatLink ᵐˢᴸ https://stat.link/or0a2n

Sweden

Foreign-born population – 2021	20.1% of the population	Main countries of birth:
Size: 2 million, 50% of women	Evolution since 2011: +48%	Syria (9%), Iraq (7%), Finland (7%)

In 2020, Sweden received 79 000 new immigrants on a long-term or permanent basis (including changes of status and free mobility), -18.8% compared to 2019. This figure comprises 28% immigrants benefitting from free mobility, 15.8% labour migrants, 43% family members (including accompanying family) and 13.2% humanitarian migrants. Around 6 600 permits were issued to tertiary-level international students and 5 100 to temporary and seasonal labour migrants (excluding intra-EU migration). In addition, 61 000 intra-EU postings were recorded in 2020, a decrease of -28% compared to 2019. These posted workers are generally on short-term contracts.

India, Syria and Afghanistan were the top three nationalities of newcomers in 2020. Among the top 15 countries of origin, Denmark registered the strongest increase (25) and Afghanistan the largest decrease (-5 300) in flows to Sweden compared to the previous year.

In 2021, the number of first asylum applicants decreased by -25.3% to reach around 10 000. The majority of applicants came from Syria (2 200), Afghanistan (1 000) and Ukraine (400). The largest increase since 2020 concerned nationals of Syria (400) and the largest decrease nationals of Uzbekistan (-560). Of the 10 000 decisions taken in 2021, 28% were positive.

In June 2021, the parliament adopted amendments to regulations in the Aliens Act, which came into force in July 2021. According to the new legislation, all residence permits issued are temporary. First time-limited permits can vary in length, but a two-year permit is the main rule. Permanent residence permits can only be granted if certain requirements are met, including a maintenance requirement. The amendment also includes stricter requirements for family migration: the relative in Sweden must be able to support both themselves and the family members and have a home sufficient in size and standard to host everyone.

In June 2022, the parliament adopted new regulations on tightening and improving the current regulations on labour migration. The regulations intend to counter exploitation of labour migrants and attract and retain international expertise and counter the expulsion of skilled workers. This was the first in a series of forthcoming proposed amendments to regulations on labour migration. The government has further tasked an inquiry to investigate the potential to introduce labour market tests to address social dumping and worker's exploitation.

In June 2022, the government tasked an inquiry to investigate how language and social skills requirements for permanent residence permits should be designed in a way that is appropriate, legally secure and effective.

In June 2022, the parliament adopted further amendments to regulations in the Aliens Act, which will come into force in August 2022, making it possible to expel aliens who commit criminal offences in more cases than presently.

The government has tasked an inquiry to propose new regulations for the initial reception of asylum seekers. One of the aims of the inquiry is to investigate to what extent refugees can be incentivised to live in state-provided accommodation during their first time in Sweden. New regulations to limit the share of refugees living in own accommodation were introduced already in 2020, to prevent asylum seekers to move to areas with socio-economic challenges.

In April 2021, the Public Employment Service started implementing the Intensive Year for newly arrived immigrants. The aim of the initiative is that highly motived newly arrived immigrants get a job within one year, by taking part in a combination of integration measures. The focus is on language training, measures that are closely tied to a workplace and shorter training courses. New measures within the Intensive Year are intensive internship and a mentorship programme with an economic compensation to employers who offer mentorships. Furthermore, Entry Agreements, a new model for getting long-term unemployed and newly arrived immigrants into the labour market and to ease future skills supply for employers, are expected to be introduced in 2022.

As of April 2022, travellers from outside the EU and the EEA will no longer be subject to COVID-19 related entry requirements when entering Sweden. The COVID-19 entry requirements for the EU, the EEA and the Nordic countries were lifted in February 2022.

For further information: www.migrationsverket.se | www.scb.se | www.regeringen.se

Key figures on immigration and emigration – Sweden

Long-term immigration flows
2020 (Source: OECD)

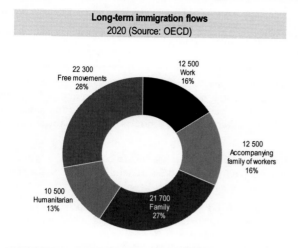

Temporary migration
(Sources: OECD, Eurostat)

Temporary labour migration (non-EU citizens)

	2020	2020/19
Working holidaymakers	1 580	- 23%
Seasonal workers	3 490	- 43%
Intra-company transfers	..	..
Other temporary workers	..	..

Education (non-EU citizens)

	2020	2020/19
International students	6 630	- 38%
Trainees	..	..

Humanitarian

	2021	2021/20
Asylum seekers	10 180	- 25%

Inflows of top 10 nationalities
(national definition)

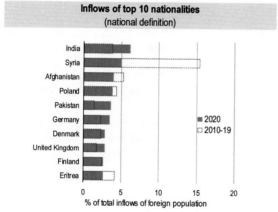

Emigration of Swedes to OECD countries
(national definition)

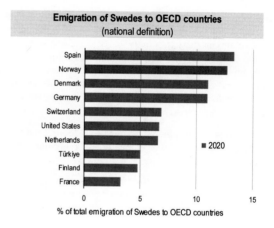

Components of population growth

	2021 Per 1 000 inhabitants	2021/20 difference
Total	7.0	+2.0
Natural increase	2.1	+0.7
Net migration plus statistical adjustments	4.9	+1.4

Annual remittances

	Million current USD	Annual change %	Share in GDP %
Inflows (2021)	3 338	+7.5	+0.5
Outflows (2021)	2 140	+21.2	+0.3

Labour market outcomes
2021

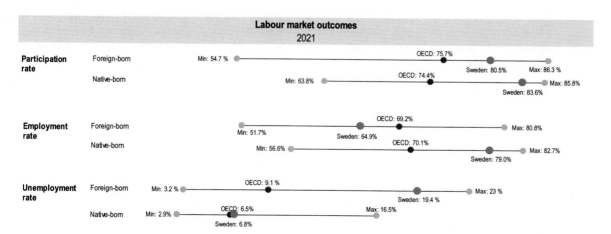

StatLink https://stat.link/6egnwi

Switzerland

Foreign-born population – 2021	30.2% of the population	Main countries of birth:
Size: 2.6 million, 51% of women	Evolution since 2011: +27%	Germany (14%), Italy (10%), Portugal (8%)

In 2020, Switzerland received 118 000 new immigrants on a long-term or permanent basis (including changes of status), -3.6% compared to 2019. This figure comprises 75.4% immigrants benefitting from free mobility, 1.5% labour migrants, 14.5% family members (including accompanying family) and 5.6% humanitarian migrants. Around 11 000 permits were issued to tertiary-level international students. In addition, 177 000 intra-EU/EFTA postings were recorded in 2020, a decrease of -28% compared to 2019. These posted workers are generally on short-term contracts.

Germany, Italy and France were the top three nationalities of newcomers in 2020. Among the top 15 countries of origin, France registered the strongest increase (1 800) and Portugal the largest decrease (-800) in flows to Switzerland compared to the previous year.

In 2021, the number of first asylum applicants increased by 36.1% to reach around 13 000. The majority of applicants came from Afghanistan (2 000), Eritrea (1 700) and Algeria (1 000). The largest increase since 2020 concerned nationals of Afghanistan (1 300) and the largest decrease nationals of Sri Lanka (-70). Of the 9 940 decisions taken in 2021, 91% were positive.

In the context of a complementary mandate of the Swiss Integration Agenda – launched in 2019, the asylum financing system will be reformed in order to harmonise the tasks of the Confederation and the cantons concerning care, social assistance and the promotion of integration, starting 1 January 2023. Specifically, to increase incentives for young individuals to take on vocational training, the Confederation will pay cantons a lump sum for refugees and temporarily admitted persons aged 18 to 25 regardless of their employment or training status. In addition, a "low income" correction factor will be introduced for refugees and temporarily admitted persons aged 25 to 60 to avoid disincentives for vocational training or part-time employment in these age groups. A lump sum will no longer be deducted for persons with an income of CHF 600 or less, thereby reducing the financial burden on the cantons. The current financing system will be maintained for asylum seekers.

Protection against discrimination has been guaranteed by the Federal Act on Foreigners and Integration (LEI) since 2019 and efforts have mainly focused on raising awareness in ordinary structures. From 2022, anti-discrimination efforts will also aim at strengthening the authorities and institutions in a targeted manner, especially regarding discriminations in job searches.

Since 1 January 2022, the government has granted freedom of movement to Croatian citizens, who now follow the same immigration procedure as EU nationals and face fewer requirements to work in Switzerland. However, if it causes serious disturbances to the labour market, the government will be allowed to limit the number of work permits issued to Croatian nationals from 2023 to the end of 2026.

The Federal Council amended the Ordinance on Entry and the Granting of Visas (EGVO) to allow Australian nationals to enter the country without a visa, beginning 1 January 2022, regardless of the purpose and duration of their stay, nonetheless, they have to require a permit if they plan to stay in Switzerland for more than three months or if they intend to work in Switzerland. In addition, Swiss nationals have been granted access to the Australian Work and Holiday Programme.

The quotas on work permits, which increased in 2019 for non-EU/EFTA nationals, have remained unchanged in 2020, 2021 and 2022 for EU/EFTA service providers, non-EU/EFTA and UK nationals.

Regarding COVID-19-related measures, Switzerland and the EU have mutually recognised their vaccination certificates to facilitate travel procedures. Since October 2021, submitting a COVID-19 test has become mandatory for persons who are forced to leave Switzerland to ensure the execution of removal orders. If necessary, tests can also be carried out against their will. This regulation of the LEI is valid until 31 December 2022. As of 17 February 2022, Switzerland has lifted its entry restrictions for all travellers except for those coming from high-risk countries.

For further information: www.sem.admin.ch

Key figures on immigration and emigration – Switzerland

Long-term immigration flows
2020 (Source: OECD)

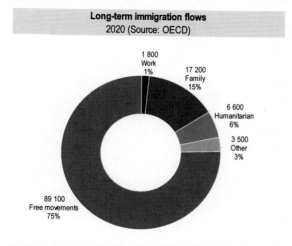

- 1 800 Work 1%
- 17 200 Family 15%
- 6 600 Humanitarian 6%
- 3 500 Other 3%
- 89 100 Free movements 75%

Temporary migration
(Sources: OECD, Eurostat)

Temporary labour migration

	2020	2020/19
Working holidaymakers	..	..
Seasonal workers	..	..
Intra-company transfers	..	..
Other temporary workers	..	..

Education

	2020	2020/19
International students	11 350	- 0%
Trainees	90	- 37%

Humanitarian

	2021	2021/20
Asylum seekers	13 300	+ 36%

Inflows of top 10 nationalities
(national definition)

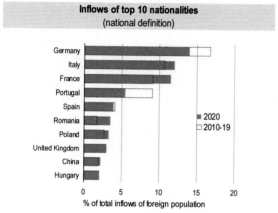

Germany, Italy, France, Portugal, Spain, Romania, Poland, United Kingdom, China, Hungary

■ 2020
□ 2010-19

% of total inflows of foreign population

Emigration of Swiss to OECD countries
(national definition)

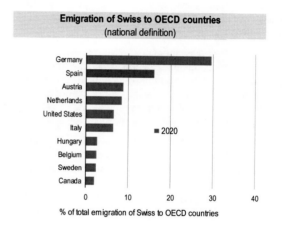

Germany, Spain, Austria, Netherlands, United States, Italy, Hungary, Belgium, Sweden, Canada

■ 2020

% of total emigration of Swiss to OECD countries

Components of population growth

	2021 Per 1 000 inhabitants	2021/20 difference
Total	7.6	+0.2
Natural increase	2.1	+1.0
Net migration plus statistical adjustments	5.5	-0.8

Annual remittances

	Million current USD	Annual change %	Share in GDP %
Inflows (2021)	3 019	+18.4	+0.4
Outflows (2020)	27 965	-0.8	+3.7

Labour market outcomes
2021

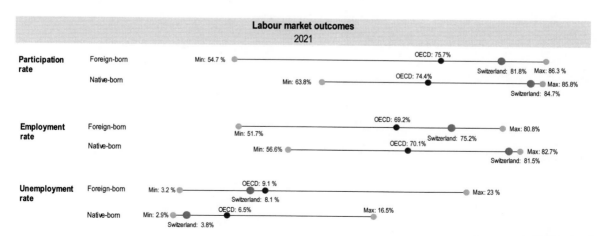

Participation rate
- Foreign-born: Min: 54.7 % | OECD: 75.7% | Switzerland: 81.8% | Max: 86.3 %
- Native-born: Min: 63.8% | OECD: 74.4% | Max: 85.8% | Switzerland: 84.7%

Employment rate
- Foreign-born: Min: 51.7% | OECD: 69.2% | Switzerland: 75.2% | Max: 80.8%
- Native-born: Min: 56.6% | OECD: 70.1% | Max: 82.7% | Switzerland: 81.5%

Unemployment rate
- Foreign-born: Min: 3.2 % | OECD: 9.1 % | Switzerland: 8.1 % | Max: 23 %
- Native-born: Min: 2.9% | OECD: 6.5% | Switzerland: 3.8% | Max: 16.5%

StatLink ᐸᔑᓬ https://stat.link/icn63h

Türkiye

Foreign-born population – 2021	3.7% of the population	Main countries of birth:
Size: 3.1 million, 52% of women	Evolution since 2014: +115%	Bulgaria (11%), Germany (11%), Iraq (10%)

In 2021, the number of first asylum applicants decreased by -6.6% to reach around 29 000. The majority of applicants came from Afghanistan (22 000), Iraq (4 000) and Iran (1 000). The largest decrease concerned nationals of Iraq (-900). Of the 46 000 decisions taken in 2021, 28% were positive.

The years 2020-21 were characterised by major developments in migration policy as a result of the COVID-19 pandemic and issues concerning Syrians under temporary protection, asylum, irregular migration and return.

In February 2020, Türkiye declared that it could no longer deal with the number of people fleeing Syria's civil war and would open its borders to facilitate the refugees who wished to leave the country for Europe. The 2016 "EU-Türkiye Statement" or "EU-Türkiye Deal" was suspended allowing irregular migrants to exit Türkiye with the aim of crossing to Greece and Bulgaria. In response, Greece and Bulgaria closed their borders resulting in many migrants staying in limbo at the border.

Additionally, the debate about voluntary return intensified in 2021 with safe zone discussions. A protocol was signed in September 2020 by the Directorate General for Migration Management, the Turkish Co-operation and Co-ordination Agency, the Ministry of Foreign Affairs and the Turkish Red Crescent for operational co-operation in the conduct of a National Assisted Voluntary Return (NAVR) mechanism.

Since 2019, the government of Türkiye has been implementing a policy to relocate Syrian refugees based on their province of initial registration. In January 2021, the Istanbul Directorate General for Migration Management announced that no new residence applications could be made in districts hosting the highest number of registered Syrian and non-Syrian residents in Istanbul and Ankara. In February 2022, the Minister of Interior extended the policy to reduce the number of Syrian refugees and other foreigners in districts where Syrian refugees represent 25% of the population. Relocation policies will be implemented alongside policies halting new registrations or residence applications for Syrians and non-Syrian residents.

Turkish authorities decided not to pursue overstay penalties against foreign nationals who were unable to depart due to COVID-19 measures, if they departed Türkiye within one month of the international border opening date. Migrants whose residential status expired during the pandemic and official closure of the borders were allowed to prolong their stay.

For further information:
www.goc.gov.tr | www.iskur.gov.tr | www.nvi.gov.tr | www.mfa.gov.tr | www.tuik.gov.tr | www.yok.gov.tr | www.denklik.yok.gov.tr

Key figures on immigration and emigration – Türkiye

Inflows of top 10 nationalities
(national definition)

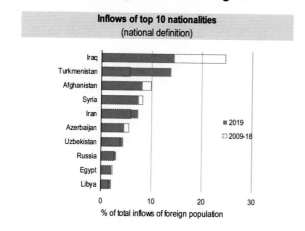

Emigration of Turks to OECD countries
(national definition)

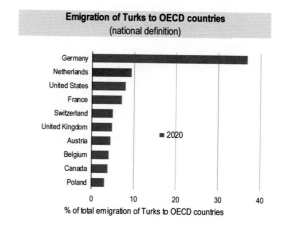

Components of population growth		
	2021 Per 1 000 inhabitants	2021/20 difference
Total	12.7	+7.2
Natural increase	..	..
Net migration plus statistical adjustments	..	..

Annual remittances			
	Million current USD	Annual change %	Share in GDP %
Inflows (2021)	704	-23.3	+0.1
Outflows (2021)	1 491	+10.9	+0.2

Labour market outcomes
Data for Türkiye refer to 2020, OECD minimum, maximum and average refer to countries with 2021 data

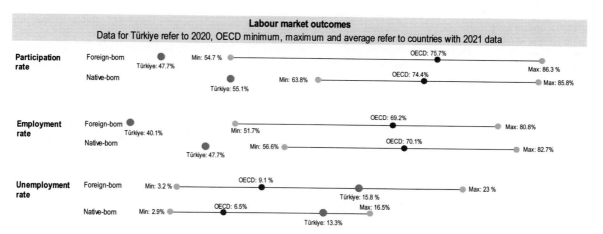

StatLink ⧉ https://stat.link/zpjtde

United Kingdom

Foreign-born population – 2019	14% of the population	Main countries of birth:
Size: 9.5 million, 52% of women	Evolution since 2011: +28%	India (9%), Poland (8%), Pakistan (5%)

In 2020, the United Kingdom received 223 000 new immigrants on a long-term or permanent basis (including changes of status and free mobility), -35.5% compared to 2019. This figure comprises 20.4% immigrants benefitting from free mobility, 18% labour migrants, 41.2% family members (including accompanying family) and 14.3% humanitarian migrants. Around 222 000 permits were issued to tertiary-level international students and 24 000 to temporary and seasonal labour migrants (excluding intra-EU migration). In addition, 62 000 intra-EU postings were recorded in 2020, a decrease of -53% compared to 2019. These posted workers are generally on short-term contracts.

In 2021, the number of first asylum applicants increased by 57% to reach around 56 000. The majority of applicants came from Iran (10 000), Iraq (7 700) and Eritrea (5 000).The largest increase since 2020 concerned nationals of Iran (6 250) and the largest decrease nationals of Pakistan (-370). Of the 24 000 decisions taken in 2021, 62% were positive.

In May 2021, the United Kingdom set out its border control strategy for subsequent years. It envisages a digital control system with a universal permission to travel requirement and a more flexible approach to recruitment from overseas for skilled jobs with an identified national shortage. Particular attention was paid to changing the asylum system to deter illegal entry.

For economic migrants, a series of changes and new routes have been announced. These include the introduction of a Health and Care Worker route in August 2020, a new Graduate route in summer 2021, and in spring 2022, a new High Potential Individual route was introduced. Changes were also made to the quota-based Seasonal Worker visa to allow for a temporarily extension to include poultry workers in November 2021 and will again be extended to poultry workers in the run up to Christmas 2022. A new Scale-up route will be operational from summer 2022, allowing high-growth companies to sponsor workers in high skilled roles. The Tier 1 (Investor) route was closed in February 2022.

In January 2022, the Afghan Citizens Resettlement Scheme (ACRS) opened and will provide up to 20 000 Afghan women, children, and others most at risk with a safe and legal route to resettle in the United Kingdom. It is separate from the Afghan Relocations and Assistance Policy (ARAP) which offers relocation to the United Kingdom for eligible Afghan citizens who were employed by the UK Government locally in Afghanistan in exposed, meaningful or enabling roles, and assessed to be at serious risk because of their work.

The Nationality and Borders Act was passed in April 2022. Its main aims are to deter illegal entry into the United Kingdom, break the business model of people-smuggling networks, and speed up the removal of those with no right to be in the United Kingdom. It puts into law that those who arrive in the United Kingdom and who are granted refugee status having travelled through a safe third country where they could have reasonably been expected to claim asylum, or did not claim asylum without delay, may be deemed to have entered illegally and can be considered inadmissible to the United Kingdom asylum system. Other measures include tougher penalties for smugglers and new approaches to legal challenges and methods for age assessment.

In April 2022 the United Kingdom announced a new Migration and Economic Development Partnership with Rwanda. The partnership addresses the shared international challenge of irregular migration and intends to break the business model of people smuggling gangs. Under this partnership, those who travel to the United Kingdom by illegal and dangerous routes, including by small boat across the English Channel, and are deemed inadmissible to the United Kingdom asylum system, may be relocated to Rwanda where they will have their asylum claim considered. Those whose claims are accepted will then be supported to build a new life in Rwanda.

In response to the war in Ukraine, special visa-controlled schemes for Ukrainian refugees were opened in March 2022 including the Ukraine Family Scheme and the Homes for Ukraine Scheme.

For further information: www.gov.uk/government/organisations/home-office | www.ons.gov.uk

Key figures on immigration and emigration – United Kingdom

Long-term immigration flows
2020 (Source: OECD)

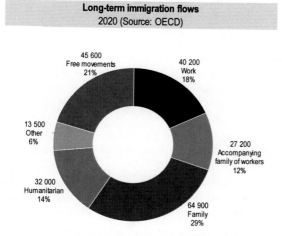

- 45 600 Free movements 21%
- 40 200 Work 18%
- 13 500 Other 6%
- 27 200 Accompanying family of workers 12%
- 32 000 Humanitarian 14%
- 64 900 Family 29%

Temporary migration
(Sources: OECD, UNHCR)

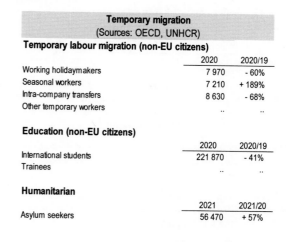

Temporary labour migration (non-EU citizens)

	2020	2020/19
Working holidaymakers	7 970	- 60%
Seasonal workers	7 210	+ 189%
Intra-company transfers	8 630	- 68%
Other temporary workers	..	..

Education (non-EU citizens)

	2020	2020/19
International students	221 870	- 41%
Trainees	..	..

Humanitarian

	2021	2021/20
Asylum seekers	56 470	+ 57%

Inflows of top 10 nationalities
(national definition)

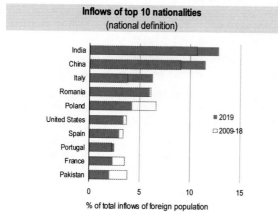

% of total inflows of foreign population

Emigration of British to OECD countries
(national definition)

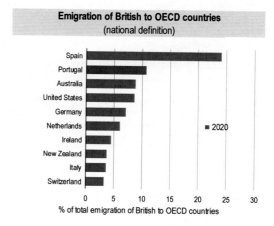

% of total emigration of British to OECD countries

Components of population growth

	2020 Per 1 000 inhabitants	2020/19 difference
Total	5.4	..
Natural increase	-0.1	..
Net migration plus statistical adjustments	5.5	..

Annual remittances

	Million current USD	Annual change %	Share in GDP %
Inflows (2021)	3 523	-16.6	+0.1
Outflows (2021)	10 083	+7.5	+0.3

Labour market outcomes
2021

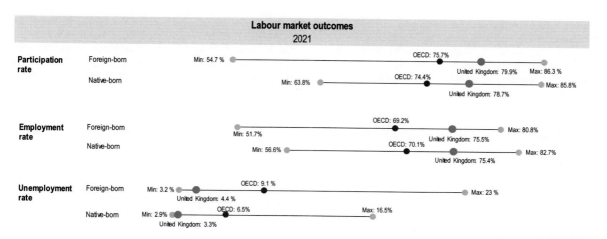

StatLink ⌐ıSL https://stat.link/h310vy

United States

Foreign-born population – 2021	13.6% of the population	Main countries of birth:
Size: 45.3 million, 51% of women	Evolution since 2011: +12%	Mexico (26%), India (7%), China (4%)

In 2020, the United States received 582 000 new immigrants on a long-term or permanent basis (including changes of status), - 43.6% compared to 2019. This figure comprises 11.1% labour migrants, 71.9% family members (including accompanying family) and 10.9% humanitarian migrants. Around 111 000 permits were issued to tertiary-level international students and 486 000 to temporary and seasonal labour migrants.

Mexico, India and China were the top three nationalities of newcomers in 2020. Among the top 15 countries of origin, Afghanistan registered the strongest increase (1 200) and Mexico the largest decrease (-55 000) in flows to the United States compared to the previous year.

In 2021, the number of first asylum applicants decreased by -24.7% to reach around 189 000. The majority of applicants came from Venezuela (27 000), Guatemala (23 000) and Honduras (20 000). The largest increase since 2020 concerned nationals of Colombia (7 400) and the largest decrease nationals of Guatemala (-13 500). Of the 114 000 decisions taken in 2021, 18% were positive.

Increasing access and reducing barriers to the legal immigration system and naturalisation remained a priority for the U.S. Citizenship and Immigration Services (USCIS) in 2022. The agency took significant steps to address processing delays caused by COVID-19 and other factors, including by waiving certain interview requirements and extending the validity of certain employment authorisation documents. USCIS also published a notice of proposed rulemaking addressing the public charge ground of inadmissibility.

In January 2022, the Department of Homeland Security (DHS) and the Department of State (DOS) announced policy initiatives to increase pathways for international STEM scholars, students, and researchers to study and work in the United States.

In 2022, DHS announced Temporary Protected Status (TPS) designations for nationals of Afghanistan, Ukraine, Cameroon, South Sudan and Sudan. DHS also continued to lead the Operation Allies Welcome initiative to support Afghan evacuees, and launched Uniting for Ukraine, committing to welcoming 100 000 Ukrainian refugees through a variety of legal channels.

DOS and DHS reinstated and expanded the Central American Minors (CAM) programme. On 29 March 2022, DHS and the Department of Justice published a final rule to enhance processing of asylum claims made by noncitizens subject to expedited removal.

Deferred action (which can confer employment authorisation) is offered for Special Immigrant Juveniles who cannot adjust to lawful permanent resident because a visa number is not available. Certain U visa (crime victims) holders are also now eligible for a four-year, renewable grant of deferred action.

In December 2021, DHS and Department of Labour authorised an additional 20 000 H-2B visas for temporary non-agricultural employment in the first half of FY 2022, with 6 500 reserved for nationals of Haiti, El Salvador, Guatemala, and Honduras They published another joint temporary final rule on 31 March 2022 to meet demand in the labour market, making an additional 35 000 H-2B visas available for the second half of FY 2022, with 11 500 reserved for nationals of those countries.

In November 2021, DHS clarified that E (Treaty Traders and Investors) and L (Intracompany Transferee) accompanying spouses are employment-authorised based on valid non-immigrant visa status, as evidenced by an unexpired entry document (the Form I-94), and do not need to apply for a employment authorisation document.

Certain policies are likely to be clarified in 2022 through judicial action. On 16 July 2021, a federal judge blocked DHS from adjudicating new applications under the Deferred Action for Childhood Arrivals (DACA) programme but granted temporary permission to continue processing of renewal requests for existing recipients. On 30 June 2022, the U.S. Supreme Court upheld the rescission of the Migrant Protection Protocols, which required certain migrants with pending asylum claims to be returned to Mexico to wait their immigration proceeding. The matter is now under review by the lower courts. Litigation also continues over the Title 42 public health order requiring the expulsion of asylum seekers during the COVID-19 pandemic. The immigration enforcement priorities announced by DHS were vacated by a federal judge in June 2022.

For further information: www.whitehouse.gov/priorities | www.dhs.gov | www.uscis.gov/ | www.state.gov

Key figures on immigration and emigration – United States

Long-term immigration flows
2020 (Source: OECD)

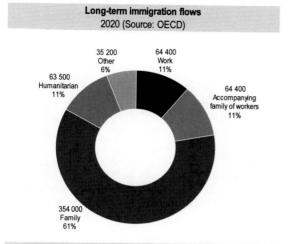

Temporary migration
(Sources: OECD, UNHCR)

Temporary labour migration

	2020	2020/19
Working holidaymakers	4 950	- 95%
Seasonal workers	213 390	+ 4%
Intra-company transfers	35 940	- 53%
Other temporary workers	231 530	- 38%

Education

	2020	2020/19
International students	111 390	- 69%
Trainees	480	- 54%

Humanitarian

	2021	2021/20
Asylum seekers	188 860	- 25%

Inflows of top 10 nationalities
(national definition)

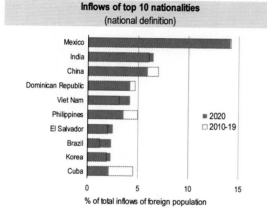

Emigration of Americans to OECD countries
(national definition)

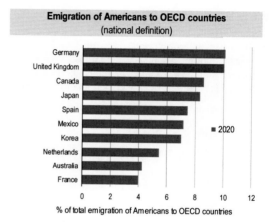

Components of population growth

	2021 Per 1 000 inhabitants	2021/20 difference
Total	7.0	-0.1
Natural increase	4.0	-0.1
Net migration plus statistical adjustments	3.0	-0.0

Annual remittances

	Million current USD	Annual change %	Share in GDP %
Inflows (2021)	6 699	-6.5	+0.0
Outflows (2021)	74 577	+6.7	+0.3

Labour market outcomes
2021

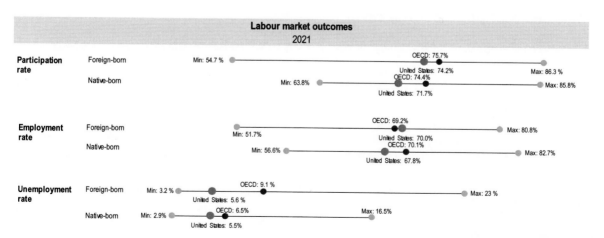

StatLink https://stat.link/27tp4y

Notes and data sources

Foreign-born population

National sources and Secretariat estimates. Sources and notes are available in the statistical annex (see metadata for Tables A.4 and B.4).

Long-term immigration flows

The statistics are generally based on residence and work permit data and have been standardised, to the extent possible, except for Bulgaria, the Czech Republic, Estonia, Greece, Hungary, Latvia, Lithuania, Poland, Romania, the Slovak Republic and Slovenia, for which the source is Eurostat's database on first permits by reason, length of validity and citizenship (Table migr_resfirst).

Temporary migration

Residence or work permit data. Data on temporary workers do not generally cover workers who benefit from a free circulation agreement. Students exclude secondary education and vocational training. For Belgium, Bulgaria, the Czech Republic, Estonia, Greece, Hungary, Latvia, Lithuania, the Netherlands, Portugal, Romania, the Slovak Republic and Slovenia, the source is Eurostat's database on first permits by reason, length of validity and citizenship (migr_resfirst).

Inflows of asylum seekers. United Nations High Commission for Refugees (www.unhcr.org/statistics); Eurostat.

Inflows of top 10 nationalities

OECD countries: sources and notes are available in the statistical annex (metadata related to Tables A.1 and B.1).

Bulgaria: Number of new permanent and long-term residence permits granted (Source: Ministry of the Interior); Romania: Changes in permanent residence (Source: Romanian Statistical Yearbook).

Emigration of nationals to OECD countries

Sum of the inflows of the country's citizens to OECD countries.

Components of population growth

European countries: Population change – Demographic balance and crude rates at national level (Eurostat); other countries: national sources.

Annual remittances

World Bank calculation based on data from IMF Balance of Payments Statistics database and data releases from central banks, national statistical agencies, and World Bank country desks.

Labour market outcomes

European countries and Türkiye: Labour Force Surveys (Eurostat).

Australia, Canada, Israel, New Zealand: Labour Force Surveys.

Chile: Encuesta de Caracterización Socioeconómica Nacional (CASEN).

Japan: Population census 2015.

Korea: Survey on Immigrants' Living Conditions and Labour Force and Economically Active Population Survey of Korean nationals (the rates refer to the long term resident foreign born population aged 15-59 who is foreign or was naturalised within the last five years).

Mexico: Encuesta Nacional de Ocupación y Empleo (ENOE).

United States: Current Population Surveys.

The OECD average excludes Chile, Japan and Korea.

Annex A. Statistical annex

Inflows and outflows of foreign population

A.1. Inflows of foreign population into OECD countries

B.1. Inflows of foreign population by nationality

A.2. Outflows of foreign population from selected OECD countries

Metadata relative to Tables A.1, B.1. and A.2. Inflows and outflows of foreign population

Inflows of asylum seekers

A.3. Inflows of asylum seekers into OECD countries

B.3. Inflows of asylum seekers by nationality

Metadata relative to Tables A.3. and B.3. Inflows of asylum seekers

Stocks of foreign and foreign-born populations

A.4. Stocks of foreign-born population in OECD countries

B.4. Stocks of foreign-born population by country of birth

Metadata relative to Tables A.4. and B.4. Stocks of foreign-born population

A.5. Stocks of foreign population by nationality in OECD countries

B.5. Stocks of foreign population by nationality

Metadata relative to Tables A.5. and B.5. Stocks of foreign population

Acquisitions of nationality

A.6. Acquisitions of nationality in OECD countries

B.6. Acquisitions of nationality by country of former nationality

Metadata relative to Tables A.6. and B.6. Acquisitions of nationality

Introduction

Most of the data published in this annex have been provided by national correspondents of the OECD Expert Group on Migration appointed by the OECD Secretariat with the approval of the authorities of member countries. Consequently, these data are not necessarily based on common definitions. Countries under review in this annex are OECD countries for which data are available. The OECD Expert Group on Migration has no authority to impose changes in data collection procedures. It is an observatory which, by its very nature, has to use existing statistics. However, it does play an active role in suggesting what it considers to be essential improvements in data collection and makes every effort to present consistent and well-documented statistics.

The purpose of this annex is to describe the "immigrant" population (generally the foreign-born population). The information gathered concerns the flows and stocks of the total immigrant population as well as the acquisition of nationality. These data have not been standardised and are therefore not fully comparable across countries. In particular, the criteria for registering persons in population registers and the conditions for granting residence permits, for example, vary across countries, which means that measurements may differ greatly even if the same type of source is being used.

In addition to the problem of the comparability of statistics, there is the difficulty of the very partial coverage of unauthorised migrants. Part of this population may be counted in censuses. Regularisation programmes, when they exist, make it possible to identify and enumerate a far from negligible fraction of unauthorised immigrants after the fact. In terms of measurement, this makes it possible to better measure the volume of the foreign-born population at a given time, even if it is not always possible to determine the year these immigrants entered the country.

Each series in the annex is preceded by an explanatory note concerning the data presented. A summary table then follows (series A, giving the total for each destination country), and finally the tables by nationality or country of birth, as the case may be (series B). At the end of each series, a table provides the sources and notes for the data presented in the tables for each country.

General comments

The tables provide annual series covering the period 2010-20 or 2011-21.

- The series A tables are presented in alphabetical order by the name of the country. In the other tables, nationalities or countries of birth are ranked by decreasing order of frequency for the last year available.
- In the tables by country of origin (series B), only the 15 main countries are shown. "Other countries" is a residual calculated as the difference between the total foreign or foreign-born population and the sum for all countries indicated in the table. For some countries, data are not available for all years and this is reflected in the residual entry of "Other countries". This must be borne in mind when interpreting changes in this category.
- There is no table by nationality for the series on outflows of the foreign population (series A.2). These statistics, as well as data by gender, are available online (http://www.oecd.org/els/mig/keystat.htm).
- The rounding of data cells may cause totals to differ slightly from the sum of the component cells.
- The symbol ".." used in the tables means that the data are not available.
- Figures in italic are estimated by the Secretariat.

Inflows and outflows of foreign population

OECD countries seldom have tools specifically designed to measure the inflows and outflows of the foreign population, and national estimates are generally based either on population registers or residence permit data. This note describes more systematically what is measured by each of the sources used.

Flows derived from population registers

Population registers can usually produce inflow and outflow data for both nationals and foreigners. To register, foreigners may have to indicate possession of an appropriate residence and/or work permit valid for at least as long as the minimum registration period. Emigrants are usually identified by a stated intention to leave the country, although the period of (intended) absence is not always specified.

In population registers, departures tend to be less well recorded than arrivals. Indeed, the emigrant who plans to return to the host country in the future may be reluctant to inform about his departure to avoid losing rights related to the presence on the register. Registration criteria vary considerably across countries; in particular the minimum duration of stay for individuals to be registered ranges from three months to one year, which poses major problems of international comparisons. For example, in some countries, register data cover many temporary migrants, in some cases including asylum seekers when they live in private households (as opposed to reception centres or hostels for immigrants) and international students.

Flows derived from residence and/or work permits

Statistics on permits are generally based on the number of permits issued during a given period and depend on the types of permits used. The so-called "settlement countries" (Australia, Canada, New Zealand and the United States) consider as immigrants persons who have been granted the right of permanent residence, and this right is often granted upon arrival. Statistics on temporary immigrants are also published in this annex for these countries. In the case of France, the permits covered are those valid for at least one year (excluding students).

Another characteristic of permit data is that flows of nationals are not recorded. Some flows of foreigners may also not be recorded, either because the type of permit they hold is not included in the statistics or because they are not required to have a permit (freedom of movement agreements). In addition, permit data do not necessarily reflect physical flows or actual lengths of stay since: i) permits may be issued overseas but individuals may decide not to use them, or delay their arrival; ii) permits may be issued to persons who have in fact been resident in the country for some time, the permit indicating a change of status.

Flows estimated from specific surveys

Ireland provides estimates based on the results of Quarterly National Household Surveys and other sources such as permit data and asylum applications. These estimates are revised periodically on the basis of census data. One of the aims of this survey is to estimate the number and characteristics of migrants. The survey is based on a random sample of approximately one out of every 500 passengers. The figures were revised significantly following the latest census in each of these two countries, which seems to indicate that these estimates do not constitute an "ideal" source either. Australia and New Zealand also conduct passenger surveys, which enable them to establish the length of stay on the basis of migrants' stated intentions when they enter or exit the country.

Table A.1. Inflows of foreign population into selected OECD countries

Thousands

	2010	2011	2012	2013	2014	2015	2016	2017	2018	2019	2020
Australia	202.2	206.4	236.0	244.8	233.9	223.7	218.5	224.2	186.6	155.8	137.5
Austria	96.9	109.9	125.6	135.2	154.3	198.7	158.7	139.3	131.7	135.0	121.3
Belgium	116.7	133.6	116.1	105.5	106.3	128.8	106.1	109.2	119.7	129.5	101.6
Canada	280.7	248.7	257.8	259.0	260.3	271.8	296.7	286.4	321.0	341.2	184.6
Chile	41.4	50.7	65.2	84.4	83.5	101.9	135.5	207.2	339.4	254.1	153.8
Colombia	..	..	..	..	..	..	..	148.6	245.2	206.7	91.1
Costa Rica	..	..	..	..	..	15.7	6.6	8.6	9.2	7.8	..
Czech Republic	28.0	20.7	28.6	27.8	38.5	31.6	34.8	43.5	55.9	63.3	53.8
Denmark	33.4	34.6	35.5	41.3	49.0	58.7	54.6	49.0	45.3	42.3	37.8
Estonia	1.2	1.7	1.1	1.6	1.3	7.4	7.7	9.1	9.7	11.0	10.3
Finland	18.2	20.4	23.3	23.9	23.6	21.4	27.3	23.7	23.1	24.2	23.3
France	145.8	142.1	151.6	251.3	251.8	242.7	245.7	246.2	255.4	254.2	200.5
Germany	683.5	841.7	965.9	1 108.1	1 342.5	2 016.2	1 719.1	1 384.0	1 383.6	1 345.9	994.8
Greece	35.4	33.0	32.0	31.3	29.5	34.0	86.1	80.5	87.3	95.4	63.4
Hungary	23.9	22.5	20.3	21.3	26.0	25.8	23.8	36.5	49.3	55.3	43.8
Iceland	3.0	2.8	2.8	3.9	4.3	5.0	7.9	11.8	11.5	9.5	7.6
Ireland	23.9	33.7	37.2	41.0	43.7	49.3	53.9	57.2	61.9	61.7	56.5
Israel	16.6	16.9	16.6	16.9	24.1	27.9	26.0	26.4	28.1	33.2	19.7
Italy	424.5	354.3	321.3	279.0	248.4	250.0	262.9	301.1	285.5	264.6	191.8
Japan	287.1	266.9	303.9	306.7	336.5	391.2	427.6	475.0	519.7	592.0	220.6
Korea	293.1	307.2	300.2	360.5	407.1	372.9	402.2	452.7	495.1	438.2	233.1
Latvia	2.8	2.9	3.7	3.5	4.5	4.5	3.4	5.1	6.5	6.6	4.6
Lithuania	1.1	1.7	2.5	3.0	4.8	3.7	6.0	10.2	12.3	19.7	22.3
Luxembourg	15.8	19.1	19.4	19.8	21.0	22.6	21.6	23.2	23.3	25.1	22.5
Mexico	26.2	22.0	18.2	63.0	43.5	34.4	35.9	32.8	38.7	40.5	58.4
Netherlands	110.2	118.5	115.7	122.3	139.3	159.5	182.2	183.9	191.0	215.2	170.6
New Zealand	69.9	71.8	71.7	75.4	90.7	101.5	104.0	103.4	104.2	124.7	53.7
Norway	65.1	70.8	70.0	66.9	61.4	59.1	58.5	49.8	44.4	44.6	30.8
Poland	41.1	41.3	47.1	46.6	32.0	86.1	107.0	128.0	137.6	163.2	163.5
Portugal	50.7	45.4	38.5	33.2	35.3	37.9	46.9	61.4	93.2	129.2	118.1
Slovak Republic	4.2	3.8	2.9	2.5	2.4	3.8	3.6	2.9	2.9	2.5	2.8
Slovenia	12.7	10.8	12.3	11.6	11.3	12.7	13.8	15.5	24.1	27.6	24.8
Spain	330.3	335.9	272.5	248.4	264.5	290.0	352.2	454.0	560.0	664.6	415.2
Sweden	79.0	75.9	82.6	95.4	106.1	113.9	143.0	125.0	114.4	98.2	65.8
Switzerland	134.2	142.5	143.8	155.4	152.1	150.4	143.1	137.8	140.1	140.6	137.0
Türkiye	29.9	..	..	..	..	..	273.9	364.6	466.9	578.5	..
United Kingdom	352.7	279.6	236.4	283.4	343.9	369.6	354.7	345.4	346.5	346.4	223.4
United States	1 042.6	1 062.0	1 031.6	990.6	1 016.5	1 051.0	1 183.5	1 127.2	1 096.6	1 031.8	707.4

Note: For details on definitions and sources, refer to the metadata at the end of Table A.2.

StatLink ⬛ᴵˢᴸ https://stat.link/wlvo42

Table B.1. Inflows of foreign population by nationality – Australia (permanent)

Thousands

	2010	2011	2012	2013	2014	2015	2016	2017	2018	2019	2020	Of which: Women 2020 (%)
India	23.5	21.9	27.8	38.1	39.6	34.7	38.6	40.0	33.1	32.6	24.5	49
China	24.5	28.7	25.3	27.9	27.1	27.9	29.1	29.3	25.7	25.5	18.8	56
United Kingdom	26.7	21.5	27.0	23.1	23.8	22.2	19.0	17.6	14.1	13.3	10.8	47
Philippines	10.2	10.7	12.8	11.0	10.3	11.9	12.0	12.1	10.9	9.2	8.5	59
Viet Nam	3.8	4.8	4.8	5.7	5.2	5.1	5.4	5.5	5.2	5.5	5.1	60
New Zealand	24.4	34.6	44.3	41.2	27.3	22.4	19.7	12.6	15.2	14.2	4.7	46
Nepal	1.3	2.1	2.5	4.0	4.4	4.2	5.1	4.4	3.0	3.8	4.7	50
South Africa	11.1	8.1	8.0	5.8	4.9	4.7	4.0	4.8	4.3	4.0	3.8	50
Pakistan	1.8	1.8	3.9	3.6	5.7	8.0	7.0	6.8	6.3	4.7	3.8	49
United States	3.2	3.0	3.3	3.8	3.8	3.5	3.5	3.6	2.7	3.6	3.2	55
Korea	4.3	4.3	5.0	5.4	3.8	3.6	3.3	3.2	2.2	2.5	2.6	57
Iran	1.8	2.6	3.0	3.1	2.7	3.9	2.8	2.8	2.6	2.2	2.4	50
Sri Lanka	5.2	4.5	5.7	5.3	4.5	3.9	3.8	3.2	2.7	2.7	2.4	52
Brazil	1.2	0.9	1.1	1.3	1.5	1.3	1.4	1.7	1.6	2.2	2.3	56
Afghanistan	1.6	2.0	1.6	2.2	5.7	3.3	3.2	3.6	3.8	2.2	2.2	61
Other countries	57.4	55.0	59.8	63.1	63.6	63.1	60.9	73.0	53.2	27.7	37.7	
Total	**202.2**	**206.4**	**236.0**	**244.8**	**233.9**	**223.7**	**218.5**	**224.2**	**186.6**	**155.8**	**137.5**	**54**

Note: For details on definitions and sources, refer to the metadata at the end of the tables.

StatLink 🔢 https://stat.link/x2hli8

Table B.1. Inflows of foreign population by nationality – Austria

Thousands

	2010	2011	2012	2013	2014	2015	2016	2017	2018	2019	2020	Of which: Women 2020 (%)
Germany	18.0	17.4	17.8	17.7	16.8	17.0	16.1	16.2	17.0	18.3	19.0	48
Romania	11.3	12.9	13.4	13.5	20.7	17.5	16.7	17.9	19.2	20.3	17.5	43
Hungary	6.4	9.3	13.1	14.9	14.5	14.4	13.3	13.1	12.6	12.1	10.1	46
Croatia	1.9	1.9	2.0	4.2	6.0	5.8	5.1	5.1	5.4	5.5	7.2	40
Serbia	7.1	6.1	6.7	7.1	7.4	7.6	7.3	7.2	6.8	6.5	5.3	45
Bulgaria	3.1	3.2	3.6	3.9	5.8	5.2	4.9	5.0	5.3	5.7	4.4	44
Poland	4.0	6.4	7.1	7.3	6.9	6.1	5.4	5.2	4.8	4.7	4.4	36
Italy	2.2	2.3	3.1	4.0	4.1	4.6	4.2	4.4	4.4	4.5	4.2	42
Slovak Republic	4.0	5.3	6.0	6.2	6.5	6.1	5.6	5.1	4.8	4.6	4.2	49
Syria	0.2	0.4	0.9	1.7	7.4	22.6	9.0	6.7	2.1	1.6	3.7	17
Bosnia and Herzegovina	2.5	3.9	4.1	5.0	5.2	5.2	4.3	4.2	4.1	3.9	3.3	44
Türkiye	4.3	3.8	4.1	4.5	3.7	3.7	3.7	3.3	3.0	3.3	2.5	40
Russia	2.2	2.6	3.4	3.5	3.1	2.9	2.7	2.4	2.1	2.2	1.8	57
United Kingdom	1.2	1.3	1.2	1.4	1.4	1.4	1.5	1.5	1.6	1.6	1.7	38
Slovenia	0.8	1.3	1.9	2.5	3.1	2.8	2.7	2.5	2.2	2.2	1.6	42
Other countries	27.6	31.7	37.2	37.8	41.6	75.6	56.2	39.5	36.6	37.9	30.3	
Total	**96.9**	**109.9**	**125.6**	**135.2**	**154.3**	**198.7**	**158.7**	**139.3**	**131.7**	**135.0**	**121.3**	**44**

Note: For details on definitions and sources, refer to the metadata at the end of the tables.

StatLink 🔢 https://stat.link/x2hli8

Table B.1. Inflows of foreign population by nationality – Belgium

Thousands

	2010	2011	2012	2013	2014	2015	2016	2017	2018	2019	2020	Of which: Women 2020 (%)
Romania	6.4	9.9	10.0	8.7	11.3	10.6	10.9	11.9	13.4	14.3	11.3	36
France	12.2	12.8	12.4	12.6	12.0	12.0	11.3	11.3	11.7	12.0	11.3	52
Netherlands	8.4	8.5	8.1	7.9	8.1	8.1	7.9	7.8	7.8	7.8	6.9	49
Italy	3.6	4.3	4.8	5.1	5.3	5.1	4.8	4.9	5.4	5.5	4.7	46
Morocco	9.4	8.6	5.8	4.5	4.7	4.8	4.7	4.5	5.0	5.8	4.7	55
Spain	3.5	4.9	5.5	5.5	5.0	4.1	3.6	4.0	4.2	4.7	4.5	48
Bulgaria	3.7	4.0	4.0	3.5	4.2	3.8	3.5	3.7	3.9	4.7	4.1	43
Poland	9.6	8.2	7.7	6.6	5.8	5.3	4.6	4.3	4.2	4.3	3.3	46
Afghanistan	1.2	3.1	2.1	1.1	1.1	7.5	2.6	1.6	2.2	3.8	3.2	27
Portugal	2.7	2.8	3.9	3.8	3.0	2.9	3.0	2.7	2.9	3.2	2.9	39
Germany	3.1	2.8	2.6	2.6	2.5	2.5	2.4	2.4	2.5	2.6	2.4	50
Türkiye	3.3	3.2	2.2	1.8	1.6	1.7	1.8	1.9	2.4	2.8	2.2	39
India	1.4	2.1	1.9	2.1	1.9	2.2	2.4	3.0	3.3	3.3	2.0	49
United Kingdom	1.9	1.9	1.8	1.8	1.6	1.7	1.6	1.6	1.8	2.1	2.0	37
Cameroon	1.4	1.7	1.6	1.3	1.4	1.5	1.6	1.7	1.8	1.8	1.7	52
Other countries	44.7	54.9	41.6	36.8	36.7	54.9	39.4	42.0	47.2	50.7	34.5	
Total	**116.7**	**133.6**	**116.1**	**105.5**	**106.3**	**128.8**	**106.1**	**109.2**	**119.7**	**129.5**	**101.6**	**47**

Note: For details on definitions and sources, refer to the metadata at the end of the tables.

StatLink https://stat.link/x2hli8

Table B.1. Inflows of foreign population by nationality – Canada (permanent)

Thousands

	2010	2011	2012	2013	2014	2015	2016	2017	2018	2019	2020	Of which: Women 2016 (%)
India	34.2	27.5	30.9	33.1	38.3	39.5	39.8	51.7	70.0	85.6	42.9	49
China	30.4	28.5	33.0	34.1	24.6	19.5	26.9	30.3	29.7	30.2	16.5	55
Philippines	38.6	36.8	34.3	29.5	40.0	50.8	41.8	40.9	35.1	27.8	11.0	54
United States	8.1	7.7	7.9	8.5	8.5	7.5	8.4	9.1	10.9	10.8	6.4	51
Nigeria	3.9	3.1	3.4	4.2	4.2	4.1	4.4	5.5	10.9	12.6	6.4	48
Pakistan	6.8	7.5	11.2	12.6	9.1	11.3	11.3	7.7	9.5	10.8	6.2	51
Syria	1.0	1.0	0.6	1.0	2.1	9.9	34.9	12.0	12.0	10.1	4.9	49
France	4.6	4.1	6.3	5.6	4.7	5.8	6.4	6.6	6.2	5.0	4.6	47
Iran	7.5	7.5	7.5	11.3	16.8	11.7	6.5	4.7	5.5	6.1	3.8	52
Brazil	2.6	1.5	1.6	1.7	1.9	1.8	1.7	2.8	4.0	5.3	3.7	54
United Kingdom	8.7	6.1	6.2	5.8	5.8	5.5	5.8	5.3	5.7	5.6	3.4	41
Korea	5.5	4.6	5.3	4.5	4.5	4.1	4.0	4.0	4.8	6.1	3.3	58
Morocco	6.2	4.4	3.9	3.3	2.5	2.7	2.1	2.3	2.8	3.0	3.0	53
Algeria	4.8	4.3	3.8	4.3	3.7	2.8	2.8	2.6	3.2	3.7	2.7	50
Eritrea	0.9	1.2	1.3	1.7	2.0	2.2	4.6	4.7	5.7	7.0	2.6	43
Other countries	116.7	103.0	100.5	97.8	91.7	92.6	95.2	96.4	105.2	111.4	63.2	
Total	**280.7**	**248.7**	**257.8**	**259.0**	**260.3**	**271.8**	**296.7**	**286.4**	**321.0**	**341.2**	**184.6**	**51**

Note: For details on definitions and sources, refer to the metadata at the end of the tables.

StatLink https://stat.link/x2hli8

Table B.1. Inflows of foreign population by nationality – Chile

Thousands

	2010	2011	2012	2013	2014	2015	2016	2017	2018	2019	2020	Of which: Women 2020 (%)
Venezuela	0.5	0.8	0.8	1.0	2.3	7.4	21.9	65.9	122.8	135.8	69.0	..
Haiti	0.5	0.7	1.1	1.2	2.2	6.4	23.0	42.1	108.7	32.2	28.6	..
Colombia	5.5	9.4	12.1	16.7	15.4	19.5	26.9	28.5	28.1	21.7	16.1	..
Bolivia	4.6	6.2	10.8	23.6	21.6	19.8	14.8	20.1	27.1	19.6	11.7	..
Peru	14.7	16.4	18.9	18.9	19.8	24.7	25.5	24.7	26.5	17.8	11.4	..
Ecuador	1.6	1.9	2.0	2.3	2.2	2.8	4.3	5.8	6.1	4.6	3.1	
Argentina	2.8	2.8	3.3	4.3	4.5	4.9	4.1	4.2	3.5	5.8	2.7	..
Brazil	1.0	1.1	1.2	1.2	1.2	1.7	2.0	2.2	2.0	2.3	1.5	..
Cuba	0.3	0.3	0.3	0.3	0.5	0.8	0.7	2.0	2.7	2.6	1.3	
China	0.8	1.0	1.0	1.1	1.4	1.7	1.7	2.1	1.9	1.6	0.9	..
Spain	0.7	1.0	2.1	4.1	3.4	2.5	1.9	1.4	0.9	0.9	0.8	..
Dominican Republic	0.8	1.2	2.9	0.7	0.4	0.6	0.8	0.8	2.2	2.4	0.7	
United States	2.2	2.1	2.3	2.3	2.1	1.7	1.4	1.2	0.9	0.9	0.6	..
Mexico	0.5	0.6	0.8	0.7	0.7	0.8	0.8	0.7	0.6	0.5	0.5	..
Paraguay	0.4	0.6	0.6	0.7	0.7	0.8	0.8	0.8	0.8	0.7	0.4	..
Other countries	4.5	4.6	4.9	5.2	5.3	5.9	5.0	5.0	5.0	5.0	5.0	
Total	**41.4**	**50.7**	**65.2**	**84.4**	**83.5**	**101.9**	**135.5**	**207.2**	**339.4**	**254.1**	**153.8**	..

Note: For details on definitions and sources, refer to the metadata at the end of the tables.

StatLink ᵐˢᴸ https://stat.link/x2hli8

Table B.1. Inflows of foreign population by nationality – Colombia

Thousands

	2010	2011	2012	2013	2014	2015	2016	2017	2018	2019	2020	Of which: Women 2020 (%)
Venezuela	..	..	..	..	..	..	..	88.9	201.7	206.6	63.7	..
Ecuador	..	..	..	..	..	..	..	4.8	4.5	4.7	2.3	..
United States	..	..	..	..	..	..	..	2.2	2.7	3.1	1.6	..
Peru	..	..	..	..	..	..	..	0.9	0.9	1.4	1.0	..
Chile	..	..	..	..	..	..	..	0.7	0.9	1.1	1.0	..
Argentina	..	..	..	..	..	..	..	0.6	0.8	1.0	0.7	..
Brazil	..	..	..	..	..	..	..	1.3	1.3	1.3	0.5	..
Mexico	..	..	..	..	..	..	..	0.6	0.5	0.7	0.5	..
Spain	..	..	..	..	..	..	..	0.4	0.4	0.7	0.5	..
Dominican Republic	..	..	..	..	..	..	..	0.6	0.4	0.8	0.4	..
Panama	..	..	..	..	..	..	..	0.4	0.3	0.4	0.3	..
Canada	..	..	..	..	..	..	..	0.2	0.1	0.2	0.2	..
Italy	..	..	..	..	..	..	..	0.1	0.1	0.2	0.2	..
Bolivia	..	..	..	..	..	..	..	0.2	0.3	0.4	0.2	..
France	..	..	..	..	..	..	..	0.2	0.2	0.3	0.1	..
Other countries	..	..	..	..	..	..	..	2.4	2.6	3.0	1.5	
Total	..	..	..	..	..	..	..	**104.5**	**217.9**	**225.8**	**74.8**	..

Note: For details on definitions and sources, refer to the metadata at the end of the tables.

StatLink ᵐˢᴸ https://stat.link/x2hli8

Table B.1. Inflows of foreign population by nationality – Czech Republic

Thousands

	2010	2011	2012	2013	2014	2015	2016	2017	2018	2019	2020	Of which: Women 2020 (%)
Ukraine	3.5	2.0	5.9	3.7	8.4	5.5	5.8	10.3	16.7	22.8	21.1	38
Slovak Republic	5.1	4.4	4.8	6.5	6.9	6.7	6.7	6.3	6.7	5.8	7.2	48
Russia	3.7	2.1	3.2	3.1	4.9	2.9	2.4	2.9	3.4	4.3	3.4	52
Romania	0.4	0.4	0.7	0.9	1.2	1.3	1.6	1.8	2.2	2.1	1.6	32
Viet Nam	1.4	0.7	1.6	1.2	1.7	1.3	1.8	2.2	2.3	1.9	1.4	59
Hungary	0.1	0.1	0.1	0.4	0.7	0.8	0.9	1.2	1.3	1.1	1.2	39
Bulgaria	0.6	0.5	0.7	1.0	1.1	1.0	1.3	1.6	2.0	1.7	1.1	39
Poland	0.7	0.6	0.6	0.6	0.6	0.6	0.7	0.8	1.0	0.8	1.0	44
Kazakhstan	0.7	0.5	0.6	0.6	1.0	0.7	0.6	0.6	0.8	1.0	1.0	53
Germany	2.0	1.3	1.3	1.7	1.6	1.1	1.0	0.6	0.6	0.6	1.0	28
United Kingdom	0.3	0.3	0.3	0.4	0.4	0.3	0.4	0.4	0.5	1.3	0.9	27
India	0.2	0.2	0.3	0.3	0.4	0.6	0.8	1.0	1.2	1.5	0.9	33
United States	1.7	1.3	1.1	0.8	0.9	0.8	1.1	1.1	1.1	1.0	0.7	42
Mongolia	0.3	0.2	0.3	0.1	0.2	0.6	0.7	1.2	1.5	1.3	0.7	47
Serbia	0.2	0.1	0.2	0.2	0.2	0.2	0.2	0.4	1.0	1.8	0.7	30
Other countries	7.1	5.9	6.9	6.5	8.1	7.3	8.8	10.9	13.6	14.2	10.0	
Total	**28.0**	**20.7**	**28.6**	**27.8**	**38.5**	**31.6**	**34.8**	**43.5**	**55.9**	**63.3**	**53.8**	**41**

Note: For details on definitions and sources, refer to the metadata at the end of the tables.

StatLink https://stat.link/x2hli8

Table B.1. Inflows of foreign population by nationality – Denmark

Thousands

	2010	2011	2012	2013	2014	2015	2016	2017	2018	2019	2020	Of which: Women 2020 (%)
Romania	2.0	2.7	3.2	3.6	4.2	4.3	4.2	4.1	4.1	3.9	3.6	36
Poland	2.9	3.2	3.3	3.6	4.0	4.1	3.8	3.7	3.4	3.0	2.8	37
Germany	1.9	1.9	1.8	1.8	2.0	2.0	2.1	2.3	2.4	2.4	2.5	53
Italy	0.7	0.7	0.9	1.1	1.4	1.5	1.5	1.5	1.5	1.7	1.7	43
Sweden	1.1	1.1	1.1	1.3	1.4	1.3	1.4	1.5	1.5	1.4	1.6	53
United Kingdom	1.0	1.1	1.0	1.1	1.2	1.4	1.6	1.7	1.6	1.5	1.5	40
Norway	1.4	1.5	1.4	1.4	1.7	1.6	1.5	1.5	1.4	1.4	1.4	61
Ukraine	1.2	1.2	1.2	1.3	1.5	1.1	1.3	1.6	1.9	2.0	1.3	45
India	0.9	1.1	0.9	1.1	1.4	1.6	1.9	1.9	2.1	2.1	1.3	43
Spain	0.7	0.8	0.9	1.0	1.1	1.0	1.1	1.1	1.1	1.1	1.2	47
Bulgaria	0.9	1.0	1.2	1.4	1.4	1.4	1.4	1.3	1.2	1.3	1.2	37
Lithuania	1.5	1.6	1.5	1.4	1.5	1.5	1.7	1.9	1.9	1.4	1.2	42
China	0.8	0.8	0.8	1.2	1.2	1.3	1.4	1.2	1.3	1.4	1.0	53
France	0.7	0.7	0.7	0.7	0.7	0.8	0.9	0.8	1.0	0.9	0.9	48
United States	0.9	0.9	0.9	0.9	1.0	1.1	1.1	1.2	1.2	0.9	0.9	52
Other countries	14.9	14.5	14.7	18.4	23.4	32.6	27.8	21.7	17.7	15.7	13.7	
Total	**33.4**	**34.6**	**35.5**	**41.3**	**49.0**	**58.7**	**54.6**	**49.0**	**45.3**	**42.3**	**37.8**	**48**

Note: For details on definitions and sources, refer to the metadata at the end of the tables.

StatLink https://stat.link/x2hli8

Table B.1. Inflows of foreign population by nationality – Estonia

Thousands

	2010	2011	2012	2013	2014	2015	2016	2017	2018	2019	2020	Of which: Women 2020 (%)
Ukraine	0.1	0.3	0.2	0.3	0.4	1.2	1.1	1.0	1.5	1.8	1.6	37
Russia	0.4	0.9	0.5	0.5	0.4	1.3	1.3	1.3	1.5	1.7	1.4	52
Finland	0.2	0.0	0.0	0.0	0.0	0.9	0.9	0.9	0.8	0.7	0.7	38
Latvia	0.1	0.0	0.0	0.0	0.1	0.3	0.4	0.9	0.8	0.7	0.5	40
Germany	0.0	0.0	0.0	0.0	0.0	0.4	0.5	0.5	0.5	0.5	0.4	49
Stateless	0.0	0.0	0.0	0.0	0.0	0.5	0.0	0.0	0.0	0.4	0.3	30
Other countries	0.5	0.5	0.4	0.7	0.4	2.7	3.5	4.5	4.7	5.2	5.4	
Total	**1.2**	**1.7**	**1.1**	**1.6**	**1.3**	**7.4**	**7.7**	**9.1**	**9.7**	**11.0**	**10.3**	37

Note: For details on definitions and sources, refer to the metadata at the end of the tables.

StatLink https://stat.link/x2hli8

Table B.1. Inflows of foreign population by nationality – Finland

Thousands

	2010	2011	2012	2013	2014	2015	2016	2017	2018	2019	2020	Of which: Women 2020 (%)
Russia	2.3	2.8	3.1	2.9	2.4	2.1	2.5	1.5	1.7	2.2	2.3	53
Estonia	3.9	4.7	6.0	5.9	4.7	3.4	2.6	2.2	2.0	1.6	1.6	39
Iraq	1.1	0.7	0.6	0.9	0.8	0.8	3.2	2.6	1.9	1.3	1.3	37
India	0.5	0.6	0.6	0.7	0.8	0.8	0.7	0.7	1.0	1.4	1.0	43
Ukraine	0.2	0.3	0.3	0.4	0.4	0.5	0.5	0.5	0.7	0.8	0.9	44
China	0.6	0.8	0.7	0.8	0.7	0.7	0.8	0.7	0.8	1.0	0.9	48
Sweden	0.7	0.7	0.6	0.6	0.6	0.5	0.6	0.6	0.6	0.7	0.7	41
Türkiye	0.3	0.3	0.4	0.4	0.3	0.3	0.3	0.3	0.4	0.7	0.7	44
Philippines	0.2	0.2	0.3	0.3	0.5	0.4	0.4	0.4	0.5	0.8	0.6	66
Afghanistan	0.3	0.4	0.6	0.6	0.5	0.4	1.9	0.9	0.7	0.7	0.6	33
Romania	0.2	0.3	0.3	0.3	0.4	0.4	0.4	0.4	0.5	0.6	0.5	41
Viet Nam	0.3	0.4	0.4	0.4	0.5	0.7	0.9	0.6	0.6	0.7	0.5	51
Serbia and Montenegro	0.0	0.0	0.0	0.0	0.0	0.0	0.0	0.3	0.0	0.5	0.5	32
Germany	0.3	0.3	0.3	0.3	0.3	0.3	0.3	0.3	0.4	0.4	0.5	43
Somalia	1.0	0.7	0.4	0.7	0.6	0.7	0.7	0.5	0.5	0.4	0.5	56
Other countries	6.4	7.3	8.7	8.7	10.0	9.6	11.4	11.1	10.9	10.4	10.3	
Total	**18.2**	**20.4**	**23.3**	**23.9**	**23.6**	**21.4**	**27.3**	**23.7**	**23.1**	**24.2**	**23.3**	44

Note: For details on definitions and sources, refer to the metadata at the end of the tables.

StatLink https://stat.link/x2hli8

Table B.1. Inflows of foreign population by nationality – France

Thousands

	2010	2011	2012	2013	2014	2015	2016	2017	2018	2019	2020	Of which: Women 2020 (%)
Algeria	21.4	21.2	23.7	23.6	22.0	22.4	21.8	21.8	22.6	21.8	17.9	50
Morocco	20.1	18.8	19.8	20.0	18.1	18.4	18.8	19.1	20.8	22.5	17.5	56
Italy	..	..	..	12.2	12.7	13.2	13.9	13.6	14.4	14.6	11.5	45
Tunisia	10.7	10.3	11.3	11.6	10.8	10.5	11.3	11.9	14.2	15.0	11.4	44
Spain	..	..	..	13.7	12.9	12.4	10.7	10.9	12.7	10.5	8.2	49
Romania	..	..	..	6.1	8.1	10.1	8.5	8.1	8.4	8.6	6.8	48
Côte d'Ivoire	3.3	3.2	3.4	3.6	4.0	3.7	3.9	4.2	5.3	6.8	6.6	42
Portugal	..	..	..	18.8	14.7	11.6	12.4	8.3	8.0	7.6	6.0	48
Guinea	1.6	1.7	1.9	2.0	2.1	2.3	2.5	2.7	3.4	4.7	5.8	23
Belgium	..	..	..	6.6	6.5	6.4	6.7	6.6	7.4	6.8	5.3	52
Afghanistan	0.4	0.4	0.6	0.9	0.8	0.6	1.7	5.0	5.3	5.5	5.2	10
Germany	..	..	..	7.7	6.4	7.1	6.2	5.7	6.1	5.7	4.5	53
Comoros	2.9	2.5	3.1	4.8	5.5	7.3	3.9	4.2	5.0	6.6	4.4	59
Mali	4.9	4.6	3.6	3.9	3.9	3.5	3.8	3.7	4.0	4.1	4.3	18
Senegal	4.0	4.0	4.2	4.4	3.7	3.7	3.9	4.2	4.4	4.9	3.9	42
Other countries	76.5	75.3	80.1	111.3	119.7	109.3	115.7	116.3	113.6	108.5	81.2	
Total	**145.8**	**142.1**	**151.6**	**251.3**	**251.8**	**242.7**	**245.7**	**246.2**	**255.4**	**254.2**	**200.5**	**52**

Note: For details on definitions and sources, refer to the metadata at the end of the tables.

StatLink ᴹˢᴸ https://stat.link/x2hli8

Table B.1. Inflows of foreign population by nationality – Germany

Thousands

	2010	2011	2012	2013	2014	2015	2016	2017	2018	2019	2020	Of which: Women 2020 (%)
Romania	75.5	97.5	120.5	139.5	198.7	221.4	222.3	230.6	252.0	245.0	198.4	34
Poland	115.6	164.7	177.8	190.4	192.2	190.8	160.7	149.7	143.6	128.6	101.9	33
Bulgaria	39.8	52.4	60.2	60.9	80.1	86.3	83.0	81.6	85.7	87.4	76.2	39
Italy	23.9	28.1	36.9	47.5	56.7	57.2	52.6	51.5	53.3	50.4	36.6	40
Croatia	10.2	11.5	12.9	25.8	46.1	61.0	62.1	58.6	57.7	48.4	33.1	36
Syria	3.0	4.6	8.5	19.0	69.1	309.7	179.4	76.4	49.0	44.1	31.1	39
Türkiye	27.6	28.6	26.2	23.2	22.1	23.7	28.6	33.7	40.6	43.8	30.4	31
Hungary	29.3	41.1	54.5	60.0	58.8	58.1	51.6	48.1	43.9	36.7	28.4	34
India	13.2	15.4	18.1	19.5	22.4	26.1	27.7	29.5	33.7	39.1	20.5	38
Serbia	16.7	16.5	22.1	27.3	38.4	39.7	22.9	24.5	25.6	26.2	20.5	39
Greece	12.3	23.0	32.7	32.1	28.8	28.3	27.1	26.1	25.6	23.5	18.3	38
Bosnia and Herzegovina	6.9	9.5	12.2	15.1	20.7	21.7	22.4	24.0	22.7	24.9	16.4	42
Spain	10.7	16.2	23.3	29.0	27.1	23.6	21.9	18.5	18.6	18.7	16.3	45
Albania	0.9	1.4	2.2	4.1	15.2	69.4	13.0	14.9	17.3	19.1	14.5	43
Afghanistan	7.4	9.3	8.6	9.1	12.9	84.9	75.8	12.5	12.5	13.0	14.1	32
Other countries	290.7	321.8	349.2	405.6	453.5	714.4	668.0	503.8	501.6	497.1	338.1	
Total	**683.5**	**841.7**	**965.9**	**1 108.1**	**1 342.5**	**2 016.2**	**1 719.1**	**1 384.0**	**1 383.6**	**1 345.9**	**994.8**	**39**

Note: For details on definitions and sources, refer to the metadata at the end of the tables.

StatLink ᴹˢᴸ https://stat.link/x2hli8

Table B.1. Inflows of foreign population by nationality – Hungary

Thousands

	2010	2011	2012	2013	2014	2015	2016	2017	2018	2019	2020	Of which: Women 2020 (%)
Ukraine	1.6	1.3	0.9	0.6	0.7	1.1	1.2	6.3	16.7	21.2	8.9	33
Slovak Republic	1.2	1.1	1.0	1.1	1.2	1.3	1.3	1.5	1.5	1.5	6.0	52
Germany	2.4	2.4	2.1	2.0	2.0	2.0	2.3	2.5	2.5	2.6	3.7	47
Romania	6.6	5.8	4.2	4.0	3.7	3.5	3.1	2.9	2.9	2.7	2.3	39
Viet Nam	0.2	0.2	0.3	0.3	0.3	0.3	0.3	0.7	1.3	2.0	1.8	44
Austria	0.6	0.5	0.5	0.5	0.5	0.4	0.4	0.5	0.4	0.4	1.7	42
Korea	0.4	0.4	0.3	0.3	0.4	0.3	0.3	0.6	0.8	1.2	1.4	20
China	1.1	0.9	1.1	2.2	4.7	3.5	1.5	2.3	2.0	2.4	1.2	45
India	0.3	0.4	0.3	0.2	0.4	0.5	0.5	0.8	1.4	1.2	0.9	33
Türkiye	0.5	0.6	0.6	0.5	0.6	0.6	0.7	1.0	1.0	1.2	0.9	30
Serbia	1.0	0.9	0.6	0.5	0.5	0.6	0.6	1.7	2.9	2.5	0.7	29
United States	1.1	1.0	1.0	1.0	1.1	1.2	1.1	1.4	1.3	1.4	0.7	49
Russia	0.4	0.4	0.5	0.6	1.0	0.9	0.7	0.8	0.9	0.9	0.6	60
France	0.3	0.3	0.3	0.3	0.4	0.4	0.4	0.4	0.4	0.4	0.6	45
United Kingdom	0.3	0.4	0.3	0.4	0.4	0.4	0.4	0.5	0.5	0.6	0.5	25
Other countries	5.7	5.9	6.3	6.8	8.3	8.8	9.0	12.6	13.0	13.2	11.9	
Total	**23.9**	**22.5**	**20.3**	**21.3**	**26.0**	**25.8**	**23.8**	**36.5**	**49.3**	**55.3**	**43.8**	41

Note: For details on definitions and sources, refer to the metadata at the end of the tables.

StatLink https://stat.link/x2hli8

Table B.1. Inflows of foreign population by nationality – Iceland

Thousands

	2010	2011	2012	2013	2014	2015	2016	2017	2018	2019	2020	Of which: Women 2020 (%)
Poland	0.8	0.8	0.9	1.3	1.4	1.6	2.9	4.5	3.9	2.8	2.0	43
Lithuania	0.3	0.2	0.1	0.2	0.2	0.3	0.7	1.3	1.2	0.9	0.6	33
Romania	0.0	0.0	0.1	0.1	0.1	0.2	0.3	0.5	0.6	0.6	0.5	26
Latvia	0.1	0.1	0.1	0.1	0.1	0.1	0.2	0.6	0.6	0.4	0.4	23
Germany	0.2	0.2	0.1	0.2	0.2	0.2	0.3	0.3	0.3	0.2	0.3	68
United States	0.1	0.1	0.2	0.2	0.2	0.2	0.3	0.3	0.3	0.3	0.2	57
United Kingdom	0.1	0.1	0.1	0.1	0.1	0.2	0.2	0.2	0.2	0.2	0.2	33
Spain	0.1	0.1	0.1	0.2	0.2	0.2	0.2	0.3	0.3	0.3	0.2	40
Czech Republic	0.0	0.0	0.0	0.1	0.1	0.1	0.2	0.3	0.4	0.4	0.2	44
Portugal	0.0	0.0	0.0	0.1	0.1	0.1	0.2	0.3	0.3	0.3	0.2	33
Philippines	0.1	0.1	0.1	0.1	0.0	0.1	0.1	0.2	0.3	0.2	0.2	74
France	0.1	0.1	0.0	0.1	0.1	0.1	0.2	0.2	0.2	0.2	0.2	46
Croatia	0.0	0.0	0.0	0.0	0.0	0.0	0.1	0.2	0.3	0.3	0.1	36
Venezuela	0.0	0.0	0.0	0.0	0.0	0.0	0.0	0.0	0.0	0.1	0.1	40
Denmark	0.1	0.1	0.1	0.1	0.1	0.2	0.2	0.2	0.2	0.1	0.1	45
Other countries	0.9	0.9	0.9	1.1	1.3	1.4	2.0	2.3	2.4	2.3	2.1	
Total	**3.0**	**2.8**	**2.8**	**3.9**	**4.3**	**5.0**	**7.9**	**11.8**	**11.5**	**9.5**	**7.6**	43

Note: For details on definitions and sources, refer to the metadata at the end of the tables.

StatLink https://stat.link/x2hli8

Table B.1. Inflows of foreign population by nationality – Israel

Thousands

	2010	2011	2012	2013	2014	2015	2016	2017	2018	2019	2020	Of which: Women 2020 (%)
Russia	3.4	3.7	3.5	4.0	4.6	6.6	7.0	7.1	10.5	15.8	6.6	0
Ukraine	1.8	2.1	2.0	1.9	5.7	6.9	5.8	7.0	6.4	6.2	2.9	0
France	1.8	1.6	1.7	2.9	6.5	6.6	4.2	3.2	2.4	2.2	2.4	51
United States	2.5	2.4	2.3	2.2	2.4	2.5	2.7	2.6	2.5	2.5	2.3	54
Belarus	0.3	..	..	..	..	0.3	0.6	0.9	0.9	..	0.6	0
Argentina	0.3	0.2	0.2	0.3	0.3	0.3	0.3	0.2	0.3	0.4	0.6	50
Brazil	0.2	0.2	0.2	0.2	0.3	0.4	0.6	0.6	0.6	0.6	0.5	55
United Kingdom	0.6	0.5	0.6	0.4	0.5	0.6	0.6	0.5	0.5	0.5	0.5	49
South Africa	0.2	0.2	0.1	0.2	0.1	0.2	0.2	0.3	0.3	0.3	0.3	49
Canada	0.3	0.2	0.2	0.2	0.3	0.3	0.3	0.3	0.2	0.2	0.2	52
Georgia	0.4	0.2	..	..	..	..	..	..	0.2	0.3	0.2	0
Mexico	0.1	0.1	0.1	0.1	0.1	0.1	0.1	0.1	0.1	0.1	0.2	51
Uzbekistan	0.3	0.3	..	..	..	..	..	..	0.2	0.2	0.1	0
Kazakhstan	0.2	..	..	..	..	..	..	..	..	..	0.1	0
Moldova	0.2	..	..	..	..	..	..	..	..	..	0.1	0
Other countries	3.9	5.4	5.6	4.6	3.3	3.1	3.5	3.5	3.1	3.8	1.9	
Total	**16.6**	**16.9**	**16.6**	**16.9**	**24.1**	**27.9**	**26.0**	**26.4**	**28.1**	**33.2**	**19.7**	**52**

Note: For details on definitions and sources, refer to the metadata at the end of the tables.

StatLink ᵍᵐˢ⌐ https://stat.link/x2hli8

Table B.1. Inflows of foreign population by nationality – Italy

Thousands

	2010	2011	2012	2013	2014	2015	2016	2017	2018	2019	2020	Of which: Women 2020 (%)
Romania	92.1	90.1	81.7	58.2	50.7	46.4	45.2	43.5	40.1	39.2	28.7	61
Albania	22.6	16.6	14.1	12.2	11.4	11.5	13.0	15.4	18.0	22.2	17.2	51
Morocco	30.0	23.9	19.6	19.6	17.6	15.0	14.7	15.7	16.9	20.3	12.5	52
Pakistan	10.8	7.5	8.8	7.8	9.6	11.4	14.7	15.0	13.2	9.9	9.7	20
Brazil	8.6	7.1	5.7	5.0	5.0	7.0	10.5	15.7	18.0	20.6	8.7	54
Bangladesh	9.7	10.3	10.1	10.5	12.7	12.4	10.7	14.6	13.4	11.8	7.8	40
India	15.2	13.3	11.2	10.8	11.1	11.2	10.0	7.7	11.1	12.0	7.3	45
Nigeria	4.8	4.5	6.7	6.3	5.3	8.9	14.7	23.3	17.9	5.7	7.2	45
Egypt	9.3	9.6	8.6	9.8	8.7	7.4	6.6	7.7	7.4	9.0	5.7	38
Ukraine	30.4	17.9	11.5	12.8	9.7	9.3	8.7	7.9	7.7	6.6	5.2	76
China	22.9	20.1	20.5	17.6	15.8	14.9	12.4	11.3	10.0	10.8	4.9	54
Senegal	8.9	6.6	5.5	6.5	6.3	7.5	8.5	10.9	8.8	5.8	4.6	27
United Kingdom	1.6	1.6	1.5	1.2	1.3	1.5	1.7	2.0	2.1	3.5	4.5	44
Tunisia	6.0	5.9	5.4	4.3	3.7	3.9	3.7	3.6	3.7	4.9	3.3	44
Peru	12.2	8.7	5.6	4.3	2.8	1.9	1.7	2.2	2.4	3.2	2.7	56
Other countries	139.5	110.7	104.7	92.2	76.8	79.7	86.1	104.9	94.9	79.2	62.0	
Total	**424.5**	**354.3**	**321.3**	**279.0**	**248.4**	**250.0**	**262.9**	**301.1**	**285.5**	**264.6**	**191.8**	**50**

Note: For details on definitions and sources, refer to the metadata at the end of the tables.

StatLink ᵍᵐˢ⌐ https://stat.link/x2hli8

Table B.1. Inflows of foreign population by nationality – Japan

Thousands

	2010	2011	2012	2013	2014	2015	2016	2017	2018	2019	2020	Of which: Women 2020 (%)
Viet Nam	11.9	13.9	19.5	31.7	43.0	65.9	77.5	98.6	123.3	148.2	71.1	..
China	107.9	100.4	107.0	93.0	98.6	100.6	103.3	109.8	114.9	131.6	45.2	..
Indonesia	8.3	8.4	9.3	9.6	11.8	14.3	16.8	19.6	23.2	28.8	13.7	..
Philippines	13.3	13.6	15.4	16.4	19.9	24.0	26.2	29.6	31.3	34.7	12.7	..
Korea	27.9	23.4	25.7	24.2	21.1	22.6	25.6	28.0	32.4	33.9	8.3	..
Thailand	10.9	13.6	15.4	15.4	14.3	14.5	15.4	16.4	17.1	17.9	6.4	..
Myanmar	1.1	1.1	1.5	2.1	3.3	5.2	6.1	7.6	8.1	11.6	6.2	..
United States	22.7	19.3	21.0	21.1	22.0	21.5	22.2	22.0	22.9	24.1	6.2	..
Chinese Taipei	6.6	5.6	6.6	6.6	7.7	10.8	12.2	13.7	14.9	16.3	4.2	..
Nepal	2.9	3.5	4.8	8.3	11.5	13.4	14.1	14.5	13.0	13.1	4.2	..
Brazil	4.7	4.5	5.8	4.8	6.1	9.1	12.8	14.2	15.8	16.6	4.1	..
Cambodia	1.1	1.1	1.1	1.3	2.3	3.7	4.2	4.8	5.0	6.3	3.7	..
India	4.9	4.7	5.6	5.6	6.9	6.9	7.0	7.9	9.6	11.0	3.7	..
Sri Lanka	1.2	1.4	1.5	1.5	2.2	3.1	4.7	5.6	4.0	3.3	2.9	..
Mongolia	1.2	1.3	1.5	1.5	2.0	2.3	2.5	3.2	3.7	4.1	2.3	..
Other countries	60.6	51.2	62.2	63.5	63.8	73.4	76.7	79.6	80.5	90.4	25.6	
Total	**287.1**	**266.9**	**303.9**	**306.7**	**336.5**	**391.2**	**427.6**	**475.0**	**519.7**	**592.0**	**220.6**	..

Note: For details on definitions and sources, refer to the metadata at the end of the tables.

StatLink 📊 https://stat.link/x2hli8

Table B.1. Inflows of foreign population by nationality – Korea

Thousands

	2010	2011	2012	2013	2014	2015	2016	2017	2018	2019	2020	Of which: Women 2020 (%)
China	155.3	149.2	127.3	178.6	192.9	177.0	165.5	156.8	169.3	138.7	96.3	50
Viet Nam	22.9	27.9	24.7	22.2	28.0	30.2	40.1	48.0	56.0	61.3	28.0	62
United States	28.3	28.1	28.9	26.6	24.5	22.7	21.8	19.8	21.2	20.8	21.3	53
Thailand	6.9	10.3	13.8	18.3	48.3	20.1	28.5	71.5	80.3	53.3	8.7	74
Uzbekistan	8.6	8.2	11.4	12.3	12.9	14.2	16.2	18.5	18.8	26.0	8.0	36
Mongolia	5.4	4.3	5.7	4.3	4.0	8.3	8.2	11.8	10.2	8.7	7.1	55
Russia	2.6	2.6	2.7	2.8	3.2	6.8	15.0	18.6	18.7	18.0	6.7	56
Japan	4.7	5.5	5.8	5.9	4.7	4.6	4.7	4.5	5.2	5.1	4.5	71
Canada	6.5	6.0	6.0	5.6	5.5	5.3	5.3	4.6	4.6	4.4	3.9	56
Kazakhstan	0.8	0.8	1.1	1.1	1.4	3.5	7.7	13.4	15.7	12.5	3.5	46
Cambodia	3.7	6.4	9.5	10.5	9.5	9.6	10.2	9.5	8.7	9.9	3.5	38
Indonesia	5.3	8.1	8.3	11.8	10.5	8.5	9.0	6.9	10.7	9.8	3.4	25
Nepal	2.7	4.3	6.9	6.0	6.8	6.5	8.7	8.6	9.8	8.8	3.0	19
Philippines	9.1	9.6	9.9	12.0	10.7	9.9	9.5	9.0	10.1	9.1	2.9	57
India	2.3	2.4	2.6	2.9	3.4	3.1	3.2	3.8	3.5	3.4	2.8	29
Other countries	28.0	33.7	35.7	39.4	40.7	42.5	48.7	47.3	52.2	48.4	29.4	
Total	**293.1**	**307.2**	**300.2**	**360.5**	**407.1**	**372.9**	**402.2**	**452.7**	**495.1**	**438.2**	**233.1**	51

Note: For details on definitions and sources, refer to the metadata at the end of the tables.

StatLink 📊 https://stat.link/x2hli8

Table B.1. Inflows of foreign population by nationality – Latvia

Thousands

	2010	2011	2012	2013	2014	2015	2016	2017	2018	2019	2020	Of which: Women 2020 (%)
Ukraine	0.1	..	..	..	0.5	..	..	0.9	1.4	1.6	1.1	17
Russia	0.9	..	..	..	1.3	..	..	0.9	0.9	0.9	0.6	47
Uzbekistan	0.0	..	..	..	0.1	..	..	0.3	0.5	0.6	0.4	11
India	0.0	..	..	..	0.1	..	..	0.6	0.9	0.8	0.4	20
Belarus	0.0	..	..	..	0.3	..	..	0.3	0.4	0.4	0.2	24
Lithuania	0.1	..	..	..	0.2	..	..	0.2	0.1	0.1	0.1	27
Kazakhstan	0.0	..	..	..	0.0	..	..	0.1	0.1	0.1	0.1	26
Sri Lanka	0.0	..	..	..	0.0	..	..	0.1	0.1	0.1	0.1	22
Germany	0.2	..	..	..	0.2	..	..	0.1	0.1	0.1	0.1	40
Türkiye	0.0	..	..	..	0.0	..	..	0.0	0.1	0.1	0.1	26
Azerbaijan	0.0	..	..	..	0.0	..	..	0.1	0.1	0.1	0.1	15
Viet Nam	0.0	..	..	..	0.0	..	..	0.0	0.1	0.1	0.1	48
China	0.0	..	..	..	0.1	..	..	0.1	0.1	0.1	0.0	40
Estonia	0.0	..	..	..	0.0	..	..	0.0	0.0	0.1	0.0	46
France	0.1	..	..	..	0.0	..	..	0.0	0.1	0.1	0.0	18
Other countries	1.3	..	..	..	1.6	..	..	1.4	1.6	1.4	1.1	
Total	**2.8**	**2.9**	**3.7**	**3.5**	**4.5**	**4.5**	**3.4**	**5.1**	**6.5**	**6.6**	**4.6**	**25**

Note: For details on definitions and sources, refer to the metadata at the end of the tables.

StatLink ⏤ https://stat.link/x2hli8

Table B.1. Inflows of foreign population by nationality – Lithuania

Thousands

	2010	2011	2012	2013	2014	2015	2016	2017	2018	2019	2020	Of which: Women 2020 (%)
Ukraine	0.1	0.2	0.4	0.4	1.1	1.1	1.6	4.3	5.7	8.9	9.3	7
Belarus	0.3	0.3	0.4	0.5	0.5	0.4	1.2	2.7	3.3	6.4	7.3	5
Russia	0.2	0.4	0.5	0.8	1.5	0.7	0.8	0.7	0.8	1.0	1.0	25
Uzbekistan	0.0	..	..	..	0.0	..	0.0	0.0	0.0	0.1	0.5	1
India	0.0	0.0	..	0.0	0.1	0.1	0.3	0.3	0.4	0.3	0.3	17
Moldova	0.0	0.0	..	0.0	0.0	0.0	0.1	0.1	0.1	0.3	0.3	6
Kyrgyzstan	..	..	..	..	..	..	..	..	..	0.1	0.3	6
Kazakhstan	0.0	0.0	..	0.1	0.0	0.0	0.1	0.0	0.1	0.1	0.3	16
Georgia	0.0	0.0	..	0.1	0.1	0.1	0.1	0.1	0.1	0.2	0.2	13
Azerbaijan	0.0	0.0	..	0.0	0.1	0.0	0.1	0.1	0.1	0.1	0.2	11
United Kingdom	0.0	0.0	0.0	0.0	0.0	0.0	0.0	0.1	0.1	0.1	0.2	25
Tajikistan	..	..	..	..	..	..	0.0	0.0	0.1	0.1	0.2	3
Germany	0.0	0.1	0.1	0.1	0.1	0.1	0.1	0.1	0.1	0.1	0.1	29
Latvia	0.0	0.1	0.1	0.1	0.1	0.1	0.1	0.1	0.1	0.1	0.1	47
United States	0.0	0.0	0.0	0.0	0.0	0.0	0.1	0.1	0.1	0.1	0.1	39
Other countries	0.3	0.6	1.0	0.9	1.0	0.9	1.4	1.4	1.4	1.7	1.9	
Total	**1.1**	**1.7**	**2.5**	**3.0**	**4.8**	**3.7**	**6.0**	**10.2**	**12.3**	**19.7**	**22.3**	**10**

Note: For details on definitions and sources, refer to the metadata at the end of the tables.

StatLink ⏤ https://stat.link/x2hli8

Table B.1. Inflows of foreign population by nationality – Luxembourg

Thousands

	2010	2011	2012	2013	2014	2015	2016	2017	2018	2019	2020	Of which: Women 2020 (%)
France	2.9	3.2	3.5	3.5	3.9	4.1	4.0	4.2	4.0	4.1	3.6	43
Portugal	3.8	5.0	5.2	4.6	3.8	3.5	3.4	3.3	3.5	3.8	3.3	42
Italy	0.8	1.0	1.1	1.3	1.6	1.6	1.8	1.8	1.9	2.0	1.7	42
Belgium	1.2	1.2	1.3	1.5	1.6	1.5	1.3	1.4	1.2	1.2	1.0	42
Germany	1.0	1.1	1.0	1.0	1.0	1.0	0.9	1.0	1.0	1.0	0.9	47
Spain	0.3	0.5	0.5	0.6	0.6	0.7	0.8	0.8	0.7	0.8	0.8	43
Romania	0.3	0.5	0.4	0.4	0.8	0.7	0.6	0.7	0.8	0.8	0.7	49
United Kingdom	0.4	0.4	0.4	0.5	0.5	0.5	0.5	0.6	0.6	0.6	0.6	43
India	0.1	0.2	0.1	0.1	0.2	0.3	0.4	0.6	0.7	0.8	0.5	46
United States	0.3	0.3	0.4	0.5	0.7	0.5	0.4	0.5	0.5	0.6	0.4	50
Poland	0.4	0.4	0.4	0.4	0.5	0.5	0.4	0.4	0.5	0.4	0.3	52
Brazil	0.2	0.2	0.2	0.3	0.2	0.2	0.2	0.3	0.4	0.4	0.3	62
Greece	0.1	0.2	0.3	0.3	0.3	0.4	0.4	0.5	0.4	0.5	0.3	48
China	0.1	0.2	0.2	0.4	0.3	0.4	0.4	0.5	0.5	0.5	0.3	59
Syria	0.0	0.0	0.0	0.0	0.1	0.7	0.4	0.5	0.2	0.3	0.3	38
Other countries	3.8	4.9	4.3	4.5	4.9	5.8	5.6	6.0	6.5	7.3	7.3	
Total	**15.8**	**19.1**	**19.4**	**19.8**	**21.0**	**22.6**	**21.6**	**23.2**	**23.3**	**25.1**	**22.5**	46

Note: For details on definitions and sources, refer to the metadata at the end of the tables.

StatLink ᔍᔎᔏ https://stat.link/x2hli8

Table B.1. Inflows of foreign population by nationality – Mexico

Thousands

	2010	2011	2012	2013	2014	2015	2016	2017	2018	2019	2020	Of which: Women 2019 (%)
Venezuela	1.7	1.3	1.2	2.8	2.6	2.2	2.5	3.4	6.3	7.4	11.0	55
Honduras	1.5	1.0	0.4	2.4	2.3	1.8	2.6	2.5	3.4	3.6	7.9	44
United States	4.0	4.3	4.0	14.4	9.4	7.1	6.8	5.4	5.2	5.0	5.3	50
Cuba	1.8	1.7	1.8	3.2	2.7	2.6	2.4	2.1	2.3	2.7	5.1	47
Colombia	2.3	1.8	1.4	3.2	2.5	2.1	2.2	2.2	2.8	2.7	3.9	53
El Salvador	0.7	0.7	0.4	1.6	1.2	1.1	1.8	2.3	2.8	2.5	3.6	46
Guatemala	1.8	1.3	0.5	3.1	2.6	1.6	1.7	1.8	2.3	1.9	2.5	40
China	1.7	1.1	0.8	5.2	2.6	2.2	2.1	1.5	1.8	1.9	1.7	50
Spain	1.0	0.8	1.0	2.6	1.8	1.6	1.7	1.5	1.5	1.3	1.4	46
Canada	0.7	0.8	0.8	3.5	2.0	1.8	1.7	1.3	1.4	1.3	1.4	38
Haiti	0.1	0.1	0.1	0.1	0.1	0.1	0.1	0.1	0.2	0.3	1.4	45
Argentina	1.4	1.0	0.9	3.2	2.1	1.4	1.4	1.0	1.1	1.1	1.3	49
Brazil	0.5	0.4	0.3	1.1	0.7	0.6	0.6	0.5	0.5	0.6	0.9	42
Korea	0.5	0.4	0.4	1.3	0.8	0.5	0.6	0.5	0.5	0.6	0.8	44
Nicaragua	0.4	0.2	0.1	0.6	0.5	0.3	0.3	0.2	0.3	0.5	0.7	32
Other countries	6.1	5.1	4.1	14.7	9.6	7.4	7.4	6.5	6.3	7.1	9.5	
Total	**26.2**	**22.0**	**18.2**	**63.0**	**43.5**	**34.4**	**35.9**	**32.8**	**38.7**	**40.5**	**58.4**	47

Note: For details on definitions and sources, refer to the metadata at the end of the tables.

StatLink ᔍᔎᔏ https://stat.link/x2hli8

Table B.1. Inflows of foreign population by nationality – Netherlands

Thousands

	2010	2011	2012	2013	2014	2015	2016	2017	2018	2019	2020	Of which: Women 2020 (%)
Poland	14.5	18.6	18.3	20.4	23.8	23.0	23.1	23.8	25.5	27.3	24.4	43
Romania	2.6	2.7	2.5	2.5	4.6	4.3	5.2	7.5	9.4	11.8	10.7	40
Germany	9.8	9.6	8.7	8.1	8.2	8.6	9.4	10.5	10.9	11.7	10.4	58
Bulgaria	4.3	5.4	5.0	4.5	5.2	4.8	5.0	6.0	6.9	9.2	9.2	42
Italy	2.8	3.1	3.6	4.2	5.1	5.7	6.5	7.6	8.5	9.4	7.7	44
United Kingdom	4.4	4.4	4.7	5.1	5.3	5.8	6.5	7.2	7.7	8.7	7.5	40
Spain	3.1	3.7	4.6	5.3	5.0	5.0	5.2	5.9	6.5	7.6	6.3	49
India	3.2	3.8	4.0	4.5	5.1	6.1	7.2	8.6	10.6	12.3	5.9	45
Syria	0.1	0.1	0.1	0.6	6.9	17.3	25.1	15.3	5.3	5.7	5.7	34
Türkiye	3.7	3.4	3.2	3.0	2.8	2.8	3.2	4.4	5.5	6.6	5.2	46
France	2.9	2.9	3.0	3.2	3.6	4.0	4.5	5.0	5.5	5.9	5.0	51
China	4.5	5.5	5.2	4.7	4.8	5.4	5.7	6.5	6.8	7.5	4.4	51
United States	3.3	3.7	3.7	3.6	3.8	4.7	4.7	5.6	5.8	6.0	4.0	55
Greece	1.8	2.7	3.3	2.9	2.6	2.8	3.1	3.6	4.0	4.7	4.0	41
Belgium	2.1	2.3	2.6	2.5	2.7	2.7	3.2	3.5	3.5	3.7	3.5	51
Other countries	47.1	46.6	43.0	47.1	49.9	56.4	64.3	62.8	68.5	77.2	56.7	
Total	**110.2**	**118.5**	**115.7**	**122.3**	**139.3**	**159.5**	**182.2**	**183.9**	**191.0**	**215.2**	**170.6**	**47**

Note: For details on definitions and sources, refer to the metadata at the end of the tables.

StatLink ⧈ https://stat.link/x2hli8

Table B.1. Inflows of foreign population by nationality – New Zealand

Thousands

	2010	2011	2012	2013	2014	2015	2016	2017	2018	2019	2020	Of which: Women 2020 (%)
India	9.6	8.4	8.6	9.1	16.2	19.5	14.7	14.0	14.3	15.1	9.1	50
United Kingdom	8.8	9.2	8.8	8.8	8.7	8.6	8.8	8.8	8.1	9.6	4.6	48
South Africa	2.2	2.1	1.9	2.2	2.5	3.4	5.8	5.8	7.0	12.2	3.9	52
China	7.6	9.6	10.0	10.6	13.0	15.0	16.4	15.5	14.9	15.2	3.8	56
Australia	5.0	4.8	4.7	5.6	6.1	6.6	6.9	6.8	6.6	7.5	3.1	50
Philippines	3.3	3.7	4.2	4.5	6.5	8.4	8.2	9.1	9.1	10.6	3.0	46
United States	2.7	3.0	2.9	3.0	2.8	3.1	3.0	3.4	3.4	4.4	2.8	53
Samoa	1.6	2.0	2.0	1.8	2.1	2.3	2.4	2.7	2.8	3.4	1.8	26
France	1.1	1.3	1.0	1.3	1.5	1.7	1.7	1.7	1.7	2.7	1.4	50
Korea	3.3	2.7	2.2	2.1	2.5	2.6	3.1	2.9	2.7	3.0	1.4	59
Tonga	1.2	1.1	0.9	1.0	1.0	1.3	1.3	1.3	1.4	2.2	1.2	28
Fiji	2.3	2.1	2.5	2.4	2.4	2.4	2.9	2.5	2.4	2.9	1.2	44
Germany	1.2	1.2	1.3	1.3	1.3	1.5	1.5	1.6	1.5	1.9	1.1	54
Vanuatu	0.0	0.1	0.0	0.1	0.1	0.0	0.1	0.1	0.1	0.6	1.0	9
Malaysia	1.7	1.7	1.5	1.4	1.6	1.6	1.8	1.8	1.8	1.9	0.9	55
Other countries	18.2	18.9	19.3	20.1	22.4	23.4	25.3	25.5	26.7	31.6	13.4	
Total	**69.9**	**71.8**	**71.7**	**75.4**	**90.7**	**101.5**	**104.0**	**103.4**	**104.2**	**124.7**	**53.7**	**49**

Note: For details on definitions and sources, refer to the metadata at the end of the tables.

StatLink ⧈ https://stat.link/x2hli8

Table B.1. Inflows of foreign population by nationality – Norway

Thousands

	2010	2011	2012	2013	2014	2015	2016	2017	2018	2019	2020	Of which: Women 2020 (%)
Poland	11.3	12.9	11.5	10.5	9.9	8.2	6.0	5.2	5.0	5.0	3.7	36
Sweden	7.6	8.2	5.7	5.3	4.6	3.6	2.5	2.2	2.1	2.0	1.8	47
Lithuania	6.6	7.7	6.6	5.6	4.4	3.3	2.5	2.7	2.8	2.5	1.8	42
Syria	0.1	0.1	0.4	0.8	2.1	4.0	11.2	7.0	3.8	1.5	1.5	44
Germany	2.7	2.3	1.8	1.6	1.5	1.3	1.3	1.2	1.3	1.3	1.1	53
India	0.8	1.2	1.5	1.5	1.8	1.7	1.4	1.6	2.0	2.4	1.0	42
Denmark	1.4	1.6	1.8	2.0	1.7	1.4	1.3	1.2	1.2	1.1	1.0	46
United Kingdom	1.5	1.5	1.4	1.3	1.3	1.0	0.9	0.9	1.1	1.2	1.0	34
Romania	1.3	1.4	2.0	2.5	2.1	1.9	1.2	1.2	1.1	1.3	0.9	35
Philippines	2.1	2.6	2.5	2.8	2.2	2.2	2.1	1.9	1.8	1.8	0.9	82
United States	0.9	1.0	1.1	1.0	0.9	0.9	0.9	0.9	0.9	1.1	0.8	51
Spain	0.8	1.0	1.4	1.5	1.4	1.3	1.1	1.0	0.9	1.0	0.7	43
Eritrea	2.0	2.0	2.4	2.7	2.8	3.3	2.7	2.1	1.1	0.7	0.7	59
Latvia	2.3	2.1	1.7	1.3	1.1	0.8	0.7	0.7	0.8	0.8	0.7	35
Türkiye	0.3	0.3	0.3	0.3	0.3	0.2	0.3	0.4	0.4	1.0	0.6	41
Other countries	23.5	25.0	28.0	26.0	23.2	23.9	22.4	19.8	18.0	20.1	12.7	
Total	65.1	70.8	70.0	66.9	61.4	59.1	58.5	49.8	44.4	44.6	30.8	47

Note: For details on definitions and sources, refer to the metadata at the end of the tables.

StatLink ᐧᐧᐧ https://stat.link/x2hli8

Table B.1. Inflows of foreign population by nationality – Poland

Thousands

	2010	2011	2012	2013	2014	2015	2016	2017	2018	2019	2020	Of which: Women 2020 (%)
Ukraine	10.3	10.1	11.8	11.9	7.8	45.2	63.8	79.0	88.7	108.4	111.0	46
Belarus	2.9	2.5	2.6	2.3	1.4	3.2	3.5	6.2	7.9	9.1	8.1	44
India	1.2	1.1	1.2	1.2	0.8	1.9	2.8	4.1	4.5	4.9	4.9	26
Georgia	0.2	0.2	0.3	0.2	0.2	0.5	0.6	0.7	1.9	4.1	4.3	17
Russia	1.6	1.6	1.9	1.9	1.1	2.5	2.6	2.7	3.0	3.4	3.4	54
Viet Nam	2.4	2.1	4.0	2.8	2.0	3.3	3.2	4.0	3.0	2.6	2.7	44
China	2.3	2.8	2.9	3.0	1.6	3.8	3.9	4.2	2.9	2.5	2.3	45
Moldova	0.4	0.4	0.4	0.4	0.3	0.5	0.7	0.9	1.1	1.8	2.0	35
Türkiye	1.1	1.2	1.3	1.4	0.9	1.7	1.7	2.0	1.9	1.9	1.7	25
Korea	1.1	1.0	1.0	1.1	0.6	1.0	0.8	0.7	0.7	0.8	1.2	35
Uzbekistan	0.2	0.2	0.2	0.2	0.2	0.5	0.9	0.8	0.5	0.6	1.1	10
United Kingdom	0.5	0.5	0.5	0.5	0.5	0.6	0.6	0.7	0.5	1.0	1.1	19
Germany	1.8	1.9	2.3	2.0	2.0	2.3	2.3	2.2	1.8	1.8	1.0	19
Azerbaijan	0.1	0.1	0.1	0.2	0.1	0.3	0.5	0.4	0.5	0.7	0.9	22
Bangladesh	0.1	0.1	0.1	0.1	0.1	0.2	0.3	0.6	0.6	0.9	0.8	11
Other countries	15.1	15.5	16.5	17.3	12.4	18.6	18.6	18.9	17.9	18.8	17.1	
Total	41.1	41.3	47.1	46.6	32.0	86.1	107.0	128.0	137.6	163.2	163.5	42

Note: For details on definitions and sources, refer to the metadata at the end of the tables.

StatLink ᐧᐧᐧ https://stat.link/x2hli8

Table B.1. Inflows of foreign population by nationality – Portugal

Thousands

	2010	2011	2012	2013	2014	2015	2016	2017	2018	2019	2020	Of which: Women 2020 (%)
Brazil	16.2	12.9	11.7	6.7	5.6	5.7	7.1	11.6	28.2	48.8	42.2	52
United Kingdom	1.8	1.7	1.2	1.4	1.5	1.9	3.1	3.8	5.1	8.4	13.2	41
India	0.9	1.1	0.9	1.0	0.9	1.1	1.0	1.8	4.1	6.3	7.2	17
Angola	1.3	1.4	1.3	1.5	1.5	1.3	1.5	1.8	2.9	4.5	4.8	57
Italy	1.0	0.8	0.7	0.8	1.1	1.6	3.1	5.3	7.0	7.9	4.5	44
Cape Verde	4.2	4.6	3.4	2.7	2.2	2.0	2.0	2.1	2.6	4.4	4.2	54
France	0.7	0.7	0.5	0.7	1.9	2.5	3.5	4.7	5.3	4.4	4.1	48
Nepal	0.2	0.4	0.5	0.8	0.9	1.4	1.3	1.7	4.2	5.0	3.9	37
Guinea-Bissau	1.6	1.7	1.6	1.2	1.2	1.1	1.0	1.1	1.9	3.5	3.4	45
Spain	1.7	1.5	1.4	1.5	1.5	1.7	2.2	2.7	2.9	3.2	2.8	48
Germany	1.0	0.8	0.6	0.8	1.0	1.0	1.6	1.9	2.5	2.8	2.6	47
Bangladesh	0.2	0.3	0.3	0.5	0.4	0.7	0.4	0.7	2.0	2.4	2.2	27
Sao Tome and Principe	1.3	1.3	1.0	0.8	0.6	0.5	0.5	0.8	1.2	1.5	1.6	53
Venezuela	0.1	0.1	0.1	0.1	0.1	0.2	0.5	0.9	1.7	1.9	1.4	58
China	1.7	1.5	1.4	1.9	3.7	2.6	2.8	2.6	2.3	2.2	1.4	54
Other countries	17.0	14.5	11.7	10.9	11.1	12.6	15.3	17.8	19.4	22.1	18.8	
Total	**50.7**	**45.4**	**38.5**	**33.2**	**35.3**	**37.9**	**46.9**	**61.4**	**93.2**	**129.2**	**118.1**	**47**

Note: For details on definitions and sources, refer to the metadata at the end of the tables.

StatLink ᯤ鬱 https://stat.link/x2hli8

Table B.1. Inflows of foreign population by nationality – Slovak Republic

Thousands

	2010	2011	2012	2013	2014	2015	2016	2017	2018	2019	2020	Of which: Women 2020 (%)
Czech Republic	0.8	0.6	0.5	0.4	0.4	0.6	0.5	0.5	0.5	0.4	0.7	49
Hungary	0.7	0.7	0.7	0.4	0.5	0.6	0.6	0.4	0.5	0.4	0.5	37
Ukraine	0.1	0.1	0.1	0.1	0.1	0.2	0.2	0.2	0.2	0.3	0.3	50
Poland	0.3	0.2	0.1	0.2	0.1	0.2	0.2	0.2	0.2	0.2	0.2	47
Germany	0.2	0.2	0.1	0.1	0.1	0.1	0.1	0.1	0.1	0.1	0.1	29
Romania	0.4	0.5	0.3	0.3	0.3	0.5	0.5	0.2	0.4	0.2	0.1	37
Italy	0.2	0.2	0.2	0.2	0.1	0.2	0.2	0.2	0.1	0.1	0.1	31
Austria	0.2	0.1	0.1	0.0	0.0	0.1	0.1	0.1	0.0	0.0	0.1	24
Russia	0.1	0.0	0.0	0.0	0.0	0.1	0.0	0.1	0.1	0.1	0.1	56
United Kingdom	0.1	0.2	0.1	0.0	0.1	0.1	0.1	0.1	0.1	0.2	0.1	26
Spain	0.1	0.1	0.1	0.0	0.0	0.1	0.1	0.1	0.1	0.1	0.1	49
France	0.1	0.1	0.1	0.1	0.1	0.1	0.1	0.1	0.0	0.0	0.1	46
Croatia	0.0	0.0	0.0	0.1	0.1	0.2	0.1	0.1	0.1	0.0	0.0	32
Viet Nam	0.0	0.1	0.1	0.1	0.0	0.0	0.0	0.0	0.0	0.0	0.0	41
Bulgaria	0.1	0.2	0.2	0.1	0.1	0.1	0.1	0.1	0.1	0.0	0.0	58
Other countries	0.7	0.6	0.5	0.5	0.4	0.6	0.6	0.5	0.4	0.4	0.4	
Total	**4.2**	**3.8**	**2.9**	**2.5**	**2.4**	**3.8**	**3.6**	**2.9**	**2.9**	**2.5**	**2.8**	**41**

Note: For details on definitions and sources, refer to the metadata at the end of the tables.

StatLink ᯤ鬱 https://stat.link/x2hli8

Table B.1. Inflows of foreign population by nationality – Slovenia

Thousands

	2010	2011	2012	2013	2014	2015	2016	2017	2018	2019	2020	Of which: Women 2020 (%)
Bosnia and Herzegovina	4.4	3.4	4.0	3.8	3.4	4.7	4.8	6.2	11.7	13.8	9.7	34
Serbia	1.1	1.2	1.3	1.4	1.3	1.3	1.6	2.0	3.2	3.8	2.9	32
Croatia	0.9	0.9	1.1	1.2	1.1	0.8	1.1	1.1	1.2	1.3	1.6	40
North Macedonia	1.1	1.0	1.1	0.8	0.7	0.7	0.9	1.0	1.5	1.6	1.4	41
Italy	0.3	0.3	0.4	0.4	0.5	0.5	0.6	0.5	0.5	0.4	0.9	39
Bulgaria	0.6	0.7	0.7	0.7	0.8	0.7	0.7	0.8	0.7	0.6	0.6	28
Russia	0.1	0.1	0.2	0.3	0.5	0.6	0.5	0.5	0.6	0.5	0.4	55
Spain	0.0	0.0	0.0	0.0	0.0	0.0	0.0	0.0	0.0	0.0	0.3	46
Germany	0.2	0.2	0.2	0.1	0.1	0.1	0.1	0.1	0.1	0.1	0.3	50
Ukraine	0.3	0.2	0.2	0.2	0.2	0.3	0.3	0.3	0.3	0.3	0.3	53
Montenegro	0.1	0.1	0.1	0.1	0.1	0.1	0.1	0.1	0.1	0.1	0.2	34
Türkiye	0.0	0.0	0.0	0.0	0.0	0.0	0.0	0.0	0.1	0.1	0.2	10
France	0.1	0.1	0.1	0.1	0.0	0.1	0.1	0.1	0.1	0.1	0.2	47
United Kingdom	0.1	0.1	0.1	0.1	0.1	0.1	0.1	0.1	0.1	0.1	0.2	34
Hungary	0.1	0.0	0.1	0.1	0.1	0.1	0.2	0.2	0.2	0.1	0.2	47
Other countries	3.3	2.5	2.7	2.3	2.4	2.6	2.7	2.5	3.7	4.7	5.4	
Total	12.7	10.8	12.3	11.6	11.3	12.7	13.8	15.5	24.1	27.6	24.8	36

Note: For details on definitions and sources, refer to the metadata at the end of the tables.

StatLink 🔗 https://stat.link/x2hli8

Table B.1. Inflows of foreign population by nationality – Spain

Thousands

	2010	2011	2012	2013	2014	2015	2016	2017	2018	2019	2020	Of which: Women 2020 (%)
Colombia	13.7	13.2	10.0	8.7	8.5	9.4	22.6	34.1	53.3	76.5	51.4	55
Morocco	30.2	28.0	22.4	20.5	20.0	23.8	29.7	39.8	60.9	72.8	44.9	42
Venezuela	6.5	6.8	4.6	4.7	7.2	10.5	18.5	31.6	47.1	57.7	29.7	54
United Kingdom	16.2	15.7	16.4	14.1	14.2	15.0	18.5	21.2	24.0	29.3	29.5	46
Italy	11.2	11.6	12.0	12.2	14.9	18.6	21.7	28.8	31.3	33.3	21.3	46
Honduras	4.7	6.3	5.3	4.3	5.7	7.6	10.9	18.3	23.4	29.0	18.7	65
Peru	8.0	7.7	5.6	4.8	4.7	5.3	8.0	13.9	19.3	28.5	18.1	56
Romania	51.9	50.8	27.3	22.8	29.7	28.8	28.6	31.0	29.1	27.1	15.7	47
Argentina	5.4	4.9	3.6	3.8	4.2	5.0	6.4	8.8	11.1	17.9	10.7	52
France	7.8	7.8	7.4	7.3	8.1	9.0	9.3	11.4	11.7	12.1	10.2	48
Nicaragua	3.0	3.6	2.8	2.1	2.7	3.1	4.1	6.2	11.4	17.1	9.2	65
Brazil	8.7	7.9	6.4	5.1	5.6	7.1	9.7	12.5	15.5	16.5	8.7	57
Germany	8.3	8.3	8.0	7.2	6.8	6.7	7.3	9.1	9.4	9.4	7.9	50
Pakistan	15.3	11.5	8.3	6.5	5.3	4.8	6.4	6.6	8.7	11.6	7.4	29
Paraguay	9.4	8.2	4.8	3.8	4.2	4.7	7.2	8.4	9.3	11.9	6.5	61
Other countries	130.1	143.6	127.6	120.4	122.7	130.6	143.4	172.3	194.3	213.8	125.1	
Total	330.3	335.9	272.5	248.4	264.5	290.0	352.2	454.0	560.0	664.6	415.2	50

Note: For details on definitions and sources, refer to the metadata at the end of the tables.

StatLink 🔗 https://stat.link/x2hli8

Table B.1. Inflows of foreign population by nationality – Sweden

Thousands

	2010	2011	2012	2013	2014	2015	2016	2017	2018	2019	2020	Of which: Women 2020 (%)
India	2.2	1.7	2.0	2.4	3.0	3.5	4.2	5.7	7.3	7.4	4.0	43
Syria	1.0	1.5	4.7	11.7	21.7	28.0	49.0	20.9	13.9	6.0	3.2	52
Afghanistan	1.9	3.4	4.7	4.2	3.8	3.4	4.1	11.3	9.6	7.9	2.6	46
Poland	4.4	4.4	4.4	4.6	5.1	5.6	5.0	4.4	3.8	3.2	2.5	38
Pakistan	1.6	0.9	0.9	0.8	0.8	1.1	1.2	1.7	2.5	3.1	2.4	40
Germany	2.2	2.2	2.2	2.2	2.2	2.3	2.5	2.4	2.4	2.5	2.3	54
Denmark	3.4	3.2	2.6	2.5	2.0	2.1	2.1	1.9	1.9	1.9	1.9	45
United Kingdom	1.4	1.8	1.5	1.6	1.8	1.7	1.9	2.0	2.1	1.9	1.8	36
Finland	2.3	2.3	2.3	2.3	2.6	2.8	3.0	2.9	2.6	2.2	1.7	59
Eritrea	1.6	2.1	2.2	3.3	5.9	7.6	7.6	4.8	3.8	3.9	1.7	46
China	3.2	2.6	2.5	2.1	2.4	2.3	2.2	2.7	2.9	2.8	1.7	51
Serbia	0.9	1.0	1.3	1.0	1.7	1.7	1.6	2.0	2.1	2.0	1.7	50
Iraq	4.5	4.5	3.6	2.3	2.4	2.8	3.4	6.0	3.9	2.8	1.6	46
Türkiye	2.2	2.0	1.8	1.3	1.2	1.2	1.1	1.5	2.2	2.2	1.6	43
Iran	2.8	2.2	2.1	2.0	1.7	1.3	1.7	2.3	2.5	2.3	1.5	48
Other countries	43.3	40.0	43.7	51.1	47.8	46.5	52.4	52.4	50.9	46.6	33.5	
Total	**79.0**	**75.9**	**82.6**	**95.4**	**106.1**	**113.9**	**143.0**	**125.0**	**114.4**	**98.2**	**65.8**	**48**

Note: For details on definitions and sources, refer to the metadata at the end of the tables.

StatLink ᴍsʟ https://stat.link/x2hli8

Table B.1. Inflows of foreign population by nationality – Switzerland

Thousands

	2010	2011	2012	2013	2014	2015	2016	2017	2018	2019	2020	Of which: Women 2020 (%)
Germany	30.7	30.5	27.1	26.6	23.8	22.1	20.9	19.7	20.2	19.9	19.2	44
Italy	10.1	10.8	13.6	17.5	17.8	18.2	18.1	15.5	16.5	15.9	16.5	41
France	11.5	11.5	11.4	13.5	13.8	14.8	13.8	14.1	13.8	14.0	15.7	43
Portugal	12.8	15.4	18.6	19.9	14.9	12.6	10.1	9.2	8.7	8.3	7.6	42
Spain	3.3	4.6	6.5	8.8	7.6	7.0	5.8	5.2	5.6	5.2	5.4	46
Romania	1.4	1.7	2.3	2.7	2.4	2.0	2.9	2.9	2.4	4.5	4.8	47
Poland	2.0	3.4	3.3	2.9	4.8	4.8	4.1	4.1	4.7	4.7	4.6	41
United Kingdom	5.5	5.4	4.4	4.6	4.2	3.9	3.6	3.8	3.8	4.0	4.0	42
China	1.9	2.1	2.4	2.9	2.9	3.3	3.2	3.1	3.1	3.3	3.1	54
Hungary	1.2	2.1	2.5	2.5	4.2	3.9	3.6	3.3	3.2	3.1	2.8	45
Türkiye	2.0	1.8	1.6	1.7	1.7	1.5	1.5	1.6	1.7	2.0	2.7	45
Austria	2.6	2.9	3.1	2.9	3.0	3.2	2.9	2.8	2.8	2.9	2.7	44
India	2.4	2.4	2.6	2.5	2.6	2.9	2.9	3.1	3.1	3.0	2.5	44
United States	4.0	4.2	3.5	3.4	3.1	2.9	2.9	3.0	3.0	2.7	2.3	54
Bulgaria	0.6	0.9	1.0	1.1	0.9	1.0	1.8	1.7	1.3	2.3	2.1	36
Other countries	42.2	42.8	39.9	42.0	44.4	46.2	45.1	44.8	46.3	44.9	40.9	
Total	**134.2**	**142.5**	**143.8**	**155.4**	**152.1**	**150.4**	**143.1**	**137.8**	**140.1**	**140.6**	**137.0**	**46**

Note: For details on definitions and sources, refer to the metadata at the end of the tables.

StatLink ᴍsʟ https://stat.link/x2hli8

Table B.1. Inflows of foreign population by nationality – Türkiye

Thousands

	2010	2011	2012	2013	2014	2015	2016	2017	2018	2019	2020	Of which: Women 2019 (%)
Iraq	1.2	..	..	..	..	..	70.9	97.1	110.3	83.8	..	46
Turkmenistan	1.2	..	..	..	..	..	8.4	20.3	34.9	80.0	..	35
Afghanistan	2.2	..	..	..	..	..	27.9	37.7	45.0	47.2	..	40
Syria	0.9	..	..	..	..	..	25.7	28.2	39.0	43.2	..	45
Iran	1.5	..	..	..	..	..	15.5	17.8	31.9	42.4	..	44
Azerbaijan	2.5	..	..	..	..	..	15.3	20.9	23.2	26.6	..	49
Uzbekistan	0.6	..	..	..	..	..	9.0	17.9	15.2	25.1	..	67
Russia	1.8	..	..	..	..	..	6.4	7.3	13.8	17.3	..	61
Egypt	0.1	..	..	..	..	..	4.1	8.6	13.5	12.5	..	39
Libya	0.0	..	..	..	..	..	4.3	6.0	7.4	12.1	..	37
Jordan	0.1	..	..	..	..	..	1.7	2.9	8.0	11.3	..	38
Somalia	0.2	..	..	..	..	..	0.7	1.5	4.5	10.3	..	47
West Bank and Gaza Strip	0.2	..	..	..	..	..	2.0	4.8	8.6	10.0	..	37
Kyrgyzstan	1.0	..	..	..	..	..	6.0	9.0	9.1	10.0	..	73
Kazakhstan	1.4	..	..	..	..	..	3.6	4.3	7.4	10.0	..	57
Other countries	15.1	..	..	..	..	..	72.3	80.3	95.1	136.9	..	
Total	29.9	..	..	..	..	..	273.9	364.6	466.9	578.5	..	46

Note: For details on definitions and sources, refer to the metadata at the end of the tables.

StatLink https://stat.link/x2hli8

Table B.1. Inflows of foreign population by nationality – United States (permanent)

Thousands

	2010	2011	2012	2013	2014	2015	2016	2017	2018	2019	2020	Of which: Women 2020 (%)
Mexico	138.3	143.0	146.0	135.1	133.2	158.3	173.5	170.1	161.6	155.7	100.0	54
India	67.5	67.4	64.7	67.3	76.3	62.8	63.0	59.1	58.9	53.8	45.8	49
China	71.4	87.9	82.4	72.1	75.9	74.4	81.9	71.8	65.6	62.3	41.7	58
Dominican Republic	53.3	45.7	41.2	41.2	43.7	50.0	59.9	58.1	57.0	49.4	29.7	53
Viet Nam	30.0	33.5	27.6	26.5	29.4	30.4	40.1	37.9	33.4	39.2	29.5	57
Philippines	57.6	56.6	56.9	54.3	49.2	56.0	52.2	48.7	46.9	45.6	25.2	65
El Salvador	18.6	18.5	16.1	18.2	19.2	19.4	23.1	24.9	28.1	27.5	17.8	54
Brazil	12.0	11.5	11.2	10.8	10.2	11.2	13.5	14.7	15.1	19.4	16.3	57
Korea	22.1	22.6	20.7	23.0	20.2	17.0	21.7	19.0	17.5	18.3	16.1	56
Cuba	33.4	36.1	32.4	31.8	45.9	53.6	65.6	64.5	75.5	39.4	15.1	51
Canada	20.4	20.2	20.6	21.0	18.5	20.1	20.3	18.8	16.1	17.8	14.5	52
Jamaica	19.3	19.3	20.4	19.1	18.7	17.4	22.9	21.7	20.2	21.5	12.7	55
Nigeria	13.1	11.6	13.2	13.5	12.6	11.3	14.1	13.4	13.8	15.7	12.2	49
Dem. Rep. of the Congo	0.8	1.5	2.9	2.2	4.6	5.8	7.7	10.9	14.7	13.8	11.8	50
Afghanistan	2.1	1.7	1.7	2.2	10.6	8.5	12.5	19.8	13.7	10.5	11.7	48
Other countries	482.6	485.0	473.8	452.2	448.4	454.8	511.6	473.8	458.5	441.9	307.2	
Total	1 042.6	1 062.0	1 031.6	990.6	1 016.5	1 051.0	1 183.5	1 127.2	1 096.6	1 031.8	707.4	54

Note: For details on definitions and sources, refer to the metadata at the end of the tables.

StatLink https://stat.link/x2hli8

Table A.2. Outflows of foreign population from selected OECD countries

Thousands

	2010	2011	2012	2013	2014	2015	2016	2017	2018	2019	2020
Australia	29.3	31.2	29.9	31.7	32.6	33.9	33.2	..	..	..	..
Austria	68.4	72.8	74.4	74.5	76.5	80.1	89.0	89.6	91.7	90.0	79.4
Belgium	43.4	52.7	60.4	69.7	64.9	59.8	61.8	58.6	56.8	46.5	52.0
Czech Republic	12.5	2.5	16.7	27.2	16.1	15.0	13.4	14.4	16.2	17.5	26.8
Denmark	27.1	26.6	29.1	29.7	30.4	30.6	37.4	41.5	45.4	52.4	41.7
Estonia	0.6	0.6	0.4	0.3	0.3	3.3	3.4	4.3	3.9	6.2	5.5
Finland	3.1	3.3	4.2	4.2	5.5	6.7	7.5	6.8	7.6	7.2	6.6
France	8.1	37.9	40.9	38.4	49.3	51.9	50.2	21.5	30.1	29.9	21.7
Germany	529.6	538.8	578.8	657.6	765.6	859.3	1 083.8	885.5	923.6	961.3	746.2
Greece	33.7	39.2	59.4	55.0	51.2	53.4	51.8	49.7	53.1	49.5	44.3
Hungary	6.0	2.7	9.9	13.1	10.8	10.4	10.5	12.9	24.4	27.9	48.0
Iceland	3.4	2.8	2.2	2.3	2.5	2.2	3.6	3.9	4.9	4.4	5.8
Ireland	40.3	38.6	33.3	33.0	30.0	27.5	29.1	34.0	28.0	25.9	28.2
Italy	32.8	32.4	38.2	43.6	47.5	44.7	42.6	40.6	40.2	57.5	38.9
Japan	242.6	230.9	219.4	213.4	212.9	223.5	233.5	259.2	292.1	333.6	173.0
Korea	196.1	217.7	290.0	268.1	270.5	301.0	325.0	348.7	365.1	425.6	361.6
Latvia	..	6.7	4.7	3.4	1.4	2.6	3.0	2.3	2.9	4.1	3.8
Lithuania	3.8	2.4	2.6	3.3	3.5	7.6	4.3	2.6	3.2	4.8	7.8
Luxembourg	7.7	7.5	8.6	8.9	9.5	10.4	11.3	11.6	11.6	13.0	14.9
Netherlands	64.0	70.2	80.8	83.1	83.4	85.2	89.9	96.4	102.8	109.9	113.2
New Zealand	43.8	45.2	41.5	37.3	35.7	37.0	38.9	45.3	47.0	55.1	35.0
Norway	22.5	22.9	21.3	25.0	23.3	27.4	30.7	26.6	24.5	17.6	19.9
Poland	48.6	51.0	68.9	49.5	68.6	89.5	40.1	45.8	43.0	43.9	57.5
Portugal	2.0	2.6	2.5	3.0	1.9	0.5	1.1	0.6	2.3	0.8	2.0
Slovak Republic	0.4	0.2	0.1	0.0	0.1	0.0	0.1	0.0	0.0	0.0	0.0
Slovenia	11.7	7.3	6.2	5.6	6.2	6.3	6.8	7.7	6.9	8.5	11.9
Spain	363.2	353.6	389.3	459.0	320.0	249.2	237.5	282.0	230.3	220.0	183.1
Sweden	22.1	23.7	26.6	24.6	26.4	31.3	23.5	23.4	24.1	25.3	26.7
Switzerland	65.5	64.0	65.9	70.0	69.2	73.4	77.6	79.1	80.7	80.0	70.3
Türkiye	..	..	..	..	..	..	178.0	253.6	323.9	245.4	..
United Kingdom	185.0	190.0	165.0	170.0	171.0	164.0	195.0	222.0	203.0	202.0	..

Note: For details on definitions and sources, refer to the metadata in the following table.

StatLink ᵐˢ▇ https://stat.link/mr4c5q

Metadata related to Tables A.1., B.1. and A.2. **Inflows and outflows of foreign population**

Country	Types of migrants recorded in the data	Other comments	Source
Australia	Includes persons who are entitled to stay permanently in Australia at arrival (Settler Arrivals) as well as those who changed status from temporary to permanent residence. Settler arrivals include holders of a permanent visa, holders of a temporary (provisional) visa where there is a clear intention to settle, citizens of New Zealand indicating an intention to settle and persons otherwise eligible to settle. *Outflows:* People leaving Australia for 12 months or more in a 16-month period. Net Overseas Migration (NOM).	Data refer to the fiscal year (July to June of the year indicated). From 2014, figures inferior to 5 individuals are not shown.	Department of Immigration and Border Protection.
Austria	*Inflows and outflows:* Foreigners holding a residence permit and who have actually stayed for at least 3 months.	Outflows include administrative corrections.	Population Registers, Statistics Austria.
Belgium	*Inflows:* Foreigners holding a residence permit and intending to stay in the country for at least 3 months. *Outflows:* Include administrative corrections.	From 2012, asylum seekers are included in inflow and outflow data.	Population Register, Directorate for Statistics and Economic Information (DGSIE).
Canada	Total number of people who have been granted permanent resident status in Canada.	Country of origin refers to country of last permanent residence. Due to privacy considerations, the figures have been subjected to random rounding. Under this method, all figures in the table are randomly rounded either up or down to multiples of 5.	Immigration, Refugees and Citizenship Canada.
Chile	Total number of people who obtained a temporary visa for the first time.	Estimations for the years 2017 and 2018.	Register of residence permits, Department of Foreigners and Migration, Ministry of the Interior.
Colombia	Inflows of all foreign nationals who entered Colombia in the given year and subsequently stayed for at least 90 days.		Migration Colombia.
Costa Rica			Dirección General de Migración y Extranjería
Czech Republic	*Inflows:* Foreigners holding a permanent or a long-term residence permit (visa over 90 days) or who were granted asylum in the given year. Excludes nationals of EU countries if they intend to stay for less than 30 days in the country. *Outflows:* Departures of foreigners who were staying in the country on a permanent or temporary basis.	Country of origin refers to country of last permanent or temporary residence. Inflows and outflows of nationals of EU countries are likely to be underestimated.	Register of Foreigners, Czech Statistical Office.
Denmark	*Inflows:* Foreigners who live legally in Denmark are registered in the Central population register, and have been living in the country for at least one year. *Outflows:* Include administrative corrections.	Excludes asylum seekers and all those with temporary residence permits.	Central Population Register, Statistics Denmark.
Estonia	*Inflows and outflows:* Foreigners expecting to stay in the country (out of the country in the case outflows) for at least 12 months.	The number of nationals from other EU countries who are staying temporarily in the country for at least 12 months may be underestimated.	Statistics Estonia.
Finland	*Inflows and outflows:* Foreign nationals with a residence permit valid for more than one year and nationals of EU countries who intend to stay in the country for more than 12 months. Nordic citizens who are moving for less than 6 months are not included.	Includes foreign persons of Finnish origin. Excludes asylum seekers and persons with temporary residence permits. Inflows and outflows of nationals of EU countries can be underestimated.	Central Population Register, Statistics Finland.

Country	Types of migrants recorded in the data	Other comments	Source
France	Inflows of non-EU nationals are first issuances of permanent-type permits. They include status changes from a temporary-type permit to a permanent-type permit. Inflows of EU nationals included from 2013 onwards are extracted from the permanent census.		Ministry of the Interior and INSEE.
Germany	*Inflows:* Foreigners who had previously no registered address in Germany and intend to stay at least one week in the country. *Outflows:* Deregistrations from population registers of persons who move out of their address without taking a new address in the country and administrative deregistrations.	Includes asylum seekers living in private households. Excludes inflows of ethnic Germans (*Aussiedler*). In 2008, local authorities started to purge registers of inactive records. As a result, higher emigration figures were reported from this year.	Central Population Register, Federal Statistical Office.
Greece	*Inflows:* Permits valid for more than 12 months delivered to third country nationals. *Outflows:* Departures of usual residents for a period that is, or is expected to be, of at least 12 months.		Eurostat.
Hungary	*Inflows:* Foreigners expecting to stay in the country for at least 90 days. *Outflows:* Foreign citizens having a residence or a settlement document and who left Hungary in the given year with no intention to return, or whose permission's validity has expired and did not apply for a new one or whose permission was invalidated by authority due to withdrawal. From 2012 on, includes estimations.		Population Register, Office of Immigration and Nationality, Central Statistical Office.
Iceland	*Inflows and outflows:* Foreigners expecting to stay in the country (out of the country in the case outflows) for at least 12 months.		Register of Migration Data, Statistics Iceland.
Ireland	*Inflows:* The estimates derive from the quarterly National Household Survey (QNHS) and relate to those persons resident in the country at the time of the survey and who were living abroad one year earlier. *Outflows:* The estimates derive from the quarterly National Household Survey (QNHS) and relate to the persons who were resident in the country at a point in the previous twelve-month period who are now living abroad.	Figures for Tables A.1. and A.2. are based on May to April of the year indicated.	Central Statistics Office.
Israel	Data refer to permanent immigrants by last country of residence.	The statistical data for Israel are supplied by and under the responsibility of the relevant Israeli authorities. The use of such data by the OECD is without prejudice to the status of the Golan Heights, East Jerusalem and Israeli settlements in the West Bank under the terms of international law.	Population register, Central Bureau of Statistics.
Italy	*Inflows and outflows:* Changes of residence.	Excludes seasonal workers. Administrative corrections are made following censuses (the last census took place in 2011).	Administrative Population Register (Anagrafe) analysed by ISTAT.
Japan	*Inflows:* Foreigners who entered the country, excluding temporary visitors and re-entries. *Outflows:* Foreigners who left Japan without re-entry permission. Excludes temporary visitors.		Ministry of Justice, Immigration Bureau.

Country	Types of migrants recorded in the data	Other comments	Source
Korea	*Inflows and outflows:* Data refer to long-term inflows/outflows (more than 90 days).		Ministry of Justice.
Latvia	*Inflows and outflows:* Long-term migration (permanent change of residence or for a period of at least one year).		Population Register, Central Statistical Office.
Lithuania	*Inflows and outflows:* Foreign citizens who have been residing in the country for at least 6 months.		Lithuanian Department of Migration.
Luxembourg	*Inflows:* Foreigners holding a residence permit and intending to stay in the country for at least 12 months. *Outflows:* Foreigners who left the country with the intention to live abroad for at least 12 months.		Central Population Register, Central Office of Statistics and Economic Studies (Statec).
Mexico	Until 2012, number of foreigners who are issued an immigrant permit for the first time *("inmigrante" FM2)*. 2011 and 2012 also include new and former refugees who obtained immigrant status *("inmigrado")*. From 2013 on, number of foreigners who are issued a permanent residence card, as the 2011 Migration Act came into effect.	The sharp increase in the numbers of 2013 is explained by administrative changes with the implementation of the 2011 Migration Act. Most of these "new residents" are foreigners already in the country on a temporary status.	National Migration Institute, Unit for Migration Policy, Ministry of Interior.
Netherlands	*Inflows:* Foreigners holding a residence permit and intending to stay in the country for at least four of the next six months. *Outflows:* Outflows include the "net administrative corrections", i.e. unreported emigration of foreigners.	Inflows exclude asylum seekers who are staying in reception centres.	Population Register, Central Bureau of Statistics.
New Zealand	*Inflows:* Permanent and long-term arrivals to live in the country for 12 months or more. *Outflows:* Permanent and long-term departures: Foreign-born returning to live overseas after a stay of 12 months or more in New Zealand.	Revised series due to a change in methodology.	Statistics New Zealand.
Norway	*Inflows:* Foreigners holding a residence or work permit and intending to stay in the country for at least 6 months. Include EU/EFTA foreigners. *Outflows:* Foreigners holding a residence or work permit and who stayed in the country for at least 6 months.	Asylum seekers are registered as immigrants only after having settled in a Norwegian municipality following a positive outcome of their application. An asylum seeker whose application has been rejected will not be registered as an 'immigrant', even if the application process has taken a long time and return to the home country is delayed for a significant period.	Central Population Register, Statistics Norway.
Poland	*Inflows:* Number of permanent and "fixed-term" residence permits issued. Since 26 August 2006, nationals of EU member states and their family members are no longer issued residence permits. However, they still need to register their stay in Poland, provided that they are planning to stay in Poland for more than 3 months. *Outflows:* Departures of usual residents for a period that is, or is expected to be, of at least 12 months.		*Inflows:* Office for Foreigners. *Outflows:* Eurostat.
Portugal	Data based on residence permits. Following the new legislation, the data include the new residence permits delivered to every foreigner with a citizenship from an EU or non-EU country. Includes continuous regularisation.		Immigration and Border Control Office (SEF); National Statistical Institute (INE); Ministry of Foreign Affairs (before 2008).

Country	Types of migrants recorded in the data	Other comments	Source
Slovak Republic	*Inflows and outflows:* Includes permanent, temporary, and tolerated residents.		Register of Foreigners, Statistical Office of the Slovak Republic.
Slovenia			Eurostat.
Spain	*Inflows and outflows:* Changes in regular residence for at least 12 months declared by foreigners.	From 2008 on, data correspond to Migration Statistics estimates that are based on the number of registrations and cancellations in the Municipal Registers by all foreigners, irrespective of their legal status.	Municipal Population Registers *(Padron municipal de habitantes),* National Statistical Institute (INE).
Sweden	*Inflows:* Foreigners holding a residence permit and intending to stay in the country for at least one year (including nationals of EU countries). *Outflows:* Departures of foreigners who have the intention to live abroad for at least one year.	Excludes asylum seekers and temporary workers.	Population Register, Statistics Sweden.
Switzerland	*Inflows:* Foreigners holding a permanent or an annual residence permit. Holders of an L-permit (short duration) are also included if their stay in the country is longer than 12 months. *Outflows:* Departures of foreigners holding a permanent or an annual residence permit and of holders of an L-permit who stayed in the country for at least one year. The data include administrative corrections, so that, for example, foreigners whose permit expired are considered to have left the country.		Register of Foreigners, Federal Office of Migration.
Türkiye	*Inflows:* Residence permits issued for the first time to foreigners intending to stay 12 months or more in the country (long-term residents). *Outflows:* Departures of long-term residents.		General Directorate of Security, Ministry of the Interior.
United Kingdom	*Inflows:* Non-British citizens admitted to the United Kingdom. *Outflows:* Non-British citizens leaving the United Kingdom.	Calculations of the Secretariat based on Home Office datasets on entry clearance visas granted outside the UK, extensions and settlement, and on the International Passenger Survey.	Managed migration datasets, Home Office, International Passenger Survey, Office for National Statistics.
United States	*Permanent migrants:* Lawful Permanent Residents (LPRs) ("green card" recipients).	Includes persons already present in the United States who changed status. Certain LPRs are admitted conditionally and are required to remove their conditional status after two years; they are counted as LPRs when they first enter. Data cover the fiscal year (October to September of the year indicated).	Office of Immigration Statistics, Department of Homeland Security; Citizenship and Immigration Services, Department of Homeland Security.

Note: Data for Serbia include persons from Serbia and Montenegro. Some statements may refer to nationalities/countries of birth not shown in this annex but available on line at: http://stats.oecd.org/.

Inflows of asylum seekers

Statistics on asylum seekers published in this annex are based on data provided by Eurostat and the United Nations High Commission for Refugees. Since 1950, the UNHCR, which has a mission of conducting and co-ordinating international initiatives on behalf of refugees, has regularly produced complete statistics on refugees and asylum seekers in OECD countries and other countries of the world (https://www.unhcr.org/data.html).

These statistics are most often derived from administrative sources, but there are differences depending on the nature of the data provided. In some countries, asylum seekers are enumerated when the application is accepted. Consequently, they are shown in the statistics at that time rather than at the date when they arrived in the country. Acceptance of the application means that the administrative authorities will review the applicants' claims and grant them certain rights during this review procedure. In other countries, the data do not include the applicants' family members, who are admitted under different provisions (France), while other countries count the entire family (Switzerland).

The figures presented in the summary table (Table A.3) generally concern initial applications (primary processing stage) and sometimes differ significantly from the totals presented in Tables B.3, which give data by country of origin. This is because the data received by the UNHCR by country of origin combine both initial applications and appeals, and it is sometimes difficult to separate these two categories retrospectively. The reference for total asylum applications remains the figures shown in summary Table A.3.

Table A.3. New asylum requests in OECD countries

	2011	2012	2013	2014	2015	2016	2017	2018	2019	2020	2021
Australia	11 510	15 790	11 740	8 960	12 360	27 630	36 250	28 840	27 400	19 220	14 150
Austria	14 420	17 410	17 500	28 060	85 620	39 950	22 470	11 610	11 010	13 420	36 750
Belgium	26 000	18 530	12 500	13 870	38 700	14 670	14 060	18 160	23 140	12 930	19 610
Canada	24 990	20 220	10 360	13 450	16 070	23 830	49 430	55 390	58 340	19 050	23 370
Chile	310	170	250	280	630	2 300	5 660	5 780	770	1 680	2 500
Colombia	80	100	230	..	..	..	630	2 710	10 620	11 920	15 940
Costa Rica	960	1 170	950	1 370	2 180	4 490	6 320	27 980	59 180	21 130	108 430
Czech Republic	760	750	500	920	1 250	1 210	1 140	1 360	1 580	800	1 060
Denmark	3 810	6 190	7 560	14 820	21 230	6 240	3 140	3 500	2 650	1 440	2 020
Estonia	70	80	100	150	230	70	180	90	100	50	80
Finland	3 090	2 920	3 020	3 520	32 270	5 320	4 350	2 960	2 460	1 460	1 370
France	52 150	55 070	60 230	59 030	74 300	70 750	91 970	111 420	138 290	81 740	103 810
Germany	45 740	64 540	109 580	173 070	441 900	722 360	198 310	161 930	142 510	102 580	148 240
Greece	9 310	9 580	8 220	9 450	11 370	49 850	56 950	64 990	74 920	37 860	22 660
Hungary	1 690	2 160	18 570	41 370	174 430	28 070	3 120	640	470	90	40
Iceland	80	110	170	160	360	1 130	1 070	730	810	630	870
Ireland	1 420	1 100	950	1 440	3 280	2 240	2 910	3 660	4 740	1 540	2 620
Israel	6 460	5 700	4 760	5 560	5 010	8 150	15 370	16 260	9 450	1 890	1 930
Italy	34 120	17 350	25 720	63 660	83 240	122 120	126 560	53 440	35 010	21 340	43 910
Japan	1 870	2 550	3 260	5 000	7 580	10 900	19 250	10 490	10 380	3 940	2 410
Korea	1 010	1 140	1 570	2 900	5 710	7 540	9 940	16 150	15 430	6 670	2 330
Latvia	340	190	190	360	330	340	360	180	180	150	580
Lithuania	410	530	280	390	290	320	520	390	630	260	3 910
Luxembourg	2 080	2 000	990	970	2 300	1 940	2 330	2 230	2 200	1 300	1 360
Mexico	750	810	1 300	1 520	3 420	8 780	14 600	29 620	70 370	41 200	131 420
Netherlands	11 590	9 660	14 400	23 850	43 100	18 410	16 090	20 470	22 540	13 720	24 830
New Zealand	310	320	290	290	350	390	560	460	540	440	420
Norway	9 050	9 790	11 470	12 640	30 520	3 200	3 390	2 550	2 210	1 340	1 620
Poland	5 090	9 170	13 760	6 810	10 250	9 840	3 010	2 410	2 770	1 510	6 240
Portugal	280	300	510	440	900	1 460	1 020	1 240	1 740	900	1 350
Slovak Republic	490	730	280	230	270	100	160	160	220	270	330
Slovenia	370	310	240	360	260	1 260	1 440	2 800	3 620	3 470	5 220
Spain	3 410	2 580	4 510	5 900	13 370	16 270	30 450	52 750	115 190	86 390	62 070
Sweden	29 650	43 880	54 260	75 090	156 460	22 410	22 230	18 110	23 150	13 630	10 180
Switzerland	19 440	25 950	19 440	22 110	38 120	25 870	16 670	13 540	12 600	9 770	13 300
Türkiye	16 020	26 470	44 810	87 820	133 590	77 850	123 600	83 820	56 420	31 330	29 260
United Kingdom	25 900	27 980	29 400	31 260	39 970	38 380	33 380	37 370	44 470	36 030	56 470
United States	70 030	78 410	84 400	121 160	172 740	261 970	331 700	254 300	301 070	250 940	188 860
OECD	**435 060**	**481 710**	**578 270**	**838 240**	**1 663 960**	**1 637 610**	**1 270 590**	**1 120 490**	**1 289 170**	**854 030**	**1 091 360**

Note: For details on definitions and sources, refer to the metadata at the end of the Tables B.3.

StatLink ᵐˢ▶ https://stat.link/e2iq6o

Table B.3. New asylum requests by nationality – Australia

	2011	2012	2013	2014	2015	2016	2017	2018	2019	2020	2021
Malaysia	182	173	209	704	2 767	7 258	7 983	9 791	7 065	4 010	2 149
China	1 189	1 155	1 537	1 541	1 456	1 914	6 638	6 586	5 058	2 296	1 975
Afghanistan	1 720	3 064	370	123	567	2 563	1 478	453	697	346	1 138
Iran	2 152	1 851	967	262	844	2 971	5 075	744	1 069	1 289	846
India	769	949	1 163	964	652	1 117	1 299	1 813	2 495	1 762	833
Viet Nam	130	81	128	264	223	772	1 263	812	959	1 165	764
Thailand	17	24	22	16	98	204	301	1 481	919	636	515
Myanmar	60	71	58	11	5	60	208	..	74	156	499
Sri Lanka	370	2 468	806	176	806	2 662	2 184	451	836	534	432
Pakistan	817	1 538	1 104	828	642	1 334	1 404	657	801	495	392
Indonesia	174	126	190	152	208	318	510	618	752	605	384
Iraq	490	778	362	422	1 043	1 378	854	264	353	288	152
Hong Kong (China)	12	23	27	0	57	46	..	..	..	188	129
Timor-Leste	0	2	4	0	0	0	5	..	..	318	118
Korea	78	70	112	128	78	52	52	72	75	51	115
Other countries	3 345	3 413	4 682	3 397	2 914	4 983	7 048	5 169	6 246	5 082	3 712
Total	**11 505**	**15 786**	**11 741**	**8 988**	**12 360**	**27 632**	**36 245**	**28 839**	**27 399**	**19 221**	**14 153**

Note: For details on definitions and sources, refer to the metadata at the end of the tables.

StatLink https://stat.link/hovm34

Table B.3. New asylum requests by nationality – Austria

	2011	2012	2013	2014	2015	2016	2017	2018	2019	2020	2021
Syria	422	922	1 991	7 661	24 314	8 723	7 255	3 300	2 675	5 080	15 710
Afghanistan	3 609	4 003	2 589	4 916	25 143	11 506	3 525	1 765	2 585	2 825	7 830
Morocco	313	353	516	220	666	953	205	90	110	705	1 810
Somalia	610	483	433	1 152	2 040	1 500	655	475	600	615	1 510
Pakistan	949	1 827	1 037	330	2 892	2 414	1 445	160	255	145	1 285
Bangladesh	87	212	278	88	709	290	125	95	205	215	970
Egypt	124	124	184	83	175	200	130	85	45	165	930
Iraq	484	491	468	1 051	13 285	2 737	1 345	650	605	625	915
Türkiye	414	273	302	165	190	310	260	175	245	280	860
India	476	401	339	266	371	407	310	195	295	140	855
Tunisia	182	198	225	128	150	125	70	35	55	145	485
Algeria	447	573	949	442	821	867	220	80	120	325	410
Iran	457	761	595	726	3 381	2 415	950	1 050	660	310	390
Russia	2 314	3 098	2 841	1 484	1 340	1 235	1 035	690	550	360	340
Moldova	79	54	35	5	20	10	25	40	10	15	190
Other countries	3 449	3 640	4 721	9 343	10 468	6 885	4 915	2 725	1 995	1 465	2 260
Total	**14 416**	**17 413**	**17 503**	**28 060**	**85 620**	**39 952**	**22 470**	**11 610**	**11 010**	**13 415**	**36 750**

Note: For details on definitions and sources, refer to the metadata at the end of the tables.

StatLink https://stat.link/hovm34

Table B.3. New asylum requests by nationality – Belgium

	2011	2012	2013	2014	2015	2016	2017	2018	2019	2020	2021
Afghanistan	2 774	2 349	892	744	7 562	2 227	995	1 045	2 245	2 310	5 155
Syria	494	798	944	2 524	10 185	2 612	2 625	2 770	2 730	1 320	1 765
Eritrea	62	65	57	745	333	331	665	725	1 155	805	1 505
West Bank and Gaza Strip	55	26	27	0	51	139	815	2 420	2 320	455	1 200
Somalia	454	293	156	260	1 994	727	295	380	765	600	935
Türkiye	430	340	204	144	182	652	465	785	1 000	585	560
Guinea	2 046	1 370	1 023	657	619	721	750	1 000	830	455	535
Georgia	347	386	229	280	199	184	415	640	500	210	485
Burundi	149	133	133	51	251	271	235	400	620	320	480
Iraq	2 005	636	295	965	9 180	759	600	895	845	405	460
Albania	1 152	607	472	487	599	649	670	505	540	270	440
Moldova	7	17	10	9	5	6	5	5	5	170	435
Cameroon	451	457	360	345	278	257	350	355	390	270	400
Dem. Rep. of the Congo	1 080	1 392	1 166	632	620	503	550	405	520	385	275
Nigeria	165	167	158	109	114	89	120	100	180	135	245
Other countries	14 332	9 489	6 374	5 924	6 528	4 543	4 500	5 730	8 495	4 235	4 730
Total	**26 003**	**18 525**	**12 500**	**13 876**	**38 700**	**14 670**	**14 055**	**18 160**	**23 140**	**12 930**	**19 605**

Note: For details on definitions and sources, refer to the metadata at the end of the tables.

StatLink 🔗 https://stat.link/hovm34

Table B.3. New asylum requests by nationality – Canada

	2011	2012	2013	2014	2015	2016	2017	2018	2019	2020	2021
Mexico	763	324	84	73	110	259	1 511	3 156	5 061	1 776	2 292
India	632	765	228	294	374	557	1 484	4 524	5 150	1 564	1 705
Colombia	904	724	597	579	701	848	1 413	2 571	3 040	974	1 441
Iran	318	264	201	161	149	286	684	2 483	3 663	689	1 396
Türkiye	332	369	178	174	263	1 096	2 194	1 820	1 548	312	842
Haiti	523	419	329	364	295	616	7 921	1 403	1 374	1 056	755
Pakistan	882	808	630	776	897	1 137	1 746	2 031	2 059	684	521
Venezuela	111	106	27	161	257	565	1 245	1 254	1 199	289	485
China	1 922	1 741	762	1 189	1 500	1 180	1 078	1 865	1 394	279	436
Lebanon	122	92	105	116	150	280	284	315	357	190	354
Afghanistan	373	362	386	461	494	638	664	634	437	190	337
Nigeria	696	700	468	578	793	1 493	5 840	9 599	3 976	646	326
Bangladesh	120	109	156	321	222	282	489	813	731	194	235
Dem. Rep. of the Congo	347	357	308	346	281	411	621	1 167	1 312	274	235
Sri Lanka	635	414	190	198	237	192	379	524	664	267	228
Other countries	16 305	12 669	5 707	7 870	9 347	13 993	21 872	21 226	26 373	9 661	11 777
Total	**24 985**	**20 223**	**10 356**	**13 661**	**16 070**	**23 833**	**49 425**	**55 385**	**58 338**	**19 045**	**23 365**

Note: For details on definitions and sources, refer to the metadata at the end of the tables.

StatLink 🔗 https://stat.link/hovm34

Table B.3. New asylum requests by nationality – Chile

	2011	2012	2013	2014	2015	2016	2017	2018	2019	2020	2021
Venezuela	2	..	..	..	..	245	1 345	1 666	226	394	2 065
Cuba	9	..	..	..	..	56	1 603	2 764	272	531	158
Colombia	267	..	..	..	..	1 804	2 516	1 157	252	670	98
Afghanistan	0	..	..	..	..	0	..	0	0	0	74
Peru	1	..	..	..	..	13	..	0	0	0	36
Haiti	2	..	..	..	..	23	..	5	0	0	29
Dominican Republic	0	..	..	..	..	64	..	59	10	0	12
Other countries	24	..	..	..	..	94	192	133	10	80	26
Total	**305**	**168**	**249**	**282**	**630**	**2 299**	**5 656**	**5 784**	**770**	**1 675**	**2 498**

Note: For details on definitions and sources, refer to the metadata at the end of the tables.

StatLink https://stat.link/hovm34

Table B.3. New asylum requests by nationality – Colombia

	2011	2012	2013	2014	2015	2016	2017	2018	2019	2020	2021
Venezuela	..	..	..	..	..	..	..	2 592	10 479	11 832	15 811
Cuba	..	..	..	..	..	..	..	..	24	57	111
Ecuador	..	..	..	..	..	..	..	..	0	5	7
Egypt	..	..	..	..	..	..	..	..	..	0	5
Syria	..	..	..	..	..	..	..	..	0	0	5
Haiti	..	..	..	..	..	..	..	..	0	0	5
Other countries	..	..	..	..	..	..	..	118	118	26	0
Total	**84**	**99**	**229**	**..**	**..**	**..**	**630**	**2 710**	**10 621**	**11 920**	**15 939**

Note: For details on definitions and sources, refer to the metadata at the end of the tables.

StatLink https://stat.link/hovm34

Table B.3. New asylum requests by nationality – Costa Rica

	2011	2012	2013	2014	2015	2016	2017	2018	2019	2020	2021
Nicaragua	..	..	..	..	38	66	78	23 138	31 624	9 416	101 962
Venezuela	..	..	..	..	280	1 423	3 175	2 884	2 626	742	2 928
Haiti	..	..	..	..	7	68	62	0	92	73	902
Colombia	..	..	..	..	583	669	778	533	1 137	377	789
Cuba	..	..	..	..	129	89	172	42	1 856	1 644	344
El Salvador	..	..	..	..	801	1 471	1 644	1 059	1 149	152	335
Honduras	..	..	..	..	82	149	225	188	436	129	325
Brazil	..	..	..	..	5	0	0	0	10	5	175
China	..	..	..	..	0	0	5	12	153	60	113
Guatemala	..	..	..	..	6	9	26	13	37	8	76
Panama	..	..	..	..	5	0	6	5	9	5	57
Peru	..	..	..	..	0	0	0	5	0	7	47
Chile	..	..	..	..	0	0	0	0	11	7	45
Ecuador	..	..	..	..	0	0	5	5	5	0	44
Dominican Republic	..	..	..	..	0	0	0	0	67	21	41
Other countries	..	..	..	..	253	542	146	88	19 968	8 481	244
Total	**964**	**1 170**	**954**	**1 373**	**2 189**	**4 486**	**6 322**	**27 972**	**59 180**	**21 127**	**108 427**

Note: For details on definitions and sources, refer to the metadata at the end of the tables.

StatLink https://stat.link/hovm34

Table B.3. New asylum requests by nationality – Czech Republic

	2011	2012	2013	2014	2015	2016	2017	2018	2019	2020	2021
Ukraine	152	101	68	416	574	356	295	280	215	240	265
Georgia	17	6	12	0	5	46	110	140	190	85	185
Afghanistan	26	10	8	6	6	36	15	20	20	5	175
Moldova	8	6	10	7	0	5	15	10	40	45	55
Viet Nam	46	35	37	42	37	53	60	75	120	40	50
Türkiye	32	10	11	0	0	23	25	35	20	25	35
Belarus	71	33	13	0	0	8	15	10	10	60	35
Syria	23	57	69	102	121	73	70	30	35	20	30
Uzbekistan	26	9	6	0	0	17	10	90	65	35	25
Algeria	10	8	4	0	0	8	5	15	10	5	20
Somalia	0	0	0	0	0	2	0	5	0	0	15
Russia	47	29	40	5	12	53	40	70	80	30	15
Mongolia	41	12	8	0	5	8	5	20	20	10	15
Iraq	9	5	11	6	22	141	45	60	15	5	10
Tunisia	3	1	2	0	0	7	5	10	5	5	10
Other countries	245	431	204	330	468	378	425	490	730	185	120
Total	**756**	**753**	**503**	**914**	**1 250**	**1 214**	**1 140**	**1 360**	**1 575**	**795**	**1 060**

Note: For details on definitions and sources, refer to the metadata at the end of the tables.

StatLink https://stat.link/hovm34

Table B.3. New asylum requests by nationality – Denmark

	2011	2012	2013	2014	2015	2016	2017	2018	2019	2020	2021
Afghanistan	903	576	425	321	2 288	1 122	170	115	90	70	555
Eritrea	20	57	98	2 293	1 738	267	295	675	480	165	380
Syria	428	907	1 702	7 185	8 604	1 251	765	600	490	340	320
Iraq	115	133	115	148	1 531	449	130	120	115	55	65
Iran	461	548	374	285	2 771	299	145	195	135	80	65
Morocco	45	108	162	226	183	347	300	175	155	100	65
Georgia	19	75	69	104	94	73	70	405	65	35	45
Somalia	107	914	964	688	259	262	85	105	160	40	40
Türkiye	25	54	18	5	24	18	35	25	25	35	35
Algeria	103	134	111	120	92	164	80	70	40	45	25
Tunisia	56	69	84	49	33	54	20	40	15	15	20
Belarus	23	148	52	55	68	44	50	30	30	15	20
Nigeria	52	115	142	93	110	121	65	25	20	15	20
Serbia	325	689	551	180	196	86	30	10	20	10	15
India	32	39	30	10	21	27	25	20	40	20	15
Other countries	1 097	1 620	2 660	3 012	3 218	1 651	905	885	765	395	330
Total	**3 811**	**6 186**	**7 557**	**14 774**	**21 230**	**6 235**	**3 140**	**3 495**	**2 645**	**1 435**	**2 015**

Note: For details on definitions and sources, refer to the metadata at the end of the tables.

StatLink https://stat.link/hovm34

Table B.3. New asylum requests by nationality – Estonia

	2011	2012	2013	2014	2015	2016	2017	2018	2019	2020	2021
Afghanistan	8	3	1	0	11	0	5	0	5	0	15
Russia	4	8	15	0	6	8	15	10	30	15	10
Türkiye	1	3	1	0	0	5	0	0	20	5	10
Armenia	7	5	0	0	7	6	0	0	0	0	5
Iraq	2	0	0	0	11	0	5	0	5	0	5
Egypt	0	2	0	0	0	0	5	10	0	0	5
Belarus	4	4	3	0	0	1	5	0	0	0	5
Ukraine	2	0	0	37	84	9	10	15	5	0	5
Other countries	39	52	77	106	111	40	135	55	35	25	15
Total	**67**	**77**	**97**	**143**	**230**	**69**	**180**	**90**	**100**	**45**	**75**

Note: For details on definitions and sources, refer to the metadata at the end of the tables.

StatLink https://stat.link/hovm34

Table B.3. New asylum requests by nationality – Finland

	2011	2012	2013	2014	2015	2016	2017	2018	2019	2020	2021
Afghanistan	292	188	172	198	5 198	697	305	135	125	190	225
Iraq	588	784	764	807	20 427	1 083	1 000	565	270	475	150
Somalia	365	173	196	407	1 974	426	100	155	140	180	140
Türkiye	74	56	55	13	40	98	110	285	360	80	125
Syria	109	180	148	146	876	600	740	105	95	55	85
Russia	294	199	219	167	160	174	395	455	285	95	70
Nigeria	105	93	202	157	153	162	95	90	105	35	55
Georgia	70	29	14	16	0	19	120	70	60	5	50
Nicaragua	0	0	0	0	0	0	0	25	30	5	35
Iran	125	121	147	84	601	141	90	230	95	25	30
Cameroon	21	22	37	29	28	86	45	55	60	25	25
Rwanda	9	4	6	0	0	6	15	5	20	0	20
Algeria	55	54	81	79	81	28	55	15	15	5	20
Ethiopia	28	13	23	18	65	34	20	20	10	10	15
Honduras	1	1	0	0	0	4	5	5	30	0	15
Other countries	950	1 005	959	1 396	2 667	1 761	1 255	740	755	270	305
Total	**3 086**	**2 922**	**3 023**	**3 517**	**32 270**	**5 319**	**4 350**	**2 955**	**2 455**	**1 455**	**1 365**

Note: For details on definitions and sources, refer to the metadata at the end of the tables.

StatLink https://stat.link/hovm34

Table B.3. New asylum requests by nationality – France

	2011	2012	2013	2014	2015	2016	2017	2018	2019	2020	2021
Afghanistan	653	522	526	605	2 453	5 466	6 600	10 255	11 685	10 000	16 005
Côte d'Ivoire	1 671	986	968	949	1 278	1 504	3 620	5 295	6 725	4 635	6 210
Bangladesh	3 572	1 093	3 069	2 646	3 358	2 198	2 620	3 920	6 705	4 615	6 200
Guinea	2 033	1 884	2 445	2 166	2 131	2 387	4 130	6 685	7 045	4 690	5 250
Türkiye	1 737	2 054	1 682	1 391	1 030	907	1 290	2 050	4 110	3 095	4 965
Albania	477	2 647	5 016	2 843	3 228	5 769	11 425	8 300	8 510	2 010	4 885
Georgia	1 645	2 552	2 456	1 369	1 084	833	1 895	6 755	7 985	1 805	4 580
Pakistan	1 433	1 941	1 735	2 130	1 810	1 691	1 500	2 100	4 610	3 555	3 730
Nigeria	802	967	1 306	1 375	1 586	1 612	2 030	2 985	5 720	3 100	3 160
Comoros	1 381	662	528	642	383	229	355	380	1 585	1 830	3 155
Somalia	762	511	479	787	1 350	829	905	2 270	3 160	2 390	3 145
Dem. Rep. of the Congo	3 845	5 321	5 263	5 170	3 984	3 063	3 805	3 965	4 545	3 120	2 750
Haiti	2 016	1 602	1 473	1 854	3 198	4 936	5 600	2 305	4 720	2 830	2 620
Mali	739	938	1 663	1 473	1 546	1 425	1 720	3 070	4 870	1 675	2 310
Ukraine	91	129	122	1 386	1 623	486	530	735	1 175	2 110	2 240
Other countries	29 290	31 259	31 503	32 255	44 258	37 413	43 940	50 345	55 140	30 275	32 605
Total	**52 147**	**55 068**	**60 234**	**59 041**	**74 300**	**70 748**	**91 965**	**111 415**	**138 290**	**81 735**	**103 810**

Note: For details on definitions and sources, refer to the metadata at the end of the tables.

StatLink 〰️🖙 https://stat.link/hovm34

Table B.3. New asylum requests by nationality – Germany

	2011	2012	2013	2014	2015	2016	2017	2018	2019	2020	2021
Syria	2 634	6 201	11 851	39 332	158 657	266 248	48 970	44 165	39 270	36 435	54 905
Afghanistan	7 767	7 498	7 735	9 115	31 382	127 011	16 425	9 945	9 520	9 900	23 275
Iraq	5 831	5 352	3 958	5 345	29 784	96 115	21 930	16 330	13 740	9 845	15 605
Türkiye	1 578	1 457	1 521	1 565	1 500	5 383	8 025	10 160	10 785	5 780	7 065
Georgia	471	1 298	2 336	2 873	2 782	3 448	3 080	3 765	3 330	2 050	3 685
Somalia	984	1 243	3 786	5 528	5 126	9 851	6 835	5 075	3 570	2 605	3 650
Eritrea	632	650	3 616	13 198	10 876	18 854	10 225	5 570	3 520	2 560	3 170
Iran	3 352	4 348	4 424	3 194	5 394	26 426	8 610	10 855	8 405	3 120	2 695
Nigeria	759	892	1 923	3 924	5 207	12 709	7 810	10 170	9 070	3 305	2 510
Moldova	21	30	68	255	1 561	3 346	890	1 780	1 770	1 285	2 390
North Macedonia	1 131	4 546	6 208	5 614	9 083	4 835	2 465	1 245	1 115	410	2 330
Algeria	487	489	1 056	2 176	2 041	3 563	1 950	1 200	1 060	1 205	1 520
Russia	1 689	3 202	14 887	4 411	5 257	10 985	4 885	3 940	3 145	1 700	1 440
Pakistan	2 539	3 412	4 101	3 968	8 199	14 484	3 670	2 210	2 175	1 015	1 255
Albania	78	232	1 247	7 865	53 805	14 853	3 775	1 875	1 695	815	1 210
Other countries	15 788	23 689	40 863	64 709	111 246	104 253	48 765	33 645	30 340	20 550	21 530
Total	**45 741**	**64 539**	**109 580**	**173 072**	**441 900**	**722 364**	**198 310**	**161 930**	**142 510**	**102 580**	**148 235**

Note: For details on definitions and sources, refer to the metadata at the end of the tables.

StatLink 〰️🖙 https://stat.link/hovm34

Table B.3. New asylum requests by nationality – Greece

	2011	2012	2013	2014	2015	2016	2017	2018	2019	2020	2021
Pakistan	2 309	2 339	1 358	1 623	1 503	4 417	8 345	7 185	6 420	3 515	3 415
Afghanistan	637	584	1 223	1 711	1 544	4 293	7 480	11 820	23 665	11 100	3 195
Syria	352	275	485	791	3 319	26 614	16 305	13 145	10 750	7 415	2 945
Bangladesh	615	1 007	727	635	536	1 053	1 255	1 435	2 375	1 625	2 480
Türkiye	34	32	30	26	20	182	1 820	4 820	3 795	1 590	1 910
Somalia	68	60	122	109	90	123	230	715	2 270	1 530	1 485
Albania	276	384	579	570	913	1 295	2 345	3 125	2 795	1 025	1 125
Iraq	257	315	145	175	579	4 773	7 870	9 640	5 590	1 465	990
Egypt	306	249	308	280	233	259	810	915	1 695	710	775
West Bank and Gaza Strip	27	28	41	61	48	848	1 305	1 515	2 140	1 260	760
Iran	247	211	188	358	187	1 084	1 295	1 730	2 325	835	575
Dem. Rep. of the Congo	12	20	153	75	112	224	1 085	1 450	3 570	1 850	565
Georgia	1 121	893	532	350	297	583	985	1 340	1 460	750	545
India	179	165	81	30	24	64	170	210	370	255	220
Cameroon	39	24	84	281	155	211	455	1 035	855	395	190
Other countries	2 832	2 991	2 168	2 357	1 810	3 824	5 195	4 905	4 840	2 540	1 485
Total	**9 311**	**9 577**	**8 224**	**9 432**	**11 370**	**49 847**	**56 950**	**64 985**	**74 915**	**37 860**	**22 660**

Note: For details on definitions and sources, refer to the metadata at the end of the tables.

StatLink ᗧᵢₛᴾ https://stat.link/hovm34

Table B.3. New asylum requests by nationality – Hungary

	2011	2012	2013	2014	2015	2016	2017	2018	2019	2020	2021
Iran	33	45	59	247	1 780	1 248	95	30	20	5	10
Ethiopia	1	2	5	0	38	30	5	5	0	0	5
Afghanistan	649	880	2 279	8 539	45 560	10 774	1 365	270	185	15	5
Other countries	1 010	1 230	16 222	32 325	127 052	16 018	1 655	330	265	70	20
Total	**1 693**	**2 157**	**18 565**	**41 111**	**174 430**	**28 070**	**3 120**	**635**	**470**	**90**	**40**

Note: For details on definitions and sources, refer to the metadata at the end of the tables.

StatLink ᗧᵢₛᴾ https://stat.link/hovm34

Table B.3. New asylum requests by nationality – Iceland

	2011	2012	2013	2014	2015	2016	2017	2018	2019	2020	2021
Venezuela		0	0	0	0	0	0	15	180	105	355
West Bank and Gaza Strip	2	2	0	0	0	15	15	25	20	120	90
Afghanistan	3	9	4	0	14	23	15	45	45	30	90
Syria	1	3	5	5	13	37	30	40	20	60	65
Iraq	5	3	6	5	19	73	110	110	135	110	60
Nigeria	7	17	2	0	0	21	10	35	50	35	50
Somalia	2	1	1	0	0	21	30	50	35	40	40
Iran	3	12	1	0	0	20	25	30	35	15	20
Colombia	2	1	0	5	0	2	0	5	10	5	15
Albania	2	11	22	10	103	231	255	90	45	10	10
Ethiopia	4	0	0	0	0	2	0	0	0	0	10
North Macedonia	2	0	2	5	10	468	50	0	0	5	5
Uganda	1	1	0	0	0	1	0	0	5	0	5
Serbia	2	1	0	0	7	15	20	10	15	0	5
Chile	0	0	0	0	0	0	0	0	5	0	5
Other countries	40	52	129	140	194	203	525	275	205	90	40
Total	**76**	**113**	**172**	**170**	**360**	**1 132**	**1 065**	**730**	**805**	**625**	**865**

Note: For details on definitions and sources, refer to the metadata at the end of the tables.

StatLink https://stat.link/hovm34

Table B.3. New asylum requests by nationality – Ireland

	2011	2012	2013	2014	2015	2016	2017	2018	2019	2020	2021
Nigeria	205	181	129	139	186	176	185	250	385	210	450
Somalia	24	8	10	5	0	29	20	55	135	165	335
Georgia	18	20	15	0	9	75	300	450	635	35	330
Afghanistan	74	50	32	7	119	121	75	95	105	70	200
Zimbabwe	69	50	70	74	88	192	260	280	445	80	145
Algeria	53	39	51	73	77	63	80	95	95	70	135
South Africa	47	35	28	33	39	94	105	200	315	80	115
Botswana	0	1	0	0	0	1	15	10	25	5	70
Albania	35	46	48	91	214	221	280	460	970	40	65
Pakistan	197	123	91	291	1 353	233	195	240	205	85	55
Syria	11	16	38	5	68	244	545	330	85	45	55
Brazil	8	12	5	0	0	32	35	110	115	70	40
El Salvador	0	0	0	0	0	1	0	5	20	20	40
Bangladesh	22	32	31	93	285	55	60	55	60	30	35
Eritrea	9	8	1	0	0	6	5	30	15	5	30
Other countries	647	483	397	637	842	694	750	990	1 130	525	515
Total	**1 419**	**1 104**	**946**	**1 448**	**3 280**	**2 237**	**2 910**	**3 655**	**4 740**	**1 535**	**2 615**

Note: For details on definitions and sources, refer to the metadata at the end of the tables.

StatLink https://stat.link/hovm34

Table B.3. New asylum requests by nationality – Israel

	2011	2012	2013	2014	2015	2016	2017	2018	2019	2020	2021
China	..	..	..	..	..	..	..	..	248	88	405
India	..	..	..	..	..	..	322	671	636	189	268
Moldova	..	..	..	..	..	..	332	436	242	75	193
Sri Lanka	..	..	..	..	..	..	430	540	446	134	174
Eritrea	..	..	..	..	..	..	2 299	6 348	129	88	138
Republic of Türkiye	..	..	..	..	..	..	..	169	322	89	128
Ukraine	..	..	..	..	..	..	7 711	1 765	633	217	117
Myanmar	..	..	..	..	..	..	..	..	5	0	76
Nepal	..	..	..	..	..	..	..	..	59	31	63
Philippines	..	..	..	..	..	..	..	..	20	0	62
Russia	..	..	..	..	..	..	635	2 772	4 477	325	53
Uganda	..	..	..	..	..	..	..	..	55	30	43
Ethiopia	..	..	..	..	..	..	195	136	133	43	28
Sudan	..	..	..	..	..	..	936	766	41	13	25
Thailand	..	..	..	..	..	..	..	..	10	5	20
Other countries	..	..	..	..	..	..	2 508	2 660	1 988	559	134
Total	**5 700**	**4 760**	**5 560**	**226**	**5 010**	**8 150**	**15 368**	**16 263**	**9 444**	**1 886**	**1 927**

Note: For details on definitions and sources, refer to the metadata at the end of the tables.

StatLink 🔗 https://stat.link/hovm34

Table B.3. New asylum requests by nationality – Italy

	2011	2012	2013	2014	2015	2016	2017	2018	2019	2020	2021
Pakistan	2 058	2 601	3 175	7 095	10 287	13 516	9 470	7 445	7 305	4 960	6 885
Bangladesh	1 595	566	460	4 524	6 017	6 611	12 125	4 165	1 340	2 275	6 640
Tunisia	4 558	893	502	465	295	332	445	1 005	705	1 000	6 375
Afghanistan	1 289	1 495	2 049	3 104	3 986	2 843	1 010	495	590	640	4 410
Egypt	249	445	905	678	560	783	810	740	805	360	2 680
Morocco	265	282	307	312	576	1 554	1 860	1 875	1 510	475	1 585
Georgia	29	65	107	79	135	194	540	1 155	970	495	1 335
Nigeria	6 208	1 613	3 170	9 689	17 779	26 698	24 950	5 510	1 255	855	1 280
Somalia	1 205	807	2 761	807	719	2 405	2 010	605	405	750	1 150
Côte d'Ivoire	1 938	629	237	1 481	3 084	7 464	8 380	1 685	405	500	1 010
Mali	2 582	785	1 714	9 758	5 446	6 347	7 495	2 075	185	320	805
Albania	39	66	114	175	420	364	465	1 290	1 545	450	765
El Salvador	9	35	44	101	209	1 060	1 365	2 270	2 520	1 060	610
Peru	2	19	13	5	16	41	120	750	2 445	735	570
Ukraine	17	37	34	2 071	4 681	2 567	2 720	3 015	1 775	380	530
Other countries	12 074	7 014	10 128	23 313	29 030	49 345	52 795	19 360	11 245	6 085	7 275
Total	**34 117**	**17 352**	**25 720**	**63 657**	**83 240**	**122 124**	**126 560**	**53 440**	**35 005**	**21 340**	**43 905**

Note: For details on definitions and sources, refer to the metadata at the end of the tables.

StatLink 🔗 https://stat.link/hovm34

Table B.3. New asylum requests by nationality – Japan

	2011	2012	2013	2014	2015	2016	2017	2018	2019	2020	2021
Sri Lanka	224	255	346	485	468	939	2 226	1 551	1 530	..	..
Türkiye	234	422	655	845	925	1 143	1 198	563	1 331	..	..
Cambodia	..	0	0	0	61	318	772	961	1 321	..	..
Nepal	251	320	544	1 293	1 768	1 451	1 451	1 713	1 256	..	..
Pakistan	169	298	241	212	296	289	469	720	971	..	..
Myanmar	491	368	380	434	808	651	962	656	788	..	..
India	51	125	163	225	228	470	603	549	730	..	..
Bangladesh	98	169	190	284	244	241	438	542	662	..	..
Cameroon	48	58	99	56	51	66	98	203	234	..	..
Sénegal	4	2	7	7	0	45	..	..	223	..	..
Uganda	30	24	31	11	20	39	..	..	193	..	..
China	20	32	35	43	159	156	315	308	134	..	..
Nigeria	51	112	68	79	148	108	..	..	120	..	..
Philippines	15	18	57	73	295	1 412	4 897	860	108	..	..
Tunisia	5	15	21	5	11	63	..	..	86	..	..
Other countries	176	327	423	948	2 098	3 510	5 821	1 867	688	..	..
Total	**1 867**	**2 545**	**3 260**	**5 000**	**7 580**	**10 901**	**19 250**	**10 493**	**10 375**	**3 936**	**..**

Note: For details on definitions and sources, refer to the metadata at the end of the tables.

StatLink https://stat.link/hovm34

Table B.3. New asylum requests by nationality – Korea

	2011	2012	2013	2014	2015	2016	2017	2018	2019	2020	2021
China	8	3	46	359	401	1 062	1 413	1 199	2 000	311	301
Bangladesh	38	32	45	52	388	335	383	608	491	435	233
Nigeria	39	102	206	203	265	324	486	390	270	147	164
India	15	7	2	34	292	218	691	1 120	959	420	148
Pakistan	434	244	275	396	1 143	809	667	1 120	790	303	131
Egypt	4	6	97	568	812	1 002	741	870	114	718	117
Nepal	14	43	90	79	230	217	149	175	291	260	108
Philippines	1	4	2	0	128	260	246	507	229	154	105
Myanmar	64	32	11	5	26	52	48	27	59	37	73
Uzbekistan	2	3	1	0	71	145	43	146	235	168	64
Liberia	20	28	42	59	68	155	175	250	144	61	53
Ghana	0	9	22	87	175	121	150	203	143	70	52
Ethiopia	6	15	68	6	15	92	62	75	76	74	51
Iraq	4	2	1	10	41	22	13	16	27	23	51
Kyrgyzstan	28	0	0	0	12	92	71	112	86	41	49
Other countries	334	613	666	1 038	1 643	2 636	4 841	9 447	9 519	3 444	628
Total	**1 011**	**1 143**	**1 574**	**2 896**	**5 710**	**7 542**	**9 942**	**16 147**	**15 433**	**6 666**	**2 328**

Note: For details on definitions and sources, refer to the metadata at the end of the tables.

StatLink https://stat.link/hovm34

Table B.3. New asylum requests by nationality – Latvia

	2011	2012	2013	2014	2015	2016	2017	2018	2019	2020	2021
Iraq	..	0	2	15	85	6	5	20	5	5	350
Afghanistan	..	4	0	5	33	35	15	5	5	10	70
Belarus	..	0	2	0	0	4	5	0	5	45	55
Russia	..	8	5	0	0	27	25	50	25	10	30
Azerbaijan	..	2	0	0	5	4	5	15	35	10	15
Uzbekistan	..	0	3	0	0	2	5	0	5	5	5
Türkiye	..	2	1	0	0	4	10	10	5	5	5
India	..	0	0	0	0	20	5	5	15	5	5
Iran	..	6	1	0	0	1	0	0	5	5	5
Cameroon	..	0	0	0	0	0	0	0	0	0	5
Pakistan	..	2	0	0	5	17	0	5	5	5	5
Cuba	..	0	0	0	0	0	0	5	5	0	5
Sri Lanka	..	0	1	0	0	6	0	5	0	0	5
Dem. Rep. of the Congo	..	23	0	0	0	1	0	0	0	0	5
Ukraine	..	0	0	66	39	6	5	5	10	0	5
Other countries	..	142	170	278	163	211	275	50	55	40	10
Total	335	189	185	364	330	344	355	175	180	145	580

Note: For details on definitions and sources, refer to the metadata at the end of the tables.

StatLink 🔗 https://stat.link/hovm34

Table B.3. New asylum requests by nationality – Lithuania

	2011	2012	2013	2014	2015	2016	2017	2018	2019	2020	2021
Iraq	1	..	..	..	25	40	0	35	10	15	2 370
Belarus	12	..	..	..	15	10	35	15	15	80	245
Congo	0	..	..	..	0	0	0	0	0	0	150
Cameroon	0	..	..	..	0	0	0	0	0	0	120
Russia	58	..	..	..	35	50	80	50	275	65	115
Afghanistan	45	..	..	..	30	30	15	20	10	10	115
Syria	1	..	..	..	5	165	170	15	15	5	110
Guinea	1	..	..	..	0	0	0	0	0	0	80
Iran	0	..	..	..	0	0	0	15	5	0	75
Sri Lanka	0	..	..	..	0	5	20	15	0	5	65
India	0	..	..	..	10	0	0	0	5	0	65
Dem. Rep. of the Congo	2	..	..	..	0	0	0	0	0	0	40
Nigeria	1	..	..	..	0	0	0	10	5	0	35
Tajikistan	4	..	..	..	5	20	50	120	205	40	35
Pakistan	0	..	..	..	0	5	10	0	0	0	30
Other countries	281	..	..	..	150	90	140	90	80	40	255
Total	406	526	275	406	275	415	520	385	625	260	3 905

Note: For details on definitions and sources, refer to the metadata at the end of the tables.

StatLink 🔗 https://stat.link/hovm34

Table B.3. New asylum requests by nationality – Luxembourg

	2011	2012	2013	2014	2015	2016	2017	2018	2019	2020	2021
Syria	10	14	24	78	635	289	405	280	375	360	445
Eritrea	14	7	5	15	23	105	230	410	565	255	320
Afghanistan	22	11	17	0	211	56	40	180	170	100	115
Iraq	41	31	27	0	527	161	140	185	130	65	50
Sudan	1	2	4	0	0	14	30	65	40	15	40
Venezuela	0	0	0	0	0	1	0	10	65	45	35
Ethiopia	6	5	4	0	0	13	25	30	25	10	30
Cameroon	5	6	4	0	0	18	15	15	25	20	25
Türkiye	21	10	3	0	8	15	10	45	60	45	25
Iran	22	30	22	0	55	50	20	50	55	55	25
Algeria	30	33	38	26	6	75	160	75	75	35	20
Somalia	12	13	7	0	0	21	20	30	45	20	15
Tunisia	42	46	52	18	0	38	100	90	30	20	15
Guinea	3	10	5	0	0	18	35	50	40	25	15
Morocco	4	8	25	0	6	74	205	90	45	25	15
Other countries	1 843	1 777	752	836	829	990	890	620	455	200	170
Total	**2 076**	**2 003**	**989**	**973**	**2 300**	**1 938**	**2 325**	**2 225**	**2 200**	**1 295**	**1 360**

Note: For details on definitions and sources, refer to the metadata at the end of the tables.

StatLink ᵐˢ᠍ᵖ https://stat.link/hovm34

Table B.3. New asylum requests by nationality – Mexico

	2011	2012	2013	2014	2015	2016	2017	2018	2019	2020	2021
Haiti	38	..	..	..	..	47	436	82	5 536	5 964	51 827
Honduras	168	..	..	..	..	4 119	4 272	13 631	30 093	15 469	36 361
Cuba	48	..	..	..	..	43	796	212	8 683	5 758	8 319
Chile	1	..	..	..	..	0	5	5	418	808	6 970
Venezuela	2	..	..	..	..	361	4 042	6 344	7 665	3 292	6 223
El Salvador	181	..	..	..	..	3 488	3 708	6 186	8 999	4 053	6 037
Guatemala	69	..	..	..	..	437	676	1 383	3 778	3 005	4 149
Brazil	1	..	..	..	..	3	5	5	552	372	3 836
Nicaragua	6	..	..	..	..	70	62	1 246	2 232	802	2 919
Colombia	43	..	..	..	..	44	96	204	558	501	1 275
Senegal	0	..	..	..	..	1	0	5	0	13	334
Ghana	14	..	..	..	..	16	24	19	86	105	309
Ecuador	6	..	..	..	..	20	23	22	78	85	245
Dem. Rep. of the Congo	9	..	..	..	..	5	0	5	221	128	209
Argentina	6	..	..	..	..	2	0	7	30	50	201
Other countries	161	..	..	..	..	125	508	417	1 437	799	2 204
Total	**753**	**811**	**1 296**	**1 524**	**3 420**	**8 781**	**14 596**	**29 623**	**70 366**	**41 204**	**131 418**

Note: For details on definitions and sources, refer to the metadata at the end of the tables.

StatLink ᵐˢ᠍ᵖ https://stat.link/hovm34

Table B.3. New asylum requests by nationality – Netherlands

	2011	2012	2013	2014	2015	2016	2017	2018	2019	2020	2021
Syria	168	454	2 673	8 748	18 675	2 226	2 965	2 960	3 675	4 070	8 395
Afghanistan	1 885	1 022	673	452	2 550	1 045	320	325	435	390	3 025
Türkiye	96	89	59	35	33	298	480	1 300	1 250	990	2 465
Yemen	12	26	39	18	33	45	170	530	645	410	1 190
Algeria	13	28	29	0	29	992	890	1 270	1 210	995	1 105
Morocco	22	24	69	42	76	1 274	980	1 065	1 060	775	915
Somalia	1 415	877	3 078	349	257	157	125	135	220	200	905
Eritrea	458	424	978	3 833	7 344	1 523	1 590	1 410	500	370	775
Iraq	1 435	1 391	1 094	616	3 009	952	845	745	620	335	750
Pakistan	94	150	150	181	157	162	180	310	395	265	440
Nigeria	129	106	136	223	216	201	245	560	2 105	635	420
Tunisia	22	16	20	0	5	205	170	385	295	240	265
Iran	929	834	728	505	1 890	890	720	1 870	1 535	370	265
Russia	451	743	263	163	126	123	315	295	400	180	205
Colombia	7	4	12	6	0	36	35	45	160	105	185
Other countries	4 454	3 476	4 398	8 679	8 700	8 285	6 060	7 260	8 035	3 390	3 525
Total	**11 590**	**9 664**	**14 399**	**23 850**	**43 100**	**18 414**	**16 090**	**20 465**	**22 540**	**13 720**	**24 830**

Note: For details on definitions and sources, refer to the metadata at the end of the tables.

StatLink ᴹˢᴾ https://stat.link/hovm34

Table B.3. New asylum requests by nationality – New Zealand

	2011	2012	2013	2014	2015	2016	2017	2018	2019	2020	2021
India	1	9	2	0	0	31	43	49	66	43	140
China	20	33	21	6	7	64	76	103	91	60	68
Sri Lanka	19	25	41	6	7	11	30	42	50	25	29
Indonesia	1	2	8	0	0	5	0	0	5	111	26
Myanmar	1	3	4	0	0	0	5	10	0	0	17
Russia	1	1	0	0	0	5	22	5	11	11	15
Bangladesh	8	8	6	0	0	11	27	12	21	7	12
Malaysia	1	4	1	0	0	12	10	18	36	38	11
South Africa	14	0	9	0	11	15	5	5	14	8	10
Philippines	1	2	2	0	0	3	10	5	11	11	9
United States	0	2	3	0	0	0	5	0	5	5	7
Thailand	1	0	0	0	0	3	0	0	0	0	6
Colombia	4	1	1	0	0	8	5	10	14	12	6
Uruguay	1	0	0	0	0	0	0	5	0	5	5
Egypt	22	4	7	0	0	2	5	0	10	0	5
Other countries	210	230	186	276	325	217	317	191	204	99	50
Total	**305**	**324**	**291**	**288**	**350**	**387**	**560**	**455**	**538**	**435**	**416**

Note: For details on definitions and sources, refer to the metadata at the end of the tables.

StatLink ᴹˢᴾ https://stat.link/hovm34

Table B.3. New asylum requests by nationality – Norway

	2011	2012	2013	2014	2015	2016	2017	2018	2019	2020	2021
Syria	198	312	868	1 978	10 520	510	1 000	415	535	540	585
Afghanistan	979	987	720	549	6 916	373	135	90	95	55	250
Eritrea	1 256	1 600	3 766	2 805	2 785	353	840	220	180	150	185
China	101	85	98	12	53	23	25	15	15	15	100
Türkiye	42	38	62	34	78	89	160	770	360	85	100
Colombia	5	0	6	0	0	8	15	10	35	25	45
Ethiopia	293	221	356	365	662	157	85	40	40	20	35
Iraq	357	229	179	165	2 939	214	140	95	50	35	30
Iran	355	435	274	84	1 308	132	85	110	70	45	30
Venezuela	0	0	0	0	0	8	10	20	20	15	30
Albania	43	167	179	202	431	130	85	65	60	15	15
Somalia	2 216	2 803	2 530	756	501	154	45	45	30	20	15
Russia	365	294	339	172	105	76	45	50	80	25	10
Yemen	47	34	37	14	54	12	10	10	30	10	10
Belarus	52	136	46	17	5	9	10	5	0	5	10
Other countries	2 744	2 444	2 007	5 487	4 163	954	695	590	605	280	165
Total	**9 053**	**9 785**	**11 467**	**12 640**	**30 520**	**3 202**	**3 385**	**2 550**	**2 205**	**1 340**	**1 615**

Note: For details on definitions and sources, refer to the metadata at the end of the tables.

StatLink 🔗 https://stat.link/hovm34

Table B.3. New asylum requests by nationality – Poland

	2011	2012	2013	2014	2015	2016	2017	2018	2019	2020	2021
Belarus	64	61	23	0	0	35	30	25	30	385	2 130
Afghanistan	35	88	43	14	5	19	25	40	55	120	1 595
Iraq	25	25	24	19	33	41	40	65	30	40	1 280
Russia	3 034	4 940	11 933	2 079	6 985	7 488	2 120	1 600	1 770	495	340
Syria	11	107	255	98	278	42	40	25	25	35	125
Ukraine	43	58	32	2 147	1 573	589	300	225	215	95	115
Tajikistan	0	9	5	107	526	835	85	35	80	45	95
Iran	10	15	9	0	0	15	10	30	35	10	60
Türkiye	11	8	12	0	10	65	45	55	115	70	60
Somalia	9	7	25	0	0	1	5	0	5	5	55
Georgia	1 427	2 960	1 057	561	232	56	20	20	50	20	45
San Marino	0	0	0	0	0	0	0	0	0	0	40
Yemen	0	0	0	0	6	2	0	10	5	10	30
Cuba	2	0	0	0	0	2	5	0	30	0	25
India	1	6	5	0	0	5	10	15	20	5	15
Other countries	414	883	335	1 785	602	645	270	260	300	175	230
Total	**5 086**	**9 167**	**13 758**	**6 810**	**10 250**	**9 840**	**3 005**	**2 405**	**2 765**	**1 510**	**6 240**

Note: For details on definitions and sources, refer to the metadata at the end of the tables.

StatLink 🔗 https://stat.link/hovm34

Table B.3. New asylum requests by nationality – Portugal

	2011	2012	2013	2014	2015	2016	2017	2018	2019	2020	2021
Afghanistan	4	5	2	0	0	18	30	5	20	10	595
Morocco	5	4	15	6	6	4	10	30	35	85	115
India	0	1	1	0	0	2	0	0	5	0	80
Gambia	2	1	6	0	0	22	20	20	175	150	65
Guinea	46	64	81	0	25	52	45	70	120	80	50
Guinea-Bissau	11	19	17	0	0	5	10	50	155	90	50
Senegal	5	7	36	0	0	26	25	20	70	80	45
Angola	5	4	2	5	7	30	120	225	305	115	45
Türkiye	1	1	0	0	0	4	5	25	10	5	25
Sierra Leone	7	4	5	0	0	24	35	15	45	15	25
Ghana	1	2	0	0	0	3	10	10	20	15	20
Nigeria	22	27	37	0	0	4	10	20	60	35	15
Pakistan	11	9	26	0	44	25	20	50	10	5	15
Venezuela	0	0	0	0	0	16	35	40	95	15	15
Algeria	0	0	1	0	0	10	20	5	15	5	15
Other countries	155	151	278	431	818	1 218	620	655	595	195	175
Total	**275**	**299**	**507**	**442**	**900**	**1 463**	**1 015**	**1 240**	**1 735**	**900**	**1 350**

Note: For details on definitions and sources, refer to the metadata at the end of the tables.

StatLink ▓▒▒▒ https://stat.link/hovm34

Table B.3. New asylum requests by nationality – Slovak Republic

	2011	2012	2013	2014	2015	2016	2017	2018	2019	2020	2021
Morocco	0	6	0	0	0	1	5	0	5	40	105
Afghanistan	75	63	84	67	23	8	25	30	85	50	90
Algeria	8	13	1	0	0	6	5	0	5	20	20
India	24	1	0	0	0	5	0	0	5	10	15
Sri Lanka	1	0	0	0	0	1	5	0	0	10	10
Syria	10	4	13	27	0	10	10	10	5	35	10
Türkiye	12	11	3	0	0	0	5	5	5	20	10
Pakistan	15	5	8	0	0	13	10	10	5	5	10
Libya	1	1	3	0	0	7	5	0	0	15	10
Egypt	2	2	1	0	0	1	0	0	0	5	5
Nepal	0	0	0	0	0	0	0	0	0	0	5
West Bank and Gaza Strip	2	5	1	0	0	0	0	0	0	0	5
Bangladesh	8	3	1	5	0	1	5	0	15	15	5
Tunisia	1	3	0	0	0	0	0	0	0	10	5
Cameroon	1	9	2	0	0	0	0	0	0	0	5
Other countries	331	606	164	129	247	47	80	100	85	30	20
Total	**491**	**732**	**281**	**228**	**270**	**100**	**155**	**155**	**215**	**265**	**330**

Note: For details on definitions and sources, refer to the metadata at the end of the tables.

StatLink ▓▒▒▒ https://stat.link/hovm34

Table B.3. New asylum requests by nationality – Slovenia

	2011	2012	2013	2014	2015	2016	2017	2018	2019	2020	2021
Afghanistan	69	50	14	58	31	409	575	455	415	740	2 590
Pakistan	29	6	19	20	17	104	140	775	520	490	490
Iran	11	2	6	6	5	73	50	160	120	50	325
Türkiye	51	26	11	5	0	60	100	65	65	55	275
Bangladesh	0	0	3	0	0	2	5	60	175	150	265
Iraq	8	1	0	0	32	108	20	95	85	85	255
Morocco	9	7	9	0	0	38	40	170	720	1 215	160
Egypt	6	1	1	5	0	1	10	15	40	145	105
Syria	11	32	56	77	8	273	90	155	60	55	90
Algeria	11	23	14	0	0	41	190	470	1 010	275	80
Tunisia	25	8	3	0	0	11	15	40	130	30	55
Nepal		0	0	0	0	0	5	25	0	10	55
Gambia	2	2	2	0	0	4	0	5	5	0	45
Cuba	0	7	7	0	0	4	10	0	30	0	40
India	3	0	0	0	0	7	5	35	25	20	35
Other countries	138	140	98	190	167	128	185	275	215	145	355
Total	**373**	**305**	**243**	**361**	**260**	**1 263**	**1 440**	**2 800**	**3 615**	**3 465**	**5 220**

Note: For details on definitions and sources, refer to the metadata at the end of the tables.

StatLink https://stat.link/hovm34

Table B.3. New asylum requests by nationality – Spain

	2011	2012	2013	2014	2015	2016	2017	2018	2019	2020	2021
Venezuela	52	28	35	122	515	4 099	10 325	19 070	40 305	28 065	15 655
Colombia	104	60	62	91	87	641	2 410	8 465	28 880	27 180	11 100
Morocco	37	47	46	91	397	343	510	1 280	1 190	1 440	4 470
Mali	41	101	1 478	619	176	229	265	650	1 190	665	3 145
Senegal	21	26	45	14	10	47	190	435	720	665	3 145
Peru	1	5	7	0	0	32	200	525	3 965	5 145	2 235
Honduras	45	41	38	39	111	397	960	2 400	6 730	5 465	2 195
Afghanistan	30	46	66	89	26	69	95	70	115	30	1 580
Pakistan	78	88	102	137	62	181	185	360	495	700	1 415
Nicaragua	11	6	13	0	0	20	30	1 360	5 840	3 680	1 195
Cuba	440	64	58	0	21	64	125	355	1 295	1 485	1 065
Syria	97	255	725	1 666	5 627	3 052	4 150	2 725	2 315	330	1 060
El Salvador	21	36	23	48	90	439	1 100	2 240	4 715	2 475	815
Ukraine	12	21	14	937	2 570	2 422	2 185	1 880	2 240	1 010	800
Algeria	122	202	351	302	650	752	1 140	1 215	1 275	650	700
Other countries	2 302	1 553	1 450	1 792	3 028	3 487	6 575	9 715	12 640	7 120	8 195
Total	**3 414**	**2 579**	**4 513**	**5 947**	**13 370**	**16 274**	**30 445**	**52 745**	**115 190**	**86 385**	**62 065**

Note: For details on definitions and sources, refer to the metadata at the end of the tables.

StatLink https://stat.link/hovm34

Table B.3. New asylum requests by nationality – Sweden

	2011	2012	2013	2014	2015	2016	2017	2018	2019	2020	2021
Syria	640	7 814	16 317	30 313	50 909	4 731	5 250	2 615	5 015	1 760	2 165
Afghanistan	4 122	4 755	3 011	2 882	41 281	2 144	1 245	615	745	850	990
Eritrea	1 647	2 356	4 844	11 057	6 513	744	1 540	750	1 155	1 205	665
Iraq	1 633	1 322	1 476	1 743	20 259	2 046	1 475	1 065	940	765	515
Türkiye	139	149	187	152	222	690	825	440	635	395	495
Somalia	3 981	5 644	3 901	3 783	4 695	1 279	550	430	730	615	490
Ukraine	194	133	173	1 278	1 327	543	460	500	835	515	445
Iran	1 120	1 529	1 172	799	4 281	935	905	1 095	985	580	310
Ethiopia	269	339	383	467	1 602	376	295	280	265	345	260
Georgia	280	748	625	735	782	638	1 005	1 040	905	355	225
Russia	933	941	1 036	712	497	261	315	300	305	110	165
West Bank and Gaza Strip	0	0	0	22	407	165	270	340	595	290	160
Uzbekistan	377	366	349	279	282	221	280	665	965	720	160
Albania	263	1 490	1 156	1 636	2 559	729	685	570	490	190	145
Nigeria	340	501	601	438	409	303	320	320	300	205	135
Other countries	13 710	15 789	19 028	18 800	20 435	6 606	6 805	7 085	8 285	4 730	2 855
Total	**29 648**	**43 876**	**54 259**	**75 096**	**156 460**	**22 411**	**22 225**	**18 110**	**23 150**	**13 630**	**10 180**

Note: For details on definitions and sources, refer to the metadata at the end of the tables.

StatLink 🔗 https://stat.link/hovm34

Table B.3. New asylum requests by nationality – Switzerland

	2011	2012	2013	2014	2015	2016	2017	2018	2019	2020	2021
Afghanistan	1 006	1 349	863	727	7 800	3 183	1 180	1 125	1 350	1 630	2 960
Türkiye	508	515	373	264	387	475	770	925	1 225	1 130	2 245
Eritrea	3 225	4 295	2 490	6 820	9 859	5 040	3 155	2 495	2 500	1 635	1 725
Algeria	464	681	714	337	284	521	515	710	780	935	960
Syria	688	1 146	1 852	3 768	4 649	2 040	1 810	1 195	945	755	905
Morocco	429	860	974	666	372	793	420	440	320	370	510
Iraq	378	382	351	279	2 286	1 251	545	520	490	270	495
Somalia	558	762	552	769	1 214	1 530	795	510	360	260	395
Georgia	281	614	565	402	365	396	615	805	530	205	335
Sri Lanka	433	443	455	906	1 777	1 317	730	500	475	340	270
Iran	326	315	178	117	570	529	280	455	490	255	260
Ethiopia	184	293	221	312	565	1 008	305	190	145	100	175
Tunisia	2 324	1 993	1 565	664	283	213	180	245	125	135	170
Libya	243	183	140	161	122	199	140	155	115	130	165
China	688	801	671	376	578	333	255	260	225	125	140
Other countries	7 704	11 316	7 476	5 545	7 009	7 044	4 975	3 005	2 525	1 490	1 585
Total	**19 439**	**25 948**	**19 440**	**22 113**	**38 120**	**25 872**	**16 670**	**13 535**	**12 600**	**9 765**	**13 295**

Note: For details on definitions and sources, refer to the metadata at the end of the tables.

StatLink 🔗 https://stat.link/hovm34

Table B.3. New asylum requests by nationality – Türkiye

	2011	2012	2013	2014	2015	2016	2017	2018	2019	2020	2021
Afghanistan	2 486	14 146	8 726	15 652	63 292	34 669	66 459	53 029	35 042	22 606	21 926
Iraq	7 912	6 942	25 280	50 510	56 332	28 479	43 711	19 959	15 532	5 875	4 961
Iran	3 411	3 589	5 897	8 202	11 023	11 856	8 828	6 387	3 558	1 425	1 032
Other countries	2 212	1 793	4 904	13 456	2 943	2 847	4 599	4 443	2 285	1 428	1 337
Total	**16 021**	**26 470**	**44 807**	**87 820**	**133 590**	**77 851**	**123 597**	**83 818**	**56 417**	**31 334**	**29 256**

Note: For details on definitions and sources, refer to the metadata at the end of the tables.

StatLink https://stat.link/hovm34

Table B.3. New asylum requests by nationality – United Kingdom

	2011	2012	2013	2014	2015	2016	2017	2018	2019	2020	2021
Iran	3 047	3 155	2 967	2 499	3 716	4 780	3 050	3 955	5 464	4 199	10 446
Iraq	367	411	450	911	2 648	3 644	3 260	3 595	3 901	3 281	7 721
Eritrea	836	764	1 431	3 291	3 756	1 278	1 125	2 195	1 927	2 604	5 019
Albania	427	987	1 641	1 972	1 998	1 756	1 690	2 370	3 970	3 071	4 754
Syria	499	1 289	2 020	2 353	2 794	1 587	795	915	1 374	1 746	3 895
Afghanistan	1 528	1 234	1 456	1 753	2 852	3 099	1 915	2 095	2 135	1 546	3 088
Sudan	791	732	834	1 615	3 018	1 462	1 830	1 770	1 784	2 153	2 385
Viet Nam	329	412	466	400	620	774	1 085	1 230	1 584	982	1 844
El Salvador	1	8	20	12	11	89	75	205	1 186	1 043	1 310
Pakistan	3 947	4 783	4 576	3 976	3 365	3 701	3 125	2 575	2 566	1 525	1 159
India	611	1 180	1 111	922	1 324	2 008	1 770	1 615	1 910	1 046	1 125
Nigeria	1 058	1 428	1 450	1 519	1 590	1 827	1 580	1 350	1 430	1 015	1 027
Bangladesh	666	1 155	1 246	919	1 320	2 226	1 980	1 440	1 364	876	887
Ethiopia	118	145	172	267	769	350	450	505	327	334	843
Kuwait	112	97	88	58	86	178	170	650	296	290	798
Other countries	11 561	10 198	9 467	9 877	10 103	9 621	9 480	10 900	13 249	10 316	10 165
Total	**25 898**	**27 978**	**29 395**	**32 344**	**39 970**	**38 380**	**33 380**	**37 365**	**44 467**	**36 027**	**56 466**

Note: For details on definitions and sources, refer to the metadata at the end of the tables.

StatLink https://stat.link/hovm34

Table B.3. New asylum requests by nationality – United States

	2011	2012	2013	2014	2015	2016	2017	2018	2019	2020	2021
Venezuela	764	716	882	3 113	7 354	18 312	29 926	27 483	25 664	23 530	27 020
Guatemala	3 671	4 152	4 865	9 098	16 419	25 723	35 318	33 073	51 502	36 490	23 008
Honduras	1 559	2 115	3 165	6 798	14 255	19 470	28 806	24 435	39 466	30 815	19 596
El Salvador	4 324	4 587	5 692	10 093	18 883	33 620	49 459	33 391	33 619	23 352	14 913
Cuba	242	195	185	155	112	147	730	1 512	9 155	9 497	12 879
Mexico	8 304	11 067	10 077	13 987	19 294	27 879	26 065	20 026	22 525	15 402	12 135
Colombia	642	574	631	817	1 058	1 767	3 204	2 678	3 334	3 852	11 263
Haiti	1 377	1 612	1 879	2 196	2 220	3 969	8 643	4 112	3 945	7 116	10 038
Ecuador	807	1 394	1 848	3 545	3 732	4 423	3 884	2 386	2 748	3 378	5 625
Brazil	340	444	311	492	983	1 454	2 625	2 282	2 798	4 593	4 915
India	2 477	1 998	1 633	3 395	3 650	6 162	7 435	9 440	10 607	5 599	4 886
Nicaragua	312	280	259	349	387	518	857	1 527	5 474	3 736	4 724
China	15 649	15 884	12 295	13 716	15 083	19 868	17 374	9 426	10 267	10 144	4 418
Russia	888	881	950	1 103	1 699	2 158	2 936	1 900	2 595	2 775	3 831
Nigeria	260	337	289	548	770	1 308	3 052	3 464	2 764	2 437	2 928
Other countries	18 971	19 865	23 282	51 755	66 841	95 192	111 386	77 165	74 602	68 224	26 681
Total	**60 587**	**66 101**	**68 243**	**121 160**	**172 740**	**261 970**	**331 700**	**254 300**	**301 065**	**250 940**	**188 860**

Note: For details on definitions and sources, refer to the metadata at the end of the tables.

StatLink ᵐˢᴾ https://stat.link/hovm34

Metadata related to Tables A.3. and B.3. **Inflows of asylum seekers**

Totals in Table A.3 might differ from the tables by nationality (Tables B.3) because the former totals get revised retroactively while the origin breakdown does not. Data for Table A.3 generally refer to first instance/new applications only and exclude repeat/review/appeal applications while data by origin (Tables B.3) may include some repeat/review/appeal applications. Data by country of origin since 2014 may be slightly underestimated as they are the sum of monthly data where only cells with 5 people and above were filled.

Comments on countries of asylum:

France: Data include unaccompanied minors.

Germany: Germany has a pre-registration system (EASY system). Asylum requests officially registered and presented in this section are lower than the pre-registrations in the EASY system (1.1 million in 2015).

EU countries and United Kingdom: Figures are rounded to the nearest multiple of 5.

United States: In Table B.3, data are a combination of the United States Citizenship and Immigration Service (USCIS – number of cases) affirmative asylum applications, and of the Executive Office for Immigration Review (EOIR – number of persons) defensive asylum applications, if the person is under threat of removal. Factors have been applied to totals since 2010 in both Table A.3. and Table B.3 to reflect the estimated number of cases.

Comments on countries of origin:

Serbia (and Kosovo): Data may include asylum seekers from Serbia, Montenegroand/or Former Yugoslavia.

Source for all countries: European countries: Eurostat; other countries: governments, compiled by the United Nations High Commissioner for Refugees, Population Data Unit (https://popstats.unhcr.org/refugee-statistics/download/).

Stocks of foreign and foreign-born populations

Who is an immigrant?

There are major differences in how immigrants are defined across OECD countries. Some countries have traditionally focused on producing data on foreign residents (European countries, Japan and Korea), whilst others refer to the foreign-born (settlement countries, i.e. Australia, Canada, New Zealand and the United States). This difference in focus relates in part to the nature and history of immigration systems and legislation on citizenship and naturalisation.

The foreign-born population can be viewed as representing first-generation migrants, and may consist of both foreign and national citizens. The size and composition of the foreign-born population is influenced by the history of migration flows and mortality amongst the foreign-born. For example, where inflows have been declining over time, the stock of the foreign-born will tend to age and represent an increasingly established community.

The concept of foreign population may include persons born abroad who retained the nationality of their country of origin but also second and third generations born in the host country. The characteristics of the population of foreign nationals depend on a number of factors: the history of migration flows, natural increase in the foreign population and naturalisations. Both the nature of legislation on citizenship and the incentives to naturalise play a role in determining the extent to which native-born persons may or may not be foreign nationals.

Sources for and problems in measuring the immigrant population

Four types of sources are used: population registers, residence permits, labour force surveys and censuses. In countries which have a population register and in those which use residence permit data, stocks and flows of immigrants are most often calculated using the same source. There are exceptions, however, with some countries using census or labour force survey data to estimate the stock of the immigrant population. In studying stocks and flows, the same problems are encountered whether population register or permit data are used (in particular, the risk of underestimation when minors are registered on the permit of one of the parents or if the migrants are not required to have permits because of a free movement agreement). To this must be added the difficulty of purging the files regularly to remove the records of persons who have left the country.

Census data enable comprehensive, albeit infrequent analysis of the stock of immigrants (censuses are generally conducted every five to ten years). In addition, many labour force surveys now include questions about nationality and place of birth, thus providing a source of annual stock data. The OECD produces estimates of stocks for some countries.

Some care has to be taken with detailed breakdowns of the immigrant population from survey data since sample sizes can be small. Both census and survey data may underestimate the number of immigrants because they can be missed in the census or because they do not live in private households (labour force surveys may not cover those living in collective dwelling such as reception centres and hostels for immigrants). Both these sources may cover a portion of the unauthorised population, which is by definition excluded from population registers and residence permit systems.

Table A.4. Stocks of foreign-born population in OECD countries

Thousands and percentages

	2011	2012	2013	2014	2015	2016	2017	2018	2019	2020	2021
Australia	6 018	6 214	6 409	6 570	6 730	6 912	7 139	7 333	7 533	7 653	7 529
% of total population	26.7	27.1	27.6	27.8	28.1	28.5	29.0	29.5	29.9	30.0	29.2
Austria	1 295	1 323	1 365	1 415	1 485	1 595	1 656	1 697	1 729	1 765	1 797
% of total population	15.3	15.6	16.0	16.4	17.1	18.2	18.8	19.1	19.3	19.6	19.9
Belgium	1 629	1 644	1 748	1 776	1 786	1 849	1 893	1 933	1 981	2 056	2 079
% of total population	14.8	14.8	15.7	15.8	15.8	16.3	16.6	16.8	17.2	17.7	17.9
Canada	6 776	6 914	7 029	7 156	7 287	7 541	7 714	7 896	..	..	..
% of total population	19.6	19.8	19.9	20.1	20.2	20.7	21.0	21.3	..	..	..
Chile	369	388	416	442	465	..	746	..	1 252	1 493	..
% of total population	2.1	2.2	2.4	2.5	2.6	..	4.0	..	6.6	7.8	..
Czech Republic	745	744	745	755	770	798	829	833	903	..	..
% of total population	7.1	7.0	7.0	7.1	7.3	7.5	7.8	7.8	8.5	..	..
Denmark	429	442	456	476	501	541	571	592	608	614	617
% of total population	7.7	7.9	8.1	8.4	8.8	9.5	10.0	10.3	10.5	10.6	10.6
Estonia	212.7	210.8	199.0	196.9	194.7	193.9	192.6	196.3	198.1	199.0	198.2
% of total population	16.0	15.9	15.0	14.9	14.8	14.7	14.6	14.8	14.9	14.9	15.0
Finland	248	266	285	304	322	337	358	373	387	404	421
% of total population	4.6	4.9	5.2	5.6	5.9	6.1	6.5	6.8	7.0	7.3	7.6
France	7 373	7 475	7 591	7 715	7 847	8 028	8 099	8 200	8 429	8 522	8 571
% of total population	11.7	11.8	11.9	12.0	12.2	12.4	12.5	12.6	12.9	13.1	13.3
Germany	10 503	9 752	10 047	10 401	10 792	11 392	12 609	13 043	13 457	13 682	13 561
% of total population	13.0	12.0	12.4	12.8	13.2	13.9	15.3	15.7	16.1	16.3	16.2
Greece	1 325	1 313	1 280	1 265	1 243	1 220	1 251	1 278	1 307	1 348	1 362
% of total population	12.2	12.2	11.9	11.8	11.7	11.5	11.8	12.1	12.5	12.9	13.1
Hungary	441	403	424	448	476	504	514	537	565	594	598
% of total population	4.5	4.1	4.3	4.6	4.9	5.2	5.3	5.5	5.8	6.2	6.2
Iceland	35	35	35	37	39	42	47	55	61	67	69
% of total population	10.7	10.6	10.8	11.3	11.9	12.6	13.9	16.2	18.1	19.6	20.1
Ireland	767	771	779	790	805	810	818	834	868	..	..
% of total population	16.7	16.7	16.9	17.1	17.3	17.3	17.2	17.3	17.8	..	..
Israel	1 869	1 850	1 835	1 821	1 817	1 818	1 812	1 811	1 809	1 812	1 797
% of total population	25.0	24.3	23.7	23.2	22.8	22.4	22.0	21.6	21.2	20.9	20.4
Italy	5 759	5 715	5 696	5 737	5 805	5 907	6 054	6 175	6 069	6 161	6 262
% of total population	9.7	9.5	9.5	9.5	9.6	9.7	10.0	10.2	10.0	10.2	10.4
Latvia	303	289	279	271	265	259	251	246	242	237	230
% of total population	14.5	14.0	13.7	13.4	13.3	13.1	12.9	12.8	12.7	12.6	12.3
Lithuania	208	207	..	137	136	130	127	131	138	153	165
% of total population	6.7	6.8	..	4.6	4.6	4.5	4.5	4.7	5.0	5.6	6.1
Luxembourg	205	215	226	238	249	261	271	281	291	302	302
% of total population	39.5	40.6	41.7	42.9	43.9	45.0	45.7	46.5	47.3	48.2	48.2
Mexico	967	974	991	940	1 007	..	..	1 075	..	1 212	..
% of total population	0.8	0.8	0.8	0.8	0.8	..	..	0.9	..	0.9	..
Netherlands	1 869	1 906	1 928	1 953	1 996	2 057	2 137	2 216	2 299	2 400	2 451
% of total population	11.2	11.4	11.4	11.6	11.8	12.1	12.6	13.0	13.4	14.0	14.3
New Zealand	956	965	1 002	1 050	1 108	1 169	1 231	1 272	..	..	..
% of total population	21.6	21.6	22.2	23.0	24.0	25.1	26.2	27.4	..	..	..
Norway	569	616	664	705	742	772	800	822	842	868	878
% of total population	11.5	12.3	13.1	13.7	14.3	14.7	15.1	15.4	15.6	16.0	16.1

	2011	2012	2013	2014	2015	2016	2017	2018	2019	2020	2021
Poland	675	631	625	620	612	626	652	696	761	849	..
% of total population	1.8	1.6	1.6	1.6	1.6	1.6	1.7	1.8	2.0	2.2	..
Portugal	872	983	1 017	991	998	1 007	1 011	1 050	1 107	1 263	..
% of total population	8.2	9.3	9.7	9.5	9.6	9.8	9.8	10.2	10.8	12.4	..
Slovak Republic	146	170	173	175	178	182	186	190	194	198	202
% of total population	2.7	3.1	3.2	3.2	3.3	3.3	3.4	3.5	3.6	3.6	3.7
Slovenia	229	230	233	235	238	241	245	250	265	282	293
% of total population	11.1	11.2	11.3	11.4	11.5	11.6	11.8	12.0	12.8	13.5	14.1
Spain	6 282	6 295	6 175	5 958	5 891	5 918	6 025	6 201	6 539	6 997	7 215
% of total population	13.3	13.4	13.2	12.7	12.6	12.7	12.9	13.3	14.0	15.0	15.4
Sweden	1 385	1 427	1 473	1 533	1 604	1 676	1 784	1 877	1 956	2 020	2 047
% of total population	14.6	15.0	15.3	15.8	16.4	17.0	18.0	18.8	19.5	20.0	20.1
Switzerland	2 075	2 158	2 218	2 290	2 355	2 416	2 480	2 519	2 553	2 590	2 630
% of total population	26.2	27.0	27.4	27.9	28.4	28.8	29.3	29.5	29.7	29.9	30.2
Türkiye	..	..	..	1 460	1 592	1 777	1 924	2 278	2 669	2 610	3 141
% of total population	..	..	..	1.9	2.0	2.2	2.4	2.8	3.2	3.1	3.7
United Kingdom	7 430	7 588	7 860	8 064	8 482	8 988	9 369	9 183	9 482	9 539	..
% of total population	11.6	11.8	12.1	12.3	12.9	13.6	14.0	13.7	14.0	14.0	..
United States	40 382	40 738	41 344	42 391	43 290	43 739	44 525	44 729	44 933	44 258	45 273
% of total population	13.0	13.0	13.1	13.3	13.5	13.5	13.7	13.7	13.7	13.4	13.5

Note: For details on definitions and sources, refer to the metadata at the end of the Tables B.4. The percentage of total population is based on the UN estimates of the total population and may differ from national estimates.

StatLink 🖳 https://stat.link/k6lfds

Table B.4. Stocks of foreign-born population by country of birth – Australia

Thousands

	2011	2012	2013	2014	2015	2016	2017	2018	2019	2020	2021	Of which: Women 2021 (%)
United Kingdom	1196.0	1211.5	1220.2	1216.3	1209.1	1202.1	1196.0	1188.1	1180.6	1172.7	1180.6	49
China	387.4	406.4	432.4	466.5	508.9	557.7	606.3	649.4	677.2	650.6	677.2	55
India	337.1	355.4	378.5	411.2	449.0	489.4	538.1	592.8	660.4	721.1	660.4	45
New Zealand	544.0	569.6	585.4	583.7	575.4	568.2	567.3	567.7	569.5	564.8	569.5	49
Philippines	193.0	206.1	218.9	230.2	241.1	252.7	265.8	277.6	293.8	310.1	293.8	61
Viet Nam	207.6	212.1	219.9	228.5	235.6	243.2	250.6	257.0	262.9	270.3	262.9	56
South Africa	161.6	167.6	172.2	174.9	177.4	180.5	185.5	189.3	193.9	200.2	193.9	50
Italy	201.7	200.4	200.7	200.4	198.5	195.8	191.5	187.0	182.5	177.8	182.5	49
Malaysia	134.1	136.6	138.4	139.4	143.4	152.9	164.7	173.6	175.9	177.5	175.9	53
Sri Lanka	99.7	105.0	110.7	115.1	119.7	124.5	129.5	134.4	140.3	147.0	140.3	47
Nepal	27.8	30.7	34.8	42.9	50.2	59.0	73.8	94.8	117.9	131.8	117.9	45
Korea	85.9	91.6	97.9	101.9	106.6	111.6	114.8	116.4	116.0	111.5	116.0	54
Germany	125.8	124.7	123.1	120.8	119.1	116.7	115.9	114.3	112.4	111.0	112.4	53
United States	90.1	96.7	100.8	102.7	104.7	105.8	108.1	108.4	108.6	110.2	108.6	52
Greece	121.2	120.5	119.8	118.3	115.8	113.4	111.5	109.1	106.7	103.7	106.7	52
Other countries	2 105.1	2 179.2	2 255.3	2 317.6	2 375.3	2 438.8	2 519.4	2 572.8	2 634.5	2 692.8	2 631.1	
Total	**6 018.2**	**6 214.0**	**6 408.7**	**6 570.2**	**6 729.7**	**6 912.1**	**7 138.6**	**7 332.6**	**7 533.0**	**7 653.2**	**7 529.6**	**51**

Note: For details on definitions and sources, refer to the metadata at the end of the tables.

StatLink ⬛ https://stat.link/5cmqi8

Table B.4. Stocks of foreign-born population by country of birth – Austria

Thousands

	2011	2012	2013	2014	2015	2016	2017	2018	2019	2020	2021	Of which: Women 2021 (%)
Germany	196.9	201.4	205.9	210.7	215.0	219.9	224.0	227.8	232.2	237.8	244.9	52
Bosnia and Herzegovina	149.7	150.5	151.7	155.1	158.9	162.0	164.3	166.8	168.5	170.5	172.4	50
Türkiye	158.5	158.7	159.2	160.0	160.0	160.2	160.4	160.3	159.7	159.6	159.1	48
Serbia	130.9	130.2	130.9	132.6	134.7	137.1	139.1	141.9	143.2	144.4	144.4	52
Romania	64.5	69.1	73.9	79.3	91.3	98.7	105.6	113.3	121.1	128.8	134.2	52
Hungary	39.3	42.6	48.1	55.0	61.5	67.7	72.4	75.8	79.0	81.9	83.9	54
Poland	57.8	60.5	63.2	66.8	69.9	72.2	73.8	75.1	75.6	76.1	76.6	51
Syria	3.0	3.4	4.2	5.2	12.3	33.6	41.6	47.0	48.5	49.7	52.3	40
Croatia	39.3	39.1	39.0	39.8	41.7	43.3	44.5	45.2	46.7	48.1	50.6	52
Slovak Republic	26.0	27.7	30.0	32.6	35.5	38.0	40.0	41.5	42.7	43.8	44.9	62
Afghanistan	8.4	11.0	13.6	18.2	20.3	36.6	44.7	44.4	43.1	42.2	42.2	34
Italy	25.2	25.3	26.2	27.7	29.3	31.2	32.3	33.3	34.1	35.1	35.9	45
Russia	26.4	27.5	29.4	30.2	31.7	33.0	33.9	34.4	34.7	35.2	35.8	60
Czech Republic	43.6	42.5	41.6	40.8	40.3	39.6	38.7	37.8	37.0	36.3	35.5	63
Bulgaria	14.6	15.7	17.0	18.5	21.6	23.8	25.7	27.4	29.2	31.1	32.2	54
Other countries	310.5	317.8	330.8	342.1	360.6	397.7	415.4	425.3	433.2	444.5	452.6	
Total	**1 294.7**	**1 323.1**	**1 364.8**	**1 414.6**	**1 484.6**	**1 594.7**	**1 656.3**	**1 697.1**	**1 728.6**	**1 765.3**	**1 797.6**	**51**

Note: For details on definitions and sources, refer to the metadata at the end of the tables.

StatLink ⬛ https://stat.link/5cmqi8

Table B.4. Stocks of foreign-born population by country of birth – Belgium

Thousands

	2011	2012	2013	2014	2015	2016	2017	2018	2019	2020	2021	Of which: Women 2021 (%)
Morocco	189.1	197.1	201.9	204.8	208.1	211.2	214.1	217.4	221.0	226.5	229.7	50
France	175.0	176.9	179.2	180.8	182.2	183.7	184.5	184.9	186.1	189.2	191.0	54
Netherlands	126.4	126.9	127.4	127.9	128.5	129.4	129.8	130.0	130.7	131.6	131.8	50
Italy	120.2	119.7	119.5	119.7	120.0	120.1	119.7	119.1	119.1	119.5	118.3	49
Romania	37.7	45.0	52.7	57.9	65.2	71.7	77.3	83.5	90.9	99.9	104.7	45
Türkiye	97.0	98.0	98.5	98.4	98.3	98.3	98.5	99.1	100.1	102.0	102.6	48
Dem. Rep. of the Congo	81.3	82.0	83.1	83.5	83.6	84.1	84.4	84.9	85.4	86.4	86.7	54
Germany	84.2	83.9	83.2	82.4	81.5	81.1	80.6	80.2	80.2	80.2	79.8	54
Poland	57.7	63.0	67.8	70.9	73.4	75.5	76.3	76.9	77.4	78.2	77.5	57
Former USSR	51.1	51.0	51.5	51.1	51.8	51.2	51.7	53.1	54.6	58.5	58.2	60
Spain	38.8	40.5	42.8	44.7	46.0	47.0	47.2	47.9	48.9	50.5	51.7	53
Former Yugoslavia	47.3	45.7	44.2	43.1	43.1	42.9	42.9	43.1	43.8	46.9	44.9	50
Bulgaria	18.7	21.1	23.9	26.1	28.7	31.3	32.9	34.8	36.9	40.4	42.6	50
Portugal	28.3	29.4	31.5	33.3	34.3	35.2	36.1	36.4	36.8	37.7	38.0	48
Syria	5.8	6.2	7.2	8.1	10.9	21.3	25.1	30.0	33.1	35.7	36.4	43
Other countries	470.7	493.6	509.9	518.1	530.4	565.2	579.7	599.2	628.2	673.3	685.9	
Total	**1 629.4**	**1 679.8**	**1 724.4**	**1 750.8**	**1 786.1**	**1 849.3**	**1 880.8**	**1 920.5**	**1 973.0**	**2 056.4**	**2 079.8**	**51**

Note: For details on definitions and sources, refer to the metadata at the end of the tables.

StatLink ⬛⬛ https://stat.link/5cmqi8

Table B.4. Stocks of foreign-born population by country of birth – Canada

Thousands

	2011	2012	2013	2014	2015	2016	2017	2018	2019	2020	2021	Of which: Women 2016 (%)
India	547.9	..	..	..	..	668.6	..	..	..	..	..	50
China	545.5	..	..	..	..	649.3	..	..	..	..	..	55
Philippines	454.3	..	..	..	..	588.3	..	..	..	..	..	58
United Kingdom	537.0	..	..	..	..	499.1	..	..	..	..	..	51
United States	263.5	..	..	..	..	253.7	..	..	..	..	..	55
Italy	256.8	..	..	..	..	236.6	..	..	..	..	..	50
Hong Kong (China)	205.4	..	..	..	..	208.9	..	..	..	..	..	53
Pakistan	156.9	..	..	..	..	202.3	..	..	..	..	..	49
Viet Nam	165.1	..	..	..	..	169.3	..	..	..	..	..	54
Iran	120.7	..	..	..	..	154.4	..	..	..	..	..	50
Poland	152.3	..	..	..	..	146.5	..	..	..	..	..	55
Germany	152.3	..	..	..	..	145.8	..	..	..	..	..	52
Portugal	138.5	..	..	..	..	139.5	..	..	..	..	..	51
Jamaica	126.0	..	..	..	..	138.3	..	..	..	..	..	57
Sri Lanka	132.1	..	..	..	..	132.0	..	..	..	..	..	51
Other countries	2 821.2	..	..	..	..	3 208.3	..	..	..	..	..	
Total	**6 775.8**	**..**	**..**	**..**	**..**	**7 540.8**	**..**	**..**	**..**	**..**	**..**	**52**

Note: For details on definitions and sources, refer to the metadata at the end of the tables.

StatLink ⬛⬛ https://stat.link/5cmqi8

Table B.4. Stocks of foreign-born population by country of birth – Chile

Thousands

	2011	2012	2013	2014	2015	2016	2017	2018	2019	2020	2021	Of which: Women 2020 (%)
Venezuela	..	..	..	..	..	..	83.0	..	287.9	455.5	..	50
Peru	138.5	146.6	157.7	..	..	..	187.8	..	223.9	235.2	..	52
Haiti	..	..	..	..	..	..	62.7	..	178.8	185.9	..	36
Colombia	14.4	16.1	19.1	..	..	..	105.4	..	147.4	161.2	..	53
Bolivia	25.1	26.7	30.5	..	..	..	73.8	..	107.5	120.1	..	54
Argentina	61.9	63.2	64.9	..	..	..	66.5	..	74.4	79.5	..	49
Ecuador	20.0	20.9	21.9	..	..	..	27.7	..	36.8	41.4	..	51
Spain	11.3	11.6	12.1	..	..	..	16.7	..	20.6	22.5	..	45
Dominican Republic	..	..	..	..	..	..	11.9	..	20.5	20.1	..	59
Brazil	10.1	10.5	11.2	..	..	..	14.2	..	18.1	20.0	..	54
United States	10.0	10.4	10.9	..	..	..	12.3	..	16.2	18.5	..	50
Cuba	..	..	..	..	..	..	6.7	..	15.8	16.3	..	42
China	5.2	5.9	6.6	..	..	..	10.1	..	13.6	15.7	..	42
France	..	..	..	..	..	..	5.4	..	8.7	10.5	..	48
Mexico	..	..	..	..	..	..	5.8	..	8.8	10.4	..	53
Other countries	73.0	76.3	80.6	..	..	..	56.3	..	72.6	80.0	..	
Total	**369.4**	**388.2**	**415.5**	**441.5**	**465.3**	**..**	**746.4**	**..**	**1 251.6**	**1 492.5**	**..**	**49**

Note: For details on definitions and sources, refer to the metadata at the end of the tables.

StatLink 🔢 https://stat.link/5cmqi8

Table B.4. Stocks of foreign-born population by country of birth – Czech Republic

Thousands

	2011	2012	2013	2014	2015	2016	2017	2018	2019	2020	2021	Of which: Women 2021 (%)
Ukraine	..	109.7	99.8	94.2	100.7	104.1	110.3	107.5	122.9	136.8	156.6	43
Slovak Republic	..	76.2	80.3	84.7	89.3	94.0	98.9	102.4	106.6	110.1	112.7	47
Viet Nam	..	48.4	46.2	45.9	45.5	45.6	46.6	46.1	47.2	47.7	48.0	46
Russia	..	29.0	29.2	30.6	32.7	33.7	36.2	33.4	35.1	35.3	39.3	55
Poland	..	18.2	18.4	18.6	18.8	19.0	19.4	19.7	20.3	20.7	19.6	52
Germany	..	12.6	13.6	14.7	15.6	16.2	16.8	16.8	16.9	17.1	16.6	19
Bulgaria	..	7.0	7.7	8.5	9.3	10.1	11.2	12.6	14.2	15.6	16.2	37
Moldova	..	7.4	6.3	6.2	6.8	7.3	8.3	8.3	9.5	10.5	11.4	40
Romania	..	4.5	5.0	5.0	5.4	6.1	7.1	8.0	9.1	9.9	10.5	29
Kazakhstan	..	5.2	5.7	6.1	6.6	7.0	7.8	7.1	7.5	7.5	8.4	50
Mongolia	..	4.6	4.4	4.4	4.6	5.1	5.8	6.4	7.3	8.0	8.1	54
United Kingdom	..	4.3	4.5	4.6	4.9	5.1	5.3	5.6	6.0	7.0	7.6	23
China	..	4.5	4.5	4.6	4.8	4.9	5.4	5.7	6.2	6.4	6.8	47
Belarus	..	3.9	3.9	4.0	4.1	4.2	4.5	4.6	5.5	6.3	6.3	50
United States	..	3.5	3.8	5.5	5.2	5.4	7.7	7.6	7.6	5.6	6.2	39
Other countries	..	51.9	54.0	58.6	62.2	65.6	73.7	75.9	85.1	89.1	95.8	
Total	**..**	**390.8**	**387.3**	**396.2**	**416.5**	**433.3**	**465.1**	**467.6**	**507.1**	**533.6**	**570.1**	**42**

Note: For details on definitions and sources, refer to the metadata at the end of the tables.

StatLink 🔢 https://stat.link/5cmqi8

Table B.4. Stocks of foreign-born population by country of birth – Denmark

Thousands

	2011	2012	2013	2014	2015	2016	2017	2018	2019	2020	2021	Of which: Women 2021 (%)
Poland	26.6	28.0	29.9	32.0	34.5	37.1	39.1	40.6	41.5	41.5	41.9	47
Syria	2.4	3.1	4.0	5.8	11.6	24.1	33.6	35.4	35.9	35.5	35.7	44
Türkiye	32.5	32.4	32.2	32.4	32.4	32.5	32.6	32.9	33.1	33.1	33.2	48
Germany	28.5	28.6	28.7	28.7	28.7	29.1	29.6	29.8	30.3	30.6	30.9	52
Romania	7.7	10.1	12.9	15.7	18.7	21.9	24.3	26.3	28.5	29.4	30.3	43
Iraq	21.3	21.2	21.2	21.1	21.2	21.2	21.4	21.6	21.9	21.8	21.9	45
Iran	12.5	12.9	13.3	14.1	14.9	15.6	16.0	16.8	17.1	17.2	17.6	43
Bosnia and Herzegovina	17.8	17.6	17.4	17.3	17.3	17.2	17.1	17.1	17.0	16.8	16.6	50
United Kingdom	12.1	12.2	12.5	12.8	13.0	13.4	14.1	14.8	15.3	15.5	15.8	35
Norway	14.7	14.9	14.9	14.9	15.1	15.6	15.8	15.8	15.7	15.7	15.6	65
Sweden	13.2	13.1	13.1	13.2	13.4	13.6	13.8	14.2	14.3	14.4	14.6	61
Pakistan	11.7	12.1	12.3	12.9	13.5	13.8	14.0	14.2	14.4	14.5	14.5	48
Afghanistan	10.6	11.1	11.6	12.1	12.6	12.8	13.0	13.5	13.8	13.9	13.9	45
Lithuania	6.3	7.3	8.3	9.0	9.7	10.6	11.3	12.4	13.2	13.2	13.2	48
Lebanon	12.1	12.0	12.1	12.2	12.3	12.6	12.7	12.8	12.9	13.0	13.1	46
Other countries	199.1	204.9	212.0	221.8	232.3	249.5	262.2	273.5	282.9	288.2	289.0	
Total	**428.9**	**441.5**	**456.4**	**476.1**	**501.1**	**540.5**	**570.6**	**591.7**	**607.6**	**614.4**	**617.8**	**50**

Note: For details on definitions and sources, refer to the metadata at the end of the tables.

StatLink https://stat.link/5cmqi8

Table B.4. Stocks of foreign-born population by country of birth – Estonia

Thousands

	2011	2012	2013	2014	2015	2016	2017	2018	2019	2020	2021	Of which: Women 2020 (%)
Russia	..	83.8	138.5	136.4	129.2	126.2	122.9	120.6	118.1	115.9	113.1	63
Ukraine	..	15.7	21.7	21.5	21.8	22.4	22.7	23.2	24.0	25.0	26.4	47
Belarus	..	9.1	11.6	11.5	11.1	10.9	10.7	10.6	10.4	10.4	10.3	61
Latvia	..	2.7	4.1	4.2	4.7	4.8	4.9	5.5	6.0	6.1	6.2	49
Finland	..	4.1	2.4	2.3	3.9	4.3	4.7	5.4	5.9	6.0	6.1	41
Kazakhstan	..	2.6	3.8	4.0	3.8	3.7	3.7	3.7	3.7	3.8	3.8	57
Lithuania	..	1.5	1.9	1.8	2.0	2.0	2.1	2.1	2.2	2.1	2.1	55
Germany	..	1.5	1.3	1.3	1.8	1.9	2.0	2.4	2.5	2.4	2.0	56
Georgia	..	0.8	1.5	1.5	1.6	1.7	1.7	1.7	1.8	1.8	1.8	49
Azerbaijan	..	1.2	1.5	1.5	1.5	1.5	1.5	1.5	1.6	1.7	1.7	41
United Kingdom	..	0.6	0.6	0.6	0.7	0.7	0.8	1.2	1.3	1.4	..	31
United States	..	0.3	0.7	0.8	0.6	0.7	0.7	1.1	1.2	1.2	..	38
Italy	..	0.5	0.3	0.3	0.6	0.7	0.8	1.1	1.2	1.2	..	34
Moldova	..	0.6	0.8	0.9	0.9	0.9	1.0	1.0	1.1	1.1	..	41
Uzbekistan	..	0.7	1.1	1.1	1.1	1.1	1.1	1.1	1.1	1.1	..	56
Other countries	..	85.1	7.0	7.2	9.4	10.4	11.4	14.1	16.0	18.0	24.9	
Total	**212.7**	**210.8**	**199.0**	**196.9**	**194.7**	**193.9**	**192.6**	**196.3**	**198.1**	**199.0**	**198.2**	**56**

Note: For details on definitions and sources, refer to the metadata at the end of the tables.

StatLink https://stat.link/5cmqi8

Table B.4. Stocks of foreign-born population by country of birth – Finland

Thousands

	2011	2012	2013	2014	2015	2016	2017	2018	2019	2020	2021	Of which: Women 2021 (%)
Estonia	25.0	29.5	35.0	39.5	42.7	44.5	45.7	46.0	46.2	46.0	46.2	50
Sweden	31.2	31.4	31.6	31.8	31.9	32.0	32.1	32.4	32.7	32.9	33.4	48
Iraq	7.2	7.9	8.4	9.3	10.0	10.7	13.8	16.3	17.9	19.0	20.1	36
Russia	8.0	9.0	10.0	11.1	12.0	12.8	13.7	14.2	14.9	15.7	16.6	54
China	7.0	7.7	8.3	8.9	9.4	10.0	10.4	10.9	11.4	11.9	12.6	57
Somalia	8.1	8.8	9.1	9.6	10.1	10.6	11.1	11.4	11.8	12.1	12.4	48
Thailand	6.7	7.4	8.1	8.7	9.2	9.7	10.2	10.5	10.9	11.3	11.7	79
Viet Nam	4.5	4.8	5.2	5.5	6.0	6.6	7.5	8.0	8.5	9.0	9.4	55
Türkiye	5.1	5.4	5.7	6.1	6.3	6.5	6.8	7.1	7.5	8.2	8.8	34
India	4.0	4.3	4.6	4.9	5.4	5.7	5.8	6.2	6.8	7.9	8.4	42
Iran	4.1	4.4	4.9	5.3	5.8	6.1	6.8	7.2	7.4	7.9	8.3	44
Afghanistan	2.6	2.9	3.3	3.7	4.0	4.3	5.7	6.4	6.9	7.3	7.8	38
Syria	0.4	0.5	0.6	0.8	1.4	2.0	3.6	5.4	6.1	6.8	7.1	44
Germany	5.9	6.1	6.2	6.4	6.5	6.6	6.6	6.6	6.7	6.9	7.1	44
United Kingdom	4.5	4.8	5.1	5.3	5.5	5.7	5.9	6.1	6.3	6.7	6.9	28
Other countries	123.7	131.3	139.5	147.5	155.8	163.4	171.7	178.1	185.5	194.6	204.0	
Total	**248.1**	**266.1**	**285.5**	**304.3**	**322.0**	**337.2**	**357.5**	**372.8**	**387.2**	**404.2**	**420.8**	48

Note: For details on definitions and sources, refer to the metadata at the end of the tables.

StatLink 🔗 https://stat.link/5cmqi8

Table B.4. Stocks of foreign-born population by country of birth – France

Thousands

	2011	2012	2013	2014	2015	2016	2017	2018	2019	2020	2021	Of which: Women 2020 (%)
Algeria	1 357.5	1 359.8	1 363.9	1 368.4	1 375.3	1 383.7	1 386.4	1 390.3	1 386.2	1 397.4		51
Morocco	895.6	907.8	924.0	935.4	953.5	967.2	981.2	992.1	1 009.6	1 019.5		51
Portugal	618.3	625.2	633.2	642.1	648.1	648.1	644.2	624.2	614.2	614.2		50
Tunisia	377.3	381.2	387.6	393.9	397.8	403.7	410.7	415.6	427.8	427.0		46
Italy	337.5	331.7	327.6	325.0	323.9	322.7	322.0	314.9	315.4	315.4		51
Spain	282.5	282.5	283.4	284.6	286.2	285.2	284.1	275.8	274.1	274.1		56
Türkiye	257.6	259.5	260.2	261.2	260.5	258.2	257.7	256.7	264.0	257.6		47
Germany	217.6	213.8	211.6	209.9	208.3	206.4	204.3	198.3	190.3	190.3		57
United Kingdom	169.9	170.1	168.0	167.0	166.5	165.6	165.0	162.3	163.6	163.6		51
Belgium	148.2	148.5	149.7	151.2	152.7	154.1	155.6	154.3	163.6	163.6		54
Senegal	116.4	119.6	124.1	127.7	132.7	137.3	143.6	148.4	156.3	158.9		47
Madagascar	118.1	120.1	122.3	124.7	127.1	134.8	137.9	140.3	141.3	149.8		60
Comoros	38.0	39.3	40.3	42.5	45.0	108.4	131.4	137.6	143.3	149.7		55
Côte d'Ivoire	91.6	96.0	99.9	104.4	109.0	114.6	120.5	127.5	133.7	143.5		53
Romania	79.5	87.3	96.7	108.8	117.3	124.6	131.9	135.7	141.2	141.2		52
Other countries	2 267.3	2 332.2	2 398.6	2 468.5	2 543.5	2 613.7	2 622.5	2 725.6	2 904.1	2 955.9		
Total	**7 372.7**	**7 474.7**	**7 590.9**	**7 715.1**	**7 847.5**	**8 028.2**	**8 098.9**	**8 199.7**	**8 428.7**	**8 521.8**		52

Note: For details on definitions and sources, refer to the metadata at the end of the tables.

StatLink 🔗 https://stat.link/5cmqi8

Table B.4. Stocks of foreign-born population by country of birth – Germany

Thousands

	2011	2012	2013	2014	2015	2016	2017	2018	2019	2020	2021	Of which: Women 2021 (%)
Poland	1 113	1 076	1 147	1 203	1 253	1 328	1 460	1 553	1 668	1 638	1 445	54
Türkiye	1 471	1 298	1 292	1 313	1 343	1 362	1 321	1 194	1 319	1 339	1 276	49
Russia	980	961	950	959	936	954	955	1 057	1 076	1 076	948	56
Syria	41	35	42	53	70	141	453	620	711	721	864	40
Kazakhstan	697	735	728	728	725	735	735	909	946	926	824	52
Romania	371	377	422	460	484	545	653	670	779	813	734	51
Italy	414	372	371	417	425	439	506	467	508	522	512	40
Bosnia and Herzegovina	154	134	148	148	157	164	171	263	289	304	332	49
Greece	229	198	211	221	233	256	281	264	298	294	291	46
Croatia	225	199	205	208	219	254	305	242	278	297	282	52
Ukraine	227	205	205	210	214	211	222	255	269	264	265	61
Iraq	87	74	75	88	97	104	151	193	233	245	250	43
Afghanistan	93	88	83	90	101	111	176	179	209	233	249	39
Austria	192	165	179	186	185	189	189	192	209	207	246	49
Serbia	183	158	174	180	185	183	187	205	207	223	231	52
Other countries	4 026	3 677	3 815	3 937	4 165	4 416	4 844	4 780	4 458	4 580	4 812	
Total	10 503	9 752	10 047	10 401	10 792	11 392	12 609	13 043	13 457	13 682	13 561	49

Note: For details on definitions and sources, refer to the metadata at the end of the tables.

StatLink https://stat.link/5cmqi8

Table B.4. Stocks of foreign-born population by country of birth – Greece

Thousands

	2011	2012	2013	2014	2015	2016	2017	2018	2019	2020	2021	Of which: Women 2016 (%)
Albania	346.2	357.1	..	337.7	..	312.7	..	..	..	..	..	49
Georgia	53.0	54.2	..	45.1	..	43.3	..	..	..	..	..	62
Russia	44.4	37.8	..	43.0	..	35.3	..	..	..	..	..	67
Bulgaria	43.9	35.0	..	40.9	..	31.0	..	..	..	..	..	71
Germany	25.1	21.2	..	25.7	..	26.7	..	..	..	..	..	61
Romania	34.9	32.7	..	27.2	..	22.1	..	..	..	..	..	58
Ukraine	13.5	11.5	..	10.7	..	16.6	..	..	..	..	..	78
Pakistan	22.5	24.0	..	18.0	..	16.5	..	..	..	..	..	5
Armenia	10.6	9.6	..	7.7	..	11.4	..	..	..	..	..	63
Poland	7.3	9.4	..	16.6	..	10.8	..	..	..	..	..	61
Cyprus	12.8	10.3	..	10.9	..	9.8	..	..	..	..	..	50
Türkiye	6.1	9.4	..	12.5	..	9.4	..	..	..	..	..	50
United States	6.2	7.4	..	5.3	..	8.7	..	..	..	..	..	58
Egypt	13.6	11.4	..	9.8	..	7.7	..	..	..	..	..	49
Moldova	3.4	1.8	..	4.9	..	6.3	..	..	..	..	..	72
Other countries	107.3	97.3	..	111.5	..	80.2	..	..	..	..	..	
Total	750.7	729.9	..	727.5	..	648.5	..	..	..	..	..	54

Note: For details on definitions and sources, refer to the metadata at the end of the tables.

StatLink https://stat.link/5cmqi8

Table B.4. Stocks of foreign-born population by country of birth – Hungary

Thousands

	2011	2012	2013	2014	2015	2016	2017	2018	2019	2020	2021	Of which: Women 2021 (%)
Romania	201.9	183.1	190.9	198.4	203.4	208.4	206.3	207.4	207.1	210.4	208.0	51
Ukraine	13.4	25.5	28.8	33.3	42.0	50.2	55.8	61.6	68.5	72.2	71.5	49
Serbia	8.2	24.1	27.1	30.0	32.4	34.0	34.7	39.4	42.2	43.0	41.0	44
Germany	29.4	25.7	27.3	29.2	30.2	31.7	32.4	33.6	34.4	37.9	39.0	49
Former USSR	30.7	13.1	14.1	13.5	13.2	13.3	12.7	14.6	23.4	27.6	27.1	47
Slovak Republic	5.7	21.1	21.3	21.3	21.1	21.1	21.1	20.9	20.3	20.5	21.3	60
United Kingdom	4.7	4.9	5.6	6.8	7.9	9.4	11.2	12.9	14.6	16.7	18.0	46
China	10.9	9.0	9.9	11.1	14.8	18.2	17.5	18.2	17.0	17.8	16.8	49
Austria	7.8	7.6	8.1	8.8	9.3	9.9	10.3	10.6	10.8	11.5	13.0	46
United States	6.9	7.0	7.2	7.4	7.8	8.2	8.4	8.7	9.0	9.4	9.1	47
Former Czechoslovakia	24.1	5.6	5.8	6.0	6.2	6.2	5.8	5.5	5.5	5.8	8.6	59
Viet Nam	3.3	2.8	3.2	3.2	3.3	3.5	3.6	4.1	5.1	6.3	7.4	47
Italy	3.5	3.4	3.9	4.3	4.7	5.3	5.6	5.9	6.0	6.4	6.1	37
Former Yugoslavia	33.0	10.9	8.5	7.3	7.1	7.2	7.0	4.2	4.1	3.9	5.0	45
France	3.6	3.5	3.7	3.9	4.2	4.4	4.4	4.6	4.7	4.9	4.8	46
Other countries	53.6	55.5	58.8	63.0	68.5	73.3	77.3	84.3	92.5	100.1	101.3	
Total	**441.0**	**402.7**	**424.2**	**447.7**	**476.1**	**504.3**	**514.1**	**536.6**	**565.1**	**594.3**	**597.6**	**49**

Note: For details on definitions and sources, refer to the metadata at the end of the tables.

StatLink ⫘⫘ https://stat.link/5cmqi8

Table B.4. Stocks of foreign-born population by country of birth – Iceland

Thousands

	2011	2012	2013	2014	2015	2016	2017	2018	2019	2020	2021	Of which: Women 2021 (%)
Poland	9.5	9.3	9.4	10.2	11.0	12.0	13.8	17.0	19.2	20.5	20.6	42
Denmark	2.9	3.0	3.1	3.2	3.3	3.3	3.4	3.5	3.6	3.6	3.7	50
Lithuania	1.5	1.4	1.4	1.5	1.5	1.6	1.9	2.4	2.9	3.3	3.3	39
United States	1.8	1.8	2.0	2.0	2.0	2.1	2.2	2.3	2.4	2.5	2.7	49
Philippines	1.4	1.5	1.5	1.5	1.6	1.6	1.7	1.9	2.1	2.2	2.3	66
Sweden	1.8	1.9	1.9	1.9	1.9	2.0	2.0	2.1	2.2	2.2	2.2	51
Germany	1.7	1.6	1.5	1.6	1.6	1.7	1.8	1.9	2.0	2.1	2.2	63
Romania	0.2	0.2	0.3	0.3	0.4	0.5	0.7	1.1	1.5	2.0	2.1	32
Latvia	0.7	0.7	0.7	0.7	0.7	0.8	0.9	1.4	1.8	2.0	2.1	33
United Kingdom	1.1	1.2	1.2	1.2	1.3	1.4	1.5	1.6	1.7	1.8	2.0	39
Thailand	1.1	1.1	1.1	1.2	1.2	1.2	1.3	1.3	1.4	1.4	1.5	74
Norway	1.0	1.0	1.0	1.0	1.0	1.1	1.1	1.2	1.3	1.3	1.3	52
Spain	0.3	0.3	0.3	0.4	0.5	0.6	0.7	0.8	0.9	1.1	1.2	41
Portugal	0.5	0.4	0.5	0.5	0.6	0.6	0.7	0.8	1.0	1.1	1.0	35
Viet Nam	0.5	0.5	0.6	0.6	0.6	0.7	0.7	0.8	0.8	0.9	1.0	55
Other countries	8.6	8.7	9.0	9.4	9.9	10.7	12.1	14.5	16.7	18.7	19.9	
Total	**34.7**	**34.7**	**35.4**	**37.2**	**39.2**	**42.0**	**46.5**	**54.6**	**61.4**	**66.8**	**68.9**	**46**

Note: For details on definitions and sources, refer to the metadata at the end of the tables.

StatLink ⫘⫘ https://stat.link/5cmqi8

Table B.4. Stocks of foreign-born population by country of birth – Ireland

Thousands

	2011	2012	2013	2014	2015	2016	2017	2018	2019	2020	2021	Of which: Women 2016 (%)
United Kingdom	288.6	..	..	..	..	277.2	..	..	..	..	..	51
Poland	115.2	..	..	..	..	115.2	..	..	..	..	..	50
Lithuania	34.8	..	..	..	..	33.3	..	..	..	..	..	54
Romania	18.0	..	..	..	..	28.7	..	..	..	..	..	49
United States	27.7	..	..	..	..	28.7	..	..	..	..	..	55
India	17.9	..	..	..	..	21.0	..	..	..	..	..	45
Latvia	20.0	..	..	..	..	19.0	..	..	..	..	..	57
Nigeria	19.8	..	..	..	..	16.6	..	..	..	..	..	53
Brazil	9.3	..	..	..	..	15.8	..	..	..	..	..	53
Philippines	13.8	..	..	..	..	14.7	..	..	..	..	..	59
Germany	13.0	..	..	..	..	13.0	..	..	..	..	..	56
Pakistan	8.3	..	..	..	..	12.9	..	..	..	..	..	35
France	10.1	..	..	..	..	11.9	..	..	..	..	..	50
Spain	7.0	..	..	..	..	11.8	..	..	..	..	..	60
China	11.5	..	..	..	..	11.3	..	..	..	..	..	56
Other countries	151.8	..	..	..	..	179.5	..	..	..	..	..	
Total	**766.8**	..	..	..	..	**810.4**	..	..	..	..	..	**51**

Note: For details on definitions and sources, refer to the metadata at the end of the tables.

StatLink https://stat.link/5cmqi8

Table B.4. Stocks of foreign-born population by country of birth – Israel

Thousands

	2011	2012	2013	2014	2015	2016	2017	2018	2019	2020	2021	Of which: Women 2021 (%)
Former USSR	875.5	867.0	862.4	858.7	859.4	863.1	867.1	873.3	882.2	895.6	891.0	56
Morocco	152.0	149.6	147.2	145.4	143.1	140.9	138.8	136.1	133.2	130.3	126.9	53
United States	82.7	84.8	86.2	88.0	90.5	92.6	94.6	96.9	98.8	101.4	103.5	52
Ethiopia	78.9	81.9	84.6	85.9	85.6	85.7	85.5	87.0	86.9	87.5	88.6	51
France	42.9	43.5	44.2	46.3	51.1	57.0	60.1	62.6	64.0	65.3	66.5	54
Romania	93.1	90.0	87.0	84.0	80.8	77.8	74.8	71.8	68.8	66.0	63.2	56
Iraq	61.8	60.0	58.5	56.8	54.9	53.0	51.1	49.3	47.4	45.4	43.4	54
Iran	48.9	48.1	47.4	46.7	46.0	45.2	44.4	43.5	42.7	41.8	40.9	52
Argentina	37.5	37.6	36.8	36.3	36.0	35.6	35.4	35.1	34.8	34.9	35.1	53
Poland	50.7	48.0	45.0	42.2	39.7	37.2	34.8	32.6	30.5	28.6	26.8	58
United Kingdom	22.5	23.0	23.0	23.2	23.5	24.0	24.4	24.6	24.8	25.2	25.3	52
Tunisia	29.9	29.2	28.8	28.4	28.6	28.3	27.7	27.1	26.4	25.6	24.9	55
Türkiye	25.6	24.9	24.1	23.4	22.8	22.1	21.6	21.2	20.6	20.0	19.2	53
Yemen	27.9	26.9	24.1	25.4	22.5	21.6	22.7	21.7	20.9	19.9	18.9	57
India	17.6	17.5	17.4	17.5	18.0	18.0	17.8	17.9	18.1	17.9	17.8	53
Other countries	221.5	218.0	218.3	213.0	214.6	215.5	211.7	210.6	208.9	207.0	205.5	
Total	**1 869.0**	**1 850.0**	**1 835.0**	**1 821.0**	**1 817.0**	**1 817.5**	**1 812.4**	**1 811.2**	**1 808.9**	**1 812.2**	**1 797.3**	**55**

Note: For details on definitions and sources, refer to the metadata at the end of the tables.

StatLink https://stat.link/5cmqi8

Table B.4. Stocks of foreign-born population by country of birth – Italy

Thousands

	2011	2012	2013	2014	2015	2016	2017	2018	2019	2020	2021	Of which: Women 2021 (%)
Romania	1 011.7	1 003.7	1 000.1	1 004.6	1 016.0	1 024.1	1 036.0	1 033.0	984.5	979.1	913.2	60
Albania	438.0	434.3	432.7	440.1	446.6	449.7	458.2	467.9	463.0	478.3	505.3	49
Former USSR	..	..	..	..	..	..	..	..	..	448.2	462.8	80
Morocco	414.5	411.1	409.6	418.1	424.1	428.9	434.5	437.8	432.4	442.4	457.0	46
China	193.5	192.0	191.3	197.1	200.4	212.2	220.1	223.7	218.3	222.4	259.1	51
Germany	221.5	219.9	220.0	216.3	214.3	211.6	210.4	209.0	205.5	204.7	198.3	57
Former Yugoslavia	..	..	..	..	..	..	..	..	..	185.7	188.9	50
Switzerland	193.5	192.1	191.5	194.9	194.0	192.8	192.1	191.7	190.4	190.1	187.3	54
India	128.3	127.3	126.8	134.1	139.1	149.5	155.6	157.8	154.4	160.6	172.0	40
Philippines	137.0	135.9	135.4	141.1	143.2	145.5	147.8	148.5	140.8	141.6	149.0	60
Bangladesh	88.6	87.9	87.5	95.4	105.5	111.3	119.5	128.5	125.9	129.5	146.7	25
Egypt	106.6	105.8	105.5	106.7	108.9	112.8	117.7	121.8	120.9	127.5	137.3	31
Pakistan	77.9	77.3	77.1	83.4	89.5	97.8	108.9	116.7	117.9	121.5	135.0	26
Brazil	110.0	109.2	108.9	102.5	100.0	104.8	111.8	121.8	129.4	140.7	128.9	63
France	137.3	136.5	136.7	132.2	127.9	128.4	128.1	127.4	124.8	124.3	122.8	60
Other countries	2 500.5	2 482.0	2 472.8	2 470.8	2 495.8	2 538.1	2 613.2	2 689.8	2 660.8	2 064.9	2 098.6	
Total	**5 759.0**	**5 715.1**	**5 695.9**	**5 737.2**	**5 805.3**	**5 907.5**	**6 054.0**	**6 175.3**	**6 069.0**	**6 161.4**	**6 262.2**	53

Note: For details on definitions and sources, refer to the metadata at the end of the tables.

StatLink 🔢 https://stat.link/5cmqi8

Table B.4. Stocks of foreign-born population by country of birth – Latvia

Thousands

	2011	2012	2013	2014	2015	2016	2017	2018	2019	2020	2021	Of which: Women 2021 (%)
Russia	159.9	152.3	146.3	140.7	136.4	131.8	126.9	122.4	117.8	113.8	109.5	..
Belarus	55.1	53.2	51.5	50.0	48.6	47.2	45.5	43.9	42.6	41.3	39.8	..
Ukraine	38.4	36.8	35.7	34.7	34.1	34.0	33.0	32.5	32.6	32.4	31.7	..
Lithuania	19.7	18.6	17.9	17.2	16.7	16.1	15.4	14.9	14.3	13.9	13.4	..
Kazakhstan	6.7	6.4	6.2	6.0	5.9	5.9	5.8	5.7	5.7	5.6	5.5	..
United Kingdom	1.0	1.0	1.2	1.7	2.2	2.6	3.2	3.5	3.7	4.1	4.3	..
Uzbekistan	2.2	2.1	2.0	2.0	2.1	2.1	2.1	2.3	2.6	2.9	2.9	..
Estonia	3.2	3.1	3.1	3.1	3.1	3.0	3.0	2.9	2.9	2.8	2.8	..
Germany	2.5	2.2	2.1	2.3	2.4	2.1	2.1	2.1	2.2	2.2	2.2	..
Azerbaijan	2.2	2.1	2.0	2.0	1.9	1.9	1.9	1.9	2.0	2.0	1.9	..
Moldova	1.9	1.8	1.8	1.7	1.7	1.7	1.7	1.7	1.7	1.8	1.7	..
India	0.1	0.1	0.1	0.1	0.1	0.2	0.2	0.8	1.3	1.5	1.3	..
Georgia	1.5	1.4	1.4	1.3	1.3	1.3	1.3	1.3	1.3	1.3	1.3	..
Ireland	0.5	0.5	0.5	0.6	0.7	0.8	0.9	0.9	0.9	1.0	1.0	..
Kyrgyzstan	..	0.9	0.9	0.8	0.8	0.8	0.8	0.8	0.8	0.8	0.7	..
Other countries	8.1	6.6	6.5	6.9	7.4	7.4	7.7	8.3	9.3	9.8	10.0	
Total	**302.8**	**289.0**	**279.2**	**271.1**	**265.4**	**258.9**	**251.5**	**246.0**	**241.8**	**237.0**	**230.1**	..

Note: For details on definitions and sources, refer to the metadata at the end of the tables.

StatLink 🔢 https://stat.link/5cmqi8

Table B.4. Stocks of foreign-born population by country of birth – Lithuania

Thousands

	2011	2012	2013	2014	2015	2016	2017	2018	2019	2020	2021	Of which: Women 2021 (%)
Russia	88.9	86.3	..	60.1	58.5	54.9	52.3	50.5	49.1	48.3	47.2	58
Belarus	49.6	47.8	..	35.4	33.6	31.1	30.0	30.8	32.2	36.0	39.6	43
Ukraine	18.0	17.4	..	12.4	12.3	11.3	12.4	15.4	19.6	25.7	30.6	20
United Kingdom	..	10.3	..	3.3	4.3	5.2	5.0	5.4	6.3	8.0	9.1	48
Latvia	9.4	9.2	..	5.7	5.6	5.6	5.5	5.4	5.4	5.5	5.5	57
Kazakhstan	..	7.7	..	4.6	4.5	4.2	4.1	4.0	4.0	4.2	4.5	50
Norway	..		..	1.0	1.4	2.0	2.2	2.3	2.6	3.1	3.4	47
Germany	3.2	3.3	..	1.5	1.6	1.8	1.7	1.8	2.0	2.3	2.6	44
Ireland	..	3.9	..	1.3	1.5	1.6	1.6	1.6	1.7	1.9	2.1	49
Poland	3.3	3.2	..	2.3	2.2	2.1	2.0	1.9	1.8	1.8	1.7	56
Moldova	..		..	0.6	0.6	0.6	0.7	0.8	0.9	1.1	1.4	17
Uzbekistan	..	1.6	..	1.0	0.9	0.8	0.8	0.8	0.8	0.9	1.3	31
Spain	..	1.2	..	0.6	0.6	0.7	0.7	0.7	0.8	0.9	1.0	43
Estonia	..	1.3	..	0.8	0.8	0.8	0.8	0.8	0.8	0.8	0.8	55
Azerbaijan	..	1.3	..	0.9	0.9	0.7	0.7	0.7	0.7	0.7	0.8	34
Other countries	35.5	12.1	..	6.1	6.6	6.4	7.0	8.1	9.5	11.4	13.6	
Total	**207.9**	**206.6**	..	**137.4**	**136.0**	**129.7**	**127.4**	**131.0**	**138.2**	**152.6**	**165.2**	**44**

Note: For details on definitions and sources, refer to the metadata at the end of the tables.

StatLink ᵐˢ🔗 https://stat.link/5cmqi8

Table B.4. Stocks of foreign-born population by country of birth – Luxembourg

Thousands

	2011	2012	2013	2014	2015	2016	2017	2018	2019	2020	2021	Of which: Women 2021 (%)
Portugal	60.9	..	..	..	..	..	72.5	72.8	73.2	73.3	73.1	48
France	28.1	..	..	..	..	..	39.0	40.6	41.9	43.2	44.0	47
Belgium	16.8	..	..	..	..	..	20.5	20.8	21.0	21.3	21.4	46
Italy	13.2	..	..	..	..	..	17.0	17.7	18.4	19.0	19.3	42
Germany	14.8	..	..	..	..	..	16.5	16.5	16.7	16.7	16.7	53
Cape Verde	4.6	..	..	..	..	..	6.4	6.6	6.9	7.4	7.7	53
Spain	2.9	..	..	..	..	..	4.9	5.2	5.5	5.8	6.1	48
United Kingdom	4.2	..	..	..	..	..	5.1	5.3	5.5	5.5	5.8	43
Romania	1.9	..	..	..	..	..	4.2	4.6	5.1	5.5	5.8	58
Poland	2.9	..	..	..	..	..	4.5	4.6	4.9	5.1	5.2	58
China	1.9	..	..	..	..	..	3.3	3.7	4.0	4.5	4.5	56
Brazil	1.8	..	..	..	..	..	2.9	3.2	3.6	4.2	4.6	60
Netherlands	3.5	..	..	..	..	..	3.9	3.9	3.9	3.9	3.8	46
Greece	1.2	..	..	..	..	..	2.5	2.8	3.1	3.3	3.5	49
India	0.9	..	..	..	..	..	1.8	2.2	2.7	3.3	3.6	46
Other countries	45.5	215.3	226.1	237.7	248.9	260.6	65.8	70.0	74.7	79.9	84.4	
Total	**205.2**	**215.3**	**226.1**	**237.7**	**248.9**	**260.6**	**270.7**	**280.8**	**291.2**	**301.7**	**309.6**	**49**

Note: For details on definitions and sources, refer to the metadata at the end of the tables.

StatLink ᵐˢ🔗 https://stat.link/5cmqi8

Table B.4. Stocks of foreign-born population by country of birth – Mexico

Thousands

	2011	2012	2013	2014	2015	2016	2017	2018	2019	2020	2021	Of which: Women 2018 (%)
United States	..	..	..	..	739.2	..	..	799.1	..	797.3	..	50
Guatemala	..	..	..	..	42.9	..	..	32.4	..	56.8	..	51
Colombia	..	..	..	..	18.7	..	..	27.9	..	..	..	61
Venezuela	..	..	..	..	15.7	..	..	24.4	..	..	..	60
Spain	..	..	..	..	22.6	..	..	19.7	..	..	..	58
Honduras	..	..	..	..	14.5	..	..	18.4	..	..	..	51
Cuba	..	..	..	..	12.8	..	..	18.2	..	..	..	39
Canada	..	..	..	..	9.8	..	..	14.8	..	..	..	11
France	..	..	..	..	8.6	..	..	14.2	..	..	..	56
El Salvador	..	..	..	..	10.6	..	..	13.6	..	..	..	52
Argentina	..	..	..	..	14.7	..	..	10.5	..	..	..	69
Other countries	..	..	..	..	120.1	..	..	81.5	..	..	..	
Total	966.8	973.7	991.2	939.9	1 007.1	..	..	1 074.8	..	1 212	..	50

Note: For details on definitions and sources, refer to the metadata at the end of the tables.

StatLink https://stat.link/5cmqi8

Table B.4. Stocks of foreign-born population by country of birth – Netherlands

Thousands

	2011	2012	2013	2014	2015	2016	2017	2018	2019	2020	2021	Of which: Women 2021 (%)
Türkiye	197.4	197.4	196.5	195.1	192.7	191.0	190.8	192.0	194.3	198.0	200.0	49
Suriname	186.2	185.5	184.1	182.6	181.0	179.5	178.6	178.2	178.3	178.8	178.4	56
Morocco	167.7	168.3	168.2	168.5	168.6	168.5	168.7	169.2	170.5	172.2	172.7	49
Poland	66.6	78.2	86.5	96.2	108.5	117.9	126.6	135.6	145.2	155.2	164.2	52
Germany	122.3	122.8	121.8	120.5	119.1	118.6	118.8	119.5	120.6	122.0	122.5	58
Indonesia	137.8	135.1	132.0	129.2	126.4	123.5	120.8	117.9	115.1	112.5	108.8	57
Syria	7.1	7.3	7.7	9.5	17.9	38.5	65.9	81.8	86.7	91.9	97.4	44
Former USSR	45.6	49.2	51.8	53.7	56.4	59.1	62.2	66.6	72.1	78.9	82.5	62
China	44.7	47.5	49.7	51.3	52.5	54.4	56.1	58.3	61.1	64.2	63.8	57
Belgium	50.0	50.9	51.9	52.8	54.0	55.3	56.9	58.6	60.2	61.8	63.5	54
United Kingdom	47.2	47.5	47.8	48.4	49.1	50.2	51.7	53.4	55.8	59.0	61.1	44
Former Yugoslavia	52.7	52.7	52.5	52.5	52.6	52.7	53.1	53.5	54.3	55.6	56.0	53
India	18.2	19.5	20.7	22.2	24.3	27.0	30.6	35.3	41.2	48.2	49.2	44
Iraq	41.0	40.8	40.6	40.5	40.7	40.9	43.1	43.9	44.8	45.4	45.9	44
Italy	20.8	21.6	22.5	23.9	25.7	27.6	29.9	32.4	35.0	38.0	39.0	41
Other countries	663.4	682.0	693.4	706.5	726.8	751.8	783.4	819.7	863.5	918.1	946.2	
Total	1 868.7	1 906.3	1 927.7	1 953.4	1 996.3	2 056.5	2 137.2	2 215.9	2 298.7	2 399.8	2 451.2	52

Note: For details on definitions and sources, refer to the metadata at the end of the tables.

StatLink https://stat.link/5cmqi8

Table B.4. Stocks of foreign-born population by country of birth – New Zealand

Thousands

	2011	2012	2013	2014	2015	2016	2017	2018	2019	2020	2021	Of which: Women 2018 (%)
United Kingdom	..	..	255.0	..	..	..	..	265.5	..	..	..	49
China	..	..	89.1	..	..	..	..	132.9	..	..	..	55
India	..	..	67.2	..	..	..	..	117.3	..	..	..	42
Australia	..	..	62.7	..	..	..	..	75.8	..	..	..	53
South Africa	..	..	54.3	..	..	..	..	71.4	..	..	..	51
Philippines	..	..	37.3	..	..	..	..	67.6	..	..	..	52
Fiji	..	..	52.8	..	..	..	..	62.3	..	..	..	51
Samoa	..	..	50.7	..	..	..	..	55.5	..	..	..	51
Korea	..	..	26.6	..	..	..	..	31.0	..	..	..	54
United States	..	..	22.1	..	..	..	..	27.7	..	..	..	54
Tonga	..	..	22.4	..	..	..	..	26.9	..	..	..	48
Malaysia	..	..	16.4	..	..	..	..	19.9	..	..	..	54
Netherlands	..	..	19.9	..	..	..	..	19.3	..	..	..	50
Germany	..	..	12.9	..	..	..	..	16.6	..	..	..	57
Sri Lanka	..	..	9.6	..	..	..	..	14.3	..	..	..	47
Other countries	..	..	202.8	..	..	..	..	267.7	..	..	..	
Total	..	..	**1 001.8**	..	..	..	..	**1 271.8**	..	..	..	**51**

Note: For details on definitions and sources, refer to the metadata at the end of the tables.

StatLink ⏭ https://stat.link/5cmqi8

Table B.4. Stocks of foreign-born population by country of birth – Norway

Thousands

	2011	2012	2013	2014	2015	2016	2017	2018	2019	2020	2021	Of which: Women 2021 (%)
Poland	57.1	67.6	76.9	84.2	91.2	96.1	97.6	98.6	99.1	101.5	102.5	37
Sweden	44.6	47.0	47.8	48.6	49.2	49.1	48.3	47.9	47.7	47.7	47.8	49
Lithuania	15.6	22.7	28.6	33.0	35.9	37.4	37.7	38.4	39.4	40.7	41.4	42
Syria	1.5	1.6	2.0	3.1	5.5	9.7	20.8	27.4	30.8	32.0	32.8	41
Germany	26.2	27.3	27.8	27.9	28.2	28.2	28.0	27.8	28.0	28.4	28.7	48
Somalia	19.4	20.7	23.7	25.9	27.0	28.3	28.7	28.8	28.7	28.6	28.4	48
Philippines	14.7	16.3	17.8	19.5	20.6	21.4	22.2	23.1	24.1	25.1	25.0	76
Denmark	22.9	23.3	23.8	24.4	25.3	25.1	24.8	24.6	24.5	24.4	24.3	48
Eritrea	6.6	8.2	10.1	12.4	14.8	17.7	20.1	21.9	22.7	23.2	23.6	42
Thailand	14.1	15.2	16.4	17.3	18.0	18.9	20.1	21.1	22.0	22.8	23.3	81
Iraq	21.4	22.0	22.1	22.1	22.2	22.2	22.5	23.1	23.3	23.3	23.3	44
Pakistan	17.6	18.0	18.6	19.0	19.4	19.7	20.1	20.6	20.9	21.3	21.6	48
United Kingdom	17.5	18.1	18.6	19.0	19.3	19.5	19.4	19.4	19.7	20.3	20.8	39
United States	16.3	16.6	17.0	17.3	17.5	17.6	17.7	17.9	18.4	18.9	19.1	51
Russia	14.6	15.3	16.2	16.8	17.2	17.5	17.7	17.9	18.3	18.7	18.9	67
Other countries	259.0	276.6	296.4	313.9	330.4	344.0	354.1	363.8	374.3	390.8	396.6	
Total	**569.1**	**616.3**	**663.9**	**704.5**	**741.8**	**772.5**	**799.8**	**822.4**	**841.6**	**867.8**	**878.2**	**48**

Note: For details on definitions and sources, refer to the metadata at the end of the tables.

StatLink ⏭ https://stat.link/5cmqi8

Table B.4. Stocks of foreign-born population by country of birth – Poland

Thousands

	2011	2012	2013	2014	2015	2016	2017	2018	2019	2020	2021	Of which: Women 2011 (%)
Ukraine	227.5	..	..	..	..	..	..	..	..	..		..
Germany	84.0	..	..	..	..	..	..	..	..	..		..
Belarus	83.6	..	..	..	..	..	..	..	..	..		..
Lithuania	55.6	..	..	..	..	..	..	..	..	..		..
United Kingdom	38.0	..	..	..	..	..	..	..	..	..		..
Ireland	8.4	..	..	..	..	..	..	..	..	..		..
Other countries	177.8	..	..	..	..	..	..	..	..	..	..	
Total	675.0	631	625	620	612	626	652	696	761	849	..	59

Note: For details on definitions and sources, refer to the metadata at the end of the tables.

StatLink https://stat.link/5cmqi8

Table B.4. Stocks of foreign-born population by country of birth – Portugal

Thousands

	2011	2012	2013	2014	2015	2016	2017	2018	2019	2020	2021	Of which: Women 2011 (%)
Angola	162.6	..	..	..	..	..	..	..	..	..	..	54
Brazil	139.7	..	..	..	..	..	..	..	..	..	..	58
France	94.5	..	..	..	..	..	..	..	..	..	..	54
Mozambique	73.1	..	..	..	..	..	..	..	..	..	..	54
Cape Verde	62.0	..	..	..	..	..	..	..	..	..	..	53
Guinea-Bissau	29.6	..	..	..	..	..	..	..	..	..	..	44
Germany	28.0	..	..	..	..	..	..	..	..	..	..	52
Venezuela	25.2	..	..	..	..	..	..	..	..	..	..	54
Romania	23.7	..	..	..	..	..	..	..	..	..	..	49
United Kingdom	19.1	..	..	..	..	..	..	..	..	..	..	50
Sao Tome and Principe	18.6	..	..	..	..	..	..	..	..	..	..	56
Spain	16.5	..	..	..	..	..	..	..	..	..	..	57
Switzerland	16.5	..	..	..	..	..	..	..	..	..	..	49
South Africa	11.5	..	..	..	..	..	..	..	..	..	..	53
China	10.9	..	..	..	..	..	..	..	..	..	..	48
Other countries	140.5	..	..	..	..	..	..	..	..	..	..	
Total	871.8	..	..	..	..	..	..	..	..	..	..	53

Note: For details on definitions and sources, refer to the metadata at the end of the tables.

StatLink https://stat.link/5cmqi8

Table B.4. Stocks of foreign-born population by country of birth – Slovak Republic

Thousands

	2011	2012	2013	2014	2015	2016	2017	2018	2019	2020	2021	Of which: Women 2021 (%)
Czech Republic	..	88.7	88.6	88.2	88.0	87.8	88.0	88.0	88.1	88.2	88.2	55
Hungary	..	17.6	17.7	17.3	17.1	16.8	16.6	16.3	16.1	15.8	15.7	47
Ukraine	..	9.8	9.8	9.9	10.1	10.5	10.7	11.1	11.4	11.8	12.1	58
United Kingdom	..	3.7	4.2	4.8	5.5	6.3	7.2	8.1	9.1	10.2	11.0	44
Romania	..	7.6	7.8	8.1	8.3	8.7	9.1	9.3	9.6	9.7	9.8	35
Poland	..	6.5	6.5	6.7	6.7	6.9	7.0	7.1	7.3	7.4	7.5	51
Germany	..	4.2	4.4	4.6	4.8	5.1	5.4	5.8	6.1	6.5	6.9	35
Austria	..	2.8	3.0	3.1	3.4	3.7	4.0	4.3	4.7	5.0	5.3	42
Italy	..	2.2	2.4	2.7	2.8	3.1	3.4	3.7	3.9	4.0	4.2	27
Russia	..	2.7	2.7	2.7	2.8	2.9	2.9	3.0	3.1	3.1	3.2	63
France	..	3.0	2.9	2.9	2.9	3.0	3.0	3.0	3.0	3.0	3.0	42
United States	..	1.9	2.0	2.1	2.2	2.3	2.4	2.5	2.6	2.7	2.9	45
Bulgaria	..	2.0	2.2	2.2	2.2	2.3	2.5	2.5	2.6	2.6	2.6	31
Serbia	..	1.7	1.8	1.9	1.9	2.0	2.2	2.3	2.4	2.5	2.6	35
Viet Nam	..	1.9	2.0	2.1	2.1	2.2	2.2	2.3	2.3	2.4	2.4	40
Other countries	..	13.6	14.6	15.7	16.8	18.2	19.7	21.0	22.2	23.4	24.6	
Total	**145.7**	**169.8**	**172.6**	**174.9**	**177.6**	**181.6**	**186.2**	**190.3**	**194.4**	**198.4**	**201.9**	**48**

Note: For details on definitions and sources, refer to the metadata at the end of the tables.

StatLink ᠁ᓯᒷ https://stat.link/5cmqi8

Table B.4. Stocks of foreign-born population by country of birth – Slovenia

Thousands

	2011	2012	2013	2014	2015	2016	2017	2018	2019	2020	2021	Of which: Women 2021 (%)
Bosnia and Herzegovina	96.9	97.2	98.5	100.0	100.9	102.8	104.7	107.7	116.4	126.4	132.6	37
Croatia	49.2	48.8	48.3	47.7	47.0	46.1	45.6	45.0	44.4	43.9	43.3	52
Serbia	26.4	26.4	26.7	26.9	27.1	24.3	24.6	25.4	27.4	29.5	30.2	38
North Macedonia	13.7	14.2	14.7	15.1	15.6	15.9	16.5	17.1	18.2	19.3	19.8	42
Germany	8.5	8.4	8.0	7.7	7.6	7.4	7.4	7.3	7.3	7.3	7.6	48
Italy	3.1	3.2	3.4	3.5	3.6	3.8	4.0	4.1	4.3	4.3	4.6	40
Russia	1.1	1.2	1.4	1.7	2.1	2.6	2.8	3.0	3.4	3.7	4.0	58
Montenegro	2.8	2.8	2.8	2.8	2.8	2.9	3.4	3.3	3.4	3.4	3.4	46
Ukraine	1.4	1.5	1.6	1.7	1.8	2.0	2.3	2.5	2.7	2.8	2.9	65
Austria	3.2	3.1	3.0	2.9	2.8	2.7	2.7	2.6	2.7	2.7	2.8	50
Serbia and Montenegro	0.0	0.0	0.0	0.0	0.0	0.0	0.0	0.0	0.0	0.0	1.8	47
China	0.8	0.8	0.8	0.9	0.9	0.9	0.9	1.0	1.1	1.2	1.2	45
Bulgaria	0.8	0.9	1.1	1.2	1.2	1.2	1.2	1.2	1.3	1.5	1.2	43
France	1.2	1.2	1.2	1.2	1.2	1.1	1.1	1.1	1.1	1.1	1.1	50
Switzerland	1.1	1.1	1.0	1.0	1.0	1.0	1.0	0.9	0.9	1.0	1.0	47
Other countries	18.5	19.2	20.0	21.0	22.1	26.4	27.1	27.9	30.3	33.6	35.2	
Total	**228.6**	**230.1**	**232.7**	**235.3**	**237.6**	**241.2**	**245.4**	**250.2**	**265.1**	**281.6**	**292.8**	**41**

Note: For details on definitions and sources, refer to the metadata at the end of the tables.

StatLink ᠁ᓯᒷ https://stat.link/5cmqi8

Table B.4. Stocks of foreign-born population by country of birth – Spain

Thousands

	2011	2012	2013	2014	2015	2016	2017	2018	2019	2020	2021	Of which: Women 2021 (%)
Morocco	767.0	762.4	740.1	712.5	699.9	696.8	699.5	713.8	752.2	803.8	828.0	45
Romania	736.3	750.4	715.0	670.1	646.2	627.8	611.9	595.7	587.1	579.3	568.9	51
Colombia	375.9	373.6	366.0	353.2	347.5	347.2	361.5	386.1	431.1	499.2	541.6	58
Ecuador	484.8	471.3	452.4	429.4	416.4	409.4	408.2	408.7	411.9	418.9	420.8	53
Venezuela	151.9	155.8	156.3	154.3	160.5	174.0	199.4	245.0	311.8	383.5	415.3	54
United Kingdom	317.5	318.7	321.1	314.4	306.0	300.3	296.8	288.4	290.2	304.0	316.9	50
Argentina	276.4	270.9	264.0	255.3	251.8	252.1	255.5	261.0	272.8	296.0	309.5	50
Peru	198.6	198.0	193.6	186.9	184.8	185.8	190.5	200.5	216.8	241.5	255.5	57
France	208.3	209.2	208.4	205.4	203.7	204.4	205.7	207.9	211.9	216.1	219.2	51
Germany	210.8	210.2	209.6	204.5	200.6	197.2	195.7	193.1	192.1	192.3	192.4	51
Dominican Rep.	141.2	148.0	152.9	154.1	156.9	159.7	164.3	170.5	176.9	183.7	186.6	60
China	161.0	163.7	160.5	155.7	155.7	158.7	161.9	165.9	171.5	176.7	176.1	55
Cuba	109.5	118.6	124.0	127.5	131.1	134.8	139.0	145.0	155.4	169.8	174.2	54
Italy	89.9	94.8	99.3	102.1	106.3	114.2	123.7	135.3	147.0	157.6	161.8	42
Bolivia	201.6	188.7	174.3	157.5	150.7	148.3	148.6	150.2	153.1	156.6	157.7	61
Other countries	1 851.6	1 860.5	1 837.1	1 775.3	1 773.1	1 807.6	1 862.4	1 931.7	2 057.0	2 217.9	2 290.2	
Total	**6 282.2**	**6 295.0**	**6 174.7**	**5 958.3**	**5 891.2**	**5 918.3**	**6 024.5**	**6 198.8**	**6 539.0**	**6 996.8**	**7 214.9**	**52**

Note: For details on definitions and sources, refer to the metadata at the end of the tables.

StatLink ᐧᐧᐧ https://stat.link/5cmqi8

Table B.4. Stocks of foreign-born population by country of birth – Sweden

Thousands

	2011	2012	2013	2014	2015	2016	2017	2018	2019	2020	2021	Of which: Women 2021 (%)
Syria	20.8	22.4	27.5	41.7	67.7	98.2	149.4	172.3	186.0	191.5	193.6	44
Iraq	121.8	125.5	127.9	128.9	130.2	131.9	135.1	140.8	144.0	146.0	146.4	46
Finland	169.5	166.7	163.9	161.1	158.5	156.0	153.6	150.9	147.9	144.6	140.3	61
Poland	70.3	72.9	75.3	78.2	81.7	85.5	88.7	91.2	92.8	93.7	93.8	53
Iran	62.1	63.8	65.6	67.2	68.4	69.1	70.6	74.1	77.4	80.1	81.3	47
Somalia	37.8	40.2	44.0	54.2	57.9	60.6	63.9	66.4	68.7	70.2	70.2	51
Former Yugoslavia	70.8	70.1	69.3	68.6	67.9	67.2	66.5	65.9	65.1	64.3	63.4	50
Afghanistan	14.4	17.5	21.5	25.1	28.4	31.3	34.8	44.0	52.0	58.8	60.9	35
Bosnia and Herzegovina	56.2	56.3	56.6	56.8	57.3	57.7	58.2	58.9	59.4	60.0	60.2	50
Türkiye	42.5	43.9	45.1	45.7	46.1	46.4	47.1	48.3	49.9	51.7	52.6	45
Germany	48.2	48.4	48.7	49.0	49.4	49.6	50.2	50.9	51.1	51.4	51.4	53
Eritrea	10.3	12.0	13.7	16.6	21.8	28.6	35.1	39.1	42.3	45.7	47.2	45
Thailand	31.4	33.6	35.6	37.0	38.1	38.8	39.9	41.2	42.4	43.6	44.3	78
India	17.9	18.6	19.4	20.6	21.9	23.2	25.7	29.7	35.2	40.6	42.8	46
Norway	43.4	43.1	42.9	42.5	42.3	42.1	42.1	42.0	41.7	41.6	41.1	55
Other countries	567.6	592.4	616.3	640.2	665.9	690.1	723.6	761.5	799.6	835.8	857.3	
Total	**1 384.9**	**1 427.3**	**1 473.3**	**1 533.5**	**1 603.6**	**1 676.3**	**1 784.5**	**1 877.1**	**1 955.6**	**2 019.7**	**2 046.7**	**50**

Note: For details on definitions and sources, refer to the metadata at the end of the tables.

StatLink ᐧᐧᐧ https://stat.link/5cmqi8

Table B.4. Stocks of foreign-born population by country of birth – Switzerland

Thousands

	2011	2012	2013	2014	2015	2016	2017	2018	2019	2020	2021	Of which: Women 2021 (%)
Germany	318.9	330.0	337.4	343.6	348.1	350.5	352.2	353.4	355.3	357.4	360.5	50
Italy	233.1	241.0	244.7	251.3	258.3	263.3	267.3	267.9	268.8	268.9	270.0	44
Portugal	172.3	187.4	199.2	211.5	218.7	222.3	223.1	220.9	217.7	214.1	210.7	46
France	132.3	138.4	141.4	146.8	153.1	158.6	162.5	166.3	169.4	172.8	178.5	50
Türkiye	76.0	76.9	77.4	77.9	78.2	78.7	79.2	79.8	80.4	81.6	82.8	47
North Macedonia	51.7	53.5	55.1	57.0	59.2	61.4	64.3	66.9	69.3	72.3	74.8	48
Spain	53.5	57.2	59.8	64.1	67.1	68.9	69.4	68.9	68.6	68.3	69.0	49
Serbia	56.5	59.2	60.1	62.9	63.4	64.6	65.3	65.7	65.9	66.8	67.2	52
Austria	58.8	59.2	59.7	59.9	60.0	60.1	59.8	59.6	59.2	58.8	58.5	59
Bosnia and Herzegovina	51.1	52.4	53.2	54.1	55.4	56.4	56.9	57.1	57.4	57.7	57.8	53
United Kingdom	41.1	43.7	44.2	44.8	45.2	45.2	45.0	45.3	45.7	46.3	47.4	46
Brazil	32.3	33.4	34.4	35.5	36.6	37.8	39.1	40.9	42.5	44.0	45.4	69
Poland	21.5	24.0	26.2	28.1	31.6	34.7	36.7	38.7	40.8	42.9	44.8	53
United States	33.7	34.9	35.4	35.9	36.3	36.6	37.0	37.6	38.6	39.0	40.0	52
Sri Lanka	28.6	29.6	30.0	30.6	31.3	32.6	34.2	35.1	35.6	35.8	35.9	47
Other countries	713.9	737.4	760.3	785.6	812.5	844.6	888.0	914.9	938.2	963.2	987.1	
Total	**2 075.2**	**2 158.4**	**2 218.4**	**2 289.6**	**2 354.8**	**2 416.4**	**2 480.0**	**2 519.1**	**2 553.4**	**2 590.0**	**2 630.4**	**51**

Note: For details on definitions and sources, refer to the metadata at the end of the tables.

StatLink 🔗 https://stat.link/5cmqi8

Table B.4. Stocks of foreign-born population by country of birth – Türkiye

Thousands

	2011	2012	2013	2014	2015	2016	2017	2018	2019	2020	2021	Of which: Women 2021 (%)
Bulgaria	..	..	..	382.1	378.7	374.0	366.2	362.7	361.9	365.1	358.5	55
Germany	..	..	..	259.1	263.3	272.7	277.9	281.9	292.4	316.6	330.3	53
Iraq	..	..	..	52.2	97.5	146.1	199.7	283.8	313.8	285.7	327.9	48
Syria	..	..	..	66.1	76.4	98.1	109.4	163.8	217.9	225.4	276.9	48
Afghanistan	..	..	..	33.8	38.7	59.3	78.7	115.2	142.4	153.9	180.5	42
Iran	..	..	..	30.2	36.2	47.5	53.8	80.2	108.5	89.4	155.0	50
Turkmenistan	..	..	..	19.9	24.9	30.3	45.2	71.2	136.9	97.3	130.3	48
Uzbekistan	..	..	..	29.6	36.1	43.7	52.1	63.2	78.0	72.7	109.9	63
Azerbaijan	..	..	..	46.1	52.8	64.2	71.2	85.3	97.8	85.0	107.1	59
Russia	..	..	..	30.3	34.5	37.8	37.4	47.2	57.0	64.3	86.8	64
Kazakhstan	..	..	..	19.3	21.5	23.1	21.6	29.5	36.2	41.1	58.8	59
Saudi Arabia	..	..	..	12.6	14.6	17.3	25.6	41.3	53.2	49.8	55.7	47
France	..	..	..	28.1	28.5	33.3	35.3	33.9	37.5	39.5	46.0	51
Netherlands	..	..	..	32.0	32.3	34.1	34.1	34.6	35.7	38.6	41.5	54
Kyrgyzstan	..	..	..	13.6	17.2	20.6	23.0	26.7	32.7	29.2	39.5	70
Other countries	..	..	..	404.8	439.1	475.3	492.8	558.2	666.6	656.4	836.9	
Total	**..**	**..**	**..**	**1 459.8**	**1 592.4**	**1 777.3**	**1 923.9**	**2 278.5**	**2 668.6**	**2 610.0**	**3 141.4**	**52**

Note: For details on definitions and sources, refer to the metadata at the end of the tables.

StatLink 🔗 https://stat.link/5cmqi8

Table B.4. Stocks of foreign-born population by country of birth – United Kingdom

Thousands

	2011	2012	2013	2014	2015	2016	2017	2018	2019	2020	2021	Of which: Women 2020 (%)
India	686	750	746	733	784	807	809	862	837	847	..	51
Poland	617	658	650	764	783	883	907	889	827	746	..	55
Pakistan	441	432	476	419	510	525	523	529	533	519	..	49
Romania	82	118	151	162	220	264	340	410	434	370	..	45
Ireland	429	429	400	346	372	391	398	380	358	364	..	54
Germany	292	303	343	279	252	299	299	309	305	310	..	56
Bangladesh	219	191	184	187	198	220	247	259	259	251	..	49
Italy	150	135	142	159	168	188	220	237	246	240	..	47
South Africa	208	208	224	201	178	200	245	235	255	229	..	52
Nigeria	203	162	202	170	206	212	190	205	207	219	..	51
China	148	99	116	118	114	209	226	210	198	211	..	55
Portugal	104	84	114	111	141	141	142	132	149	175	..	50
France	132	146	128	127	174	146	164	178	183	169	..	56
United States	159	203	216	186	158	179	163	159	174	168	..	55
Philippines	140	134	129	124	150	148	143	144	144	167	..	64
Other countries	3 420	3 536	3 639	3 978	4 074	4 086	4 301	4 250	4 289	4 167	..	
Total	**7 430**	**7 588**	**7 860**	**8 064**	**8 482**	**8 988**	**9 369**	**9 183**	**9 482**	**9 539**	..	..

Note: For details on definitions and sources, refer to the metadata at the end of the tables.

StatLink 🔗 https://stat.link/5cmqi8

Table B.4. Stocks of foreign-born population by country of birth – United States

Thousands

	2011	2012	2013	2014	2015	2016	2017	2018	2019	2020	2021	Of which: Women 2021 (%)
Mexico	11 691.6	11 489.4	11 556.5	11 714.5	11 643.3	11 573.7	11 269.9	11 171.9	10 931.9	11 295.3	11 780.9	48
India	1 855.7	1 974.3	2 036.3	2 205.9	2 389.6	2 434.5	2 610.5	2 652.9	2 688.1	3 075.1	3 020.6	48
China	1 651.5	1 719.8	1 786.1	1 929.5	2 065.4	2 130.4	2 216.8	2 221.9	2 250.2	1 943.0	1 952.8	57
Philippines	1 814.9	1 862.0	1 863.5	1 926.3	1 982.4	1 941.7	2 008.1	2 013.8	2 045.2	1 704.0	1 747.2	62
Cuba	1 090.6	1 114.9	1 138.2	1 172.9	1 210.7	1 271.6	1 311.8	1 344.0	1 360.0	1 430.0	1 465.9	50
El Salvador	1 245.5	1 254.5	1 247.5	1 315.5	1 352.4	1 387.0	1 401.8	1 419.3	1 412.1	1 484.3	1 424.9	51
Dominican Republic	878.9	960.2	1 010.7	997.7	1 063.2	1 085.3	1 162.6	1 177.9	1 169.4	1 244.8	1 248.0	56
Guatemala	844.3	880.9	900.5	915.6	927.6	935.7	958.8	1 007.0	1 111.5	1 082.1	1 136.7	45
Honduras	500.0	535.7	539.2	588.3	599.0	651.1	655.4	646.3	745.8	831.1	900.7	49
Korea	1 095.1	1 105.7	1 081.2	1 079.8	1 060.0	1 041.7	1 063.1	1 039.1	1 038.9	891.9	816.8	55
Haiti	602.7	616.0	599.6	628.0	675.5	668.2	679.8	687.2	701.7	735.8	732.0	55
Jamaica	694.6	668.8	705.3	705.8	711.1	736.3	744.7	733.4	772.2	680.2	721.9	55
Canada	787.5	799.1	841.1	806.4	830.6	783.2	809.3	813.7	797.2	609.2	671.1	53
Venezuela	198.5	198.6	195.5	216.2	255.5	290.2	351.1	393.8	465.2	527.8	582.6	56
Brazil	334.1	325.5	337.1	335.6	361.4	409.6	451.1	472.6	502.1	489.1	526.0	57
Other countries	15 096.1	15 232.9	15 505.9	15 852.7	16 161.8	16 398.7	16 830.7	16 933.8	16 941.2	16 234.7	16 544.8	
Total	**40 381.6**	**40 738.2**	**41 344.4**	**42 390.7**	**43 289.6**	**43 738.9**	**44 525.5**	**44 728.5**	**44 932.8**	**44 258.3**	**45 272.9**	52

Note: For details on definitions and sources, refer to the metadata at the end of the tables.

StatLink 🔗 https://stat.link/5cmqi8

Metadata related to Tables A.4. and B.4. **Stocks of foreign-born population**

Country	Comments	Source
Australia	® Estimated residential population. *Reference date:* 30 June.	Australian Bureau of Statistics (ABS).
Austria	® Stock of foreign-born residents recorded in the population register. *Reference date:* 1 January.	Population Register, Statistics Austria.
Belgium	® From 2011 on, includes persons who have lived in Belgium for a continuous period of at least 12 months and persons who arrived in Belgium less than 12 months before the reference time with the intention of staying there for at least one year; also includes asylum seekers. Up to 2010, includes persons whose main place of residence is in Belgium and who are registered in a municipality (aliens' register or register of aliens with a privileged status or register of European Union officials) so excludes asylum seekers, persons who have been residing in the Belgian territory for less than three months or are in an irregular situation. The series include breaks in 2011 and in 2012, and data for the year 2019 are provisional.	Population Register, Eurostat.
Canada	® 2011: National Household Survey. The foreign-born population covers all persons who are or have ever been a landed immigrant/permanent resident in Canada. The foreign-born population does not include non-permanent residents, on employment or student authorizations, or who are refugee claimants. ® 2016: 2016 Census, 25% sample data. ε PM for other years.	Statistics Canada.
Chile	® Up to 2017: register of residence permits. ε From 2018 on: estimates for the total and for selected countries.	Department of Foreigners and Migration, Ministry of the Interior and Public Security.
Czech Republic	® 2011 Census. ε CM for other years. In table B4, data broken down by nationality from 2012 to 2021 are from Eurostat (permanent residents only).	Czech Statistical Office, Eurostat.
Denmark	® Immigrants according to the national definition, e.g. persons born abroad to parents both foreigner or born abroad. When no information is available on the parents' nationality/country of birth, foreign-born persons are classified as immigrants.	Statistics Denmark.
Estonia	® National population register.	Ministry of the Interior.
Finland	® Population register. Includes foreign-born persons of Finnish origin.	Central Population Register, Statistics Finland.
France	® From 2006 on, annual censuses. From 2016 on estimated totals are based on Eurostat data. Includes the département of Mayotte from 2014. Includes persons who were born French abroad.	National Institute for Statistics and Economic Studies (INSEE).
Germany	® 2011 Census. ε Other years, estimation based on the 2011 census. Up to 2016, data refers to country of citizenship or former citizenship; from 2017 on, it refers to country of birth. Includes ethnic Germans (Aussiedler). Excludes people in shared/community accommodation.	Federal Statistical Office.
Greece	® Totals in Table A.4 (Eurostat dataset) are not comparable to data presented in Table B.4 by country of birth (Labour Force Survey data, foreign-born population aged 15 and above; 4th quarter prior to 2014; 2nd quarter from 2014 on).	Eurostat and Hellenic Statistical authority.
Hungary	® From 2010 on, includes third-country nationals holding a temporary residence permit (for a year or more). From 2011 on, includes persons under subsidiary protection. Data for 2011 were adjusted to match the October census results. *Reference date:* 1 January.	Office of Immigration and Nationality; Central Office Administrative and Electronic Public Services (Central Population Register); Central Statistical Office.
Iceland	® National population register. Numbers from the register are likely to be overestimated. *Reference date:* 1 January.	Statistics Iceland.
Ireland	® 2011 and 2016 Censuses. Persons usually resident and present in their usual residence on census night. ε PM for other years.	Central Statistics Office.

Country	Comments	Source
Israel	® Estimates are based on the results of the Population Censuses and on the changes that occurred in the population after the Censuses, as recorded in the Population Register. They include Jews and foreign-born members of other religions (usually family members of Jewish immigrants). The statistical data for Israel are supplied by and under the responsibility of the relevant Israeli authorities. The use of such data by the OECD is without prejudice to the status of the Golan Heights, East Jerusalem and Israeli settlements in the West Bank under the terms of international law.	Central Bureau of Statistics.
Italy	® Population register. From 2019 on, the data on foreign resident population takes into account the results of the permanent population census. *Reference date:* 1 January.	National Institute of Statistics (ISTAT).
Latvia	® Population register. *Reference date:* 1 January.	Central Statistical Office.
Lithuania	*Reference date:* 1 January.	Department of Migration.
Luxembourg	® 2011: Census. ε CM for other years.	Central Office of Statistics and Economic Studies (Statec).
Mexico	® 2010 census; 2015 Intercensal Survey. ε Other years, estimation from the National Survey on Occupation and Employment (ENOE).	National Institute of Statistics and Geography (INEGI).
Netherlands	® *Reference date:* 1 January.	Population register, Central Bureau of Statistics (CBS).
New Zealand	® 2013 and 2018 Censuses. ε PM for other years.	Statistics New Zealand.
Norway	® *Reference date:* 1 January.	Central Population Register, Statistics Norway.
Poland	® 2011 Census. Excluding foreign temporary residents who, at the time of the census, had been staying at a given address in Poland for less than 12 months. Country of birth in accordance with administrative boundaries at the time of the census. From 2012 on, estimates based on Eurostat data.	Central Statistical Office and Eurostat.
Portugal	® 2011 census. From 2012 on, estimates based on Eurostat data.	National Statistical Institute (INE).
Slovak Republic	® Population Register.	Ministry of the Interior.
Slovenia		Eurostat.
Spain	® Population register. Foreign-born recorded in the Municipal Registers irrespective of their legal status. *Reference date:* 1 January.	Municipal Registers, National Statistics Institute (INE).
Sweden	® *Reference date:* 1 January.	Population Register, Statistics Sweden.
Switzerland	® Population Register of the Confederation. ε CM for other years.	Federal Statistical Office.
Türkiye		Ministry of Labour and Social Security.
United Kingdom	® Until 2019: Foreign-born residents in the Labour Force Survey. 2020: Estimates from the Annual Population Survey.	Office for National Statistics.
United States	® Includes persons who are naturalised and persons who are in an unauthorised status. Excludes children born abroad to US citizen parents. Break in series in 2020: for 2020 and 2021, CPS instead of ACS.	American Community Survey and Current Population Survey, Census Bureau.

Notes: ® Observed figures. ε Estimates (in italic) made by means of the complement method (CM) or the parametric method (PM). No estimate is made by country of birth (Tables B.4). Data for Serbia include persons from Serbia and Montenegro. Some statements may refer to nationalities/countries of birth not shown in this annex but available on line at: http://stats.oecd.org/.

Table A.5. Stocks of foreign population by nationality in OECD countries

Thousands and percentages

	2011	2012	2013	2014	2015	2016	2017	2018	2019	2020	2021
Austria	913.2	951.4	1 004.3	1 066.1	1 146.1	1 267.7	1 341.9	1 395.9	1 438.9	1 486.2	1 531.1
% of total population	10.8	11.2	11.7	12.4	13.2	14.5	15.2	15.7	16.1	16.5	16.9
Belgium	1 168.6	1 206.5	1 231.3	1 241.2	1 276.9	1 333.2	1 353.8	1 376.4	1 413.8	1 478.8	1 489.2
% of total population	10.6	10.9	11.0	11.1	11.3	11.7	11.9	12.0	12.3	12.8	12.8
Canada	1 957.0	..	..	..	..	2 404.8	..	..	..	..	..
% of total population	5.9	..	..	..	..	6.8	..	..	..	..	..
Chile	..	..	..	..	..	..	952.7	..	1 251.2	1 492.5	..
% of total population	..	..	..	..	..	..	5.4	..	6.9	8.1	..
Czech Republic	424.3	434.2	435.9	439.2	449.4	464.7	493.4	524.1	564.3	593.4	632.6
% of total population	4.0	4.1	4.1	4.1	4.2	4.4	4.6	4.9	5.3	5.5	5.9
Denmark	346.0	358.9	374.7	397.3	422.6	463.1	485.0	506.0	525.8	537.1	539.5
% of total population	6.2	6.4	6.6	7.0	7.4	8.1	8.5	8.8	9.1	9.3	9.3
Estonia	..	211.1	210.9	211.7	211.4	211.5	212.2	213.7	216.4	215.6	..
% of total population	..	16.0	16.0	16.1	16.1	16.1	16.1	16.2	16.3	16.3	..
Finland	168.0	183.1	195.5	207.5	219.7	229.8	243.6	249.5	257.6	267.6	278.9
% of total population	3.1	3.4	3.6	3.8	4.0	4.2	4.4	4.5	4.7	4.8	5.0
France	3 889.0	3 980.0	4 084.0	4 289.0	4 428.0	4 542.0	4 704.0	4 769.4	4 986.9	5 150.0	5 226.0
% of total population	6.3	6.4	6.5	6.8	7.0	7.1	7.3	7.4	7.7	7.9	8.0
Germany	6 753.6	6 930.9	7 213.7	7 633.6	8 153.0	9 107.9	10 039.1	10 623.9	10 915.5	11 228.3	11 432.5
% of total population	8.4	8.6	8.9	9.4	10.0	11.1	12.1	12.8	13.1	13.4	13.6
Greece	934.4	921.4	886.5	855.0	822.0	798.4	810.0	816.1	831.7	906.3	921.5
% of total population	8.5	8.4	8.1	7.9	7.6	7.4	7.6	7.7	7.8	8.6	8.8
Hungary	206.9	143.4	141.4	140.5	146.0	156.6	151.1	161.8	180.8	200.0	194.5
% of total population	2.1	1.5	1.4	1.4	1.5	1.6	1.6	1.7	1.9	2.1	2.0
Iceland	21.1	21.0	21.4	22.7	24.3	26.5	30.3	37.8	44.3	49.4	51.3
% of total population	6.5	6.4	6.6	6.9	7.4	8.0	9.1	11.2	13.1	14.5	15.0
Ireland	598.1	599.9	601.8	603.7	605.5	607.4	566.6	593.5	622.7	644.4	645.6
% of total population	13.5	13.3	13.2	13.1	13.1	13.2	12.2	12.8	13.3	13.6	13.4
Italy	3 879.2	4 052.1	4 387.7	4 921.3	5 014.4	5 026.9	5 047.0	5 144.4	4 996.2	5 039.6	5 171.9
% of total population	6.5	6.8	7.3	8.1	8.3	8.3	8.3	8.5	8.3	8.3	8.6
Japan	2 132.9	2 078.5	2 033.7	2 066.4	2 121.8	2 232.2	2 382.8	2 561.8	2 731.1	2 933.1	2 887.1
% of total population	1.7	1.6	1.6	1.6	1.7	1.7	1.9	2.0	2.2	2.3	2.3
Korea	1 088.6	1 200.1	1 202.3	1 303.8	1 488.9	1 594.8	1 662.8	1 749.6	1 951.1	2 024.6	1 889.5
% of total population	2.2	2.4	2.4	2.6	2.9	3.1	3.3	3.4	3.8	4.0	3.7
Latvia	342.8	324.3	315.4	304.8	298.4	288.9	279.4	272.5	266.6	260.4	252.4
% of total population	16.4	15.7	15.4	15.1	14.9	14.6	14.3	14.1	14.0	13.8	13.5
Lithuania	24.0	22.9	22.2	21.6	22.5	18.7	20.1	27.3	47.2	65.8	79.9
% of total population	0.8	0.8	0.7	0.7	0.8	0.6	0.7	1.0	1.7	2.4	3.0
Luxembourg	220.5	229.9	238.8	248.9	258.7	269.2	281.5	288.2	291.5	296.5	299.4
% of total population	42.5	43.3	44.0	44.9	45.6	46.5	47.6	47.7	47.3	47.4	47.2
Mexico	303.9	296.4	..	326.0	355.2	381.8	423.9	462.0	480.3	..	..
% of total population	0.3	0.3	..	0.3	0.3	0.3	0.3	0.4	0.4	..	..
Netherlands	760.4	786.1	796.2	816.0	847.3	900.5	972.3	1 040.8	1 110.9	1 192.3	1 203.0
% of total population	4.5	4.7	4.7	4.8	5.0	5.3	5.7	6.1	6.5	7.0	7.0
Norway	369.2	407.3	448.8	483.2	512.2	538.2	559.2	567.8	584.2	604.5	601.6
% of total population	7.5	8.1	8.8	9.4	9.8	10.3	10.6	10.6	10.9	11.2	11.0
Poland	79.3	85.8	93.3	101.2	108.3	149.6	210.3	239.2	289.8	358.2	..
of total population	0.2	0.2	0.2	0.3	0.3	0.4	0.6	0.6	0.8	0.9	..

	2011	2012	2013	2014	2015	2016	2017	2018	2019	2020	2021
Portugal	445.3	436.8	417.0	401.3	395.2	388.7	397.7	421.7	480.3	590.3	662.1
% of total population	4.2	4.1	4.0	3.9	3.8	3.8	3.9	4.1	4.7	5.8	6.5
Slovak Republic	68.0	53.4	56.5	59.2	61.8	65.8	69.7	72.9	76.1	78.9	82.1
% of total population	1.3	1.0	1.0	1.1	1.1	1.2	1.3	1.3	1.4	1.4	1.5
Slovenia	82.7	85.6	91.4	96.6	101.5	107.8	114.4	121.9	138.2	156.4	168.7
% of total population	4.0	4.2	4.4	4.7	4.9	5.2	5.5	5.9	6.6	7.5	8.1
Spain	5 312.4	5 236.0	5 072.7	4 677.1	4 454.4	4 417.5	4 419.5	4 563.0	4 840.2	5 226.9	5 368.3
% of total population	11.3	11.1	10.8	10.0	9.5	9.5	9.5	9.8	10.4	11.2	11.5
Sweden	633.3	655.1	667.2	694.7	739.4	782.8	851.9	897.3	932.3	940.6	905.3
% of total population	6.7	6.9	6.9	7.2	7.6	8.0	8.6	9.0	9.3	9.3	8.9
Switzerland	1 720.4	1 772.3	1 825.1	1 886.6	1 947.0	1 993.9	2 029.5	2 053.6	2 081.2	2 111.4	2 151.9
% of total population	21.8	22.1	22.5	23.0	23.5	23.8	24.0	24.1	24.2	24.4	24.7
Türkiye	190.5	242.1	278.7	456.5	518.3	650.3	816.4	919.1	1 211.0	1 531.2	..
% of total population	0.3	0.3	0.4	0.6	0.7	0.8	1.0	1.1	1.5	1.8	..
United Kingdom	4 785.0	4 788.0	4 941.0	5 154.0	5 592.0	5 951.0	6 137.0	5 991.0	6 227.0	..	..
% of total population	7.5	7.4	7.6	7.9	8.5	9.0	9.2	8.9	9.2	..	..
United States	22 225.5	22 115.0	22 016.4	22 263.4	22 426.2	22 415.3	22 459.7	22 081.1	21 693.3	20 219.3	..
% of total population	7.1	7.0	6.9	6.9	6.9	6.9	6.9	6.8	6.6	6.1	..

Note: For details on definitions and sources, refer to the metadata at the end of the Tables B.5.

StatLink https://stat.link/z9w8ck

Table B.5. Stocks of foreign population by nationality – Austria

Thousands

	2011	2012	2013	2014	2015	2016	2017	2018	2019	2020	2021	Of which: Women 2021 (%)
Germany	144.1	150.9	157.8	164.8	170.5	176.5	181.6	186.8	192.4	200.0	208.7	50
Romania	41.6	47.3	53.3	59.7	73.4	82.9	92.1	102.3	112.7	123.5	131.8	50
Serbia	110.5	110.4	111.3	112.5	114.3	116.6	118.5	120.2	121.3	122.1	122.0	49
Türkiye	112.5	112.9	113.7	114.7	115.4	116.0	116.8	117.3	117.2	117.6	117.6	49
Bosnia and Herzegovina	89.6	89.6	89.9	91.0	92.5	94.0	94.6	95.2	95.8	96.6	97.0	46
Hungary	25.6	29.8	37.0	46.3	54.9	63.6	70.6	77.1	82.7	87.5	91.4	52
Croatia	58.3	58.3	58.6	62.0	66.5	70.2	73.3	76.7	80.0	83.6	89.0	47
Poland	38.6	42.1	46.0	50.3	54.3	57.6	60.1	62.2	63.4	64.4	65.6	47
Syria	1.6	1.9	2.7	4.3	11.3	33.3	41.7	48.1	49.8	51.5	55.4	41
Slovak Republic	20.4	22.5	25.3	28.6	32.1	35.3	38.1	40.2	42.0	43.6	45.4	60
Afghanistan	6.7	9.4	12.4	14.0	16.8	35.6	45.3	45.7	44.4	43.7	44.0	35
Italy	15.4	16.2	17.8	20.2	22.5	25.3	27.3	29.2	30.9	32.5	34.3	42
Bulgaria	11.2	12.5	14.1	15.9	19.6	22.4	24.9	27.4	29.9	32.5	34.2	51
Russia	24.2	25.5	27.3	28.8	30.0	31.2	32.0	32.4	32.6	32.9	33.3	58
North Macedonia	18.6	18.9	19.4	20.1	20.9	21.7	22.4	23.1	23.4	24.1	24.6	49
Other countries	194.5	203.3	217.7	233.0	251.3	285.3	302.7	312.0	320.3	330.2	336.8	
Total	913.2	951.4	1 004.3	1 066.1	1 146.1	1 267.7	1 341.9	1 395.9	1 438.9	1 486.2	1 531.1	49

Note: For details on definitions and sources, refer to the metadata at the end of the tables.

StatLink 🔒 https://stat.link/am1o6l

Table B.5. Stocks of foreign population by nationality – Belgium

Thousands

	2011	2012	2013	2014	2015	2016	2017	2018	2019	2020	2021	Of which: Women 2021 (%)
France	145.3	149.8	153.3	155.9	158.8	161.8	163.7	164.9	166.9	170.9	173.8	52
Netherlands	137.8	141.1	143.8	146.0	148.9	151.7	153.2	154.7	157.1	159.5	160.9	48
Italy	162.8	159.6	157.4	156.4	156.6	156.8	156.3	155.6	155.5	155.7	154.7	46
Romania	34.2	42.4	50.9	56.7	65.3	73.2	79.8	86.6	94.9	105.5	111.3	44
Morocco	84.8	86.2	83.4	80.9	82.3	83.0	82.6	81.3	80.3	80.9	80.9	53
Poland	49.7	55.9	61.4	64.9	68.1	70.4	71.1	71.2	71.0	71.0	70.1	52
Spain	48.0	50.8	54.3	57.3	59.9	61.7	62.6	63.6	65.1	67.9	70.0	49
Portugal	34.5	36.0	38.7	41.1	42.6	44.2	45.6	46.4	47.5	49.1	50.2	47
Bulgaria	17.8	20.4	23.4	25.6	28.6	31.3	32.9	34.8	37.0	40.6	43.1	48
Germany	39.8	39.9	39.7	39.4	39.1	39.3	39.3	39.2	39.5	39.7	40.0	52
Türkiye	40.8	40.1	38.7	37.4	37.2	37.1	37.0	37.0	37.5	38.8	39.0	48
Syria	2.9	3.1	3.8	4.6	7.4	18.0	22.1	27.5	30.8	33.1	32.8	45
Afghanistan	4.8	7.2	8.8	8.5	9.6	17.5	19.0	19.2	19.7	22.7	23.3	30
Dem. Rep. of the Congo	22.5	22.6	22.5	22.0	22.1	22.3	22.3	22.5	22.5	22.8	22.7	51
United Kingdom	25.0	24.8	24.5	24.1	23.9	23.5	22.8	21.2	20.2	19.1	18.6	42
Other countries	317.9	326.7	326.6	320.3	326.6	341.7	343.5	350.8	368.3	401.7	397.7	
Total	1 168.6	1 206.5	1 231.3	1 241.2	1 276.9	1 333.2	1 353.8	1 376.4	1 413.8	1 478.8	1 489.2	49

Note: For details on definitions and sources, refer to the metadata at the end of the tables.

StatLink 🔒 https://stat.link/am1o6l

Table B.5. Stocks of foreign population by nationality – Canada

Thousands

	2011	2012	2013	2014	2015	2016	2017	2018	2019	2020	2021	Of which: Women 2016 (%)
China	..	..	..	..	..	340.6	..	..	..	..	..	53
India	..	..	..	..	..	274.2	..	..	..	..	..	47
Philippines	..	..	..	..	..	259.2	..	..	..	..	..	58
United States	..	..	..	..	..	149.7	..	..	..	..	..	55
United Kingdom	..	..	..	..	..	113.9	..	..	..	..	..	48
France	..	..	..	..	..	65.2	..	..	..	..	..	46
Korea	..	..	..	..	..	60.5	..	..	..	..	..	56
Pakistan	..	..	..	..	..	59.2	..	..	..	..	..	49
Iran	..	..	..	..	..	52.2	..	..	..	..	..	50
Germany	..	..	..	..	..	46.6	..	..	..	..	..	52
Syria	..	..	..	..	..	35.9	..	..	..	..	..	49
Mexico	..	..	..	..	..	35.6	..	..	..	..	..	49
Haiti	..	..	..	..	..	27.7	..	..	..	..	..	54
Nigeria	..	..	..	..	..	27.2	..	..	..	..	..	47
Italy	..	..	..	..	..	27.2	..	..	..	..	..	51
Other countries	..	..	..	..	..	829.9	..	..	..	..	..	
Total	**1 957.0**	..	..	..	..	**2 404.8**	..	..	..	..	..	**52**

Note: For details on definitions and sources, refer to the metadata at the end of the tables.

StatLink ᐃᔑᕵᐳ https://stat.link/am1o6l

Table B.5. Stocks of foreign population by nationality – Chile

Thousands

	2011	2012	2013	2014	2015	2016	2017	2018	2019	2020	2021	Of which: Women 2017 (%)
Argentina	..	..	..	..	..	..	501.3	..	..	..	..	..
Venezuela	..	..	..	..	..	..	117.1	..	..	..	..	
Haiti	..	..	..	..	..	..	108.9	..	..	..	..	
Bolivia	..	..	..	..	..	..	81.1	..	..	..	..	
Peru	..	..	..	..	..	..	52.4	..	..	..	..	
Colombia	..	..	..	..	..	..	33.7	..	..	..	..	..
Brazil	..	..	..	..	..	..	20.9	..	..	..	..	
Ecuador	..	..	..	..	..	..	7.2	..	..	..	..	
Australia	..	..	..	..	..	..	2.9	..	..	..	..	
China	..	..	..	..	..	..	2.6	..	..	..	..	
Uruguay	..	..	..	..	..	..	2.5	..	..	..	..	
France	..	..	..	..	..	..	2.3	..	..	..	..	..
Spain	..	..	..	..	..	..	2.3	..	..	..	..	..
Germany	..	..	..	..	..	..	1.8	..	..	..	..	..
Israel	..	..	..	..	..	..	1.3	..	..	..	..	..
Other countries	..	..	..	..	..	..	14.4	..	..	..	..	
Total	..	..	..	..	..	..	**952.7**	..	**1 251.2**	**1 492.5**	..	..

Note: For details on definitions and sources, refer to the metadata at the end of the tables.

StatLink ᐃᔑᕵᐳ https://stat.link/am1o6l

Table B.5. Stocks of foreign population by nationality – Czech Republic

Thousands

	2011	2012	2013	2014	2015	2016	2017	2018	2019	2020	2021	Of which: Women 2021 (%)
Ukraine	124.3	118.9	112.5	105.1	104.2	105.6	109.9	117.1	131.3	145.2	165.4	44
Slovak Republic	71.8	81.3	85.8	90.9	96.2	101.6	107.3	111.8	116.8	121.3	124.5	47
Viet Nam	60.3	58.2	57.3	57.3	56.6	56.9	58.0	59.8	61.1	61.9	62.8	46
Russia	31.8	32.4	33.0	33.1	34.4	34.7	35.8	36.6	38.0	38.0	41.7	56
Germany	13.9	15.8	17.1	18.5	19.7	20.5	21.2	21.3	21.3	21.5	20.9	20
Poland	18.2	19.1	19.2	19.5	19.6	19.8	20.3	20.7	21.3	21.8	20.7	52
Romania	4.4	4.8	5.7	6.8	7.7	9.1	10.8	12.6	14.7	16.8	18.4	33
Bulgaria	6.9	7.4	8.2	9.1	10.1	11.0	12.3	13.8	15.6	17.2	17.9	37
Mongolia	5.6	5.4	5.3	5.3	5.5	6.0	6.8	7.9	9.1	9.8	10.1	53
United Kingdom	4.4	4.9	5.2	5.4	5.6	6.0	6.3	6.7	7.1	8.3	9.1	25
Hungary	0.7	0.8	1.0	1.5	2.3	3.1	4.1	5.4	6.6	7.7	8.9	37
China	5.5	5.6	5.6	5.5	5.6	5.7	6.1	6.9	7.5	7.7	7.9	47
United States	6.1	7.3	7.0	7.1	6.5	6.5	8.8	9.6	9.5	7.2	7.5	40
Belarus	4.2	4.2	4.3	4.3	4.4	4.5	4.7	5.2	6.2	6.9	7.0	51
Kazakhstan	4.2	4.5	4.8	4.8	5.0	5.1	5.5	5.7	6.0	5.9	6.9	56
Other countries	62.0	63.5	63.9	64.8	66.0	68.5	75.7	83.3	92.3	96.1	102.7	
Total	**424.3**	**434.2**	**435.9**	**439.2**	**449.4**	**464.7**	**493.4**	**524.1**	**564.3**	**593.4**	**632.6**	**43**

Note: For details on definitions and sources, refer to the metadata at the end of the tables.

StatLink https://stat.link/am1o6l

Table B.5. Stocks of foreign population by nationality – Denmark

Thousands

	2011	2012	2013	2014	2015	2016	2017	2018	2019	2020	2021	Of which: Women 2021 (%)
Poland	22.6	24.5	26.8	29.3	32.3	35.3	37.6	39.3	40.5	40.8	41.2	45
Syria	1.3	1.9	2.7	4.4	9.8	21.6	31.0	33.6	34.7	34.9	35.6	45
Romania	6.9	9.5	12.4	15.4	18.8	22.4	25.3	27.8	30.7	32.4	33.8	43
Türkiye	29.2	29.0	28.8	28.9	28.8	28.8	28.1	28.2	28.3	28.4	28.4	49
Germany	21.6	22.1	22.4	22.7	23.0	23.7	24.4	24.8	25.5	26.1	26.5	50
United Kingdom	14.7	15.0	15.4	15.8	16.1	16.7	17.6	18.3	18.8	19.0	18.7	35
Sweden	12.9	13.1	13.4	13.9	14.4	14.9	15.1	15.7	16.1	16.5	17.0	56
Norway	15.1	15.3	15.3	15.5	15.8	16.4	16.7	16.8	16.8	17.0	17.0	61
Lithuania	6.5	7.7	8.7	9.7	10.4	11.5	12.4	13.5	14.5	14.7	14.7	49
Ukraine	6.1	6.3	6.6	7.0	7.9	8.6	9.2	10.2	11.7	12.7	12.8	50
India	4.5	4.9	5.1	5.6	6.3	7.5	8.7	9.6	10.9	12.0	11.9	44
Italy	4.8	5.1	5.7	6.4	7.2	8.1	9.0	9.6	10.2	10.9	11.7	40
Bulgaria	3.2	4.0	5.0	6.1	7.2	8.2	9.0	9.7	10.4	10.8	11.2	42
China	7.6	7.5	7.8	8.4	8.9	9.6	10.1	10.5	10.9	11.3	10.9	57
Thailand	8.3	8.6	8.8	9.2	9.5	9.8	10.0	10.2	10.4	10.5	10.5	85
Other countries	180.8	184.7	189.9	199.1	206.0	220.0	220.7	228.2	235.3	239.1	237.7	
Total	**346.0**	**358.9**	**374.7**	**397.3**	**422.6**	**463.1**	**485.0**	**506.0**	**525.8**	**537.1**	**539.5**	**49**

Note: For details on definitions and sources, refer to the metadata at the end of the tables.

StatLink https://stat.link/am1o6l

Table B.5. Stocks of foreign population by nationality – Estonia

Thousands

	2011	2012	2013	2014	2015	2016	2017	2018	2019	2020	2021	Of which: Women 2020 (%)
Russia	..	96.5	95.1	93.6	92.6	91.4	90.3	89.0	88.1	86.0	..	53
Ukraine	..	5.4	5.5	5.7	6.3	7.2	7.8	8.3	9.3	10.4	..	41
Finland	..	4.3	5.0	5.7	6.3	6.9	7.6	8.2	8.8	9.2	..	35
Latvia	..	2.6	2.9	3.3	3.6	3.9	4.2	5.0	5.6	6.3	..	41
Germany	..	1.4	1.7	1.9	2.2	2.6	3.0	3.3	3.6	3.9	..	45
Lithuania	..	1.8	1.8	2.0	2.1	2.2	2.3	2.4	2.5	2.6	..	43
Italy	..	0.6	0.8	0.9	1.1	1.3	1.5	1.7	2.0	2.2	..	36
Belarus	..	1.6	1.6	1.6	1.6	1.6	1.7	1.8	1.9	2.0	..	52
France	..	0.5	0.6	0.8	0.9	1.1	1.3	1.5	1.7	2.0	..	40
United Kingdom	..	0.7	0.8	0.9	0.9	1.1	1.2	1.3	1.4	1.6	..	23
Sweden	..	0.8	0.9	1.0	0.9	1.0	1.1	1.3	1.4	1.5	..	22
Spain	..	0.3	0.4	0.6	0.7	0.8	1.0	1.1	1.3	1.4	..	42
Poland	..	0.5	0.6	0.7	0.8	0.9	0.9	1.0	1.0	1.1	..	42
Romania	..	0.1	0.1	0.4	0.5	0.5	0.6	0.7	0.8	1.0	..	21
India	..	0.1	0.2	0.2	0.3	0.3	0.4	0.5	0.6	0.9	..	29
Other countries	..	93.9	93.0	92.5	90.7	88.8	87.4	86.7	86.1	83.6	..	
Total	..	**211.1**	**210.9**	**211.7**	**211.4**	**211.5**	**212.2**	**213.7**	**216.4**	**215.6**	..	47

Note: For details on definitions and sources, refer to the metadata at the end of the tables.

StatLink 🖳 https://stat.link/am1o6l

Table B.5. Stocks of foreign population by nationality – Finland

Thousands

	2011	2012	2013	2014	2015	2016	2017	2018	2019	2020	2021	Of which: Women 2021 (%)
Estonia	29.1	34.0	39.8	44.8	48.4	50.4	51.5	51.5	51.5	50.9	50.9	48
Russia	28.4	29.6	30.2	30.8	30.6	30.8	31.0	29.2	28.7	28.5	28.9	54
Iraq	5.0	5.7	5.9	6.4	6.8	7.1	9.8	11.7	13.1	13.9	14.7	35
China	5.6	6.2	6.6	7.1	7.6	8.0	8.5	8.7	9.2	9.8	10.5	54
Sweden	8.5	8.5	8.4	8.4	8.3	8.2	8.0	8.0	8.0	8.0	8.0	40
Thailand	5.0	5.5	6.0	6.5	6.9	7.2	7.5	7.5	7.6	7.8	7.9	85
India	3.5	3.8	4.0	4.4	4.7	5.0	5.0	5.2	5.7	6.8	7.2	40
Afghanistan	2.5	2.8	3.0	3.2	3.5	3.7	5.3	5.8	6.2	6.7	7.1	37
Syria	0.2	0.2	0.3	0.5	1.0	1.6	3.4	5.3	6.0	6.6	6.9	46
Viet Nam	2.8	3.1	3.3	3.6	4.0	4.6	5.3	5.6	5.9	6.4	6.6	53
Somalia	6.6	7.4	7.5	7.5	7.4	7.3	7.0	6.7	6.4	6.4	6.5	49
Ukraine	2.1	2.3	2.5	2.7	3.0	3.4	3.8	4.0	4.6	5.1	5.8	47
Türkiye	4.0	4.2	4.3	4.4	4.5	4.6	4.7	4.7	4.8	5.2	5.7	38
United Kingdom	3.5	3.7	3.9	4.0	4.3	4.4	4.6	4.5	4.6	4.7	4.8	20
Philippines	1.3	1.5	1.7	2.0	2.4	2.7	3.0	3.3	3.5	4.2	4.7	64
Other countries	60.0	64.7	68.1	71.4	76.3	80.8	85.4	87.7	91.5	96.7	102.8	
Total	**168.0**	**183.1**	**195.5**	**207.5**	**219.7**	**229.8**	**243.6**	**249.5**	**257.6**	**267.6**	**278.9**	45

Note: For details on definitions and sources, refer to the metadata at the end of the tables.

StatLink 🖳 https://stat.link/am1o6l

Table B.5. Stocks of foreign population by nationality – France

Thousands

	2011	2012	2013	2014	2015	2016	2017	2018	2019	2020	2021	Of which: Women 2015 (%)
Portugal	501.8	509.3	519.5	530.6	541.6	546.1	548.7	..	..	..	..	47
Algeria	466.6	469.6	476.5	483.8	495.7	505.6	518.1	..	..	..	..	48
Morocco	433.4	436.4	443.4	448.5	458.2	464.9	472.6	..	..	..	..	49
Türkiye	219.8	217.8	216.4	215.7	215.5	212.5	211.8	..	..	..	..	47
Italy	172.6	174.9	177.2	181.3	187.9	194.6	202.6	..	..	..	..	45
Tunisia	150.4	155.0	161.5	168.0	173.0	178.9	187.1	..	..	..	..	41
Spain	129.1	133.4	138.7	144.4	152.2	157.4	163.6	..	..	..	..	50
United Kingdom	157.0	156.4	153.6	151.8	150.4	148.2	146.1	..	..	..	..	49
China	90.1	93.8	96.2	97.6	100.6	100.4	102.1	..	..	..	..	57
Belgium	94.7	95.1	96.1	97.4	99.2	100.4	101.7	..	..	..	..	52
Romania	57.6	64.8	74.3	86.9	96.9	106.2	116.8	..	..	..	..	50
Germany	93.7	93.4	91.7	90.8	89.8	88.2	86.6	..	..	..	..	55
Mali	64.9	66.8	69.7	71.0	73.4	75.5	78.1	..	..	..	..	40
Haiti	62.7	64.2	65.8	68.6	72.5	74.6	77.5	..	..	..	..	55
Senegal	52.6	54.8	57.4	59.8	62.8	65.2	69.2	..	..	..	..	44
Other countries	1 145.8	1 194.9	1 245.9	1 303.9	1 365.7	1 523.3	1 621.4	..	..	..	..	
Total	**3 892.8**	**3 980.6**	**4 083.9**	**4 199.9**	**4 335.4**	**4 542.0**	**4 704.0**	**4 769.4**	**4 986.9**	**5 150.0**	**5 226.0**	**50**

Note: For details on definitions and sources, refer to the metadata at the end of the tables.

StatLink https://stat.link/am1o6l

Table B.5. Stocks of foreign population by nationality – Germany

Thousands

	2011	2012	2013	2014	2015	2016	2017	2018	2019	2020	2021	Of which: Women 2021 (%)
Türkiye	1 629.5	1 607.2	1 575.7	1 549.8	1 527.1	1 506.1	1 492.6	1 483.5	1 476.4	1 472.4	1 461.9	48
Poland	419.4	468.5	532.4	609.9	674.2	741.0	783.1	866.9	860.1	862.5	866.7	46
Syria	30.1	32.9	40.4	56.9	118.2	366.6	637.8	699.0	745.6	789.5	818.5	41
Romania	126.5	159.2	205.0	267.4	355.3	452.7	533.7	622.8	696.3	748.2	799.2	43
Italy	517.5	520.2	529.4	552.9	574.5	596.1	611.5	643.1	643.5	646.5	648.4	42
Croatia	220.2	223.0	225.0	240.5	263.3	297.9	332.6	367.9	395.7	414.9	426.8	47
Bulgaria	74.9	93.9	118.8	146.8	183.3	226.9	263.3	310.4	337.0	360.2	388.7	46
Greece	276.7	283.7	298.3	316.3	328.6	339.9	348.5	362.2	363.2	363.7	364.3	46
Afghanistan	51.3	56.6	61.8	67.0	75.4	131.5	253.5	251.6	257.1	263.4	271.8	36
Russia	191.3	195.3	202.1	216.3	221.4	231.0	245.4	249.2	254.3	260.4	263.3	63
Iraq	81.3	82.4	84.1	85.5	88.7	136.4	227.2	237.4	247.8	255.1	259.5	42
Serbia	179.0	198.0	202.5	205.0	220.9	230.4	223.1	225.5	231.2	237.8	242.6	49
Hungary	68.9	82.8	107.4	135.6	156.8	178.2	192.3	207.0	212.4	211.7	211.5	43
Bosnia and Herzegovina	152.4	153.5	155.3	157.5	163.5	168.0	172.6	181.0	190.5	203.3	211.3	47
Austria	175.2	175.9	176.3	178.8	179.8	181.8	183.6	191.3	187.4	186.7	186.9	49
Other countries	2 559.3	2 598.0	2 699.3	2 847.4	3 021.9	3 323.4	3 538.4	3 725.2	3 816.9	3 952.2	4 011.1	
Total	**6 753.6**	**6 930.9**	**7 213.7**	**7 633.6**	**8 153.0**	**9 107.9**	**10 039.1**	**10 623.9**	**10 915.5**	**11 228.3**	**11 432.5**	**47**

Note: For details on definitions and sources, refer to the metadata at the end of the tables.

StatLink https://stat.link/am1o6l

Table B.5. Stocks of foreign population by nationality – Greece

Thousands

	2011	2012	2013	2014	2015	2016	2017	2018	2019	2020	2021	Of which: Women 2021 (%)
EU	203.7	202.1	196.1	192.6	198.7	206.7	205.2	211.2	213.2	191.1	168.6	63
Non-EU	730.7	719.4	690.3	662.4	623.2	584.7	604.8	604.9	618.5	715.2	752.9	48
Total	**934.4**	**921.4**	**886.5**	**855.0**	**822.0**	**798.4**	**810.0**	**816.1**	**831.7**	**906.3**	**921.5**	**51**

Note: For details on definitions and sources, refer to the metadata at the end of the tables.

StatLink ᐧᐧᓯᐧ https://stat.link/am1o6l

Table B.5. Stocks of foreign population by nationality – Hungary

Thousands

	2011	2012	2013	2014	2015	2016	2017	2018	2019	2020	2021	Of which: Women 2021 (%)
Ukraine	16.5	11.9	10.8	8.3	6.9	6.7	5.8	10.5	24.2	30.3	27.4	36
China	11.8	10.1	11.5	12.7	16.5	19.8	19.1	19.9	18.9	19.7	18.6	49
Romania	76.9	41.6	34.8	30.9	28.6	29.7	24.0	22.7	21.0	22.2	18.2	34
Germany	20.2	15.8	17.4	18.7	18.8	19.4	18.6	17.9	16.5	18.3	17.5	47
Slovak Republic	7.3	6.7	7.6	8.3	8.7	9.4	9.5	9.7	9.6	10.6	14.7	55
Viet Nam	3.1	2.6	3.1	3.1	3.1	3.2	3.3	3.7	4.7	5.7	6.7	47
Russia	3.5	2.9	3.4	3.7	4.3	4.9	4.9	4.8	5.1	5.3	5.0	61
Austria	3.9	3.3	3.7	3.9	4.0	4.0	4.0	3.7	3.1	3.3	4.1	38
Italy	1.8	1.6	2.0	2.3	2.7	3.1	3.4	3.6	3.6	4.0	3.7	28
Serbia	16.3	8.3	4.9	3.1	2.4	2.4	2.3	3.4	5.3	5.0	3.5	30
United Kingdom	2.5	2.1	2.4	2.6	2.8	3.0	3.1	3.2	3.1	3.5	3.4	33
India	0.8	0.9	0.9	0.9	1.0	1.3	1.5	2.0	2.9	3.2	3.3	31
Korea	1.1	1.1	1.0	1.1	1.2	1.1	1.1	1.4	1.8	2.4	3.2	31
Türkiye	1.7	1.7	1.7	1.7	1.8	1.9	2.1	2.3	2.8	3.2	3.2	28
Netherlands	1.9	1.9	2.2	2.4	2.5	2.7	2.8	2.9	2.8	3.2	3.1	40
Other countries	37.5	30.9	34.0	36.9	40.6	43.9	45.6	50.2	55.3	60.0	59.0	
Total	**206.9**	**143.4**	**141.4**	**140.5**	**146.0**	**156.6**	**151.1**	**161.8**	**180.8**	**200.0**	**194.5**	**42**

Note: For details on definitions and sources, refer to the metadata at the end of the tables.

StatLink ᐧᐧᓯᐧ https://stat.link/am1o6l

Table B.5. Stocks of foreign population by nationality – Iceland

Thousands

	2011	2012	2013	2014	2015	2016	2017	2018	2019	2020	2021	Of which: Women 2021 (%)
Poland	9.1	9.0	9.4	10.2	11.1	12.1	13.8	17.0	19.3	20.6	20.8	41
Lithuania	1.6	1.6	1.6	1.7	1.7	1.8	2.3	3.4	4.1	4.6	4.6	35
Romania	0.1	0.2	0.2	0.2	0.3	0.4	0.6	1.0	1.5	2.1	2.2	29
Latvia	0.6	0.7	0.7	0.7	0.7	0.8	0.9	1.4	1.9	2.1	2.2	31
Germany	1.0	0.9	0.8	0.9	1.0	1.0	1.1	1.2	1.3	1.4	1.5	67
Portugal	0.5	0.5	0.5	0.5	0.6	0.7	0.8	1.0	1.2	1.4	1.3	35
United Kingdom	0.6	0.6	0.6	0.6	0.7	0.8	0.8	0.9	1.0	1.2	1.3	33
Spain	0.2	0.2	0.2	0.3	0.5	0.6	0.6	0.8	0.9	1.1	1.2	41
Philippines	0.6	0.6	0.6	0.6	0.5	0.5	0.6	0.7	0.9	1.0	1.0	62
Croatia	0.0	0.0	0.0	0.0	0.0	0.1	0.2	0.4	0.7	0.9	0.9	27
Denmark	0.9	0.9	0.9	0.9	0.9	0.9	0.9	0.9	0.9	0.9	0.9	53
United States	0.5	0.5	0.6	0.6	0.6	0.6	0.6	0.7	0.7	0.8	0.9	51
France	0.3	0.3	0.3	0.3	0.4	0.5	0.5	0.6	0.7	0.7	0.8	46
Czech Republic	0.1	0.1	0.1	0.2	0.2	0.3	0.3	0.5	0.7	0.8	0.7	46
Italy	0.2	0.2	0.2	0.2	0.2	0.3	0.3	0.4	0.5	0.6	0.6	41
Other countries	4.7	4.7	4.8	4.8	5.0	5.3	6.0	7.1	8.0	9.2	10.4	
Total	**21.1**	**21.0**	**21.4**	**22.7**	**24.3**	**26.5**	**30.3**	**37.8**	**44.3**	**49.4**	**51.3**	**42**

Note: For details on definitions and sources, refer to the metadata at the end of the tables.

StatLink https://stat.link/am1o6l

Table B.5. Stocks of foreign population by nationality – Ireland

Thousands

	2011	2012	2013	2014	2015	2016	2017	2018	2019	2020	2021	Of which: Women 2016 (%)
Poland	122.6	..	..	..	..	122.5	..	..	..	..	..	50
United Kingdom	112.3	113.0	113.4	114.9	115.5	103.1	107.7	110.8	114.5	116.9	118.2	49
Lithuania	36.7	..	..	..	..	36.6	..	..	..	..	..	54
Romania	17.3	..	..	..	..	29.2	..	..	..	..	..	48
Latvia	20.6	..	..	..	..	19.9	..	..	..	..	..	57
Brazil	8.7	..	..	..	..	13.6	..	..	..	..	..	53
Spain	6.8	..	..	..	..	12.1	..	..	..	..	..	60
Italy	7.7	..	..	..	..	11.7	..	..	..	..	..	45
France	9.7	..	..	..	..	11.7	..	..	..	..	..	50
Germany	11.3	..	..	..	..	11.5	..	..	..	..	..	57
India	17.0	..	..	..	..	11.5	..	..	..	..	..	37
United States	11.0	..	..	..	..	10.5	..	..	..	..	..	58
Slovak Republic	10.8	..	..	..	..	9.7	..	..	..	..	..	50
Hungary	8.0	..	..	..	..	9.3	..	..	..	..	..	49
Pakistan	6.8	..	..	..	..	7.4	..	..	..	..	..	31
Other countries	190.8	..	..	..	..	187.1	..	..	..	..	..	
Total	**598.1**	**600.0**	**601.8**	**603.7**	**605.6**	**607.4**	**566.6**	**593.5**	**622.7**	**644.4**	**645.6**	**50**

Note: For details on definitions and sources, refer to the metadata at the end of the tables.

StatLink https://stat.link/am1o6l

Table B.5. Stocks of foreign population by nationality – Italy

Thousands

	2011	2012	2013	2014	2015	2016	2017	2018	2019	2020	2021	Of which: Women 2021 (%)
Romania	782.0	834.5	933.4	1 081.4	1 131.8	1 151.4	1 168.6	1 190.1	1 143.9	1 145.7	1 076.4	58
Albania	450.2	450.9	465.0	495.7	490.5	467.7	448.4	440.5	423.2	421.6	433.2	49
Morocco	400.7	408.7	426.8	454.8	449.1	437.5	420.7	416.5	406.1	414.2	428.9	46
China	184.2	197.1	223.4	256.8	265.8	271.3	282.0	290.7	283.4	288.9	330.5	50
Ukraine	171.6	180.1	191.7	219.1	226.1	230.7	234.4	237.0	227.9	228.6	236.0	78
India	109.2	118.4	128.9	142.5	147.8	150.5	151.4	151.8	147.2	153.2	165.5	41
Philippines	120.0	129.2	139.8	162.7	168.2	165.9	166.5	167.9	158.0	157.7	165.4	57
Bangladesh	73.8	81.7	92.7	111.2	115.3	118.8	122.4	132.0	131.0	138.9	158.0	28
Egypt	62.4	66.9	76.7	96.0	103.7	109.9	112.8	119.5	119.9	128.1	139.6	33
Pakistan	66.3	71.0	80.7	90.6	96.2	101.8	108.2	114.2	116.6	121.6	135.5	29
Moldova	122.4	132.2	139.7	149.4	147.4	142.3	135.7	131.8	122.8	118.5	122.7	66
Nigeria	44.7	48.2	56.5	66.8	71.2	77.3	88.5	106.1	114.1	113.0	119.1	42
Sri Lanka	65.3	71.6	79.5	95.0	100.6	102.3	104.9	108.0	104.8	107.6	112.0	47
Senegal	69.5	73.7	80.3	90.9	94.0	98.2	101.2	105.9	105.3	106.2	111.1	26
Tunisia	81.1	83.0	88.3	97.3	96.0	95.6	94.1	93.8	90.6	93.4	97.4	38
Other countries	1 076.0	1 104.9	1 184.4	1 311.1	1 310.8	1 305.8	1 307.4	1 338.7	1 301.4	1 302.4	1 340.6	
Total	**3 879.2**	**4 052.1**	**4 387.7**	**4 921.3**	**5 014.4**	**5 026.9**	**5 047.0**	**5 144.4**	**4 996.2**	**5 039.6**	**5 171.9**	51

Note: For details on definitions and sources, refer to the metadata at the end of the tables.

StatLink https://stat.link/am1o6l

Table B.5. Stocks of foreign population by nationality – Japan

Thousands

	2011	2012	2013	2014	2015	2016	2017	2018	2019	2020	2021	Of which: Women 2021 (%)
China	687.2	674.9	652.6	649.1	654.8	665.8	695.5	730.9	764.7	813.7	778.1	54
Korea	566.0	545.4	530.0	519.7	501.2	457.8	453.1	450.7	449.6	446.4	426.9	54
Viet Nam	41.8	44.7	52.4	72.3	99.9	147.0	200.0	262.4	330.8	412.0	448.1	44
Philippines	210.2	209.4	203.0	209.2	217.6	229.6	243.7	260.6	271.3	282.8	279.7	70
Brazil	230.6	210.0	190.6	181.3	175.4	173.4	180.9	191.4	201.9	211.7	208.5	46
Nepal	17.5	20.4	24.1	31.5	42.3	54.8	67.5	80.0	89.0	96.8	96.0	43
Indonesia	24.9	24.7	25.5	27.2	30.2	35.9	42.9	50.0	56.3	66.9	66.8	33
Chinese Taipei	..	..	22.8	33.3	40.2	48.7	52.8	56.7	60.7	64.8	55.9	67
United States	50.7	49.8	48.4	50.0	51.3	52.3	53.7	55.7	57.5	59.2	55.8	32
Thailand	41.3	42.8	40.1	41.2	43.1	45.4	47.6	50.2	52.3	54.8	53.4	72
Peru	54.6	52.8	49.2	48.6	48.0	47.7	47.7	48.0	48.4	48.7	48.3	48
India	22.5	21.5	21.7	22.5	24.5	26.2	28.7	31.7	35.4	40.2	38.6	31
Myanmar	8.6	8.7	8.0	8.6	10.3	13.7	17.8	22.5	26.5	32.0	35.0	54
Dem. People's Rep. of Korea	..	..	..	..	..	33.9	32.5	30.9	29.6	28.1	27.2	45
Sri Lanka	9.1	9.3	8.4	9.2	10.7	13.2	17.3	23.3	25.4	27.4	29.3	27
Other countries	168.1	164.2	156.9	162.7	172.4	186.7	201.2	217.0	231.7	247.8	239.7	
Total	**2 132.9**	**2 078.5**	**2 033.7**	**2 066.4**	**2 121.8**	**2 232.2**	**2 382.8**	**2 561.8**	**2 731.1**	**2 933.1**	**2 887.1**	50

Note: For details on definitions and sources, refer to the metadata at the end of the tables.

StatLink https://stat.link/am1o6l

Table B.5. Stocks of foreign population by nationality – Korea

Thousands

	2011	2012	2013	2014	2015	2016	2017	2018	2019	2020	2021	Of which: Women 2021 (%)
China	537.6	610.7	591.8	650.3	755.1	809.1	824.5	837.1	886.1	887.1	816.9	51
Viet Nam	98.2	110.6	114.2	113.8	122.6	128.0	137.8	151.4	170.7	187.3	181.4	52
United States	64.3	67.0	67.8	69.0	71.1	70.6	69.7	69.1	69.3	71.3	69.5	52
Uzbekistan	21.2	25.8	30.9	34.5	39.3	42.5	49.3	56.7	63.1	68.1	61.1	35
Philippines	39.5	38.4	33.2	38.8	43.2	45.3	46.1	45.2	45.3	45.4	40.7	46
Cambodia	11.7	16.8	23.4	30.7	37.3	42.0	44.5	45.7	45.3	45.0	40.2	33
Russia	6.6	7.2	8.0	9.0	9.8	13.2	21.5	28.7	35.3	40.5	38.9	51
Nepal	9.2	12.6	17.8	20.7	25.5	29.2	33.1	35.4	38.9	40.9	38.5	12
Indonesia	27.5	29.7	29.9	33.3	38.9	40.2	39.3	37.1	37.6	37.3	33.5	10
Thailand	27.6	26.0	21.4	26.2	26.8	27.9	29.3	30.2	31.4	32.6	30.8	35
Myanmar	3.8	5.6	8.3	11.5	14.7	18.1	21.3	23.5	26.7	27.5	25.0	5
Mongolia	21.8	21.3	19.8	18.4	17.3	18.5	20.1	22.6	24.2	24.8	24.5	52
Japan	19.9	21.8	23.4	23.9	24.0	23.8	24.1	24.1	24.7	25.1	23.5	77
Sri Lanka	17.4	20.5	21.0	21.9	24.6	25.2	26.0	25.3	24.3	23.5	21.2	3
Kazakhstan	1.4	1.7	2.1	2.5	3.0	3.9	7.6	12.7	18.5	22.7	19.9	46
Other countries	180.8	184.5	189.3	199.4	235.9	257.3	268.6	304.7	409.7	445.3	423.7	
Total	**1 088.6**	**1 200.1**	**1 202.3**	**1 303.8**	**1 488.9**	**1 594.8**	**1 662.8**	**1 749.6**	**1 951.1**	**2 024.6**	**1 889.5**	**45**

Note: For details on definitions and sources, refer to the metadata at the end of the tables.

StatLink 📊 https://stat.link/am1o6l

Table B.5. Stocks of foreign population by nationality – Latvia

Thousands

	2011	2012	2013	2014	2015	2016	2017	2018	2019	2020	2021	Of which: Women 2021 (%)
Russia	33.8	37.0	36.1	38.8	51.6	56.0	55.4	54.7	53.9	53.1	52.3	..
Ukraine	2.5	2.4	2.3	2.4	4.1	5.9	6.4	7.0	8.2	9.2	9.4	..
Lithuania	3.0	3.0	2.9	2.9	4.3	4.6	4.8	5.0	5.1	5.1	5.2	..
Belarus	1.7	1.6	1.6	1.7	2.6	2.9	3.0	3.2	3.5	3.9	3.9	..
Germany	0.5	0.4	0.4	0.6	1.8	2.2	2.4	2.6	2.5	2.6	2.7	..
Uzbekistan	..	..	..	..	1.0	1.6	1.6	1.6	1.7	2.3	2.4	..
India	..	..	..	..	..	0.6	0.9	1.3	2.2	2.7	2.4	..
Estonia	0.7	0.7	0.7	0.7	1.1	1.2	1.2	1.2	1.2	1.3	1.3	..
United Kingdom	..	..	..	..	..	0.8	0.9	1.0	1.1	1.2	1.3	..
Bulgaria	..	..	..	..	0.8	0.8	0.9	0.9	0.9	0.9	0.9	..
Sweden	..	..	..	..	0.7	0.8	0.9	0.9	0.9	0.9	0.9	..
China	..	..	..	..	0.9	1.3	1.2	1.1	1.0	0.9	0.9	..
Italy	..	..	..	..	0.4	0.5	0.6	0.7	0.8	0.8	0.9	..
France	..	..	..	..	0.4	0.5	0.6	0.6	0.7	0.8	0.9	..
Poland	0.3	0.2	0.2	0.2	0.6	0.6	0.7	0.7	0.7	0.8	0.8	..
Other countries	300.4	279.0	271.1	257.5	228.2	208.6	197.9	190.0	182.2	173.9	166.4	
Total	**342.8**	**324.3**	**315.4**	**304.8**	**298.4**	**288.9**	**279.4**	**272.5**	**266.6**	**260.4**	**252.4**	**52**

Note: For details on definitions and sources, refer to the metadata at the end of the tables.

StatLink 📊 https://stat.link/am1o6l

Table B.5. Stocks of foreign population by nationality – Lithuania

Thousands

	2011	2012	2013	2014	2015	2016	2017	2018	2019	2020	2021	Of which: Women 2021 (%)
Ukraine	1.3	2.1	1.9	1.7	2.1	1.5	2.5	6.2	13.9	21.4	26.9	11
Belarus	2.3	3.4	3.0	2.3	1.9	0.8	0.9	3.2	8.9	15.6	20.8	11
Russia	11.2	10.8	10.5	10.3	10.7	8.9	8.3	8.1	10.9	12.3	12.6	46
Poland	0.4	1.1	1.1	1.2	1.3	1.3	1.4	1.4	1.5	1.5	1.5	49
Latvia	0.3	0.5	0.5	0.7	0.7	0.9	0.9	1.1	1.2	1.3	1.4	51
United Kingdom	..	..	..	0.1	0.2	0.2	0.2	0.3	0.6	0.8	0.9	44
India	..	..	..	0.0	0.0	0.0	0.1	0.4	0.5	0.8	0.9	27
Germany	0.3	0.4	0.3	0.4	0.4	0.5	0.6	0.6	0.7	0.8	0.9	30
Moldova	..	..	..	0.1	0.0	0.0	0.1	0.2	0.4	0.6	0.9	13
Kazakhstan	..	..	..	0.2	0.2	0.2	0.2	0.2	0.4	0.5	0.7	39
Ireland	..	..	..	0.1	0.1	0.1	0.1	0.1	0.6	0.7	0.7	49
United States	0.2	0.3	0.3	0.1	0.1	0.0	0.0	0.1	..	0.6	0.7	47
Uzbekistan	..	..	..	0.1	0.1	0.1	0.0	0.0	0.0	0.6	0.7	7
Romania	..	..	..	0.2	0.3	0.4	0.5	0.5	0.5	0.2	0.6	15
Stateless	3.5	2.5	2.3	1.8	1.6	1.4	1.3	1.2	1.0	0.9	0.8	55
Other countries	4.5	1.8	2.3	2.3	2.8	2.4	3.0	3.7	6.1	7.2	9.0	
Total	**24.0**	**22.9**	**22.2**	**21.6**	**22.5**	**18.7**	**20.1**	**27.3**	**47.2**	**65.8**	**79.9**	22

Note: For details on definitions and sources, refer to the metadata at the end of the tables.

StatLink ᵐˢᴾ https://stat.link/am1o6l

Table B.5. Stocks of foreign population by nationality – Luxembourg

Thousands

	2011	2012	2013	2014	2015	2016	2017	2018	2019	2020	2021	Of which: Women 2021 (%)
Portugal	82.4	85.3	88.2	90.8	92.1	93.1	96.8	96.5	95.5	95.1	94.3	47
France	31.5	33.1	35.2	37.2	39.4	41.7	44.3	45.8	46.9	47.8	48.5	47
Italy	18.1	18.1	18.3	18.8	19.5	20.3	21.3	22.0	22.5	23.0	23.5	44
Belgium	16.9	17.2	17.6	18.2	18.8	19.4	20.0	20.2	20.0	19.8	19.6	45
Germany	12.0	12.3	12.4	12.7	12.8	12.8	13.1	13.1	13.0	12.8	12.8	50
Spain	3.7	4.0	4.3	4.7	5.1	5.5	6.1	6.5	6.8	7.2	7.7	48
Romania	1.6	1.9	2.2	2.5	3.2	3.8	4.1	4.7	5.2	5.7	6.1	57
Poland	2.7	3.0	3.2	3.4	3.8	4.1	4.3	4.5	4.7	4.8	4.9	56
United Kingdom	5.5	5.6	5.7	5.9	6.0	6.1	6.1	5.9	5.8	5.3	4.6	43
Netherlands	3.9	3.9	3.9	4.0	4.0	4.0	4.3	4.3	4.2	4.2	4.1	46
China	1.6	1.7	1.8	2.2	2.5	2.8	3.2	3.5	3.7	3.9	4.1	55
Greece	1.5	1.7	1.9	2.1	2.3	2.6	2.9	3.3	3.4	3.7	3.8	50
India	0.6	0.7	0.8	0.8	1.0	1.2	1.4	1.9	2.3	2.8	3.1	45
Montenegro	3.8	3.8	3.9	3.9	3.9	3.8	4.4	4.2	3.6	3.2	2.9	48
Brazil	1.2	1.3	1.4	1.6	1.7	1.8	1.8	2.0	2.2	2.4	2.6	67
Other countries	33.6	36.3	38.0	40.3	42.7	46.2	47.3	49.8	51.6	54.7	56.7	
Total	**220.5**	**229.9**	**238.8**	**248.9**	**258.7**	**269.2**	**281.5**	**288.2**	**291.5**	**296.5**	**299.4**	48

Note: For details on definitions and sources, refer to the metadata at the end of the tables.

StatLink ᵐˢᴾ https://stat.link/am1o6l

Table B.5. Stocks of foreign population by nationality – Mexico

Thousands

	2011	2012	2013	2014	2015	2016	2017	2018	2019	2020	2021	Of which: Women 2019 (%)
United States	68.5	63.4	..	65.3	67.5	68.9	74.6	79.6	82.5	..	..	44
Venezuela	12.8	12.9	..	15.3	18.6	22.3	28.2	35.1	39.3	..	..	55
Colombia	16.9	16.7	..	18.3	20.6	23.0	26.3	30.0	32.0	..	..	55
Cuba	14.0	14.5	..	17.0	18.4	20.5	24.3	26.5	27.9	..	..	50
Spain	19.6	20.7	..	24.7	26.7	27.7	28.5	28.9	26.9	..	..	40
China	15.2	15.6	..	18.3	20.5	21.5	22.7	23.5	24.5	..	..	42
Honduras	7.6	6.9	..	7.8	9.3	12.0	15.6	19.5	22.5	..	..	54
Argentina	15.8	15.3	..	16.8	18.0	19.0	19.8	20.7	20.8	..	..	47
Guatemala	10.9	9.7	..	10.3	11.6	13.2	15.8	18.5	19.9	..	..	55
Canada	13.6	12.9	..	13.2	14.1	14.6	16.0	17.2	18.3	..	..	46
El Salvador	6.0	5.7	..	6.2	7.2	9.0	12.2	15.3	17.3	..	..	50
France	9.1	9.0	..	9.8	10.5	10.9	11.7	12.1	11.8	..	..	45
Brazil	7.1	6.5	..	7.2	8.2	9.3	10.5	11.4	11.6	..	..	53
Germany	9.0	8.8	..	9.5	10.5	10.9	11.2	11.4	11.0	..	..	42
Japan	5.2	5.6	..	8.0	9.0	9.9	10.8	11.2	11.0	..	..	40
Other countries	72.7	72.1	..	78.3	84.5	89.2	95.8	101.1	103.0	..	..	
Total	303.9	296.4	..	326.0	355.2	381.8	423.9	462.0	480.3	..	..	47

Note: For details on definitions and sources, refer to the metadata at the end of the tables.

StatLink ᔕᒷ https://stat.link/am1o6l

Table B.5. Stocks of foreign population by nationality – Netherlands

Thousands

	2011	2012	2013	2014	2015	2016	2017	2018	2019	2020	2021	Of which: Women 2021 (%)
Poland	52.5	65.1	74.6	85.8	99.6	110.9	121.4	132.4	144.0	155.9	164.9	50
Germany	71.4	72.8	72.6	72.2	71.8	72.3	73.3	75.0	77.1	79.5	80.6	56
Türkiye	88.0	84.8	81.9	80.1	77.5	75.4	74.1	73.8	74.8	77.0	77.3	48
Syria	0.6	0.6	0.8	1.4	8.2	25.4	51.4	67.5	74.1	79.5	71.2	44
United Kingdom	41.4	41.4	41.7	42.3	43.0	44.2	45.3	46.0	47.3	47.9	48.8	41
Italy	21.9	22.6	23.6	25.0	27.1	29.5	32.3	35.5	39.1	43.3	45.1	42
Bulgaria	14.1	16.8	17.6	17.8	19.8	21.9	24.1	27.3	31.2	36.8	41.8	48
China	21.4	23.9	25.9	27.2	28.2	29.7	31.4	33.9	36.5	39.4	38.9	52
Spain	19.2	20.3	21.9	23.9	25.3	26.8	28.3	30.3	32.7	35.6	37.4	50
India	9.6	10.8	11.7	13.1	14.7	17.1	20.4	24.9	30.6	37.4	37.1	43
Belgium	27.2	27.6	28.2	28.8	29.6	30.6	31.9	33.2	34.4	35.9	37.0	53
Romania	8.3	9.1	9.5	10.0	11.9	13.7	16.1	20.0	24.9	30.7	34.6	47
Morocco	61.9	56.6	51.0	48.1	44.9	42.3	39.9	38.0	36.5	35.8	33.8	49
Eritrea	0.3	0.3	0.3	0.4	3.2	9.1	15.7	21.0	26.0	30.4	30.0	46
France	17.8	18.1	18.3	18.7	19.7	20.9	22.6	24.2	25.8	27.8	29.0	52
Other countries	304.8	315.3	316.6	321.2	322.8	330.7	344.1	357.8	375.9	399.4	395.5	
Total	760.4	786.1	796.2	816.0	847.3	900.5	972.3	1 040.8	1 110.9	1 192.3	1 203.0	50

Note: For details on definitions and sources, refer to the metadata at the end of the tables.

StatLink ᔕᒷ https://stat.link/am1o6l

Table B.5. Stocks of foreign population by nationality – Norway

Thousands

	2011	2012	2013	2014	2015	2016	2017	2018	2019	2020	2021	Of which: Women 2021 (%)
Poland	55.2	66.6	77.1	85.6	93.6	99.6	102.0	103.8	105.2	108.6	110.3	37
Lithuania	16.4	24.1	30.7	35.8	39.5	41.7	42.5	43.7	45.1	46.9	47.9	43
Sweden	39.2	42.0	43.1	44.2	45.1	45.1	44.4	44.0	44.0	44.2	43.6	48
Syria	0.4	0.4	0.7	1.5	3.6	7.6	18.9	26.0	30.2	32.0	32.8	42
Germany	22.4	23.7	24.4	24.6	25.0	25.2	24.9	24.7	24.8	25.3	25.6	42
Denmark	20.9	21.4	21.9	22.6	23.5	23.3	23.0	22.8	22.8	22.9	22.3	47
United Kingdom	14.0	14.7	15.5	15.8	16.3	16.3	16.3	16.2	16.5	17.2	17.5	45
Romania	4.5	5.7	7.5	10.0	12.0	13.8	14.5	15.0	15.6	16.6	17.2	35
Eritrea	5.7	7.6	10.0	12.7	15.2	17.7	19.0	18.6	19.1	18.9	17.1	42
Latvia	4.9	6.9	8.5	9.4	10.3	10.8	11.0	11.1	11.5	12.1	12.5	42
Philippines	7.8	8.9	10.1	11.4	11.7	11.8	12.1	11.7	12.3	12.8	12.1	42
Thailand	9.3	10.0	10.8	11.4	11.5	11.6	12.1	11.3	11.9	12.0	11.9	76
Russia	10.8	10.9	11.2	11.4	11.5	11.5	11.4	11.3	11.9	12.0	11.9	85
Spain	2.7	3.4	4.6	5.8	6.9	7.6	8.1	8.5	8.8	9.5	9.8	66
United States	8.6	8.8	9.2	9.3	9.3	9.3	9.2	9.2	9.5	9.9	9.8	44
Other countries	146.4	152.2	163.5	171.7	177.2	185.3	189.8	190.0	195.6	204.0	199.7	51
Total	**369.2**	**407.3**	**448.8**	**483.2**	**512.2**	**538.2**	**559.2**	**567.8**	**584.2**	**604.5**	**601.6**	**46**

Note: For details on definitions and sources, refer to the metadata at the end of the tables.

StatLink ᵐˢᵖ https://stat.link/am1o6l

Table B.5. Stocks of foreign population by nationality – Poland

Thousands

	2010	2011	2012	2013	2014	2015	2016	2017	2018	2019	2020	Of which: Women 2010 (%)
Ukraine	10.2	..	13.4	..	..	..	..	..	..	..	..	..
Germany	4.4	..	5.2	..	..	..	..	..	..	..	..	..
Russia	4.2	..	4.2	..	..	..	..	..	..	..	..	..
Belarus	3.2	..	3.8	..	..	..	..	..	..	..	..	..
Viet Nam	2.9	..	2.6	..	..	..	..	..	..	..	..	..
Armenia	1.4	..	1.8	..	..	..	..	..	..	..	..	..
Sweden	1.3	..	..	..	..	..	..	..	..	..	..	..
Bulgaria	1.1	..	..	..	..	..	..	..	..	..	..	..
United States	1.1	..	..	..	..	..	..	..	..	..	..	..
Former USSR	1.0	..	..	..	..	..	..	..	..	..	..	..
Austria	1.0	..	..	..	..	..	..	..	..	..	..	..
Greece	0.9	..	..	..	..	..	..	..	..	..	..	..
United Kingdom	0.8	..	..	..	..	..	..	..	..	..	..	..
France	0.7	..	..	..	..	..	..	..	..	..	..	..
Czech Republic	0.7	..	..	..	..	..	..	..	..	..	..	..
Other countries	40.4	..	54.8	..	..	..	..	..	..	..	..	..
Total	**75.2**	**79.3**	**85.8**	**93.3**	**101.2**	**108.3**	**149.6**	**210.3**	**239.2**	**289.8**	**358.2**	**47**

Note: For details on definitions and sources, refer to the metadata at the end of the tables.

StatLink ᵐˢᵖ https://stat.link/am1o6l

Table B.5. Stocks of foreign population by nationality – Portugal

Thousands

	2011	2012	2013	2014	2015	2016	2017	2018	2019	2020	2021	Of which: Women 2021 (%)
Brazil	119.4	111.4	105.6	92.1	87.5	82.6	81.3	85.4	105.4	151.3	184.0	56
United Kingdom	17.2	17.7	16.7	16.5	16.6	17.2	19.4	22.4	26.4	34.4	46.2	45
Cape Verde	44.0	43.9	42.9	42.4	40.9	38.7	36.6	35.0	34.7	37.4	36.6	53
Romania	36.8	39.3	35.2	34.2	31.5	30.5	30.4	30.8	30.9	31.1	30.1	46
Ukraine	49.5	48.0	44.1	41.1	37.9	35.8	34.5	32.5	29.2	29.7	28.6	55
Italy	5.1	5.3	5.2	5.1	5.3	6.1	8.5	12.9	18.9	25.4	28.2	42
China	15.7	16.8	17.5	18.7	21.5	21.4	22.6	23.2	25.4	27.9	26.1	50
France	5.1	5.3	5.2	5.3	6.5	8.4	11.3	15.3	19.8	23.1	24.9	47
India	5.3	5.4	5.7	6.0	6.4	6.9	7.2	8.0	11.4	17.6	24.6	22
Angola	23.5	21.6	20.4	20.2	19.7	18.2	17.0	16.9	18.4	22.7	24.4	57
Nepal	0.8	1.1	1.7	2.6	3.5	4.8	5.8	7.4	11.5	16.8	21.0	37
Guinea-Bissau	19.8	18.5	17.8	17.8	18.0	17.1	15.7	15.2	16.2	18.9	19.7	47
Spain	8.9	9.3	9.4	9.5	9.7	10.0	11.1	12.5	14.1	15.8	17.0	49
Germany	9.0	9.1	8.6	8.6	8.8	9.0	10.0	11.2	12.8	14.7	16.0	47
Sao Tome and Principe	10.5	10.5	10.4	10.3	10.2	9.6	9.0	8.6	9.2	10.2	10.7	55
Other countries	74.7	73.6	70.9	70.9	71.3	72.3	77.4	84.4	96.1	113.2	124.0	
Total	**445.3**	**436.8**	**417.0**	**401.3**	**395.2**	**388.7**	**397.7**	**421.7**	**480.3**	**590.3**	**662.1**	**49**

Note: For details on definitions and sources, refer to the metadata at the end of the tables.

StatLink ᴍⓈ☞ https://stat.link/am1o6l

Table B.5. Stocks of foreign population by nationality – Slovak Republic

Thousands

	2011	2012	2013	2014	2015	2016	2017	2018	2019	2020	2021	Of which: Women 2021 (%)
Czech Republic	9.0	10.6	11.0	11.4	11.9	12.5	13.0	13.5	14.0	14.4	15.1	48
Hungary	5.3	7.1	7.8	8.1	8.6	9.2	9.8	10.2	10.7	11.1	11.6	34
Romania	5.8	4.4	4.7	4.9	5.3	5.8	6.3	6.5	6.9	7.1	7.3	29
Poland	5.6	4.8	4.9	5.1	5.2	5.4	5.6	5.8	5.9	6.1	6.3	47
Ukraine	6.3	2.6	2.7	2.7	2.8	3.1	3.2	3.5	3.7	4.1	4.4	61
Germany	4.1	3.4	3.5	3.6	3.7	3.8	3.9	4.1	4.2	4.3	4.4	26
Italy	1.7	1.7	1.9	2.0	2.1	2.4	2.6	2.8	2.9	3.0	3.1	20
United Kingdom	1.5	1.4	1.5	1.6	1.6	1.7	1.9	2.0	2.2	2.4	2.5	29
Austria	2.2	1.7	1.8	1.8	1.9	1.9	2.0	2.1	2.1	2.1	2.2	25
Bulgaria	1.7	1.4	1.5	1.6	1.6	1.8	1.9	2.0	2.1	2.1	2.2	26
Russia	2.2	1.3	1.3	1.4	1.4	1.5	1.5	1.6	1.7	1.7	1.8	62
France	1.7	1.2	1.3	1.4	1.4	1.5	1.6	1.7	1.7	1.7	1.8	30
Viet Nam	2.3	1.2	1.3	1.4	1.4	1.5	1.5	1.6	1.7	1.7	1.8	44
Croatia	0.5	0.3	0.3	0.5	0.6	0.7	0.9	0.9	1.0	1.1	1.1	24
Spain	0.5	0.5	0.5	0.6	0.6	0.7	0.8	0.9	0.9	1.0	1.1	39
Other countries	17.6	9.9	10.6	11.1	11.7	12.4	13.2	13.8	14.4	14.9	15.4	
Total	**68.0**	**53.4**	**56.5**	**59.2**	**61.8**	**65.8**	**69.7**	**72.9**	**76.1**	**78.9**	**82.1**	**38**

Note: For details on definitions and sources, refer to the metadata at the end of the tables.

StatLink ᴍⓈ☞ https://stat.link/am1o6l

Table B.5. Stocks of foreign population by nationality – Slovenia

Thousands

	2011	2012	2013	2014	2015	2016	2017	2018	2019	2020	2021	Of which: Women 2021 (%)
Bosnia and Herzegovina	38.8	39.3	41.3	43.3	44.9	47.7	50.4	54.0	62.9	73.2	79.6	29
Serbia	7.6	7.3	7.8	9.8	9.7	9.8	10.6	11.8	14.0	16.2	17.3	27
North Macedonia	8.8	9.1	9.6	9.8	10.1	10.4	10.8	11.3	12.3	13.3	14.0	45
Croatia	7.7	8.0	8.3	8.7	8.8	8.9	9.2	9.5	9.8	10.1	10.2	39
Russia	0.6	0.7	0.8	1.1	1.5	2.0	2.3	2.6	3.0	3.3	3.5	55
Bulgaria	1.1	1.5	1.8	2.1	2.5	2.6	2.9	3.2	3.4	3.6	3.3	30
Italy	0.9	1.0	1.2	1.4	1.6	1.8	2.1	2.2	2.4	2.5	2.8	34
Ukraine	1.2	1.3	1.4	1.4	1.5	1.7	1.9	2.0	2.2	2.3	2.4	62
China	0.9	0.9	1.0	1.0	1.0	1.0	1.1	1.1	1.2	1.3	1.4	44
Germany	0.8	0.8	0.9	0.9	0.9	0.9	0.9	0.9	0.9	0.9	1.0	48
Montenegro	0.6	0.7	0.7	0.7	0.8	0.8	0.8	0.8	0.8	0.9	0.9	44
United Kingdom	0.4	0.4	0.4	0.4	0.4	0.4	0.5	0.5	0.6	0.6	0.7	37
Hungary	0.2	0.2	0.2	0.3	0.4	0.4	0.5	0.6	0.6	0.7	0.7	46
Austria	0.4	0.4	0.4	0.4	0.4	0.4	0.4	0.4	0.4	0.4	0.5	42
Slovak Republic	0.5	0.4	0.4	0.5	0.5	0.5	0.5	0.5	0.5	0.5	0.5	65
Other countries	12.4	13.7	15.2	14.9	16.6	18.3	19.6	20.4	23.0	26.5	29.9	
Total	**82.7**	**85.6**	**91.4**	**96.6**	**101.5**	**107.8**	**114.4**	**121.9**	**138.2**	**156.4**	**168.7**	**34**

Note: For details on definitions and sources, refer to the metadata at the end of the tables.

StatLink https://stat.link/am1o6l

Table B.5. Stocks of foreign population by nationality – Spain

Thousands

	2011	2012	2013	2014	2015	2016	2017	2018	2019	2020	2021	Of which: Women 2021 (%)
Morocco	774.2	771.6	759.3	718.0	688.7	680.5	665.6	682.0	713.8	760.7	775.3	47
Romania	783.2	799.0	769.6	728.3	708.4	695.0	683.8	673.6	670.2	665.9	658.0	51
United Kingdom	312.2	313.0	316.4	310.1	301.8	296.4	293.5	285.0	286.8	300.6	314.0	49
Colombia	265.8	245.8	223.1	173.2	145.5	135.9	138.4	159.6	199.2	261.2	297.7	56
Italy	172.1	178.2	181.0	180.8	182.7	191.6	203.8	221.4	243.7	267.7	279.7	45
Venezuela	55.1	53.8	52.0	44.4	44.2	50.0	63.3	91.1	134.0	187.2	209.0	56
China	167.6	170.8	169.6	166.0	167.5	172.2	177.5	183.5	190.6	197.2	197.6	51
Germany	154.2	153.6	153.4	148.5	145.0	142.1	141.1	138.8	138.3	139.0	139.6	51
Ecuador	350.3	309.8	269.4	214.0	174.4	159.0	145.2	139.4	134.9	132.6	126.9	47
Honduras	28.1	32.2	35.0	34.3	35.9	40.8	48.1	64.1	84.8	109.5	123.1	69
France	100.4	101.1	101.5	99.5	98.7	100.7	103.2	106.2	111.5	117.1	121.7	50
Bulgaria	149.3	151.5	147.3	139.9	134.4	130.5	127.4	125.0	123.3	122.8	120.8	50
Peru	130.9	122.0	109.6	84.2	66.4	61.3	59.5	66.7	79.9	101.0	112.0	57
Ukraine	83.3	84.4	84.1	81.8	84.1	90.8	94.5	99.0	103.6	107.6	107.2	57
Portugal	123.8	121.3	116.4	109.0	103.8	101.8	100.9	100.1	102.8	106.1	106.9	42
Other countries	1 662.0	1 628.0	1 584.8	1 445.1	1 372.6	1 369.0	1 373.7	1 427.5	1 522.9	1 650.7	1 678.5	
Total	**5 312.4**	**5 236.0**	**5 072.7**	**4 677.1**	**4 454.4**	**4 417.5**	**4 419.5**	**4 563.0**	**4 840.2**	**5 226.9**	**5 368.3**	**51**

Note: For details on definitions and sources, refer to the metadata at the end of the tables.

StatLink https://stat.link/am1o6l

Table B.5. Stocks of foreign population by nationality – Sweden

Thousands

	2011	2012	2013	2014	2015	2016	2017	2018	2019	2020	2021	Of which: Women 2021 (%)
Syria	4.1	5.0	9.1	20.5	42.2	70.0	116.4	132.1	137.1	116.4	95.1	45
Poland	40.9	42.7	44.6	46.1	48.2	50.8	52.5	54.0	54.9	55.5	53.8	44
Afghanistan	9.8	12.7	16.7	20.3	23.6	26.0	28.0	37.4	45.4	49.6	48.5	33
Finland	70.6	67.9	65.3	62.8	59.7	57.6	55.8	53.8	51.0	48.7	46.1	58
Eritrea	6.4	8.4	10.0	12.8	18.0	25.1	32.1	36.4	39.7	43.0	43.5	44
Norway	34.9	34.8	34.8	34.6	34.5	34.4	34.6	34.7	34.5	34.5	32.6	52
Denmark	40.5	40.5	40.2	39.3	38.4	37.1	35.2	33.4	31.5	30.2	29.1	42
Germany	27.6	27.8	28.0	28.1	28.2	28.2	28.7	29.0	29.2	29.5	29.0	50
Somalia	30.8	33.0	36.1	45.0	47.1	46.2	41.3	36.4	32.4	30.9	28.9	50
India	7.1	7.7	8.4	9.2	10.4	11.4	13.5	17.1	22.2	27.0	28.3	41
Iraq	56.6	55.8	43.2	31.2	25.9	23.2	22.7	25.3	26.4	25.9	23.4	41
China	14.1	15.5	16.3	17.1	17.5	16.6	17.3	18.6	20.2	21.9	22.3	53
Romania	8.8	10.2	11.2	12.0	13.0	14.4	15.5	16.9	18.2	19.3	18.9	44
Lithuania	6.6	7.7	8.7	9.5	10.4	11.3	12.2	13.6	14.6	15.5	15.6	45
Iran	13.5	14.3	14.5	14.8	14.9	14.1	14.2	14.6	15.2	15.9	15.6	45
Other countries	260.9	271.1	280.2	291.4	307.5	316.4	332.0	344.0	360.0	376.7	374.9	
Total	**633.3**	**655.1**	**667.2**	**694.7**	**739.4**	**782.8**	**851.9**	**897.3**	**932.3**	**940.6**	**905.3**	**46**

Note: For details on definitions and sources, refer to the metadata at the end of the tables.

StatLink 🔗 https://stat.link/am1o6l

Table B.5. Stocks of foreign population by nationality – Switzerland

Thousands

	2011	2012	2013	2014	2015	2016	2017	2018	2019	2020	2021	Of which: Women 2021 (%)
Italy	289.1	290.5	294.4	301.3	308.6	313.7	318.7	319.4	322.1	323.7	328.3	42
Germany	264.2	276.8	285.4	293.2	298.6	301.5	304.7	305.8	307.9	309.4	311.5	45
Portugal	213.2	224.2	238.4	253.8	263.0	268.1	269.5	268.0	265.5	262.9	260.9	45
France	95.1	99.5	103.9	110.2	116.8	123.1	127.3	131.5	135.3	139.6	146.4	45
Spain	64.2	66.0	69.8	75.4	79.5	82.4	83.5	83.7	84.3	85.2	87.2	46
North Macedonia	60.2	60.8	61.6	62.5	63.3	64.2	65.2	65.8	66.5	67.0	67.6	51
Türkiye	70.6	70.2	69.6	69.2	69.1	68.6	68.0	67.3	66.7	66.3	67.1	47
Serbia	113.3	103.0	94.9	79.3	69.7	65.3	64.3	63.2	61.9	60.7	59.7	50
Austria	37.2	38.2	39.0	39.6	40.4	41.3	42.1	42.7	43.2	43.9	44.5	47
United Kingdom	36.4	38.6	39.4	40.4	41.1	41.3	41.0	41.0	41.0	41.4	42.4	43
Poland	11.5	13.9	16.2	17.9	21.4	24.7	26.9	29.2	31.6	33.9	36.2	49
Eritrea	8.4	8.4	9.8	11.7	14.0	16.6	19.8	23.2	26.2	29.0	30.9	45
Bosnia and Herzegovina	34.6	33.5	32.9	32.2	31.8	31.3	30.8	30.2	29.6	29.0	28.5	49
Croatia	33.8	32.8	31.8	30.7	30.2	29.6	29.0	28.5	28.5	28.3	28.3	50
Sri Lanka	24.6	24.6	23.9	23.7	24.5	25.4	25.8	25.9	26.0	26.2	26.5	48
Other countries	364.2	391.4	414.2	445.5	474.9	497.0	513.0	528.3	544.9	564.9	586.0	
Total	**1 720.4**	**1 772.3**	**1 825.1**	**1 886.6**	**1 947.0**	**1 993.9**	**2 029.5**	**2 053.6**	**2 081.2**	**2 111.4**	**2 151.9**	**47**

Note: For details on definitions and sources, refer to the metadata at the end of the tables.

StatLink 🔗 https://stat.link/am1o6l

Table B.5. Stocks of foreign population by nationality – Türkiye

Thousands

	2011	2012	2013	2014	2015	2016	2017	2018	2019	2020	2021	Of which: Women 2020 (%)
Iraq	8.1	11.8	19.1	31.1	47.2	93.7	149.7	201.1	283.9	313.8	..	47
Afghanistan	7.4	10.7	19.5	27.9	33.6	38.5	59.9	79.6	120.4	152.2	..	42
Turkmenistan	3.9	5.8	11.7	13.4	18.4	23.4	28.3	42.8	68.1	133.7	..	44
Syria	2.9	5.1	10.1	57.9	50.9	56.6	75.2	64.6	88.0	114.3	..	42
Iran	5.2	7.9	12.2	16.8	21.9	27.8	37.9	44.9	68.8	92.7	..	47
Germany	32.6	43.6	25.6	59.0	63.2	69.9	75.1	77.2	82.0	88.5	..	52
Azerbaijan	9.9	14.8	18.9	26.2	30.2	36.5	47.0	51.6	61.8	68.5	..	53
Uzbekistan	2.7	3.4	6.5	7.9	11.0	16.1	21.7	31.6	34.1	44.9	..	71
Russia	10.7	14.4	15.6	20.7	21.6	25.3	27.7	24.3	33.4	40.2	..	67
Egypt	0.3	0.4	0.6	1.2	2.7	4.4	7.6	14.5	26.2	31.1	..	38
Libya	0.2	0.3	1.3	1.0	6.2	14.5	13.8	15.8	19.5	24.3	..	38
Kyrgyzstan	3.3	4.8	6.1	8.4	10.6	14.0	17.1	18.6	19.6	23.5	..	74
Georgia	1.7	2.4	15.7	13.5	19.1	19.8	22.1	23.2	19.9	22.1	..	81
West Bank and Gaza Strip	0.6	0.8	1.3	1.9	2.5	3.3	4.8	8.3	15.7	21.5	..	38
Kazakhstan	5.8	6.9	8.4	11.1	11.9	13.7	14.9	12.6	16.8	21.2	..	61
Other countries	95.3	109.0	106.0	158.6	167.4	192.8	213.6	208.3	252.7	338.7	..	
Total	**190.5**	**242.1**	**278.7**	**456.5**	**518.3**	**650.3**	**816.4**	**919.1**	**1 211.0**	**1 531.2**	**..**	**49**

Note: For details on definitions and sources, refer to the metadata at the end of the tables.

StatLink https://stat.link/am1o6l

Table B.5. Stocks of foreign population by nationality – United Kingdom

Thousands

	2010	2011	2012	2013	2014	2015	2016	2017	2018	2019	2020	Of which: Women 2018 (%)
Poland	550	658	713	679	826	855	1 006	994	829	..	..	52
Romania	72	79	117	148	165	219	324	382	478	..	..	45
India	354	332	360	336	354	379	347	317	370	..	..	54
Ireland	344	386	356	345	309	329	330	343	350	..	..	56
Italy	117	153	125	138	182	212	262	296	311	..	..	42
Portugal	104	123	106	138	140	235	247	269	195	..	..	46
Pakistan	137	166	163	194	197	184	175	167	186	..	..	48
Lithuania	99	129	126	153	158	192	204	196	181	..	..	57
France	116	114	132	132	135	189	181	186	179	..	..	54
Spain	61	55	82	75	130	167	162	191	156	..	..	46
United States	133	109	146	149	145	132	127	130	149	..	..	58
China	107	106	87	93	106	122	113	132	148	..	..	65
Netherlands	58	56	59	83	85	81	102	97	125	..	..	55
Germany	129	132	137	153	110	119	166	131	120	..	..	61
Bulgaria	34	47	33	62	45	68	81	109	105	..	..	50
Other countries	2 109	2 140	2 047	2 063	2 067	2 109	2 124	2 197	2 109	..	..	
Total	**4 524**	**4 785**	**4 788**	**4 941**	**5 154**	**5 592**	**5 951**	**6 137**	**5 991**	**6 227**	**..**	**52**

Note: For details on definitions and sources, refer to the metadata at the end of the tables.

StatLink https://stat.link/am1o6l

Table B.5. Stocks of foreign population by nationality – United States

Thousands

	2011	2012	2013	2014	2015	2016	2017	2018	2019	2020	2021	Of which: Women 2017 (%)
Mexico	..	..	..	8 579.5	8 327.0	8 256.8	7 791.9	7 581.3	7 172.9	6 530.2	..	47
India	..	..	..	1159.0	1296.9	1325.7	1469.8	1446.0	1433.2	1311.5	..	46
China	..	..	..	963.6	1079.0	1118.9	1148.0	1124.8	1139.3	1083.3	..	53
El Salvador	..	..	..	913.6	927.4	912.3	923.4	919.5	951.4	823.0	..	46
Guatemala	..	..	..	670.0	679.6	674.0	685.8	713.1	805.4	621.2	..	38
Philippines	..	..	..	596.1	615.2	563.8	593.5	585.3	559.3	539.9	..	60
Dominican Republic	..	..	..	474.4	493.6	513.3	553.9	538.5	502.2	500.2	..	46
Honduras	..	..	..	441.3	462.8	518.7	486.7	492.5	574.7	464.3	..	47
Cuba	..	..	..	502.1	491.4	536.8	545.3	541.2	529.7	407.1	..	52
Canada	..	..	..	422.0	445.9	405.1	419.3	418.4	393.5	406.1	..	52
Korea	..	..	..	418.0	409.5	389.9	401.2	366.5	353.1	350.4	..	56
Brazil	..	..	..	207.9	224.9	253.8	296.5	291.2	330.0	335.8	..	45
Venezuela	..	..	..	129.1	145.0	162.6	229.7	261.6	299.7	330.1	..	58
Colombia	..	..	..	294.3	304.1	280.3	319.5	302.0	307.4	328.3	..	54
Viet Nam	..	..	..	318.0	320.0	307.4	303.2	286.9	330.0	312.5	..	57
Other countries	..	..	..	6 174.6	6 204.0	6 195.9	6 291.9	6 212.2	6 011.5	5 875.5	..	
Total	..	..	..	**22 263.4**	**22 426.2**	**22 415.3**	**22 459.7**	**22 081.1**	**21 693.3**	**20 219.3**	..	**49**

Note: For details on definitions and sources, refer to the metadata at the end of the tables.

StatLink ᴍᴤᴾ https://stat.link/am1o6l

Metadata related to Tables A.5. and B.5. **Stocks of foreign population**

Country	Comments	Source
Austria	Stock of foreign citizens recorded in the population register. *Reference date:* 1 January.	Population Register, Statistics Austria.
Belgium	From 2011 on, includes foreigners who have lived in Belgium for a continuous period of at least 12 months and persons who arrived in Belgium less than 12 months before the reference time with the intention of staying there for at least one year; also includes asylum seekers. Up to 2010, includes foreigners whose main place of residence is in Belgium and who are registered in a municipality (aliens' register or register of aliens with a privileged status or register of European Union officials) so excludes asylum seekers, persons who have been residing in the Belgian territory for less than three months or are in an irregular situation. The series include breaks in 2011 and in 2012, and data for the year 2019 are provisional. *Reference date:* 1 January.	Population Register, Eurostat.
Canada	2011 and 2016 Censuses.	Statistics Canada.
Chile	Estimation of the resident foreign population in the 2017 Census.	
Czech Republic	Numbers of foreigners residing in the country on the basis of permanent or temporary residence permits (i.e. long-term visa, long-term residence permit or temporary residence permit of EU nationals). *Reference date:* 1 January.	Ministry of the Interior, Directorate of Alien Police.
Denmark	Stock of foreign citizens recorded in the population register. Excludes asylum seekers and all persons with temporary residence permits. *Reference date:* 1 January.	Central Population Register, Statistics Denmark.
Estonia	Population register. *Reference date:* 1 January.	Ministry of the Interior.
Finland	Stock of foreign citizens recorded in the population register. Includes foreign persons of Finnish origin. *Reference date:* 1 January.	Central Population Register, Statistics Finland.
France	Foreigners with permanent residence in France. Including trainees, students and illegal migrants who accept to be interviewed. Excluding seasonal and cross-border workers. 2018 to 2021 totals are estimated based on INSEE data. Includes the département of Mayotte from 2014.	Censuses, National Institute for Statistics and Economic Studies (INSEE).
Germany	Stock of foreign citizens recorded in the population register. Includes all foreigners regardless of their housing situation (private or non-private dwelling). Excludes ethnic Germans *(Aussiedler)*. *Reference date:* 1 January.	Central Population Register, Federal Office of Statistics.
Greece	Estimated population by group of citizenship. *Reference date:* 1 January.	Hellenic Statistical authority.
Hungary	Foreigners having a residence or a settlement document. From 2010 on, includes third-country nationals holding a temporary residence permit (for a year or more). From 2012 on, includes persons under subsidiary protection. Data for 2011 were adjusted to match the October census results. *Reference date:* 1 January.	Office of Immigration and Nationality, Central Statistical Office.
Iceland	Data are from the National Register of Persons. It is to be expected that figures are overestimates. *Reference date:* 1 January.	Statistics Iceland.
Ireland	Census data for 2011 and 2016.	Central Statistics Office (CSO).
Italy	Data refer to resident foreigners (registered in municipal registry offices). Excludes children under 18 who are registered on their parents' permit. Includes foreigners who were regularised following the 2009 programme. From 2019 on, the data takes into account the results of the permanent population census. *Reference date:* 1 January.	National Statistical Institute (ISTAT).
Japan	Foreigners staying in Japan for the mid- to long-term with a resident status under the Immigration Control and Refugee Recognition Act. *Reference date:* 1 January.	Ministry of Justice, Immigration Bureau.
Korea	Foreigners staying in Korea more than 90 days and registered in the population registers. Includes foreign residents, ethnic Koreans holding a F-4 visa, and illegal stayers with short-term visas (under the unknown citizenship category).	Ministry of Justice.

Country	Comments	Source
Latvia	Population register. *Reference date:* 1 January.	Office of Citizenship and Migration Affairs.
Lithuania	*Reference date:* 1 January.	Department of Migration.
Luxembourg	Stock of foreign citizens recorded in population register. Excludes visitors (staying for less than 3 months) and cross-border workers. *Reference date:* 1 January. 2010 figures are extracted from the February 2011 census.	Population Register, Central Office of Statistics and Economic Studies (Statec).
Mexico	Number of foreigners who hold a valid permit for permanent or temporary residence. Data until 2013 are estimates under the terms of the 1974 Act; they include immigrants FM2 "inmigrante" and "inmigrado" (boths categories refer to permanent residence) and non-immigrants FM3 with specific categories (temporary residence). Data from 2015 are estimates under the terms of the 2011 Migration Act.	National Migration Institute, Unit for Migration Policy, Ministry of Interior.
Netherlands	Stock of foreign citizens recorded in the population register. Figures include administrative corrections and asylum seekers (except those staying in reception centres). *Reference date:* 1 January.	Population Register, Central Bureau of Statistics (CBS).
Norway	Stock of foreign citizens recorded in the population register. It excludes visitors (staying for less than six months) and cross-border workers. *Reference date:* 1 January.	Central Population Register, Statistics Norway.
Poland		Central Population Register, Central Statistical Office.
Portugal	Figures include holders of a valid residence permit and holders of a renewed long-term visa.	Immigration and Border Control Office (SEF); National Statistical Institute (INE).
Slovak Republic	Holders of a permanent or long-term residence permit.	Register of Foreigners, Ministry of the Interior.
Slovenia	Number of valid residence permits, regardless of the administrative status of the foreign national. *Reference date:* 1 January.	Central Population Register, Ministry of the Interior.
Spain	All foreign citizens in the Municipal Registers irrespective of their legal status. *Reference date:* 1 January.	Municipal Registers, National Statistics Institute (INE).
Sweden	Stock of foreign citizens recorded in the population register. *Reference date:* 1 January.	Population Register, Statistics Sweden.
Switzerland	Stock of all those with residence or settlement permits (permits B and C, respectively). Holders of an L-permit (short duration) are also included if their stay in the country is longer than 12 months. Does not include seasonal or cross-border workers. *Reference date:* 1 January.	Register of Foreigners, Federal Office of Migration.
Türkiye	*Reference date:* 1 January.	Eurostat.
United Kingdom	Foreign residents. Those with unknown nationality from the New Commonwealth are not included (around 10 000 to 15 000 persons). *Reference date:* 1 January.	Labour Force Survey, Home Office.
United States	Foreigners born abroad.	Current Population Survey, Census Bureau.

Note: Data for Serbia include persons from Serbia, Montenegro and Serbia and Montenegro. Some statements may refer to nationalities/countries of birth not shown in this annex but available on line at: http://stats.oecd.org/.

Acquisitions of nationality

Nationality law can have a significant impact on the measurement of the national and foreign populations. In France and Belgium, for example, where foreigners can fairly easily acquire the nationality of the country, increases in the foreign population through immigration and births can eventually contribute to a significant rise in the population of nationals. On the other hand, in countries where naturalisation is more difficult, increases in immigration and births among foreigners manifest themselves almost exclusively as growth in the foreign population. In addition, changes in rules regarding naturalisation can have significant impact. For example, during the 1980s, a number of OECD countries made naturalisation easier and this resulted in noticeable falls in the foreign population (and rises in the population of nationals).

However, host-country legislation is not the only factor affecting naturalisation. For example, where naturalisation involves forfeiting citizenship of the country of origin, there may be incentives to remain a foreign citizen. Where the difference between remaining a foreign citizen and becoming a national is marginal, naturalisation may largely be influenced by the time and effort required to make the application, and the symbolic and political value individuals attach to being citizens of one country or another.

Data on naturalisations are usually readily available from administrative sources. The statistics generally cover all means of acquiring the nationality of a country. These include standard naturalisation procedures subject to criteria such as age or residency, etc., as well as situations where nationality is acquired through a declaration or by option (following marriage, adoption or other situations related to residency or descent), recovery of former nationality and other special means of acquiring the nationality of the country.

Table A.6. Acquisitions of nationality in OECD countries

Numbers and percentages

	2010	2011	2012	2013	2014	2015	2016	2017	2018	2019	2020
Australia	119 383	95 235	83 698	123 438	162 002	135 596	133 126	137 750	80 562	127 674	204 817
% of foreign population	..	..	..	..	..	..	..	..	..	..	..
Austria	6 135	6 690	7 043	7 354	7 570	8 144	8 530	9 271	9 450	10 606	8 996
% of foreign population	0.7	0.8	0.8	0.8	0.8	0.8	0.7	0.7	0.7	0.8	0.6
Belgium	34 636	29 786	38 612	34 801	18 726	27 071	31 935	37 399	36 200	40 594	33 915
% of foreign population	3.4	2.8	3.3	2.9	1.5	2.2	2.5	2.8	2.7	2.9	2.4
Canada	143 579	179 451	111 923	127 470	259 274	251 144	147 267	105 813	176 487	250 498	110 835
% of foreign population	..	..	5.7	..	..	..	..	4.4	..	..	..
Chile	741	1 030	1 226	678	1 048	691	792	2 991	1 801	354	487
% of foreign population	..	..	..	..	..	..	..	..	0.2	..	0.0
Czech Republic	1 495	1 936	2 036	2 514	5 114	4 925	5 536	6 440	5 260	4 456	4 214
% of foreign population	0.3	0.4	0.5	0.6	1.2	1.1	1.2	1.4	1.1	0.9	0.7
Denmark	3 006	3 911	3 489	1 750	4 747	11 745	15 028	7 272	2 836	1 781	7 076
% of foreign population	0.9	1.2	1.0	0.5	1.3	3.0	3.6	1.6	0.6	0.4	1.3
Estonia	1 189	1 518	1 340	1 330	1 614	897	1 775	882	766	779	770
% of foreign population	..	..	..	0.6	0.8	0.4	0.8	0.4	0.4	0.4	0.4
Finland	4 334	4 558	9 087	8 930	8 260	7 921	9 375	12 219	9 211	9 649	7 816
% of foreign population	3.0	2.9	5.4	4.9	4.2	3.8	4.3	5.3	3.8	3.9	3.0
France	143 261	114 569	96 050	97 276	105 613	113 608	119 152	114 274	110 014	109 821	86 483
% of foreign population	3.8	3.0	2.5	2.4	2.6	2.6	2.7	2.5	2.3	2.3	1.7
Germany	101 570	106 897	112 348	112 353	108 422	107 317	110 383	112 211	112 340	128 905	109 880
% of foreign population	1.5	1.6	1.7	1.6	1.5	1.4	1.4	1.2	1.1	1.2	1.0
Greece	9 387	17 533	20 302	29 462	21 829	12 837	32 819	34 305	27 857	16 328	13 272
% of foreign population	1.0	1.9	2.2	3.2	2.5	1.5	4.0	4.3	3.4	2.0	1.6
Hungary	6 086	20 554	18 379	9 178	8 745	4 048	4 315	2 787	3 508	3 255	2 139
% of foreign population	3.3	10.4	8.9	6.4	6.2	2.9	3.0	1.8	2.3	2.0	1.2
Iceland	450	370	413	597	595	801	703	637	569	437	395
% of foreign population	1.8	1.7	2.0	2.8	2.8	3.5	2.9	2.4	1.9	1.2	0.9
Ireland	6 387	10 749	25 039	24 263	21 090	13 565	10 044	8 195	8 223	5 791	5 475
% of foreign population	1.1	1.9	4.2	4.0	3.5	2.2	1.7	1.3	1.5	1.0	0.9
Italy	65 938	56 153	65 383	100 712	129 887	178 035	201 591	146 605	112 523	127 001	131 803
% of foreign population	1.9	1.5	1.7	2.5	3.0	3.6	4.0	2.9	2.2	2.5	2.6
Japan	13 072	10 359	10 622	8 646	9 277	9 469	9 554	10 315	9 074	8 453	9 079
% of foreign population	0.6	0.5	0.5	0.4	0.5	0.5	0.5	0.5	0.4	0.3	0.3
Korea	17 323	18 400	12 527	13 956	14 200	13 934	12 854	13 293	14 758	12 875	16 065
% of foreign population	1.7	1.7	1.0	1.2	1.1	0.9	0.8	0.8	0.8	0.7	0.8
Latvia	3 660	2 467	3 784	3 083	2 141	1 897	1 957	962	930	808	725
% of foreign population	1.0	0.7	1.1	1.0	0.7	0.6	0.7	0.3	0.3	0.3	0.3
Lithuania	162	311	183	173	179	177	173	166	196	123	176
% of foreign population	0.5	1.1	0.8	0.8	0.8	0.8	0.8	0.9	1.0	0.4	0.4
Luxembourg	4 311	3 405	4 680	4 411	4 991	5 306	7 140	9 030	11 864	11 450	9 387
% of foreign population	2.0	1.6	2.1	1.9	2.1	2.1	2.8	3.4	4.2	4.0	3.2
Mexico	2 150	2 633	3 590	3 581	2 341	2 736	2 940	3 067	3 872	3 070	..
% of foreign population	0.8	0.9	1.2	1.2	..	0.8	0.8	0.8	0.9	0.7	..
Netherlands	26 275	28 598	30 955	25 882	32 578	27 877	28 534	27 663	27 851	34 191	55 943
% of foreign population	3.7	3.9	4.1	3.3	4.1	3.4	3.4	3.1	2.9	3.3	5.0
New Zealand	15 331	19 513	27 607	28 468	28 759	28 468	32 862	37 464	36 840	31 977	23 528
% of foreign population	..	..	..	..	..	..	..	..	..	..	..
Norway	11 903	14 637	12 384	13 223	15 336	12 432	14 676	21 648	10 268	13 201	19 698

	2010	2011	2012	2013	2014	2015	2016	2017	2018	2019	2020
% of foreign population	3.9	4.4	3.4	3.2	3.4	2.6	2.9	4.0	1.8	2.3	3.4
Poland	2 926	2 325	3 792	3 462	4 518	4 048	4 086	4 259	4 593	12 917	7 159
% of foreign population	4.8	3.1	4.8	4.0	4.8	4.0	3.8	2.8	2.2	5.4	2.5
Portugal	21 750	23 238	21 819	24 476	21 124	20 396	25 104	18 022	21 333	21 099	32 147
% of foreign population	4.9	5.1	4.9	5.6	5.1	5.1	6.4	4.6	5.4	5.0	6.7
Slovak Republic	239	272	255	207	234	309	484	645	721	586	548
% of foreign population	0.5	0.4	0.4	0.4	0.4	0.5	0.8	1.0	1.0	0.8	0.7
Slovenia	1 840	1 775	1 490	1 470	1 057	1 255	1 297	1 563	1 978	1 911	1 725
% of foreign population	2.6	2.2	1.8	1.7	1.2	1.3	1.3	1.5	1.7	1.6	1.2
Spain	123 721	114 599	115 557	225 793	205 880	114 351	150 944	66 498	90 774	98 954	126 266
% of foreign population	2.3	2.1	2.2	4.3	4.1	2.4	3.4	1.5	2.1	2.2	2.6
Sweden	32 197	36 328	49 746	49 632	42 918	48 249	60 343	68 898	63 818	64 206	80 175
% of foreign population	5.7	6.0	7.9	7.6	6.4	6.9	8.2	8.8	7.5	7.2	8.6
Switzerland	39 314	36 757	34 121	34 332	33 325	40 888	41 587	44 515	42 630	40 277	34 062
% of foreign population	2.4	2.2	2.0	1.9	1.8	2.2	2.1	2.2	2.1	2.0	1.6
Türkiye	9 488	9 216	..	..	..	..	..	..	..	..	..
% of foreign population	9.1	5.5	..	..	..	..	..	..	..	..	..
United Kingdom	195 014	177 866	194 288	208 021	125 715	118 054	149 378	123 207	157 004	159 356	130 551
% of foreign population	4.5	3.9	4.1	4.3	2.5	2.3	2.7	2.1	2.6	2.7	2.1
United States	619 913	694 193	757 434	779 929	653 416	730 259	753 060	707 265	761 901	843 593	628 254
% of foreign population	2.9	3.2	3.4	3.5	3.0	3.3	3.4	3.2	3.4	3.7	2.8

Note: For details on definitions and sources, refer to the metadata at the end of the Tables B.6.

StatLink 🔗 https://stat.link/43vlae

Table B.6. Acquisitions of nationality by country of former nationality – Australia

	2010	2011	2012	2013	2014	2015	2016	2017	2018	2019	2020	Of which: Women 2020 (%)
India	17 788	12 948	10 076	19 217	27 827	24 236	21 989	24 181	17 716	28 470	38 209	51
United Kingdom	22 284	19 101	16 401	20 478	25 884	20 583	20 949	21 069	13 875	13 366	25 018	48
China	11 109	8 898	6 876	8 979	9 203	7 549	6 931	6 578	1 720	7 974	14 764	58
Philippines	4 505	4 051	5 592	9 090	11 628	8 996	8 333	9 112	4 921	9 267	12 838	58
Pakistan	1 728	1 057	990	2 100	2 739	2 341	3 077	4 480	919	3 360	8 821	45
Viet Nam	2 000	1 688	1 929	2 568	3 514	3 835	4 173	3 859	1 216	3 501	6 804	65
Sri Lanka	3 412	2 520	1 671	2 746	3 957	3 179	3 752	4 487	3 262	4 861	6 195	52
South Africa	5 218	4 389	4 206	7 900	9 286	6 211	5 629	4 906	3 370	2 680	5 438	50
New Zealand	4 165	4 304	3 458	3 794	5 361	4 091	4 390	3 593	1 840	3 027	5 367	50
Afghanistan	1 342	941	889	1 253	2 620	2 103	991	1 102	387	620	5 102	48
Iran	918	779	1 024	1 657	2 155	2 198	2 416	3 182	1 108	2 770	4 634	49
Ireland	1 280	1 302	1 145	1 796	2 843	3 092	3 943	4 286	2 670	2 991	4 301	46
Iraq	1 538	875	1 103	2 739	3 150	2 054	1 417	1 930	788	3 087	3 883	51
Nepal	550	520	589	1 384	1 810	2 401	2 959	2 402	1 665	3 294	3 676	50
Malaysia	2 216	2 207	1 487	1 841	2 788	2 213	2 827	2 734	1 979	2 480	3 633	55
Other countries	39 330	29 655	26 262	35 896	47 237	40 514	39 350	39 849	23 126	35 926	56 134	
Total	**119 383**	**95 235**	**83 698**	**123 438**	**162 002**	**135 596**	**133 126**	**137 750**	**80 562**	**127 674**	**204 817**	**53**

Note: For details on definitions and sources, refer to the metadata at the end of the tables.

StatLink https://stat.link/lmp2jh

Table B.6. Acquisitions of nationality by country of former nationality – Austria

	2010	2011	2012	2013	2014	2015	2016	2017	2018	2019	2020	Of which: Women 2020 (%)
Bosnia and Herzegovina	1 278	1 174	1 131	1 039	1 120	1 216	1 261	1 288	1 032	1 183	967	54
Serbia	1 265	1 090	709	823	671	633	751	557	625	1 008	943	59
Türkiye	937	1 178	1 198	1 108	885	997	818	778	828	911	847	49
Russia	137	296	316	427	431	298	337	323	373	463	355	59
Iran	111	138	168	18	159	182	226	217	306	325	355	48
Romania	114	223	275	224	244	221	257	291	456	376	301	64
Afghanistan	113	157	179	28	232	187	332	424	328	372	298	40
North Macedonia	150	182	163	182	210	224	297	296	453	313	250	51
Germany	132	117	110	127	187	148	182	234	265	239	227	54
Hungary	68	66	71	83	111	119	154	227	258	236	221	62
Syria	28	61	53	83	95	79	134	98	103	164	211	35
Croatia	456	363	401	224	184	143	160	168	251	236	195	65
India	84	82	171	165	207	233	277	342	238	250	185	48
Ukraine	75	106	99	134	136	298	225	181	220	360	184	77
Egypt	94	97	152	174	189	214	169	196	247	236	180	46
Other countries	1 093	1 360	1 847	2 515	2 509	2 952	2 950	3 651	3 467	3 934	3 277	
Total	**6 135**	**6 690**	**7 043**	**7 354**	**7 570**	**8 144**	**8 530**	**9 271**	**9 450**	**10 606**	**8 996**	**54**

Note: For details on definitions and sources, refer to the metadata at the end of the tables.

StatLink https://stat.link/lmp2jh

Table B.6. Acquisitions of nationality by country of former nationality – Belgium

	2010	2011	2012	2013	2014	2015	2016	2017	2018	2019	2020	Of which: Women 2020 (%)
Morocco	7 380	7 035	7 879	5 926	2 408	3 170	3 996	5 084	4 856	4 975	3 756	52
Romania	395	356	777	1 155	824	1 192	1 535	2 031	2 219	2 409	2 079	52
Afghanistan	370	174	260	283	194	326	534	875	1 067	1 418	1 464	31
Syria	259	186	246	205	92	185	253	243	474	979	1 431	37
Italy	2 833	3 697	3 203	1 856	1 199	1 067	1 048	1 174	1 352	1 589	1 217	48
Dem. Rep. of the Congo	1 604	1 158	1 936	1 526	713	1 061	1 016	1 201	1 191	1 359	1 178	60
Poland	523	394	729	888	742	1 136	1 243	1 498	1 528	1 710	1 096	61
Cameroon	490	600	924	915	546	738	845	872	955	1 046	945	54
Netherlands	641	495	961	1 272	705	993	1 390	1 368	1 064	1 296	939	48
Iraq	322	184	397	612	377	546	655	930	672	759	888	37
Türkiye	2 760	2 359	2 517	1 857	691	843	989	1 061	985	1 073	882	47
United Kingdom	111	114	99	141	110	127	506	1 381	1 045	1 630	868	44
France	717	638	903	973	586	647	673	795	869	952	862	51
Russia	1 641	1 032	1 439	1 525	641	950	1 029	973	896	1 059	835	61
Guinea	291	228	757	941	416	635	681	972	855	832	711	51
Other countries	14 299	11 136	15 585	14 726	8 482	13 455	15 542	16 941	16 172	17 508	14 764	
Total	**34 636**	**29 786**	**38 612**	**34 801**	**18 726**	**27 071**	**31 935**	**37 399**	**36 200**	**40 594**	**33 915**	50

Note: For details on definitions and sources, refer to the metadata at the end of the tables.

StatLink https://stat.link/lmp2jh

Table B.6. Acquisitions of nationality by country of former nationality – Canada

	2010	2011	2012	2013	2014	2015	2016	2017	2018	2019	2020	Of which: Women 2020 (%)
Philippines	11 586	15 902	10 392	14 583	27 416	31 729	23 875	14 050	19 647	33 922	15 991	..
India	18 958	22 043	13 319	15 246	26 320	28 048	16 601	9 978	19 486	31 337	15 418	..
Syria	674	763	481	412	1 084	1 252	657	587	1 597	6 434	7 179	..
Iran	3 585	4 923	3 506	3 337	9 357	8 959	3 927	3 523	10 037	14 041	4 887	..
Pakistan	8 060	9 812	5 526	5 197	8 988	8 628	5 779	5 089	9 406	11 187	4 740	..
China	13 464	15 503	10 382	10 053	21 620	20 081	10 786	5 949	9 716	13 456	4 705	..
United States	3 713	5 010	3 797	4 424	7 249	6 627	4 405	3 283	4 229	5 623	2 479	..
France	1 971	2 702	1 441	2 089	5 755	4 590	2 252	2 112	3 836	5 502	2 316	..
Nigeria	1 405	2 184	1 238	1 318	2 978	4 210	2 158	1 883	4 398	5 021	2 285	..
United Kingdom	4 506	5 971	4 298	4 721	7 293	6 255	4 158	3 005	3 515	4 844	2 020	..
Iraq	1 056	1 581	1 298	2 359	4 556	5 175	2 983	2 238	3 951	5 056	2 003	..
Algeria	2 456	3 296	1 585	1 837	7 173	5 679	2 468	2 004	3 340	4 245	1 595	..
Mexico	1 798	2 392	1 423	1 599	3 558	3 477	2 079	1 505	2 433	3 770	1 536	..
Bangladesh	2 281	2 846	1 468	1 674	4 261	3 526	1 731	1 330	3 239	3 602	1 515	..
Egypt	1 047	1 458	990	1 135	3 471	4 729	2 392	2 284	4 115	4 109	1 505	..
Other countries	67 019	83 065	50 779	57 486	118 195	108 179	61 016	46 993	73 542	98 349	40 661	
Total	**143 579**	**179 451**	**111 923**	**127 470**	**259 274**	**251 144**	**147 267**	**105 813**	**176 487**	**250 498**	**110 835**	..

Note: For details on definitions and sources, refer to the metadata at the end of the tables.

StatLink https://stat.link/lmp2jh

Table B.6. Acquisitions of nationality by country of former nationality – Chile

	2010	2011	2012	2013	2014	2015	2016	2017	2018	2019	2020	Of which: Women 2020 (%)
Colombia	54	98	149	105	168	121	121	597	155	68	108	59
Peru	156	241	307	153	236	142	167	944	223	74	87	71
Ecuador	89	116	174	95	127	83	95	272	268	53	64	55
Venezuela	17	26	21	8	23	24	42	93	143	25	56	59
Bolivia	94	135	119	58	92	54	63	224	241	29	31	61
Dominican Republic	6	4	17	2	14	10	15	103	42	20	30	57
Cuba	119	158	159	88	115	85	69	183	178	12	18	61
Argentina	16	26	33	21	31	27	28	67	69	14	15	47
Haiti	1	2	1	1	6	4	14	43	86	3	11	27
Spain	9	5	14	8	17	8	6	34	24	6	8	25
Russia	4	8	14	4	6	7	4	28	30	3	7	86
Brazil	6	7	9	5	6	6	8	25	20	3	6	33
India	9	23	15	8	23	12	18	48	25	7	5	20
Mexico	2	6	4	3	7	1	5	11	19	1	4	75
Türkiye	4	2	4	1	6	2	3	7	11	2	3	33
Other countries	155	173	186	118	171	105	134	312	267	34	34	
Total	**741**	**1 030**	**1 226**	**678**	**1 048**	**691**	**792**	**2 991**	**1 801**	**354**	**487**	**58**

Note: For details on definitions and sources, refer to the metadata at the end of the tables.

StatLink ᐧᐧᑦ https://stat.link/lmp2jh

Table B.6. Acquisitions of nationality by country of former nationality – Czech Republic

	2010	2011	2012	2013	2014	2015	2016	2017	2018	2019	2020	Of which: Women 2020 (%)
Ukraine	396	501	518	948	2 075	1 044	1 429	1 891	1 319	1 002	940	..
Russia	50	68	173	162	463	305	563	752	633	574	516	..
Slovak Republic	377	378	331	270	574	111	372	630	501	421	365	..
Belarus	15	38	49	53	137	94	135	215	139	107	115	..
Viet Nam	52	86	80	166	298	271	405	223	231	129	89	..
Kazakhstan	17	48	30	65	122	48	50	64	53	41	60	..
Moldova	15	32	25	41	175	55	93	138	118	92	58	..
Poland	63	198	180	176	105	34	96	110	60	58	54	..
Serbia	..	..	..	..	57	65	66	90	57	38	47	..
Armenia	11	47	74	46	144	49	35	41	19	30	33	..
Romania	36	76	70	30	311	111	115	108	82	69	33	..
Bosnia and Herzegovina	9	16	27	11	59	47	49	51	38	28	32	..
Bulgaria	21	28	19	27	52	51	65	87	53	30	31	..
North Macedonia	2	9	6	14	20	23	28	47	31	22	15	..
Croatia	7	8	12	5	20	38	20	30	22	25	11	..
Other countries	424	403	442	500	502	2 579	2 015	1 963	1 904	1 790	1 815	
Total	**1 495**	**1 936**	**2 036**	**2 514**	**5 114**	**4 925**	**5 536**	**6 440**	**5 260**	**4 456**	**4 214**	**..**

Note: For details on definitions and sources, refer to the metadata at the end of the tables.

StatLink ᐧᐧᑦ https://stat.link/lmp2jh

Table B.6. Acquisitions of nationality by country of former nationality – Denmark

	2010	2011	2012	2013	2014	2015	2016	2017	2018	2019	2020	Of which: Women 2020 (%)
United Kingdom	34	26	21	17	21	20	85	164	143	118	692	41
Pakistan	21	73	89	77	38	191	641	199	82	43	630	39
Poland	36	33	41	39	29	45	174	372	122	78	384	71
Germany	81	55	80	41	27	38	110	248	168	129	375	57
Ukraine	16	35	44	32	10	72	228	329	73	79	362	54
United States	13	12	11	15	6	23	110	248	114	54	254	56
India	25	27	27	9	34	31	211	85	48	45	241	38
Russia	74	55	85	62	31	76	232	330	110	62	209	74
Romania	22	18	34	23	8	43	101	164	49	38	197	61
Iraq	368	838	730	356	1 588	1 131	2 917	357	96	82	195	46
Türkiye	239	227	300	166	150	193	977	353	113	71	192	51
Bosnia and Herzegovina	131	110	82	39	59	96	493	374	94	53	164	46
Afghanistan	354	576	463	151	917	408	1 621	297	67	62	164	43
Sweden	58	64	57	33	47	105	277	164	185	117	140	61
Stateless	182	205	109	46	161	130	415	274	92	14	353	48
Other countries	1 352	1 557	1 316	644	1 621	9 143	6 436	3 314	1 280	736	2 524	
Total	**3 006**	**3 911**	**3 489**	**1 750**	**4 747**	**11 745**	**15 028**	**7 272**	**2 836**	**1 781**	**7 076**	53

Note: For details on definitions and sources, refer to the metadata at the end of the tables.

StatLink ᐧᐧᐧ https://stat.link/lmp2jh

Table B.6. Acquisitions of nationality by country of former nationality – Estonia

	2010	2011	2012	2013	2014	2015	2016	2017	2018	2019	2020	Of which: Women 2020 (%)
Russia	77	156	174	169	204	132	244	225	199	230	198	55
Ukraine	18	10	24	18	30	19	29	30	26	33	19	79
Other countries	1 094	1 352	1 142	1 143	1 380	746	1 502	627	541	516	553	
Total	**1 189**	**1 518**	**1 340**	**1 330**	**1 614**	**897**	**1 775**	**882**	**766**	**779**	**770**	52

Note: For details on definitions and sources, refer to the metadata at the end of the tables.

StatLink ᐧᐧᐧ https://stat.link/lmp2jh

Table B.6. Acquisitions of nationality by country of former nationality – Finland

	2010	2011	2012	2013	2014	2015	2016	2017	2018	2019	2020	Of which: Women 2020 (%)
Russia	1 925	1 652	2 477	2 103	2 317	1 728	2 028	2 758	1 766	1 946	1 546	62
Iraq	78	106	457	521	405	560	534	742	621	589	602	32
Somalia	131	96	609	814	834	955	1 066	957	856	583	541	48
Estonia	243	302	521	436	382	420	459	705	541	658	516	59
Thailand	41	50	75	104	125	150	193	261	249	281	304	82
Afghanistan	108	100	510	479	251	242	376	469	339	309	264	49
Ukraine	92	95	148	157	141	145	163	281	202	255	220	63
Syria	6	23	20	22	16	28	47	118	118	299	205	38
Sweden	104	196	190	146	186	165	206	212	210	248	196	41
India	73	76	117	99	152	137	193	245	154	174	181	57
Türkiye	132	166	278	271	257	229	264	313	210	260	172	50
Iran	137	145	451	341	219	140	222	309	244	205	156	44
Viet Nam	54	82	150	150	114	146	225	249	197	221	148	61
Serbia and Montenegro	109	106	297	209	94	73	108	42	183	214	134	49
United Kingdom	20	16	20	20	13	26	31	147	134	211	126	29
Other countries	1 081	1 347	2 767	3 058	2 754	2 777	3 260	4 411	3 187	3 196	2 505	
Total	**4 334**	**4 558**	**9 087**	**8 930**	**8 260**	**7 921**	**9 375**	**12 219**	**9 211**	**9 649**	**7 816**	**53**

Note: For details on definitions and sources, refer to the metadata at the end of the tables.

StatLink 🔗 https://stat.link/lmp2jh

Table B.6. Acquisitions of nationality by country of former nationality – France

	2010	2011	2012	2013	2014	2015	2016	2017	2018	2019	2020	Of which: Women 2020 (%)
Morocco	28 919	22 612	18 325	16 662	18 051	19 110	17 769	16 687	15 390	15 776	12 759	50
Algeria	21 299	15 527	12 991	13 408	15 142	17 377	17 662	16 283	14 867	14 785	11 072	50
Tunisia	9 008	6 828	5 546	5 569	6 274	7 018	7 663	7 045	6 687	6 640	5 346	47
Türkiye	9 667	8 277	6 920	5 873	5 835	5 595	5 757	5 332	5 101	5 198	3 982	48
United Kingdom	205	261	335	354	279	374	517	1 733	3 268	4 088	3 146	52
Mali	3 214	2 616	2 201	2 645	3 345	3 621	4 111	4 057	3 662	3 638	2 666	48
Côte d'Ivoire	3 096	2 257	1 766	2 513	3 055	3 188	3 652	3 363	3 012	2 863	2 399	53
Congo	3 417	2 018	1 326	1 808	1 797	2 089	2 181	2 967	2 935	2 994	2 248	53
Senegal	3 839	3 168	2 755	2 823	3 048	3 382	3 369	3 249	2 949	2 940	2 224	49
Cameroon	2 890	2 425	1 926	2 579	3 010	3 125	3 377	3 137	2 502	2 463	2 108	59
Haiti	3 166	2 204	1 799	2 121	2 181	2 228	2 922	2 574	2 496	2 603	2 059	53
Comoros	1 546	1 828	1 778	2 307	2 175	1 881	2 869	2 917	3 903	2 613	1 834	51
Russia	4 507	3 390	2 203	2 517	3 040	2 654	4 094	3 550	2 011	2 414	1 775	71
Guinea	1 465	1 270	974	1 208	1 457	1 678	1 820	1 995	1 828	1 878	1 545	43
Romania	1 024	1 233	1 268	1 409	1 486	1 557	1 695	1 882	1 956	1 896	1 522	60
Other countries	45 999	38 655	33 937	33 480	35 438	38 731	39 694	37 503	37 447	37 032	30 179	
Total	**143 261**	**114 569**	**96 050**	**97 276**	**105 613**	**113 608**	**119 152**	**114 274**	**110 014**	**109 821**	**86 864**	**52**

Note: For details on definitions and sources, refer to the metadata at the end of the tables.

StatLink 🔗 https://stat.link/lmp2jh

Table B.6. Acquisitions of nationality by country of former nationality – Germany

	2010	2011	2012	2013	2014	2015	2016	2017	2018	2019	2020	Of which: Women 2020 (%)
Türkiye	26 192	28 103	33 246	27 970	22 463	19 695	16 290	14 984	16 700	16 235	11 630	48
Syria	1 401	1 454	1 321	1 508	1 820	2 027	2 263	2 479	2 880	3 860	6 700	38
Romania	2 523	2 399	2 343	2 504	2 566	3 001	3 828	4 238	4 325	5 830	5 930	61
Poland	3 789	4 281	4 496	5 462	5 932	5 957	6 632	6 613	6 220	6 020	5 000	69
United Kingdom	256	284	325	460	515	622	2 865	7 493	6 640	14 600	4 930	39
Iraq	5 228	4 790	3 510	3 150	3 172	3 450	3 553	3 480	4 080	4 645	4 770	44
Italy	1 305	1 707	2 202	2 754	3 245	3 406	3 597	4 256	4 050	4 475	4 075	49
Iran	3 046	2 728	2 463	2 560	2 546	2 533	2 661	2 689	3 080	3 805	3 965	50
Afghanistan	3 520	2 711	2 717	3 054	3 000	2 572	2 482	2 400	2 545	2 675	2 880	41
Serbia	3 285	2 878	2 611	2 586	2 223	1 941	2 596	1 950	2 475	3 115	2 765	54
Greece	1 450	2 290	4 167	3 498	2 800	3 058	3 444	3 424	3 235	3 130	2 650	49
Morocco	2 806	3 011	2 852	2 710	2 689	2 551	2 450	2 390	2 365	2 390	2 320	48
Ukraine	3 118	4 264	3 691	4 539	3 142	4 168	4 048	2 718	2 455	4 260	2 260	68
India	928	865	946	1 190	1 295	1 343	1 549	1 619	1 760	2 130	2 235	44
Bulgaria	1 447	1 540	1 691	1 790	1 718	1 619	1 676	1 739	1 830	1 990	2 040	61
Other countries	41 276	43 592	43 767	46 618	49 296	49 374	50 449	49 739	47 700	49 745	45 730	
Total	**101 570**	**106 897**	**112 348**	**112 353**	**108 422**	**107 317**	**110 383**	**112 211**	**112 340**	**128 905**	**109 880**	**52**

Note: For details on definitions and sources, refer to the metadata at the end of the tables.

StatLink https://stat.link/lmp2jh

Table B.6. Acquisitions of nationality by country of former nationality – Greece

	2010	2011	2012	2013	2014	2015	2016	2017	2018	2019	2020	Of which: Women 2020 (%)
Albania	6 059	15 452	17 396	25 830	18 409	10 665	28 251	29 769	24 203	14 050	10 795	48
Romania	57	56	76	129	156	136	234	306	291	205	273	64
Bulgaria	70	101	75	192	200	142	287	329	220	136	230	68
Ukraine	178	130	235	246	231	188	504	449	388	171	223	69
Russia	611		1	2	309	289	386	345	353	184	186	60
India	6	35	122	16	18	18	255	278	245	190	171	32
Georgia	763	252	152	359	226	189	331	323	300	207	148	58
United Kingdom	47	15	29	41	43	43	31	58	52	30	118	63
Moldova	44	91	131	159	124	114	365	378	241	137	115	63
Türkiye	71	49	70	167	151	139	141	107	106	63	84	37
Armenia	199	150	210	189	150	109	296	287	240	154	82	61
Egypt	36	65	332	58	57	45	358	283	144	114	78	45
Cyprus	61	46	41	118	93	73	95	76	38	46	61	61
Poland	38	25	27	52	33	46	66	89	78	51	48	56
Serbia	20	277	201	372	59	35	120	86	59	42	48	67
Other countries	1 127	789	1 204	1 532	1 570	606	1 099	1 142	899	548	612	
Total	**9 387**	**17 533**	**20 302**	**29 462**	**21 829**	**12 837**	**32 819**	**34 305**	**27 857**	**16 328**	**13 272**	**50**

Note: For details on definitions and sources, refer to the metadata at the end of the tables.

StatLink https://stat.link/lmp2jh

Table B.6. Acquisitions of nationality by country of former nationality – Hungary

	2010	2011	2012	2013	2014	2015	2016	2017	2018	2019	2020	Of which: Women 2020 (%)
Romania	3 805	3 939	15 658	14 392	6 999	6 200	2 605	2 874	1 757	2 123	1 822	46
Slovak Republic	97	97	414	307	202	310	208	282	136	223	260	60
Ukraine	558	646	2 189	1 765	894	858	386	365	186	192	142	64
Venezuela	0	0	1	1	2	3	1	0	2	46	129	53
Egypt	5	3	2	6	9	81	93	101	119	191	103	39
Viet Nam	39	75	38	29	15	67	39	36	46	87	100	53
Russia	119	111	168	151	97	170	131	119	75	89	93	67
Germany	35	25	55	67	35	59	29	15	38	50	59	49
United Kingdom	2	4	6	8	7	4	3	11	14	22	52	23
Türkiye	10	9	12	8	20	58	19	20	23	20	26	15
United States	9	2	17	13	9	25	13	17	10	17	25	52
Poland	13	9	27	18	11	45	15	18	22	19	21	76
Iran	18	14	7	14	11	16	10	21	10	11	21	38
Israel	5	4	9	10	6	10	15	13	7	9	16	37
Greece	0	0	1	2	2	0	2	2	1	7	15	13
Other countries	1 148	262	256	211	432	328	287	248	306	308	198	
Total	**6 086**	**20 554**	**18 379**	**9 178**	**8 745**	**4 048**	**4 315**	**2 787**	**3 508**	**3 255**	**2 139**	**49**

Note: For details on definitions and sources, refer to the metadata at the end of the tables.

StatLink https://stat.link/lmp2jh

Table B.6. Acquisitions of nationality by country of former nationality – Iceland

	2010	2011	2012	2013	2014	2015	2016	2017	2018	2019	2020	Of which: Women 2020 (%)
Poland	50	35	30	89	149	265	224	223	149	131	134	57
Thailand	28	27	26	26	43	42	48	34	37	19	19	84
Viet Nam	39	14	8	39	33	33	26	22	27	30	18	61
Lithuania	11	8	6	7	16	10	16	15	13	4	15	67
Philippines	67	35	49	89	52	74	55	41	20	27	13	77
Norway	0	1	1	0	0	0	1	3	0	2	13	62
Sweden	3	6	11	3	6	11	17	10	15	5	12	58
Latvia	2	1	4	18	4	21	22	24	19	16	11	45
United Kingdom	5	7	3	2	1	3	2	5	6	8	9	56
United States	19	11	12	13	14	18	11	17	28	12	9	67
Ukraine	15	10	21	18	12	17	12	11	7	11	8	63
Czech Republic	0	2	1	1	1	4	3	7	10	8	7	43
Russia	21	12	21	18	13	25	14	20	10	11	7	71
Denmark	2	6	1	0	5	11	35	22	9	9	6	50
Italy	1	2	0	3	3	0	3	3	2	1	6	50
Other countries	187	193	219	271	243	267	214	180	217	143	108	
Total	**450**	**370**	**413**	**597**	**595**	**801**	**703**	**637**	**569**	**437**	**395**	**57**

Note: For details on definitions and sources, refer to the metadata at the end of the tables.

StatLink https://stat.link/lmp2jh

Table B.6. Acquisitions of nationality by country of former nationality – Ireland

	2010	2011	2012	2013	2014	2015	2016	2017	2018	2019	2020	Of which: Women 2020 (%)
United Kingdom	59	68	84	55	51	54	98	529	687	665	945	47
Poland	29	25	359	508	939	1 161	1 326	1 357	1 464	925	758	53
Romania	143	135	457	564	1 029	901	756	763	819	552	538	50
India	443	944	2 617	3 009	2 939	1 611	1 028	665	629	515	465	37
Nigeria	1 012	1 204	5 689	5 792	3 293	1 360	776	509	478	305	227	58
Brazil	31	86	203	245	459	393	304	264	220	188	180	53
Philippines	630	1 755	3 830	2 486	2 184	1 167	729	362	320	191	157	60
Latvia	22	19	98	150	226	327	379	392	308	221	146	66
Pakistan	306	428	1 288	1 807	1 244	732	419	341	364	125	136	45
United States	112	148	263	217	304	246	233	177	195	154	132	66
China	258	403	798	656	576	494	304	225	234	162	129	60
South Africa	343	418	708	489	563	0	213	140	143	97	85	58
Hungary	2	1	38	77	137	172	216	163	142	102	80	58
Russia	253	288	464	328	320	154	109	96	91	70	66	68
Ukraine	202	432	815	695	536	323	200	130	99	87	62	58
Other countries	2 542	4 395	7 328	7 185	6 290	4 470	2 954	2 082	2 030	1 432	1 369	
Total	6 387	10 749	25 039	24 263	21 090	13 565	10 044	8 195	8 223	5 791	5 475	52

Note: For details on definitions and sources, refer to the metadata at the end of the tables.

StatLink 🔗 https://stat.link/lmp2jh

Table B.6. Acquisitions of nationality by country of former nationality – Italy

	2010	2011	2012	2013	2014	2015	2016	2017	2018	2019	2020	Of which: Women 2020 (%)
Albania	9 129	8 101	9 493	13 671	21 148	35 134	36 920	27 112	21 841	26 033	28 107	47
Morocco	11 350	10 732	14 728	25 421	29 025	32 448	35 212	22 645	15 496	15 812	18 024	49
Romania	4 707	3 921	3 272	4 386	6 442	14 403	12 967	8 042	6 542	10 201	11 449	58
Brazil	2 099	1 960	1 442	1 786	1 579	1 458	5 799	9 936	10 660	10 762	7 149	51
Bangladesh	822	972	1 460	3 511	5 323	5 953	8 442	4 411	1 873	1 541	5 661	38
Pakistan	535	601	1 522	3 532	4 216	5 617	7 678	6 170	1 974	2 722	5 629	37
India	1 261	1 051	2 366	4 863	5 015	6 176	9 527	8 200	5 425	4 683	5 602	42
Moldova	1 060	846	1 222	1 430	1 475	2 464	5 605	3 827	3 068	3 788	4 340	62
Senegal	689	797	1 070	2 263	4 037	4 144	5 091	4 489	2 918	2 869	4 005	33
North Macedonia	923	1 141	1 219	2 089	2 847	5 455	6 771	3 845	3 487	4 966	3 230	43
Egypt	1 431	2 352	1 342	2 130	3 138	4 422	3 438	1 477	1 122	1 245	2 791	41
Tunisia	2 003	2 067	2 555	3 521	4 411	5 585	4 882	3 187	2 484	2 471	2 718	47
Ecuador	951	599	677	854	1 182	2 660	4 604	3 426	2 306	3 041	2 579	61
Peru	2 235	1 726	1 589	2 055	3 136	5 503	5 783	3 689	2 421	2 685	2 553	61
Ukraine	1 820	1 199	1 580	1 806	1 443	1 822	2 890	2 698	2 423	2 400	2 305	72
Other countries	24 923	18 088	19 846	27 394	35 470	44 791	45 982	33 451	28 483	31 782	25 661	
Total	65 938	56 153	65 383	100 712	129 887	178 035	201 591	146 605	112 523	127 001	131 803	49

Note: For details on definitions and sources, refer to the metadata at the end of the tables.

StatLink 🔗 https://stat.link/lmp2jh

Table B.6. Acquisitions of nationality by country of former nationality – Japan

	2010	2011	2012	2013	2014	2015	2016	2017	2018	2019	2020	Of which: Women 2020 (%)
Korea	6 668	5 656	5 581	4 331	4 744	5 247	5 434	5 631	4 357	4 360	4 113	..
China	4 816	3 259	3 598	2 845	3 060	2 813	2 626	3 088	3 025	2 374	2 881	..
Brazil	..	..	..	..	..	..	..	..	..	383	409	..
Philippines	..	..	..	..	..	..	..	..	..	235	301	..
Viet Nam	..	..	..	..	..	..	..	..	..	264	301	..
Peru	..	..	..	..	..	..	..	..	..	168	172	..
Bangladesh	..	..	..	..	..	..	..	..	..	81	125	..
Nepal	..	..	..	..	..	..	..	..	..	..	100	..
India	..	..	..	..	..	..	..	..	..	..	66	..
Sri Lanka	..	..	..	..	..	..	..	..	..	46	55	..
Other countries	1 588	1 444	1 443	1 470	1 473	1 409	1 494	1 596	1 692	542	556	
Total	**13 072**	**10 359**	**10 622**	**8 646**	**9 277**	**9 469**	**9 554**	**10 315**	**9 074**	**8 453**	**9 079**	**..**

Note: For details on definitions and sources, refer to the metadata at the end of the tables.

StatLink 🔗 https://stat.link/lmp2jh

Table B.6. Acquisitions of nationality by country of former nationality – Korea

	2010	2011	2012	2013	2014	2015	2016	2017	2018	2019	2020	Of which: Women 2020 (%)
China	..	..	6 282	5 801	7 052	6 753	5 328	5 095	5 089	4 617	8 115	..
Viet Nam	..	..	3 011	4 034	3 044	2 834	3 429	3 894	4 988	4 008	4 194	..
United States	..	..	1 414	1 587	1 764	1 681	1 498	1 667	1 694	1 490	1 069	..
Philippines	..	..	339	532	400	412	476	496	750	612	500	..
Chinese Taipei	..	..	224	274	286	479	303	249	279	388	418	..
Cambodia	..	..	362	509	404	427	503	418	464	365	327	..
Canada	..	..	158	226	250	305	289	359	339	280	222	..
Mongolia	..	..	110	123	133	119	125	121	125	117	159	..
Uzbekistan	..	..	75	110	96	120	87	82	86	93	151	..
Thailand	..	..	72	91	84	81	75	94	99	115	116	..
Russia	..	..	99	125	93	134	138	100	77	119	88	..
Japan	..	..	57	84	82	95	68	68	71	59	72	..
Australia	..	..	53	87	95	96	102	112	116	122	64	..
Nepal	..	..	34	60	66	71	65	68	85	57	60	..
Bangladesh	..	..	14	22	32	17	13	30	33	17	59	..
Other countries	..	..	223	291	319	310	355	440	463	416	451	
Total	**17 323**	**18 400**	**12 527**	**13 956**	**14 200**	**13 934**	**12 854**	**13 293**	**14 758**	**12 875**	**16 065**	**..**

Note: For details on definitions and sources, refer to the metadata at the end of the tables.

StatLink 🔗 https://stat.link/lmp2jh

Table B.6. Acquisitions of nationality by country of former nationality – Latvia

	2010	2011	2012	2013	2014	2015	2016	2017	2018	2019	2020	Of which: Women 2020 (%)
Russia	67	49	82	71	109	70	127	53	50	59	92	..
Belarus	10	12	14	12	15	12	14	5	13	12	11	..
Ukraine	34	13	8	51	54	32	39	9	8	22	10	..
Armenia	2	4	6	3	4	5	5	3	3	1	5	..
United States	6		4	23	25	10	20	2	0	3	4	..
Other countries	3 541	2 389	3 670	2 923	1 934	1 768	1 752	890	856	711	603	
Total	**3 660**	**2 467**	**3 784**	**3 083**	**2 141**	**1 897**	**1 957**	**962**	**930**	**808**	**725**	..

Note: For details on definitions and sources, refer to the metadata at the end of the tables.

StatLink 🔗 https://stat.link/lmp2jh

Table B.6. Acquisitions of nationality by country of former nationality – Lithuania

	2010	2011	2012	2013	2014	2015	2016	2017	2018	2019	2020	Of which: Women 2020 (%)
Russia	43	97	39	53	49	38	49	43	39	34	47	..
Belarus	11	17	14	14	12	14	16	22	29	9	20	..
Ukraine	19	44	19	19	26	28	36	29	26	16	20	..
Kazakhstan	2	5	4	2	7	5	7	2	1	2	6	..
Armenia	2	6	7	8	6	9	5	8	7	5	5	..
Türkiye	1	1	1	4	2	..	2	6	8	0	4	..
Lebanon	..	4	2	3	1	2	2	3	1	2	4	..
Moldova	1	3	1	2	3	2	1	3	2	2	2	..
Uzbekistan	..	..	..	..	..	3	1	..	2	1	2	..
Israel	..	..	..	1	..	2	1	2	..	..	2	..
Azerbaijan	1	..	1	..	..	..	1	1	2	5	2	..
Viet Nam	..	..	..	1	2	4	1	2	4	..	2	..
Egypt	..	..	1	1	1	2	3	1	7	3	2	..
Georgia	1	..	1	3	1	2	5	1	3	..	2	..
Stateless	78	125	86	57	61	50	33	31	50	38	45	..
Other countries	3	9	7	5	8	16	10	12	15	6	11	..
Total	**162**	**311**	**183**	**173**	**179**	**177**	**173**	**166**	**196**	**123**	**176**	..

Note: For details on definitions and sources, refer to the metadata at the end of the tables.

StatLink 🔗 https://stat.link/lmp2jh

Table B.6. Acquisitions of nationality by country of former nationality – Luxembourg

	2010	2011	2012	2013	2014	2015	2016	2017	2018	2019	2020	Of which: Women 2020 (%)
France	342	314	462	639	860	1 205	2 262	2 468	2 784	2 466	2 264	50
Brazil	3	7	12	18	15	30	100	280	931	2 116	1 799	54
Belgium	258	450	1 581	1 577	1 346	1 264	1 836	1 624	1 598	1 335	1 013	50
Portugal	1 351	1 085	1 155	982	1 211	1 168	1 089	1 328	1 594	1 067	981	50
United States	44	32	42	48	80	100	233	412	665	730	438	55
Germany	333	208	201	195	209	279	246	288	364	360	360	55
United Kingdom	53	44	56	37	66	75	128	384	440	431	291	42
Montenegro	218	148	126	99	118	127	134	264	490	372	260	50
Italy	665	425	411	314	418	313	304	379	461	339	256	40
Serbia	194	80	68	49	79	55	55	97	225	201	149	47
Cape Verde	40	60	41	44	27	47	33	142	220	167	129	57
Bosnia and Herzegovina	202	114	74	60	56	70	71	161	394	186	100	58
Russia	50	30	17	22	30	40	31	60	77	95	88	72
Spain	58	35	38	30	48	42	44	85	124	90	79	49
Greece	14	11	14	15	21	23	33	59	99	73	73	53
Other countries	486	362	382	282	407	468	541	999	1 398	1 422	1 107	
Total	**4 311**	**3 405**	**4 680**	**4 411**	**4 991**	**5 306**	**7 140**	**9 030**	**11 864**	**11 450**	**9 387**	**52**

Note: For details on definitions and sources, refer to the metadata at the end of the tables.

StatLink ᴍᴵˢᴸ https://stat.link/lmp2jh

Table B.6. Acquisitions of nationality by country of former nationality – Mexico

	2010	2011	2012	2013	2014	2015	2016	2017	2018	2019	2020	Of which: Women 2019 (%)
Venezuela	126	162	279	334	259	484	580	725	1 245	1 096	..	57
Cuba	240	408	579	531	287	305	341	403	467	376	..	48
Colombia	305	486	634	601	397	378	358	346	364	265	..	53
United States	117	79	108	119	120	136	119	127	189	139	..	46
Spain	121	152	180	163	119	169	166	165	173	116	..	34
Argentina	170	178	271	304	130	126	172	141	147	93	..	49
El Salvador	81	82	99	109	66	66	75	73	100	79	..	53
Honduras	55	92	143	129	60	74	89	66	94	78	..	56
Guatemala	95	117	196	141	62	57	98	84	75	62	..	52
Peru	107	138	182	159	100	93	79	79	72	58	..	50
Nigeria	0	7	8	3	5	39	63	56	59	56	..	27
Dominican Republic	29	22	75	59	53	63	81	72	69	52	..	37
Ecuador	41	46	63	59	40	62	56	63	78	49	..	55
Russia	24	36	42	36	44	29	28	38	41	45	..	73
Italy	39	45	53	66	31	38	59	60	61	43	..	28
Other countries	600	583	678	768	568	617	576	569	638	463	..	
Total	**2 150**	**2 633**	**3 590**	**3 581**	**2 341**	**2 736**	**2 940**	**3 067**	**3 872**	**3 070**	**..**	**50**

Note: For details on definitions and sources, refer to the metadata at the end of the tables.

StatLink ᴍᴵˢᴸ https://stat.link/lmp2jh

Table B.6. Acquisitions of nationality by country of former nationality – Netherlands

	2010	2011	2012	2013	2014	2015	2016	2017	2018	2019	2020	Of which: Women 2020 (%)
Syria	80	82	126	236	235	210	86	94	214	1 587	15 177	40
Eritrea	36	45	46	30	52	70	51	63	70	237	3 659	36
Türkiye	4 984	5 029	4 292	2 872	3 119	2 824	2 764	2 947	2 675	2 828	3 025	49
Morocco	5 797	6 824	6 238	3 886	4 251	3 272	3 364	2 944	3 005	2 582	2 961	53
India	193	292	406	415	794	638	574	616	661	756	2 029	44
United Kingdom	208	207	198	165	162	166	636	1 241	1 250	2 588	1 360	48
Iraq	288	289	525	929	1 331	909	922	738	761	849	1 223	50
Iran	217	281	361	848	690	464	449	492	443	463	1 007	55
Somalia	69	108	105	64	86	249	440	468	517	427	804	55
Russia	275	295	427	291	446	355	403	376	399	409	799	72
Afghanistan	402	371	567	1 341	1 027	510	477	453	392	390	789	52
Suriname	967	934	875	659	828	594	601	536	560	593	717	59
Ukraine	189	223	276	228	337	277	256	277	304	343	697	68
Philippines	263	330	381	263	457	319	331	349	334	327	620	79
Pakistan	208	279	388	248	384	322	242	226	231	303	531	46
Other countries	12 099	13 009	15 744	13 407	18 379	16 698	16 938	15 843	16 035	19 509	20 545	
Total	**26 275**	**28 598**	**30 955**	**25 882**	**32 578**	**27 877**	**28 534**	**27 663**	**27 851**	**34 191**	**55 943**	**49**

Note: For details on definitions and sources, refer to the metadata at the end of the tables.

StatLink https://stat.link/lmp2jh

Table B.6. Acquisitions of nationality by country of former nationality – New Zealand

	2010	2011	2012	2013	2014	2015	2016	2017	2018	2019	2020	Of which: Women 2020 (%)
United Kingdom	2 814	4 808	6 039	5 299	4 883	4 382	5 405	6 552	6 074	4 896	4 147	49
India	1 573	1 664	2 249	2 225	2 235	2 429	3 412	4 745	4 948	4 798	3 413	42
Philippines	852	676	2 240	2 822	2 757	3 048	3 060	3 633	3 164	2 625	2 076	55
South Africa	1 375	2 156	2 910	3 389	3 871	3 713	3 819	3 051	2 830	2 534	1 803	50
Samoa	1 946	2 074	3 018	2 988	2 647	2 776	3 086	3 008	3 291	2 873	1 627	47
Fiji	1 309	1 219	2 097	2 124	2 270	2 422	2 752	3 307	2 583	2 059	1 323	51
China	693	852	1 158	1 190	1 239	922	1 138	1 209	1 092	1 046	668	52
Australia	118	116	179	232	287	317	564	764	881	667	633	53
United States	324	448	587	605	602	558	659	830	889	722	577	53
Pakistan	42	47	112	135	149	161	190	195	361	571	499	50
Tonga	384	328	466	531	500	516	783	705	865	723	398	52
Sri Lanka	242	164	204	271	350	445	537	704	654	555	339	47
Russia	102	150	191	244	225	235	311	325	417	356	270	55
Malaysia	464	398	467	398	392	386	477	495	472	358	256	55
Ireland	85	117	153	206	189	204	211	324	329	338	256	49
Other countries	3 008	4 296	5 537	5 809	6 163	5 954	6 458	7 617	7 990	6 856	5 243	
Total	**15 331**	**19 513**	**27 607**	**28 468**	**28 759**	**28 468**	**32 862**	**37 464**	**36 840**	**31 977**	**23 528**	**50**

Note: For details on definitions and sources, refer to the metadata at the end of the tables.

StatLink https://stat.link/lmp2jh

Table B.6. Acquisitions of nationality by country of former nationality – Norway

	2010	2011	2012	2013	2014	2015	2016	2017	2018	2019	2020	Of which: Women 2020 (%)
Somalia	1 528	2 131	1 571	1 667	1 138	451	1 250	1 746	1 879	2 986	3 051	50
Eritrea	248	254	199	323	563	1 114	1 911	2 971	1 089	1 406	2 790	44
Sweden	248	300	213	229	253	300	483	257	209	133	1 172	49
Syria	49	61	54	57	65	84	112	289	141	253	817	41
Philippines	322	421	341	479	851	704	603	1 389	410	682	718	69
Russia	673	644	629	418	401	444	482	464	351	186	638	64
Iran	554	539	297	307	336	353	420	626	365	333	621	47
Thailand	267	380	265	346	547	683	707	1 666	300	583	586	87
Denmark	171	152	126	207	161	120	96	77	53	26	487	43
Sudan	90	122	72	58	80	57	180	293	125	404	467	38
India	152	209	130	132	313	382	391	636	167	373	425	47
Ethiopia	225	341	236	195	362	336	440	709	191	436	403	56
Pakistan	430	526	478	424	503	714	482	592	437	222	400	50
Afghanistan	1 054	1 281	1 013	1 005	1 371	1 088	1 004	1 264	448	655	360	43
Stateless	..	..	..	..	..	..	..	605	682	684	545	46
Other countries	5 892	7 276	6 760	7 376	8 392	5 602	6 115	8 064	3 421	3 839	6 218	
Total	**11 903**	**14 637**	**12 384**	**13 223**	**15 336**	**12 432**	**14 676**	**21 648**	**10 268**	**13 201**	**19 698**	**52**

Note: For details on definitions and sources, refer to the metadata at the end of the tables.

StatLink ⟨ᴍˢ⟩ https://stat.link/lmp2jh

Table B.6. Acquisitions of nationality by country of former nationality – Poland

	2010	2011	2012	2013	2014	2015	2016	2017	2018	2019	2020	Of which: Women 2020 (%)
Ukraine	992	800	1 196	908	1 911	2 010	1 432	900	2 608	7 072	3 985	..
Belarus	418	320	456	390	741	527	512	229	833	2 145	2 010	..
Russia	215	200	244	171	370	251	112	63	219	367	311	..
Viet Nam	97	104	150	105	289	222	68	120	136	246	93	..
Armenia	101	103	163	111	367	285	160	113	119	120	90	..
Türkiye	33	12	72	17	33	36	34	22	33	57	43	..
United Kingdom	9	7	9	16	7	8	6	7	29	47	40	..
Egypt	38	4	76	11	5	15	9	2	30	36	27	..
Kazakhstan	38	42	44	41	36	36	17	13	40	32	27	..
Georgia	11	17	11	11	14	8	13	8	3	16	21	..
India	24	12	55	12	14	36	6	10	23	33	20	..
Lithuania	14	19	26	28	13	21	9	19	19	17	20	..
Uzbekistan	10	11	12	8	15	11	8	3	8	28	18	..
Czech Republic	9	12	10	8	23	22	7	5	13	17	17	..
Bulgaria	21	38	29	25	27	36	18	13	13	21	17	..
Other countries	896	624	1 239	1 600	653	524	1 675	2 732	467	2 663	420	
Total	**2 926**	**2 325**	**3 792**	**3 462**	**4 518**	**4 048**	**4 086**	**4 259**	**4 593**	**12 917**	**7 159**	**..**

Note: For details on definitions and sources, refer to the metadata at the end of the tables.

StatLink ⟨ᴍˢ⟩ https://stat.link/lmp2jh

Table B.6. Acquisitions of nationality by country of former nationality – Portugal

	2010	2011	2012	2013	2014	2015	2016	2017	2018	2019	2020	Of which: Women 2020 (%)
Brazil	4 007	5 352	4 596	5 102	4 656	6 394	7 804	6 084	6 928	6 468	10 109	62
Cape Verde	3 982	3 502	3 230	3 821	3 200	2 854	3 607	2 591	3 640	3 462	4 701	58
Guinea-Bissau	1 847	1 815	1 753	2 082	1 915	1 676	1 884	1 226	1 542	1 451	2 257	45
Angola	1 953	1 870	1 857	2 131	1 630	1 316	1 507	1 225	1 438	1 387	2 118	56
Ukraine	1 358	2 336	3 322	4 007	3 310	2 895	3 240	1 909	1 752	1 620	2 111	56
India	919	860	628	539	490	454	1 002	693	855	747	1 326	28
Sao Tome and Principe	1 097	1 156	869	1 027	938	809	1 061	753	1 006	951	1 271	55
Nepal		51	36	33	53	102	293	319	426	1 103	1 249	30
Pakistan	388	476	443	346	333	189	407	239	285	291	688	26
Bangladesh	340	193	110	93	71	98	230	189	284	629	678	24
Romania	303	469	492	796	687	515	621	412	434	484	582	57
Venezuela	76	87	68	45	80	51	127	90	188	283	449	63
Moldova	2 675	2 324	2 043	1 816	1 363	964	815	453	400	356	422	55
Russia	580	590	506	515	395	327	359	194	272	196	368	63
Mozambique	208	204	193	199	148	148	206	158	175	161	283	65
Other countries	2 017	1 953	1 673	1 924	1 855	1 604	1 941	1 487	1 708	1 510	3 535	
Total	**21 750**	**23 238**	**21 819**	**24 476**	**21 124**	**20 396**	**25 104**	**18 022**	**21 333**	**21 099**	**32 147**	53

Note: For details on definitions and sources, refer to the metadata at the end of the tables.

StatLink https://stat.link/lmp2jh

Table B.6. Acquisitions of nationality by country of former nationality – Slovak Republic

	2010	2011	2012	2013	2014	2015	2016	2017	2018	2019	2020	Of which: Women 2020 (%)
Czech Republic	45	45	36	24	37	70	105	91	119	88	98	57
Ukraine	44	61	60	63	62	73	77	129	127	76	90	64
Serbia	57	53	55	9	5	8	94	124	42	26	55	47
Viet Nam	15	5	11	15	49	20	26	53	54	46	40	53
United States	7	6	6	2	5	31	19	16	39	35	35	43
United Kingdom	..	..	..	..	..	2	15	33	60	70	30	60
Germany	3	3	2	1	1	11	38	35	41	33	23	52
Romania	10	18	25	9	7	5	26	24	25	17	17	41
Australia	..	..	..	..	..	..	4	12	10	20	16	31
Afghanistan	..	..	..	1	2	..	1	1	6	5	12	25
Poland	5	4	4	4	2	4	4	6	9	7	9	56
Hungary	12	9	8	5	1	4	6	13	15	8	8	38
Russia	8	8	3	20	5	5	7	6	27	21	8	38
North Macedonia	..	..	..	1	5	3	2	10	3	6	7	29
Türkiye	1	1	3	1	1	3	2	6	5	4	6	0
Other countries	32	59	42	52	52	70	58	86	139	124	94	
Total	**239**	**272**	**255**	**207**	**234**	**309**	**484**	**645**	**721**	**586**	**548**	49

Note: For details on definitions and sources, refer to the metadata at the end of the tables.

StatLink https://stat.link/lmp2jh

Table B.6. Acquisitions of nationality by country of former nationality – Slovenia

	2010	2011	2012	2013	2014	2015	2016	2017	2018	2019	2020	Of which: Women 2020 (%)
Bosnia and Herzegovina	565	635	587	545	570	741	724	918	1 321	1 215	1 144	41
Serbia	211	169	139	184	155	127	159	153	179	262	186	52
North Macedonia	197	165	155	122	117	145	166	208	222	192	158	44
Croatia	154	164	134	93	34	30	30	22	40	48	33	58
Ukraine	25	31	30	35	17	21	29	23	24	33	21	76
Bulgaria	3	2	5	1	1	4	1	5	3	12	19	32
Russia	6	19	13	12	26	8	11	17	7	13	17	53
Moldova	4	10	9	7	10	6	6	7	3	6	9	67
Italy	206	204	156	186	11	23	18	27	13	7	7	43
Romania	4	3	1	3	2	2	3	2	3	1	6	50
Montenegro	28	22	22	32	9	20	25	24	22	16	5	40
United Kingdom	0	0	1	0	0	0	0	2	1	5	4	50
Hungary	0	5	3	4	1	1	2	1	1	1	4	75
Albania	1	1	3	1	1	1	0	1	1	3	4	0
Egypt	6	3	3	2	1	2	0	0	1	2	3	33
Other countries	430	342	229	243	102	124	123	153	137	95	105	
Total	**1 840**	**1 775**	**1 490**	**1 470**	**1 057**	**1 255**	**1 297**	**1 563**	**1 978**	**1 911**	**1 725**	**44**

Note: For details on definitions and sources, refer to the metadata at the end of the tables.

StatLink ⏹ https://stat.link/lmp2jh

Table B.6. Acquisitions of nationality by country of former nationality – Spain

	2010	2011	2012	2013	2014	2015	2016	2017	2018	2019	2020	Of which: Women 2020 (%)
Morocco	10 703	14 427	16 163	31 674	34 806	24 286	37 010	17 082	25 315	24 527	28 240	42
Colombia	23 995	19 803	19 396	39 332	25 114	11 881	14 299	5 647	6 826	7 515	9 021	60
Ecuador	43 091	32 026	23 763	39 226	32 756	13 950	15 255	7 301	7 988	8 157	8 336	52
Bolivia	4 778	5 333	7 424	19 278	20 895	11 164	15 802	6 124	8 157	7 417	7 794	63
Dominican Rep.	3 801	4 985	6 028	14 611	14 110	8 171	9 176	4 107	4 940	5 366	6 897	59
Venezuela	2 730	2 596	2 823	6 217	4 302	2 332	3 127	1 068	2 034	2 554	5 817	58
Cuba	3 546	3 088	2 921	7 026	5 618	3 072	4 353	1 429	2 688	3 105	5 405	57
Pakistan	375	491	596	1 949	3 326	2 798	3 148	1 708	2 054	3 057	4 458	28
Peru	8 291	9 255	12 008	19 225	16 601	6 954	6 933	3 224	3 273	3 798	4 219	58
Honduras	473	440	578	1 702	2 142	1 632	2 525	1 267	1 783	2 739	3 868	79
Paraguay	766	864	1 297	2 958	3 003	1 935	3 358	1 265	2 500	2 726	3 647	78
Argentina	6 395	5 482	5 217	8 843	7 059	3 054	3 716	1 445	2 043	2 493	3 581	53
Brazil	1 738	1 854	2 540	4 698	4 017	2 273	3 427	1 294	2 153	2 737	3 382	66
Romania	319	416	528	1 174	1 608	966	1 469	696	991	1 696	2 771	60
Ukraine	221	262	318	746	1 032	662	1 164	378	981	1 558	2 254	58
Other countries	12 499	13 277	13 957	27 134	29 491	19 221	26 182	12 463	17 048	19 509	26 576	
Total	**123 721**	**114 599**	**115 557**	**225 793**	**205 880**	**114 351**	**150 944**	**66 498**	**90 774**	**98 954**	**126 266**	**53**

Note: For details on definitions and sources, refer to the metadata at the end of the tables.

StatLink ⏹ https://stat.link/lmp2jh

Table B.6. Acquisitions of nationality by country of former nationality – Sweden

	2010	2011	2012	2013	2014	2015	2016	2017	2018	2019	2020	Of which: Women 2020 (%)
Syria	418	675	666	540	495	1 370	4 479	8 635	10 626	20 066	24 472	39
Iraq	4 354	6 164	16 582	14 317	7 271	4 955	3 694	3 272	2 579	2 260	3 610	55
Afghanistan	848	636	851	776	785	1 198	2 330	2 316	1 912	2 793	2 820	35
Poland	1 477	1 787	1 645	2 473	2 417	2 333	2 702	2 083	1 783	1 209	2 722	52
Eritrea	326	396	743	836	997	1 113	1 451	1 677	1 836	1 865	2 307	49
United Kingdom	392	277	296	288	424	444	960	1 228	1 340	4 495	2 151	27
Somalia	1 075	1 087	1 547	2 482	2 925	4 776	9 069	8 140	6 746	2 952	2 120	48
Thailand	1 426	1 537	1 903	2 038	2 070	2 928	2 675	2 517	1 620	1 391	1 921	84
Norway	381	342	317	302	370	331	355	384	431	346	1 725	54
Iran	958	1 021	1 392	1 305	1 128	1 331	1 420	1 788	1 736	1 399	1 584	54
Finland	2 966	2 227	2 245	2 255	3 023	2 133	2 182	1 974	2 522	1 730	1 582	63
Romania	237	195	350	744	781	736	886	822	779	573	1 431	50
Türkiye	1 036	1 322	1 303	1 124	1 005	1 182	1 320	1 488	796	915	1 431	46
Germany	912	770	654	837	920	918	858	854	893	694	1 419	50
Stateless	1 139	1 517	1 450	2 005	1 710	3 264	4 395	7 072	5 629	3 197	3 227	47
Other countries	14 252	16 375	17 802	17 310	16 597	19 237	21 567	24 648	22 590	18 321	25 653	
Total	**32 197**	**36 328**	**49 746**	**49 632**	**42 918**	**48 249**	**60 343**	**68 898**	**63 818**	**64 206**	**80 175**	**47**

Note: For details on definitions and sources, refer to the metadata at the end of the tables.

StatLink ≋≋ https://stat.link/lmp2jh

Table B.6. Acquisitions of nationality by country of former nationality – Switzerland

	2010	2011	2012	2013	2014	2015	2016	2017	2018	2019	2020	Of which: Women 2020 (%)
Germany	3 617	3 544	3 401	3 835	4 120	5 255	4 658	6 021	6 212	6 640	6 924	50
Italy	4 111	4 109	4 045	4 401	4 495	5 496	5 134	5 863	5 233	4 839	3 946	47
France	1 084	1 325	1 229	1 580	1 750	2 598	3 134	2 964	2 699	2 747	2 756	50
Portugal	2 217	2 298	2 110	2 201	2 458	3 626	3 941	3 920	3 352	2 801	2 055	53
Türkiye	2 091	1 886	1 662	1 628	1 399	1 808	1 729	1 796	1 678	1 802	1 363	48
North Macedonia	1 586	1 337	1 223	1 272	1 288	1 306	1 554	1 721	1 626	1 706	1 270	50
Serbia	6 859	4 359	3 463	2 562	1 865	1 677	1 568	1 543	1 493	1 364	1 069	52
Spain	1 120	1 091	1 055	1 054	1 071	1 501	1 564	1 585	1 491	1 280	994	49
United Kingdom	298	351	396	328	449	617	665	883	1 006	844	727	48
Bosnia and Herzegovina	1 924	1 628	1 163	1 173	966	1 103	965	972	995	847	566	48
Sri Lanka	..	..	..	..	781	768	761	825	793	657	531	50
Russia	..	361	369	397	397	562	614	589	514	536	485	68
Croatia	1 483	1 273	1 201	1 126	838	904	737	730	649	560	454	58
Brazil	..	..	..	..	455	596	538	618	595	480	350	71
Poland	148	169	172	202	218	258	248	292	283	313	279	65
Other countries	12 776	13 387	13 001	12 573	10 775	12 813	13 777	14 193	14 011	12 861	10 293	
Total	**39 314**	**36 757**	**34 121**	**34 332**	**33 325**	**40 888**	**41 587**	**44 515**	**42 630**	**40 277**	**34 062**	**52**

Note: For details on definitions and sources, refer to the metadata at the end of the tables.

StatLink ≋≋ https://stat.link/lmp2jh

Table B.6. Acquisitions of nationality by country of former nationality – United Kingdom

	2010	2011	2012	2013	2014	2015	2016	2017	2018	2019	2020	Of which: Women 2020 (%)
Pakistan	22 049	17 639	18 437	21 647	12 995	13 083	16 737	10 379	11 802	12 914	11 459	46
India	29 397	26 278	28 343	36 349	22 425	18 391	24 615	16 687	15 104	14 680	11 444	48
Nigeria	7 870	7 932	8 878	9 268	8 074	8 049	9 810	6 941	8 696	8 839	8 065	48
Italy	356	297	555	808	479	846	1 282	3 515	5 255	5 774	6 049	47
Romania	1 009	565	678	2 487	1 501	1 673	1 979	3 022	5 527	5 604	5 483	53
Poland	1 419	1 862	3 041	6 063	3 161	3 777	4 435	7 113	9 626	8 802	5 430	59
France	511	490	630	744	411	728	1 163	2 824	4 103	4 472	3 465	55
Bangladesh	7 965	5 147	5 701	8 900	3 891	3 611	4 648	3 080	3 572	3 780	3 424	48
Germany	339	400	479	569	311	584	992	2 635	4 759	4 331	3 244	60
South Africa	7 442	6 351	6 925	6 447	5 294	4 771	5 059	3 103	3 582	4 797	3 008	50
United States	2 923	2 589	3 345	3 117	3 761	2 961	4 024	3 182	3 270	3 496	2 749	61
Bulgaria	1 930	969	746	1 941	1 314	995	1 246	1 818	2 640	2 914	2 561	53
Spain	165	158	260	328	260	402	614	1 624	2 401	2 604	2 529	51
Ghana	4 550	3 935	4 744	4 676	3 138	2 978	3 562	2 591	3 179	2 719	2 415	51
Iran	2 587	5 539	4 135	2 389	1 542	1 518	2 097	1 797	2 854	2 960	2 342	42
Other countries	104 502	97 715	107 391	102 288	57 158	53 687	67 115	52 896	70 641	70 670	56 884	
Total	**195 014**	**177 866**	**194 288**	**208 021**	**125 715**	**118 054**	**149 378**	**123 207**	**157 011**	**159 356**	**130 551**	**52**

Note: For details on definitions and sources, refer to the metadata at the end of the tables.

StatLink 🔗 https://stat.link/lmp2jh

Table B.6. Acquisitions of nationality by country of former nationality – United States

	2010	2011	2012	2013	2014	2015	2016	2017	2018	2019	2020	Of which: Women 2020 (%)
Mexico	66 941	94 721	102 121	99 330	94 843	105 910	103 487	118 469	131 950	121 973	83 436	56
India	60 049	45 087	41 916	48 945	36 931	41 178	45 183	49 815	51 325	63 578	47 233	51
Philippines	35 121	42 122	44 508	43 076	34 277	40 438	40 973	36 573	38 519	43 260	33 079	67
Cuba	13 910	20 903	31 071	30 299	23 975	25 674	31 939	25 836	31 940	35 969	31 013	53
China	34 532	33 666	32 608	36 011	30 840	31 819	36 300	37 836	39 800	39 716	26 453	60
Viet Nam	18 832	20 416	23 106	23 798	18 451	21 624	24 405	18 989	20 658	25 192	22 302	63
Dominican Rep.	15 405	20 402	33 225	39 448	23 694	26 582	31 216	29 598	22 891	22 976	18 494	58
Canada	14 131	14 723	14 443	14 931	13 878	14 969	15 170	13 649	15 796	18 495	13 588	53
Jamaica	11 892	14 385	15 314	16 278	13 387	16 370	16 541	14 889	16 998	17 719	13 202	59
Colombia	18 234	22 478	23 733	21 942	16 283	17 024	18 374	16 012	17 402	16 914	12 562	63
El Salvador	10 314	13 830	16 679	18 363	15 568	16 886	17 189	16 893	17 260	18 206	12 514	56
Iraq	3 327	3 194	3 351	7 636	12 310	14 897	11 996	7 701	12 340	18 314	12 200	47
Korea	11 065	12 623	13 732	15 697	13 513	14 119	14 251	14 470	15 922	16 149	11 223	57
Haiti	12 253	14 170	19 097	23 444	13 635	14 037	15 223	12 723	14 343	14 227	10 726	54
United Kingdom	10 023	10 945	10 814	11 066	10 333	11 638	11 052	10 485	12 165	13 907	10 126	46
Other countries	283 884	310 528	331 716	329 665	281 498	317 094	319 761	283 327	302 592	356 998	270 103	
Total	**619 913**	**694 193**	**757 434**	**779 929**	**653 416**	**730 259**	**753 060**	**707 265**	**761 901**	**843 593**	**628 254**	**55**

Note: For details on definitions and sources, refer to the metadata at the end of the tables.

StatLink 🔗 https://stat.link/lmp2jh

Metadata related to Tables A.6. and B.6. **Acquisitions of nationality**

Country	Comments	Source
Australia	Data from 2007 to 2010 are based on the former Reporting Assurance Section. Data from 2011 are sourced from Citizenship Programme Management. From 2014, figures inferior to 5 individuals are not shown.	Department of Immigration and Border Protection.
Austria	Data refer to persons living in Austria at the time of acquisition.	Statistics Austria and BMI (Ministry of the Interior).
Belgium	Data refer to all acquisitions of Belgian nationality, irrespective of the type of procedure. Data only take into account those residing in Belgium at the time of the acquisition.	Directorate for Statistics and Economic Information (DGSEI) and Ministry of Justice.
Canada	Data refer to country of birth, not to country of previous nationality. Persons who acquire Canadian citizenship may also hold other citizenships at the same time if allowed by the country of previous nationality.	Immigration, Refugees and Citizenship Canada.
Chile	Register of residence permits.	Department of Foreigners and Migration, Ministry of the Interior.
Czech Republic	Acquisitions of nationality by declaration or by naturalisation.	Ministry of the Interior.
Denmark	The decrease in 2013 can be explained by the change in the naturalisation conditions that year.	Statistics Denmark.
Estonia	Acquisitions of citizenship by naturalisation.	Police and Border Guard Board.
Finland	Includes naturalisations of persons of Finnish origin.	Central Population Register, Statistics Finland.
France		Ministry of the Interior and Ministry of Justice.
Germany	Figures do not include ethnic Germans (Aussiedler). From 2018 on, figures are rounded to the nearest multiple of five.	Federal Office of Statistics.
Greece	Data refer to all possible types of citizenship acquisition: naturalisation, declaration (for Greek descents), adoption by a Greek, etc.	Ministry of Interior and Administrative Reconstruction.
Hungary	Person naturalised in Hungary: naturalisation (the person was born foreign) or renaturalisation (his/her former Hungarian citizenship was abolished). The rules of naturalisation in Hungary were modified by the Act XLIV of 2010. The act introduced the simplified naturalisation procedure from 1 January 2011, and made it possible to obtain citizenship without residence in Hungary for the foreign citizens who have Hungarian ancestors. This data refer only to those new Hungarian citizens who have an address in Hungary.	Central Office Administrative and Electronic Public Services (Central Population Register), Central Statistical Office.
Iceland	Includes children who receive Icelandic citizenship with their parents.	Statistics Iceland.
Ireland	Figures include naturalisations and post nuptial citizenship figures.	Department of Justice and Equality.
Italy		Ministry of the Interior.
Japan		Ministry of Justice, Civil Affairs Bureau.
Korea		Ministry of Justice.
Latvia	Acquisition of citizenship by naturalisation including children who receive Latvian citizenship with their parents.	Office of Citizenship and Migration Affairs.
Lithuania		Eurostat.
Luxembourg	Includes non-residents. Excludes children acquiring nationality as a consequence of the naturalisation of their parents.	Ministry of Justice.
Mexico		Ministry of Foreign Affairs (SRE).
Netherlands		Central Bureau of Statistics (CBS).
New Zealand	Before 2016, the country of origin refers to the country of birth if birth documentation is available (if not, the country of origin is the country of citizenship as shown on the person's passport).	Department of Internal Affairs.
Norway	The statistics are based on population register data.	Statistics Norway.
Poland	Data include naturalisations by marriage and acknowledgment of persons of Polish descent, in addition to naturalisation by ordinary procedure.	Office for Repatriation and Aliens.
Portugal	Acquisition of nationality by foreigners living in Portugal.	Institute of registers and notarial regulations, Directorate General for Justice Policy (DGPJ).
Slovak Republic	Data refer to persons living in Slovak Republic at the time of acquisition.	Ministry of the Interior.

Country	Comments	Source
Slovenia	Include all grounds on which the citizenship was obtained.	Internal Administrative Affairs, Migration and Naturalisation Directorate, Ministry of the Interior.
Spain	Includes only naturalisations on the ground of residence in Spain. Excludes individuals recovering their former (Spanish) nationality. The large increase in the number of naturalisations in 2013 is due to the Intensive File Processing Nationality Plan *(Plan Intensivo de tramitación de expedientes de Nacionalidad)* carried out by the Ministry of Justice.	Ministry of Employment and Social Security, based on naturalisations registered by the Ministry of Justice.
Sweden		Statistics Sweden.
Switzerland		Federal Office of Migration.
Türkiye		General Directorate for population and citizenship, Ministry of the Interior.
United Kingdom	The increase in 2009 is partly due to the processing of a backlog of applications filled prior to 2009.	Home Office.
United States	Data by country of birth refer to fiscal years (October to September of the year indicated).	Department of Homeland Security.

Note: Data for Serbia include persons from Serbia and Montenegro. Some statements may refer to nationalities/countries of birth not shown in this annex but available on line at: http://stats.oecd.org/.

List of the members of the OECD Expert Group on Migration

Australia	John NAPIER, Australian Home Affairs, Canberra
Austria	Gudrun BIFFL and Isabella SKRIVANEK, Danube University, Krems
Belgium	Sarah DECLERCQ and Koen DEWULF, Federal Migration Center, Brussels
Bulgaria	Daniela BOBEVA, Academy of Sciences, Sofia
Canada	Cédric DE CHARDON, Immigration, Refugees and Citizenship, Canada, Ottawa
Chile	Alvaro BELLOLIO and Carolina CALVO ASENCIO, Ministry of the Interior, Santiago
China	Zhao HAISHAN, National Immigration Administration, Beijing
Czech Republic	Jarmila MAREŠOVÁ, Czech Statistical Office, Prague
Denmark	Henrik Torp ANDERSEN, Ministry of immigration and integration, Copenhagen
Estonia	Mari NELJAS, Ministry of the Interior, Tallinn
Finland	Pipa Turvanen, Ministry of Economic Affairs and Employment, Helsinki
France	Jean-Baptiste HERBET, Ministry of the Interior, Paris
Germany	Jürgen SCHRODER, Federal Ministry of Labour and Social Affairs, Berlin
Greece	Eda GEMI, European University of Tirana
Hungary	Vető GÁBOR, Ministry of the Interior, Budapest
Ireland	Philip O'CONNELL, The Economic and Social Research Institute, Dublin
Israel	Gilad NATHAN, Ruppin Academic Center, Jerusalem
Italy	Ugo MELCHIONDA, Member of the Board of Directors, Religions for Peace – Europe, Rome
Japan	Arisa ASANO and Keiichi SHIMIZU, Ministry of Health, Labour and Welfare, Yu KOREKAWA, National Institute of Population and Social Security Research
Korea	Dong-Hoon SEOL, Chonbuk National University, Jeonju
Latvia	Ilze SILIŅA-OSMANE, Office of Citizenship and Migration Affairs, Riga
Lithuania	Audra SIPAVIČIENE, International Organization for Migration, Vilnius Office
Luxembourg	Adolfo Jose SOMMARIBAS ARIAS, Research Associate EMN Luxembourg, University of Luxembourg, and Pietro LOMBARDINI, Ministry of Foreign Affairs, Luxembourg
Mexico	Carlos HEREDIA, División de Estudios Internacionales, Centro de Investigación y Docencia Económicas, Mexico
Netherlands	Arend ODÉ and Jeanine KLAVER, Regioplan Policy Research, Amsterdam
New Zealand	David PATERSON, Ministry of Business Innovation and Employment, Wellington
Norway	Espen THORUD, Norwegian Ministry of Education and Research, Oslo
Poland	Pawel KACZMARCZYK, University of Warsaw, Warsaw
Portugal	Jorge MALHEIROS, University of Lisbon, Lisbon
Romania	Mihaela MATEI, Bucharest
Russian Federation	Olga CHUDINOVSKIKH, Centre for Population Studies, Lomonosov Moscow State University, Moscow
Slovak Republic	Martina LUBYOVÁ and Lubica GAJDOŠOVÁ, Centre of Social and Psychological Sciences SAS, Bratislava
Slovenia	Grega MALEC, Ministry of Labour, Family, and Social Affairs and Equal Opportunities, Ljubljana
Spain	Juan Carlos DOMINGO, Ministry of Labour, Migrations and Social Security, Madrid
Sweden	Elin JANSSON, Ministry of Justice, Stockholm and Binniam KIDANE, Ministry of Employment, Stockholm
Switzerland	Clovis VOISARD, Kathrin GAÜMANN and Claire de COULON, Federal Office of State Secretary for Migration, Bern
Türkiye	Ahmet ICDUYGU, Koç University, Istanbul
United Kingdom	Bex NEWELL and Jon SIMMONS, Home Office Analysis and Insight, Croydon
United States	Amanda BARAN, Department of Homeland Security, Washington

Composition of OECD International Migration Division

Mona AHMED, Administrator

Lisa ANDERSSON, Administrator

Dominika ANDRZEJCZAK, Assistant

Charlotte BAER, Assistant

Yves BREEM, Administrator

Jonathan CHALOFF, Principal Administrator

Ana DAMAS DE MATOS, Administrator

Jean-Christophe DUMONT, Head of Division

Philippe HERVÉ, Statistician

Elisabeth KAMM, Junior Analyst

Ave LAUREN, Administrator

Jongmi LEE, Statistician

Thomas LIEBIG, Principal Administrator

Lauren MATHERNE, Administrator

Christopher MCDONALD, Administrator

Sara MOUHOUD, Junior Analyst

Nicolas ORTEGA, Statistician

Géraldine RENAUDIÈRE, Administrator

Gilles SPIELVOGEL, Administrator

Cécile THOREAU, Administrator

Marcela VALDIVIA, Administrator

Alina WINTER, Junior Analyst

Rieke WÖNIG, Junior Analyst

Kristýna BLAHOVÁ, Intern

Penda-Ba DIALLO, Intern

Helen EWALD, Intern

Alžbeta JANECKOVÁ, Intern

Kowovi HANTO, Intern

Yukiko NUKINA, Intern